COMPANION TO SEXUALITY STUDIES

Companion to Sexuality Studies

EDITED BY
NANCY A. NAPLES

WILEY Blackwell

This edition first published 2020
© 2020 John Wiley & Sons Ltd

All rights reserved. No part of this publication may be reproduced, stored in a retrieval system, or transmitted, in any form or by any means, electronic, mechanical, photocopying, recording or otherwise, except as permitted by law. Advice on how to obtain permission to reuse material from this title is available at http://www.wiley.com/go/permissions.

The right of Nancy A. Naples to be identified as the author of this editorial material in this work and has been asserted in accordance with law.

Registered Office(s)
John Wiley & Sons, Inc., 111 River Street, Hoboken, NJ 07030, USA

Editorial Office
9600 Garsington Road, Oxford, OX4 2DQ, UK

For details of our global editorial offices, customer services, and more information about Wiley products visit us at www.wiley.com.

Wiley also publishes its books in a variety of electronic formats and by print-on-demand. Some content that appears in standard print versions of this book may not be available in other formats.

Limit of Liability/Disclaimer of Warranty
While the publisher and authors have used their best efforts in preparing this work, they make no representations or warranties with respect to the accuracy or completeness of the contents of this work and specifically disclaim all warranties, including without limitation any implied warranties of merchantability or fitness for a particular purpose. No warranty may be created or extended by sales representatives, written sales materials or promotional statements for this work. The fact that an organization, website, or product is referred to in this work as a citation and/or potential source of further information does not mean that the publisher and authors endorse the information or services the organization, website, or product may provide or recommendations it may make. This work is sold with the understanding that the publisher is not engaged in rendering professional services. The advice and strategies contained herein may not be suitable for your situation. You should consult with a specialist where appropriate. Further, readers should be aware that websites listed in this work may have changed or disappeared between when this work was written and when it is read. Neither the publisher nor authors shall be liable for any loss of profit or any other commercial damages, including but not limited to special, incidental, consequential, or other damages.

Library of Congress Cataloging-in-Publication Data
Name: Naples, Nancy A., editor.
Title: Companion to sexuality studies / edited by
 Nancy A. Naples.
Description: Hoboken, NJ: Wiley, [2020] | Includes bibliographical
 references and index.
Identifiers: LCCN 2019052319 (print) | LCCN 2019052320 (ebook) | ISBN
 9781119314998 (hardback) | ISBN 9781119315032 (adobe pdf) | ISBN
 9781119315056 (epub)
Subjects: LCSH: Sexology.
Classification: LCC HQ60 .W55 2020 (print) | LCC HQ60 (ebook) | DDC
 306.7–dc23
LC record available at https://lccn.loc.gov/2019052319
LC ebook record available at https://lccn.loc.gov/2019052320

Cover Design: Wiley
Cover Image: © oxygen/Getty Images

Set in 10/12.5pt Sabon by SPi Global, Pondicherry, India

Printed and bound by CPI Group (UK) Ltd, Croydon, CR0 4YY

10 9 8 7 6 5 4 3 2 1

Contents

Editors		vii
Notes on Contributors		ix
Acknowledgments		xv
PART I	INTRODUCTION	1
	1 The Diversity and Academic Institutionalization of Sexuality Studies *Nancy A. Naples*	3
PART II	THEORETICAL AND METHODOLOGICAL DIVERSITY	19
	2 Sexology *Agnieszka Kościańska*	21
	3 Sexualities in Historical Comparative Perspective *Mathew Kuefler*	40
	4 Postcolonial Sexualities *Vrushali Patil and Jyoti Puri*	61
	5 Queer Theory *J. Michael Ryan*	79
	6 Queer Methodologies and Social Science *Stuti Das*	95
	7 Queer Pedagogies *Leigh Potvin*	122
PART III	HEALTH, SCIENCE, AND PSYCHOLOGY	141
	8 Sexuality, Science, and Technology *Donna J. Drucker*	143
	9 Sexuality and Socialization *Leah R. Warner, Emily A. Leskinen, and Janelle Leyva*	160
	10 LGBTQ Reproduction and Parenting *Kate Luxion*	179

PART IV SEXUALITY AND INSTITUTIONS — 203

11 Sexuality and Religion — 205
    Kelsy Burke and Brandi Woodell

12 Sexuality Education — 225
    Louisa Allen

13 Sexuality, Employment, and Discrimination — 242
    Patti Giuffre and Courtney Caviness

14 Commodification of Intimacy and Sexuality — 258
    Julia Meszaros

PART V POPULAR CULTURE — 279

15 Sexuality and Popular Culture — 281
    Diane Grossman

16 LGBT Literature — 299
    Julie Beaulieu

17 Queer Comics and LGBT in Comparative Perspective — 318
    Helis Sikk

PART VI CITIZENSHIP, POLICY, AND LAW — 335

18 Sexual Citizenship in Comparative Perspective — 337
    Carol Johnson and Vera Mackie

19 Sexuality and Migration — 357
    Shweta M. Adur

20 Sexuality and Criminal Justice — 371
    Sharon Hayes and Cristina Khan

21 Sexual Harassment Policy in the US and Comparative Perspective — 389
    Jennifer Ann Drobac

22 Sex Work and Sex Trafficking — 409
    Kamala Kempadoo and Elya M. Durisin

PART VII HUMAN RIGHTS AND SOCIAL JUSTICE MOVEMENTS — 427

23 Sexual Rights and Globalization — 429
    Shweta M. Adur

24 The Global LGBT Workplace Equality Movement — 445
    Apoorva Ghosh

25 Reproductive Justice — 464
    Michele Eggers-Barison and Crystal M. Hayes

Index — 482

Editors

Editor

Nancy A. Naples is Board of Trustees Distinguished Professor of Sociology and Women's, Gender, and Sexuality Studies. She served as president of the *Society for the Study of Social Problems*, *Sociologists for Women in Society*, and the *Eastern Sociological Society*. Her publications includes over 50 book chapters and journal articles in a wide array of interdisciplinary and sociological journals. She is author of *Grassroots Warriors: Community Work, Activist Mothering and the War on Poverty* and *Feminism and Method: Ethnography, Discourse Analysis, and Activist Research*. She is editor of *Community Activism and Feminist Politics: Organizing Across Race, Class, and Gender*; and coeditor of *Border Politics: Social Movements, Collective Identities, and Globalization*; *Teaching Feminist Praxis*; *Women's Activism and Globalization: Linking Local Struggles and Transnational Politics*; and *The Sexuality of Migration: Border Crossings and Mexican Immigrant Men* by Lionel Cantú. She is series editor for *Praxis: Theory in Action* published by SUNY Press and Editor-in-Chief of the five-volume Wiley Blackwell *Encyclopedia of Gender and Sexuality Studies*. Her awards include the 2015 Jessie Bernard Award for distinguished contributions women and gender studies from the American Sociological Association and the 2014 Lee Founders Award from the Society for the Study of Social Problems. She also received the 2010 Distinguished Feminist Lecturer Award and the 2011 Feminist Mentor Award from *Sociologists for Women in Society* and College of Liberal Arts and Sciences' 2011 Excellence in Research for Social Sciences and Alumni Association's 2008 Faculty Excellence Award in Research from the University of Connecticut. She is currently working on a book on *Sexual Citizenship*.

Managing Editor

Cristina Khan is a lecturer in the Department of Women's, Gender, and Sexuality Studies at Stony Brook University. She received her PhD from the Department of Sociology at the University of Connecticut in 2019 with a certificate in Feminist

Studies. Her specializations include race, ethnicity, embodiment, sexualities, and qualitative research methods. Her dissertation, "Undoing Borders: A Feminist Exploration of Erotic Performance by Lesbian Women of Color," draws on two years of ethnographic fieldwork and 40 in-depth interviews with a collective of lesbian exotic dancers, uncovering how race and sexuality, together, shape women's potential to enact agency over the conditions of their participation in exotic dance. Her research on "Constructing Eroticized Latinidad: Negotiating Profitability in the Stripping Industry" has been published in *Gender & Society*. She is also coauthor of *Race and Sexuality* (Polity Press, 2018). Her research experience includes serving as a consultant on diversity and equity initiatives at the New York City Department of Education, and as a research assistant on cochlear implant usage and experience amongst families under the supervision of Dr. Laura Mauldin.

Notes on Contributors

Shweta M. Adur, PhD, is an Assistant Professor of Sociology at California State University, Los Angeles. Before this, she served as an Assistant Professor of Women and Gender Studies at California State University, Fullerton. She completed her PhD in Sociology from the University of Connecticut and has received a Master's in International Development from the University of Pittsburgh. Her research interests include gender, sexuality, human rights and immigration. She is the coauthor of the book *As the Leaves Turn Gold: Asian Americans and Experiences of Aging* (Rowman & Littlefield, 2012) that engages with issues surrounding aging and social inequality from a transnational perspective. Her publications have appeared in peer-reviewed journals (most recent ones were featured in *Current Sociology* and *Journal of Gender Studies*) and edited collections.

Louisa Allen is a Professor of Education at the *University of Auckland*, New Zealand. She specializes in research in the areas of sexuality, education, and young people. These topics are explored through the theoretical frameworks of queer theory and feminist new materialisms. She has published eight books in these areas the most recent of which is *Sexuality Education and New Materialism: Queer Things* (Palgrave, 2018).

Julie Beaulieu is a Lecturer for the Gender, Sexuality, and Women's Studies Program at the University of Pittsburgh. She received her PhD in Literature with a certificate in Gender, Sexuality, and Women's Studies from the University of Pittsburgh. Her research and teaching interests include the history of sexuality, LGBTQ studies, eighteenth-century British literature, queer theory, and affect theory. She is currently working on her first book manuscript, entitled, *Obsessive Love: A Queer History*.

Kelsy Burke is an Assistant Professor of Sociology at the University of Nebraska-Lincoln where she researches the relationship between religion and sexuality in contemporary America. Her first book is *Christians under Covers: Evangelicals and Sexual Pleasure on the Internet* (University of California Press, 2016). Her research has also appeared in *Sexualities*, *Sociological Compass*, the *Journal for the Scientific Study of Religion*, and the *Journal for Religion and Popular Culture*.

Courtney Caviness is a PhD candidate in sociology at the University of California, Davis. Her research focus is in areas of gender, sexuality, and work, as primarily viewed through feminist and critical theory lenses. Her current research relies on interviews with current and former LGBTQ military personnel to examine how they experience the increasingly inclusionary US military workplace following the repeal of "Don't Ask Don't Tell" and most recently, the ban on transgender service.

Stuti Das is a PhD student in the Department of Sociology at Boston University. She received her M.Phil. from the Department of Sociology, University of Hyderabad, India in 2019. Her research interests lie in the areas of gender, sexualities, migration, and global health.

Jennifer Ann Drobac is the Samuel R. Rosen Professor of Law at the Indiana University, Robert H. McKinney School of Law. Her recent work includes: *Sexual Exploitation of Teenagers: Adolescent Development, Discrimination, and Consent Law* (University of Chicago Press, 2016) and two forthcoming books, *Sexual Harassment Law: History, Cases, and Practice* 2nd ed., with co-authors Carrie N. Baker and Rigel C. Oliveri (Carolina Academic Press, 2020) and *The Myth of Consent* (Cambridge University Press, anticipated 2021). She anticipates the completion of *Rule10b-5 Financial Reporting of Sexual Harassment: The Empirical Evidence for A New Approach* (with Dr. Mark Russell) – an article on the corporate disclosure of the costs of sexual harassment.

Donna J. Drucker is Senior Advisor, English as the Language of Instruction at Technische Universität Darmstadt, Germany. She is the author of *The Classification of Sex: Alfred Kinsey and the Organization of Knowledge* (Pittsburgh, 2014), *The Machines of Sex Research: Technology and the Politics of Identity, 1945–1985* (Springer, 2014), and *Contraception: A Concise History* (MIT, forthcoming 2020). Her next monograph project is a history of barrier contraceptives for women. She thanks the 2017 Berliner Colloquium zur Geschichte der Sexualität for their feedback on an earlier version of the chapter in this volume.

Elya M. Durisin holds a PhD in Political Science from York University, Canada. Her research focused on sexualized nationalism in narratives of sex trafficking in government discourse. She has been involved in the sex worker rights movement locally and internationally, and she is a coeditor, with Emily van der Meulen and Chris Bruckert, of *Red Light Labour: Sex Work Regulation, Agency, and Resistance* (UBC Press, 2018).

Michele Eggers-Barison is an Assistant Professor at Chico State University. Her work focuses on addressing global reproductive inequities and the interrelated issues of environmental and economic exploitation, poverty, and repression, linking broader constructs of violence to lived experience. She is currently working on a book manuscript based on her dissertation, *Embodying Inequality: The Criminalization of Women for Abortion in Chile*. She is a documentary filmmaker, producing multiple shorts on gender-based violence and environmental and human rights abuses, the producer of the Eugene Environmental Film Festival, and activist on these issues.

NOTES ON CONTRIBUTORS

Apoorva Ghosh is a PhD candidate in Sociology at the University of California, Irvine. His research is located at the intersection of sociology of sexualities, family, social movements, globalization, and organizations. He has authored papers in these areas for *Gender, Work & Organizations, Indian Journal of Industrial Relations, Management and Labour Studies, Sexualities, Sociology Compass*, and *South Asian Journal of Management*. Ghosh has held fellowships from the US Department of State (Fulbright 2012–2013), University of Maastricht, the Netherlands (METEOR Visiting Doctoral Student 2010), XLRI- Xavier School of Management, India (Fellow Program in Management 2009–2013), and the University of California, Irvine (Social Science Merit Fellowship 2015–2021). In addition to doing research, Ghosh teaches upper division undergraduate sociology courses on gender and globalization.

Patti Giuffre is a Professor of Sociology at Texas State University. She conducts research on gender, sexuality, inequality, and work. She has co-authored articles on sexual harassment, gender inequality in workplaces, homophobia in workplaces, "gay-friendly" workplaces, qualitative methods, globalization, women's workplace solidarity, and gender inequality in the culinary industry in *Gender & Society, Gender Issues, Sociology Compass, Research in the Sociology of Work, Sexuality Research & Social Policy, Sociology Compass, Sociological Spectrum*, and *Teaching Sociology*. Her recent book, with Deborah A. Harris, *Taking the Heat: Women Chefs and Gender Inequality in the Professional Kitchen* (2015; Rutgers University Press) examines why the occupation of chef—a job based on the feminized skill of cooking—is male-dominated and considered a masculine occupation.

Diane Grossman received her PhD in Philosophy from New York University, where she was an Ida Parker Bowne Scholar. She is Professor of Women's and Gender Studies and Philosophy at Simmons University, Chair of the Philosophy Department, and Director of the Honors Program. Dr. Grossman has served Simmons as Chair of both departments, as Director of Academic Advising, and as Associate Dean and Dean of the College of Arts and Sciences. She is the author of *Existentialism and the Philosophical Tradition, Looking at Gay and Lesbian Life*, and numerous articles and essays on ethics, feminist theory, and cultural studies. In addition, she is part of a cross-disciplinary research team that studies girls' and women's perceived confidence; the team has published several articles on that subject.

Crystal M. Hayes, MSW, is a PhD candidate at the University of Connecticut School of Social Work. Her research focuses on reproductive justice issues for incarcerated women. Crystal's work promotes the need for gender-responsive, healing-centered, comprehensive reproductive healthcare for incarcerated women. She works closely with human rights groups working to end reproductive oppression globally. Crystal is the recipient of numerous awards and fellowships as well as the author of numerous publications and blogs on related topics.

Sharon Hayes is an Adjunct in the School of Criminology and Criminal Justice at Griffith University, Brisbane. She has been researching in the areas of criminal justice, criminology, and ethics for the past thirty years and has developed a focused research profile in the areas of sexuality/gender studies, specifically sex and crime, domestic violence and violence against women. Recent books include *Romantic Terrorism: An Auto-ethnography of Domestic Violence Victimization and Survival* (Palgrave 2015), and *Sex Love and Abuse: Discourses on Domestic Violence and Sexual Assault* (Palgrave 2014). Sharon is also Co-Curator of the Routledge Critical Studies in Crime, Diversity and Criminal Justice books series.

Carol Johnson is an Emerita Professor in the Department of Politics and International Studies at the University of Adelaide. She has written extensively on issues of sexuality, including specifically on issues of comparative sexual citizenship. She is a co-editor, with Manon Tremblay and David Paternotte of *The Lesbian and Gay Movement and the State: Comparative Insights into a Transformed Relationship* (Ashgate, Farnham, 2011). Her most recent book on *Social Democracy and the Crisis of Equality: Australian Social Democracy in a Changing World*, (Springer 2019), also contains a key chapter on international social democracy and sexual equality.

Kamala Kempadoo is Professor of Social Science at York University, Toronto, Canada. She publishes and speaks widely on migrant and sex worker's rights, and anti-trafficking discourses from antiracist and transnational feminist perspectives. One of her most influential books, co-edited with Jo Doezema. is *Global Sex Workers: Rights, Resistance and Redefinition*. She received the 2017 "Distinguished Scientific Award" from the Society from the Scientific Study of Sexuality for her research on sex work.

Cristina Khan is Lecturer in the Women's, Gender, and Sexuality Studies Department at SUNY Stony Brook. She earned her PhD from the Department of Sociology at the University of Connecticut. Her specializations include race and ethnicity, embodiment, sexualities, and qualitative research methods. Her dissertation, "Undoing Borders: A Feminist Exploration of Erotic Performance by Lesbian Women of Color," draws on two years of ethnographic fieldwork and 40 in-depth interviews with a collective of lesbian exotic dancers, uncovering how race and sexuality, together, shape women's potential to enact agency over the conditions of their participation in exotic dance. She is coauthor of *Race and Sexuality* (Polity Press, 2018).

Agnieszka Kościańska is an Associate Professor at the Department of Ethnology and Cultural Anthropology, University of Warsaw. She is the author and (co)editor of several volumes on gender, sexuality, and sexology, including the monographs, *Gender, Pleasure, and Violence: The Construction of Expert Knowledge of Sexuality in Poland* (forthcoming with Indiana University Press; Polish version: University of Warsaw Press, 2014) and *To See a Moose: The History of Polish Sex Education from the First Lesson to the Internet* (forthcoming with Berghahn Books; Polish version: Czarne, 2017), and the special issue of *Sexualities*, "The Science of Sex in a Space of Uncertainty: Naturalizing and Modernizing Europe's East, Past and Present" (no. 1–2, 2016, coedited with Hadley Renkin).

Mathew Kuefler is professor of history at San Diego State University. He is the author of *The History of Sexuality Sourcebook* (Toronto, 2007) and multiple books and articles on gender and sexuality in late Roman antiquity and the European Middle Ages on topics ranging from homoeroticism and castration to marriage regulations and childhood. From 2004 to 2014 he was editor of the *Journal of the History of*

Sexuality. His current research is on gender, sexuality, and holiness in the Christian tradition. Together with Merry Wiesner-Hanks he is now also editing a four-volume *Cambridge World History of Sexualities*.

Emily A. Leskinen, PhD, MSW, is an Assistant Professor of Social Science and she is affiliated with the Women's, Gender, and Sexuality Studies program in the School of Social Science and Human Services at Ramapo College of New Jersey. Her research takes an interdisciplinary approach to examining social inequalities and injustices, primarily from the target's perspective. Using an intersectional framework, she has three lines of research related to these core interests: (i) sex-based harassment, (ii) stereotyping and prejudice, and (iii) social attitudes and health behaviors.

Janelle Leyva holds a BA in Psychology from Ramapo College of New Jersey, with minors in Women's and Gender Studies and Substance Abuse. She investigates perceptions of criminal defendants, law enforcement, and victims, and she conducts social psychological research on emotion perception.

Kate Luxion is a genderqueer/nonbinary researcher focusing on LGBTQ+ inclusive reproduction and parenting. Presently, they are pursuing a PhD in Social Science at University College London, teaching college courses, and serving as Executive Director of Journal of Reproductive Justice. Their PhD research centers on the interplay of vulnerability and resilience, while also assessing how each factor may influence parent and infant health outcomes. As Executive Director, Luxion helps the organization provide inclusive resources and education for LGBTQ+ families and the providers who serve them. Mx. Luxion can also be found volunteering for like-minded organizations and working on art with their partner and kiddo.

Vera Mackie is Senior Professor of Asian and International Studies in the Faculty of Law, Humanities and the Arts at the University of Wollongong. She is coauthor, with Sharon Crozier-De Rosa, of *Remembering Women's Activism* (Routledge, 2019), coeditor, with Mark McLelland, of the *Routledge Handbook of Sexuality Studies in East Asia* (Routledge, 2015), and coeditor, with Nicola J. Marks and Sarah Ferber, of The Reproductive Industry: Intimate Experiences and Global Processes (Lexington Books, 2019).

Julia Meszaros is an Assistant Professor at Texas A&M University Commerce. Her research interrogates the international dating and marriage industry, commonly known as the "mail order bride" industry, and the role of commodified intimacies in the global economy. Her work on this topic is published at *Gender, Place and Culture and Women's Studies Quarterly*. Please visit her website juliameszaros.com.

Nancy A. Naples is Board of Trustees Distinguished Professor of Sociology and Women's, Gender, and Sexuality Studies. Her publications includes seven books and over 50 book chapters and journal articles in a wide array of interdisciplinary and sociological journals. She is series editor for *Praxis: Theory in Action* published by SUNY Press and Editor-in-Chief of the five-volume Wiley Blackwell *Encyclopedia of Gender and Sexuality Studies*.

Vrushali Patil is Associate Professor of Sociology at Florida International University. She writes and teaches on the interconnections among race, gender, and sexuality, in historical and transnational perspective. She is currently working on a book entitled *Empire and the Sociologies of Sex, Gender and Sexuality: From Societies to Webbed Connectivities*. Her previous book is *Negotiating Decolonization in the United Nations: Politics of Space, Identity and International Community* (Routledge, 2008).

Leigh Potvin is an Assistant Professor at Cape Breton University in Sydney, Nova Scotia (Canada). Her research focuses on straight allyship, queer pedagogies, fat activism, and food sovereignty/justice.

Jyoti Puri is Hazel Dick Leonard Chair and Professor of Sociology at Simmons University. She writes and researches at the crossroads of sociology, sexuality/queer studies, and postcolonial feminist theory. Her recent book, *Sexual States: Governance and the Struggle against the Antisodomy Law in India's Present* (Duke University Press, 2016), won the outstanding book award given by the Sexualities Section of the American Sociological Association. Her previous books include *Woman, Body, Desire in Post-Colonial India* (Routledge, 1999) and *Encountering Nationalism*, (Blackwell, 2004). She is working on a project on death and migration.

J. Michael Ryan, PhD, is an Assistant Professor of Sociology at Nazarbayev University in Kazakhstan. Dr. Ryan was previously a researcher for the TRANSRIGHTS Project at The University of Lisbon (Portugal) and has taught courses at The American University in Cairo (Egypt), Facultad Latinoamericana de Ciencias Sociales (FLACSO) (Ecuador), and the University of Maryland. Before returning to academia, Dr. Ryan worked as a research methodologist at the National Center for Health Statistics in Washington, DC. He is the editor of multiple volumes, including *Trans Lives in a Global(-izing) World: Rights, Identities, and Politics* (Routledge, 2020), and *Core Concepts in Sociology* (Wiley, 2018). Dr. Ryan also served as an advisory editor on *The Wiley Blackwell Encyclopedia of Gender and Sexuality Studies*.

Helis Sikk is a Visiting Assistant Professor in Women's and Gender Studies at the University of South Florida Tampa. Her research takes a feral multidisciplinary approach in exploring the relationships between queerness, affect, the built environment, communities, media, and visual cultures. She co-edited a collection of essays, *The Legacies of Matthew Shepard* (Routledge 2019) and is currently working on her monograph, *Mainstreaming Violence: Affect, Activism, and Queer Politics of Representation*.

Leah R. Warner, PhD, is an Associate Professor of Psychology and she is affiliated with the Women's, Gender, and Sexuality Studies program in the School of Social Science and Human Services at Ramapo College of New Jersey. Her research explores how emotion perception processes reflect, produce, and reproduce status and power structures, as well as interdisciplinary scholarship on integrating intersectionality theory into psychological research.

Brandi Woodell is an Assistant Professor of Sociology and Criminal Justice at Old Dominion University. Her research examines the disparities between sexual minorities and heterosexuals within the social contexts of religion, family, and health. Her recent work on sexual minority health disparities examines how gender and rurality shape the experiences of community resources and social support.

Acknowledgments

I am grateful to all the authors, reviewers, and editors who have made this ambitious interdisciplinary volume possible. The authors bring a wide range of expertise from different academic training and activist backgrounds to their chapters with a commitment to sharing their visions and knowledge of the diverse topics and themes that shape the *Companion* on *Sexuality Studies*. Many of my colleagues in Women's, Gender and Sexuality Studies at the University of Connecticut and other academic sites around the world have generously supported the project in the important role of anonymous reviewers, often providing a quick turnaround to facilitate the demanding production deadlines. I am grateful for their extremely insightful reviews and their understanding of the international and interdisciplinary goals of the *Companion*. Special thanks to Shweta M. Adur, Françoise Dussart, Michele Eggers-Barison, Vrshali Patil, and Barbara Sutton for sharing their expertise on various chapters. J. Michael Ryan also graciously offered his editorial and academic knowledge whenever asked and without hesitation. I would also like to thank the Wiley Blackwell editorial and production team – Merryl Le Roux, Richard Samson, Elisha Benjamin, and Justin Vaughan – for their commitment and dedication to this project. Thanks also go to copy-editor Katherine Carr. My appreciation to M.J. Taylor who assisted at the very early and crucial stage of identification and outreach to authors and organization of manuscripts. Managing Editor Cristina Khan was an extremely valuable collaborator who has assisted in reviewing and editing all the chapters as well as co-authoring a chapter in this volume to advance the coverage of important topics in the *Companion*. Cristina signed on as Managing Editor at the early stages, not expecting, I suspect, all that this would entail. She was able to see it through to completion even as she started a new position in Women's, Gender and Sexuality Studies at Stoney Brook University in New York. I could not have done this massive editorial project without her.

Part I
Introduction

1

The Diversity and Academic Institutionalization of Sexuality Studies

NANCY A. NAPLES

The Companion to Sexuality Studies captures the history and the institutional regulatory processes that socially construct sex and sexuality over different periods of time and in different social and national contexts. It attends to the diverse knowledges produced by sexuality researchers since the late nineteenth century through the present. This chapter also offers a brief overview of the history and academic institutionalization of sexuality studies. The second half of the chapter provides an introduction to the remaining 24 chapters that constitute this volume to demonstrate both the richness and diversity of fields and institutional formation in the areas of science, health, psychology, culture, social and economic institutions, policy, law, and social justice movements.

History of Sexuality Studies

While the field of Sexuality Studies spans over a century and a half, sexuality has been a central concern for all institutions from religion to politics and science long before that time. In writing this history, the work of sexologists became the dominant approach to sexuality research from the mid-1880s. Sexology viewed sex and sexuality through methods informed by a strong attachment to scientific principles that were also infused with assumptions of heterosexuality and, binary gender difference as the norm.

Sociobiology influenced much of early Sexuality Studies and continues to influence many scientists interested in explaining differences in genders, sexual identities, and sexual practices (Wilson 1975; Kessler 1990). Evolutionary psychologists and neurologists continue to explore evolutionary processes in contemporary gender and sexuality research. For example, in a 1995 article on "Brain Research, Gender and Sexual Orientation," authors Dick Swaab, Louis Gooren and Michel Hofman of the

Netherlands Institute for Brain Research in Amsterdam wrote that "recent brain research revealed structural differences in the hypothalamous in relation to biological sex and sexual orientation" (p. 283). Writing over a decade later, Fernano Saravi (2008) notes that:

> Activity, connectivity and structure of certain regions [of the brain] have been repeatedly shown to considerably differ between gay and straight people (insert a snarky joke about bisexual erasure) as well as cis- and transgenders. But, as with so many things in neuroscience, it is yet not 100% clear in which way the connection goes -- did these neural differences predetermine who you like or did your experiences and behaviour gradually shape these structures the way they are now? Still, a lot of scientists think these differences have been there from the very beginning, influenced by hormonal or genetic factors.

Andrea Ganna et al. (2019) found that "both biology and one's environment may be a factor that influences sexuality" and that "a range of experiences in a person's development as well as social and cultural factors that all could affect behavior" (Ennis 2019, n.p.). Their findings indicate the impossibility of disentangling the biological and environmental factors in shaping an individual's sexuality (see also Davis 2015).

Research on sexualities was also conducted by scientists and psychologists who adapted findings from animal studies of gender and sexuality. In 1938, Zoology professor Alfred C. Kinsey was approached to teach the first class on human sexuality at Indiana University. The class was designed to cover the topics of sexuality, contraception, and reproduction. Rebecca Clay (2015) reports that Kinsey found a lack of "scientific literature on human sexual behavior" and that the few research studies he found were primarily "based on small numbers of patients or were judgmental in tone" (n.p.). As a consequence, he launched a long and notable career interviewing diverse people about their sex lives. He and his colleagues collected close to 18,000 sexual histories that revealed the complicated ways people experience and express their sexuality. Kinsey is best known for developing a scale that places heterosexuality and homosexuality on a six-point continuum to reflect his research findings that many people's desires and behaviors cannot be categorized as either heterosexual or homosexual (Kinsey, Pomeroy, and Martin. 1948 [1998]). In fact, he found that while some people exhibit traits or identities that can be considered exclusively one or the other, others express mixes of both homosexuality and heterosexuality. Those who have an equal mix of both were placed at the center of the scale.

In the late 1950s and 1960s, US sex researchers William Masters and Virginia Johnson (1966) faced a backlash from the medical profession on their research into sexual response using techniques including videotaping couples' sexual encounters and individuals masturbating. Their work subsequently inspired the expansion of sexuality research that continues to this day through the Institute of Sex Research established at Indiana University and renamed the Kinsey Institute in 1981.

Beginning in the 1970s, gay and lesbian social movement activists and their allies inside and outside of the academy pushed for incorporation of more critical and interdisciplinary analyses to challenge longstanding scientific, psychological, and criminological approaches which had pathologized sexual desire, expression and behaviors which did not adhere to heterosexuality. Early courses often included co-teaching by faculty from different disciplines to offer broad understanding of sexual diversity and sexual practices over time and place. While the courses on Human Sexuality that were offered in universities before that time were more likely to be taught by scientists and psychologists, academic faculty in Sociology, Anthropology, and History brought attention to the powerful role of socialization, culture, and historical context for producing and reproducing sexual norms and behaviors (Leacock 1981; Lerner 1977; Rossi 1973). Faculty trained in the Humanities fostered recognition of the role of language and discourse for constructing what counts as legitimate sexual expression and whose experiences and artistic expressions have been devalued or ignored in academic curricula and research (Cixous and Sellers 1994; Nochlin 1971).

Michel Foucault's (1978) now classic work on the *History of Sexuality* identified hidden regulatory processes that included repression of sexuality. Foucault notes how Sigmund Freud made some progress in opening up sexuality as a fundamental site for understanding identify formation and psychopathology but accomplished this by "normalizing the functions of psychoanalysis" (p. 5) as the site for analysis of sexual "perversions" (p. 42).

By the late 1970s, the women's movement organized and organized against gender inequality in marriage and other social and economic institutions, and the gay and lesbian movement was effectively pushing against the presumption of heteronormativity and the pathologizing of so-called nonnormative sexualities in academic research and social policy. Furthermore, as feminist anthropologist Gayle Rubin explains,

> as soon as you get away from the presumptions of heterosexuality, or a simple hetero-homo opposition, differences in sexual conduct are not very intelligible in terms of binary models. Even the notion of a continuum is not a good model for sexual variations.
> (Rubin with Butler 1997, 76–77; also see Rubin 1984)

Lesbian feminist scholars also challenged the presumption of heterosexuality and marginalization of lesbian sexuality within the feminist movement (see, for example, Poirot 2009) and paved the way for both the possibility of separate institutional academic formations as well as theorizing complex intersections between sexuality and gender.

One of the many contributions of feminist analysis of gender was recognition of its social construction, rather than the biological essentialist understanding found in the dominant research paradigm. As Mary Crawford (2006) explains:

> Distinguishing sex from gender was a very important step in recognizing that biology is not destiny – that many of the apparent differences between women and men might be societally imposed rather than natural or inevitable.
> (p. 26, quoted in Muehlenhard and Peterson 2011, n.p.)

In the late 1980s, feminists, began to reconsider the distinction between sex and gender. As Chalene Muehlenhard and Zoe Peterson point out in their assessment of the diversity of ways in which psychologists use the terms, sex can be socially constructed as well (see, also, Gatens 1991; Davis 2015; Kessler 1990).

> Individuals are born with a wide distribution of biological indicators of sex (Fausto-Sterling 2000). In many Western societies, surgery and hormones are used to make bodies fit as neatly as possible into two nonoverlapping categories (Fausto-Sterling 2000). Social expectations and taboos continue to create difference in these two categories, such as by encouraging boys and men, but not girls and women, to engage in sports and work that develops their muscles.
>
> (Hubbard 1990)

Gayle Rubin (1984) also complicated the distinction between sex and gender in her influential article, "Thinking Sex: Note for a Radical Theory of the Politics of Sexuality." In an interview with philosopher Judith Butler, Rubin clarifies that, in that essay:

> I never claimed that sexuality and gender were always unconnected, only that they are not identical. Moreover, their relationships are situational, not universal, and must be determined in particular situations.
>
> (Rubin with Butler 1997, p. 104)

Butler (1997) further notes that:

> What separates the putative object of feminism – gender, construed as sex—from the putative object of lesbian and gay studies – sex, construed as sexuality – is a chiasmic confusion in which the constitutive ambiguity of "sex" is denied in order to make arbitrary territorial respectful claims… In this sense, the very formulation of lesbian and gay studies depends upon the evacuation of a sexual discourse from feminism. And what passes as a benign, even respectful, analogy with feminism is the means by which the fields are separated, where that separation requires the desexualization of the feminist project and the appropriation of sexuality as the "proper" object of lesbian/gay studies.
>
> (pp. 8–9)

She subsequently argues that:

> Indeed, according to Rubin's logic, sexuality is no more likely to receive a thorough analysis under the rubric of lesbian and gay studies than it is under that of feminist studies. Not only do central notions like the racialization of sexuality get dropped or domesticated as "instances" of either feminism or lesbian and gay studies, but the notion of sexual minorities, which include sex workers, transexuals, and cross-generational partners, cannot be adequately approached through a framework of lesbian and gay studies.
>
> (p. 13)

Trans terminology has changed over the years so that terms "transgender" and "trans" are more acceptable usage than the "transsexual" that Butler used 20 years ago. Trans activists and scholars raised further awareness of the intersectional investments of gender and sexuality. Although trans scholarship has been influenced by both queer theory and feminism (Weed and Schor 1997), it has pushed these frameworks further in challenging the deep reliance on the gender binary in both theory and practice (see Khan and Kolbe in *The Companion to Women's and Gender Studies* (2020)]). Intersex scholars have also challenged the biological gender essentialism and terminology that continue to shape the medical profession's practices and cultural attitudes (Davis 2015; Kessler 1990; Malatino 2019).

What constitutes the "proper objects" of feminism and queer studies was further fractured by challenges from feminist and queer scholars of color and those from non-Western contexts (Butler 1997, p. 20). African and African American Studies scholar Evelynn Hammonds argued that "white feminists must refigure (white) female sexualities so that they are not theoretically dependent upon an absent yet ever-present pathologized black female sexuality" (1997, p. 141). She also called for black feminist scholars to "reclaim sexuality through the creation of a counternarrative that can reconstitute a present black female subjectivity and that includes an analysis of power relations between white and black women and among different groups of black women" (p.97). Chong-Suk Han (2019) recently applied a queer and critical race analysis to explore "sexual racism" and revealed how Asian and Asian American men's sexuality is made invisible by the dominance of whiteness in the gay male community (see also Han 2015). Transnational scholars have also examined sexuality in international and comparative perspective to further reveal the diversity of sexual identities, norms, behaviors, regulatory practices, and sexual politics (see, for example, Cantú 2009; Hunter 2010; Puri 2016).

Structural analyses of sexuality have also been enriched by engagement with postcolonial theories that demonstrate the power of colonial processes to shape gender and sexual relations which "continue to unfold in the ex-colonies as well as in the heart of the erstwhile empires" as Vrushali Patil and Jyoti Puri consider in Chapter Four of this volume. I now turn to provide an overview of the diverse chapters included in *The Companion to Sexuality Studies* that further elaborate the history, debates, and object of study that form contemporary Sexuality Studies.

Diversity within Sexuality Studies

Part II Theoretical and methodological diversity

Writing in Germany in the late 1880s, early sex researcher Richard von Krafft-Ebing (1894) argued for the significance of sexuality in shaping individual lives and societal beliefs. He also viewed any sexual activity that did not lead to procreation as pathological. As Agnieszka Kościańska notes in Chapter 2, one of the first influential texts that established the field of Sexology, Krafft-Ebing's *Psychopathia Sexualis*, was published in 1866 (see also Drucker in this volume). Sexology reflected and in turn reinforced societal fears already infused in religious institutions into the new institutional formations of medicine and science. Kościańska explains that Michel Foucault (1978) and queer scholars view sexology as "one of the major tools of modern power." While sexologists "often assumed the pathological character of nonnormative sexuality, they started the process of the construction of sexual identities and made sexual activism possible (Oosterhuis 2000)."

Some early researchers like Magnus Hirschfeld (1897) who organized the Scientific Humanitarian Committee that organized against the criminalization of homosexuality and faced intense backlash. In 1929 the International League for Sexual Reform made an attempt to legitimize extramarital birth, provide birth control and necessary information regarding sexual health, prevention and transmission of STIs" (Adur, Chapter 23 in this volume). Furthermore, as Shweta Adur points out, "it even sought to medicalize homosexuality in a bid to protect against criminal prosecutions prevalent at the time." This shift also continued to construct nonheterosexual sexuality as pathological.

In Chapter 3, Mathew Kuefler reviews the historical and cultural shifts in ideology, practices and regulation of sexuality. He notes variations and alternative genders and sexualities across time and space. Kuefler explains the significance for the development of sexuality studies of the new field of social history that focused on "ordinary people of the past" rather than exclusively center major political and economic events and religious and political leaders. Even then, historians of sexuality met with resistance from academic colleagues as the sexuality researchers attempted to legitimize their field in the 1970s. Scholars are still trying to understand the complex relationship between past and present sexual behaviors and identities. He concludes that the "modern, third generation of historians of sexuality, is profoundly interested in how sexuality overlaps with other aspects of the self: gender identity, race [racialized identity] and ethnicity, nationality, social position."

In Chapter 4, Patil and Puri show the power of feminist and queer scholarship for enriching postcolonial analyses of sexualities; but also note the persistence of colonial constructions in queer politics including the uncritical application of assumptions about constructions of sexual identity and sexual norms developed in the Global North toward the Global South (see, also, Boellstorff 2005; McLelland and Mackie 2015; and Johnson and Mackie, Chapter 18 in this volume). The chapter is enriched by the authors' use of diverse case studies derived from multiple national and regional contexts to illustrate their complex analysis.

Similar to feminist theory that developed through insights from women's movement activism, queer theory is a form of praxis informed by the activist projects organized in response to the HIV/AIDS crisis and the rise in antigay violence in the late 1980s. For example, the naming of the activist group Queer Nation was designed to reflect a wide embrace of nonnormative gender and sexual identities. In the academy, it is understood as a theoretical approach that challenge heteronormativity, homonormativity, and gender and sexual binaries. The influence of queer theory resonates throughout *The Companion to Sexuality Studies*. J. Michael Ryan (Chapter 5) discusses the development of queer theory in academia and its engagement with gay and lesbian studies. He shows its intellectual origins in the work of social constructionist and poststructuralist scholars, most notably Eve Kosofsky Sedgwick (1985) Judith Butler (1990), and Teresa de Lauretis (1991). As Ryan explains, queer theorists argue against rigid binaries associated with gender and sexuality and for the significance of "the discursive production of identities." He unpacks the complex intellectual projects associated with queer theory and explains how the latter postmodern approach has opened up queer theory to critiques that it erases "the lived experiences of individual actors who suffer material oppressions ... that exist outside the realm of discourse (Seidman 1996)." Ryan concludes by arguing that while queer theory has "drastically change[d] many a field, ... as an 'independent' entity [it] seems to have largely receded from the spotlight." It continues, however, to contour debates in a variety of other arenas including the debates in critical methodologies that Stuti Das reviews in Chapter 6 (also see Ghaziani and Brim 2019).

Das opens her chapter titled "Queer Methodologies and Social Science" with an introduction to social research methods. She also considers what counts as methodology, and analyzes the impact of queer theory in social science research. She notes that "queer conceptualizations ... in the social sciences [were] prompted by efforts to address and reverse the tremendous hold of positivistic scientific methods over qualitative methodologies." Das observes, quoting Catherine Nash (2010, p. 133), that "queer epistemological and ontological perspectives help focus attention on how social categories of being and lived experience, are constituted within certain historical, cultural and spatialized contexts, including normative ideas about what are deemed to be embodied gendered and sexual practices and behaviours." In this chapter, Das also examines the significance of positionality of the researcher, reflexivity in research practice, and the ethics or research from the point of view of queer methodology.

Queer theory has also contoured how scholars envision and enact pedagogical practice. Like Das, Leigh Potvin (Chapter 7) opens with an articulation of key terms and then emphasizes the importance of acknowledging the positionality of the researcher and the research community for shaping and queering classroom interactions. Queer pedagogical practice includes destabilizing binary constructions of gender and sexuality, creating community, encouraging creativity, recognizing the diversity of identities, and teaching for social change.

Part III Health, science, and psychology

The second section of *The Companion to Sexuality Studies* addresses the important intersecting fields of health, science, and psychology. The first chapter in this section provides an overview of how sexuality has been manipulated within science and technology. In Chapter 8, Donna J. Drucker provides an historical analysis of sexology that adds to Kościańska's discussion in Chapter 2. Drucker details how reproductive technologies also contour family, gender, and sexuality. She pays attention to the ways in which technologies have been used as a tool for research methodologies to study sexuality. These include "electromechanical technologies such as photography, cardiographs, and electroencephalograms"; the "orgone box" developed by Wilhelm Reich ([1942] 1986; and the "dildo-camera" used by Williams Masters and Virginia Johnson (1996). Drucker notes that "queer feminist science studies is just one example of how scholars are reformulating and producing new schools of thought for thinking and acting as sexual beings." She concludes that: "issues of power, agency, and subjectivity, not to mention the intersectionality of racial, gender, and class identities, will continue to shed light on the deep embeddedness of sciences and technologies in everyday sexual life."

In Chapter 9, Leah R. Warner, Emily A. Leskinen, and Janelle Leyva shift attention from science and technology, broadly defined, to the institutional practices that contribute to social psychological processes which influence individual understandings and expressions of identity and erotic expression. They outline "the process of acquiring knowledge, norms, attitudes, cultural symbols, codes of conduct, and value relative to sex and sexuality." They describe three different approaches adopted by feminist psychologists to explain the socialization of sexuality in everyday life: symbolic interactionism, scripting theory, and intersectionality. Warner et al. highlight the role of parents, friends, and peers as well as social institutions, especially the educational system, the media, religion and government, in constructing and reinforcing heteronormative expressions of sex and sexuality.

Technological innovations have effectively reshaped understandings and expressions of family by providing greater access to reproduction for gay and lesbian families. In Chapter 10, "LGBTQ Reproduction and Parenting," Kate Luxion provides a global analysis of this topic that includes analyses of adoption, in vitro fertilization, and surrogacy. Although research indicates that LGBTQ+ families often face discrimination and stigmatization, Luxion reports that the well-being of children who grow up in LGBT homes is equal if not better than children of heterosexual parents (see also, Mackie, Marks, and Ferber 2019).

Part IV Sexuality and institutions

The next section of *The Companion to Sexuality Studies* focuses on the institutions of religion, education and the economy to uncover the ways that these sites impact constructions of and policies towards sexuality. In Chapter 11, Kelsy Burke and Brandi Woodell examine how "practices, beliefs, and institutions influence cultural ideas about sex and sexuality across time and place." Since religious ideology is a powerful framework through which sex and sexuality are constructed and regulated, many progressive movement must challenge these prescriptions to effect social change.

The institution of education also forms a powerful context for the construction and socialization of sex and sexuality. In Chapter 12, Louisa Allen demonstrates the important role of sexual education in sexuality socialization. Allen analyzes sexuality education over the last 10 years in different locales to consider the conceptual and programmatic debates in the field. She explores different perspectives on sexuality education from the vantage point of students, teachers, and parents to illustrate the tensions in understanding how and what should be taught. One significant challenge is how to ensure that young people put the knowledge they receive into practice. Parents and community members often have strong opinions concerning at what age student should be introduced to this information and what should be highlighted or left out. The conservative emphasis on abstinence-only approaches, for example, has gained hold in many communities across the US.

The last two chapters in this section foreground the economy and analyze how sexuality shapes experiences and opportunities in the workplace and the ways in which intimate labor is commodified (see, for example, Boris and Parreñas 2010). In Chapter 13, Patti Giuffre and Courtney Caviness provide an overview of crosscultural analyses of law and social policies designed to address employment discrimination based on sexual orientation. They also examine how the presumption of heterosexuality infuses workplace cultures that, in turn, provide informal constraints on those who do not fit into the heterosexual and I should add, monogamous cultural norm. They also document how much has changed in many workplaces in this regard and note that "the move toward greater workplace inclusion of historically marginalized workers presents opportunities to shape new institutional and interactional workplace arrangements." Giuffre and Caviness conclude by emphasizing the need for future research to take into account the intersection of racialized position, gender, and sexuality in understanding workers' experiences of workplace discrimination.

In the closing chapter of this section, Julia Meszaros considers the ways in which intimate labor, such as domestic labor, reproductive labor, sexual or erotic labor, and cross-border marriage have become increasingly commodified through processes of neoliberal globalization. She applies a transnational feminist analysis "that connects intimate, micro processes of relationships to the larger transnational processes of migration, globalization, and economic development." Meszaros highlights women's agency in this context and contests approaches "that consider various forms of intimate labor examples of involuntary labor trafficking, particularly domestic labor, sexual labor, and marriage migration." Furthermore, she concludes, "While the state [broadly defined] presents its antitrafficking policies as a means of protecting vulnerable populations, these policies often place women and migrants in more vulnerable positions, as their dependence upon third-party actors increases."

Part V Popular culture

The next section includes three chapters on another important arena in which sexuality is constructed and reproduced. In Chapter 15, Diane Grossman demonstrates the powerful role of popular culture in shaping ideologies and practices of sex and sexuality. She contrasts the critics of media representation of sex and sexuality who offer objectifying and regressive depictions of LGBT subjects with queer theorists' arguments that texts and films involve multivocal and oppositional interpretations, depending on the reader's social location. In Chapter 16, Julie Beaulieu highlights the role of LGBT literature in providing alternative readings that decenter heteronormative representations in mainstream texts. She begins by outlining different definitions of LGBT. She then considers LGBT literature in comparative context and introduces key scholars in "Western formations" of LGBT literature and queer literary studies. Beaulieu concludes by noting the increasing mainstreaming of LGBT literature.

In Chapter 17, Helis Sikk argues for the significance of queer comics for activism in the US and Japan. Queer comics began as an underground enterprise that moved into visibility and wide acceptance. The context for the development of queer comics differed between the US and Japan. In Japan, Sikk explains, queer comics and graphic novels (manga) were born in the underground press during the 1950s and were initially dominated by a "male-focused hypermasculine culture." In contrast, women led the way in "expanding the topics beyond the sexuality explicit" in the US context. In addition to their role as artistic forms of expression, Sikk points out the changing ways that comics engage with politics over time. In the 1980s politics was addressed through "direct political commentary." According to Sikk, contemporary comics take up politics more "implicitly through affective personal narratives."

Part VI Citizenship, policy, and law

The next section includes five chapters, beginning with Chapter 18 by Carol Johnson and Vera Mackie, titled "Sexual Citizenship in Comparative Perspective," which traces the origin and the diverse meanings of the term. They also discuss the contestations over the centering of the state and the failure to incorporate attention to "the economy, society and the cultural rights of minority sexual groups." Johnson and Mackie note that the concept was first defined in 1993 by David Evans and expanded from its early application to same-sex rights to a broader understanding of the different ways in which we are all sexual citizens. As Johnson and Mackie point out, however, quoting David Bell and Jon Binnie (2000, p. 142), we are all sexual citizens, but "we are not all '*equal* sexual citizens.'"

In Chapter 19, Shweta Adur examines the ways in which immigration policy reinforces as well as reenvisions conceptualizations of sexual citizenship. She takes an historical and intersectional feminist perspective that foregrounds the Global South and reveals Western hegemony in the policies, practices, and assumptions about sexuality found in diverse colonial and postcolonial countries. In doing so, she analyzes "the temporal continuity between the colonial era and contemporary era" and points out "that many of the 'changes' introduced during the colonial period continue to resonate through the contemporary era of globalization."

Chapter 20 by Sharon Hayes and Cristina Khan offers an overview of how sex and sexuality are regulated through the criminal justice system. The authors take an intersectional approach to explicate how differences based on gender, racialized positions, and class contour criminal law and justice. Hayes and Khan also demonstrate how the wider political, moral, and religious context influence "the governance of sex and sexuality across time."

In Chapter 21, Jennifer Ann Drobac examines "Sexual Harassment Policy in the US and Comparative Perspective." Drobac begins by defining what is considered sex-based harassment and provides an overview of its prevalence. She discusses US employment law and compares the US and Israel. She notes that recent efforts to address the problem include extralegal approaches of education and training. Drobac concludes with a call for legal reforms to broaden the "narrow definitions of sex-based harassment" that are currently shaping traditional legal approaches.

In the closing chapter of this section (Chapter 22), Kamala Kempadoo and Elya M. Durisin explore one of the most controversial topics in feminist scholarship, "Sex Work and Sex Trafficking." Kempadoo and Durisin outline the debates and explain the different understandings of who can make claim to rights and protections, the role of criminalization, and how to conceptualize economic and social justice. The tensions between the sexual libertarian and feminist materialist approach to sex work and the radical feminist view of such work as prostitution situate young people under 18 in a particularly vulnerable position in the context of criminalization. However, instead of an approach that emphasizes law enforcement and punishment, especially as it is applied to young people, they argue for a "more nuanced, youth-centered" approach to "research and theorizing that addresses difficult matters surrounding young people and sex, as that intersects with persistent (neo)colonialisms, economic survival, violence, desire, and subjectivity."

Part VII Human rights and social justice movements

The final section comprises three chapters on the political claims-making and activism for expansion of sexual rights in a global context. In Chapter 23, Shweta Adur's second contribution to this volume, she provides an historical overview of the promotion of sexual rights in United Nations platforms. She concludes that "definitional inconsistencies, problems with implementation, Western hegemony, pushback in the name of tradition and culture, and the rise of extremist movements continue to hold it [sexual rights legislation] hostage." The final two chapters address two important arenas for the expansion of sexual rights: workplace equality and reproductive justice.

In Chapter 24, Apoorva Ghosh situates his analysis of "The Global LGBT Workplace Equality Movement" in a global and cross-national context and points out the importance of developing organizing strategies that are responsive to the local political, cultural, and economic context. In the closing chapter to *The Companion to Sexuality Studies*, Michele Eggers-Barison and Crystal M. Hayes offer a comparison of activism for reproductive justice in the US and Chile. They emphasize that reproductive justice as a political framework developed in the context of activism by and for black women and girls and other marginalized women. Contemporary struggles include ensuring that reproductive justice struggles continue to:

> empower them [Black women] and other Women of Color who live under the constant threat of violence and the daily violation to their human rights. In this new era of reproductive politics, we also need to reaffirm our commitment to poor women, undocumented women, and immigrant women, indigenous women, and trans-women, and other gender nonbinary people who are constantly mis-gendered and often the victims of violence at a higher rate than all other women.

Like many of the authors in *The Companion to Sexuality Studies*, Barison and Hayes adopt transnational and intersectional lenses in their analysis to enhance "understanding of the multiple systems of inequity (social construction of laws, policies, cultural attitudes, poverty, discriminatory practices, violent harms against women) that impact women helps to be able to deconstruct inequity in order to change it."

At the time of this writing, gender, sexual and reproductive rights are under attack in some countries while, in others, there have been significant legal advances. For example, in the US nine states passed bills to limit access to abortion, six of whom passed the "so-called heartbeat bills that effectively prohibit abortions after six to eight weeks of pregnancy, when doctors can usually start detecting a fetal heartbeat" (Lai 2019, n.p.). Paradoxically, in countries where one might not expect liberalization due to, for example, the major role of conservative religions, abortion rights and other legal protections have been achieved. Ireland has had "one of the most restrictive abortion laws in Europe, codified in a 1983 constitutional amendment that effectively banned the practice" (Vogelstein and Turkington, 2019, n. p.). In 2018, however, "the Irish Parliament legalized pregnancy termination before twelve weeks, as well as in cases in which the health of the mother is at stake" (ibid).

The visibility of the problem of sexual harassment and sexual abuse has been enhanced by the #MeToo movement that originated in the US and expanded quickly to become a worldwide mobilization. It has also given rise to a backlash that has taken a number of forms, among which is the meme "#HimToo" that became "a reactionary response to the #MeToo movement, propagated by those who maintain that false accusations of rape against men are exceptionally common and a threat to men everywhere" (*Guardian* 2018, n. p.) and "was cheered by many in [US President Donald] Trump's base; and won support from like-minded lawmakers" (Asimov 2018, n.p.).

In his article on "The Global Backlash Against Gay Rights: How Homophobia Became a Political Tool," Omar Encarnación (2017) analyzes the antigay rights backlash that is evident "in Western Europe and the Americas, home to the world's most democratically advanced states and the largest and most sophisticated gay rights movements" (n.p.). He notes, "across Africa, the Middle East, and much of the post-Communist world, the parts of the globe where democracy, civil society, and human rights are either in short supply or struggling, ... the gay backlash involves passing legislation that criminalizes or re-criminalizes homosexuality and that bans the promotion of homosexuality (n.p.; see, also, Altman and Symons 2016).

Queer postcolonial scholars challenge the presumption that all countries in the Global South consistently lag behind those in the Global North in granting lesbian, gay, and transgender rights (Hawley 2001; Ruvalcaba 2016). For example, gay rights movements continue to achieve important successes in Latin America despite the long tradition of Catholicism and machismo (Encarnación 2016, p. 75). Brazil's Psychology Federal Council banned reparative therapy designed to convert gay men and lesbians to heterosexuality in 1999 (p. 153; Movement Advancement Project 2019). Encarnación notes that same sex marriage was recognized in Argentina in 2010, earlier than many countries in the Global North including France, Britain, and the US. Latin American countries are also in the forefront of expanding laws to support rights for transgender people (p. 35). Encarnación explains that the achievement of gay rights successes in Latin American is partially a result of the inspired ways that gay rights activists crafted campaigns that drew on external gay politics and strategies and events that are grounded in regional and local politics (p. 189). Such analyses call for more complex exploration and understanding of the diverse ways that gender, reproductive, and sexual rights are expanded or resisted in different locales and political contexts.

Conclusion

Many of the first interdisciplinary courses in sexuality in the US were offered by faculty associated with Women's and Gender Studies [WGS]. With the expansion of the interdisciplinary critical and queer literature on sexuality came the push for the institutionalization of sexuality studies as an academic unit separate from WGS. Many WGS faculty, however, saw their work as speaking to both the fields of women's and gender studies and sexuality studies, or understood sexuality studies as part of a larger effort to incorporate and institutionalize intersectionality across the curriculum and strongly advocated for a reconceptualization of their mission and title to incorporate sexuality studies. In other cases, the decision to remain within WGS was more strategic or fiscal than conceptual and theoretical in that insufficient institutional support and financial resources were made available to support two separate units. Another model is offered by The Ohio State University [OSU] that institutionalized a Department of Women's, Gender and Sexuality Studies that offers a Master of Arts and a PhD, but also offers sexuality studies as a separate major and graduate concentration. Their undergraduate Sexuality Studies major

> explores the historical, political, biological, cultural, sociological, educational, legal, health, aesthetic, and psychological contexts of human sexuality. The Sexuality Studies program at OSU pays particular attention to processes and practices of normalization in different cultures and times through which certain sexual behaviors, expressions, or identities are esteemed and others devalued. It also investigates the ways in which sexuality is shaped by other social differences such as race, gender, class, dis/ability, religion, nationality, and ethnicity.
>
> (The Ohio State University 2019)

In keeping with the diversity in the institutional investments, histories, scholarship, and activism in the area of sexuality studies, this volume offers the reader a window into different aspects of this exciting interdisciplinary field. Given that new scholarship, policies, and artistic expressions are developed on a daily basis, it is fully impossible to capture the ongoing research findings, literatures, policy changes, cultural innovations, and activist achievements that expand daily. We also recognize that there are many other rich and varied perspectives, experiences, and institutional contexts especially in the Global South that are shaping constructions of sexuality, sexual citizenship, and cultural expressions which remain unexamined in this text. We do hope that the information, and analyses offered here encourage readers to delve deeper into questions unanswered and topics unexamined as well as build on the insights offered in *The Companion*.

References

Altman, Dennis and Jonathan Symons. 2016. *Queer Wars: The New Global Polarization over Gay Rights*. Malden, MA: Polity Press.

Asimov, Nanette. 2018. "#MeToo Movement Spurs #HimToo Backlash: 'People don't want to believe.'" San Francisco Chronicle, October 13. Available at: https://www.sfchronicle.com/nation/article/MeToo-movement-spurs-HimToo-backlash-People-13304270.php

Bell, David and Jon Binnie. 2000. *The Sexual Citizen: Queer Politics and Beyond*. Cambridge: Polity Press.

Boellstorff, Tom. 2005. *The Gay Archipelago: Sexuality and Nation in Indonesia*. Princeton, NJ: Princeton University Press.

Boris, Eileen and Rachel Parreñas, eds. 2010. *Intimate Labor: Cultures, Technologies, and Politics of Care*. Stanford, CA: Stanford University Press.

Butler, Judith. 1990. *Gender Trouble: Feminism and the Subversion of Identity*. New York, NY: Routledge.

Butler, Judith, 1997. "Against Proper Objects." In *Feminism Meets Queer Theory*, edited by Elizabeth Weed and Naomi Schor, 1–30. Bloomington, IN: Indiana University Press.

Cantú, Lionel. 2009. "The Sexuality of migration: Border crossings and Mexican immigrant men" edited by Nancy A. Naples and Salvador Vidal-Ortiz. New York: New York University Press.

Cixous, Hélène. and S. Sellers. 1994. *The Hélène Cixous Reader*. New York, NY: Routledge.

Clay, Rebecca A. 2015. "Sex Research at the Kinsey Institute: Psychologists Have Long Played a Major Role at the Kinsey Institute. Here's What They Are Exploring Now." *Monitor* 46(9): 49. Available at: https://www.apa.org/monitor/2015/10/research-kinsey.

Davis, Georgiann. 2015. *Contesting Intersex: The Dubious Diagnosis*. NY, NY: New York University Press.

de Lauretis, Teresa. 1991. "Queer Theory: Lesbian and Gay Sexualities." *differences: A journal of Feminist Cultural Studies* 3(2): iii–xviii.

Encarnación, Omar G. 2016. *Out in the Periphery: Latin America's Gay Rights Revolution*. New York, NY: Oxford University Press.

Encarnación, Omar G. 2017. "The Global Backlash Against Gay Rights: How Homophobia Became a Political Tool." *Foreign Affairs*, May 2.

Ennis, Dawn. 2019. "The 'Gay Gene' is a Myth but Being Gay is 'Natural' Say Scientists." *Forbes*, August 30.

Evans, David T. 1993. *Sexual Citizenship: The Material Construction of Sexualities*. London: Routledge.

Fausto-Sterling, Anne. 2000. *Sexing the Body: Gender Politics and the Construction of Sexuality*. New York, NY: Basic Books.

Foucault, Michel. 1978. *The History of Sexuality, Vol. 1: The Will to Knowledge*, translated by R. Hurley. New York, NY: Pantheon Books.

Ganna, Andrea, Karin J.H. Verweij, Michel G. Nivard et al. 2019. "Large-scale GWAS Reveals Insights Into the Genetic Architecture of Same-Sex Sexual Behavior." *Science* 365(6456) eaat7693.

Gatens, Moira. 1991. *Feminism and Philosophy: Perspectives on Difference and Equality*. Bloomington: Indiana University Press.

Ghaziani, Amin and Matt Brim, eds. 2019. *Imagining Queer Methods*. New York, NY: New York University Press.

Guardian. 2018. "#HimToo: How An Attempt To Criticize #Metoo Went Delightfully Wrong." October 9. Available at: https://www.theguardian.com/technology/2018/oct/09/himtoo-metoo-tweet-pieter-hanson-mothers-attack-on-feminism-movement-goes-wrong

Hammonds, Evelynn. 1997. "Black (W)holes and the Geometry of Black Female Sexuality." In *Feminism Meets Queer Theory*, edited by Elizabeth Weed and Naomi Schor, 136–156. Bloomington, IN: Indiana University Press.

Han, C. Winter. 2015. *Geisha of a Different Kind: Race and Sexuality in Gaysian America*. New York, NY: NYU Press.

Han, Chong-Suk. 2019. *They Don't Want to Cruise Your Types: Gay Men of Color and the Racial Politics of Exclusion*. Unpublished PhD dissertation, University of Connecticut.

Hawley, John C. 2001. *Postcolonial and Queer Theories: Intersections and Essays*. Westport, CT Greenwood Press.

Hubbard, R. 1990. "The Political Nature of Human Nature." In *Theoretical Perspectives on Sexual Difference*, edited by D.L. Rhode, 63–73. New Haven: Yale University Press.

Hunter, Mark. 2010. *Love in the Time of AIDS: Inequality, Gender, and Rights in South Africa*. Bloomington: Indiana University Press.

Kinsey, Alfred C., Wardell Pomeroy, and Clyde Martin. (1948 [1998]). *Sexual Behavior in the Human Male*. Philadelphia, PA: W.B. Saunders; Bloomington: Indiana University Press. [First publication of Kinsey's Heterosexual–Homosexual Rating Scale. Discusses Kinsey Scale, pp. 636–659.]

Kessler, Suzanne J. 1990. *Lessons from the Intersexed*. New Brusnwick, NJ: Rutgers University Press.

Krafft-Ebing, Richard von. 1894 [1886]. *Psychopathia Sexualis*, Contrary Sexual Instinct: A Medico-Legal Study, trans. Charles Gilbert Chaddock, Philadelphia, PA: F.A. Davis.

Lai, K. K. Rebecca. 2019. "Abortion Bans: 9 States Have Passed Bills to Limit the Procedure This Year." *New York Times*, May 29.

Leacock, Eleanor. 1981. *Myths of Male Dominance: Collected Articles on Women Cross-Culturally*. New York, NY: Monthly Review Press.

Lerner, Gerda. 1977. *The Female Experience: An American Documentary*, 1st edn., American Heritage Series (New York, NY); no. 90). Indianapolis, IN: Bobbs-Merrill.

Mackie, Vera, Nicola J. Marks, and Sarah Ferber, eds. 2019. *The Reproductive Industry: Intimate Experiences and Global Processes*. Lanham, MD: Lexington.

Malatino, Hilary. 2019. "Queer embodiment: Monstrosity, medical violence, and intersex experience." Lincoln: University of Nebraska Press.

Masters, William H. and Virginia E. Johnson. 1966. *Human Sexual Response*. Boston, MA: Little, Brown.

McLelland, Mark and Vera Mackie, eds. 2015. *The Routledge Handbook of Sexuality Studies in East Asia*. Oxford: Routledge.

Movement Advancement Project. 2019. "Equality Maps: Conversion Therapy Laws." Available at: http://www.lgbtmap.org/equality-maps/conversion_therapy.

Muehlenhard, Charlene L. and Zoe D. Peterson. 2011. "Distinguishing Between Sex and Gender: History, Current Conceptualizations, and Implications." *Sex Roles* 64(11–12): 791–803.

Nash, Catherine J. 2010. "Queer Conversations: Old-Time Lesbians, Transmen and the Politics of Queer Research." In *Queer Methods and Methodologies: Intersecting Queer Theories and Social Science Research*, edited by Kath Browne and Catherine J. Nash, 129–142. Farnham: Ashgate.

Nochlin, Linda. 1971. "Why Have There Been No Great Women Artists?" *ARTnews* 39: 67–71.

Oosterhuis, Harry. 2000. *Stepchildren of Nature. Krafft-Ebing, Psychiatry, and the Making of Sexual Identity*. Chicago, IL: University of Chicago Press.

Poirot, Kristan. 2009. "Domesticating the Liberated Woman: Containment Rhetorics of Second Wave Radical/Lesbian Feminism." *Women's Studies in Communication* 32(3): 263–292.

Puri, Jyoti. 2016. "Sexual States: Governance and the decriminalization of sodomy in India's present." Durham: Duke University Press.

Reich, Wilhelm. 1942 [1986]. *The Function of the Orgasm: Discovery of the Orgone*, vol. 1. New York, NY: Farrar, Straus, and Giroux.

Rossi, Alice. 1973. *The Feminist Papers: From Adams to de Beauvoir*. New York, NY: Columbia University Press.

Rubin, Gayle. 1984. "Thinking Sex: Note for a Radical Theory of the Politics of Sexuality." In *Pleasure and Danger: Exploring Female Sexuality*. 267–319 Boston, MA: Routledge.

Rubin, Gayle, with Judith Butler. 1997. "Sexual Traffic, Interview." In *Feminism Meets Queer Theory*, edited by Elizabeth Weed and Naomi Schor, 31–67. Bloomington, IN: Indiana University Press.

Ruvalcaba, Héctor Domínguez. 2016. *Translating the Queer. Body Politics and Trans-national Conversations*. London: Zed Books.

Saravi, Fernando. 2008. "Elusive Search for a 'Gay' Gene." In *Tall Tales about the Mind and Brain: Separating Fact from Fiction*, edited by Sergio Della Sala, 461–477. New York, NY: Oxford University Press.

Sedgwick, Eve Kosofsky. 1985. *Between Men: English Literature and Male Homosocial Desire*. New York, NY: Columbia University Press.

Seidman, Steven, ed. 1996. *Queer Theory, Sociology*. London: Wiley Blackwell.

Swaab, Dick F., Louis J. Gooren, and Michel A. Hofman. 1995. "Brain Research, Gender and Sexual Orientation." *Journal of Homosexuality* 28(2–3):283–301.

The Ohio State University. 2019. Sexuality Studies: Undergraduate Major (Bachelor of Arts). Available at: https://sexualitystudies.osu.edu/Academics/Undergraduate/Major.

Vogelstein, Rachel B. and Rebecca Turkington. 2019. "Abortion Law: Global Comparisons." *Council on Foreign Relations*, July 15. Available at: https://www.cfr.org/article/abortion-law-global-comparisons.

Weed, Elizabeth and Naomi Schor, eds. 1997. *Feminism Meets Queer Theory*. Bloomington, IN: Indiana University Press.

Wilson, E.O. 1975/2000. *Sociobiology: The New Synthesis*. Cambridge, MA: Harvard University Press.

Part II
Theoretical and Methodological Diversity

2

Sexology

AGNIESZKA KOŚCIAŃSKA

Introduction

"Very few ever fully appreciate the powerful influence which sexuality exercises over feeling, thought, and conduct, both in the individual and in society," wrote the Viennese doctor Richard von Krafft-Ebing in a preface to the first, 1886, edition of his hallmark volume *Psychopathia Sexualis* (Krafft-Ebing 1894 p. iii), which marked the foundation of sexology. He complained that philosophers and psychologists either ignored the existence of sexuality, or they saw the study of it to be distasteful. Only poets, like Schiller, recognized the meaning of sexuality, continued Kraff-Ebing. But poets, he reasoned, "are men of feelings rather than understanding" (Krafft-Ebing 1894, p. iii). Therefore, there was a need for the science of sex.

He was indeed right. As the historian of sexuality and a major specialist on Krafft-Ebing's work and life, Harry Oosterhuis (2000), suggested, "nineteenth-century medical interest in sexuality was dictated by wider social anxieties" (Oosterhuis 2000, p. 27). He pointed to neo-Malthusian interest in birth control, middle-class stress on morality and respectability, concerns about health, race, and same-sex relations (Oosterhuis 2000, pp. 27–31), the development of a new concept of marriage based on romantic love (so difficult for sexual "others"), and the growing visibility of sexual subcultures due to the expansion of metropolitan life and consumer culture (Oosterhuis 2000, pp. 245–254).

The science of sex, namely sexology, developed under the sociocultural conditions of the late nineteenth century. Since its foundation, it constituted more than just a description of sexuality: it also influenced how modern sexuality was experienced, understood, and managed (Foucault 1978; Weeks 1985, 2010). For Michel Foucault, sexology was one of the major tools of modern power (Foucault 1978). Scholars like Foucault and Jeffrey Weeks also claimed that, in fact, it was the sexologists (along with other nineteenth-century experts) who invented modern sexuality: they made it

---

Companion to Sexuality Studies, First Edition. Edited by Nancy A. Naples.
© 2020 John Wiley & Sons Ltd. Published 2020 by John Wiley & Sons Ltd.

significant, and gave us language to describe our bodily pleasure and identities. The foundation of sexology moved sexuality from the jurisdiction of religion to the jurisdiction of science and medicine. In conservative societies, the scientific character of sexology was often the condition of its existence; science was the only way to speak about sexuality.

Early sexological classifications of people were based on their sexual behaviors. Although sexologists often assumed the pathological character of nonnormative sexuality, they started the process of the construction of sexual identities and made sexual activism possible (Oosterhuis 2000). Sexual others took over sexological classification: initial pathologizing led to rights claims. As people were characterized based on their sexuality, for instance homosexuals, they could build group identity and start to organize themselves. For decades, sexologists, who also often became the first sexuality activists, stressed the congenital character of nonnormative sexuality. This naturalness made rights claims possible, but at the same time, it caused the development of essentialist thinking about sexuality. Such was the case not only within sexology, but also within activism that often did not give enough attention to social and cultural factors (Vance 1988; Weeks 2010). Sexology set the stage for sexual activism. Even activists of today struggle with issues that are rooted in early sexology, such as in its link to colonialism and the equalization of progress with colonization (Bauer 2017).

This chapter has two aims. The first is to discuss the development of sexology from the time of its foundation in the second part of the nineteenth century to today. The second aim is to give an overview of social scientific and historical research on sexology so as to allow us to see the broader social significance of sexology and how it was entangled in various forms of power: fascism and colonialism (and their racial hygiene), communism, and, recently, neoliberalism.

The chapter is divided into six sections. The first section shows the development of sexology in two ways: firstly, the standard way, as it was always told to have been established by white, male, European medical doctors; secondly, its development in an alternative way, possible thanks to new research on the transnational history of sexology. The chapter then describes the complicated relations between sexology and the state. Drawing on examples from various authoritarian contexts, it shows that on the one hand, as Foucault demonstrated, sexology was embedded in power relations. On the other hand, sexologists resisted power. The third section of the chapter traces the development of sexology vis-à-vis race. It shows it complicated relations with colonialism and how its foundation was bound with racism. This is followed by a section that focuses on mechanisms of sexological knowledge production. It is based on new research on the development of sexology that points to the active role of patients in the creation of sexological knowledge. The fifth section deals with the issue of progress. On the one hand, sexologists usually see themselves as progressive agents fighting for sexual freedom and against backwardness. On the other, Foucault presented sexology as a disciplining knowledge, or a tool used by power to control its subjects. This section posits that none of these approaches properly describes the meaning of sexology as a conservative or progressive power. Instead, it traces the role of sexology in building social policies, both conservative and progressive. Finally, it shows that progress and regress in sexual liberalization might develop in various ways, not necessarily following the assumption of constant progress. The chapter's last section is devoted to new developments in sexology, namely the invention of so-called sexuopharmaceuticals and their influence on both sexology itself and wider culture.

The Development of Sexology: Two Narratives

The second part of the nineteenth century and the beginning of the twentieth century marked the rapid development of sexology. Apart from Krafft-Ebing's *Psychopathia Sexualis*, there are several other salient publications from that period, including Karl Heinrich Ulrichs's *The Riddle of "Man-Manly Love"* (12 volumes, published in Leipzig between 1864 and 1870), Iwan Bloch's *The Sexual Life of Our Time in its Relations to Modern Civilization* (published in Berlin in 1907), Magnus Hirschfeld's *The Transvestite* (published in Berlin in 1910), Havelock Ellis's *Sexual Inversion* (published in 1897, coauthored with John Addington Symonds) and *Man and Woman* (1894), and Stanisław Kurkiewicz's *Inquires into Sexual Life* (2 volumes, published in Krakow in 1905 and 1906). The authors of these volumes were the pioneers of sexology. They expressed a special interest in nonnormative sexuality, called "perversions" or "deviations", considered pathological at the time, and focused on developing their descriptions, explanations, and names. It was the work of early sexologists that "invented" and popularized the modern language of sexuality. Terms such as homosexuality and heterosexuality were first used by the Hungarian activist and journalist Karl Maria Kertbeny, but it was Kraff-Ebing who popularized their use. Furthermore, Kraff-Ebing invented several other terms, such as sadism, masochism, zoophilia, and pedophilia (Oosterhuis 2000, pp. 49–50). As *Psychopathia Sexualis* was translated into multiple languages, those terms found their way into multiple languages and cultures. As a result, attempts to introduce sexual terms in local languages often failed, as for instance in the Polish language. *Psychopathia Sexualis* was translated into Polish in 1888 (just two years after its first German edition). Not even two decades later, the sexologist Stanisław Kurkiewicz offered a compendium of the Polish language of sexuality, drawing on multiple sources from the history of ancient Greece to Slavic folk culture, but his attempts failed completely as Kafft-Ebing's sexual vocabulary was already well established in the Polish language (Kościańska 2017, pp. 209–220).

These terms and medical classifications, homosexuality especially, brought relief to many readers across Europe as they saw that they were not alone, and that their desire was congenital, and therefore natural. Thanks to these terms, the process of the formation of modern sexual identities began. Krafft-Ebing was instrumental in establishing sexology as a medical and scientific discipline, which was essential at the time for sexology to be established at all in the late nineteenth century (Oosterhuis 2000). The next generation of sexologists (those working in the early twentieth century), was interested not only in developing sexual classification, but also in reforming laws and morality. Magnus Hirschfeld was a major figure among second-generation sexologists. He is mostly known from his pioneering research on transvestitism, sexual reform activism, the establishment of the first institute of sex research in 1919 in Berlin, his fight against the German paragraph 175 penalizing homosexuality, the foundation of the World League of Sexual Reform in 1921 and the Scientific-Humanitarian Committee in 1897, which was the first organization focused on the rights of "sexual others" (on Hirschfeld see, for example, Wolff 1986; Bauer 2017).

Until very recently, this was how researchers of the history of sexology described its beginnings: as scientific, linked to studies on nonnormative sexuality and, because of its Western orientation, placed in the context of German-speaking Europe, mostly in Vienna and Berlin, as well as in Great Britain (on British sexology see for instance Porter and Hall 1995), with people like Krafft-Ebing, Hirschfeld, or Ellis as the pioneers. In the last few years, a new body of work has broadened the focus by asking about the non-European roots of sexology, women in the development of modern sexology (Leng 2015; Rusterholz 2018), the role of clergy (Fisher 2018), the relation between sexology and issues of birth control (Fisher 2018), and about the nonmedical elements of the new science (for instance the role of material culture, Funke et al. 2017).

Recently, two groundbreaking volumes on the history of sexology have been published: *Sexology and Translation* edited by Heike Bauer and *A Global History of Sexual Science (1880–1960)* edited by Veronika Fuechtner, Douglas E. Haynes and Ryan M. Jones. Bauer draws on Ann L. Stoler's (2005) work on sexuality, race, and the empire. Stoler argues that "the discursive and practical field in which nineteenth-century bourgeois sexuality emerged was situated on an imperial landscape where the cultural accoutrements of bourgeois distinction were partially shaped through contrasts forged in the politics and language of race" (quoted in Bauer 2015, p. 4). Given the colonial sources of the construction of sexuality in following Stoler, is it at all possible to talk about sexology, past and present, without the context of colonialism and race? This question is further exacerbated by the fact that when it comes to sexuality, colonial legacies are visible throughout contemporary political discourses (Stoler 2016). Studies of sexology should not, then, be kept outside of the transnational turn in sexuality studies visible since the 1900s (see Povinelly and Chauncey 1999). Bauer and the contributors to her volume use the framework of translation, drawing on and extending Susan Bassnett's definition of translation "as a process of negotiation between texts and between cultures" (quoted in Bauer 2015, p. 7, see the fourth section, "In Response to Patients' Concerns", of this chapter). They also employ postcolonial theoretical perspective about translation in relation to "the unequal distribution of power and its relationship to subjectivity and identity formation" (Bauer 2015, p. 7) and the work of literary scholars who stress the role of translators in cultural production. In similar fashion, Fuechtner, Haynes, and Jones (2018) conclude that "sexual science ... was globally a formation that simultaneously emerged in multiple sites and that took multiple shapes," wherein scientific exchange on sexuality had become "circular in nature" by the beginning of the twentieth century (Fuechtner, Haynes, and Jones 2018, p. 2).

These new studies have definitively weakened the claim that sexology was produced in Vienna and Berlin. There were other important centers, even within Central Europe itself. The Institute for the Study of Sexual Pathology was established in 1921 in Prague, just two years after the Hirschfeld's institute in Berlin (Lišková 2018, p. 13). In revolutionary Russia, psychiatrists discussed and researched the etiology of same-sex desire and cross-dressing. While some of them were much influenced by Hirschfeld's work and his biological explanations, others challenged it and "emphasized the social environment in which sexualities developed" (Healy 2001, p. 139).

Furthermore, there were multiple networks of scientific exchange in and outside of Europe. The first European sexological journal was published in 1896 in Naples. Its editor, Paquale Penta, made an effort to attract international authors, including the major British sexologist Ellis (Beccalossi 2018). Chiara Beccalossi describes extensive links among scholars in Italy, Spain and Argentina. These were supported by the requirements of medical education: "physicians were expected to speak a range of different languages, and during their medical training they often spent a year abroad" (Beccalossi 2018, p. 307).

In the early twentieth century, knowledge traveled globally in various directions. For instance, the Japanese writer Sueo Iwaya

> published an article on masculinity and homosexuality in traditional Japanese culture in the German-language *Yearbook for Sexual Intermediaries*. His writings, influenced by European scholarship, shaped how German sexologists like Hirschfeld ... came to conceive ... the 'erotic exotic' (i.e., the nexus between 'Others,' empire, and sexual desire).
> (Fuechtner et al. 2018, p. 2)

As a result, when Hirschfeld went to India, what he knew about "the East" was based on what he had read on Japan. Hirschfeld was also invited to China by Chinese sexual researchers, who not only drew on European works on sexuality, but also discussed sex and studied it themselves in reference to multiple cultural sources and social practices. The first Chinese sexological journal appeared in 1935. Chinese sex debates were also enriched through dialog with the wider public. According to Howard Chiang, "Sexology in Republican China was indeed a new system of knowledge in which, literally, new [homosexual] subjects were made" (Chiang 2015, p. 77). Chiang's research stands in stark contrast to the work of scholar-activists like Dennis Altman (1997), who claimed that both "gay identity" and "scientia sexualis" came to China with postsocialism (on sexology in China see also McMillan 2006).

These new studies of sexology also point to translation between disciplines. Second-generation sexologists gradually distanced themselves from the strictly medical approach represented by Kraff-Ebing, in seeing "alterative forms of expertise and cross-disciplinary contributions ... [as] essential to a fully comprehensive and scientific understanding of sexuality" (Fisher and Funke 2015, p. 97). Kate Fisher and Jana Funke analyze the processes behind this shift. In their view, it came about because some second-generation sexologists were more liberal and engaged in the social project of sexual reform than their "forefathers." Fisher and Funke argue that for second-generation sexologists, the pathologizing perspective was too narrow; sexuality as a whole could not be understood through the lens of pathology. John Addington Symonds (1840–1893), who co-authored *Sexual Inversion* with Havelock Ellis, serves to illustrate this point. Symonds was highly critical of the Russian physician Benjamin Tarnowsky, "whose practice in St. Petersburg has brought him into close professional relations with the male prostitutes and habitual paederasts of the capital. ... I cannot but think that the very peculiarities of his experience have led him to form incomplete theories" (quoted in Fisher and Funke 2015, p. 100). Symonds did not have any training in medicine or science. He was a poet, translator of poetry, literary critic, and cultural historian. Fisher and Funke argue that it was precisely people like him who inspired physicians to go beyond the medical perspective. Along with other nonmedical writers like Edward Carpenter (1844–1929, a socialist and sex reformer with a degree in mathematics and the experience of being a Church of England curate), Symonds inspired sexologists in Germany and Britain, such as Ellis and Ivan Bloch, to go beyond the framework set by Kraff-Ebing.

In their reconstruction of the collaboration between Ellis and Symonds, Fisher and Funke point to the role of cross-disciplinary and cross-cultural translation. Researchers maintain that Symonds approached Ellis and collaborated with him to "gain access to medical credentials and scientific authority" (Fisher and Funke 2015, p. 107). But the detailed study of their correspondence suggests that at the beginning, Symonds had much more exhaustive knowledge about sexual science than Ellis. Symonds encouraged Ellis to read Albert Moll and others; thus in terms of medical knowledge, the two authors dialoged as equals. According to Fisher and Funke, the most important effect of this collaboration was the establishment of British sexual science as based on cross-disciplinary translation. Symonds, who was interested in ancient Greece, "believed that the history of ancient Greece provided an important corrective to pathological readings of homosexuality presented in first generation of sexual science" (Fisher and Funke 2015, p. 108). Although the chapter on ancient Greece written by Symonds was initially moved to the appendix of *Sexual Inversion* (as it contradicted a congenial model of homosexuality, which they both agreed was strategic to use in an oppressive society), the discussion between Ellis and Symonds established historical and anthropological materials as legitimate sources for sexual science. This allowed second-generation sexologists to work on the nonpathological dimension of homosexuality (as in ancient Greece) and, more broadly, "sexual diversity through cross-historical and cross-cultural comparison" (Fisher and Funke 2015, p. 109).

World War II brought significant reconfigurations to the field of sexology. North American – not European – sexology became the primary reference point for sexologists all over the world. Already before World War II, Alfred Kinsey, a taxonomist and professor of zoology at Indiana University, began coordinating a marriage course for his students (Irvine 2005, p. 19). Janice Irvine describes: "he was dismayed by the dearth of scientific literature on sex and his consequent inability to answer his students' questions" (p. 19). He criticized existing sex research as "methodically unsounded" and "too narrow in scope" (p.19). Thus, Kinsey started collecting his own data.

Kinsey struggled to make sexology scientific, which is what made him more like Kraff-Ebing than like the second-generation sexologists. In her pioneering work on the history of sexology (first published in 1990), Janice Irvine argues that it was his way to make the study of sex a legitimate field of study under the conditions of highly conservative American society of the time. Kinsey never took any "public stands on political or social issues of the day" (Irvine 2005, p. 20) and he carefully designed his large-scale research of human (read white American) sexuality. Kinsey had very specific requirements when hiring his interviewers (Irvine 2005, p. 25): "His staff, then, consisted of male, heterosexual, white Anglo-Saxon Protestants (*WASPs*), since for Kinsey these characteristics represented the yardstick of normality" (p. 25).

According to Irvine, Kinsey's "approach was so based in numbers and frequencies that he inevitably viewed the characteristics of any numerical majority as 'natural,' normative, or good. Since male WASPs represent, if not statistical, at least the cultural, norm in the United States, Kinsey considered them to be natural researchers. With enough scientific training in the fine points of interviewing, he believed they could be neutral, win the trust of their subjects, and elicit information from anyone" (pp. 25–26). This method was intended to achieve what he saw as scientific, objective results (for more on Kinsey see Drucker 2014).

These efforts were continued by William Masters and Virginia Johnson, who likewise wanted to present their research of sexuality as scientific. They did not build wild scales, but measured the body's reactions to sexual stimulation. As a result, they saw sexual pleasure as purely placed in the body, and described it in the form of a universal human sexual response cycle for both genders, consisting of four phases: excitement, plateau, orgasm, and resolution. By omitting social, cultural, and economic factors, they set the stage for the current commodification of sexuality (Tiefer 2000, see the last section, "Sexology Today," of this chapter). Meanwhile, studies on sexology and the Cold War show that on the other side of the Iron Curtain sexology (and sexuality) developed away from the influence of the dominant biomedical model and away from the logic of the capitalist market. Here, sexology grew out of often unexpected collaborations, for example in Catholic and socialist Poland, where in the 1980s a sexology unit hired a Catholic priest to help its transsexual patients to transition spiritually. Furthermore, in the 1970s, Masters and Johnson's work was well-known among Polish sexologists (it was published in Polish translation in 1975), but they were critical toward its focus on effective stimulation as the way to sexual satisfaction. They believed that a sexologist should place his/her patients' problems in the broad perspective of the social, the cultural, the political, and the psychological (Kościańska 2014; McLellan 2011; on the various aspects of the development of sexology see also Bland and Doan 1998, 1999).

Sexology and the State

Drawing on examples from Western Europe, and France in particular, Michel Foucault argued that the science of sex was crucial for the construction of modern power (Foucault 1978). Empirical studies on sexology in various cultural and political contexts show the complexity of the relationship between sexology and the state. Studies on the development of sexology under conditions of the authoritarian state, especially fascist and communist, provide particularly interesting examples of both sexological contribution to state power and sexological opposition therein.

The development of sexology in fascist Italy serves as a good example of sexological collaboration with the state. Extensive networks between scientists in Italy and Argentina resulted in the development of what was called "biotypology." Invented by prominent Italian eugenicist and Cesare Lombroso's follower, Nicola Pende, biotypology combined criminal anthropology with endocrinology and various psychological approaches. Its aim was to "control the physical, psychological, and sexual development so that 'normality' could be ensured and abnormalities prevented" (Beccalossi 2018, p. 316). In 1926, Pende founded the Institute of Biotypology in Genoa. Soon after its establishment, the Institute offered sex education, marriage and eugenic advice, and tried to cure impotence and infertility. With its interest in "a modern management of sexuality" and "demographic optimization," the Institute "fitted Mussolini's plans for national cohesion" (Beccalossi 2018, p. 317). The Institute developed "biotypological cards," which contained information about "the individual's morphology, psychology, and general behavior" (Beccalossi 2018, p. 317). Similar cards were in use in Argentina, Brazil, and Mexico. Members of the Opera Nazionale Balilla (an Italian Fascist youth organization) had cards that indicated no "symptoms of deviance" (Beccalossi 2018, p. 318). Homosexuals, meanwhile, could be sent to Pende's Institute for correction.

Kateřina Lišková's research on of sexological approaches towards "sexual deviants," called "delinquents" in communist Czechoslovakia, suggests a direct link between the development of sexology and the state's political aims, which explains why during the first decade of communism in Czechoslovakia (the 1950s) sexologists were not really interested in treating sexual pathology. This interest came later, in the 1970s, when for political and demographic reasons, the state wanted to develop the family and keep its citizens at home. Those who did not fit in were confined in sexology wards:

> Sexologists collaborated with the courts striving to bring the sexological terminology of diagnoses and aberrations in line with the criminological lexicon of law breaking and misconduct. Thus a fuzzy category of sexual delinquency was born, one that captured men who were deemed unwilling or unable to live a family life.
> (Lišková 2018, p. 252)

But sometimes, sexologists contested the state. Sabine Frühstück shows that sexology contributed to the formation of the nation-state in Japan in the 1870s and:

> brought about new concepts of the populace as a social organism to be protected, nurtured, and improved by a public health system borrowed primary from Prussia and other European countries. By the 1880s, the state had developed powerful instruments with which to investigate, manage, and control the health (more precisely, the sexual health) of the populace in order to build a modern health regime.
> (Frühstück 2003, p. 6)

One of these instruments was sexology. But "from the 1920s onward, sexologists were lumped together with pacifists, socialists, communists, and anarchists and regarded as a nuisance or even a danger to the imperialist state" (Frühstück 2003, p. 13). In the 1930s and 1940s they were silenced, arrested and even killed when they protested Japanese imperial politics and its racial hygiene. The state censored sexology, afraid that after reading about birth control the middle class would not reproduce. Sexologists who wanted to liberate sex from both tradition and state control were seen as a threat to "the colonialist and militarist state" (Frühstück 2003, p. 196).

Similar processes of sexological resistance to the state accrued in the USSR. Although homosexuality was decriminalized after the October revolution, it become illegal again in 1934 when Stalin took over (Healey 2001).[1] Although the law only concerned male homosexuality, women who were reported as lesbians were forced to undergo psychiatric treatment (Essig 1999). The sociologist Francesca Stella showed "forced psychiatric treatment may not have been a universally accepted practice among medical practitioners" (Stella 2015, p. 47). Stella conducted in-depth interviews with lesbians about their experiences of contacts with medicine during the late Soviet period. Her interview partners who sought treatment from psychiatrists were not cured from homosexuality but from the psychiatric problems, with which they struggled.

Sexology, Race, and Processes of "Othering"

Since its foundation, sexual science was entangled with racism in various ways. At least until World War II, many sexologists as well as birth control activists were proponents of eugenics and the concept of racial hygiene.[2] Although they often did not support negative eugenic methods, like many progressive thinkers of the time, they saw racial hygiene as a way of eradicating poverty. But some, like the biotypologists, participated actively in state-sponsored racial hygiene policies. The study of sexuality and the study of race were intertwined in the various ways of constructing the other.

In her classical analysis of race and sexology in the United States, Siobhan B. Somerville (1998 [1994]) asks: "is it merely a historical coincidence that classification of bodies as either 'homosexual' or 'heterosexual' emerged at the same time as the United States was aggressively policing the imagery boundary between 'black' and 'white'?" (Somerville 1998, p. 61). Although in sexological writings of the time, very little explicitly concerned race, on the whole these writings were rooted in the racial ideologies of the time. Somerville tries to make sense of things that are neither named nor explicitly stated and offers "speculations" on how sexologists drew on scientific racism in their late nineteenth and early twentieth century texts. Sexologists used methods such as comparative anatomy "to position the 'homosexual' body as anatomically distinguishable from the 'normal' body." They built the model of the racially "mixed body as a way to make sense of the 'invert'" (Somerville 1998, p. 72).

Recently, Somerville's method and analysis was taken up Heike Bauer, who also draws on Stoler's work. Bauer looks at Magnus Hirschfeld's lack of attention to racial issues. Hirschfeld has long been celebrated as a progressive pioneer of lesbian, gay, bisexual, transgender, and queer/questioning (LGBTQ) rights activism. Bauer examines Hirschfeld's approach to race and possible connections between sexuality, race, and emancipation.

Bauer exposes Hirschfeld's ambivalent attitude towards race. On the one hand, as a Jew, he was a victim of sexualized racism. He had been attacked across Europe for his sexual activism and his opponents drew heavily on anti-Semitic rhetoric, "even going as far as to insist that 'we must make an end of people like Dr Hirschfeld'" (Bauer 2017, p. 26). Later, his Institute was burned by the Nazis. On the other hand, Hirschfeld was brought up as a German patriot (Wolff 1986). Bauer reveals his admiration of the German Empire and its colonialism, which as many argued, "paved the way for the rise of Nazism" (Bauer 2017, p. 14). This could be seen on various levels. People directly involved in colonization were present at a small party organized to celebrate the opening of the Scientific Humanitarian Committee. Hirschfeld's journal, the first journal on same-sex relations, reproduced some of the scientific racism of the time when it published anthropological studies of 'pederasty and tribadism' among *Naturvölkern* (primitive people) to support its argument that same-sex sexuality was a naturally occurring phenomenon in the distinct group of *Kulturevölkern* (civilized people).

(Bauer 2017, p. 25)

Furthermore, Bauer shows that Hirschfeld was aware of the brutality of colonial rule, but seemed to ignore it, as in the case of the Herero genocide in southwest Africa. In *Sexualpsychologie und Volkspsychologie* (Sexual psychology and national psychology), he mentioned a patient-prisoner who told him that he was traumatized because of his own cruel acts committed during the Herero uprising. In contrast to the prisoner, Bauer comments, Hirschfeld "had nothing to say about the atrocities committed on indigenous people in the name of the German Empire" (Bauer 2017, p. 29). Sometimes, Hirschfeld went even further and praised the German Empire, for example in *Warum Hassen uns die Völker?* (Why do other nations hate us?), published in 1915. The pamphlet claims that "it was the country's success as a colonial nation that had prompted its envious neighbors to start the war" (Bauer 2017, p. 32). Finally, in his writings on sexuality in Africa, Hirschfeld equals colonialism with progress. For example, while discussing same-sex sexuality among Hausa women (to prove the universality of homosexuality), he wrote that "before English colonial rule these women would have been punished by death if found to have engaged in same-sex acts" (Bauer 2017, p. 30). Bauer notes:

> This argument anticipates later debates about the role played by sexual rights discourses in cultural imperialism and political and military attacks against regions that are seen to fail certain sexual rights standards of progress and colonialism.
>
> (Bauer 2017, p. 31)

This makes Hirschfeld not only a pioneer in sexology and sex activism, but also a representative of Eurocentric, "evolutionary" thinking, with which queer activists continue to struggle today (see, for instance, discussions around Altman 1997). Similar processes were observed and analyzed by the anthropologist Hadley Z. Renkin, who focused on Géza Róheim, a Hungarian folklorist and a follower of Freud. Renkin shows how Róheim's work on sexuality in the context of folklore, ethnography, and psychoanalysis contributed to the construction of Eastern Europe as "a space of failed, non-modern, non-European societies" (Renkin 2016, p. 182) that were sexually backward and "naturally" homophobic. Renkin shows how those ideas of Eastern Europe mask "the presence of homophobia in the West" (Renkin 2016, p. 184) and make it impossible to understand and combat the root causes in the East.

In Response to Patients' Concerns: Agency in the Construction of Sexological Knowledge

In the Foucauldian vision of power, there is no space for individual or collective agency.[3] Any possible resistance is perceived as belonging to the discourse of power. In his view, power produces resistance, but this opposition is only possible within the framework set by power. For instance, sexology (being part of power's discourse) described and pathologized homosexuality in the nineteenth century. Even if homosexuals referred to themselves using the sexological term homosexuality to claim their rights, they did so under the limits set by power, without transforming the system of power. Foucault described this process using a term "'reverse' discourse," within which "homosexuality began to speak in its own behalf" as just a part of the controlling discourse of power (Foucault 1978, pp. 101–102). In this section, I argue for a more nuanced picture. In various political and cultural conditions, sexologists followed their patients' ideas and needs while constructing their theories and writing their sex manuals. I demonstrate that sexological knowledge resulted from interactions between doctors and their patients, and it was later further transformed by other social actors. Therefore, the process of sexological knowledge construction cannot be seen, as with Foucault, to be lacking human agency: sexological patients, readers of sexological texts, sexological research participants, and novelists drawing on sexological work wielded agency in this process.

Inspired by the Foucauldian constructivist approach to sexuality, but simultaneously critical of the concept of reverse discourse, the anthropologist Jennifer Terry (1999) pointed to research subjects' agency in her research on the Committee for the Study of Sex Variants. The Committee was established in New York City in 1935 and was inspired by Hirschfeld's work, but also by ideas developed by people like anthropologist Margaret Mead. It undertook the first large scientific study of homosexuality in the United States. The Committee was supervised by the physiatrist George William Henry and designed to be flexible, to "allow its subjects to give rich accounts of their experiences" (Terry 1999, p. 178) and to learn what they "had to say for themselves" (Terry 1999, p. 179).

In her work, Terry traces "the interplay between, on the one hand, medical experts' intent upon identifying symptoms and prescribing remedies and on the other, the men and women who resisted such reductions even as they were drawn to scientific inquiry in hopes that it would be liberating" (Terry 1999, p. 233). Departing from Foucault's "reverse discourse," Terry proposes a new term, "variant subjectivity," that builds on the notion of "reverse discourse," but offers new understanding of the subject and his/her agency. In her view, the subjects do more than simply reverse medical discourse. For example, they spoke using a specific, subcultural language, which they "shared as dissenters from normative regimes of sex, gender and sexuality" (Terry 1999, p. 223). As a result, "the interviews published in Sex Variants feature homosexual subjects who were not merely docile victims" (Terry 1999, p. 223). Terry provided multiple examples of the subjects introducing their ideas about gender and sexuality, linking femininity with independence and even aggressiveness. Thus, in Terry's work, the subjects appear as being active/agentic in the process of knowledge building.

In his *Stepchildren of Nature: Krafft-Ebing, Psychiatry, and the Making of Sexual Identity* (2000), Harry Oosterhuis also pointed to nonnormative subjects' agency. He showed Krafft-Ebing's *Psychopathia Sexualis* as creating space for various voices, including very critical ones, in which sexual others demanded decriminalization and depathologization of same-sex sexuality. One such voice wrote to Krafft-Ebing:

> Together with the majority of urnings,[4] I claim that our sexual anomaly does not affect our mental condition or only slightly at best. Our desire may be abnormal, but it is as

intense as the normal urge and not unnatural. Therefore, legislators do not have the right to deny to us cooperative boys and men, just as they have no right to deprive paralytics of their crutches.

(quoted in Oosterhuis 2000, pp. 195–196)

Drawing on this evidence and comparing Krafft-Ebing's materials (for instance the letters he received) with their presentation in the published form, Oosterhuis argues that differently from other mid or late nineteenth century physicians, the founding father of sexology neither "generalize[d] from a small number of cases" nor "theorize[d] without retelling individual life history" (Oosterhuis 2000, p. 195). Therefore, *Psychopathia Sexualis* opened a space in which patients and correspondents could look for their own voice and identity models. Oosterhuis shows that case studies presented in the book linked often-painful individual introspections with "the conforming sense of belonging to a community of like-minded individuals" (pp. 197–198). In this way, "sexual deviants" co-wrote the most important sexological work of the nineteenth century, and there is no doubt that it contributed greatly to the construction of modern sexual identity.

The issue of agency could also be considered from another angle. The historian Katie Sutton (2015) has looked for agency in the process of translating sexological knowledge. Drawing on the works of Oosterhuis (2000) and others who search for signs of agency and emancipation in the discourse of sexuality, Sutton focuses on "the cultural mediation" or "translation" between sexologists and "inverts"/"members of 'third sex' in fin de siècle and interwar Germany" (Sutton 2015, p. 53). She examines texts and films from the era, including Minna Wettstein-Adelt's alias Aimée Duc's novel *Sind es Frauen?* (Are they women?) published in 1901, and presents writers or filmmakers as active agents who use sexology to claim sexual rights.

Wettstein-Adelt presents characters who defined themselves using categories invented or popularized by Krafft-Ebing and who simultaneously claimed their rights. She also tries to counteract any pathologizations present in *Psychopathia Sexualis*. While Kraff-Ebing linked third sex with "degeneration," one of *Sind es Frauen?* characters has a weak foot, but at the same time is a skillful cyclist. Another one of her characters discusses Krafft-Ebig directly: "'But with regard to Krafft-Ebing! Isn't he the one who stands up for the perverse people?' ... 'Certainly, it is he, the writer of the work 'Psychopathis sexualis' upon which most lay readers pounce in greed and lust'" (quoted in Sutton 2015, pp. 58–59).

Such texts, Sutton argues, "translate" the scientific into the popular and, at the same time, stress through somewhat contradictory use of medical/pathologizing categories the issues of rights and emancipation. The contradiction between the pathologizing language of medicine and the excitatory claims of novels and their authors are, as Sutton explains: "symptomatic of categories and identities in flux" (Sutton 2015, p. 61).

Sexology Between the Progressive and the Conservative

Researchers often ask: Is sexology progressive? Sexologists usually see themselves as progressive (for more, see Waters 2006). Figures like Magnus Hirschfeld are usually seen as key sex reformers. Scholars studying the development of sexual science vary in their interpretations. For instance, in his *The Modernization of Sex*, first published in 1976, Paul Robinson argues that people like Ellis, Kinsey, and Masters and Johnson were instrumental in changing social attitudes toward sex by modernizing them, bringing more openness and more acceptance of the whole spectrum of sexual behaviors including homosexuality and female pleasure. Robinson is explicit about Ellis being engaged in the depathologization of homosexuality and Masters and Johnson being feminists.

As Chris Waters (2006) shows, this approach changed fundamentally after Foucault's *The History of Sexuality*. In his chapter "Scientia sexualis," Foucault discussed sexology as inherently disciplining, pathologizing, and constitutive of the oppressive power (Foucault 1978). In a similar vein, George Chauncey (1982/1983) describes how conservative social concerns (like antifeminism) could be expressed through sexological discourse. In his view, the concept of female sexual "deviance" in the United States between the 1880s and 1920s was "part of the general ideological reaction by the medical profession to women's challenge to the [Victorian] sex/gender system" (1982/1983, p. 140).

In the long run, these critiques brought nuanced studies of how progressive and conservative or liberal and oppressive approaches intertwine. For instance, Irvine (2005) argues that although Masters and Johnson's work contributed greatly to perspectives on female sexuality by stressing the importance of the clitoral orgasm or women's ability to have multiple orgasms, for which they were praised by feminists (for example Koedt 1970), in many ways, it was far from feminist intervention. Virginia Johnson was, on many occasions, explicitly critical of feminism, and both researchers were committed to both the institution of marriage and the family. They were also blind to issues such as power or inequality (Irvine 2005, p. 64; see also Tiefer 2001). Similar dynamics can be observed in Poland. The most popular Polish sexology book, *The Art of Love* by Michalina Wisłocka, was published in 1978 and sold 7 million copies. It has been perceived as revolutionary. The author focused on female pleasure, and gave women technical advice on how to achieve it, also drawing on Masters and Johnson's research. At the same time, the book was highly conservative when it comes to gender. In socialist Poland, where gender equality was an official politics, she wrote, for instance: "One can educate herself, have an academic or other career, be an activist, but at home and when it comes to love a woman has to be a woman, and a man has to be a man, if they want to live the full life and avoid disappointments and complexes" (quoted in Kościańska 2016, p. 246). In this way, Wisłocka and other Polish sexologists contributed to sexual liberation, which was not accompanied with gender liberation, dominant on the other side of the Iron Curtain (see also Lišková 2018 on Czechoslovakia).

Irvine also describes the complexity of Kinsey's research on women's sexuality, which could be accused of overlooking women's sexual capability. Kinsey ignored social and cultural factors that could explain it and focused on the biological aspects instead. At the same time, he was a proponent of equality in marriage and "challenged the primacy of penis and sexual intercourse as a source of pleasure for women. In many ways he assessed women's sexuality on its own terms, and thus afforded it a certain importance and validity through his serious attention" (Irvine 2005, p. 40). Furthermore, as described in the section "The Development of Sexology" above, although he did not see any reason to include homosexuals among his interviewers, the role of his research findings in the process of the depathologization of homosexuality in the early 1970s cannot be ignored (Bayer 1981).

Sexology could also serve reformist ends in other cultural settings. In their study of the key figure of Indian sexology, R.D. Karve (1882–1953), Shrikant Botre and Douglas E. Haynes (2018) demonstrate that for many intellectuals in China, Japan, and India in the early twentieth century, sexology was "a vehicle for combatting 'ignorance,' the effect of stifling traditions, the patriarchal oppression of women, and attitudes towards population control that they believed were harming the nation's development" (Botre and Haynes 2018, p. 163). Karve was preoccupied with the classical Hindu concept of *brahmacharya* (self-constraint or celibacy), which in the first decades of the twentieth century was "deemed by many nationalists to be crucial to the revitalization of the Indian male and Indian nation" (p. 165). Karve drew on European sexual science to prove them wrong. For instance, in his sex manual *Adhunik Kamashastra* (Modern sexual science) he argued against *brahmacharya* by quoting extensively from European sexual scientists such as Ellis "on the adverse effects of abstinence" (Botre and Haynes 2018, p. 178). Interestingly, he "created a direct equivalence between the word 'abstinence' in English-language writings and the concept *brahmacharya*, strategically disregarding some of the cultural specificities in the latter word's meaning" (Botre and Haynes 2018, p. 178). It was meant to contest "the 'denial of coevalness' central to the colonial construction of difference" (Botre and Haynes 2018, p. 179). Karve stressed that "Europe and India were both engaged in struggles to overcome backward, religious based, unscientific attitudes to sexuality" (Botre and Haynes 2018, p. 179). Hence, Botre and Haynes show not only that Karve used sexology to challenge Indian nationalism, but also to break colonial imageries.

There is yet another dimension to the debate on the progressive versus the conservative. Research on sexology can serve to destabilize ideas of progress that underpin studies in the history of sexuality. Dagmar Herzog notes that current discourse around sexuality is dominated by "the liberalization paradigm," the assumption of "the gradual overcoming of obstacles to sexual freedom" (Herzog 2009, p. 1295). In her study of sexology in Czechoslovakia, Lišková (2018) departs from Herzog's observation, and contends that in communist Czechoslovakia things developed quite differently. While in the 1950s sexologists in Czechoslovakia focused on women's emancipation and conducted studies on female orgasm, in the 1970s they contributed to "the normalization" after the Prague Spring, meaning the promotion of so-called traditional gender roles and marriage. Lišková shows how sexological knowledge followed state regulation. After World War II, communists in Czechoslovakia introduced new laws that made marriage a union of equals. Authors representing the Sexological Institute relied on the works Marx, Engels and Lenin to criticize the bourgeois concept of marriage. They also thought about pleasure and linked it to equality. They conducted extensive research on female orgasm and pointed to the multiple sources of women's sexual difficulties ("somatic, psychosexual and social"; Lišková 2018, p. 134). For instance, the sexologist Jiřina Knoblochová argued that "happiness in sexual life was a product of the equal involvement of both spouses in the domestic and the public spheres, of their egalitarian and respectful relationship" (Lišková 2018, p. 137). Czechoslovak sexologists in the 1950s, differently to experts in the West, expressed highly progressive ideas about sexuality and gender. They followed communist politics of gender equality and explicitly linked women's sexual pleasure with equality and their public presence.

Lišková shows that after the Prague Spring and due to the new political situation, this discourse of equality was replaced by a far less progressive, family-centered discourse. In the 1970s, Czechoslovakian sexologists would speak in a completely different fashion, stressing men's superiority over women as the key to marital happiness. Therefore, the communist Czechoslovak case shows the progress narrative to be far from universal. Sexuality here developed from one based on equality between the sexes in the 1950s to one based on traditional family and gender roles in the 1970s.

Sexology Today: (Bio)Medicalization and Commodification of Sexuality

In the mid 1990s, sexology was revolutionized by Viagra. The invention, marketization, and advertisement of Viagra brought new models of masculinity and relationships, or rather reinforced patriarchal order (Åsberg and Johnson 2009; Fishman and Mamo 2001; Potts and Tiefer 2006). Earlier, men who experienced sexual dysfunctions, as well as their partners, had to make an effort to find the root causes of their problems. It was up to them to explore together the various sexual techniques, including alternatives to penetration. Viagra advertising stressed men's independence from their partners, defined sex as penetration and men as constantly active in life, not only sexually (also during old age). After the spectacular success of Viagra and other sexuopharmaceuticals for men, the industry tried to develop a similar drug for women, a "pink Viagra." Jennifer R. Fishman describes how some sexologists actively collaborated with the industry in not only inventing drugs, but also in inventing and promoting new dysfunctions, i.e. in creating a market for new pharmaceuticals (Fishman 2004). Through ethnographic fieldwork in sexological milieus, Fishman traces interconnections and exchange networks in science, medicine, and the pharmaceutical industry. She describes mechanisms in which new diagnoses are developed and promoted.

Fishman's research examines the mechanisms of the commodification of female sexuality and the active role of both sexologists and the industry in this process. As the feminist sexologist Leonore Tiefer (2000) notes, sex researchers are prompted to collaborate with the industry because of the constant lack of funding and legitimacy (sex research is still often stigmatized). Both groups work through the media, as "information on health and illness is proliferating in many kinds of media, especially newspapers, on the Internet, in popular magazines, and through direct-to-consumer prescription and over-the-counter drug advertising" (Fishman 2004, p. 201). Fishman looks at celebrity sex experts, such as Jennifer and Laura Berman, who direct the Female Sexual Medicine Center at the University of California, Los Angeles, and are respected researchers of female sexual dysfunctions. They were instrumental to the appearance of female sexual dysfunctions in the public sphere. They use the arguments of women's rights to pleasure to advertise sexuopharmaceuticals for women and to conduct informal testing (women are asked to participate in a survey on their website). The medical sociologist Adele Clarke, who described the process of biomedicalization,[5] argues that an important element of biomedicalization is the appropriation of the achievements of social movements (in this case the women's health movement) by biomedicine. And this is exactly what is at work here. The website contains medical information that until recently, was only available to specialists (another element of biomedicalization). As such, it might be argued that their work contributes to the democratization of knowledge, but this, in following Fishman, is rather alleged since in fact it serves marketing goals.

Fishman's work shows that today's North American sexology is involved in multiple exchanges. As described in the beginning of this chapter, in the early twentieth century, sexological knowledge was based on contacts between medical doctors, historians, anthropologists, social reformers, patients, and correspondents. At the beginning of the twenty-first century, the networks cover the pharmaceutical industry, the media, and consumers (formerly called patients). But other networks also exist. The collaboration between medicine and business was challenged by a group of researchers, artists, and therapists from across the globe led by Tiefer. This group formed the New View Campaign designed to promote thinking about female sexuality beyond the logic of the market and biomedicine, through a social and cultural lens, both in the media and among specialists (Tiefer 2001).

Conclusion

Since the mid-nineteenth century, sexology has been developed as a diverse field within which the medical approach struggled with the humanist and the activist approaches. Sexology not only described, but also constructed, sexuality. It set the stage for how we understand sexuality, our sexual identity, and our sexual pleasures today. It also set the stage for sexual activism. Sexologists were often activists, working to reform how sexuality is constructed in the mainstream. Sexology has been constantly changing. Its development was trapped between state regulations and the opposition to them, conservatism and progress, patients' needs, and finally, the pathologizing language of medicine.

Although many people consider science and medicine to be objective and independent from any social or political factors, sexology has always been embedded in very complicated relations with power, the state, and society, and their ideologies. The latter concerned not only sexuality, but also gender and race. Today, under conditions of the neoliberal commodification of sexuality and the domination of sexuopharmaceuticals, we are very much in need of strong collaboration between medical sexology and the humanist and activist approaches. Further, we need more people like Symonds and Tiefer, who broadened the horizons of sexologists beyond the medical in the early twentieth and in the early twenty-first century, respectively.

Notes

1. Male homosexuality in the USSR was legalized again in 1993.
2. The term racial hygiene refers to practices and ideas associated with eugenics, which aimed at improving population. There were negative eugenic methods (for instance, the

sterilization of the poor or people of "improper" racial background, such as the Roma) and positive eugenic methods (encouraging the rich, the healthy, and those of "proper" racial background, for example whites, to procreate). Eugenics was a highly popular ideology in the first part of the twentieth century, usually associated with the Nazis, but it was also embraced by activists and scholars from progressive milieus such as feminists and birth control proponents.

3 In social science, agency is defined as a capacity of a subject to act and to cause (partial) change in social settings (see, for example, Brettell 2002).

4 The term urning, in wide use in the late nineteenth century. Drawing on Karl Heinrich Ulrichs, Richard von Krafft-Ebing defined urnings as "male individuals that felt like women toward men" (Krafft-Ebing 1894, p. 224).

5 Clarke argues that medicalization ("the processes through which aspects of life previously outside the jurisdiction of medicine come to be constructed as medical problem," Clarke et al. 2010, p. 47) is being replaced with the process of biomedicalization, meaning "the increasingly complex, multisited, multidirectional processes of medicalization that today are being both extended and reconstituted through the emergent social forms and practices of a highly and increasingly technoscientific biomedicine" (Clarke et al. 2010, p. 47).

References

Altman, Dennis. 1997. "Global Gaze/Global Gays." *GLQ* 3(4): 417–436.

Åsberg, Cecilia and Ericka Johnson. 2009. "Viagra Selfhood: Pharmaceutical Advertising and the Visual Formation of Swedish Masculinity." *Health Care Analysis* 17(2): 144–157.

Bauer, Heike. 2015. "Introduction." In *Sexology and Translation. Cultural and Scientific Encounters across the Modern World*, edited by Heike Bauer. Philadelphia, PA: Temple University Press.

Bauer, Heike. 2017. *The Hirschfeld Archives: Violence, Death, and Modern Queer Culture*. Philadelphia, PA: Temple University Press.

Bayer, Roland. 1981. *Homosexuality and American Psychiatry: The Politics of Diagnosis*. Princeton NJ: Princeton University Press.

Beccalossi, Chiara. 2018. "Latin Eugenics and Sexual Knowledge in Italy, Spain, and Argentina: International Networks across the Atlantic." In *A Global History of Sexual Science, 1880–1960*, edited by Veronika Fuechtner, Douglas E. Haynes, and Ryan M Jones, 305–330. Oakland: University of California.

Bland, Lucy and Laura Doan, eds. 1998. *Sexology Uncensored. The Documents of Sexual Science*. Chicago, IL: Chicago University Press.

Bland, Lucy and Laura Doan, eds. 1999. *Sexology in Culture: Labeling Bodies and Desires*, 1st edn. Chicago, IL: University of Chicago Press.

Botre, Shrikant and Douglas E. Haynes. 2018. "Understanding R.D. Karve: Brahmacharya, Modernity and the Appropriation of Global Sexual Science in Western India, 1927–1953." In *A Global History of Sexual Science, 1880–1960*, edited by Veronika Fuechtner, Douglas E. Haynes, and Ryan M Jones, 163–185. Oakland: University of California.

Brettell, Caroline B. 2002. "The Individual/Agent and Culture/Structure in the History of the Social Sciences." *Social Science History* 26(3): 429–445.

Chauncey, George. 1982/1983. "From Sexual Inversion to Homosexuality: Medicine and the Changing Conceptualization of Female Deviance." *Salmagundi* 58/59: 114–146.

Chiang, Howard 2015. "Data of Desire: Translating (Homo)Sexology in Republican China." In *Sexology and Translation. Cultural and Scientific Encounters across the Modern World* edited by Heike Bauer, 72–90. Philadelphia, PA: Temple University Press.

Clarke, Adele E., Janet K. Shim, Laura Mamo, Jennifer Ruth Fosket and Jennifer R. Fishman. 2010. "Biomedicalization." In *Biomedicalization* edited by Adele E. Clarke, Laura Mamo, Jennifer Ruth Fosket et al., 47–87. Durham, NC: Duke University Press.

Drucker, Donna J. 2014. *The Classification of Sex: Alfred Kinsey and the Organization of Knowledge*. Pittsburgh, PA: University of Pittsburgh Press.

Essig, Laurie. 1999. *Queer in Russia*. Durham. NC: Duke University Press.

Fisher, Kate. 2018. "'The Scientists Who … Brought Us Closer to Our Liberated Selves'. Early Sexology in the 20th Century Culture." Opening lecture presented at the International Colloquium "Sexology and Ideology in Institutionalisation Era (1960–2000)," Université Libre de Bruxelles, Belgium (March 21–23, 2018).

Fisher Kate and Jana Funke. 2015. "British Sexual Science beyond the Medical: Cross-Disciplinary. Cross-Historical, and Cross-Cultural Translations." In *Sexology and Translation. Cultural and Scientific Encounters across the Modern World* edited by Heike Bauer, 95–114.Philadelphia. PA: Temple University Press.

Fishman, Jennifer R. 2004. "Manufacturing Desire: The Commodification of Female Sexual Dysfunction." *Social Studies of Science* 34(2): 187–218.

Fishman, Jennifer R. and Laura Mamo. 2001. "What's in a Disorder: A Cultural Analysis of Medical and Pharmaceutical Constructions of Male and Female Sexual Dysfunction. *Women & Therapy* 24(1–2): 179–193.

Foucault, Michel. 1978. *The History of Sexuality, Vol. 1: The Will to Knowledge*, translated by R. Hurley). New York, NY: Pantheon Books.

Frühstück, Sabine. 2003. *Colonizing Sex: Sexology and Social Control in Modern Japan*. Berkeley: University of California Press.

Fuechtner Veronika, Douglas E. Haynes, and Ryan M Jones. 2018. *A Global History of Sexual Science*, 1880–1960. Oakland: University of California.

Funke Jana, Kate Fisher, Jen Grove, and Rebecca Langlands. 2017. "Illustrating Phallic Worship: Uses of Material Objects and the Production of Sexual Knowledge in Eighteenth-Century Antiquarianism and Early Twentieth-Century Sexual Science." *Word & Image: A Journal of Verbal/Visual Enquiry* 33(3): 324–337.

Healey, Dan. 2001. *Homosexual Desire in Revolutionary Russia*. Chicago: University of Chicago Press.

Herzog, Dagmar. 2009. "Syncopated Sex: Transforming European Sexual Cultures." *American Historical Review* 114(5): 1287–1308.

Irvine, Janice M. 2005. *Disorders of Desire. Sexuality and Gender in Modern American Sexology*. Philadelphia, PA: Temple University Press.

Koedt, Anne. 1970. *The Myth of the Vaginal Orgasm*. Boston, MA: New England Free Press.

Kościańska, Agnieszka. 2014. "Beyond Viagra: Sex Therapy in Poland." *Sociologický časopis Czech Sociological Review* 50(6): 919–938.

Kościańska, Agnieszka. 2016. "Sex on Equal Terms? Polish Sexology on Women's Emancipation and 'Good Sex' from the 1970s to Present." *Sexualities* 19(1–2): 236–256.

Kościańska, Agnieszka. 2017. *Zobaczyć łosia*, Wołowiec: Wydawnictwo Czarne.

Krafft-Ebing, Richard von. 1894 [1886]. Psychopathia Sexualis, Contrary Sexual Instinct: A Medico-Legal Study, translated by Charles Gilbert Chaddock, Philadelphia, PA: F.A. Davis.

Leng Kristen. 2015. The Personal Is Scientific: Women, Gender, and the Production of Sexological Knowledge in Germany and Austria, 1900–1931. *History of Psychology* 18(3): 238–251.

Lišková, Kateřina. 2018. *Sexual Liberation, Socialist Style. Communist Czechoslovakia and the Science of Desire, 1945–89*. Cambridge: Cambridge University Press.

McLellan, Josie. 2011. *Love in the Time of Communism: Intimacy and Sexuality in the GDR*. Cambridge and New York: Cambridge University Press.

McMillan, Joanna. 2006. *Sex, Science and Morality in China*. New York, NY: Routladge.

Oosterhuis, Harry. 2000. *Stepchildren of Nature: Krafft-Ebing, Psychiatry, and the Making of Sexual Identity*. Chicago, IL: University of Chicago Press.

Porter, Roy and Lesley A. Hall. 1995. *The Facts of Life: The Creation of Sexual Knowledge in Britain, 1650–1950*. New Haven, CT: Yale University Press.

Potts, Annie and Leonore Tiefer. 2006. "Introduction." *Sexualities* 9(3): 267–272.

Povinelli, Elizabeth A. and George Chauncey. 1999 "Thinking Sexuality Transnationally." *GLQ* 5(4): 439–450.

Renkin Hadley Z. 2016. "Biopolitical Mythologies: Róheim, Freud, (Homo)phobia, and the Sexual Science of Eastern European Otherness." *Sexualities* 19(1/2): 168–189.

Robinson, Paul. 1989. *The Modernization of Sex*, 2nd edn. Ithaca, NY: Cornell Univeristy Press.

Rusterholz, Caroline. 2018. "British Women Doctors And Sexual Disorders 1930–1970." Paper presented at the International Colloquium "Sexology and Ideology in Institutionalization Era (1960–2000), Université Libre de Bruxelles, Belgium (March 21–23, 2108).

Somerville, S. Siobhan. 1998 [1994]. *Scientific Racism and the Emergence of the Homosexual Body*. In *Sexology in Culture: Labeling Bodies and Desires*, edited by Lucy Bland and Laura Doan, 60–76. Chicago, IL: University of Chicago Press.

Stella, Francesca. 2015. *Lesbian Loves in Soviet and Post-Soviet Russia*. London: Palgrave Macmillan.

Stoler, Ann L. 2005. *Race and the Education of Desire: Foucault's History of Sexuality and the Colonial Order of Things*. Durham, NC: Duke University Press.

Stoler, Ann L. 2016. *Duress: Imperial Durabilities in our Times*. Durham, NC: Duke University Press.

Sutton, Katie. 2015. "Representing the 'Third Sex': Cultural Translations of the Sexological Encounter in Early Twentieth-Century Germany." In *Sexology and Translation. Cultural and Scientific Encounters across the Modern World*, edited by Heike Bauer, 53–77. Philadelphia, PA: Temple University Press.

Terry, Jennifer. 1999 *An American Obsession. Science, Medicine, and Homosexuality in Modern Society*. Chicago, IL: University of Chicago Press.

Tiefer, Leonore. 2000 "Sexology and the Pharmaceutical Industry: The Threat of Co-option." *Journal of Sex Research* 37(3): 273–283.

Tiefer, Leonore. 2001 "Arriving at a 'New View' of Women's Sexual Problems: Background, Theory, and Activism." *Women & Therapy* 24(1/2): 63–98.

Vance, Carole S. 1989. "Social Construction Theory: Problems in the History of Sexuality." In *Homosexuality, Which Homosexuality?*, edited by Dennis Altman, 13–33. Amsterdam: Uitgeverij An Dekker/Schorer.

Waters, Chris. 2006. "Sexology." In *The Modern History of Sexuality*, edited by H.G. Cocks and Matt Houlbrook, 41–63. Basingstoke: Palgrave Macmillan.

Weeks, Jeffrey. 1985. *Sexuality and Its Discontents: Meanings, Myths and Modern Sexualities*. London: Routledge.

Weeks, Jeffrey. 2010. *Sexuality*. London: Routledge.

Wolff, Charlotte. 1986. *Magnus Hirschfeld: A Portrait of a Pioneer in Sexology*. London: Quartet Books.

3

Sexualities in Historical Comparative Perspective

MATHEW KUEFLER

Introduction

What is the value of history? We have all heard the cliché about those who do not learn from history being condemned to repeat it. For the history of sexuality, the concept of repetition is crucial. Human sexuality has been constituted through thousands of years, cemented into custom and theorized over time into moral principles. The enduring patterns of sexual acts and attitudes we discover when we study history cannot be avoided and are worthy of study. Nonetheless, we are not only passive recipients of the past: we also transform it with the knowledge we gain from life and the choices we make because of our desires. Throughout history, human beings have done the same. Perhaps the true value of history is finding out for ourselves the surprising diversity of the past even within tradition.

Sexuality in Traditional Societies

Though every society is different, including past societies, there are general patterns that permit comparison and contrast. Foremost is the prevalence of patriarchy, the name given to male dominance in history. Patriarchy influenced most structures of sexuality in most societies about which we have any real knowledge. Why there is so little evidence for egalitarian societies or ones dominated by women is not really clear. Pastoralists overall seem to have been less patriarchal than agriculturalists, though how precisely men's and women's relationships were affected by nomadism and settlement, warfare, or variations in wealth and status is also unclear (Hodgson 1999; Bolger 2010). If some early societies were matriarchal, that is, dominated by women, they have left little trace in the historical record (Pembroke 1967; Ledgerwood 1995; Jay 1996). So what we know of traditional societies must be filtered through this patriarchal lens. In what follows, the term "traditional" will be used to describe societies, from ancient to modern, that can be characterized as patriarchal, though most cultures exhibit a range of traditional and nontraditional elements (Waters 1989; Moghadam 2004).

The seclusion of women is a good example of how patriarchal structures influenced sexual customs. In some traditional societies, women were not permitted much freedom to be outside and away from the control of fathers or husbands. Their seclusion was intended to prevent their having uncontrolled sex – that meant loss of virginity for unmarried women and adultery for married women, and for both the possibility of illegitimate heirs, but it was also linked to fears that women polluted men or their spaces by their proximity (Ortner 1978; Chamberlin 2006). In some cultures, accordingly, women spent most of their lives in "women's quarters" and only rarely appeared in public. In others, women could travel away from their homes only if accompanied by male relatives or servants, often only if they were veiled or carried in litters so that they remained isolated even out-of-doors. The bridal veil, Catholic nun's habit, and Muslim hijab represent modern remnants of these age-old traditions that preserved a women's sexual modesty in public. These customs prevented much casual interaction between men and women. Exceptions existed for women of the lower classes, who were required to farm or fetch water or purchase food or run any number of public errands – and there are many stories of encounters between women and men at the local well, since it was one of the few places where they could meet (Baron 1989; Cohen 1989).

Marriage and family life

Traditional marriages different significantly even within this patriarchal framework. Polygamy was common, mostly in the form of polygyny, the marriage of one man to multiple women (Friedman 1982; Hassig 2016). Even when polyandry existed, that is, the marriage of one woman to multiple men, it seems often to have happened because of its advantages to men: in Himalayan societies, for example, several brothers might marry the same woman so as to keep family inheritances together, and their children would be regarded as heirs to all of the brothers (Mann 1978; also Cassidy and Lee 1989; Sommer 2015). In other parts of the world, monogamous marriage was the norm. In both polygamous and monogamous marriages, men kept informal wives, usually called concubines, as well as formal wives: in traditional China, for example, it was usual for a wealthy man to have one formal wife and one informal wife (McMahon 2010; Bossler 2013). The differences between formal and informal marriage relied more often on marriage payments rather than cohabitation. Payments might be made by a bride's parents to the groom or his parents, called a dowry, or from the groom's parents to the bride or her parents, called a brideprice or reverse dowry (Spiro 1975; Tambiah et al., 1989; Testart 2013). These payments might be listed in a written contract, as in ancient Egypt (which perhaps survives among modern Jewish couples), along with other obligations or restrictions. Ceremonies, which we might consider to be essential to establishing a formal marriage, do not seem to have been as important in the distant past: they existed, to be sure, but often consisted of simple ritual actions, such as eating a cake together in ancient Rome (Hersch 2010) or the simple escorting of the bride from her father's home to her husband's after a meal, as in ancient Greece (Oakley and Sinos 1993).

The distinction between formal and informal marriages does remind us of the legal significance of marriage in traditional societies. Marriages were usually the result of negotiations between families intending economic or social or political advantages. The birth of legitimate heirs was paramount, since it both cemented these bonds between families and also provided a channel for the transference of wealth or status from one generation to the next. The typical ages of marriage depended on this vital aspect of marriage, as, for example, in ancient Rome. Women were often married as soon as they were able to bear children, that is, at puberty. Men, in contrast, frequently delayed their marriages until they had received their inheritance or had established themselves in business, and thus often married only in their thirties (Saller 1987). The gap of perhaps 20 years between a husband's and a wife's ages probably did not help their intimacy. It also meant that women were much likelier than men to be widowed. Some traditional societies permitted widows to remarry (Holmgren 1985; Stampfer 1988); in others, they were considered a burden and, as in ancient and modern India, encouraged to commit suicide at their husband's death (Stein 1988; also Fisch 2006).

Variations of all sorts can be seen in the historical record on marriage. In some societies, such as in medieval Arab Islamic lands, marriages between cousins were the norm: a custom believed to reinforce existing extended family bonds and still practiced in the Middle East today (Murphy and Kasdan 1959; also Moore 1963; Taylor and Taylor 1985). In other societies, such as in medieval Western Christian lands, marriages between any persons closely related was forbidden: at first, between anyone sharing an ancestor going back seven generations, but later revised to three generations, that is, back to one's great-grandparents (Bouchard 1981; also Morgan 1979). In a few societies, marriages between even more closely related relatives existed: uncles and nieces, fathers and daughters, and/or brothers and sisters. Ancient Egypt is one example (Middleton 1962; also Davenport 1994).

Most marriages in traditional societies were expected to be permanent, though men held the right to divorce their wives for misconduct: adultery or disobedience, or even for circumstances beyond their control like the inability to have children. Women seldom held the right to initiate a divorce from their husbands. Adultery was usually punishable in married men only if they had sex with a married woman, whereas the penalty for married women might be death (Jayasekera 1982; Roth 1988; Cohn-Haft 1995; Stacey 2002). In a few societies, temporary marriages existed. In Shia Islam, for example, parents could arrange for what was called a "marriage of joy" between a daughter and a man who would be her husband only for a designated period of time (Haeri 1989). In southwest China, the Na or Moso people enjoyed "walking marriages," where men and women established temporary sexual relationships: here, women lived with their extended families and men only visited them at night, either a man or a woman might begin or end such a relationship, and any children born to the union joined her extended family (Shih 2009). A different type of temporary marriage existed among the Azande people of central Africa: here, where polygyny was the norm and older men married most eligible women, younger men married pubescent boys who acted socially and sexually as wives. As the husbands in these same-sex marriages matured and achieved greater status, they took female wives, and as the boys matured, they abandoned the role of wife to become a husband to a new generation of boys (Evans-Pritchard 1970).

The importance of religion

Key to the maintenance of these traditional sexual customs, and likely also to their origins, were religious and philosophical beliefs. Ancient religious legends portrayed gods and goddesses as modeling human patterns of sex and marriage (O'Flaherty 1969a and 1969b). Or human customs were explained as part of a divine plan or cosmic order. The biblical story of Adam and Eve, for example, had Eve created after Adam and intended to be his helper. It also describes female subordination to men and the pain of childbirth as the punishment for Eve's sin (Kvam, Schearing, and Ziegler 1999; Crowther 2010). The ancient Chinese philosopher we call Confucius saw all of society as a set of unequal social bonds: rulers and subjects, parents and children, and husbands and wives (Gao 2003; Clark and Wang 2004). Needless to say, such ideas helped to reinforce the gender inequalities of patriarchy.

For most traditional religions, sex – and the pleasure that accompanied it, at least for men – was a natural part of human life. In the ancient Chinese belief system of Daoism, men and women each contributed a special force to the universe and to each other: *yin* is the name for the feminine energy and *yang* for the masculine. The best-lived life was one of balance between these energies, and sex between a man and a woman was one of the simplest ways of ensuring such balance (Harper 1987; Leo 2011). Among the Hindus, *kama*, usually translated as pleasure, was among the chief goals of life. Again, a manual called the *Kamasutra* ("Book of Pleasure") instructed men on how to maximize this feeling during sex (Macy 1975; Doniger 2003). Phallic worship and rituals involving an artificial and oversized penis – as seen, for example, in ancient Greek and Roman images and in modern Japanese shinto or the worship of Shiva's penis in Hinduism – were built upon the religious reverence for sexual pleasure (Stone 1976; Doniger 2011). Pleasure was also key to the ancient practice of sacred prostitution, wherein followers of a deity – usually a goddess of fertility – had sex with priestesses in temples dedicated to her (Westenholz 1989; also Vijaisri 2004).

An alternative pattern in traditional religions placed sexual renunciation above sexual expression. Even among the ancient fertility religions, for example, there is evidence for men who castrated themselves, probably meant as a self-sacrifice of individual fertility for the sake of the community (Latham 2012). The modern *hijra* of India may be the religious descendants of such individuals, since they still remove their male genitals as part of the worship of a Hindu fertility goddess (Reddy 2005). Buddhism began with Siddhartha's admonitions that his followers abandon all desires. Christianity's founder Jesus told his disciples to concern themselves with heavenly rather than earthly pursuits. In both Buddhism and Christianity, the drive to discount sex and marriage led to the institutionalization of celibacy in monasticism, where monks and nuns lived sexless lives in communities called monasteries (Faure 1998; Cabezón 2017). Among Western Christians in the Middle Ages (and still in the modern Roman Catholic Church) that impulse to abandon sex resulted also in a celibate clergy: where the willingness to give up sex is seen as a sign of one's suitability for ritual and institutional leadership (Brown 1988; Wiesner-Hanks 2010). Both Buddhism and Christianity eventually provided recognized roles for those who still engaged in sex and still married – called "householders" in the Buddhist tradition and "the laity" in the Christian tradition (Junko and Glassman 1993; Muecke 2004). Both also developed mystical traditions in which sex is seen as a metaphor for devotion: as seen in images of Siddhartha embracing Tara, the personification of enlightenment, or in the idea of the Christian soul as the "bride of Christ" (Davidson 2002; Nissinen and Uro 2008). And, in Christianity, the notion that marriage was a sacred institution, called a sacrament, gradually developed – which greatly increased the reverence for it (Reynolds 2016).

Alternative sexualities and genders

As the example of sexual renunciation demonstrates, religious ideologies provided support not only for traditional sexual and gender roles but also for alternative possibilities. Many ancient legends represented gods and goddesses as violating the norms for typical human behavior (Sienkewicz 2013). Alternative sexual arrangements often involved alternative gender identities. The Hindu god Shiva transformed himself into the goddess Mohini, and his new appearance so aroused the god Vishnu that he ejaculated spontaneously (Kalidos 1986). While imagining these possibilities in a divine realm, human cultures also generated new roles for themselves. In most societies where sacred prostitution existed, castrated priests served alongside priestesses, having sex with the men who visited the temples. These eunuch priests existed across the Mediterranean; they seem to have freely chosen their sexual and gender identities, castrating themselves as a sign of devotion to their goddess and dressing themselves in women's clothing (Roscoe 1996).

The opportunity to choose alternative gender identities and the sexual behaviors that accompanied them can be found in some, but not all, traditional human societies. Perhaps best known are the individuals who chose the so-called berdache or two-spirit role in native North American societies, though each indigenous language had its own names for the role. These persons chose to take on the appearance and activities of their nonbiological sex, including marrying and adopting children (Schnarch 1992; also Epple 1998). Similar roles existed among the peoples of the Pacific islands, Arabia, and Southeast Asia (Besnier and Alexeyeff 2014; Rowson 1991; Wikan 1977; also Peletz 2006). In other places, cross-dressing served to enhance sexual interest but was not part of the assumption of an alternative gender identity, such as the young women who cross-dressed as boys at the court of the Abbasid caliphs of Baghdad or the boys who performed as female characters on and off the Noh stage in early modern Japan (Rowson 2003; MacDuff 1996).

We might consider these identities and the sexual roles that followed from them as similar to the lives of transgender individuals today, but there are other behaviors that are less certain and sometimes without obvious modern parallels. These include the female marriages among various peoples of Africa. Among the Nuer, for example, widows without children could choose to become female husbands, marrying women and adopting children or arranging for surrogate fathers: any children born to these female marriages would be considered as the heirs to the deceased male husband. We might think of them as lesbian relationships, though there is not always a sexual component in these female marriages (Cadigan 1998). In truth, the patriarchal nature of most traditional societies restricted many women's control over their sex lives, and when we hear about same-sex relations between women, it is often through men who are worried about female sexual autonomy rather than from the women themselves (Rupp 2011).

One of the most common sexual alternatives in traditional societies was pederasty, where adult men had sex with pubescent or adolescent boys. The practice was common in many parts of the world, and survives in modern New Guinea (Herdt 1982). Most men who engaged in it were also married – indeed, given the differences in ages of marriage between men and women, many men's wives were about the same age as their male sex partners. Where it existed, boys were expected to play a penetrated role in sexual encounters until they matured, at which point they took new partners from younger males (Cantarella 2002). Sometimes pederasty was mixed with cross-dressing, so boys who were the sexual partners of older males dressed as women, as happened in ancient China, for example (Hinsch 1992). There does not seem to have been a female equivalent to pederasty.

A final alternative to marriage that existed in most traditional societies was prostitution. Prostitution can be found throughout history; only in recent centuries, with the spread of sexually transmitted diseases, have there been serious attempts to restrict it. There were both male and female prostitutes but most served male clients. Most, as today, became prostitutes because of limited opportunities otherwise; many were slaves or trafficked, also as still often happens. Given the delayed ages of marriage of men in many traditional societies, prostitutes provided sexual outlets to men between adolescence and middle age, though married men also visited prostitutes (Bullough and Bullough 1987).

Making the Modern World

History provides almost endless variations on these basic patterns of traditional sexualities, many of which have remained to this day. Yet we can also see how the various features of modern life – the growing interconnections in the world, the influence of scientific ideas about sex, and more – have changed many of these customs as well as the ideological assumptions that produced them. For some scholars, the modern age represents a new mode of human relationship to the self (Harvey 2002; Cocks 2006). What follows is a list of some of these new elements.

Intercultural connections

We in the modern era are fully aware of how different each society is. So it is probably impossible for us to understand fully how shocking it was when those who traveled outside of their own cultural zones in past eras discovered societies that operated on very different terms – social, political, and sexual – from their own. We can see some of that astonishment in the historical record, as travelers wrote of places where individuals walked about in the nude or where some men had huge harems with hundreds of wives and concubines or where women lived in essential equality with men. For some, the response was hostile: they condemned the peoples they encountered as immoral or ignorant. Others had a more positive reaction: they might have questioned the values and customs of their own societies and some even abandoned their own heritage for a new way of life, if they saw the peoples they encountered as living closer to nature or without the baggage of unwanted traditions (Bleys 1995; Nagel 2003).

An important aspect of these intercultural connections happened through immigration, when large numbers of human populations permanently settled elsewhere. Some of these migrations were voluntary: as with the settlements of Europeans in the Americas or of the Chinese around the Pacific Ocean, and some were forced, as with African slaves brought to the Americas, but all ended by introducing new customs – including sexual customs – around the globe (Manalansan 2006; Loos 2009). The different forms that immigration took also influenced how these changes happened. African slaves were taken from many different peoples, so the marriage customs that developed mixed those of many cultures, maintained as best they could while living in slavery. Jews escaping persecution in Europe mostly migrated as family groups to North America or the Middle East, and many lived in proximity to other Jewish families, and thus they preserved their traditions (Gshur and Okun 2003; Davis 2018). Chinese men, in contrast, tended to immigrate without wives or families, and so they more frequently married into and had sexual interactions with the local populations where they settled (Jiemin 2003; Lee 2010). In all of these ways, an increasing diversity of hybrid sexual traditions were formed.

The influence of science

Another feature of modern sexuality so commonplace as to go mostly unremarked is the influence of science. In premodern societies, individuals tended to go to religious leaders for answers to their questions about sex, and while traditionalists still do, more and more ask these questions of scientists, whether physicians, biologists, psychologists, geneticists, statisticians, or others. The scientific revolution of the seventeenth and eighteenth centuries provided the foundations for this shift, but it was the professionalization of the sciences in the nineteenth and twentieth centuries that made the real difference. Many scholars have written of the obsessions of nineteenth-century European medicine: sexual perversion, especially in men, hysteria, especially in women, and masturbation, especially in children (Goldstein 1982; Hunt 1998; Moore 2009). Through such medical concerns, the bulk of the population was made the subject of scientific study and made to believe that only scientists could help them. A new field of science, called sexology, was founded in the nineteenth century to legitimize these investigations (Leck 2016). In the twentieth century these ideas were disseminated across the globe (Fuechtner, Haynes, and Jones 2018).

One of the chief claims of science has been its objectivity. Scientists usually considered their knowledge as based more on fact than the assertions of religion. Recently, however, scholars have challenged some of the cultural assumptions made by scientists both for the types of questions they asked and for the answers they gave (Weis 1998). Discredited scientific ideas, like eugenics, offer especially clear opportunities for reviewing the claims of scientific objectivity, and challenges have come also from scholars influenced by feminism and postcolonialism, who see many scientific ideas as having been created by men for men, and imposed on peoples around the world as a sort of ideological colonialism (Irvine 2005; Bashford and Levine 2010).

The impact of industrialization, urbanization, and consumerism

A surprisingly critical factor in the making of modern sexualities has been the impact of industrialization. While the greatest industrial zones were in Europe and North America, much of the rest of the world participated as the suppliers of raw materials for industry and also as the consumer markets for industrial goods. Before industrialization, families generally worked together in farming or small-scale business. Rural areas or small towns offered a limited pool for marriage partners. Since married couples depended on the goodwill of their families for support and inheritances, they might well accept marriage partners chosen for them by their parents. Having many children meant more hands to do the work (Sylvester 2001; Osterud 2012). The shift to factory work changed all that. In some regions, especially in the colonies, entire families worked in collecting or processing the raw resources for industry (Mallon 1987; Schmidt 1991; Hammad 2016). But as child labor laws took hold in Europe and the Americas in the nineteenth century, factory work separated families: fathers worked outside the home, while mothers and children stayed home – though mothers often took in laundry or cared for other children to supplement the family's income. Wages meant that married couples no longer depended as much on inheritances and their families' goodwill. More children were a greater financial burden, and married couples began using contraceptives – inexpensive rubber condoms were invented in the mid-nineteenth century – to limit the size of their families (Freedman 1982; also Rao 1973; Ekong 1986). For similar reasons, polygamy declined in parts of the world where it had been practiced (Solway 1990; also Clignet and Sween 1974).

The urbanization that accompanied industrialization also impacted sexuality. Populations flocked to industrial zones or to the ports that supplied goods or materials. Growing cities provided much greater pools of potential marriage partners – as well as pools of potential sexual partners who did not demand marriage – including prostitutes – and of disrupters of marriages. The greater anonymity of the cities also allowed for more discreet sexual encounters and for greater experimentation in sex (Ni 1954; Hew 2003).

The greater availability of industrial goods stimulated a growing consumerism, which encouraged individuals to spend their wages on things that offered more than food and shelter. And at the heart of consumerism is sexuality. Men and women were encouraged to buy the latest fashions in clothing or an increasingly elaborate range of beauty products with the promise that they would provide sex appeal (Walker 2007; Manzano 2009; Wu 2009). Facial cosmetics were targeted to women from the 1920s on, for example; before then, make-up had not been commonly worn (Delano 2000; Schweitzer 2005). Consumerism also marketed venues for love and happiness, at a price: the first amusement parks and movie theaters opened at the very end of the nineteenth century, and they were later joined by nightclubs and dance halls (Callaci 2011).

By the early twentieth century women were taking increasing advantage of industrialization. Women had always worked, of course, but in the early industrial era most had been confined to their homes – or to the homes of the wealthy as servants, cooks, and nannies. Unmarried women sometimes did factory work, but often in ways that reinforced traditional gender roles, in textile or food production. Other unmarried women worked as teachers and nurses – again, reinforcing their traditional roles. But once a woman married, there were few available jobs, and even wealthy women who had servants to do their housework were denied careers (Seccombe 1986). Yet over the course of the twentieth century, women moved into the workforce in ever greater numbers, earned wages, and participated more fully in the consumer economy (Brooke 2006). Some demanded the right to vote: a right accorded to women in most countries of the world between the 1910s and 1950s. That brought its own changes, since politicians responded to women's right to vote by creating policies that appealed to women and offered them greater equality with men: in a sexual context, that meant giving women greater ability to choose their own marriage and sexual partners, gain access to contraception, initiate divorce, take custody of children, and so on (Tilly 1994; Öztimur 2007).

The ideal of romance

As men and women gained greater independence from family restraints and were likelier to live in urban areas with greater numbers of potential sexual and marital partners around them, it became increasingly important that they learn to present themselves in the best possible light. That meant not only wearing the latest fashions and using the most effective beauty accessories, though these things were supposed to help, but also behaving in romantic ways that attracted others (Reekie 1991; Stearns and Knapp 1993; Teo 2005). Romance isn't entirely a modern invention. Poems and stories about love have been written since ancient times: for example, in the devotion of Sita for Rama in the Indian legend called the *Ramayana* or in the medieval Arthurian myths of Lancelot and Guinevere. But romance was something separate from marriage, as both stories also demonstrate (Goldman 1991; Nickolaus 2002). Increasingly in the modern world, in contrast, romance has been the precursor to marriage. Historians call this the companionate marriage (Simmons 2009; Cuno 2015). Generally, men were expected to bring the passion of sexual drive to a marriage and women the tender feelings of love. Popular literature and music, made more accessible by rising literacy rates and new inventions like the phonograph and radio, touted the joys of romance – and the misery of the broken heart – throughout the twentieth century (Hogeland 1995; Puri 1997). And if romance caused a marriage to come into being, its loss might be sufficient reason to end a marriage, as seen in the rising divorce rates in the last century (Hackstaff 1999; Dommaraju and Jones 2011; Clark and Brauner-Otto 2015).

Modern sexual identities

The modern notion of romance insisted that individuals might find self-fulfillment in love. Implied in this idea was that we all have the right to the kind of love we want. Those with unconventional sexual orientations and gender identities have increasingly claimed the right to love. Again, gender and sexually nonconforming persons are nothing new to the modern era (Greenberg 1990). What is new are the categories for understanding gender and sexual difference, both as self-understanding and labeling by others. Industrialization seems to have provided the foundation for these new identities. Living in cities meant anonymity and the availability of likeminded partners; earning wages also meant independence from family control. So as cities grew, there existed places – bars and nightclubs, or secluded corners of parks and docks – where such individuals could go to find sex or companionship (Aldrich 2004). Gender and sexual nonconformity are still often easier in urban rather than rural settings (Feyisetan and Pebley 1989; Schvaneveldt and Hubler 2012).

The individuals who met in these places reflected a range of gender and sexual identities. Indeed, it is not really possible to describe such persons with our modern terms. Through the middle of the twentieth century, many of them mixed gender and sexual unconventionality, and same-sex desires were often accompanied by and perhaps made more readily visible by cross-dressing or in cross-gendered mannerisms called "mannish" in women and "effeminate" in men (Martin 1993). A group of women in early twentieth-century Paris, for example dressed in men's clothes and enjoyed sexual relationships with each other (Doan 1998; Latimer 2005). In New York City in the same period men nicknamed fairies or pansies met in nightclubs, looking for so-called "normal" men with whom to have sex, and displaying the same mix of gender and sexual variance (Chauncey 1995). Similar groups existed in many of the world's cities (Parker 1999). There were probably others, persons who were not so visible and did not therefore get noticed, but it is difficult to do more than speculate. Historians often refer to "intimate or romantic friendships" when they find same-sex couples who have not left enough of a trace to determine if their relationships were sexual or not, and who did not exhibit any gender nonconformity (Smith-Rosenberg 1975; Rotundo 1989).

It was out of this mixture that modern notions of sexual orientation and transgender identity developed, but only gradually. The word "homosexual" was coined in 1869 by a Hungarian physician, and was popularized in multiple languages by Sigmund Freud's adoption of it (Beachy 2010). In the United States the word "gay" gradually took over as a less clinical term, especially for naming oneself and especially in the 1970s, when the gay liberation movement took hold. It has since been imported both as a word and a concept into many societies. In the 1970s the term "lesbian" also became the usual term for women with same-sex desires, many of whom saw themselves as embodying an identity and a culture separate from gay men (Faderman 1992; Marcus 2002). The twentieth century also saw the rise of the bisexual identity, which came to public attention only in the 1980s, and of the queer identity, which appeared in the 1990s (Angelides 2001). Transgender identities developed slowly over the same century. The first experiments in gender confirmation surgery began in Germany in the 1920s but became more readily available in the 1950s in Europe and in the 1970s in North America (Meyerowitz 2004; Stryker 2017). Intersex persons, who have the genetic information and/or biological characteristics of both male and female, and gender nonbinary persons, who do not feel themselves to be either male or female, are only now gaining public awareness (Reis 2009; McNabb 2018). The proliferation of alternative sexual and gender identities that is represented by the labels lesbian, gay, bisexual, transgender, queer, intersex, gender fluid, and more (LGBTQI+) demonstrates that it is not easy to categorize all human beings with general labels.

Liberation

The last half-century in human history is often seen as a period of sexual liberation. Many date the beginnings of this shift with the so-called sexual revolution of the 1960s and 1970s, and it is true that these decades marked new beginnings across the globe

(Allyn 2000). Yet there were liberated spaces that existed earlier, including Paris in the late nineteenth and early twentieth centuries, or Berlin in the 1920s, or Las Vegas in the 1940s – that is, places known to individuals who wanted to live lives freer of social constraints (Baxter 2006; Gordon 2006; Gragg 2007). Perhaps it was the disruptions of the First and Second World Wars that contributed most to the broadening of sexual liberation. The wars mobilized huge numbers of young adults, who fought or provided essential services to the war efforts, and who were relocated to urban areas and ports or sent overseas. Many worried about their future: some abandoned traditional morality and engaged in sexual experimentation (Goodman 2002; Leder 2006; Cohler 2010; Roberts 2013; Smaal 2015; Todd 2017). Out of this sexual liberation has come more liberal attitudes toward cohabitation without marrying, pre- and extramarital sex, divorce and remarriage, homosexuality, and more (Herzog 2006).

Efforts to restore the old social order after both world wars were not very successful. Governments worked hard to encourage traditional family life, for example, with benefits given to couples for having children (Cousins 1999). They also tried to discourage sexual license, including with censorship laws that made sexually explicit and "obscene" literature, art, and films illegal (Semonche 2007; Strub 2011). Many local governments also banned "loitering" in public places, so as to make prostitution and gay cruising more difficult, and they closed down meeting places for those deemed to be "sex deviates" (Campbell 1999). But the shift in attitudes was impossible to stop. Policies were influenced by postwar social movements, especially the women's liberation movement or second-wave feminism, which worked toward women's equality with men both in private and public life (Gerhard 2001). Postwar courts across Europe and the Americas generally expanded individual rights, striking down laws against divorce, sexually explicit materials and sex education, contraception and abortion, homosexuality, and more (Gordon 2002; Seymour 2006; Zimmerman 2015). And the advent of television brought sexual topics into homes across the globe (Press 2009; Stadel 2014; Kutulas 2017). Colonial governments were slower than others to implement these more liberal laws, so many newly independent countries kept more restrictive laws on the books, and some have rejected the liberalization of sexual attitudes as symptoms of "modern Western decadence" – even while individuals within these societies have embraced the need for change (Keddie 1990; Epprecht 2009; O'Shaughnessy 2009; Chaudhuri 2012; Klausen 2015). Communist governments embraced these reforms in the early twentieth century – and because of it, many Western governments in the Cold War era linked sexual liberation to communism – but many freedoms were reversed as Communist governments sought to impose order on their citizens' lives (Stacey 1982; Voronina 1993; Guerra 2010; McLellan 2011).

The shift from sexual restrictions to sexual liberation has created deep divides in most modern societies. Some have welcomed the changes in sexuality and hope for even more. Other have refused to abandon traditional values about sex and marriage (Widmer, Treas, and Newcomb 1998). These political divisions have become entangled with other social concerns: about impact of immigrants with different values about sex, for example (Eichenberger 2012). What the future holds for the notion of sexual liberation is unclear. In some countries, same-sex relationships are punishable by death; in others, same-sex marriages are legal (Thoreson 2014). In some countries, reproductive rights are greatly restricted; in others, there are few restrictions

(Hartmann 2016). Globalization has made it increasingly possible for individuals in one part of the world to know what is happening in other regions, including advances in sexual rights and freedoms. How this will affect changes in law and government policies is still to be determined (Altman 2004).

Conclusion: The History of the History of Sexuality

The study of the history of sexuality is still in its infancy. It grew out of a popular twentieth-century field of history, called social history, which focused on the lives of ordinary people of the past. The first generation of scholars who studied historical sexuality in the 1970s often had to work hard to justify the legitimacy of the topic, since it was seen by many as something that should not be talked about. Many of these first scholars saw their efforts as uncovering the roots to modern trends or identities (Bullough 1976; Boswell 1980). But they were criticized by the second generation of historians of sexuality for assuming too much similarity between persons of the past and us today. We don't really have the sort of historical record that allows us to dig too deeply into the motives or impulses of historical individuals, especially in the distant past, and the documents and images that do survive often reveal very different understandings of what sexuality meant and its connection to a sense of self (Padgug 1979; Cook 2007). The debates among historians of sexuality in the 1980s and 1990s pitted social constructionists against essentialists. Social constructionists were those who concluded from the historical evidence that persons in every historical society had unique ways of expressing sexuality and that the farther back in the past you looked, the more unfamiliar these behaviors and identities were. Essentialists were not really a defined group; rather, the term was used pejoratively for those who did not take these differences into account. The debates have made historians of sexuality very careful about not presuming too much about what any sexual activities reveal about historical persons (Stein 1990; Halperin 2002). At the same time, we must use familiar words to describe even unfamiliar actions. The modern, third generation of historians of sexuality, is profoundly interested in how sexuality overlaps with other aspects of the self: gender identity, race and ethnicity, nationality, social position, and more – what scholars call intersectionality (Gottfried 1998; Valocchi 1999; Parker 2009; Patil 2013). And, as I have tried to show with varied references to scholars working in all parts of the world and in all historical periods, more and more are exploring the unique histories of each region and each era.

References

Aldrich, Robert. 2004. "Homosexuality and the City: An Historical Overview." *Urban Studies* 41(9): 1719–1737.
Allyn, David. 2000. *Make Love, Not War: The Sexual Revolution, an Unfettered History*. Boston, MA: Little, Brown.
Altman, Dennis. 2004. "Sexuality and Globalisation." *Agenda: Empowering Women for Gender Equity* 18(62): 22–28.
Angelides, Steven. 2001. *A History of Bisexuality*. Chicago, IL: University of Chicago Press.

Baron, Beth. 1989. "Unveiling in Early Twentieth Century Egypt: Practical and Symbolic Considerations." *Middle Eastern Studies* 25(3): 370–386.

Bashford, Alison and Philippa Levine, eds. 2010. *The Oxford Handbook of the History of Eugenics*. Oxford: Oxford University Press.

Baxter, John. 2006. *We'll Always Have Paris: Sex and Love in the City of Light*. New York, NY: HarperCollins.

Beachy, Robert. 2010. "The German Invention of Homosexuality." *Journal of Modern History* 82(4): 801–838.

Besnier, Niko and Kalissa Alexeyeff, eds. 2014. *Gender on the Edge: Transgender, Gay, and Other Pacific Islanders*. Honolulu: University of Hawai'i Press.

Bleys, Rudi. 1995. *The Geography of Perversion: Male-to-Male Sexual Behavior Outside the West and the Ethnographic Imagination, 1750–1918*. New York: New York University Press.

Bolger, Diane. 2010. "The Dynamics of Gender in Early Agricultural Societies of the Near East." *Signs* 35(2): 503–531.

Bossler, Beverly. 2013. *Courtesans, Concubines, and the Cult of Female Fidelity*. Cambridge, MA: Harvard University Press.

Boswell, John. 1980. *Christianity, Social Tolerance, and Homosexuality: Gay People in Western Europe from the Beginning of the Christian Era to the Fourteenth Century*. Chicago, IL: University of Chicago Press.

Bouchard, Constance B. 1981. "Consanguinity and Noble Marriages in the Tenth and Eleventh Centuries." *Speculum* 56(2): 268–287.

Brooke, Stephen. 2006. "Bodies, Sexuality and the 'Modernization' of the British Working Classes, 1920s to 1960s." *International Labor and Working-Class History* 69(1): 104–122.

Brown, Peter. 1988. *The Body and Society: Men, Women, and Sexual Renunciation in Early Christianity*. New York, NY: Columbia University Press.

Bullough, Vern L. 1976. *Sex, Society, and History*. New York, NY: Science History.

Bullough, Vern L. and Bonnie Bullough. 1987. *Women and Prostitution: A Social History*. Buffalo, NY: Prometheus.

Cabezón, José Ignacio. 2017. *Sexuality in Classical South Asian Buddhism*. Somerville, MA: Wisdom.

Cadigan, R. Jean. 1998. "Woman-to-Woman Marriage: Practices and Benefits in Sub-Saharan Africa." *Journal of Comparative Family Studies* 29(1): 89–98.

Callaci, Emily. 2011. "Dancehall Politics: Mobility, Sexuality, and Spectacles of Racial Respectability in Late Colonial Tanganyika, 1930s–1961." *Journal of African History* 52(3): 365–384.

Campbell, Robert A. 1999. "Managing the Marginal: Regulating and Negotiating Decency in Vancouver's Beer Parlours, 1925–1954." *Labour/Le Travail* 44(Fall): 109–127.

Cantarella, Eva. 2002. *Bisexuality in the Ancient World*, 2nd edn. New Haven, CT: Yale University Press.

Cassidy, Margaret L. and Gary R. Lee. 1989. "The Study of Polyandry: A Critique and Synthesis." *Journal of Comparative Family Studies* 20(1): 1–11.

Chamberlin, Ann. 2006. *A History of Women's Seclusion in the Middle East: The Veil in the Looking Glass*. New York, NY: Haworth.

Chaudhuri, Maitrayee. 2012. "Indian 'Modernity' and 'Tradition': A Gender Analysis." *Polish Sociological Review* 178(2): 281–293.

Chauncey, George. 1995. *Gay New York: Gender, Urban Culture, and the Making of the Gay Male World, 1890–1940*. New York: Basic Books.

Clark, Shelley and Sarah Brauner-Otto. 2015. "Divorce in Sub-Saharan Africa: Are Unions Becoming Less Stable?" *Population and Development Review* 41(4): 583–605.

Clark, Kelly James and Robin R. Wang. 2004. "A Confucian Defense of Gender Equity." *Journal of the American Academy of Religion* 72(2): 395–422.

Clignet, Remi and Joyce Sween. 1974. "Urbanization, Plural Marriage, and Family Size in Two African Cities." *American Ethnologist* 1(2): 221–242.

Cocks, H.G. 2006. "Modernity and the Self in the History of Sexuality." *Historical Journal* 49(4): 1211–27.

Cohen, David. 1989. "Seclusion, Separation, and the Status of Women in Classical Athens." *Greece & Rome* 36(1): 3–15.

Cohn-Haft, Louis. 1995. "Divorce in Classical Athens." *Journal of Hellenic Studies* 115: 1–14.

Cohler, Deborah. 2010. *Citizen, Invert, Queer: Lesbianism and War in Early Twentieth-Century Britain*. Minneapolis: University of Minnesota Press.

Cook, Hera. 2007. "Sexuality and Contraception in Modern England: Doing the History of Reproductive Sexuality." *Journal of Social History* 40(4): 915–932.

Cousins, Mel. 1999. "The Introduction of Children's Allowances in Ireland, 1939–1944." *Irish Economic and Social History* 26(1): 35–53.

Crowther, Kathleen M. 2010. *Adam and Eve in the Protestant Reformation*. Cambridge: Cambridge University Press.

Cuno, Kenneth M. 2015. *Modernizing Marriage: Family, Ideology, and Law in Nineteenth- and Early Twentieth-Century Egypt*. Syracuse, NY: Syracuse University Press.

Davenport, William H. 1994. *Pi'o: An Enquiry into the Marriage of Brothers and Sisters and Other Close Relatives in Old Hawai'i*. Lanham, MD: University Press of America.

Davidson, Ronald M. 2002. *Indian Esoteric Buddhism: A Social History of the Tantric Movement*. New York, NY: Columbia University Press.

Davis, Rebecca L. 2018. "Purity and Population: American Jews, Marriage, and Sexuality." In *Devotions and Desires: Histories of Sexuality and Religion in the Twentieth-Century United States*, edited by Gillian Frank, Bethany Moreton, and Heather R. White, 54–70. Chapel Hill: University of North Carolina Press.

Delano, Page Dougherty. 2000. "Making Up for War: Sexuality and Citizenship in Wartime Culture." *Feminist Studies* 26(1): 33–68.

Doan, Laura. 1998. "Passing Fashions: Reading Female Masculinities in the 1920s." *Feminist Studies* 24(3): 663–700.

Dommaraju, Premchand and Gavin Jones. 2011. "Divorce Trends in Asia." *Asian Journal of Social Science* 39(6): 725–750.

Doniger, Wendy. 2003. "The 'Kamasutra': It Isn't All About Sex." *Kenyon Review* 25(1): 18–37.

Doniger, Wendy. 2011. "God's Body, or, The Lingam made Flesh: Conflicts over the Representation of the Sexual Body of the Hindu God Shiva." *Social Research* 78(2): 485–508.

Eichenberger, Sarah L. 2012. "When For Better is For Worse: Immigration Law's Gendered Impact on Foreign Polygamous Marriage." *Duke Law Journal* 61(5): 1067–1110.

Ekong, Sheilah Clarke. 1986. "Industrialization and Kinship: A Comparative Study of Some Nigerian Ethnic Group." *Journal of Comparative Family Studies* 17(2): 197–206.

Epple, Carolyn. 1998. "Coming to Terms with Navajo 'Nádleehí': A Critique of 'Berdache,' 'Gay,' 'Alternate Gender,' and 'Two-Spirit.'" *American Ethnologist* 25(2): 267–290.

Epprecht, Marc. 2009. "Sexuality, Africa, History." *American Historical Review* 114(5): 1258–1272.

Evans-Pritchard, E.E. 1970. "Sexual Inversion among the Azande." *American Anthropologist* 72(6): 1428–1434.

Faderman, Lillian. 1992. *Odd Girls and Twilight Lovers: A History of Lesbian Life in Twentieth-Century America*. New York, NY: Penguin.

Faure, Bernard. 1998. *The Red Thread: Buddhist Approaches to Sexuality*. Princeton, NJ: Princeton University Press.

Feyisetan, Bamikale and Anne R. Pebley. 1989. "Premarital Sexuality in Urban Nigeria." *Studies in Family Planning* 20(6): 343–354.

Fisch, Jörg. 2006. *Burning Women: A Global History of Widow Sacrifice from Ancient Times to the Present*. London: Seagull.

Freedman, Estelle B. 1982. "Sexuality in Nineteenth-Century America: Behavior, Ideology, and Politics." *Reviews in American History* 10(4): 196–215.

Friedman, Mordechai A. 1982. "Polygyny in Jewish Tradition and Practice: New Sources from the Cairo Geniza." *Proceedings of the American Academy for Jewish Research* 49: 33–68.

Fuechtner, Veronika, Douglas E. Haynes, and Ryan M. Jones, eds. 2018. *A Global History of Sexual Science, 1880–1960*. Berkeley: University of California Press.

Gao, Xiongya. 2003. "Women Existing for Men: Confucianism and Social Injustice against Women in China." *Race, Gender & Class* 10(3): 114–125.

Gerhard, Jane F. 2001. *Desiring Revolution: Second-Wave Feminism and the Rewriting of American Sexual Thought, 1920 to 1982*. New York, NY: Columbia University Press.

Goldman, Robert P. 1991. "The Rāmāyana: Myth and Romance?" In *The Rāmāyaṇa of Vālmīki: An Epic of Ancient India*, vol. 3. Princeton, NJ: Princeton University Press.

Goldstein, Jan. 1982. "The Hysteria Diagnosis and the Politics of Anticlericalism in Late Nineteenth-Century France." *Journal of Modern History* 54(2): 209–239.

Goodman, Philomena. 2002. *Women, Sexuality, and War*. New York, NY: Palgrave.

Gordon, Linda. 2002. *The Moral Property of Women: A History of Birth Control Politics in America*. Urbana: University of Illinois Press.

Gordon, Mel. 2006. *Voluptuous Panic: The Erotic World of Weimar Berlin*, 2nd edn. Los Angeles, CA: Feral House.

Gottfried, Heidi. 1998. "Beyond Patriarchy? Theorising Gender and Class." *Sociology* 32(3): 451–468.

Gragg, Larry Dale. 2007. "From 'Sodom and Gomorrah' to the 'Last Frontier Town': The Changing Perceptions of Las Vegas in American Popular Culture, 1929–1941." *Studies in Popular Culture* 29(2): 43–62.

Greenberg, David F. 1990. *The Construction of Homosexuality*, 2nd edn. Chicago, IL: University of Chicago Press.

Gshur, Binyamin and Barbara K. Okun. 2003. "Generational Effects on Marriage Patterns: Jewish Immigrants and their Descendants in Israel." *Journal of Marriage and the Family* 65(2): 287–301.

Guerra, Lillian. 2010. "Gender Policing, Homosexuality and the New Patriarchy of the Cuban Revolution, 1965–70." *Social History* 35(3): 268–289.

Hackstaff, Karla B. 1999. *Marriage in a Culture of Divorce*. Philadelphia, PA: Temple University Press.

Haeri, Shahla. 1989. *Law of Desire: Temporary Marriage in Shi'i Iran*. Syracuse, NY: Syracuse University Press.

Halperin, David M. 2002. *How to Do the History of Homosexuality*. Chicago, IL: University of Chicago Press.

Hammad, Hanan. 2016. *Industrial Sexuality: Gender, Urbanization, and Social Transformation in Egypt*. Austin: University of Texas Press.

Harper, Donald. 1987. "The Sexual Arts of Ancient China as Described in a Manuscript of the Second Century B.C." *Harvard Journal of Asiatic Studies* 47(2): 539–593.

Hartmann, Betsy. 2016. *Reproductive Rights and Wrongs: The Global Politics of Population Control*, 3rd edn. Chicago, IL: Haymarket Books.

Harvey, Karen. 2002. "The Century of Sex? Gender, Bodies, and Sexuality in the Long Eighteenth Century." *Historical Journal* 45(4): 899–916.

Hassig, Ross. 2016. *Polygamy and the Rise and Demise of the Aztec Empire*. Albuquerque: University of New Mexico Press.

Herdt, Gilbert. 1982. *Rituals of Manhood: Male Initiation in Papua New Guinea*. Berkeley: University of California Press.

Hersch, Karen Klaiber. 2010. *The Roman Wedding: Ritual and Meaning in Antiquity*. Cambridge: Cambridge University Press.

Herzog, Dagmar. 2006. "Sexuality in the Postwar West." *Journal of Modern History* 78(1): 144–171.

Hew, Cheng Sim. 2003. "The Impact of Urbanization on Family Structure: The Experience of Sarawak, Malaysia." *Sojourn: Journal of Social Issues in Southeast Asia* 18(1): 89–109.

Hinsch, Bret. 1992. *Passions of the Cut Sleeve: The Male Homosexual Tradition in China*. Berkeley: University of California Press.

Hodgson, Dorothy L. 1999. "Pastoralism, Patriarchy and History: Changing Gender Relations among Maasai in Tanganyika, 1890–1940." *Journal of African History* 40(1): 41–65.

Hogeland, Lisa Marie. 1995. "Sexuality in the Consciousness-Raising Novel of the 1970s." *Journal of the History of Sexuality* 5(4): 601–632.

Holmgren, Jennifer. 1985. "The Economic Foundations of Virtue: Widow-Remarriage in Early and Modern China." *Australian Journal of Chinese Affairs* 13: 1–27.

Hunt, Alan. 1998. "The Great Masturbation Panic and the Discourses of Moral Regulation in Nineteenth- and Early Twentieth-Century Britain." *Journal of the History of Sexuality* 8(4): 575–615.

Irvine, Janice M. 2005. *Disorders of Desire: Sexuality and Gender in Modern American Sexology*. Philadelphia, PA: Temple University Press.

Jay, Jennifer W. 1996. "Imagining Matriarchy: 'Kingdoms of Women' in Tang China." *Journal of the American Oriental Society* 116(2): 220–229.

Jayasekera, M.L.S. 1982. "Marriage and Divorce in Ancient Sinhala Customary Law." *Journal of the Royal Asiatic Society Sri Lanka Branch* 26: 77–96.

Jiemin, Bao. 2003. "The Gendered Biopolitics of Marriage and Immigration: A Study of Pre-1949 Chinese Immigrants in Thailand." *Journal of Southeast Asian Studies* 34(1): 127–151.

Junko, Minamoto and Hank Glassman. 1993. "Buddhism and the Historical Construction of Sexuality in Japan." *U.S.-Japan Women's Journal: English Supplement* 5: 87–115.

Kalidos, Raju. 1986. "Viṣṇu's Mohinī Incarnation: An Iconographical and Sexological Study." *East and West* 36(1–3): 183–204.

Keddie, Nikki R. 1990. "The Past and Present of Women in the Muslim World." *Journal of World History* 1: 77–108.

Klausen, Susanne Maria. 2015. *Abortion under Apartheid: Nationalism, Sexuality, and Women's Reproductive Rights in South Africa*. Oxford: Oxford University Press.

Kutulas, Judy. 2017. "Obviously Queer: Gay-Themed Television, the Remaking of Sexual Identity, and the Family-Values Backlash." In *After Aquarius Dawned: How the Revolutions of the Sixties Became the Popular Culture of the Seventies*, 137–166. Chapel Hill: University of North Carolina.

Kvam, Kristen E., Linda S. Schearing, and Valarie H. Ziegler, eds. 1999. *Eve and Adam: Jewish, Christian, and Muslim Readings on Genesis and Gender*. Bloomington: Indiana University Press.

Latham, Jacob. 2012. "'Fabulous Clap-Trap': Roman Masculinity, the Cult of Magna Mater, and Literary Constructions of the *Galli* at Rome from the Late Republic to Late Antiquity." *Journal of Religion* 92(1): 84–122.

Latimer, Tirza True. 2005. *Women Together/Women Apart: Portraits of Lesbian Paris*. New Brunswick, NJ: Rutgers University Press.

Leck, Ralph M. 2016. *Vita Sexualis: Karl Ulrichs and the Origins of Sexual Science*. Champaign: University of Illinois Press.

Leder, Jane Mersky. 2006. *Thanks for the Memories: Love, Sex, and World War II*. Westport, CT: Praeger.

Ledgerwood, Judy L. 1995. "Khmer Kinship: The Matriliny/Matriarchy Myth." *Journal of Anthropological Research* 51(3): 247–261.

Lee, Catherine. 2010. "'Where the Danger Lies': Race, Gender, and Chinese and Japanese Exclusion in the United States, 1870–1924." *Sociological Forum* 25: 248–271.

Leo, Jessieca. 2011. *Sex in the Yellow Emperor's Basic Questions: Sex Longevity, and Medicine in Early China*. Dunedin, FL: Three Pines.

Loos, Tamara. 2009. "Transnational Histories of Sexualities in Asia." *American Historical Review* 114(5): 1309–1324.

MacDuff, William. 1996. "Beautiful Boys in Nō Drama: The Idealization of Homoerotic Desire." *Asian Theatre Journal* 13(2): 248–258.

Macy, Joanna. 1975. "The Dialectics of Desire." *Numen* 22(2): 145–160.

Mallon, Florencia E. 1987. "Patriarchy in the Transition to Capitalism: Central Peru, 1830–1950." *Feminist Studies* 13(2): 379–407.

Manalansan, Martin F. 2006. "Queer Intersections: Sexuality and Gender in Migration Studies." *International Migration Review* 40(1): 224–249.

Mann, R.S. 1978. "Ladakhi Polyandry Reinterpreted." *Indian Anthropologist* 8(1): 17–30.

Manzano, Valeria. 2009. "The Blue Jean Generation: Youth, Gender, and Sexuality in Buenos Aires, 1958–75." *Journal of Social History* 42(3): 657–676.

Marcus, Eric. 2002. *Making Gay History: The Half-Century Fight for Lesbian and Gay Rights*. New York, NY: Perennial.

Martin, Karin A. 1993. "Gender and Sexuality: Medical Opinion on Homosexuality, 1900–1950." *Gender and Society* 7(2): 246–260.

McLellan, Josie. 2011. *Love in the Time of Communism: Intimacy and Sexuality in the GDR*. Cambridge: Cambridge University Press.

McMahon, Keith. 2010. *Polygamy and Sublime Passion: Sexuality in China on the Verge of Modernity*. Honolulu: University of Hawai'i Press.

McNabb, Charlie. 2018. *Nonbinary Gender Identities: History, Culture, Resources*. Lanham, MD: Rowman & Littlefield.

Meyerowitz, Joanne. 2004. *How Sex Changed: A History of Transsexuality in the United States*. Cambridge, MA: Harvard University Press.

Middleton, Russell. 1962. "Brother-Sister and Father-Daughter Marriage in Ancient Egypt." *American Sociological Review* 27(5): 603–611.

Moghadam, Valentine M. 2004. "Patriarchy in Transition: Women and the Changing Family in the Middle East." *Journal of Comparative Family Studies* 35(2): 137–162.

Moore, Alison. 2009. "Rethinking Gendered Perversion and Degeneration in Visions of Sadism and Masochism, 1886–1930." *Journal of the History of Sexuality* 18(1): 138–157.

Moore, Sally Falk. 1963. "Oblique and Asymmetrical Cross-Cousin Marriage and Crow-Omaha Terminology." *American Anthropologist* 65(2): 296–311.

Morgan, Kenneth. 1979. "Clan Groups and Clan Exogamy among the Navajo." *Journal of Anthropological Research* 35(2): 157–169.

Muecke, Marjorie. 2004. "Female Sexuality in Thai Discourses about Maechii ('Lay Nuns')." *Culture, Health & Sexuality* 6(3): 221–238.

Murphy, Robert F. and Leonard Kasdan. 1959. "The Structure of Parallel Cousin Marriage." *American Anthropologist* 61: 17–29.

Nagel, Joanne. 2003. *Race, Ethnicity, and Sexuality: Intimate Intersections, Forbidden Frontiers*. Oxford: Oxford University Press.

Ni, Ernest. 1954. "The Family in China." *Marriage and Family Living* 16(4): 315–318.

Nickolaus, Keith. 2002. *Marriage Fictions in Old French Secular Narratives: A Critical Re-evaluation of the Courtly Love Debate Based on Secular Narratives from 1170–1250*. New York, NY: Routledge.

Nissinen, Martti, and Risto Uro, eds. 2008. *Sacred Marriages: The Divine-Human Sexual Metaphor from Sumer to Early Christianity*. Winona Lake, IN: Eisenbrauns.

Oakley, John Howard and Rebecca H. Sinos. 1993. *The Wedding in Ancient Athens*. Madison: University of Wisconsin Press.

O'Flaherty, Wendy Doniger. 1969a. "Asceticism and Sexuality in the Mythology of Śiva. Part I." *History of Religions* 8: 300–337.

O'Flaherty, Wendy Doniger. 1969b. "Asceticism and Sexuality in the Mythology of Śiva. Part II." *History of Religions* 9: 1–41.

Ortner, Sherry B. 1978. "The Virgin and the State." *Feminist Studies* 4(3): 19–35.

O'Shaughnessy, Kate. 2009. *Gender, State and Social Power in Contemporary Indonesia: Divorce and Marriage Law*. London: Routledge.

Osterud, Nancy Grey. 2012. *Putting the Barn Before the House: Women and Family Farming in Early-Twentieth-Century New York*. Ithaca, NY: Cornell University Press.

Öztimur, Neşe. 2007. "Women as Strategic Agents of Global Capitalism." *International Review of Modern Sociology* 33(1): 117–128.

Padgug, Robert. 1979. "Sexual Matters: On Conceptualizing Sexuality in History." *Radical History Review* 20: 3–24.

Parker, Richard. 1999. *Beneath the Equator: Cultures of Desire, Male Homosexuality, and Emerging Gay Communities*. New York, NY: Routledge.

Parker, Richard. 2009. "Sexuality, Culture and Society: Shifting Paradigms in Sexuality Research." *Health & Sexuality* 11(3): 251–266.

Patil, Vrushali. 2013. "From Patriarchy to Intersectionality: A Transnational Feminist Assessment of How Far We've Really Come." *Signs* 38(4): 847–867.

Peletz, Michael G. 2006. "Transgenderism and Gender Pluralism in Southeast Asia since Early Modern Times." *Current Anthropology* 47(2): 309–340.

Pembroke, Simon. 1967. "Women in Charge: The Function of Alternatives in Early Greek Tradition and the Ancient Idea of Matriarchy." *Journal of the Warburg and Courtauld Institutes* 30: 1–35.

Press, Andrea. 2009. "Gender and Family in Television's Golden Age and Beyond." *Annals of the American Academy of Political and Social Science* 625(1): 139–50.

Puri, Jyoti. 1997. "Reading Romance Novels in Postcolonial India." *Gender & Society* 11(4): 434–452.

Rao, L. Jaganmohan. 1973. "Industrialization and the Family: A World View." *International Journal of Sociology of the Family* 3: 179–189.

Reddy, Gayatri. 2005. *With Respect to Sex: Negotiating Hijra Identity in South India*. Chicago, IL: University of Chicago Press.

Reekie, Gail. 1991. "Decently Dressed? Sexualised Consumerism and the Working Woman's Wardrobe 1918–1923." *Labour History* 61: 42–56.

Reis, Elizabeth. 2009. *Bodies in Doubt: An American History of Intersex*. Baltimore, MD: Johns Hopkins University Press.

Reynolds, Philip. 2016. *How Marriage Became One of the Sacraments: The Sacramental Theology of Marriage from its Medieval Origins to the Council of Trent*. Cambridge: Cambridge University Press.

Roberts, Mary Louise. 2013. *What Soldiers Do: Sex and the American GI in World War II France*. Chicago, IL: University of Chicago Press.

Roscoe, Will. 1996. "Priests of the Goddess: Gender Transgression in Ancient Religion." *History of Religions* 35(3): 195–230.

Roth, Martha T. 1988. "'She Will Die by the Iron Dagger': Adultery and Neo-Babylonian Marriage." *Journal of the Economic and Social History of the Orient* 31(2): 186–206.

Rotundo, E. Anthony. 1989. "Romantic Friendship: Male Intimacy and Middle-Class Youth in the Northern United States, 1800–1900." *Journal of Social History* 23(1): 1–25.

Rowson, Everett K. 1991. "The Effeminates of Early Medina." *Journal of the American Oriental Society* 111(4): 671–693.

Rowson, Everett K. 2003. "Gender Irregularity as Entertainment: Institutionalized Transvestism at the Caliphal Court in Medieval Baghdad." In *Gender and Difference in the Middle Ages*, edited by Sharon Farmer and Carol Braun Pasternack, 45–72. Minneapolis: University of Minnesota Press.

Rupp, Leila J. 2011. *Sapphistries: A Global History of Love Between Women*. New York, NY: New York University Press.

Saller, R.P. 1987. "Men's Age at Marriage and its Consequences for the Roman Family." *Classical Philology* 82: 21–34.

Schmidt, Elizabeth. 1991. "Patriarchy, Capitalism, and the Colonial State in Zimbabwe." *Signs* 16(4): 732–756.

Schnarch, Brian. 1992. "Neither Man nor Woman: Berdache – A Case for Non-Dichotomous Gender Construction." *Anthropologica* 34(1): 105–121.

Schvaneveldt, Paul L. and Daniel Hubler. 2012. "Mate Selection in Bolivia: A Comparison of Rural and Urban Practices and Preferences." *Journal of Comparative Family Studies* 43(6): 837–855.

Schweitzer, Marlis. 2005. "'The Mad Search for Beauty': Actresses' Testimonials, the Cosmetics Industry, and the 'Democratization of Beauty.'" *Journal of the Gilded Age and Progressive Era* 4(3): 255–292.

Seccombe, Wally. 1986. "Patriarchy Stabilized: The Construction of the Male Breadwinner Wage Norm in Nineteenth-Century Britain." *Social History* 11(1): 53–76.

Semonche, John E. 2007. *Censoring Sex: A Historical Journey through American Media*. Lanham, MD: Rowman & Littlefield.

Seymour, Mark. 2006. *Debating Divorce in Italy: Marriage and the Making of Modern Italians, 1860–1974*. New York, NY: Palgrave Macmillan.

Shih, Chuan-Kang. 2009. *Quest for Harmony: The Moso Traditions of Sexual Union and Family Life*. Stanford, CA: Stanford California Press.

Sienkewicz, Thomas J., ed. 2013. *Critical Survey of Mythology and Folkore: Love, Sexuality, and Desire*. Ispwich, MA: Salem.

Simmons, Christina. 2009. *Making Marriage Modern: Women's Sexuality from the Progressive Era to World War II*. Oxford: Oxford University Press.

Smaal, Yorick. 2015. *Sex, Soldiers and the South Pacific, 1939–45*. New York, NY: Palgrave Macmillan.

Smith-Rosenberg, Caroll. 1975. "The Female World of Love and Ritual." *Signs* 1(1): 1–30.

Solway, Jacqueline S. 1990. "Affines and Spouses, Friends and Lovers: The Passing of Polygyny in Botswana." *Journal of Anthropological Research* 46(1): 41–66.

Sommer, Matthew. 2015. *Polyandry and Wife-Selling in Qing Dynasty China: Survival Strategies and Judicial Interventions*. Berkeley: University of California Press.

Spiro, Melford E. 1975. "Marriage Payments: A Paradigm from the Burmese Perspective." *Journal of Anthropological Research* 31(2): 89–115.

Stacey, Judith. 1982. "People's War and the New Democratic Patriarchy in China." *Journal of Comparative Family Studies* 13(3): 255–76.

Stacey, Robin Chapman. 2002. "Divorce, Medieval Welsh Style." *Speculum* 77(4): 1107–1127.

Stadel, Luke. 2014. "Cable, Pornography, and the Reinvention of Television, 1982–1989." *Cinema Journal* 53(3): 52–75.

Stampfer, Shaul. 1988. "Remarriage among Jews and Christians in Nineteenth-Century Eastern Europe." *Jewish History* 3(2): 85–114.

Stearns, Peter N. and Mark Knapp. 1993. "Men and Romantic Love: Pinpointing a 20th-Century Change." *Journal of Social History* 26(4): 769–95.

Stein, Dorothy. 1988. "Burning Widows, Burning Brides: The Perils of Daughterhood in India." *Pacific Affairs* 61(3): 465–485.

Stein, Edward, ed. 1990. *Forms of Desire: Sexual Orientation and the Social Constructionist Controversy*. New York, NY: Routledge.

Stone, Lee Alexander. 1976. *The Story of Phallicism*. New York, NY: AMS.

Strub, Whitney. 2011. *Perversion for Profit: The Politics of Pornography and the Rise of the New Right*. New York, NY: Columbia University Press.

Stryker, Susan. 2017. *Transgender History: The Roots of Today's Revolution*, 2nd edn. New York, NY: Seal.

Sylvester, Kenneth Michael. 2001. *The Limits of Rural Capitalism: Family, Culture, and Markets in Montcalm, Manitoba, 1870–1940*. Toronto: University of Toronto Press.

Tambiah, Stanley J., Mitzi Goheen, Alma Gottlieb et. al. 1989. "Bridewealth and Dowry Revisited: The Position of Women in Sub-Saharan Africa and North India." *Current Anthropology* 30(4): 413–435.

Taylor, J. Garth and Helga Taylor. 1985. "Cousin Marriage in Traditional Labrador Inuit Society." *Études/Inuit/Studies* 9(1): 183–186.

Teo, Hsu-Ming. 2005. "The Americanisation of Romantic Love in Australia." In *Connected Worlds: History in Transnational Perspective*, edited by Ann Curthoys and Marilyn Lake, 171–192. Canberra: Australian National University Press.

Testart, Alain. 2013. "Reconstructing Social and Cultural Evolution: The Case of Dowry in the Indo-European Area." *Anthropology* 54(1): 23–50.

Thoreson, Ryan. 2014. *Transnational LGBT Activism: Working for Sexual Rights Worldwide*. Minneapolis: University of Minnesota Press.

Tilly, Louise A. 1994. "Women, Women's History, and the Industrial Revolution." *Social Research* 61(1): 115–137.

Todd, Lisa M. 2017. *Sexual Treason in Germany during the First World War*. New York, NY: Palgrave Macmillan.

Valocchi, Steve. 1999. "The Class-Inflected Nature of Gay Identity." *Social Problems* 46(2): 207–224.

Vijaisri, Priyadarshini. 2004. *Recasting the Devadasi: Patterns of Sacred Prostitution in Colonial South India*. New Delhi: Kanishka.

Voronina, Olga. 1993. "Soviet Patriarchy: Past and Present." *Hypatia* 8(4): 97–112.

Walker, Susannah. 2007. *Style and Status: Selling Beauty to African American Women, 1920–1975.* Lexington: University Press of Kentucky.

Waters, Malcolm. 1989. "Patriarchy and Viriarchy: An Exploration and Reconstruction of Concepts of Masculine Domination." *Sociology* 23(2): 193–211.

Weis, David L. 1998. "The Use of Theory in Sexuality Research." *Journal of Sex Research* 35(1): 1–9.

Westenholz, Joan Goodnick. 1989. "Tamar, Qĕdēšā, Qadištu, and Sacred Prostitution in Mesopotamia." *Harvard Theological Review* 82(3): 245–265.

Widmer, Eric D., Judith Treas, and Robert Newcomb. 1998. "Attitudes toward Nonmarital Sex in 24 Countries." *Journal of Sex Research* 35(4): 349–358.

Wiesner-Hanks, Merry. 2010. *Christianity and Sexuality in the Early Modern World: Regulating Desire, Reforming Practice.* New York, NY: Routledge.

Wikan, Unni. 1977. "Man Becomes Woman: Transsexualism in Oman as a Key to Gender Roles." *Man* 12(2): 304–319.

Wu, Huaiting. 2009. "The Construction of a Consumer Population in Advertising in 1920s China." *Discourse & Society* 20(1): 147–171.

Zimmerman, Jonathan. 2015. *Too Hot to Handle: A Global History of Sex Education.* Princeton, NJ: Princeton University Press.

4

Postcolonial Sexualities

VRUSHALI PATIL AND JYOTI PURI

Introduction

In 2013, the Hawai'i state legislature legalized same-sex marriage, two years before the US Supreme Court extended this right throughout the nation. But, it was an issue that pitted Kanaka Maoli (Native Hawai'ians) against each other: those who opposed same-sex marriage and those who fought hard on behalf of lesbian, bisexual, gay, transgender and māhū Hawai'ians.[1] Describing the circumstances leading to this moment, J. Kēhaulani Kauanui (2017) notes that at heart this collision was over precolonial Hawai'ian history and the impact of colonialism. Proponents of same-sex marriage had to make the case that gender and sexual diversity was indigenous to Hawai'i, and not a colonial Western import as believed by some opponents. Indeed, they had to sway opinion by arguing that it was the imposition of Christianity and colonial rule that introduced homophobia on the island and eroded sexual and gender variation from the Hawai'ian social fabric.

In contrast, the Bahamas introduced the Sexual Offences and Domestic Violence Act in 1991 that is still in place. While ostensibly addressing matters of domestic violence, this Act, in fact, drew parallels between rape and incest and same-sex sexual activity among consenting adults. In her incisive analysis, M. Jacqui Alexander notes that it was the "first attempt to impose a veiled sexual order on the chaotic legacy of colonialism (1994, p. 8). To this purpose, the Act fixed conjugal heterosexuality as the natural foundation to the social order, while selectively criminalizing deviations from it. Thus, this draconian law equated sexual assault with same-sexual desire and practices, and also criminalized sex among women, thereby extending the purview of colonial antisodomy laws.

Despite their differences, these two examples illustrate the overarching point that sexualities, colonialisms, and postcolonialisms are tightly linked. Although Bahamas achieved independence in 1973 and Hawai'i gained statehood in 1959, the impact of colonialism is still playing out in profound ways. The Hawai'ian struggle for sovereignty continues, as does the difficult task of contending with the colonial fallout resulting in the marginalization of gender and sexually variant Native Hawai'ians. But sexuality's relevance to colonial projects extends beyond these specific examples, for it profoundly shaped how Europeans encountered and perceived colonized groups – as well as themselves. Sexuality modulated European racialized beliefs, namely that non-Europeans were more sexual and closer to nature, that they were less civilized, and that they were in need of social and sexual reform, thereby justifying colonial domination. Nationalist elites frequently internalized versions of these colonial ideologies in ways that persisted once the colonies became independent or domination was no longer articulated in terms of formal colonization, while other groups, as we see in the Hawai'ian example, continue to resist and redefine these colonial and nationalist ideologies.

Foregrounding these complexities, this chapter focuses on postcolonialisms and sexualities, or what is abbreviated as postcolonial sexualities. While we elaborate below on the meanings of postcolonialism as well as sexuality, to be noted here is that the postcolonial has to do with the process, aftermath, and ongoing legacies of Euro-American colonialisms. Thus, postcolonial sexualities include the sexual politics, knowledges, and identities that were forged or embattled during the colonial encounter and its postcolonial aftermath. To put a finer point on it, understanding postcolonial sexualities means accounting for the colonial, as much as the postcolonial, period.

This chapter aims to provide an overview of postcolonial sexualities from a feminist lens that is informed by the dynamics of race and resistance. The chapter's structure pivots around two interweaving axes: (i) an introduction to how sexuality and colonial governance intersected in a variety of sites and spaces and how these histories continue to unfold in the ex-colonies as well as in the heart of the erstwhile empires; and (ii) an overview of the feminist and sexuality/queer studies scholarship that has captured and provided critical understandings of colonial and postcolonial sexualities. The chapter begins with a synopsis of postcolonialism and sexuality (meanings, definitions, and the like), before presenting a distilled account of sexuality and colonialism, followed by a section on their persistent postcolonial legacies. Issues of resistance are integrated into both sections.

Defining Postcolonialisms and Sexualities

Although colonialism had long been an object of investigation, the field of postcolonial studies was inaugurated with Edward Said's book, *Orientalism* (Said 1979). Said argued that the notion of the Orient, including parts of Africa, Asia, and the Middle East that experienced colonial domination, were in fact European projections that had been legitimated through reports, travel writings, scientific books, and other forms of knowledge production. That is, notions of the Orient, as exotic, erotic, uncivilized, and so on, were European portrayals, which concurrently allowed Europe to constitute itself as civilized and progressive. These dualistic understandings became commonplace and even commonsensical through the one-sided histories, descriptions, academic and popular writings on colonized peoples, and other forms of knowing that were generated during colonial encounters.

Alongside the earlier contributions of scholars like Frantz Fanon and others, *Orientalism* launched a field of study that is devoted to understanding the cultural and epistemological dimensions of colonization that continue to reverberate today. Think here of the enduring beliefs in the West that the Middle East and much of Africa are culturally backward and are inherently more exotic (and erotic) than the West. In addition, there exists the belief that these ex-colonies lack the kind of modernity that distinguishes Europe or US postcolonial studies' purview ranges from settler colonialism (a form of colonial domination which seeks to replace the indigenous or existing population of a colonized territory with a new society of settlers, as in the US), colonial rule through a relatively small number of European administrators (British colonization of India), or economic and political forms of imperialism that were not strictly colonial (British imperialism in Brazil). Further, postcolonial studies takes as foundational the interconnections between economic and cultural dimensions of colonization; that is, the colonial extraction of resources and labor is inextricable from questions of cultural, educational, and legal "reform" in the colonies. And, not least, scholars seek to uncover the various modalities of colonization – be it slavery and indentured service, generating new ethnic and racial categories in the colonies, or using the colonies as laboratories of Western modernity(Cooper and Stoler 1997).

While racial difference was and continues to be significant for researchers writing on colonialism/postcolonialism, it was left to the feminist and sexuality studies scholars to highlight the significance of gender and sexuality to colonial projects and their persisting legacies. Anne McClintock's book, *Imperial Leather: Race, Gender and Sexuality in the Colonial Contest* (1995), begins with the essential insight that although European men were most directly responsible for colonization, issues of gender and sexuality have been systematically neglected in influential studies of colonialism (*Orientalism* is a case in point). Using the concept of "porno-tropics," she presents examples of Christopher Columbus and others to highlight how the European male imagination of Africa and the Americas was profoundly gendered, sexualized, and racialized, thereby mediating colonial conquest and control.

The sections below detail the numerous ways in which colonial rule was profoundly structured through matters of gender and sexuality, but two points are underscored at the outset. First, sexuality and gender need to be understood broadly. As we will see, sexuality includes not just aspects of sexual behaviors and practices, whether involving similarly or differently gendered people, but also notions of sexual propriety, child marriage, widow remarriage, issues of fertility, demography, the exotification of colonies and entire groups of people, among other aspects. Gender includes men and women, as well as a range of genders that were seen as aberrant or deviant according to prevailing European standards; here, māhū is a case in point. At the same time, since European perceptions of sexual and gender differences in the colonies were filtered through perceptions of racial hierarchies, any approach to understanding sexualities and genders in the colonial/postcolonial periods must in fact consider the relevance of race.

Second, it is helpful to grasp postcolonialism in terms of space and time. While colonial forces and those being subjugated were typically separated by physical distances, for example, the vastness between Britain and South Africa, colonialism was a form of encounter, albeit a highly unequal one, between these groups. In fact, McClintock's central contribution in *Imperial Leather* is not only that colonial projects were thoroughly mediated by gender, sexuality, and the emergent racial order, but also that these projections resonated back at home, profoundly impacting Western industrial modernity. Mary Louise Pratt's (1992) concept of contact zone – the social spaces where cultures meet, clash, and grapple with each other, typically in highly asymmetrical contexts – further encourages complex understandings of colonialisms. Also seeking to show how the ex-colonies and the West are connected, Inderpal Grewal and Caren Kaplan (1994a) emphasize the notion of *linkages*, which is to say, the asymmetric ways in which the West and the rest are bound due to colonialism and ongoing forms of imperialism.

Tying together the past and the present of the metropoles and the colonies is another significant aspect of postcolonial approaches. Although the prefix of "post" appears to emphasize the formal end of colonialism and its increasing irrelevance, this assumption requires clarification. Undeniably, most colonies gained independence in the post-World War II period, and were reincarnated into formally sovereign national states. But, as we see in the example of Bahamas, these states inherited and continue to grapple with issues and problems with antecedents in the colonial period. India's large population, in fact, can be traced back to colonial policies that resulted in landlessness, famine, and other hardships that encouraged bearing more children as a means of securing the family's survival.

The impact has been even more devastating under settler colonialism, as in the cases of Canada and the US, when considered from the perspective of First Nations. Joanne Barker's book, *Critically Sovereign: Indigenous Gender, Sexuality and Feminist Studies*, offers a trenchant criticism of the cultural appropriation of Native cultures that began with colonialism and still persists:

> The insistent repetition of the racially gendered and sexualized image…(is) a still image of a movingly malleable narrative of Indigenous womanhood/femininity and manhood/masculinity that reenacts Indigenous people's lack of knowledge and power over their own culture and identity in an inherently imperialist and colonialist world.
>
> (2017, p. 2)

The takeaway, then, is that the "colonial" is as important as the "post" in the terminology of the postcolonial. One more point about this prefix by way of disrupting notions of then and now: critical scholars have usefully noted that the prefix is best apprehended as going against the grain of the colonial, or resistance to the colonial. Seen thus, the postcolonial includes the anticolonial movements, practices, and discourses that were generated as a result of colonial domination (de Alva 1995; Loomba 1998).

Identifying the linkages between the metropoles and the colonies, making connections between the past and present, highlighting questions of resistance to colonial rule as well as contemporary national states are among the key contributions of feminist scholars focusing on issues of sexuality and gender. The trajectory of feminist scholarship, though, has been uneven as well as multistranded. Early feminist work broke new ground by foregrounding colonial and postindependence regulation of gender, while seeing sexuality as secondary to gender. It demonstrated how the "woman question" – women's access to education, mobility, age of marriage, veiling, female circumcision, among other questions – in the colonies was central to European perceptions, civilizational projects, administrative policies, as well as the justification for colonialism. Despite the fact that many dimensions of the "woman question" were directly about sexuality, feminist analyses were framed in terms of gender or, really, women. In cases where feminists did usefully accent sexuality, it was typically within heterosexual parameters (McClintock 1995, Stoler 2002).

Analyses of sexuality's significance to colonial projects emerged alongside the proliferation of sexuality and queer studies in the US academy. While sexuality is related to gender, or for that matter race, feminist and queer studies scholars honed the point that sexuality is neither the same as gender nor simply a corollary of it. Thus, M. Jacqui Alexander (1994), Inderpal Grewal and Caren Kaplan (1994b), and Elizabeth Povinelli (1998) were among those who unearthed sexuality's significance to colonialism. Arriving at this from a transnational perspective, they were at the forefront of scholarship especially committed to understanding the linkages across spatial and temporal contexts. Alexander and Povinelli also usefully shifted the needle from the overwhelming (and typically unstated) focus on heterosexuality to same-sex, queer, and other nonnormative sexualities in colonial and postcolonial contexts. The dynamic blend of decoloniality and queer studies spurred the pathbreaking contributions of Lugones, and others who sought not only to trouble the defining European impacts on sexual politics in the colonies, but also to write alternative histories of sexualities from the vantage point of the subjugated. Lugones, for example, centers colonial processes in the formation of heteronormative ideas about bodies, genders and sexualities, both in colonies and metropoles, though in distinct ways (Lugones 2007, 2010). Distinctive, then, about postcolonial sexualities scholarship are its transnational, decolonial, feminist, and queer strands, its inherent interdisciplinarity, and its commitment to challenging dominant ways of knowing and understanding social worlds – points which we purse in the sections, below.

The Sexual Histories of European Colonialism and their Postcolonial Legacies

Historically, sexuality has played a critical role in framing ethnic, racial, and cultural difference within the colonial encounter. European colonialists came from a Christian society with heteronormative, patriarchal views about sexuality and gender. On the one hand, there was some discussion of indigenous sexualities as positive or innocent. For example, the Italian historian Peter Martyr d'Anghiera, writing in the service of Spain and an important chronicler of the early Spanish experience in the Americas, wrote about indigenous Caribbean peoples as living in a "Golden Age" of innocent simplicity (Rubiés 2007, p. 133). On the other hand, Columbus himself focused on the "nakedness" of the peoples he encountered in the Caribbean, associating this nakedness with sexuality and sin (Hulme 1994). Indeed, the predominant pattern for European colonists was to understand cultural and racial difference – particularly in terms of sexual behavior – in terms of sin and aberration. European Christian conquistadors, missionaries, travelers, capitalists, settlers, and others wrote about a variety of "deviant" behaviors, from the aforementioned "nakedness" and lack of modesty, prostitution, polygamy, sex outside marriage, and sex with multiple partners or "animalistic" sex to loose or "whorish" women, and same-sex sexual practices. As this list suggests, ideas about deviant sexuality were intimately tied to ideas of deviance regarding masculinity and femininity, and marital and family forms.

Collectively, such ideas shaped Europe's encounter with the Americas and Caribbean, Asia (or "Orient"), and Africa. In the Americas and Caribbean, the "noble savage in a Golden World" of early expectations was transformed into a "savage beast in the hideous wilderness" (Smith 2011, p. 48), as indigenous peoples became associated with practices such as bestiality, sodomy, and extramarital sex. Indigenous men were seen as effeminate sodomites, while indigenous women were seen as excessively lascivious. The deeply heteronormative and patriarchal logic of the early conquistadors as well as the settler colonialists that would follow, then, read the New World in terms of savagery and sin and in requirement of Christianity and colonization (Kempadoo 2004; Mason 1990; Smith 2011).

The context of encounter between European colonialists and indigenous peoples was somewhat different in Asia, as negative stereotypes about oriental sexual deviance preceded the colonial encounter. We can identify several such stereotypes, having to do with sodomy, men's excessive oppression of women, and deviant marital and family forms such as polygamy and child marriage. Regarding sodomy, Arabic and Middle Eastern men had long been constructed as especially prone to engaging in sodomy (Bleys 1995; Boone 2014). These men were also seen as excessively domineering and oppressive over their women, as indicated by the enclosure of women in harems and the practice of purdah. Finally, polygamy and child marriage also became matters of great concern and were also associated with Asian men's oppression of women (Nussbaum 1995; Wiley 2006).

In contrast to the New World and Asia, sub-Saharan Africa was constructed somewhat differently. While the former two were associated with same-sex practices, southern Africa was associated especially with a hypersexual or "animalistic" heterosexuality (Arnfred 2004; Epprecht 2009). African women in particular were constructed as "hot constitution'd ladies" who satisfied their lust outside of marriage. Such images were produced in the service of chattel slavery, as well as settler colonialism (Morgan 2004). One powerful example of the dehumanization of black women is the case of Sara Bartmen, a Khoisan woman born in the area that is now present-day South Africa in the 1790s. Thought to possess a distinctive feature of the Khoisan, unusually large buttocks, which were associated with excessive sexuality, she was displayed in savage freak shows in Europe. Upon death, her body was dissected by European scientists (Abrahams 1998). With their focus on African sexuality as deviant, European colonizers fundamentally misunderstood a cultural context wherein there was a division between sex for procreation and sex for pleasure, with societal controls present more for the former than the latter. Colonial policies aimed to bring ideas and practices around pleasure more firmly under Church and state control (Arnfred 2004).

Given these histories of encounter, colonial entities engaged in a variety of civilizational or reform practices which have impacted sexualities. In New Spain, for example, examining the Spanish Catholic mission, Overmyer-Velasquez (2005) argues that precontact Nahua emphasized balance, centeredness and order, with sexuality seen as necessary for a happy life and women considered autonomous beings with a presence in public life and some access to power and authority. For the Church, however, these sentiments were impediments to conversion. It also did not understand the many Nahua sexualities and genders, which existed outside of its Catholic framework. Ultimately, it solved its conversion problem by translating Christian notions of gender and sexual hierarchy via Nahua moral tropes, and by connecting feminine sexuality and deceit with lack of balance, disorder, and decenteredness. In the process, it mistranslated or suppressed other Nahua sexualities. Over time, it had the effect of displacing local conceptions of balance and interdependence with hierarchical categories of good and evil, god and devil, and male and female. This served to erode the power of Nahua women and downgraded genders and sexualities that the Catholic Church did not support. Local conceptions were not entirely eradicated, but rather mixed with Catholic ideas (Overmyer-Velazquez 2005; Sigal 2007).

Another example comes from colonial dealings with prostitution. Following the discussion above, European colonialists believed that native cultures were sexually deviant and thus more prone to ills such as prostitution. Within India, for instance, British colonialists focused on *devdasis*, women dedicated to Hindu temples and married to gods, who oftentimes also made sexual alliances with high-status men, as an example of degraded native culture. Ignoring subtleties and variations in the practice, this example of so-called barbaric sexuality was used to justify a series of civilizing state interventions. At the same time, the colonial state relied on prostitutes to make the life of their men in the colonies less "morally and physically dangerous" (Levine 2004, p. 160). In fact, it actually organized and managed prostitution among local women to service its men – in ways that would be considered unacceptable within the metropole itself.

Yet another example comes from the politics of female circumcision in colonial Kenya. Christian missionaries in particular targeted female circumcision as a barbaric act with no social value. Yet, signifying the passage from girlhood to adulthood, female circumcision conferred upon the women who underwent it authority over those who did not. It also gave initiates power in other ways. By fighting the practice, then, missionaries "eroded" (Kiruthu, Musalia, and Jalang'o-Ndede 2013) this power. Furthermore, this marking out and targeting of the practice had the long-term impact of politicizing it as a "traditional cultural practice" which must be defended for the burgeoning independence movement. Jomo Kenyatta, who would become Kenya's first postindependence prime minister, defended the practice as critical for the maintenance of the community. Hence in postcolonial Kenya, as elsewhere, women's bodies and sexualities became a site in this critical contestation between European colonialists and indigenous elites (Kiruthu et al. 2013).

Perhaps the most well-known example of this sort of colonialist attempt at civilizing natives in the arena of sexuality is the antisodomy laws that Britain enacted throughout its colonies. Colonial attempts to police native desire and to segregate and protect white virtue shaped the first colonial antisodomy law, written by the British into the Indian penal code in 1860 (Hyam 1990, p. 116). Subsequently, this antisodomy law circulated in various forms to most other colonies in the British Empire, from Africa to Asia and the Caribbean (Gupta 2008). Notably, this colonial-era anti-sodomy legislation generally constituted the first such legislation in the colonies.

These processes were important in the settler colonial context of the United States as well. For example, Finley discusses the boarding schools for Native Americans created by the US state for the purposes of assimilation. The boarding schools taught sexual shame, which was deeply impactful, and which has been passed down for generations. Hence Native peoples adapted a silence around sexuality, and over the long term a number of tribal councils have adopted heterosexist marriage acts. Thus, Finley argues, "heterosexism and the structure of the nuclear family need to be thought of as a colonial system of violence" (2011, p. 32).

Beyond its utility in legitimating civilizing missions, this colonial politics of sexuality was also useful in managing and responding to challenges to colonial rule. Events as far flung as the First War for Independence in India, the later Amritsar massacre in India, the Morant Bay Rebellion in Jamaica, the "black peril" scare in South Africa, and lynchings in the US South all invoked the specter of black and brown men as violent rapists threatening the purity of white or European women. In each case, such presumed, nonverified threats were used to justify egregiously violent actions, both on the part of the racial state and nonstate white actors (Keegan 2001; Patil and Purkayastha 2015; Woollacott 2006). While there was some criticism of this sort of violence in the metropole, over time such behaviors helped reaffirm a notion of white masculinity as protective of (white) women, again in opposition to deviant and dangerous black and brown masculinity (Hall 2002; Woollacott 2006).

The colonial encounter, thus, was deeply shaped by and itself shaped beliefs, values and politics regarding sexuality. Young writes that at the heart of the colonial encounter was an ambivalence regarding racialized sexuality and especially concerning the black and brown bodies to which it was attached. That is, white men experienced an "ambivalent axis of desire and repugnance" as they moved back and forth between repulsion at the idea of racial mixing, and the expression of sexual desire for black and brown bodies (Young 1995, p. 152). Their desire would clearly become culturally and politically significant, as Dutch, French and British colonial regimes would all have to concern themselves with the growing 'problem' of mixed-race children (Stoler 2002).

In this context, civilizing efforts were certainly about regulating and uplifting colonized peoples, but they were also about shoring up the civilizational superiority of European sexuality and gender (Stoler 2002, p. 42). Colonial prescriptions on proper sexual conduct for European women and men, furthermore, did not remain in the colonies but were also directed at "recalcitrant and ambiguous participants in imperial culture" in the metropole (Stoler 1995, p. 109). In that sense, bourgeois concerns with sexual morality and respectability in the metropole which were emergent in the nineteenth century are also shaped by these racialized, colonial histories.

Hence, colonial practices and images concerning native sexualities were constructed in opposition to, and helped solidify notions of, Christian civilized monogamy, European Christian men's more enlightened masculinity, and European Christian women's greater equality. Furthermore, this vantage point of European superiority, or what may be called the civilizational gaze, was critical for producing its issues of concern. For example, the image of the black or brown rapist continues to hold power today (Patil and Purkayastha 2015). Imperial and colonial histories are also critical for the consolidation of contemporary "problematic practices" such as female genital circumcision (Nnaemeka 2005). Finally, the impetus to civilize black and brown peoples away from their "deviant" sexualities and to take up monogamous, patriarchal households would also remain powerful, long after the colonial powers were officially gone.

Consequences for Sexuality Politics in Specific Places

As Patil (2009) shows, the histories of racialized sexuality and gender within colonial politics have had important consequences for anticolonial and postcolonial processes. Examining post World War II decolonization politics in the United Nations among Euro-American apologists of colonialism and Asian and African anticolonial states, for example, Patil argues that the arguments of the largely male delegates generally turned on contending patriarchal metaphors. That is, while colonial apologists sought to legitimate the colonial project with an appeal to a colonial paternalism that emphasized the benefits of their tutelage for childlike African and Asian peoples, anticolonialists argued that this tutelage violated their patriarchal rights as "masters in their own house." In this way, elite, anticolonial men in the UN reclaimed that colonialist index of civilization, the patriarchal household, as a site for recuperating anticolonial masculinity.

Women also remain the object of social and sexual reform in postcolonial contexts in ways that trail the legacies of the colonial era.[2] The focus on regulating women's (hetero)sexualities and bodies, while managing practices and identities that exceed heteropatriarchal monogamy defines the aftermath of colonialism, as well. Indeed, the centrality of women bodies and sexualities to the founding of newly independent national states is traumatically illustrated during colonial India's partitioning into India and Pakistan in 1947. In the intense conflict that ensued, an estimated 75,000 women were raped or abducted on both sides of the newly formed borders as a means of violating the integrity of the other community. Seen as matters of national shame, the recovery of the Indian and Pakistani women who were harmed by "the other side" during the process of partition was also framed as imperatives of national honor. As Das (2007) notes, the women were recovered in their capacities as sexual and reproductive beings, even as men were construed as the legitimate inheritors of the new nations and states.

Women remain at the heart of discourses of tradition and modernity that are also spillovers from the colonial periods. The ongoing tussles over veiling by Muslim women remains a case in point (Mernissi 1991; Moghadam 1993). Although Iran was impacted by imperialism, rather than colonial occupation, the history of veiling, unveiling, and reveiling, as Hamideh Sedghi shows, sheds crucial light on how regulating women's sexuality was at the heart of imperialist and subsequent competing nationalist projects. Asking why Iranian women were veiled at the turn of the twentieth century, forced to unveil from 1936 to 1979, and then subjected to reveiling after the revolution, Sedghi argues that this control over women's sexuality and their bodies belies a tussle between those who sought to impose secular Western modernity and those who sought to impose religious tradition. Precisely because veiling is weighted by the paradoxes of modernity, tradition, Westernization, culture, religion, secularization, progress, religion, and, not least, women's agency, it continues to be a volatile symbol of nationalist politics. Elite as well as working-class women, Sedghi notes, are active participants on both sides of these debates, with elite, pro-establishment women supporting unveiling and working-class women mobilizing on the side of the *chador*.

Three points emerge regarding the endurance of tradition and modernity or Westernization and national culture that repeat insistently in postcolonial contexts. First, women in postcolonial contexts are rarely regulated outside of the mediating influences of social class, race, ethnicity, religion, and sexual identities. In other words, all women are not seen as belonging equally to the nation, thereby also requiring different strategies of regulation and control. On the one hand, middle-class and elite women from dominant communities are frequently seen as the emissaries of national sexual respectability. Puri (1999) shows that privileged heterosexual urban women in India are well aware that their sexual conduct and practices reflect not only on their families but also the national culture. Their stories reveal the awareness of national sexual norms – what *Indian* women ought or ought not to do sexually or that Indian women should confine sexual activity to marriage – even as they resist these norms in a variety of ways by, for instance, having forms of sex other than penetrative heterosexual intercourse. Bringing further nuance to this, Patricia Hill Collins (2006) and E. Frances White (2001) compellingly show the complicated effects of sexual respectability on minority nationalist projects, in this case black nationalism in the US. In this view, black heterosexual women become the bearers of sexuality respectability as a means of combatting racism, while ignoring the presence of queer black people.

On the other hand, indigent and marginalized women are frequently impacted through direct forms of bodily and sexual control. In her overview of the global politics of population control across numerous countries, Betsy Hartmann (1995) highlights the case of Bangladesh in which the US, World Bank, the Bangladeshi government, and elite Bangladeshi women colluded to exert control over indigent Muslim and minority Hindu women's fertilities in the 1970s–1980s. Deriving from pejorative assumptions that rural indigent women are traditional, backward, and unable to make informed choices, these policies used a mix of "compensation payments" (p. 228) that exploited economic desperation and intimidation to impose sterilization. Rather than wedding family planning to improvements in the lives of women who most needed them, Hartmann notes, the approach all along was, "Its all right if the poor stay as poor as ever, just as long as there are fewer of them born" (p. 224).

Women and other gendered and sexual subjects deemed to be sexually transgressive pose particular conundrums to nationalist and elitist politics. Sex work is a case in point. All-too-often, sex work is heavily stigmatized in ways that were exacerbated through colonial intervention. The British Contagious Diseases Acts passed in the latter part of the nineteenth century sought to control the spread of sexually transmitted diseases by targeting sex workers in the metropole and the British colonies. While postcolonial nations carried forward the cultural stigma against prostitution and even strengthened legal prohibitions, they also relied on it as a national development strategy. Thus, for example, sex workers are the targets of policing and bear the brunt of the violence, while governments collude with business interests to promote sex industries and sex tourism (Kempadoo 1998). At the same time, also notable are the vibrant histories of activism in numerous parts of the world, documented by Kempadoo and Doezema (1998). Encountering these examples in postcolonial contexts, be it in Cuba, Senegal, or Mexico, not only provides necessary insights into the kinds of issues around which sex workers mobilize. It also undoes persistent stereotypes of them as helpless victims requiring rescue by those from the Global North and other such neocolonial representations.

The second point to emerge is that the tensions of tradition, modernity, Westernization, and such are not limited to heterosexuality but are also salient in same-sex sexualities. For example, the contemporary claims of many southern African politicians regarding the heterosexual nature of Africans neglects various extra-heterosexual indigenous sexualities, while characterizing homosexuality in the subcontinent as a foreign import (Epprecht 2009). Likewise in the postcolonial state of the Bahamas, Alexander highlights the ways that state mangers imagine and seek to build the nation as heterosexual, granting full citizenship only to those who can inhabit the space of proper heteropatriarchal, heterosexuality (Alexander 1996). Again discussing parallel discourses of Hindu nationalism in India, Bacchetta identifies two "dual operations," one which involves the claim that queerness is not Indian and comes from the outside, from British colonialism in particular, and a second which assigns queerness to all those who are other to the nation. And here, the other par excellence has been the Muslim man (Bacchetta 1999). In many postcolonial spaces, then, sexual and gender minority groups marginalized by this sort of rhetoric must resist not only colonial histories but also postcolonial politics. The politics of collective memory and identity is key in such struggles. For example, in South Africa and Namibia, lesbian, gay, bisexual, and transgender (LGBT) activist groups struggle to navigate allegations of their foreignness and present themselves as African (Currier 2012).

To the third point, these differences and collisions exceed intranational politics, and influence international and transnational framings of nationalisms, genders, and sexualities. For example, older colonial ideas about native people's sexualities reappear in the work of contemporary development agencies and non-governmental organizations (NGOs). The reliance of the post-World War II impetus for development and population control on curbing women's fertility, for instance, reproduces the image of oversexed native women who lack the rational behaviors and lifestyles to sufficiently control their fertility. This sort of development and population control politics deflects attention from structural factors and from political economic processes having to do with powerful entities. Rather than focusing on the consumption patterns of countries like the US, for example, the focus moves to the "irrational" behaviors and lifestyles of some of the least powerful individuals in the world (Wangari 2002). Likewise, northern-based feminist NGOs that seek to eradicate practices like female genital mutilation today are also shaped by these fraught histories. As Hodgson explains in her work on the Maasai, while northern donors and NGOs focus on genital circumcision as a traditional and patriarchal relic that must be eradicated, Maasai women themselves prioritize economic and political empowerment (Hodgson 2011).

The legacies of colonial and postcolonial histories can also be seen in contemporary tensions around queer politics. For example, a number of writers critique the use of the northern dichotomy of heterosexuality versus homosexuality, with its emphasis on the closet, visibility, and identity. They argue that northern gay and lesbian groups interpret sexual practices in other parts of the world that fall outside of northern frameworks as less developed and in need of northern theorizing and politics (Hoad 2000). Massad argues that "the Gay International" exercises precisely these sorts of imperialist and orientalist tendencies in the Arab World (2008). The parallel with representations of sex workers from postcolonial contexts is striking. Focusing on same sex sexualities and politics in Uganda, Tushabe argues that colonial histories must be acknowledged, as same-sex sexualities were not criminalized prior to European control. Addressing global human rights frameworks which do not account for these histories, she writes:

> The self-identity that colonial construction of homosexuality imposed on us, supposedly, as a means of our self-knowledge, impedes our self-knowledge as it forecloses processes and avenues for a politic of decolonization. Only a human rights discourse that is invested in de-colonial practices could help change the way we think and see others.
>
> (Tushabe 2013, p. 154)

On the other hand, while also problematizing the northern produced and dominant global gay politics and sexual epistemology that circulates today, writing on lesbian activism in Singapore, Tang argues that local activists actually appropriate these discourses about sexual identity, visibility, and progress, refiguring them and transforming them in the process (2017). Speaking to similar complexities, in his ethnography of Filipino gay men in the US, Manalansan also explores how these men move back and forth between US/western gay and Filipino bakla sexual and gender identities (2003).[3]

Perhaps nothing has impacted the politics of sexual identity and activism in the last two decades more than the proliferation of HIV/AIDS, which has all too frequently enabled the repetition of older discourses and perceptions at the local, national, and global stages. HIV/AIDS have spotlighted issues of sexuality in numerous parts of the world and foregrounded not just women but also men and sexual and gender minorities in unprecedented ways. Undeniably, the spotlight has not been positive, for numerous postcolonial nations have targeted women sex workers, sexual and gender minorities, drug-injecting people, as well as working-class men who migrate for labor or have itinerant lives as truck drivers, for example, as the contagions for the spread of HIV. Pervasive anxieties resulted in national policies based on racial, religious, gender, sexual, or class stereotypes.

At the international level, racist ideas about Africa and black communities more generally led to the suspect label of "African AIDS," linking infections with unchecked, excessive heterosexual intercourse, which was contiguous with racist colonialist discourses (Patton 2002). As Cindy Patton notes, "the image of an African continent of seething sex and rampant death was simply relocated to describe America's black communities, now said to be 'like' villages in Africa" (2002, p. xiii). The reason HIV infections among sex workers in Kinshasa, African migrants in Brussels, or gay men in Los Angeles become visible to the authorities, Patton argues, is because of preexisting surveillance systems wary of "deviant" sexualities. But, the story of the HIV pandemic is incomplete without an account of the extensive forms of activism through which people banded together locally to provide care for those infected as well as to take on national governments, international bodies such as the World Health Organization, and corporations profiting from this crisis.

More recently, scholars are starting to discuss how postcolonial sexuality politics are further complicated by neoliberalism, understood in a nutshell as the expansion of market ideologies – individual as entrepreneurial and competitive, private over public – to virtually every aspect of life (Brown 2015). Insofar as sexuality is tightly linked with the private sphere, it presents particularly fertile ground for the advancement of neoliberal principles. In the metropoles, the standing concerns have been about neoliberalism's impact on sexual politics. Duggan (2002) and Richardson (2005) note how mainstream lesbian and gay politics have become about personal freedoms and private rights (for example, the emphasis on the right to marry) over the significance of collective gains (such as ending discrimination in hiring and employment related to sexual orientation). That is, what Duggan (2002) has famously come to call homonormativity, which exists alongside and in relation to rampant forms of homophobia in the US.

As in the metropoles, the postcolonies, too, are shaped by the complex interplay of neoliberalism and sexual politics. Writing about the antisodomy law in India (a colonial hangover) Puri (2016a) highlights the complex impact of the neoliberal climate on sexual activism. It shaped the strategy used to petition the state to decriminalize consensual sex among adults by inserting the caveat of privacy. This legal strategy, in effect, furthered the interests of privileged gay-identified subjects, while undermining the interests of working-class and non-English-speaking sexual and gender minorities without access to privacy. Puri (2016b) further shows that, contrary to popular assumptions, the state is not declining under neoliberal imperatives of privatization, but, in fact, regulating sexuality more closely than ever before. Discussing the Anglican Church in Africa in the context of neoliberal capital, Hoad also suggests that the vehement homophobia exhibited by the Church "is symptomatic, a strategy for deflecting attention from pressing social problems that they have been unwilling or unable to address" (2007, p 66). In her turn, Savci (2016) troubles the class divide that shapes the terrain of LGBT(I) politics in Istanbul. Contrasting two markedly different organizations, one openly political and the other avowedly commercial, she shows that neoliberalism shapes what are considered fundable and respectable queer politics.

Concluding Remarks

This chapter provides an overview of postcolonial sexualities by describing the long-standing entanglements of colonialisms, sexualities, postcolonialisms, nationalisms, and histories of resistance. While we have tried to draw on the contributions of numerous feminist and sexuality studies scholars in showing the complex histories and intersections of postcolonialisms and sexualities, we have hardly exhausted this rich and extensive field of study. Our hope is that this overview will provide readers with a foundation from which to proceed. By the same token, we have drawn examples from a variety of contexts and time periods to make some necessary generalizations.

Yet, generalizations are to an extent simplifications necessary to engaging new ideas and arguments. We encourage readers to apprehend the complexities and nuances of postcolonial sexualities that inevitably emerge once we delve more carefully into the specifics of place and time.

Presenting insight into how issues of sexuality, gender, race, social class, and religion propelled and mediated colonial conquest, this chapter shows that these issues were also foundational to ensuing forms of regulation and governance. Sexual desire and fantasy but also revulsion and anxiety figured prominently in the colonial encounter, sometimes drawing Europeans to the colonies and shaping their relationships with subjugated groups, and at other times powering the need to civilize and exert control. Seen this way, regulating, managing, and exploiting sexuality reshaped fundamental social institutions, relationships, and practices in the colonies, while also reverberating in the metropoles in significant ways. The impact in the colonies, however, was sweeping – ranging from the criminalization of select behaviors to suppressing women's sexualities, from determining lineage to adjudicating inheritance, from defining marriage to managing health and disease. The most consistent pattern across the numerous contexts that we have noted in the preceding discussion was that colonial officials and agents defined a "problem" in the colonies and then sought to reform it in the image of European white bourgeois notions of conjugal monogamous heteropatriarchy.

Colonial regulation shaped the terrain of sexual politics in ways that continue to resonate. During the colonial eras, native elites sometimes colluded with and embraced the sexual regulation of women, sexual and gender variant peoples, and other marginalized groups, while also accentuating issues of sexuality – our women, our sexual traditions – in anticolonial nationalist struggles. These politics were complex and their particular nuances were always context-specific. As we have noted, a whole range of sexual politics – demographics, sex work, criminalization of same-sex sexualities, sexual respectability, and more – became embattled at the time, spilling forward into the postcolonial period. Even as new challenges emerged on these national and regional scenes – such as HIV/AIDS, the heightening of sexual violence – they have been incorporated and interpreted through older frameworks, whether of tradition and modernity, or Westernization and national cultural traditions. At the same time, present-day international sexual politics – exemplified by the HIV/AIDS pandemic and population control – are also wrought through colonial histories and discourses.

In this sense, colonial, anticolonial, and postcolonial histories, as they affect sexuality politics, continue to reverberate through more contemporary processes having to do with development, neoliberalism, and globalization. Again then, the "post" in postcolonial sexualities is part misnomer, part elusive, yet a determined destination for postcolonial peoples the world over.

Notes

1 As Kauanui notes, translating māhū is not easy, but it can be generally understood as bein a self-identity for those assigned male at birth, who are third gender while presenting like women.

2 By "women," we do narrowly mean those who are seen as embodying normative womanhood and are presumptively heterosexual. Put another way, the reference to women intends to signal cisgender, heterosexual women who have long been objects of colonial and postcolonial regulation.
3 Bakla is a Tagalog gender and sexual identity prevalent in the Philippines.

References

Abrahams, Yvette. 1998. "Images of Sara Bartmen: Sexuality, Race and Gender in Early Nineteenth-Century Britain." In *Nation, Empire, Colony: Historicizing Gender and Race*, edited by R. R. Pierson and N. Chaudhuri, 220–236. Bloomington, IN: Indiana University Press.

Alexander, M. Jacqui. 1994. "Not Just (Any)Body Can Be a Citizen: The Politics of Law, Sexuality and Postcoloniality in Trinidad and Tobago and the Bahamas." *Feminist Review* 48: 4–23.

Alexander, M. Jacqui. 1996. "Erotic Autonomy as a Politics of Decolonization: An Anatomy of Feminist and State Practice in the Bahamas Tourist Industry." In *Feminist Genealogies, Colonial Legacies, Democratic Futures*, edited by M.J. Alexander and C.T. Mohanty, 63–100. New York, NY: Routledge.

Arnfred, Signe. 2004. "'African Sexuality'/Sexuality in Africa: Tales and Silences." In *Re-Thinking Sexualities in Africa*, edited by S. Arnfred, 59–78. Uppasala, Sweden: Nordiska Afrikainstitutet.

Bacchetta, Paola. 1999. "When the (Hindu) Nation Exiles Its Queers." *Social Text* 17(4): 141–166.

Barker, Joanne. 2017. "Introduction: Critically Sovereign." In *Critically Sovereign: Indigenous Gender, Sexuality, and Feminist Studies*, edited by Joanne Barker, 1–44. Durham, NC: Duke University Press.

Bleys, Rudi C. 1995. *The Geography of Perversion*. New York, NY: New York University Press.

Boone, Joseph Allen. 2014. *The Homoerotics of Orientalism*. New York, NY: Columbia University Press.

Brown, Wendy. 2015. *Undoing the Demos: Neoliberalism's Stealth Revolution*. New York, NY: Zone Books.

Collins, Patricia Hill. 2006. *From Black Power to Hip Hop: Racism, Nationalism, and Feminism*. Philadelphia, PA: Temple University Press.

Cooper, Frederick and Ann Laura Stoler, eds. 1997. *Tensions of Empire: Colonial Cultures in a Bourdeois World*. Berkeley: University of California Press.

Currier, Ashley. 2012. *Out in Africa: LGBT Organizing in Namibia and South Africa*. Minneapolis: University of Minnesota Press.

Das, Veena. 2007. *Life and Words: Violence and the Descent into the Ordinary*. Berkeley: University of California Press.

de Alva, J.J.K. 1995. "The Postcolonization of the (Latin) American Experience: A Reconsideration of "Colonialism", "Postcolonialism" and "Mestizaje." In *Life and Words: Violence and the Descent into the Ordinary*, edited by G. Prakash, 241–275. Princeton: Princeton University Press.

Duggan, Lisa. 2002. "The New Homonormativity: The Sexual Politics of Neoliberalism." In *Materializing Democracy: Towards a Revised Cultural Politics*, edited by D. Nelson and R. Castronovo, 175–194. Durham, NC: Duke University Press.

Epprecht, Marc. 2009. *Heterosexual Africa? The History of an Idea from the Age of Exploration to the Age of Aids*. Athens, OH: Ohio University Press.

Finley, Chris. 2011. "Decolonizing the Queer Native Body (and Recovering the Native Bull-Dyke): Bringing 'Sexy Back' and out of Native Studies' Closet." In *Queer Indigenous Studies: Critical Interventions in Theory, Politics, and Literature*, edited by Q.-L. Driskill, C. Finley, B. J. Gilley and S. L. Morgensen, 31–42. Tuscon, AZ: University of Arizona Press.

Grewal, Inderpal and Caren Kaplan. 1994a. "Introduction." In *Scattered Hegemonies: Postmodernity and Transnational Feminist Practice*, edited by I. Grewal and C. Kaplan. Minneapolis: University of Minnesota Press.

Grewal, Inderpal and Caren Kaplan, eds. 1994b. *Scattered Hegemonies: Postmodernity and Transnational Feminist Practice*. Minneapolis, MN: University of Minnesota Press.

Gupta, Alok. 2008. *This Alien Legacy: The Origins of 'Sodomy' Laws in British Colonialism*. New York, NY: Human Rights Watch.

Hall, Catherine. 2002. *Civilizing Subjects: Metropole and Colony in the English Imagination, 1830–1867*. Chicago IL: University of Chicago Press.

Hartmann, Betsy. 1995. *Reproductive Rights and Wrongs: The Global Politics of Population Control*. Boston, MA: South End Press.

Hoad, Neville. 2000. "Arrested Development of the Queerness of Savages: Resisting Evolutionary Narratives of Difference." *Postcolonial Studies* 3(2):133–158.

Hoad, Neville. 2007. *African Intimacies: Race, Homosexuality and Globalization*. Minneapolis: University of Minnesota Press.

Hodgson, Dorothy. 2011. "'These Are Not Our Priorities': Maasai Women, Human Rights, and the Problem of Culture." In *Gender and Culture at the Limit of Rights*, edited by D. Hodgson, 138–160. Philadelphia, PA: University of Pennsylvania Press.

Hulme, Peter. 1994. "Tales of Distinction: European Ethnography and the Caribbean." In *Implicit Understandings: Observing, Reporting and Reflecting on the Encounters between Europeans and Other Peoples in the Early Modern Era*, edited by S.B. Schwartz, 157–197. Cambridge: Cambridge University Press.

Hyam, Ronald. 1990. *Empire and Sexuality: The British Experience*. Manchester, UK: Manchester University Press.

Kauanui, J. Kēhaulani. 2017. "Indigenous Hawaiian Sexuality and the Politics of Nationalist Decolonization." In *Critically Sovereign: Indigenous Gender, Sexuality, and Feminist Studies*, edited by Joanne Barker, 45–68. Durham, NC: Duke University Press.

Keegan, Timothy. 2001. "Gender, Degeneration and Sexual Danger: Imagining Race and Class in South Africa, Ca 1912." *Journal of Southern African Studies* 27(3): 460–468.

Kempadoo, K. 1998. "Introduction: Global Sex Workers' Rights." In *Global Sex Workers: Rights, Resistance, and Redefinition* edited by K. Kempadoo and J. Doezema, 1–28. New York, NY: Routledge.

Kempadoo, Kempala. 2004. *Sexing the Caribbean: Gender, Race and Sexual Labor*. New York, NY: Routledge.

Kempadoo, K. and J. Doezema, eds. 1998. *Global Sex Workers: Rights, Resistance, and Redefinition*. London: Routledge.

Kiruthu, Felix, Martha Wangari Musalia, and Mildred Jalang'o-Ndede. 2013. "The Struggle for Sexual Rights among the Kikuyu Women of Central Kenya, 1918–2002." In *Women, Gender and Sexualities in Africa*, edited by T. Falola and N.A. Amponsah, 123–146. Durham, NC: Carolina Academic Press.

Levine, Philippa. 2004. "A Multitude of Unchaste Women: Prostitution in the British Empire." *Journal of Women's History* 15(4): 159–163.

Loomba, Ania. 1998. *Colonialism/Postcolonialism*. New York, NY: Routledge.
Lugones, Maria. 2007. "Heterosexualism and the Colonial/Modern Gender System." *Hypatia* 22(1): 186–209.
Lugones, Maria. 2010. "Towards a Decolonial Feminism." *Hypatia* 25(4): 742–759.
Manalansan, Martin. 2003. *Global Divas: Filipino Gay Men in the Diaspora*. Durham, NC: Duke University Press.
Mason, Peter. 1990. *Deconstructing America: Representations of the Other*. New York, NY: Routledge.
Massad, Joseph A. 2008. *Desiring Arabs*. Chicago, IL: University of Chicago Press.
McClintock, Anne. 1995. *Imperial Leather: Race, Gender and Sexuality in the Colonial Contest*. New York, NY: Routledge.
Mernissi, Fatima. 1991. *The Veil and the Male Elite: A Feminist Interpretation of Women's Rights in Islam*. Reading, MA: Addison-Wesley.
Moghadam, Valentine. 1993. "The Veil and the Male Elite: A Feminist Interpretation of Women's Rights in Islam." *Journal of World History* 4(2): 243–264.
Morgan, Jennifer L. 2004. *Laboring Women: Reproduction and Gender in New World Slavery*. Philadelphia: University of Pennsylvania Press.
Nnaemeka, Obioma, ed. 2005. *Female Circumcision and the Politics of Knowledge: African Women in Imperialist Discourses*. Westport, CN: Praeger.
Nussbaum, Felicity. 1995. *Torrid Zones: Maternity, Sexuality, and Empire in Eighteenth-Century English Narratives*. Baltimore, MD: Johns Hopkins University Press.
Overmyer-Velazquez, Rebecca. 2005. "Christian Morality in New Spain: The Nahua Woman in the Franciscan Imaginary." In *Bodies in Contact: Rethinking Colonial Encounters in World History*, edited by T. Ballantyne and Antoinette Burton, 67–83. Durham, NC: Duke University Press.
Patil, Vrushali. 2009. "Contending Masculinities: The Gendered (Re)Negotiation of Colonial Hierarchy in the United Nations Debates on Decolonization." *Theory and Society* 38(2): 195.
Patil, Vrushali and Bandana Purkayastha. 2015. "Sexual Violence, Race and Media (in) Visibility: Intersectional Complexities in a Transnational Frame." *Societies* 5(1): 598–617.
Patton, Cindy. 2002. *Globalizing Aids*. Minneapolis: University of Minnesota Press.
Povinelli, Elizabeth. 1998. "The State of Shame: Australian Multiculturalism and the Crisis on Indigenous Citizenship." *Critical Inquiry* 234(2): 576–610.
Pratt, Mary Louise. 1992. *Imperial Eyes: Travel Writing and Transculturation*. London and New York: Routledge.
Puri, Jyoti. 1999. *Woman, Body, Desire in Post-Colonial India: Narratives of Gender and Sexuality*. New York and London: Routledge.
Puri, Jyoti. 2016a. *Sexual States: Governance and the Struggle over the Antisodomy Law in India*. Durham, NC: Duke University Press.
Puri, Jyoti. 2016b. "Sexualizing Neoliberalism: Identifying Technologies of Privatization, Cleansing, and Scarcity." *Sexuality Research and Social Policy* 13(4): 308–320.
Richardson, Diane. 2005. "Desiring Sameness? The Rise of a Neoliberal Politics of Normalisation." *Antipode: A Radical Journal of Geography* 37(3): 515–535.
Rubiés, Joan-Pau 2007. "Travel Writing and Humanistic Culture." In *Bringing the World to Early Modern Europe: Travel Accounts and Their Audiences*, edited by P.C. Mancall, 131–168. Boston: Brill.
Said, Edward. 1979. *Orientalism*. New York, NY: Vintage.

Savci, Evren. 2016. "Who Speaks the Language of Queer Politics? Western Knowledge, Politico-Cultural Capital and Belonging among Urban Queers in Turkey." *Sexualities* 19(3): 369–387.

Sedghi, Hamideh. 2014. *Women and Politics in Iran: Veiling, Unveiling, and Reveiling*. Cambridge: Cambridge University Press.

Sigal, Peter. 2007. "Queer Nahuatl: Sahagún's Faggots and Sodomites, Lesbians and Hermaphrodites." *Ethnohistory* 54(1): 9–34.

Smith, Andrea. 2011. "Queer Theory and Native Studies: The Heteronormativity of Settler Colonialism." In *Queer Indigenous Studies: Critical Interventions in Theory, Politics and Literature*, edited by Q.-L. Driskill, C. Finley, B. J. Gilley and S. L. Morgensen, 43–65. Tuscon, AZ: University of Arizona Press.

Stoler, Ann Laura. 1995. *Race and the Education of Desire: Foucault's History of Sexuality and the Colonial Order of Things*. Durham, NC: Duke University Press.

Stoler, Ann Laura. 2002. *Carnal Knowledge and Imperial Power Race and the Intimate in Colonial Rule*. Oakland, CA: University of California Press.

Tang, Shawna. 2017. *Postcolonial Lesbian Identities in Singapore: Re-Thinking Global Sexualities*. London: Routledge.

Tushabe, Caroline. 2013. "Decolonizing Homosexuality in Uganda as a Human Rights Process." In *Women, Gender and Sexuality in Africa*, edited by T. Falola and N.A. Amponsah, 147–154. Durham, NC: Carolina Academic Press.

Wangari, Esther. 2002. "Reproductive Technologies: A Third World Feminist Perspective." In *Feminist Post-Development Thought : Rethinking Modernity, Post-Colonialism & Representation*, edited by K. Saunders, 298–312. London: Zed Books.

White, E. Frances. 2001. *The Dark Continent of Our Bodies: Black Feminism and the Politics of Respectability*. Philadelphia, PA: Temple University Press.

Wiley, Angela. 2006. "'Christian Nations,' 'Polygamic Races,' and Women's Rights: Toward a Genealogy of Non/Monogamy and Whiteness." *Sexualities* 9(5): 530–546.

Woollacott, Angela. 2006. *Gender and Empire*. Farnham: Palgrave Macmillan.

Young, Robert. 1995. *Colonial Desire: Hybridity in Theory, Culture and Race*. London: Routledge.

5

Queer Theory

J. Michael Ryan

There are few working in the social sciences or humanities today who have not at least heard of queer theory. That said, relatively few (not enough?) have an understanding of its theoretical and political underpinnings or of its potential for enriching our understandings of a wide variety of fields. To begin with, queer theory is not simply a code name for gay and lesbian studies nor need it necessarily even be confined to studies of sexuality (both to be discussed below). While the term "queer" has also become a shorthand for those lying outside the dominant sex/gender/sexuality paradigm, in the sense of queer theory it is meant more to imply "queering" something, that is to say questioning it, turning it inside out, and decentering it from the norm.

The term "queer" itself has been heavily contested (Giffney 2016; Marcus 2005). It has at times been simply a reference to gays and lesbians but has since transformed into a term referencing all those who fall outside the hegemonic binaries of gender and sexuality (or, according to some, those who fall outside the "norm" of any kind (Halperin 1995)). As Butler (1993) has noted, in order to avoid replicating normative claims, queer must be a category in constant formation. That said, one oft-claimed confusion of queer theory is that it is a theory which refers only to "queers," typically read as gays and lesbians.[1] It is, however, much more. To quote Warner (1993), "people want to make theory queer, not just to have a theory about queers" (p. xxvi).

In many ways queer theory is not really a theory at all. As Green (2002) has noted, "queer theory is less a formal theory with falsifiable propositions than a somewhat loosely bound, critical standpoint" (p. 524). Rather, it can perhaps be better read as a method of investigation, a political project, or a combination of the two. Thus, queer theory can be read in multiple ways.[2] In perhaps the most dominant stream, it is a theoretical and sometimes methodological project rooted in radical deconstructionism and anti-essentialism. It is, at least for many, a project of anti-identity.[3]

Companion to Sexuality Studies, First Edition. Edited by Nancy A. Naples.
© 2020 John Wiley & Sons Ltd. Published 2020 by John Wiley & Sons Ltd.

In another stream, it is a project of political subversion seeking to decenter the core and problematize the normal. It is a political project to counter the methods of an identity politics. In both such approaches, queer theory intends not so much to champion the rights of a particular minority identity but rather to challenge the very system that created the need for such championing in the first place.

At this point, I must make an apology for attempting to systematize knowledge and present a coherent picture of what exactly queer theory entails. To fail to make such an apology would reflect a misunderstanding of the very project queer theory seeks to undertake. With that apology in place, however, this chapter will indeed seek to present some coherent idea(s) about queer theory, its (multiple) origins, its significant academic and political contributions, and some critical reflections about where the field stands now and what kind of future it might have.

Theoretical and Institutional Origins

The origins of queer theory are as ambiguous and contested as many of the tenets of the theory itself. That said, there is some general agreement that the institutionalization of queer theory into academic discourse owes much to the work of Teresa de Lauretis, especially her mention of it at a conference at the University of California at Santa Cruz in 1990 and her introduction to "Queer Theory: Lesbian and Gay Sexualities," a special issue of *differences: A Journal of Feminist Cultural Studies* in 1991.[4] However, the origins of what would become known as queer theory can arguably be traced back even further, most notably to the work of Foucault and his *The History of Sexuality, Volume I* (1978) but also to other key works such as Eve Kosofsky Sedgwick's *Between Men* (1985) and *Epistemology of the Closet* (1990) and Judith Butler's *Gender Trouble* (1990).

Whatever its exact origins, if such a thing could ever even be determined, queer theory began to take a foothold, at least in the academy, in the late 1980s and early 1990s. During this time there were a number of key publications, conferences, and academic works that helped queer theory to flourish (see, for example, Seidman 1994; Jagose 1996b). Outside of the academy, the eruption of the AIDS crisis and associated movements such as ACT UP, as well as the political projects of gay and lesbian activism also served to draw attention to the potential usefulness of queer theory.[5]

The theoretical origins of queer theory can be found in a number of fields, but arguably its strongest roots are in the humanities, and also in ideas of poststructuralism, social constructionism, gay and lesbian studies, philosophy, and critical theory. Three of these – gay and lesbian studies, social constructionism, and poststructuralism – arguably exerted the greatest influence and so will be further explored in turn in this chapter.

Roots in gay and lesbian studies

The growth of gay and lesbian studies in the academy was a long, often tumultuous process. An academic interest in the homosexual as subject (or at least of homosexuality as practice) owes much its origins to the works of Krafft-Ebing (1877) and

Hirschfeld (1926–1930) who brought issues of "alternative" gender and sexualities to light in the late nineteenth and early twentieth centuries. The next great impetus arguably came with the groundbreaking work of Kinsey in the 1940s and 1950s and the political organization of homophile organizations such as the Mattachine Society and the Daughters of Bilitis. The 1960s witnessed the growth of a number of alternative movements such as the women's movements, the American Indian movement, movements by Latinos, blacks, and other peoples of color, and also by gays and lesbians. Perhaps most notably, the Stonewall Rebellion of 1969 helped consolidate the homosexual as an identity, but more importantly as a political identity with a history, a cause, and a so-called agenda framed around civil and political equality.

The field of gay and lesbian studies continued to grow through the 1970s and early 1980s with a growing body of literature, albeit one now critiqued, especially by those in queer theory, for being too narrowly focused and not critical enough of the social underpinnings of sexuality. It was in the early 1980s, however, when the field of lesbian and gay studies took a strong shaking on two fronts. First, the eruption of the AIDS crisis (initially known as GRID – Gay Related Immuno Deficiency) helped fuel the radical rights antigay backlash and brought the movement back to a more defensive posture. Second, non-White, non-middle class, non-"mainstream" gays and lesbians began to critique the movement more vocally for not representing their interests. The coherence of a gay and lesbian identity began to be questioned by those who did not fall under its hegemonic imaginary.

These shifts in the 1980s set the stage in the early 1990s for a range of new scholars, especially those rooted in French poststructuralism and Lacanian psychoanalysis, to begin to develop a new understanding of sexuality. This new understanding, which would develop loosely into what we are referring to as queer theory, was based in an understanding that identities are always multiple, unstable, and regulatory (Seidman 1994), ideas this chapter now explores.

Queer theory, in a clear affront to identity politics, argues that identities are *multiple* and that any attempt at understanding identities, even a composite of identities, necessarily leaves other identities excluded. For example, if I assert an identity as a gay, white, middle-class, educated male, I am simultaneously excluding other identities, for example those related to religion, ability, nationality, or linguistic community. Thus, it becomes difficult, nay impossible, to assert identity in the face of such multiplicity and necessarily implied exclusion.

Identities are also *unstable*, being highly dependent on context and historical moment. In this way, queer theory can be used to reveal the ways in which an identity-based method of theorizing or political action is problematic by demonstrating the unstable meanings attached to certain identities. For example, in the United States, my income would leave me being viewed as middle class whereas, in Portugal, I would be lower upper class, and in Peru, I would be a member of the upper class. My class position is dependent on context. Similarly, the possibility of having a "homosexual identity" is relatively new, arguably having origins in the explosion of discourse around sexuality during the Victorian era (Foucault 1978). Further, the identity of gay has come to mean something very different in the post-Stonewall era than it did pre-Stonewall.

Identities are also seen as *regulatory*. Rather than serving as a source of liberation and community building, identities are viewed as imposed social templates which limit the possibilities of expression and personhood. In this sense, identities come to be social scripts by which actors are prejudged and have the potential to become outsider-imposed master statuses through which the actions of actors are interpreted, assessed, and often misunderstood.

At the root of gay and lesbian studies, and many early studies of sexuality, is the idea of the homosexual as a knowable subject. Early theories posited worked with the assumption, à la arguments by Foucault but in contradiction to his project, that the "homosexual" was a stable identity and one on par with the "heterosexual." The goal was to explore such an identity, its history, its site as a means of discrimination and oppression, and its stigmatized status. They worked on the idea that sexuality was itself a key component of the social, one that had been overlooked by earlier theorists but one very much deserving of attention. Queer theory, on the other hand, seeks to deconstruct such an identity by turning attention to the regulatory framework of sexuality itself, its discursive production, and the underlying mechanisms by which sexuality influences all aspects of the social. It is not that sexuality is simply one socially constructed aspect of a larger social whole but rather than sexuality is infused, ever present, and inextricably social. As Seidman eloquently puts it:

> In this regard, queer theory is suggesting that the study of homosexuality should not be a study of a minority – the making of the lesbian/gay/bisexual subject – but a study of those knowledges and social practices which organize "society" as a whole by sexualizing – heterosexualizing or homosexualizing – bodies, desires, acts, identities, social relations, knowledges, culture, and social institutions. Queer theory aspires to transform homosexual theory into a general social theory or one standpoint from which to analyze whole societies.
>
> (Seidman 1994, p. 174)

In this way despite having roots in gay and lesbian studies, queer theory is in many ways the antithesis of what those studies used to be. While earlier incarnations of gay and lesbian studies saw the homosexual as a knowable subject position, queer theory adamantly rejects such an idea of selfhood.

Roots in social constructionism

Social constructionism argues that sex, gender, sexuality, and indeed all identities are the products of particular contexts in particular locales at particular historical moments. Queer theory throws into question the concepts of sex, gender, and sexuality to an even more radical degree than was done by social constructionism. Whereas social constructionists view each of the above categories as the result of social forces dependent on time, place, and context, queer theorists question the distinction of such categories in the first place. Thus, even though social constructionists question the essential nature of these categories as given, they still accept that once categorized, there are consequences from such labels. Instead, queer theorists assert that "because these binaries are revealed to be cultural constructions or ideological fictions, the reality of sexed bodies and gender and sexual identities are fraught with incoherence and instability" (Valocchi 2005, p. 753). In other words, according to queer theorists, social constructionists do not go far enough in questioning the formation of categorical boundaries or of categories themselves.

Additionally, whereas social constructions question the alignment between sex, gender, and sexuality, queer theorists see the categories as interrelated and question, for example, the ways in which gender is sexed or sex is gendered in nonhegemonic ways (Gagne and Tewksbury 2002).

Queer theory also challenges the heterosexual/homosexual binary in multiple ways. One such way is by emphasizing the larger regulatory framework of sexuality rather than any particular manifestation of it. In other words, by putting emphasis on how sexuality is produced discursively and effected politically, the focus falls not on the subsequent identity resultant from a set of sociopolitical discourses but on the discourses themselves. Another way in which queer theory challenges this binary is by putting into question the sex-of-object choice as the most appropriate mode by which to understand sexual identity. So, for example, sadomasochists, trans peoples, and intersexed individuals provide examples of modes of sexual practice and embodiment that complicate an understanding of sexuality as based on a dichotomous view of sex-of-object choice (Chase 1998; Hale 1997; Kessler 1998).

The idea of a core self is, in varying ways and degrees, at the heart of much theorizing in the social sciences. Even social constructionists, who are quick to recognize the importance of time, place, and context as determining the how, when, etc. of identity expression, still see some core sense of self that is acting throughout the various times, places, and contexts. In other words, if it is understood in terms of structure (an overarching sociopolitical institutionalized regime of the social) and agency (one's ability to act within and react toward said structure), the latter is the location of the core self. Queer theory challenges this notion by highlighting how such an understanding still relies on reifying social categories: a form that is constituted only by its other. In this way, queer theory collapses the structure/agency dualism (Stein 1989), instead seeing the self as "'human subject', that is, derived from the manifold social, cultural, and economic forces that construct the false notion of the autonomous self, and provide the discursive material for the conscious and unconscious enactment of the self" (Valocchi 2005, p. 755).

Roots in poststructuralism

Poststructuralism is another theoretical approach that heavily influenced queer theory, especially in its early days. With its emphasis on deconstruction, decentering, and concerns with the discursive production of categories, especially those related to identity, one could potentially make the argument that queer theory is, in many ways, an outgrowth of poststructuralism, albeit one that, at least in its initial conceptions, was largely concerned with sexuality.

Much of poststructuralism, and by extension queer theory, has origins in the work of Foucault. Most relevant to queer theory is Foucault's work on sexuality and the discursive formation of "the homosexual." In *The History of Sexuality* (1978), Foucault examines the origins of the homosexual as a knowable subject. He roots his arguments in what he terms "the repressive hypothesis." Foucault argues that during the Victorian era, sexuality was supposedly silenced, especially through legal inhibitions and a preoccupation with its repression. This attempt at repression, however, was far from the reality where sexuality was being heavily discussed, debated, and brought to the light in everyday conversations, legal regulations, and academic studies creating a type of "discursive explosion." This proliferation of discourses led to the formation of a new category of person – that of the "homosexual." Foucault does not argue that homosexual acts were something new to this era but rather that the idea of a homosexual as a knowable category and a classifiable identity was indeed something new. Thus, the attempt to repress sexuality, in fact, led to its creation as a category for identity and, "made possible the formation of a 'reverse' discourse: homosexuality began to speak in its own behalf, to demand that its legitimacy or 'naturality' be acknowledged, often in the same vocabulary, using the same categories by which it was medically disqualified" (1978, p. 101). In this way, Foucault argues that the homosexual, rather than a concrete knowable natural category, is instead the result of a discursive production of identity which engendered the understanding of a type of person, that of the homosexual. It was not that there was a sudden discovery of a new type of personage but rather that the production of discourse and knowledge about such a "type" is what came to constitute its very existence.

Poststructuralism made especially important contributions to queer theory with the idea that we must not consider the social ramifications of categories as such, but instead focus on the very production of those categories. In reaction to labeling theory and many dominant theories of deviance, queer theory asserts that we should not focus on deviant identities and communities, an act which itself only reinforces the legitimacy and hegemonic status of the "normal," but instead examine the very creation of those categories and their discursive reliance on one another. In support of a sociological queer theory, Namaste (1994) has argued, "If we focus on the 'subculture' of homosexuality, and if we never interrogate the conditions which engender its marginalization, we shall remain trapped within a theoretical framework which refuses to acknowledge its own complicity in constructing its object (or subjects) of study" (p. 228).

Another foundational work in queer theory is Fuss's (1991) edited volume *Inside/Out: Lesbian Theories, Gay Theories*. In this volume, Fuss highlights one of the central tenets of queer theory with the idea that one can neither be fully inside nor outside. Working with the idea of "the closet," Fuss notes that declaring oneself to be "out" of the closet necessarily implies that there is an "in" to the closet as well. Thus, in order to attain an identity as "out" one must first not only recognize, but also privilege by assumption the dominant category of "in" and further that that is the "natural" starting point from which one moves. Thus, coming out can be seen as "a transgression of the border which is necessary to constitute the border as such" (1991, p. 3).

Queer theory is not so much concerned with the categories of in and out, or of homosexual and heterosexual as such, but rather with the discursive production of the boundaries between those categories. The concern is less with the existence of a given boundary, or with what identities might lie on either side, and more with how such a boundary was created, how the boundary is policed, and how those on either side might contest or alter the boundary itself.

One example of such a contestation could arguably be found in the early 2010s' fad of the metrosexual and shows such as *Queer Eye for the Straight Guy*. In this show, a team of five, largely flamboyant, gay men took up the project of "helping" some poor sloppy heterosexual man with things like fashion tips, makeovers, and redecorating. The play on stereotypes, of both homosexuals and heterosexuals, simultaneously reinforced the idea of two distinct categories, but by so doing also produced a new categorical distinction, that of a well-groomed, manicured, well-smelling heterosexual man who was not homosexual. Thus, a metrosexual is a heterosexual male with "gay sensibilities." The social categorization of the metrosexual can perhaps better be read not so much about the creation of a new category of sexual identity – indeed the dominant binary of homosexual/heterosexual remains unaltered, if not reinforced by such a conception (Westerfelhaus and Lacroix 2006) – but more as a demonstration that the categories themselves are the result of a cultural discourse rooted in assumptions of particular behaviors, styles, mannerisms, and ways of being. Thus, the metrosexual is a contestation of the border between heterosexual and homosexual who, by effect of having needed to be named, highlights and disrupts the categorical distinctions of sexual identity.[6]

Queer theory, by virtue of decategorizing binary oppositions and instead interrogating their discursive production, has the advantage of opening the door to understanding "marginalized identities" (a term, which itself, reinforces normative hegemonic categorical distinctions), of those who are generally left out of sociological discourse, even those focusing on minority categories. In relation to sexuality, for example, this would mean exploring categories which are neither homosexual nor heterosexual and thereby enriching our understanding of the larger social production of sexual identity categories. Since "these binaries incompletely or imperfectly represent a broad range of complicated social processes surrounding the meaning of bodies and the social cues, practices, and subjectivities associated with gender and sexuality" (Valocchi 2005, p. 753), this attention to what is excluded, even from the inside and the out, serves to further interrogate the broader cultural production, and reproduction, of categorical distinctions and to further elucidate how the boundaries between them are created, maintained, policed, and contested.

To Be or To Question Being, That is the Project (Hallmarks of Queer Theory)

As has become clear, delineating exactly what is meant by queer theory is a project whose very undertaking undermines its objective. As Berlant and Warner (1995) have cautioned, queer theory "cannot be assimilated to a discourse, let alone a propositional program" (p. 343). Put simply, to mark out an understanding of queer theory is to demonstrate a lack of understanding for its fundamental principles. That said, there are certain ideological and theoretical underpinnings to most projects that would normatively be labeled as "queer theory" and by exploring these one can gain a better appreciation of the paradox of doing so.

Stein and Plummer (1994) offer one such set of four identifying hallmarks of that which we might call queer theory:

- "*A conceptualization of sexuality which sees sexual power embodied in different levels of social life, expressed discursively and enforced through boundaries and binary divides*" (pp. 181–182). The implication is that sexual power is present throughout the social world – the media, politics, religion, etc. – and not just restricted to the realm of "the sexual." This power is expressed through the recreation and reinforcement of a presumed binary between the homosexual and the heterosexual. This categorical division serves to maintain the privileged position of heterosexuality and to relegate homosexuality to an inferior margin. Queer theory takes aim at such a conceptualization by questioning not the positions within the division but the discursive production, recreation, and potential contestation of the socially manufactured boundary between them.

- *"Problematization of sexual and gender categories, and of identities in general. Identities are always on uncertain ground, entailing displacement of identification and knowing"* (p. 182). Building on the above, sexual categories are seen as ways of doingrather than as ways of being. Rather than taking as starting points or as independent units of analysis (as was the case for much of the research in the early days, and arguably even to the present, of gay and lesbian studies), queer theory is more interested in interrogating how such categories are the result of a particular discursive production rooted in a particular sociohistorical context. Identity, rather than being understood as something stable, is seen as something which is always shifting, not only by situation and historical moment as is the understanding of social constructionists, but also by the particular sociohistorical discourse. Thus, as discourse shifts, so too does the potential for understanding the production of social categorizations.
- *"Rejection of civil rights strategies in favor of a politics of carnival, transgression, and parody which leads to deconstruction, decentering, revisionist readings, and an anti-assimilationist politics"* (p. 182). Rooted heavily in the poststructuralist ideas of play and carnival, queer theory takes particular aim at the political project of identity politics. For example, the political aims of the gay and lesbian rights movement would be shunned on the grounds that such political contestation only serves to legitimate the very power it seeks to contest. By resisting oppression based on a politics of identity, one is, in fact, empowering the hegemonic position of a discursively produced binary that led to such oppression in the first place.
- *"A willingness to interrogate areas which normally would not be seen as the terrain of sexuality, and to conduct queer 'readings' of ostensibly heterosexual or nonsexualized texts"* (p. 182). Queer theorists explore aspects of social life which are not typically seen as being under the purview of the sexual. Thus, issues such as the media (Walters 2001), popular culture (Sullivan 2003), education (Kosciw 2004), archaeology (Dowson 2002), the health sciences (Argüello 2016), Middle East studies (Mikdashi and Puar 2016), accounting (Rumens 2016), and even teen soap operas (Jenner 2011) have all been explored using an approach of queer theory. The aim is to show how sexuality, rather than being a distinct component of the social, is inextricably intertwined with the social. There is also a willingness by queer theory to reinterpret classical texts, or those which are not seen as sexualized, in order to demonstrate how the sexual is present (see, for example Miller 1991; Doty 1993).

Other theorists have also attempted to provide similar hallmarks of queer theory. Valocchi (2005, p. 766), for example, has presented a series of conceptual and analytic tools that he advocates for empirical work in gender and sexuality.

His recommendations serve not only as useful tools for doing this kind of work but in many ways also highlight important tenets of queer theory:

- *"Queering the relationship between sex, gender, and sexuality."* For many working in gay and lesbian studies it was an important step to delineate differences between the categories of sex, gender, and sexuality. Queer theory, however, reveals these categories to be "cultural constructions or ideological fictions," highlighting instead how "the reality of sexed bodies and gender and sexual identities are fraught with incoherence and instability" (p. 753).
- *"Taking seriously the nonnormative alignments across these variables."* Queer theory looks for interrelationships between these categories exploring, for example, how gender is sexed and sexuality is gendered in ways that fall outside of the dominant paradigm (see, for example, Gagne and Tewksbury 2002).
- *"Resisting the tendency to essentialize identity or to conflate it with the broad range of gender and sexual practices."* Queer theory discounts the possibility of a knowable sexualized subject. It does so, in part, by refusing to categorize individuals by privileging their sexual, or any other, identity. It also does not conflate identity as such with the various practices, enactments, or performances of actors.
- *"Broadening an understanding of power to include identity formations as well as other discursive formations."* Power is not seen as an external force, or as something inherent to given individuals in particular social positions. It is, instead, seen as being constituted through the discursive production of particular social and identity categories. Thus, heterosexuality is not an inherently privileged position but rather its ability to be that by which other identities are positioned, to act as the center and the "against which" by which other identities come to have meaning, is the means by which heterosexuality maintains its hegemonic normalcy.
- *"Treating the construction of intersectional subjectivities as both performed and performative."* Queer theory, being heavily influenced by the work of Butler on performativity, sees identity as a performance rather than as a core attribute of individuals. Thus, for example, heterosexuality is not an inherent characteristic of a given individual but rather a social performance, one whose meaning is validated only by repetitive performances and the constitution of that which it is not.

Although the above hallmarks are simply that, hallmarks, they are useful in providing a rough sketch of many of the fundamental principles of queer theory.

Fad or Forever: The Present and Potential Future of Queer Theory

There is little doubt that queer theory has left its mark on a number of academic fields. Akin to its philosophical forerunner, poststructuralism, it has made it difficult for many who engage in any number of academic enterprises to continue to work in the same way as before. The important questions, criticisms, and contributions of queer theory have no doubt enriched fields ranging from gay and lesbian studies to sociology and even to many of the hard sciences. Most notably, the broad-based perspective of queer theory has enlarged the scope of any number of identity-based fields, including, but not limited to, gay and lesbian studies. As Marcus (2005) has noted, after the appearance of queer theory, gay and lesbian studies "analogously moved from tracing historically stable identities based on object choice to defining queerness in relation to sexual norms" (p. 195).

Green (2002) has argued that queer theory exists in two strands – one is a project of radical deconstruction (questioning the ontological basis of categories) and the other is one of radical subversion (using queer as a site from which to politically contest normative categories). He identifies the first strand, one of radical deconstructionism, as the predominant strand and one that "embraces a social constructionist project seeded by French post-structuralism and Lacanian psychoanalysis" where scholars "draw from Foucault, challenge the scientific basis of sexual identity and reduce sexual classifications (e.g. heterosexuality, homosexuality) to the effects of discourse" (p. 524). The second strain, one of radical subversion, "targets homosexuality and other non-heteronormative practices, identities, and representations as sites of queer subversion. ... the very fact of non-heterosexual desire connotes transgression and rebellion" (p. 531).

I argue that a review of the current state of queer theory points to it is being employed in three rather distinct ways: (i) those who continue to view it as a largely philosophical issue tied primarily to discourse and still rooted largely in issues of sexuality; (ii) those who remain largely true to the philosophical underpinnings of queer theory yet, in response to its multiple criticisms for failing to do so, wish to more firmly root it in the material world (e.g. Valocchi 2005); and (iii) those who seek to employ the principles of queer theory largely as a methodological approach and to move it beyond the realm of sexuality.

There are some die-hard queer theorists who still cling to its founding principles as a project of radical deconstruction wedded to a politics of anti-identity and largely rooted in issues of sexuality. They tend to reject the criticisms leveled against the theory, instead defending that material changes are less consequential than the philosophical underpinnings of categorical creation that led to material inequalities in the first place. Those in this vein are found largely in the places where queer theory first took root – the humanities, philosophy, and pedagogical studies.

The second strand, and perhaps the dominant one of the day, still holds to the basic tenets of queer theory, yet has also attempted to incorporate a more material understanding. In response to perhaps the most commonly leveled criticism of queer theory (see more on this in the section "Critiques"), those in this strand attempt to incorporate a greater understanding of the material consequences of identity, and especially of the lived everyday realities of individuals. Those in this strand tend to be more in the realm of sociology and other social sciences whose primary preoccupation has been the social.

The third strand are those who see queer theory less as a philosophical endeavor and more as a methodological approach. They attempt to utilize the precedents of queer theory as a means of approaching particular issues. Thus, they draw less on the specifically sexual tenets of the theory and more on the general approach of deconstruction, anti-identity, and a shift toward examining the discursive creation of social categories rather than the social locations per se. Such a focus more easily facilitates a utilization of queer theory beyond the realm of simply sexuality and into other fields, for example, race and ethnicity studies, and studies of disability.

The Uneasy Relationship between Queer Theory and Sociology

Much has been written about the uneasy relationship between queer theory and sociology. Most have ended arguing that, in many ways, queer theory represents a sort of antithesis to the core principles of sociological research. At heart, while sociological approaches tend to focus on selves, institutions, everyday material experiences, and, by extension, the "social," queer theory instead seeks to dismantle the idea of a knowable subject with a focus on texts, discourse, and a radical deconstructionist philosophy bent on dismantling any concept of identity. As Green (2007) has noted, "queer theory, anchored in deconstruction, is the *saboteur* of the late modern self, and in its hands the historical project of social intelligibility and the corresponding mechanisms of subjectification are gaily offered up in ritual sacrifice" (p. 42).

In reference to studies of sexuality, there are strong arguments that queer theory, while not a replacement for sociology in the study of sexuality, is at least a worthy companion. Green (2007), for example, has made a strong case for the potential benefits of drawing on both approaches and arguing that critics of their compatibility "may ultimately represent a misplaced effort to synthesize queer theory and sociology, asking too much of queer theory and, perhaps, too little of sociology" (p. 42). Green makes the case that while queer theory perhaps goes too far in its rejection of a knowable subject, sociology perhaps does not go far enough in its deconstructionist effort. Thus, he argues that the potential long-term contribution of queer theory to sexuality studies (and to sociology more generally) "lies not in uncovering subjects and selves, but, following Warner [1993], by pivoting the analysis to a broader field of normalization that invokes the terms of the social order so that it might ultimately reduce them to obsolescence" (p. 43). The relationship between the two then is really a call for "a reflexive sociology situated in a productive incommensurability with queer theory – a partnership in the study of sexualities that promises a vital dialectic between the constructionist and reifying tendencies of interpretivism, on the one hand, and the deconstructionist, negating tendencies of queer theory, on the other" (p. 43).

Queer theory has also arguably helped change the agenda of sociologists interested in studying sexuality by shifting attention from gays and lesbians as sexual subjects (often with little, or no, attention to the heterosexual subject) to a broader focus on the social order and the overarching effects of heteronormativity. Indeed, as Gamson and Moon (2004) have noted, "queer theory has helped set a different sort of agenda for sociological research in sexualities: to operationalize and then investigate the claims that sexual identities are 'discursively produced' and unstable and that the social order rests on 'heteronormativity'" (pp. 48–49). Further, Green (2002) notes that since the introduction of queer theory, rather than thinking of binary categories of heterosexual and homosexual as overarching units of analysis, "sociologists have been challenged to sharpen their analytical lenses, to grow sensitized to the discursive production of sexual identities, and to be mindful of the insidious force of heteronormativity as a fundamental organizing principle throughout the social order" (p. 521).

There is no doubt that queer theory has had an impact on sociologists, especially those interested in sexualities, but it has also failed to significantly impact the way the field as a whole goes about its business. While those who had previously been interested in sexuality only in terms of individual subjects and lived experiences are now more apt to focus on the larger social order and the mutually constitutive creation of the so-called hetero/homo binary, this shift in perspective has not made significant inroads into other areas of research. However, there are signs that a queer theoretical approach is starting to gain the attention of some working in race and ethnicity studies (see, for example, Glick 2003; Johnson and Henderson 2005) and also in disability studies (see, for example, McRuer and Wilkerson 2003; McRuer 2006), so the future of the relationship between queer theory and sociology is far from already written.

Critiques

One critique of queer theory is that it has gone too far in its own critique of identity (Kirsch 2000; Green 2002). By focusing on the discursive production of identities, rather than on their lived realities, queer theory has arguably erased the lived experiences of individual actors who suffer material oppressions, ones that exist outside the realm of discourse (Seidman 1996). Although understanding how identities come to be constructed is no doubt important, so too is the ways in which actors embedded in institutions experience lived realities. Thus, by attacking the social order, queer theory fails to account for the effects of the social on individual lived experience.

Building on the above, discounting the lived material experiences of actors, and rejecting political action based around identity, has the effect of leaving those dealing with oppression with little means for the practical amelioration of their concerns (Edwards 1998). An attitude of carnival rather than an identity-based social movement pushing for greater equality leaves the status quo in place for those more willing to play the game of institutional management. If a minority group is left without the possibility to organize and engage in meaningful political action on the basis of the very identity that has made them a minority, then what does social justice action look like and how can those who are oppressed seek to remedy the inequalities enacted against them?

As queer theory is heavily rooted in textual analysis and discourse, the language used by many who engage with it is often quite complicated. Thus, much of the knowledge generated by queer theory is left outside the realm of understanding of many lay people and academics alike. The complicated jargon used by many queer theorists has rendered its application subject to criticisms of intellectual elitism. Further, the use of such language can be read as a general disregard for transformative change outside of a privileged elite circle capable of, and interested in, understanding its complex language.

Related to the above is the criticism that much of what has come to be known as mainstream queer theory has been largely generated by a select group of white middle-class intellectuals working in university settings in economically elite countries. Just as the complicated jargon of the theory leaves it outside the realm, nay interest, of many, the production of such knowledge has also been largely limited to a narrow elite.

A rather ironic criticism of queer theory is that, as it became increasingly accepted into academic discourse, it lost its revolutionary potential. Its very success has rendered it increasingly ineffective as a source of potential change. Thus, as queer theory came to take on more normative structures (for example, being defined through intellectual projects such as this very chapter), it lost what had made it radical in the first place. As Halperin (1995) has noted, "the more it verges on becoming a normative academic discipline, the less queer 'queer theory' can plausibly claim to be" (p. 113).

Conclusion

Ritzer and Ryan (2007) have argued that postmodernism is now dead but it still lives on as an important tool in our theoretical toolkit. Thus, although there are few who still claim to be postmodernists, many of the ideas of postmodernism are still used in a variety of disciplines. Much the same can potentially be said of queer theory. The number of academics claiming to be queer theorists has arguably declined since its heyday in the 1990s, but it has still left a lasting impact and conceptual tools and frameworks that influence many throughout the academy. As Edelman (1995) has noted, "utopic in its negativity, queer theory curves endlessly toward a realization that its realization remains impossible" (p. 348).

Nearly as quickly as it exploded onto the academic scene, queer theory has arguably vanished (though, as argued above, there are some signs that this trend might be reversing as it gains popularity in fields such as race and ethnicity studies and disability studies). Although it managed to drastically change many a field, queer theory as an independent entity seems to have largely receded from the spotlight. Similar to poststructuralism, from which it took root, queer theory has left an impact but has few notable practitioners, instead most often appearing as a special interest class in a gay and lesbian studies or sociology department, or appearing as a day of inquiry on a social theory syllabus. One sees fewer special issues devoted to its treatment, fewer academic tomes investigating its merits, fewer specialized academic conferences debating its principles, and arguably fewer far-reaching ideas emerging from its bowels.[7] This, however, is not necessarily a bad thing. Following one of the critiques outlined above, one potential downfall of the successful institutionalization of queer theory was bound to be its own demise (much the same could be said of its forerunner poststructuralism). Perhaps this recession from the academic spotlight, albeit one that has left its glow on many a field, is exactly what queer theory needed in order to remain, if I may use the term, "queer."

Notes

1 There might be claims to support this confusion, especially in the early days of queer theory. Namaste (1994), for example, has claimed that "intellectuals from Teresa de Lauretis (1991) to Eve Sedgwick (1990) claim to have written a theory which is "queer," but they grant only lesbians and gay men the right to belong to that category" (p. 228).

2   Some have even argued that queer theory should more properly be stated as queer theo-*ries*. Donald Hall (2003), for example, has argued "simply put there is no 'queer' theory in the singular, only many different voices and sometimes overlapping, sometimes divergent perspectives that can loosely be called 'queer theories'" (p. 5).
3   Jagose (1996a) has taken issue with the idea of queer theory as being an attack on identity arguing instead that, "instead of theorizing queer in terms of its opposition to identity politics, it is more accurate to represent it as ceaselessly interrogating both the preconditions of identity and its effects."
4   It is interesting to note that de Lauretis would only three years later denounce the use of the term "queer theory" in the same journal in which she first helped to popularize it: "As for 'queer theory', my insistent specification lesbian may well be taken as a taking of distance from what, since I proposed it as a working hypothesis for lesbian and gay studies in this very journal (differences, 3.2), has very quickly become a conceptually vacuous creature of the publishing industry" (de Lauretis 1994).
5   For an excellent overview of the genealogy of queer theory, see Turner (2000) *A Genealogy of Queer Theory* or Sullivan *(2003) A Critical Introduction to Queer Theory*. For more general overviews, see Meeks (2006), Ryan (2007), and Fikry and Ryan (2015).
6   See Ramsey and Santiago 2004 for a counter to this argument – they argue instead that "metrosexuals on *Queer Eye* entertain Americans with their newfound love of "'product' (the feminine) without threatening to challenge the boundaries of masculinity (their 'success' is usually defined in terms of success in romantic conquests and business successes" (p. 354).
7   This is not to say that there is not still a great deal of productive and interesting work being done in the field. See, for example, Giffney and O'Rourke's (2016) edited volume *The Ashgate Research Companion to Queer Theory*, for an excellent overview of the field, including recent new directions.

References

Argüello, T.M. 2016. Fetishizing the Health Sciences: Queer Theory as an Intervention. *Journal of Gay & Lesbian Social Services* 28(3):231–244.

Berlant, L. and M. Warner. 1995. "What Does Queer Theory Teach Us About X?" *PMLA* 110(3): 343–349.

Butler, Judith. 1990. *Gender Trouble: Feminism and the Subversion of Identity*. New York, NY: Routledge.

Butler, Judith. 1993. *Bodies that Matter: On the Discursive Limits of "Sex."* New York, NY: Routledge.

Chase, Cheryl. 1998. "Hermaphrodites with Attitude: An Emergence of Intersex Political Activism." *GLQ* 4(2): 189–211.

de Lauretis, Teresa. 1991. "Queer Theory: Lesbian and Gay Sexualities." *differences: A Journal of Feminist Cultural Studies* 3(2) iii–xviii.

de Lauretis, Teresa. 1994. "Habit Changes." *differences: A Journal of Feminist Cultural Studies* 6(2–3): 296–313.

Doty, Alexander. 1993. *Making Things Perfectly Queer: Interpreting Mass Culture*. Minneapolis, MN: University of Minnesota Press.

Dowson, Thomas A. 2002. "Why Queer Archaeology? An Introduction." *World Archaeology* 12(2): 161–165.

Edelman, L. 1995. "Queer Theory: Unstating Desire." *GLQ* 2(4): 343–346.

Edwards, Tim. 1998. "Queer Fears: Against the Cultural Turn" *Sexualities* 1(4): 471–484.
Fikry, Noha and J. Michael Ryan. 2015. "Queer Theory." In *The Wiley Blackwell Encyclopedia of Gender and Sexuality Studies*, edited by Nancy Naples. Oxford: Wiley Blackwell.
Foucault, Michel. 1978. *The History of Sexuality, Volume I: An Introduction*. Translated by Robert Hurley. London: Pantheon.
Diana Fuss, ed. 1991. *Inside/Out: Lesbian Theories, Gay Theories*, New York, NY: Routledge.
Gagne, Patricia and Richard Tewksbury. 2002. *Gendered Sexualities*. Oxford: Elsevier Science.
Gamson, Joshua and Dwane Moon. 2004. "The Sociology of Sexualities: Queer and Beyond." *Annual Review of Sociology* 30: 47–64.
Giffney, Noreen. 2016. "Introduction: The 'Q' Word." In *The Ashgate Research Companion to Queer Theory*, edited by Noreen Giffney and Michael O'Rourke, 1–10. London: Routledge.
Giffney, Noreen and Michael O'Rourke. 2016. *The Ashgate Research Companion to Queer Theory*. London: Routledge.
Glick, E.F. (2003). Introduction: Defining Queer Ethnicities. *GLQ* 10(1): 123–124.
Green, Adam Isaiah. 2002. "Gay but Not Queer: Toward a Post-Queer Study of Sexuality." *Theory and Society* 31(4): 521–545.
Green, Adam Isaiah. 2007. "Queer Theory and Sociology: Locating the Subject and the Self in Sexuality Studies." *Sociological Theory* 25(1): 26–45.
Hale, C. Jacob. 1997. "Leatherdyke Boys and Their Daddies: How To Have Sex Without Women or Men." *Social Text* 15(3–4): 222–236.
Hall, D.E. 2003. *Queer Theories*. New York, NY: Palgrave Macmillan.
Halperin, David. 1995. *Saint Foucault: Towards A Gay Hagiography*. New York, NY: Oxford University Press.
Jagose, Annamarie. 1996a. "Queer Theory." *Australian Humanities Review*. Association for the Study of Australian Literature.
Jagose, Annamarie. 1996b. *Queer Theory: An Introduction*. New York, NY: New York University Press.
Jenner, Mareike. 2011. "'I Can't Even Imagine What It's Gonna Be Like Here without Him': Friendship and Queer Theory in American Teen Soap." *Spire Journal of Law, Politics and Societies* 6(1): 30–48.
Johnson, E.P. and M.G. Henderson. 2005. *Black Queer Studies: A Critical Anthology*. Durham, NC: Duke University Press.
Kessler, Suzanne. 1998. *Lessons from the Intersexed*. New Brunswick, NJ: Rutgers University Press.
Kirsch, Max H. 2000. *Queer Theory and Social Change*. London: Routledge.
Kosciw, J.G. 2004. "*The 2003 National School Climate Survey: The School-Related Experiences of Our Nation's Lesbian, Gay, Bisexual and Transgender Youth*." New York, NY: GLSEN.
Marcus, Sharon. 2005. "Queer Theory for Everyone: A Review Essay" *Signs* 31(1): 191–218.
McRuer, R. 2006. *Crip Theory: Cultural Signs of Queerness and Disability*. New York, NY: New York University Press.
McRuer, R. and A.L. Wilkerson. 2003. "Desiring Disability: Queer Theory Meets Disability Studies. *GLQ* 9(1–2): 1–24.
Meeks, Chet. 2006. "Queer Theory." In *Blackwell Encyclopedia of Sociology*, edited by George Ritzer. Oxford: Wiley Blackwell.

Mikdashi, Maya and Jasbir K. Puar. 2016. "Queer Theory and Permanent War." *GLQ* 22(2): 215–222.

Miller, D.A. 1991. "Anal Rope." In *Inside/Out: Lesbian Theories, Gay Theories*, edited by Diana Fuss, 110–141. New York, NY: Routledge.

Namaste, Ki. 1994. "The Politics of Inside-Out: Queer Theory, Poststructuralism, and a Sociological Approach to Sexuality." *Sociological Theory* 12(2): 220–231.

Ramsey, E. Michele and Gladys Santiago. 2004. "The Conflation of Male Homosexuality and Femininity in Queer Eye for the Straight Guy." *Feminist Media Studies* 4(3): 353–355.

Ritzer, George and J. Michael Ryan. 2007. "Postmodern Social Theory and Sociology: On Symbolic Exchange with a 'Dead' Theory." In *Reconstructing Postmodernism: Critical Debates*, edited by Jason Powell and Tim Owen, 41–57. New York, NY: Nova Science Publishers.

Rumens, Nick. 2016. "Sexualities and Accounting: A Queer Theory Perspective." *Critical Perspectives on Accounting* 35: 111–120.

Ryan, J. Michael. 2007. "Queer Theory." In *Modern Sociological Theory*, edited by George Ritzer, 633–640. New York, NY: McGraw-Hill.

Sedgwick, Eve Kosofsky. 1985. *Between Men: English Literature and Male Homosocial Desire*. New York, NY: Columbia University Press.

Sedgwick, Eve Kosofsky. 1990. *Epistemology of the Closet*. Berkeley, CA: University of California Press.

Seidman, Steven. 1994. "Queer-Ing Sociology, Sociologizing Queer Theory: An Introduction." *Sociological Theory* 12(2): 166–177.

Seidman, Steven, ed. 1996. *Queer Theory, Sociology*. London: Wiley Blackwell.

Stein, Arlene. 1989. "Three Models of Sexuality: Drives, Identities, and Practices." *Sociological Theory* 7(1): 1–13.

Stein, Arlene and Ken Plummer. 1994. "'I Can't Even Thinking Straight': 'Queer' Theory and the Missing Sexual Revolution in Sociology." *Sociological Theory* 12(2): 178–187.

Sullivan, Nick. 2003. *A Critical Introduction to Queer Theory*. New York, NY: New York University Press.

Turner, William Benjamin. 2000. *A Genealogy of Queer Theory*. Philadelphia, PA: Temple University Press.

Valocchi, Stephen. 2005. "Not Yet Queer Enough: The Lessons of Queer Theory for the Sociology of Gender and Sexuality." *Gender & Society* 19(6): 750–770.

Walters, Suzanna Danuta. 2001. *All the Rage: The Story of Gay Visibility in America*. Chicago, IL: University of Chicago Press.

Warner, Michael. 1993. "Introduction." In *Fear of a Queer Planet: Queer Politics and Social Theory*, edited by Michael Warner, viii–xxxi. Minnesota: University of Minnesota Press.

Westerfelhaus, Robert and Celeste Lacroix. 2006. "Seeing 'Straight' Through Queer Eye: Exposing the Strategic Rhetoric of Heteronormativity in a Mediated Ritual Of Gay Rebellion." *Critical Studies in Media Communication* 23(5): 426–444.

6

Queer Methodologies and Social Science

Stuti Das

This chapter provides a succinct yet comprehensive review of scholarship on queer methodologies, offering the reader a systematic account of what queer methodologies entail. Accordingly, efforts have been made to shed light on the need for such methodologies, their genesis, and their characteristics. The question of methods as well as issues of ethics, positionality, reflexivity, validity, and data analysis have been centered in queer methodologies. While it is possible to "queer" any discipline, that is, challenge the heteronormative biases embedded in the basic tenets of any subject, this chapter confines itself to a discussion of queer methodologies in the social sciences. In doing so, efforts have been directed at highlighting the complexities and contradictions embodied by all that can be subsumed under the term.

Setting the Premise

Prior to embarking on a discussion of queer methodologies, I would like to take a detour and focus briefly on the following questions: What is meant by "methods" in social research? What does the term "methodology" signify? What are the implications of the word "queer"? What does "queer theory" entail?

In answering the first two questions, my aim is to present the conceptual distinction between the terms 'method' and 'methodology.' The latter questions are an attempt to set the stage for an understanding of the genealogy and characteristics of 'queer methodologies,' and of the wide-ranging complexities and contradictions embodied by all that can be subsumed under the term.

Companion to Sexuality Studies, First Edition. Edited by Nancy A. Naples.
© 2020 John Wiley & Sons Ltd. Published 2020 by John Wiley & Sons Ltd.

Method and Methodology

A research method is nothing but a technique of gathering evidence through any one, or a combination of more than one, of the following means: listening to (or interrogating) informants, observing behavior, and examining historical traces and records (Harding 1987). In other words, a method entails what is done for the purpose of data collection, and includes techniques such as interviews, questionnaires, focus groups, photographs, videos, observation, and the like (Browne and Nash 2010).

In research design, "methodologies" refer to the processes by which research is undertaken consistent with a project's epistemological and ontological stance through the selection and application of technical methods of data collection for the purpose of producing knowledges that can be regarded as valid and authentic (Browne and Nash 2010), while also calling into question the authority of the knowledges produced and the accountability of the researcher for the political implications of the same (Moss 2002; Ramazanoglu and Holland 2002). In other words, the term refers to the set of rules and procedures that guides the design of research, an integral part of which involves making decisions about which methods should be used and for what purpose. Methodology, thus, is the "logic that links the project's ontological and epistemological approaches to the selection and deployment of ... methods" (Browne and Nash 2010, p. 11). Hence, methods do not embody any inherent epistemological or ontological qualities; rather it is the mode of their deployment that influences the kind of knowledges they produce (see, for example, Maynard 1994; Stanley 1990, 1997; Stanley and Wise 1983, 1993 for a discussion on the use of methods to generate feminist ways of knowing that contest masculinist forms of knowledges).

Queer, Queer Theory, Queering

A detailed discussion on the meanings and implications of queer, queer theory, and queering lies beyond the scope of this chapter. Therefore, I will provide only a brief overview of each of these terms. The purpose, as I have stated earlier, is to facilitate a nuanced understanding of the conceptual and theoretical underpinnings of queer methodologies and to contextually situate their emergence and development.

Queer

In the late nineteenth century, the word "queer" became slang for homosexual, and was used mainly as a term of homophobic abuse. Since 1990, however, as a result of political mobilization by groups such as ACT UP and Queer Nation in the USA and OutRage! in Britain, "queer" began to be accepted as a term of self-identification by sexual minority groups who wanted to reclaim the word as a sign of power, pride, and identity. In doing so, they rejected and overturned the term homosexual which, for decades, science and medicine had imposed upon them as a term of illness. This, coupled with the rapid growth of programs of lesbian and gay studies within the academy in the 1990s, and the consequent rise of queer theory, marked a major shift in queer's connotations in much of the English-speaking world: the term came to symbolize self-definition, and as such reflected a real shift in self-perception, group identity, and belonging (Casey 2011; Epstein 1994; Jagose 1996).

The word "queer" has multiple connotations and embodies several meanings. However, there exists no critical consensus on the definitional limits of queer (Jagose 1996). According to Epstein (1994), it is a term rife with connotations, some of them contradictory. While on the one hand, the invocation of the word is viewed as an act of linguistic reclamation in which a pejorative term is appropriated by the stigmatized group so as to negate the term's power to wound, thereby representing an anti-assimilationist stand in opposition to mainstream lesbian and gay politics that rely on discourses of civil liberties and civil rights, queer also serves as a marker of generational difference within sexual minority groups wherein older gays and lesbians sometimes object bitterly to the use of the term, which they consider the language of the oppressor.

Broadly speaking, queer describes those gestures or analytical models which delineate the incoherencies in the allegedly stable relations between chromosomal sex, gender, and sexual desire. In other words, queer problematizes and deconstructs normative consolidations of sex, gender, and sexuality, as well as the categories, oppositions, and equations that sustain them. Consequently, it is critical of all those versions of identity, community, and politics that are believed to evolve naturally from such consolidations. Therefore, implicit in the term is a resistance to the model of stability that claims to originate from heterosexuality, although the latter is more properly its effect (Jagose 1996).

According to Warner (1991, cited in Epstein 1994, p. 195), queer offers a comprehensive way of characterizing those whose sexuality places them in opposition to the current "normalizing regime." As explained by Gabriel Rotello, former editor of the now-defunct New York City queer magazine *Outweek* (Duggan 1992, p. 224, cited in Epstein 1994, p. 195), "When you're trying to describe the community, and you have to list gays, lesbians, bisexuals, drag queens, transsexuals (post-op and pre), it gets unwieldy. Queer says it all" [sic].

However, queer is a category in the process of formation. This implies that queer has yet to solidify and take on a more consistent profile: its definitional indeterminacy is one of its constituent characteristics shaping its radical potential. Further, by refusing to crystallize in any specific form, queer maintains a relation of resistance to whatever constitutes the "normal." But since queer does not assume for itself any specific materiality or positivity, its resistance to what it differs from is necessarily relational rather than oppositional (Jagose 1996).

Queer Theory

The term "queer theory" is attributed to Teresa de Lauretis who jokingly coined it as the title of a conference she organized in February 1990 at the University of California, Santa Cruz (Halperin 2003). Since then, however, queerness and queer theory as critical categories have undergone considerable reinvention to be encapsulated in an all-encompassing definition (Jackman 2010).

There is no single queer theory, but multiple queer theories advocated for by different thinkers (Warner 2004). Consequently, queer theory does not constitute a homogeneous or systematic school of thought, but includes a mixture of studies that focus critically on heteronormativity (Rosenberg 2008).

Queer theorists place the question of sexuality at the center of society and cultural analysis, and question the category of sex itself. They recognize that the categories of man and woman are themselves social constructions which rely on cultural-historical specificity to derive meaning, and are legitimized through the matrix of heterosexuality wherein sexuality is not merely confined to sexual acts but encompasses the appearance of the appropriate gendered identity of the subject. Thus, sexuality becomes the lens through which to comprehend the sexed subject (Anderson 2007).

Since its inception, queer theory, drawing on the "post" turn in social theory, has attempted to stretch the boundaries of sex, sexuality, and gender to accommodate the multiple possibilities in which sexuality and gender are or can be deployed, particularly in the ways these relate to queer bodies (Detamore 2010). It aims to destabilize those normative taxonomies of gendered and sexualized identity which, as central, organizing principles of society, social relations, and social institutions, function to preserve a hegemonic order (Anderson 2007). In this way, "queer theory challenges the normative social ordering of identities and subjectivities along the heterosexual/homosexual binary as well as the privileging of heterosexuality as 'natural' and homosexuality as its deviant and abhorrent 'other'" (Browne and Nash 2010, p. 5).

Jones and Adams (2010) have enlisted a number of characteristics of queer theory. Queer theory conceives of identity as a relational 'achievement' (Garfinkel 1967), thereby situating it in interaction (Hacking 1990, 1999). It foregrounds the fact that identities fluctuate across time and space, and hence, require constant attention and negotiation, and distances itself from essentialist and constructionist debates of selfhood (Watson 2005, p. 74, see also Butler 1990; Freeman 2001; Gamson 2003). Queer theory is characterized by an affinity for "definitional indeterminacy" and "conceptual elasticity" (Yep et al. 2003, p. 9; see also Haraway 2004; Henderson 2001; Thomas 2000; Wilchins 2004). This is reflected in the propensity of many queer theorists to reject "labeling philosophies" and reclaim marginal linguistic identifiers (Butler 1993a; Muscio 1998; Nicholas 2006; Watson 2005). Additionally, queer theory values "political commitment" (Yep et al. 2003, p. 9), and embraces a "politics of transgression" (Watson 2005, p. 68; Hird 2004) that revels in "symbolic disorder" (Baudrillard 2001, p. 125), pollutes established social conventions (Crawley 2002; Haraway 2004), and diffuses hegemonic categories and classifications.

Queering

Queer theory is marked by a tendency to radically question and destabilize all forms of identity that are considered to be the norm while rejecting the binarized categories of homosexuality and heterosexuality. This deconstruction of the hegemonic heteronormative social order is attained through a consideration of the historical (time) and contextual (space) (Anderson 2007; Hammers and Brown 2004).

What, then, are the methodological potentials for such a framework? Britzman (1998, p. 82) articulates what queer theory can achieve as a practice: "Queer theory is not an affirmation, but an implication. Its bothersome and unapologetic imperatives are explicitly transgressive, perverse, and political." Likewise, Detamore (2010, p. 172) argues that "as queer theory has come into its own as a set of academic discourses, its *methodological potentials* to interrogate not only the contingency and complexity of human subjectivity through an optic of sexualised/gendered constructions, but other social and political formations have become ever more apparent."

According to Detamore (2010) and Reid-Pharr (2002), queer theory has the potential to serve as a methodological tool that can facilitate an understanding of a vast array of realities that lie beyond the realms of gender, sex, and sexuality, as is evident from the works of Gibson-Graham (1999), Warner (2002), Puar, Rushbrook, and Schein (2003), Butler (2005), Puar (2007, 2001), and Floyd (2009). Thus, as Clarke (2004, p. 80) has suggested, queer theory can be utilized most successfully as "a method or practice, a set of tools which can help us re-read and over-read historical traces, spaces and gaps." In this context, Anderson (2007) refers to the concept of "queering," the phenomenon that has emerged as an appropriation of the study of nonnormative sexualities within queer theory. To queer something implies to question its normalcy by problematizing its apparent neutrality and objectivity (Manning 2009). As Childers (2003, p. 39) states, "'To queer' is to disrupt the dominant cultural understanding of the naturalness of heterosexuality and conventional gender relations. Going beyond the deconstruction of post-structuralist inquiry, queering has become a mode of teasing out the strange regulatory manner in which normalised identities regulated themselves."

According to Jones and Adams (2010), this is achieved through an intentional re/appropriation of phenomena to pollute canonical discourse by disrupting insidious, normalizing ideologies, questioning what may pass as normal, "twisting" social order (Betsky 1999, p. 18), generating counter-canonical stories (Bochner 2001, 2002) making discursive "trouble" (Butler 1990), and explicitly advocating for change.

According to Rooke (2010) and Brim and Ghaziani (2016), the emergence of queer theory in the early 1990s resulted in a shift from empirical research on homosexuality guided by social constructionist approaches to readings of literary and cultural texts, often with a French poststructuralist Foucauldian and Lacanian emphasis. Consequently, sociological scholarship has criticized queer theory's tendency toward philosophical abstraction and textual criticism, its employment of an underdeveloped concept of the social, and its lack of engagement with the material relations of inequality.

Furthermore, Nash (2010) laments the scant attention paid to the implications of queer theoretical approaches for research methodologies. In this context, the question that Brim and Ghaziani (2016, p. 15) raise is: "Why then has queer theory not staked a more pervasive, methods-oriented claim?" They attribute queer theory's lack of focus on methods to apprehensions about the potential threat such an attention might pose to the theory's constitutional claims to inter/antidisciplinarity since, in reality, the import of queer theory within the social sciences occasioned a "humanities-centered displacement" of the disciplinary innovations that were unfolding as lesbian, gay, bisexual, transgender (LGBT)/queer studies. Additionally, Brim and Ghaziani (2016, p. 16) note that "a story of methodological continuity" fails to render the kind of intellectual and historiographic value that the "dominant queer theory narrative of productively cultivating antidisciplinary irreverence" does.

In contrast, Anderson (2007) is optimistic that the fluidity and dynamism that characterizes queer thought endows it with enormous potential to radicalize and disrupt the already established methodologies of gender and sexuality, and also to facilitate a reflection on the notion of disciplinarity itself and the binaries that continue to persist. In a similar vein, drawing on the ideas of Warner (1999), Gamson (2003), Plummer (2005), Seidman (1995), and Valocchi (2005) on the futility of the attempt to reconcile the differences between critical humanism and queer theory, Browne and Nash (2010, p. 10) argue that "across social research, there is the potential to variously deploy and rework 'queer,' as well as to critically engage with and contest theories, concepts and ideas that have developed in the humanities and through particular forms of textual and linguistic analyses," while acknowledging that "what forms these engagements might take, or how they might be categorized, necessarily remains permanently blurred, contingent and multiple...."

The Need for Queer Methodologies

Browne and Nash (2010, p. 4) are of the view that any attempt to trace a "coherent lineage for 'queer' thinking is a perilous and not necessarily useful undertaking," given that "genealogies of queer theory reveal considerable disagreement over its relationship with and debt to philosophy, women's and lesbian studies, second wave and postmodern feminism and gay and lesbian studies." According to them, "queer inflected perspectives, approaches and conceptualisations have been taken up, disputed and reworked in different disciplinary contexts, reflecting the traditions of knowledge production in those disciplines" and "contemporary queer theory remains in continuous conversation with innumerable bodies of scholarship, however contested or collegial such exchanges might be."

It was in the wake of the HIV/AIDS activism in North America in the 1970s and the early 1980s that queer perspectives gained visibility, and eventually made their way into disciplines within which the tenets of postmodern thought had succeeded in finding a place, namely, architecture, literary theory and criticism, film studies, sociology, philosophy, and geography. However, the contention among most scholars is that it is within the humanities as opposed to the social sciences that queer theorizing attained higher and more rapid visibility. This development was prompted by the radical realignments taking place within the former on long-held ideas such as "the conceptualisation of the modern Enlightenment subject as rational, unified and stable," the prevalence of "a universal human condition and the linear tale of a progressive human history," and the notions of the "supposedly unassailable 'objective researcher' inexorably uncovering a knowable reality through reliance on a relational theory of truth," and of "the 'subject' of research ... as a unified, coherent and self-knowledgeable individual." These shifts resulted in reframing the understanding of certain supposedly fixed attributes of the self, such as gender and sexuality, as unstable and contingent (Jackson 2001, cited in Browne and Nash 2010, pp. 4–5).

The accommodation of queer conceptualizations within the social sciences was prompted by efforts to address and reverse the tremendous hold of positivistic scientific methods over qualitative methodologies which, in fact, were devised to address the drawbacks of the former. To challenge the power of science over qualitative methods required that qualitative methods "surrender to the postmodern influenced queer impossibility of truth and generalizability in its paradigms"

(Ferguson 2013, p. 5) and undergo a queering that could enable research to move beyond a documentation and analysis of injustice and inequality.

The ideals of the Enlightenment paved the way for the secularization of society and the development of a scientific method based on the principles of objectivity and empiricism that came to be assigned a privileged position for its ability to uncover the "Truth" (Hammers and Brown 2004). As Charmaz (2006, p. 4) notes, "mid-century positivist conceptions of scientific method and knowledge stressed objectivity, generality, replication of research and falsification of competing hypotheses and theories." Consequently, Ferguson (2013) argues, even social scientific-based qualitative methodologies, the main aim of which was to overcome the insufficiencies of quantitative methods of inquiry rooted in a strong positivistic tradition, remained shackled by an empirical scientism with an emphasis on proving a hypothesis by exposing "data" from human subjects. In this process, research subjects came to be treated as sources of data/texts or fact-based evidence to be dissected and studied.

Acknowledging the fact that a generalization of qualitative methodologies is problematic, Ferguson (2013) foregrounds the exclusionary and silencing practices often inherent in the tools, processes, and representation strategies employed in qualitative work whereby research subjects' experiences and testimonies are treated as homogeneous truths derived from observation and individual experiences, and whereby the possible qualities of human experience are reduced in order to satisfy quantifiable variables (Charmaz 2006, p. 5). This is because theories and methods in the social sciences are marked by a heterosexist bias (Honeychurch 1996, cited in Sheldon 2010), while ideas emerging from positivistic scientific endeavors have often been used to the detriment of those who fail to fit within conventional norms (Gamson 2000, cited in Sheldon 2010).

These tendencies are illustrated by Warner's (2004) discussion of psychological research on LGBT lives conducted by Evelyn Hooker during the 1950s and by James M. Cantor in 2002 both of which clearly show that methodology is not a neutral tool used to evaluate the truth of some population "out there." For instance, by drawing her sample from a group of homosexuals of "an average adjustment," Hooker constructed the "normal male homosexual" that continued to serve as the basis for the "matrix of intelligibility" that would guide research on, and policy-making pertaining to, alternative sexualities for a long time to come. This, in turn, contributed to the further solidification of homosexuality as an identity with normal and deviant strains.[1] Cantor, who represents the next generation of sexuality researchers, continued the process of differentiating normal from deviant homosexual desire, and further promoted the practice of identifying a biological substrate for all desires. Thus, as Warner (2004, p. 334) notes, "queers are spoken for by experts who seek to influence policy in their own conception of 'The Good' and 'Healthy.'" Clearly, such methodology is infused with a dichotomous thinking that limits the possibilities of what is allowed to exist, and negates queer existences because those who identify as queer live beyond the binaries of sex, gender, and sexuality (Manning 2010). Similarly, Ferguson (2013) offers a discussion of Catherine Cashore and Teresa G. Tuason's (2009) study of transgender and bisexual individuals, "Negotiating the Binary: Identity and Social Justice for Bisexual and Transgender Individuals" as an example of a qualitative-based study that undermines the fluid and kinetic subjectivities of the queer subjects, in the process, showing why contemporary qualitative methods need to consider a restructuring process. These studies clearly demonstrate that the aspiration to objectivity is "often complicit in a regulatory regime which does less to liberate homosexual desire, than to account for it, limit it, and often convert it to something 'normal'" (Warner 2004, p. 321).

Although Barney Glaser and Anselm Strauss's infusion of qualitative methods with grounded theory worked to challenge these drawbacks (Charmaz 2006, p. 5), it ended up perpetuating a positivistic assumption and linguistic obsession with "technical operations," including data, codes, categories, themes, and a constant comparative method (Barrett 1996, p. 214; Charmaz 2006, p. 5). On the other hand, qualitative work that focused on interpreting and analyzing the meanings of "research participants" encountered scientific critiques of the work being self-reflexive and/or too interpretive instead of being objective. Such aspersions cast on the "more humanities-based methods that allow for multiple levels of interpretation instead of single conclusion" by scientific rationality based on positivism "allowed science to maintain control over qualitative inquiry either through language, objection to interpretation and analysis" (Ferguson 2013, p. 3).

The notions of a singular, universal truth and "objective" knowledge were ruptured with the advent of postmodernism which propounded the idea of multiple and equally valid knowledge claims and epistemologies (Hammers and Brown 2004). As Barrett (1996, p. 153) put it, "postmodernists, in contrast, emphasize the particular and the unique, valorize the 'other' (the subjects of research), and are comfortable with an image of social life that is inherently fragmented, disjointed and incomplete." With this, it became evident that "the traditional, distinctly modern, social scientific approaches that adhere to objectivity, detachment and clear demarcations of the boundaries between researcher–researched, are inadequate to explore identity formations, such as sexualities, ethnicities, nationalities, genders and their myriad expressions that exemplify social life in these ever changing and uncertain times" (Hammers and Brown 2004, p. 85). This is evidenced in the assertions of symbolic interactionists, social psychologists, and feminists (see, for example, Smith 1972 for a critique of sociology's androcentric bias and its proclamations of being "objective" and value-free). Consequently, as Ferguson (2013, p. 3) argues, "qualitative methods, then, need to cut the cords, so to speak, from the scientific foundation that it was birthed from in the first place similar to how qualitative grew out of quantitative – qualitative inquiries require a deconstruction and reconstruction to shatter methodologies' scientific shackles."

Gamson (2003, p. 388) notes that queer theory offers qualitative studies with "interesting tools, born in part from its assumption that sexual subjects are not simply there to be represented as good or bad, but always under construction." Accordingly, queer qualitative methods accept that "the language of science is regarded as the language of oppression" (Barrett 1996, p. 164), and acknowledge a "language of difference" which is focused on the multilayered understanding of difference rather than a concern for stable identity" (Turner 2000, p. 23). This acknowledgment provides them with a "sophisticated irrationality" (Barrett 1996, p. 175) that has the ability to challenge the core foundation of scientism embedded in the language of qualitative inquiry, and equips qualitative inquiries to function as "praxis-oriented interventions in the area of social justice by surrendering all positivistic and empirical preoccupations" (Ferguson 2013, p. 5). In this way, queer qualitative methods produce, as Butler argues, "reverse discourses," which are "competing discourses (collections of stories from experience that challenge the 'truth' of the discourse)" (Watson 2005, p. 72).

According to Manning (2009), queer methodologies are "vital for exposing hegemonic linear ways of being and thinking that analyze, categorize and psychiatrize those outside of such polarized identities." For Brim and Ghaziani (2016, p. 18), "with repercussions beyond the academy, queer methods can offer a framework for 'making space for what is' as they illuminate the messy and chaotic interstices across theory, lived experience, and practice." Thus, according to them, the mandate of queer methods is: "to clarify, but not overdetermine, the conditions that make life livable" (Brim and Ghaziani 2016, p. 19).

What Constitutes Queer Methodologies?

Browne and Nash (2010, p. 4) argue that "'queer research' can be any form of research positioned within conceptual frameworks that highlight the instability of taken-for-granted meanings and resulting power relations." Consequently, "queer epistemological and ontological perspectives help focus attention on how social categories of being, and lived experience, are constituted within certain historical, cultural and spatialized contexts, including normative ideas about what are deemed to be embodied gendered and sexual practices and behaviours" (Nash 2010, p. 133).

According to Warner (1993, p. xxvi), "queer takes on its critical edge by defining itself against the normal rather than the heterosexual, and the normal includes normal business in the academy." Accordingly, the project of queering methodologies is concerned with a critical examination of the politics of knowledge production, particularly of the potential complicity of researchers in normalizing knowledge production (Nash 2010). As a result, as Browne and Nash (2010, p. 4) note, "queerly crafted scholarship in both the humanities and the social sciences has pushed analyses in new and exhilarating directions."

Characteristics of Queer Methodologies

An ontology is a theory about what the world is like, what it consists of, and why (Strega 2005, p. 201). Deeply embedded within the modernist ontology, the main basis for knowledge production and classification during the 'Age of Reason', are "systems of classification and representation, which lend themselves easily to binary oppositions, dualisms, and hierarchical orderings of the world" (Tuhiwai Smith 1999, p. 55), and consequently, a tendency to inscribe binary constructs that serve to uphold sexual and gender dominance (Manning 2009). These binary constructs are not merely confined to the areas of sex and sexualities but encompass a wide range of social phenomena (See, for example, Somerville (2000) for a discussion on how the classification and enmeshing of race and sexuality facilitate the construction of deviant, knowable and subordinate objects, and Wittig (1996) for a discussion on the need for the ontological different/other for the sciences and disciplines). Positivist science regards these classifications as objective, neutral, and universally true, an assumption that has lent itself to severe criticism (see Fausto-Sterling 1997, 2000; Foucault 1990; Hammers and Brown 2004; Tuhiwai Smith 1999; Ramazanoglu and Holland 2002; Adrienne Rich 1984).

The multiple research methodologies permeated by modernist ontology and characterized by a dualistic nature perpetuate the existing social, physical, and political hierarchies. While this is particularly true of methodologies that are located within positivist paradigms, interpretative and emancipatory methodologies are also influenced by this ontology, since even within these research paradigms, a researcher can reproduce dominant modernist representations by confining their own complexity to a binary identification as an insider or outsider (Manning 2009).[2] Evidently, then, these methodologies are engaged in a constant reaffirmation of the heteronorm "because heterosexuality is the standard from which others are seen to differ" (Hicks 2008, p. 68), and a consequent reification of the homosexual as an object of study.

On the contrary, queer methodologies, characterized by a "continuous questioning and deconstruction of all knowledge" (Hammers and Brown 2004, p. 88) and a rejection of the attempts "to legitimize and solidify shifting, mobile existences" (Manning 2009), are more likely to be rooted in ontologies that are marked by complexity, multiplicity, and inconsistency. They understand the performative nature of identity and do not view the social as rooted in the biological (Warner 2004). Thus, a queer methodology has a distinct ontology and epistemology that can pose a challenge to modernist ideas of binary, stable categories. Since ontology determines what existences are made possible and visible,[3] a queer methodology renders visible the otherwise marginalized and invisible queer and trans lives, experiences, and encounters. Thus, according to Warner (2004, p. 335), "queer methodology is a methodology of the margins that does not seek to make things intelligible in terms of the heteropatriarchy, but tries to find the words of the margins itself." It achieves this by not attempting to reify mobile, unstable "disorientations," instead seeking to expose hetero- and homonormativity (Manning 2009).[4]

Accordingly, Browne and Nash (2010) view queer research as a way of challenging those frameworks of power that derive both from the disciplinary tools at the researcher's disposal as well as the topic chosen for investigation and inquiry. Achieving this goal, however, is contingent upon undertaking the complicated task of "keeping queer permanently unclear, unstable and 'unfit' to represent any particular sexual identity" in order to maintain a nonnormative queer position within "an academy that increasingly embraces 'queer' contingencies while simultaneously requiring specific rules of rigour, clarity and truthfulness; all the while generating queer celebrities who supposedly 'get it right'" (Browne and Nash 2010, pp. 7–8).

It is important to note that since there is no singular, overarching truth about sexual identities and sexualities, there can be no singular method that can provide answers to all and any questions concerning these phenomena. Thus, as Warner (2004, p. 334) points out, "there can be no *one* queer research methodology, but many methodologies." In a similar vein, Browne and Nash (2010, p. 12) point out that "there is, in fact, no one 'queer method' (that is, 'methods' specifically as research techniques), in the sense that 'queer' lives can be addressed through a plethora of methods, and all methods can be put to the task of questioning normativities – a political positioning that infuses research processes with ethical considerations."

However, there are some basic heuristics that a queer methodology must satisfy (Warner 2004, pp. 334–335). Firstly, a queer research methodology should cultivate a reflexive awareness of the process by which it constitutes its object(s) of investigation, and eschew the positivistic assumption regarding the inherent subject–object dichotomy that obfuscates the constitutive nature of knowledge production. Rightly then, Hammers and Brown (2004, p. 87) point out, "this 'situating' of oneself, that is, the acknowledgement and awareness of one's own biases would not only re-organize the researcher (subject)–researched (object) relationship to be one that is non-hierarchal, equitable and respectful, but make as central direct, material experience and reality." In a similar vein, Nash (2010) points to the need for queer methodologies to acknowledge the impossibility of a constant between the research, the researched, and the field, and to recognize the fact that the relations between the researcher and the researched are perpetually unstable, which can considerably affect the nature of the research.[5] Although such a pursuit would most certainly help to identify the power relations operating within a research project, according to Manning (2009), merely identifying one's subjectivity is not a sufficient condition to eradicate the power dynamics inherent in any research endeavor. Secondly, queer methodologies must qualitatively account for their object of inquiry. This is because modes of inquiry aiming to generate quantitative information are characterized by a tendency to assume commonalities among subjects, thereby obscuring the highly subjective nature of individual experiences.

For queer methodologies aiming to challenge universalisms and decenter privilege through an emphasis on multiplicity, an intersectional perspective is indispensible. This is because inattention to the way the various axes of individual identity intersect and influence each other can result in the reenactment of those very exclusions and boundaries that "queer" has set out to challenge. For example, as Taylor (2010) notes, the absence of an analysis of social class in studies on sexualities has resulted in the reproduction of a middle-class LGBT experience as universal. Consequently, there is a need for "stratifying homosexualities" in research (Plummer 1998, p. 612).[6]

The Question of Methods

Methods function as productive devices (Graham 2010). Hence, any discussion on methodology remains incomplete without a reflection on methods.

Scholars have deliberated on whether certain methods can be "deemed queerer than others" (Binnie 2007, p. 33). It is important to bear in mind that no method is inherently queer. All methods can be put to queer political ends; however, they vary with respect to their usefulness in this regard (Graham 2010).[7] Hence, an awareness regarding what a method is constituted of, what it can account for, and what it excludes is crucial. In this connection, Binnie (2007, p. 33) suggests, "rather than trying to prescribe certain methods as queerer than others, we should pay attention to the queering potentialities of different types of research."[8] Further, since queer aims at destabilizing normative understandings of social processes, the "queering" of methods holds the promise of possibilities as well as poses challenges for traditional methods of data collection (Gamson 2003; Green 2007; Plummer 2005).

Jack Halberstam (1998, p. 13) conceptualizes queer methodology as "a scavenger methodology" that uses different methods – often a combination of those that are considered to be at odds with each other – "to collect and produce information on subjects who have been deliberately or accidentally excluded from traditional studies of human behavior." This refusal to yield to the academic compulsion towards disciplinary coherence necessitates a commitment to researching sites that have not previously found legitimization, as well as a willingness to draw from a range of disciplinary methods.

According to Nash (2010), adopting a queer methodological approach requires researchers to use a wide variety of qualitative methods to directly interact with their participants in various fields, while at the same time, to reexamine "those methods and their deployment within the wider historical and political context of research on sexual minorities and the more intimate and constraining spaces of interaction in the field" (Nash 2010, p. 142). Such an endeavor behooves researchers on the one hand, to recognize their participants as embodied gendered, sexualized and sexed individuals, and on the other, to cultivate an awareness of the impact of their own lived experiences on the research process, an endeavor that results in the "mutual production of knowledge across different ways of being in the world and the possibility of shared understandings across that difference" (Nash 2010, p. 134).

According to Brim and Ghaziani (2016), queer social research methods recognize the incongruence between existing conceptual categories and lived experiences and, therefore, are constantly engaged in questioning the origins and effects of concepts and categories while steering clear of all attempts at reifying them in a generalizable variable-oriented paradigm. Thus, the aim is to examine "moments of Otherness, the strange, the deviant, the disorientation" rather than solidifying or essentializing orientation within a specific research paradigm (Manning 2009). Additionally, queer social research methods are also marked by a rejection of naïve empiricism in favor of embracing multiplicity, misalignments, and silences (Brim and Ghaziani 2016). This is because what is observed is often contingent upon how a phenomenon is measured.[9]

Boellstorff (2010) has put forward two emphatically heuristic theses regarding what a queer method might look like. Firstly, he makes use of the ideas of emic and etic theory to argue that queer methods need to overturn this distinction and allow for "the emergence of theory from both 'within' and 'without'" (Browne and Nash 2010, p. 21). Secondly, he contends that queer methods need to "surf binarisms." This entails an acceptance of the fact that "binarisms are ubiquitous in all languages; no human analytic can avoid them," and that neither a complete identification nor a total deconstruction of binarisms is possible, and from there to proceed "via an implicit binarism of identification/deconstruction" (Boellstorf 2010, p. 222) to help maximize the critical potential of queer methodologies.

Qualitative and Quantitative Traditions

Studies of sexual lives demonstrate an overwhelming affinity for qualitative data (Browne 2010). This can be attributed to two reasons: on the one hand, the tendency of queer approaches to regard the self as fluid and contingent; and on the other, the greater suitability of qualitative methods to explore differences, describe fluidities, and contest rigidities (Gamson 2003, Plummer 2005). Consequently, an increasing number of researchers of queer lives rely on such research techniques as participant observation, interviews and qualitative questionnaires for the development of queer theorizations regarding the construction of bodies and spaces (See, for example, Brown 2004; Browne 2004, 2007; Johnston 2005) as well as for the deconstruction of sexual subject positions (Valocchi 2005; Gamson 2003; Green 2002; Seidman 1995), and also to address issues of deviancy that have historically pervaded scientific studies of sexualities (Gamson 2003; Reynolds 2001).

This tendency is paralleled by a shortage of critical engagements with quantitative methods and methodologies on the part of queer and sexualities researchers (Browne 2010). This could be due to the fact that quantitative methods' reliance on categories stands in direct opposition to queer's deconstructive tendencies that eschew fixities in favor of fluidities. Quite contrarily, however, within popular culture, the "gay and lesbian" figure is subjected to counting and regulation (Browne 2008; Brown and Knopp 2006), an act that results in the production of particular images of sexual and gender difference.[10]

Counting, thus, is not a neutral act that involves simply recording figures; rather it is a qualitative decision of what and how to count, and hence, can play a crucial role in the creation and legitimization of particular groups.[11] Additionally, as Reynolds (2001) argues, numbers can elicit recognition and justice from the heteronormative state that does not statistically acknowledge those who exist outside of heterosexuality. Consequently, "measuring the numbers of 'lesbians,' 'gay men' and 'bisexuals' is increasingly lobbied for as part of the tool that decides the allocation of resources in an 'equitable' way and challenges the heteronormative state to include once pathologized citizens" (Browne 2010, p. 245).

It would therefore be highly erroneous to ignore the potential of quantitative methods for antinormative politics.[12] In this connection, Browne (2010) alerts us to the dangers of asserting that queer epistemologies should be methodologically reliant on qualitative methods only.

All these necessitate a queer deconstruction of quantitative research tools in order to interrogate the normative categorization impulses inherent in quantitative techniques.[13] Such a process would entail an examination of the processes of data construction and interpretation (Brown and Knopp 2006), which, in turn, can expose the ways in which calculation participates in the very production of what it sets out to measure.

The Issues of Ethics, Positionality, Reflexivity, Validity, and Data Analysis in Queer Methodologies

Ethics

Any research involving human subjects is an ethical undertaking as it involves the researcher entering into a relationship with the researched that evokes emotional responses (Madison 2005; Detamore 2010). In this context, Detamore (2010) proposes a "queer ethics for research." This ethical imperative traces the act of co-producing knowledge horizontally between the researcher and the researched which overturns "liberal fantasies of 'emancipating' or 'redeeming' 'subjugated voices'" (Detamore 2010, p. 178) to create new trajectories of social and environmental justice and a political space – or ethical terrain – that binds one to the other. However, what makes this process a complicated one is the fact that it is influenced significantly by the researcher's own ethical formations, social anxieties, and personal reservations (see, for example, Bain and Nash (2006) for a discussion on the nature of this complexity).

For instance, what happens when nonheterosexual researchers doing sexuality research are compelled to engage in "covert queer research" through either concealing their identity or the topic of their research? According to Sheldon (2010), attempts on the part of the researcher to conceal their identity limits the transformative effects of queer research: "how can research have the kind of transformative effects a researcher might desire when they feel compelled to hide their own identities and purposes of their studies?" (Sheldon 2010, p. 13).[14]

However, he complicates the argument further by referring to the general skepticism of queer theorists about the nature of the closet, and its repeated reinforcement through the act of "outing" oneself (Butler 1993b). In this context, the question that he poses is, "If one cannot come out without reinforcing the whole notion of the closet, is it such a bad thing to creatively use strategies of concealment and revelation... Might this strategic disclosure give researchers a new sense of agency in an otherwise oppressive locale in which they are doing fieldwork?" (Sheldon 2010, p. 5). However, instead of attempting to answer this question himself, he refers to Bryson and de Castell (1998) who denounce the idea of covert research and advocate instead for the opening of spaces for out queer researchers in view of the fact that "it matters who is doing the research" (Sheldon 2010, p. 5).

Positionality

Our positionality affects what we are able to see (Charmaz 2006, p. 15). Every step of the research process right from selecting the sample to interpreting the participants' responses is influenced by the positionings of both the researcher and the researched (Haritaworn 2008). Emancipatory methodologies acknowledge this truth, and view the process of knowledge production as resulting from the negotiations between researchers, subjects, and epistemic communities (Ramazanoglu and Holland 2002). Accordingly, a queer perspective necessitates that researchers eschew positivistic paradigms in which the neutral observer comes to know an objective truth. This means that researchers need to maintain a continual skepticism about the notion of positionality and deconstruct their own identities (Rasmussen 2006).[15] Such a project enables the researcher to "directly 'touch/interact/connect' with our subjects, in ways which are less exploitative, less objectifying, and more politically relevant" (Haritaworn 2008, p. 3).

At the same time, it is important to bear in mind that within the enterprise of knowledge production, the interaction between the researcher and the researched does not take place on an equal footing (Phoenix 1994). Mary Lou Rasmussen cites Kennedy and Davis's (1996) observation that although they themselves as well as their subjects were lesbians, it "did not make positioning [themselves] in relation to the complex and powerful forces of class, race, and gender oppression – not to mention homophobia – easy" (Rasmussen 2006, p. 47, cited in Sheldon 2010, pp. 7–8).

Furthermore, to research from a queer perspective necessitates the integration of the sexual and erotic components of one's interactions with one's subjects. In other words, queer research entails attributing primacy not only to intellectual ideas but also to material bodies,[16] and this requires that researchers extend their concerns beyond publishing their findings and account for their practices in the field[17] (Sheldon 2010).

Reflexivity

The way researchers conduct themselves during the course of their research has a direct bearing on how effectively they are able to represent the life experiences of those they are studying. An awareness of this process is crucial in preventing partial, problematic representations of queer subjects that result from "constraining them into pre-constructed scientific empirical models of meaning" (Ferguson 2013, p. 8). Consequently, queer methodologies necessitate a critical reflexivity on the part of the researcher about their own power and subjectivity in relation to those they are researching (Ferguson 2013; Gorman-Murray, Johnston and Waitt 2010).

According to Adams and Jones (2011, p. 108), "reflexivity is the means – the action, the movement, the performance – by which we engage a personal and queer scholarship." It requires "the understanding, to the best of our ability, how we frame ourselves and others" (p. 113). Self-reflexivity involves accounting for "being half in and half out of identities, subject positions and discourses and having the courage to be fluid in a world relentlessly searching for stability and certainty" (p. 114). In other words, reflexivity demands recognition of the fact that "both researchers and research participants are, in fact, subjects, in that both researchers and participants enter the research relationship from the perspective of their own subjectivities" (Gorman-Murray et al. 2010, p. 98).

According to Dowling (2005, p. 25), "critical reflexivity is the most appropriate strategy for dealing with subjectivity." The subjectivity of an individual is contingent upon the multiple and spatial social traits that they possess. The value attributed to a particular social trait is determined by the social context in which it occurs which, in turn, influences the position that the possessor of the value would occupy in that context. Hence, positionality and subjectivity determine and are determined by each other.

Queer reflexivity also involves drawing attention to the "erotics of knowledge production" (Rooke 2010, p. 35). This is because attention to sexual subjectivity can facilitate an understanding of the contingent, plural, and shifting nature of the ethnographic self of both the researcher and the researched (see, Rooke 2010 for a discussion on the need to reflect on the role of performativity of erotics in the field in knowledge-making).

Validity

Conducting queer research involves "putting oneself into one's work" (Sheldon 2010). This is because, as Honeychurch (1996, p. 342–343, cited in Sheldon 2010) argued, the adoption of a queer perspective necessitates that researchers "embrace... a dynamic discursive position from which subjects of homosexualities can both name themselves and impact the conditions under which queer identities are constituted." Sheldon (2010) argues that this act of "putting oneself" into one's research begets questions regarding the validity of one's findings. For positivists, validity refers to the "appropriateness, meaningfulness, correctness, and usefulness of the inferences a researcher makes" (Fraenkel and Wallen 2009, p. 147). In order to be suitably applicable to the context of "openly ideological research" which are "designed to criticize and change the status quo" (Lather 1986, p. 67) such as those involving queer methodologies, this concept needs to be reconfigured. In this context, with the aim of initiating a dialogue on issues of interpretation by moving beyond the more usual discussion on the impediments to ensuring objectivity in research and eliminating the biases therein, Lather (1986) offers four criteria for validity, namely, triangulation, construct validity, face validity, and catalytic validity (Sheldon 2010).[18]

Lather (1986) improvised upon the traditional idea of *triangulation* as the process of making use of multiple sources to include the criterion of making use of multiple theoretical schemes (p. 67). Thus, queer researchers can utilize multiple perspectives such as feminist perspectives, Marxist theory, and/or critical race theory in their inquiries into queer lives.

Construct validity involves evaluating how well an instrument measures what it is actually supposed to measure. Lather reimagines this concept to indicate a measure of the impact of the data on the theory. She rejects the notion of using a priori theories, instead allowing for theories to be shaped by real-life experiences (p. 67). *Face validity* would entail the researcher sharing the outcomes with the research participants so as to verify them against their understanding of the phenomenon.

Finally, *catalytic validity*, which Sheldon (2010) refers to as Lather's most innovative idea blurring the lines between research and practice, refers to the extent to which research participants are transformed through their participation in the research process, that is, the degree to which the research process has helped them to gain "self-understanding" and "self-determination" (p. 67). For Sheldon (2010), this concept assumes particular significance for queer methodologies since "in socially transformative research like queer research, researchers' goal should be for subjects to be transformed by their encounters with the researcher."

Queering data analysis

Data analysis refers to "the process of systematically searching and arranging the… materials that you accumulate to increase your own understanding of them and to enable you to present what you have discovered to others" (Bogdan and Biklen 1998, p. 157). According to Sheldon (2010), the implications of queer research extend way beyond the presentation of findings. For instance, a researcher might end up participating in the reification of sexual categories in the pursuit of identifying those who do or do not belong to those categories, in the process failing to contextualize those identities (Capper 1999; Leck 2000, cited in Sheldon 2010). The result is that the categories purportedly "found" by the researcher are in fact created by them (Sheldon 2010). Hence, standard techniques of data analysis such as identifying themes, coding, drawing diagrams, speculating, and summarizing may not be suitable for queer methodologies. In this context, Sheldon (2010) considers the Foucauldian approach to data analysis expounded by Harwood and Rasmussen (2007) as a more suitable approach to analyzing data in queer research.

This approach involves four key areas, namely, discontinuity, contingency, emergences, and subjugated knowledges (p. 34). In a Foucauldian genealogy, a researcher starts with a problem in the present and then explores the history of it in an attempt to alter the problem through the reinterpretation of the past. In this process, efforts are made to identify "ruptures in thought" and the "role of chance" (p. 35), which means acknowledging the fact that there is nothing deterministic about historical processes which could have turned out differently under the influence of a different set of factors. This is also what is meant by the notion of contingency which recognizes that history is constitutive of a patchwork of factors, and not the outcome of simple cause and effect, and that the task of the researcher is to uncover the "emergences" or points of rupture in which truth was created (p. 36). Through this, attempts are made to uncover "subjugated knowledges" which were hidden by systemizing theory (p. 36). For instance, Saltmarsh's (2007) study of sexual violence at an elite boys' school in Sydney, Australia uses the Foucauldian method of analyzing discourses to explore school violence and educational marketization; in the process, it combines insights from multiple theoretical frameworks used in the analysis of interviews and media representations to highlight how representational practices and social institutions go hand-in-hand in the production of violence.

The Difficulties in Developing Queer Methodologies

According to Hegarty (2008), the anti-essentialist counter-disciplinary tendencies embodied by 'queer' are antithetical to the development of a rational and coherent 'methodology'. This is because while queer implies multiplicity and heterogeneity, methodology tends to dismiss these characteristics as error variance. Hence, Hegarty argues, the term 'queer methodologies' is inherently contradictory.

Additionally, one of the major impediments to the development of queer methods in the social sciences is what Kevin A. Clarke and David M. Primo (2012) have termed as "physics envy" (cited in Brim and Ghaziani 2016). In this context, a new paradigm is seen as deriving legitimacy from its affinity to the "scientific method" based on a hypothetico-deductive model – a framework which is deeply erroneous in its view of how research actually occurs, and consequently devalues all theoretical models that do not find empirical support.

Conclusion

A methodology is a theory and analysis of how research should proceed (Harding 1987), and includes accounts of how "the general structure of theory finds its application in particular scientific disciplines" (Caws 1967, p. 339). Queer methodologies redefine ontological views which frame everyday realities that have been relegated to the margins by normative systems of categorization (Muñoz 2010) through a critical exploration of the disciplined normative truths about gender, sexuality, and sex in order to reveal multiple positionings, normativities, and intersections (Taylor 2010).

Queer perspectives endorse the notion of fragmented and multiple realities (Benko and Strohmayer 1997). Consequently, the idea of a grand narrative that can account for all possible human experience is rejected in favor of partial, local, and situated knowledges that can reflect the specificity of lived experience (Moss 2002; Bailey 1999; Haraway 1991). Furthermore, the distinctiveness of queer research derives not only from its underlying theoretical, epistemological, and ontological starting points but also from its political commitment to progressive and radical social and political change. Thus, queer scholarship can be described as "critical scholarship" that goes beyond providing a descriptive account of reality in order to bring about material and social change (Nash 2010).

In practice, however, one of the major failings of the extant scholarship on sexualities remains that much of its theoretical and methodological premise derives from perspectives that are largely academic, Western, white, and privileged. As Jackman (2010, p. 115) notes, "sexual identities and practices in seemingly remote locales are informed by, and sometimes themselves also inform, the construction of sexualities in distant cultural contexts." Consequently, much of queer scholarship today embodies colonial and ethnocentric assumptions wherein the Anglo-US white, urban West constitutes the default point of origin and reference (Engebretsen 2008).

The result is the generation of homonormative, white, Western queer epistemologies that end up excluding the marginalized and racialized "other" and reinforcing homonormative privilege (Muñoz 2010). This, in turn, results in the proliferation of a dominant queer model of individualized sexual subjectivity based on "coming out, being out, visible and proud as self-identified gays, lesbians, queers" which perpetuates "(sub)disciplinary complacency, monolithic discourse, and hegemonic institutionalization, and not ... the multiplication of place and scale...." (Engebretsen 2008, pp. 89–90) and, consequently, fails to account for realities beyond the non-Western sociocultural contexts. Furthermore, these exclusionary practices end up creating hierarchies of knowledge wherein legitimacy is enjoyed largely by the theorizing and publishing that takes place within the United States at the expense of scholarship produced outside of it (Engebretsen 2008).

Unfortunately, the growing awareness about the current limitations in queer scholarship has not yet translated into genuine efforts toward a more inclusive, transnational, and interdisciplinary analytical and theoretical premise (Engebretsen 2008). For instance, as Taylor (2010, p. 76) has noted, "queer discussions of 'homonormativity' often call for an interrogation of class privilege, but rarely deliver on this empirically."

These realizations have prompted calls to dismantle the predominance of US-Anglo-centric queer studies (Engebretsen 2008; Castell and Bryson 1998; Clifford 1988). According to Engebretsen (2008), the task of effecting this shift needs to take place at the level of research methodologies and theoretical paradigms so that queer methodologies can move "beyond an involuntary reiteration of fixed places, conceptual regimes, and necessary Anglo-US-hegemony" (p. 93).[19] This can be achieved through a critical reexamination of the ways in which research is conducted so as to investigate "the kinds of questions we ask, to whom we address these questions, the themes we propose, the theories we consult and adapt, and the ways in which we choose to disseminate our research – including matters of writing, terminology, language and audience" (pp. 95–96).

Notes

1 See Gayle Rubin (2011) for a discussion on the "erotic pyramid" in modern Western societies based on a "hierarchical system of sexual value."
2 Several feminist theorists have complicated the insider/outsider dichotomy by blurring the line between them (see, for instance, Tang (2006), Fine (1998), and Lal (1996) who have dwelt on the impact of resisting the insider/outsider binary on subjectivity).
3 See Fausto-Sterling (2000) who exemplifies how even within science, one's politics and ontology can shift one's gaze to uncover existences obscured by the heteronormative framework that erases queer existences.
4 See the work of Welle et al. (2006) on queer youths' existence on the periphery of lesbian and trans communities as they seek services as an example of how research can trouble dominant heteronormative understandings and problematize lesbian and transgender hegemony.
5 See Nash (2010), Haritaworn (2008), and Blackwood (1998) for a discussion on the evolving nature of the field and changes within the researcher's own status as insider/outsider in the course of the research and the consequent complications arising out of these shifts.
6 See Muñoz (2010) for a discussion on the need for "queer of color" epistemologies to reconstruct practices in the field in ways that do not exclude or marginalize "queer" of color sensibilities; and Taylor (2010) for a discussion on the perils of ignoring material realities, both theoretically and methodologically, in researching and theorizing sexuality.
7 Rooke (2010) argues that field-based methods serve to counter the tendency toward high abstraction and reliance on theory that have long characterized queer research. Jackman (2010) complicates this notion by pointing out that a critical examination of the centrality of the field in shaping research relations is essential to the ability of any fieldwork-based discipline to critique the heteronormativity that constitutes its foundations. In this context, Jackman offers two preliminary suggestions for alternatives to fieldwork that can help bring forth a radical reorientation in how scholars position themselves in relation to their work, as well as in how they conceptualize their research aims: firstly, the study of queer publics; and secondly, the study of queer assemblages.
8 See Jones and Adams (2010) for a discussion on why authoethnography is a queer method; Nash (2010), Jackman (2010), Rooke (2010), Engebretsen (2008), and Blackwood (1998) on queer ethnography; Boellstorff (2007) on the role of participant observation in queer methodology; and Ahmed (2006) on queer phenomenology.
9 See Savin-Williams (2006) and Diamond (2008) to understand the perils of confining one's understanding of gender and sexuality only to empirically observable categories.
10 See, for example, Browne (2008), Fish (2008), Brown and Knopp (2006), Duncan and Smith (2006), Badgett (2003), and Brown (2000) to understand how statistical data gathered on sexuality, mainly through market research or census data on "couples", usually finds white, affluent, middle-class, men who live in specific areas.
11 See, for example, Tsika (2016) for a discussion on how computational tools and algorithms used by popular websites blur the line between quantification and interpretation; Crampton and Elden (2006) and Legg (2005) on the controlling aspect of statistical data; Prewitt (2003) on how state quantitative data collection is more than a question of how many people live where; and Nobels (2002) on the politics of census gathering.

12 See Doan (2016) who argues that counting can be a queerly radical act when the aim is to ensure social justice, and Grzanka (2016) who vouches for a multidimensional person-centered rather than variable-centered statistical approach as a distinctly queer method.
13 See, for example, Brown and Knopp (2006), Crampton and Elden (2006), Stychin (2006), Valocchi (2005), Butler (2004), and Brown (2000) on the need to explore how government quantitative social research tools produce political regimes, create identities, and shape lives through the production of exclusive and legitimate sexuality categories.
14 See, also, Pascoe (2007), Capper (1999), and Bryson and de Castell (1998) for a discussion on covert queer research in educational sites.
15 See, also, Sheldon (2010) for a discussion on the need to critically analyze one's identity during the research process.
16 Newton (1993) discusses the need for researchers to account for their own desires.
17 For instance, see, Masequesmay's (2003) study of the types of identity work facilitated by Ô-Môi, a support group for Vietnamese lesbians, bisexual women, and female-to-male transgenders, wherein she reflects on her own involvement with the organization.
18 See Sheldon (2010) for a discussion on the extent to which C.J. Pascoe's (2007) study on high school masculinity and sexuality satisfies each of these criteria.
19 See Engebretsen (2008) for a discussion on the methodological and epistemological arguments in anthropologies of nonnormative sexuality that attempt to bridge the local/global and data/theory split.

References

Adams, Tony E. and Stacy Holman Jones. 2011. "Telling Stories: Reflexivity, Queer Theory and Autoethnography." *Cultural Studies ↔ Critical Methodologies* 11: 108–116.

Ahmed, Sara. 2006. *Queer Phenomenology: Orientations, Objects, Others*. Durham, NC: Duke University Press.

Anderson, Zoe. 2007. "Queer(ing) History: Queer Methodologies, Pedagogies and Interventions in the Discipline of History." In *Student Engagement. Proceedings of the 16th Annual Teaching Learning Forum*, Perth, The University of Western Australia (30–31 January 2007). Available at: https://clt.curtin.edu.au/events/conferences/tlf/tlf2007/refereed/anderson.html.

Badgett, Lee. 2003. *Money, Myth and Change: The Economic Lives of Lesbians and Gay Men*. Chicago, IL: University of Chicago Press.

Bailey, Robert W. 1999. *Gay Politics, Urban Politics: Identity and Economics in an Urban Setting*. New York, NY: University of Columbia Press.

Bain, Alison L. and Catherine J. Nash. 2006. "Undressing the Researcher: Feminism, Embodiment and Sexuality at a Queer Bathhouse Event." *Area* 38(1): 99–106.

Barrett, Stanley R. 1996. *Anthropology: A Student's Guide to Theory and Method*. Toronto: University of Toronto Press.

Baudrillard, Jean. 2001. *Jean Baudrillard: Selected Writings*. Stanford, CA: Stanford University Press.

Benko, Georges and Ulf Strohmayer, eds. 1997. *Space and Social Theory: Interpreting Modernity and Postmodernity*. Oxford: Blackwell.

Betsky, Aaron. 1997. *Queer Space: Architecture and Same-Sex Desire*. New York, NY: William Morrow and Company.

Binnie, Jon. 2007. "Sexuality, the Erotic and Geography: Epistemology, Methodology and Pedagogy." In *Geographies of Sexualities: Theory, Practices and Politics*, edited by Kath Browne, Jason Lim, and Gavin Brown, 29–38. Aldershot: Ashgate.

Blackwood, Evelyn. 1998. "Tombois in West Sumatra: Constructing Masculinity and Erotic Desire." *Cultural Anthropology* 13(4): 491–521.

Bochner, Arthur P. 2001. "Narrative's Virtues." *Qualitative Inquiry* 7(2): 131–157.

Bochner, Arthur P. 2002. "Perspectives on Inquiry III: The Moral of Stories." In *Handbook of Interpersonal Communication*, edited by Mark L. Knapp and John A. Daly, 73–101. Thousand Oaks, CA: Sage.

Boellstorff, Tom. 2007. *A Coincidence of Desires: Anthropology, Queer Studies, Indonesia.* Durham, NC: Duke University Press.

Boellstorff, Tom. 2010. "Queer Techne: Two Theses on Methodology and Queer Studies." In *Queer Methods and Methodologies: Intersecting Queer Theories and Social Science Research*, edited by Kath Browne and Catherine J. Nash, 215–230. Aldershot: Ashgate.

Bogdan, Robert C. and Sari Knopp Biklen. 1998. *Qualitative Research in Education: An Introduction to Theory and Methods*. Needham Heights, MA: Allyn & Bacon.

Brim, Matt and Amin Ghaziani. 2016. "Introduction: Queer Methods." *Women's Studies Quarterly* 44(3/4): 14–27. doi: 10.1353/wsq.2016.0037.

Britzman, Deborah. 1998. "Queer Pedagogy and its Strange Techniques." In *Lost Subjects, Contested Objects: Toward a Psychoanalytic Inquiry of Learning*, by Deborah Britzman. Albany, NY: State University of New York Press.

Brown, Gavin. 2004. "Sites of Public (Homo)Sex and the Carnivalesque Spaces of Reclaim the Streets." In *The Emancipatory City: Paradoxes and Possibilities*, edited by Loretta Lees, 91–107. London: Sage.

Brown, Michael P. 2000. *Closet Space: Geographies of Metaphors from the Body to the Globe*. London: Routledge.

Brown, Michael and Larry Knopp. 2006. "Place or Polygons? Governmentality, Scale and the Census in the Gay and Lesbian Atlas." *Population, Space and Place* 12(2): 223–242.

Browne, Kath. 2004. "Genderism and the Bathroom Problem: (Re)Materialising Sexed Sites, (Re)Creating Sexed Bodies." *Gender, Place and Culture* 11(3): 331–346.

Browne, Kath. 2007. "A Party With Politics? (Re)Making LGBTQ Pride Spaces in Dublin and Brighton." *Social and Cultural Geography* 8(1): 63–87.

Browne, Kath. 2008. "Selling My Queer Soul or Queerying Quantitative Research?" *Sociological Research Online* 13. Available at: http://www.socresonline.org.uk/13/1/11.html.

Browne, Kath. 2010. "Queer Quantification or Queer(y)ing Quantification: Creating Lesbian, Gay, Bisexual or Heterosexual Citizens through Governmental Social Research." In *Queer Methods and Methodologies: Intersecting Queer Theories and Social Science Research*, edited by Kath Browne and Catherine J. Nash, 231–249. Aldershot: Ashgate.

Browne, Kath and Catherine J. Nash. 2010. "Queer Methods and Methodologies: An Introduction." In *Queer Methods and Methodologies: Intersecting Queer Theories and Social Science Research*, edited by Kath Browne and Catherine J. Nash, 1–23. Aldershot: Ashgate.

Bryson, Mary and Suzanne de Castell. 1998. "From the Ridiculous to the Sublime: On Finding Oneself in Educational Research." In *Queer Theory in Education*, edited by William Pinar, 245–250. Mahwah, NJ: Lawrence Erlbaum.

Butler, Judith. 1990. *Gender Trouble: Feminism and the Subversion of Identity*. London: Routledge.

Butler, Judith. 1993a. *Bodies that Matter: On the Discursive Limits of "Sex"*. London: Routledge.

Butler, Judith. 1993b. "Imitation and Gender Insubordination." In *Lesbian and Gay Studies Reader*, edited by Henry Abelove, Michele Aina Barale, and David M. Halperin, 307–320. New York, NY: Routledge.

Butler, Judith. 2004. *Undoing Gender*. London: Routledge.

Butler, Judith. 2005. *Precarious Life: The Powers of Mourning and Violence*. London: Verso.

Capper, Colleen A. 1999. "(Homo)Sexualities, Organizations, and Administration: Possibilities for In(queer)y." *Educational Researcher* 28(5): 4–11.

Casey, Mark. 2011. "Sexual Identity-Politics: Activism from Gay to Queer and Beyond." In *Routledge Handbook of Identity Studies*, edited by Anthony Elliott, 275– 290. London: Routledge.

Cashore, Catherine and Teresa G. Tuason. 2009. "Negotiating the Binary: Identity and Social Justice for Bisexual and Transgender Individuals. *Journal of Gay and Lesbian Social Services* 21(4): 374–401.

Castell, Suzanne de and Mary Bryson. 1998. "Queer Ethnography: Identity, Authority, Narrativity, and a Geopolitics of Text." In *Inside the Academy and Out: Lesbian/Gay/Queer Studies and Social Action*, edited by Janice L. Ristock and Catherine G. Taylor, 97–110. Toronto: University of Toronto Press.

Caws, Peter. 1967. "Scientific Method." In *the Encyclopedia of Philosophy*, edited by Paul Edwards, 339–343. New York, NY: Macmillan.

Charmaz, Kathy. 2006. *Constructing Grounded Theory*. Thousand Oaks, CA: Sage.

Childers, Julie. 2003. "Review of Queer Studies: An Interdisciplinary Reader." *Radical Teacher* 67(Spring): 39–42.

Clarke, Danielle. 2004. "Finding the Subject: Queering the Archive." *Feminist Theory* 5(1): 79–83.

Clifford, James. 1988. *The Predicament of Culture: Twentieth-Century Ethnography, Literature, and Art*. Cambridge, MA: Harvard University Press.

Crampton, Jeremy W. and Stuart Elden. 2006. "Space, Politics, Calculation: An Introduction." *Social and Cultural Geography* 7(5): 681–685.

Crawley, Sara L. 2002. "'They Still Don't Understand Why I Hate Wearing Dresses!' An Autoethnographic Rant on Dresses, Boats, and Butchness." *Cultural Studies ↔ Critical Methodologies* 2(1): 69–92.

Detamore, Mathias. 2010. "Queer(y)ing the Ethics of Research Methods: Toward a Politics of Intimacy in Researcher/Researched Relations." In *Queer Methods and Methodologies: Intersecting Queer Theories and Social Science Research*, edited by Kath Browne and Catherine J. Nash, 167–182. Aldershot: Ashgate.

Diamond, Lisa M. 2008. *Sexual Fluidity: Understanding Women's Love and Desire*. Cambridge, MA: Harvard University Press.

Doan, Petra L. 2016. "To Count or Not to Count: Queering Measurement and the Transgender Community." *Women's Studies Quarterly* 44(3/4): 89–110.

Dowling, Robyn. 2005. "Power, Subjectivity, and Ethics in Qualitative Research." In *Qualitative Research Methods in Human Geography*, edited by Iain Hay, 23–36. Oxford: Oxford University Press.

Duncan, Simon and Darren Smith. 2006. "Individualisation Versus the Geography of 'New' Families." *Journal of the Academy of Social Sciences* 1(2): 167–189.

Engebretsen, Elisabeth Lund. 2008. "Queer Ethnography in Theory and Practice: Reflections on Studying Sexual Globalization and Women's Queer Activism in Beijing." *Graduate Journal of Social Science* 5(2): 88–116.

Epstein, Steven. 1994. "A Queer Encounter: Sociology and the Study of Sexuality." *Sociological Theory* 12(2): 188–202.

Fausto-Sterling, Anne. 1997. "How to Build a Man." In *The Gender/Sexuality Reader*, edited by Roger Lancaster and Micaela di Leonardo, 244–248. New York, NY: Routledge.
Fausto-Sterling, Anne. 2000. *Sexing the Body: Gender Politics and the Construction of Sexuality*. New York, NY: Basic Books.
Ferguson, Joshua M. 2013. "Queering Methodologies: Challenging Scientific Constraint in the Appreciation of Queer and Trans Subjects." *The Qualitative Report* 18(13): 1–13.
Fine, Michelle. 1998. "Working the Hyphens: Reinventing Self and Other in Qualitative Research." In *The Landscape of Qualitative Research*, edited by Norman K. Denzin and Yvonna S. Lincoln, 130–155. London: Sage.
Fish, Julie. 2008. "Navigating Queer Street: Researching the Intersections of Lesbian, Gay, Bisexual and Trans (LGBT) Identities in Health Research." *Sociological Research Online* 13. Available at: http://www.socresonline.org.uk/13/1/12.html.
Floyd, K. 2009. *The Reification of Desire: Toward a Queer Marxism*. Minneapolis: University of Minnesota Press.
Foucault, Michel. 1990. *The History of Sexuality: An Introduction*, translated by Robert Hurley, vol. 1. New York, NY: Vintage Books.
Fraenkel, Jack R. and Norman E. Wallen. 2009. *How to Design and Evaluate Research in Education*, 7th edn. New York, NY: McGraw-Hill.
Freeman, Mark. 2001. "From Substance to Story: Narrative, Identity, and the Reconstruction of Self." In *Narrative and Identity: Studies in Autobiography, Self and Culture*, edited by Jens Brockmeier and Donald A. Carbaugh, 283–298. Philadelphia, PA: John Benjamins.
Gamson, Joshua. 2003. "Sexualities, Queer Theory, and Qualitative Research." In *The Landscape of Qualitative Research: Theories and Issues*, edited by Norman K. Denzin and Yvonna S. Lincoln, 540–564. London: Sage.
Gibson-Graham, J.K. 1999. "Queer(y)ing Ccapitalism In and Out of the Classroom" *Journal of Geography in Higher Education* 23(1): 80–85.
Garfinkel, Harold. 1967. *Studies in Ethnomethodology*. Englewood Cliffs, NJ: Prentice Hall.
Gorman-Murray, Andrew, Lynda Johnston, and Gordon Waitt. 2010. "Queer(ing) Communication in Research Relationships: A Conversation about Subjectivities, Methodologies and Ethics." In *Queer Methods and Methodologies: Intersecting Queer Theories and Social Science Research*, edited by Kath Browne and Catherine J. Nash, 97–112. Aldershot: Ashgate.
Graham, Mark. 2010. "Method Matters: Ethnography and Materiality." In *Queer Methods and Methodologies: Intersecting Queer Theories and Social Science Research*, edited by Kath Browne and Catherine J. Nash, 183–194. Aldershot: Ashgate.
Green, Adam Isaiah. 2002. "Gay but Not Queer: Toward a Post-Queer Study of Sexuality." *Theory and Society* 31(4): 521–545.
Green, Adam Isaiah. 2007. "Queer Theory and Sociology: Locating the Subject and the Self in Sexuality Studies." *Sociological Theory* 25(1): 26–45.
Grzanka, Patrick R. 2016. "Queer Survey Research and the Ontological Dimensions of Heterosexism." *Women's Studies Quarterly* 44(3/4): 131–149. doi: 10.1353/wsq.2016.0037.
Hacking, Ian. 1990. "Making Up People." In *Forms of Desire: Sexual Orientation and the Social Constructionist Controversy*, edited by Edward Stein, 69–88. New York, NY: Garland.
Hacking, Ian. 1999. *The Social Construction of What?* Cambridge, MA: Harvard University Press.
Halberstam, Jack. 1998. *Female Masculinity*. London: Duke University Press.

Halperin, David M. 2003. "The Normalization of Queer Theory." *Journal of Homosexuality* 45: 339–43.
Hammers, Corie and Alan D. Brown III. 2004. "Towards a Feminist–Queer Alliance: A Paradigmatic Shift in the Research Process." *Social Epistemology* 18(1): 85–101.
Haraway, Donna. 1991. *Simians, Cyborgs and Women: The Reinvention of Nature*. London: Routledge.
Haraway, Donna J. 2004. *The Haraway Reader*. New York, NY: Routledge.
Harding, Sandra, ed. 1987. *Feminism and Methodology*. Bloomington, IN: Indiana University Press.
Haritaworn, Jin. 2008. "Shifting Positionalities: Empirical Reflections on a Queer/Trans of Colour Methodology." *Sociological Research Online* 13. Available at: http://www.socresonline.org.uk/13/1/13.html.
Harwood, Valerie and Mary Louise Rasmussen. 2007. "Scrutinizing Sexuality and Psychopathology: A Foucauldian Inspired Strategy for Qualitative Data Analysis." *International Journal for Qualitative Studies in Education* 20(1): 31–50.
Hegarty, Peter. 2008. "Queer Methodologies." In *Feeling Queer or Queer Feelings: Radical Approaches to Counselling Sex, Sexualities and Genders*, edited by Lyndsey Moon, 125–140. London: Routledge.
Henderson, Lisa. 2001. "Queer Communication Studies." In *Communication Yearbook 24*, edited by William B. Gudykunst, 465–484. Thousand Oaks, CA: Sage.
Hicks, Stephen. 2008. "Thinking through Sexuality." *Journal of Social Work* 8(1): 65–82.
Hird, Myra J. 2004. "Naturally Queer." *Feminist Theory* 5(1): 85–89.
Honeychurch, Kenn Gardner. 1996. "Researching Dissident Subjectivities: Queering the Grounds of Theory and Practice." *Harvard Educational Review* 66(2): 339–355.
Jackman, Michael Connors. 2010. "The Trouble with Fieldwork: Queering Methodologies." In *Queer Methods and Methodologies: Intersecting Queer Theories and Social Science Research*, edited by Kath Browne and Catherine J. Nash, 113–128. Aldershot: Ashgate.
Jagose, Annamarie. 1996. *Queer Theory: An Introduction*, 1st edn. Melbourne: Melbourne University Press.
Johnston, Lynda. 2005. *Queering Tourism: Paradoxical Performances at Gay Pride Parades*. London: Routledge.
Jones, Stacy Holman and Tony E. Adams. 2010. "Autoethnography is a Queer Method." In *Queer Methods and Methodologies: Intersecting Queer Theories and Social Science Research*, edited by Kath Browne and Catherine J. Nash, 195–214. Aldershot: Ashgate.
Lal, Jayati. 1996. "Situating Locations: The Politics of Self, Identity, and "Other" in Living and Writing the Text." In *Feminist Dilemmas in Fieldwork*, edited by Diane L. Wolf, 185–214. Boulder, CO: Westview.
Lather, Patti. 1986. "Issues of Validity in Openly Ideological Research: Between a Rock and a Soft Place." *Interchange* 17(4): 63–84.
Legg, Stephen. 2005. "Foucault's population Geographies: Classifications, Biopolitics and Governmental Spaces." *Population, Space and Place* 11(3): 137–156.
Madison, D. Soyini. 2005. *Critical Ethnography: Method, Ethics, and Performance*. Thousand Oaks, CA: Sage.
Manning, Eli. 2009. "Queerly Disrupting Methodology." Paper presented at Feminist Research Methods – An international Conference, Stockholm, Sweden (February 4–6, 2009).
Masequesmay, Gina. 2003. "Negotiating Multiple Identities in a Queer Vietnamese Support Group." In *Queer Theory and Communication: From Disciplining Queers to Queering the Discipline(s)*, edited by Gust A. Yep, 193–216. Binghamton, NY: Harrington Park Press.

Maynard, Mary. 1994. "Methods, Practice and Epistemology: The Debate about Feminism and Research." In Researching Women's *Lives From a Feminist Perspective*, edited by Mary Maynard and June Purvis, 10–26. London: Taylor & Francis.

Moss, Pamela, ed. 2002. *Feminist Geography in Practice: Research and Methods*. Oxford: Blackwell.

Muñoz, Lorena. 2010. "Brown, Queer and Gendered: Queering the Latina/o 'Street-Scapes' in Los Angeles." In *Queer Methods and Methodologies: Intersecting Queer Theories and Social Science Research*, edited by Kath Browne and Catherine J. Nash, 55–67. Aldershot: Ashgate.

Muscio, Inga. 1998. *Cunt: A Declaration of Independence*. Seattle, WA: Seal Press.

Nash, Catherine J. 2010. "Queer Conversations: Old-Time Lesbians, Transmen and the Politics of Queer Research." In *Queer Methods and Methodologies: Intersecting Queer Theories and Social Science Research*, edited by Kath Browne and Catherine J. Nash, 129–142. Aldershot: Ashgate.

Newton, Esther. 1993. "My Best Informant's Dress: The Erotic Equation in Fieldwork." *Cultural Anthropology* 8(1): 3–23.

Nicholas, Cheryl L. 2006. "Disciplinary-Interdisciplinary GLBTQ (Identity) Studies and Hecht's Layering Perspective." *Communication Quarterly* 54(3): 305–330.

Nobles, Melissa. 2002. "Racial Categorisation and Censuses." In *Census and Identity: The Politics of Race, Ethnicity and Language in National Censuses*, edited by David I. Kertzer and Dominique Arel, 43–70. Cambridge: Cambridge University Press.

Pascoe, C.J. 2007. *Dude, You're A Fag: Masculinity and Sexuality in High School*. Berkeley, CA: University of California Press.

Phoenix, Ann. 1994. "Practicing Feminist Research: The Intersection of Gender and 'Race' in the Research Process." In *Researching Women's Lives from a Feminist Perspective*, edited by Mary Maynard and June Purvis, 49–71. London: Taylor & Francis.

Plummer, Ken. 1998. "Afterward: The Past, Present and Futures of the Sociology of Same Sex Relations." In *Social Perspectives in Lesbian and Gay Studies: A Reader*, edited by Peter M. Nardi and Beth Schneider, 605–614. London: Routledge.

Plummer, Ken. 2005. "Critical Humanism and Queer Theory: Living with the Tensions." In *The Landscape of Qualitative Research: Theories and Issues*, edited by Norman K. Denzin and Yvonna S. Lincoln, 357–373. London: Sage.

Prewitt, Kenneth. 2003. *Politics and Science in Census Taking*. New York, NY: Russell Sage Foundation and the Population Reference Bureau.

Puar, Jasbir K. 2001. "Global Circuits: Transnational Sexualities and Trinidad." *Signs* 26(4): 1039–1065.

Puar, Jasbir K. 2007. *Terrorist Assemblages: Homonationalism in Queer Times*. Durham, NC: Duke University Press.

Puar, Jasbir K., Dereka Rushbrook, and Louisa Schein. 2003. "Sexuality and Space: Queering Geographies of Globalization." *Environment and Planning D: Society and Space* 21(4): 383–387.

Rasmussen, Mary Louise. 2006. *Becoming Subjects: A Study of Sexualities and Secondary Schooling*. New York, NY: Routledge.

Ramazanoglu, Caroline and Janet Holland, eds. 2002. *Feminist Methodology: Challenges and Choices*. London: Sage.

Reid-Pharr, Robert. 2002. "Extending Queer Theory to Race and Ethnicity." *Chronicle of Higher Education* 48(7): 7–9.

Reynolds, Paul. 2001. "Accounting for Sexuality: The Scope and Limitations of Census Data on Sexual Identity and Difference." *Radical Statistics* 78: 63–76.

Rich, Adrienne. 1984. "Notes Toward the Politics of Location." In *Blood, Bread, and Poetry: Selected Prose, 1979–1985,* by Adrienne Rich, 210–231. W.W. Norton.

Rooke, Alison. 2010. "Queer in the Field: On Emotions, Temporality and Performativity in Ethnography." In *Queer Methods and Methodologies: Intersecting Queer Theories and Social Science Research*, edited by Kath Browne and Catherine J. Nash, 25–39. Aldershot: Ashgate.

Rosenberg, Tiina. 2008. "Locally Queer. A Note on the Feminist Genealogy of Queer Theory." *Graduate Journal of Social Science* 5(2): 5–18.

Rubin, Gayle. 2011. "Thinking Sex: Notes for a Radical Theory of Politics of Sexuality." In *Deviations: A Gayle Rubin Reader*, edited by Gayle S. Rubin, 137–181. London: Dunham.

Saltmarsh, Sue. 2007. "Cultural Complicities: Elitism, Heteronormativity and Violence in The Education Marketplace." *International Journal of Qualitative Studies in Education* 20: 335–354.

Savin-Williams, Ritch C. 2006. "Who's Gay? Does It Matter?" *Current Directions in Psychological Science* 15(1): 40–44.

Seidman, Steven. 1995. "Deconstructing Queer Theory or the Under-theorization of the Social and the Ethical." In *Social Postmodernism*, edited by Linda Nicholson and Steven Seidman, 116–141. Cambridge: Cambridge University Press.

Sheldon, James, R. 2010. "(Re)Searching Queer Subjects: Approaching a Queer Methodology." Paper presented at the Annual Meeting of the American Educational Research Association, Denver, CO (April 30–May 4, 2010).

Smith, Dorothy. 1972. "Women's Perspectives as a Radical Critique of Sociology." In *Feminism and Methodology*, edited by Sandra Harding, 84–86. Bloomington, IN: Open University Press.

Somerville, Siobhan B. 2000. "Scientific Racism and the Invention of the Homosexual Body." In *Queering the Color Line – Race and the Invention of Homosexuality in American Culture*, edited by Siobhan B. Somerville, 15–38. Durham, NC: Duke University Press.

Stanley, Liz. 1990. "Feminist Praxis and the Academic Mode of Production: An Editorial Introduction." In *Feminist Praxis: Research Theory and Epistemology and Feminist Sociology*, edited by Liz Stanley, 3–19. London: Routledge.

Stanley, Liz. 1997. "Methodology Matters!" In *Introducing Women's Studies*, edited by Diane Richardson and Victoria Robinson, 198–219. London: Macmillan.

Stanley, Liz and Sue Wise, ed. 1983. *Breaking Out: Feminist Consciousness and Feminist Research*. London: Routledge.

Stanley, Liz and Sue Wise, ed. 1993. *Breaking Out Again: Feminist Ontology and Epistemology*. London: Routledge.

Strega, Susan. 2005. "The View from the Poststructural Margins: Epistemology and Methodology Reconsidered." In *Research as Resistance*, edited by Leslie Brown and Susan Strega, 119–152. Toronto: Canadian Scholars Press.

Stychin, Carl F. 2006. "'Las Vegas is Not Where We Are': Queer Readings of the Civil Partnership Act." *Political Geography* 25: 899–920.

Tang, Denise Tse Shang. 2006. "The Research Pendulum: Multiple Roles and Responsibilities as a Researcher." *Journal of Lesbian Studies* 10(3–4): 11–27.

Taylor, Yvette. 2010. "The 'Outness' of Queer: Class and Sexual Intersections." In *Queer Methods and Methodologies: Intersecting Queer Theories and Social Science Research*, edited by Kath Browne and Catherine J. Nash, 69–83. Aldershot: Ashgate.

Thomas, Calvin, ed. 2000. *Straight with a Twist: Queer Theory and the Subject of Heterosexuality*. Urbana: University of Illinois Press.

Tsika, Noah. 2016. "CompuQueer: Protocological Constraints, Algorithmic Streamlining, and the Search for Queer Methods Online." *Women's Studies Quarterly* 44(3/4): 131–149. doi: 10.1353/wsq.2016.0037.

Tuhiwai Smith, Linda. 1999. *Decolonizing Methodologies: Research and Indigenous People*. London: Zed Books.

Turner, William B. 2000. *A Genealogy of Queer Theory*. Philadelphia, PA: Temple University Press.

Valocchi, Stephen. 2005. "Not Yet Queer Enough: The Lessons of Queer Theory for the Sociology of Gender and Sexuality." *Gender and Society* 19(6): 750–770.

Warner, Daniel Noam. 2004. "Towards a Queer Research Methodology." *Qualitative Research in Psychology* 1(4): 321–337.

Warner, Michael, ed. 1993. *Fear of a Queer Planet: Queer Politics and Social Theory*. Minneapolis: University of Minnesota Press.

Warner, Michael. 1999. *The Trouble with Normal: Sex, Politics, and the Ethics of Queer Life*. New York, NY: The Free Press.

Warner, Michael. 2002. *Publics and Counterpublics*. New York, NY: Zone Books.

Watson, Katherine. 2005. "Queer Theory." *Group Analysis* 38(1): 67–81.

Welle, D.L., S.S. Fuller, D. Mauk, and M.C. Clatts. 2006. "The Invisible Body Of Queer Youth: Identity And Health In The Margins Of Lesbian And Trans Communities." *Journal of Lesbian Studies* 10(1/2): 43–71.

Wilchins, Riki. 2004. *Queer Theory, Gender Theory*. Los Angeles, CA: Alyson.

Wittig, Monique. 1996. "The Straight Mind." In *The Material Queer: A LesBiGay Cultural Studies Reader*, edited by Donald Morton, 207–212. Boulder, CO: Westview Press.

Yep, Gust A., Karen E. Lovaas, and John P. Elia. 2003. "Introduction: Queering Communication: Starting the Conversation." *Journal of Homosexuality* 45(2/3/4): 1–10.

7

Queer Pedagogies

Leigh Potvin

Queer pedagogies resist dominant social norms in classrooms and schools and seek to create space for multiple ways of knowing and being to counteract the marginalization experienced by lesbian, gay, bisexual, trans, queer+ (LGBTQ+)[1] people in educational contexts. More than a framework that pursues acceptance of the queer or generic "celebrations of diversity," queer politics and pedagogies seek to transgress and even rewrite social norms, only to transgress them and rewrite them again in perpetuity, seeking spaces and realities where a multiplicity of ever-changing norms exists. In this chapter, I explore queer pedagogies, including its emergence in sociological theory and its application in educational contexts. I want to acknowledge that I am a white/settler, straight, cisgender Canadian scholar. I was born in Northwestern Ontario on the traditional territory of the Anishnaabe people and currently live in Unama'ki (Cape Breton) the traditional territory of the Mi'kmaw people. This chapter reflects my research and teaching experiences and focuses on queer pedagogies in Western contexts. But not without first acknowledging the work of scholars, activists, and educators in the Global South doing similar research and fighting similar human rights battles, including queer activism and pedagogical efforts in the Philippines, Brazil, and South Africa to advocate for and protect the rights of LGBTQ people (Francis 2012; Francis and Msibi 2011; Mountian 2014). I make this acknowledgment and situate myself in this chapter so as not to "whitestream" queer studies as Coloma (2006, 2013) warns is all too common. As Battiste (2013) suggests: settler privilege and the bias that comes with it cannot be side-stepped or eliminated, but must be situated at the fore of critical research.

Relevant Terms and Concepts

Queer pedagogies are teaching philosophies guided by queer theory. In other words, they include approaches to education that emphasize a multiplicity of identities and worldviews encapsulated by the term "queer." Those who identify as queer pedagogues, or espouse a queer pedagogy, needn't identify as queer themselves, but rather ascribe to the values that support queerness. Those include multiple ways of knowing, being, and understanding the world and supporting a proliferation of such identities in perpetuity.

Heteronormativity refers to the normalization of heterosexual privilege (Driskill et al. 2011) evident in school dances and health and physical education curriculums. For example, it is the presumed norm, not the exception, that students will attend prom and other events in straight couple pairings. In health and physical education classes, students are divided into male and female groups and are often provided sex education that presumes cisgender straightness. These examples magnify the point that heterosexism presumes the superiority and naturalness of heterosexuality (Finley 2011; Walton 2006).

The concept of allyship and straight privilege are also important to explicate in this chapter. Straight teachers can be important allies to LGBTQ+ students. According to Bishop (2002), allies are "people who recognize the unearned privilege they receive from society's patterns of injustice and take responsibility for changing these patterns" (p. 1). While Bishop's definition presents an ideal of allyship, I argue throughout this chapter that acknowledging one's own privilege is one of the most challenging tasks for allies (Potvin 2016). Bishop (2002) emphasizes the importance of allies exercising their power in ways that support social movements rather than reinscribing oppression. One way to avoid reinscribing oppression is to acknowledge one's privilege, which can be understood as a form of dominance, afforded to a group over others, that perpetuates inequities (Sensoy and DiAngelo 2012). In this context, it means exploring straight privilege in the context of queer theory. The dual actions of recognizing and taking responsibility suggest that straight allies are afforded privilege in society – at the expense of LGBTQ+ people – on account of their being heterosexual.

Queer Theory

As concepts, queer pedagogies, heteronormativity, allyship, and straight privilege are integral building blocks to understanding queer theory. Often, queer theory is defined by what it is not rather than by what it is. Outside of a queer critique, queerness is often seen as abnormal, different, other. Queerness becomes the subject of study, the focus, and the new normal. Put differently, queer theory seeks to dismantle normative constructions and envision a reality where multiple ways of knowing and being exist. As a theoretical framework, it is rooted in the resistance of social norms. Foucault's work (1978, 1986) forms the basis of queer theory's core both in his own writing and also through his cited influence on poststructuralist feminist thinkers like Butler (1990 [2011], 2004) and Sedgwick (1985, 1993). For Butler, (1990 [2011]) gender and sexuality are socially constructed and fluid parts of a person's identity. Gender and sexuality, through a poststructuralist lens, resist being essentialized, which is to be made static and unchanging. At first glance, gender or sexuality may not seem like a fluid part of oneself, not because of the innate qualities of gender or sexuality themselves, but because of the ways they are regulated in society. Schools are one site of regulation. For example, many schools are currently in the process of adapting their washrooms to provide safer facilities for trans students with gender-neutral washrooms.[2] The challenge for trans students lies in the perception of their gender by other people. The highly regulatory nature of schools can result in harassment and discrimination toward trans students seeking alternatives because of the lack of understanding and supports in place. In addition to these structural impositions, individuals and groups in schools and classrooms impose norms and values about gender and sexuality by challenging gender-nonconforming students' appearance and not using their preferred pronouns and/or name.

Sedgwick (1993) understands the notion of queerness, at the heart of queer theory, as "the open mesh of possibilities, gaps, overlaps, dissonances and resonances, lapses and excesses of meaning when the constituent elements of anyone's gender or anyone's sexuality aren't made (or can't be made) to signify monolithically" (p. 8). In other words, gender and sexuality are multilayered, diverse, and constantly changing entities. Like queer theory, schools are also complex, multilayered, and diverse spaces. Too often, however, they do not function that way. Instead, schools are highly regulated environments where identity, behavior, and codes of conduct are rigidly constructed and regulated, which limits possibilities for diversity that pedagogy guided by queer theory could offer. The potential that queer theory provides to reenvision schools as spaces where more fluid gender and sexual identities are fostered is vast and allies could play an important role in creating the conditions for change given proper training and institutional support.

The central point is that queer theory and, by extension, queer pedagogy, aim to disrupt the boundary between excluded and included. As queer theorist Britzman (1995) notes, these areas are "explicitly transgressive, perverse, and political" (p. 157). They formulate new ways of knowing and working beyond the inclusion/exclusion binary. Disruption of this kind is desirable because it is valuable to have critical discussions about straight privilege and the insidious role it can play in educational contexts.

Queer educational scholars who engage with queer pedagogy argue that it has the potential to disrupt normative discourse in schools and classrooms (Britzman1995; Linville 2009; Pinar 1998, 2007; Rodriguez 2007). Teaching guided by queer pedagogies serves not only to disrupt homophobia, but also to confront heteronormativity and heterosexism in schools (Britzman 1995; Bryson and de Castell 1993; Luhmann 1998). Teachers who espouse queer pedagogies are often guided by theory that values, alongside deeply reflective teaching practices, a multiplicity of identities and lived experiences. Strategic resistance to homophobia, guided by queer pedagogies, is more effective than ad hoc antihomophobia efforts because such resistance requires a shift away from heteronormativity (Halperin 1997; Rasmussen 2004). Martino (1999) encourages teachers to "move beyond a dominant liberal pedagogy to encourage students to think about what we take for granted as 'normal' and 'natural'" (p. 147). Queer pedagogies provide teachers with models they can examine and then apply to queer politics and content in their classrooms and lesson plans (Britzman 1995; Bryson and de Castell 1993; Kumashiro 2002).

Early sociological scholars like Weber and Durkheim in the early-to-middle twentieth century were silent on the topic of sexuality. This silence lead to a normalization of heterosexuality in the discipline, as these sites were considered private (not public) and therefore, not subject to social forces (Seidman 1994). Sociologists entered into discussions of sex and sexuality by way of so-called deviant behavior: prostitution, pornography, and homosexuality. Many sociologists studied homosexuality before heterosexuality, meaning that "a sociology of homosexuality emerged as part of the sociology of sex" (p. 169). The Kinsey Project on sex and sexuality in the 1950s and 1960s moved sex and sexuality studies away from an exclusive focus on deviance. In his groundbreaking work on human sexuality, Kinsey started to shape an understanding of sexuality as a continuum of behaviors and preferences (Seidman 1994). It is from this theoretical point that the feminist and gay liberation movements of the 1970s "fashioned elaborate social concepts of homosexuality" (p. 169). Radical lesbian feminists (see Dworkin 1989; Rich 1980) sought to normalize same-sex relationships (and attraction) and critique institutions like marriage, child-rearing, and a traditional gender division of labor normalized by heterosexuality. Around this time, Foucault entered the academic conversation about sex, sexuality, and their regulation. Foucault (1978) discusses relations of power, sex, homosexuality, and public interest/discourse. He emphasizes that relations of power (the way that power exists and is exercised in relation to others) are central to sex/sexuality. Foucault maintains that public discourse, although often covert, deploys its power to regulate people's sexual (private) lives and identities. Further, such discourse shapes notions of private and public sexualities in the first place. Foucault uses the example of the public vilification of homosexuality, and other "deviations" from the norms of so-called acceptable sexuality, as evidence of the ways in which public institutions (specifically, the State and the Church) exercise power in regulating private lives (sex/sexuality). As attitudes towards homosexuality relaxed, "homosexuality began to speak on its own behalf, to demand that its legitimacy or 'naturality' be acknowledged" (p. 101). Foucault outlines the ways in which power and public interest have regulated private lives.

Halperin (1997) builds on Foucault's theoretical contributions to queer theory and provides a framework for disrupting normative ways of being, knowing, and thinking. While queer theorists assign great influence to Foucault's work, Foucault himself did not identify as a queer theorist. In fact, as a theoretical framework, queer theory was largely formulated and conceptualized after his death. Homophobia, according to Halperin, is a systemic strategy, broad in scope, that aims to oppress queer people and those perceived as queer. It is not constituted as one simple act or even a series of acts that can be resisted with an oppositional act or set of acts. As such, it must be resisted strategically, and not simply refuted in the ways that antihomophobia efforts often attempt. Queer theory, therefore, provides a platform from which to comprehensively resist homophobia. Strategic resistance of homophobia, guided by queer theory, is more effective than ad hoc antihomophobia efforts because it requires a move away from heteronormativity. The goal of queer theory is to shift from a paradigm where heterosexuality is imbued with subjectivity, often assumed or deemed as innate or natural, whereas homosexuality occupies an objectified space. Sexualities themselves, as Foucault (1978) argued two decades earlier, are a by-product of the scientific method and the discourse surrounding it. Under such a set of heteronormative assumptions, homosexuality is never fully conceived of or assigned the agency and complexity that heterosexuality is afforded. Homophobia would see its end, Halperin argues, if this traditional binary of subject (heterosexual) and object (homosexual) could be replaced with "queer theory" – an umbrella term for a broader, systemic queer ideology that actively dismantles homophobia, heterosexism, and heteronormativity.

Berlant and Warner (1995) debunk two prevailing notions about queer theory: first, the presumption that it is monolithic; and second, that it does not comprise a set of easily compartmentalized theories. They articulate their interest in eschewing conventional definitions that "define, purify, sanitize, or otherwise entail the emerging queer commentary," instead aiming "to prevent the reduction of queer theory to a specialty or metatheory" (p. 344). The authors shed light on queer theory's multiplicities – on its many faces. In particular, they suggest the pursuit of queer publics. These spaces or publics are not exclusively for individuals who identify as queer, but are rather for those who seek an alternative to the normalized gender/sexual narrative under patriarchy. Seeking membership and belonging in queer publics is "more a matter of aspiration than it is the expression of an identity or a history" (p. 344). For those educators who espouse and employ queer pedagogies, they must contest, challenge, and rethink social norms, all while challenging their students to do the same.

Queer Pedagogy

Bryson and de Castell (1993) bring queer pedagogy into focus in their practice as university educators, and they highlight its transgressive possibilities. They argue that queer pedagogy is "teaching against the grain ... an amalgam of performative acts ... enfleshing a radical form of what we envisioned to be potentially liberatory enactments of 'gender treachery'" within the "heterosexually coded space of academic women's studies programs" (p. 288). Put differently, queer pedagogy brings the boundary-pushing qualities of queer theory into classrooms through the teacher's guiding philosophy. Britzman (1995), Bryson and de Castell (1993) believe there is a distance between queer theory and queer pedagogy, a distance they would like to decrease. Doing so is no simple task, given the heteronormative relations of power and identity that are at work in a classroom. The goal of a queer praxis, then, is to engage in a "queerying of pedagogy" (p. 299). Bryson and de Castell (1993) highlight how gender, sexuality, identity, and relations of power are subject to continual change even as they may appear stable. As a result, one exclusive definition of queer pedagogy in their conceptions defies the foundations of queer theory itself.

Where Britzman (1995) aligns with Bryson and de Castell (1993), however, is in bringing queer theory into the realm of education and pedagogy. According to Britzman, queer pedagogy posits "resistance as not outside of the subject of knowledge or the knowledge of subjects, but rather as constitutive of knowledge and its subjects" (p. 154). What she means is that queer pedagogy is not an add-on or an afterthought; it is the foundation upon which sound educational practice is built.

The limits of "thinkability," Britzman says, are to "engage the limit of thought – where thought stops, what it cannot bear to know, what it must shut out to think as it does" (p. 156). Here, Britzman seems to encourage the reader to consider the way in which the naturalization of heterosexuality creates a category of (queer) persons that are "the dismissed, the unworthy, the irrelevant" (p. 156). Those who are excluded (queer people) are defined by their relationship to those who are included (straight people). Britzman challenges educators to push themselves to know (and learn) what may be difficult to learn.

Pinar (1998) emphasizes the importance of queer theory in the context of education because "homophobia (not to mention heterosexism) is especially intense in the field of education, a highly conservative and often reactionary field" (p. 1). For Pinar, queer pedagogy displaces and decenters the curriculum away from normalized heterosexuality. A queer curriculum is multifaceted and malleable. Compulsory heterosexuality as a hegemonic practice helps elicit understandings of the naturalized norms and assumptions implicit within curriculum (Rich 1980). Evoking similar ideas as Foucault (1978) and Halperin (1997), Pinar (1998) and Rodriguez, and Pinar (2007) argue that heterosexuality's meaning is contingent on homosexuality, and that the coherence of the former idea is predicated on the exclusion, repression, and repudiation of the latter. They are interdependent concepts, but instead of meeting as equals, they are hierarchical and unequal. Elsewhere, Pinar (2007) articulates that, "queer pedagogy requires a self-reflexive examination of limitations" (p. 16). In other words, educators employing a queer pedagogy must engage in a continuous process of challenging their own (and others) barriers and shortsightedness.

Queer pedagogy, according to Luhmann (1998), "traverses identity demands central to other critical pedagogies and instead poses the question of how a 'post-identity pedagogy' becomes thinkable" (p. 120). Luhmann says that queer pedagogy must disrupt the binary of heterosexual as normal and homosexual as deficient. Presenting positive images of homosexual people (as is common in LGBT studies) is insufficient because it lacks a critical lens to challenge this position of this binary in and of itself. Can queer pedagogy resist "stable knowledge" and shift pedagogy "to an inquiry into the conditions for understanding, or refusing, knowledge" (p. 126)? Queer pedagogy is "about the process of risking the self" (p. 128). Luhmann presents pedagogues with the exciting and likely unsettling possibility of disrupting knowledge and practice in order to learn and teach differently.

Queering Traditional Pedagogical Practices

Walton (2006) focuses on strategies to equip K–12 teachers and administrators with the tools they need to adequately address homophobic bullying in schools. The three concepts that Walton outlines as significant to this process are homophobia, heterosexism, and heteronormativity. Identifying and naming these phenomena can help educators understand the broader sociological forces at work within school-based bullying and address it, instead of shying away out of fear of discussing sex with teens, and particularly anal sex which is perceived, inaccurately, by some as "gay sex." Indeed, this aversion to discussing sex in general and gay sex in particular is often cited as the reason for an educator's failure to address homophobic harassment

(Gay Lesbian & Straight Education Network [GLSEN] 2011; Taylor et al. 2011, 2015). Although sexuality is a legitimate terrain of discussion in age-appropriate ways, addressing homophobic bullying is, in fact, not tantamount to teachers having conversations with students about sex or sexual activity. Such an assertion is wilfully ignorant and homophobic. As Walton (2005) points out, understanding heterosexism and recognizing heteronormative assumptions are key to addressing the harassment in schools that arises within the matrix of sexuality and gender.

Pascoe (2007) focused on such harassment in her study called *Dude, You're a Fag*. In it, she outlines the role that gender performance, and particularly antinormative performances, can play in the regulation of straightness. Regulation of gender performance, she argues, depends upon social context and social groups. That is, what may be considered a normative masculine (straight) performance within one socioeconomic and/or cultural group may be viewed as transgressive (queer) within another. For example, her study finds that dancing is usually an encouraged and acceptable expression of masculinity among African American male students. Among most white male students, however, dancing is typically seen as abnormal and, as such, masculinity of boys is policed through homophobic epithets like "fag" and "queer." "Fag," Pascoe says, "is not only an identity linked to homosexual boys but an identity that can temporarily adhere to heterosexual boys as well" (p. 53); such is particularly apparent in instances of gender-nonconformity. Fear of homophobic responses in the form of name-calling and the threat of violence pressures males to conform to gender-normative behavior and also to bully or harass nonconforming males as a way of normalizing themselves or avoiding harassment.

Aligning with Pascoe, Jackson (2006) suggests that heterosexuality is "a gender relationship ordering not only sexual life, but also domestic and extra-domestic divisions of labour and resources" (p. 107). Jackson identifies the ways that normalized heterosexuality regulates even straight people's lives in its dominant form. For instance, straight people also should adhere to rigid norms and roles within their relationship. Although they occupy a position of social privilege, the boundaries of heterosexuality, like gender, are rigidly constructed and maintained (Butler 2004; Pascoe 2007). I present Jackson's perspective to show the way that boundaries of heterosexuality are policed even for straight people. I am not presenting this to show how straight people are oppressed on the basis of sexuality (because they are not), but rather to show the pervasive nature of heteronormativity.

One strategy to disrupt heteronormativity in school is the creation of queer schools for LGBTQ+ students exclusively. Rasmussen (2004) discusses the notion of streamed schools, what she calls queer spaces, for LGBTQ+ students. Although queer schools should provide a safer environment – one which honors and serves the student body more equitably than typical mainstream schools – they remain somewhat problematic. Queer schools, according to Rasmussen, reinscribe the heteronormative premise that pervades mainstream schooling. In other words, queer schools remain at the opposite end of the heteronormative binary from mainstream schools. They do not necessarily reenvision new spaces and ways of being, but instead exist in opposition to mainstream schools.[3] The oppositional stance from which these (queer) schools are conceived remains linked to the very forces (homophobia, heterosexism, heteronormativity) they seek to resist. Queer students continue, under this model, to occupy space outside the norm instead of rewriting and reimagining norms within the mainstream. Segregating queer youth, by their choice or otherwise, reduces the possibility for queering mainstream school environments – and despite the shadow of heteronormalization they cast, it is possible for mainstream school spaces to be subversive sites. A typical response to overt forms of homophobic harassment in schools, in the broader context of school bullying and violence as a political issue, is the emergence of safe spaces in schools. Rasmussen takes exception to this method, asserting quick fixes to homophobia like this are insufficient for truly shifting culture and subverting heteronormative realities (she also considers antihomophobia education and progressively intended segregated schools as insufficient quick fixes).

Perhaps Rasmussen gives short shrift to the importance of physical and emotional safety that is at the philosophical heart of segregated schools. Students who live with the daily emotional and physical violence that exists in schools may choose a safer reality, despite the theoretical limitations according to scholars such as Rasmussen. The goal of increased safety to learn seems like an important sentiment to foster. This does not mean that educators with queer pedagogies should stop work to shift the culture of mainstreams schools. Instead, I suggest the two could exist in tandem, ensuring the safety of students right now and in the future. Continuing work for safer, mainstream school experiences is important because many students and their families live outside the major urban centers where segregated schools tend to exist.

Short's (2013) work focuses on ways to bolster such safety by identifying further complexities in regards to heteronormativity. For instance, he outlines the ways that heteronormativity is not only hidden, but also overt within the curriculum. He emphasizes that, "the sense of heterosexual moral superiority, cultural achievement, and social privilege permeates all aspects of social life" (p. 117). Like Pinar (1998, 2007) and Rodriguez (2007), Short (2013) argues that heterosexuality's subjectivity and its constructed normalcy defines the queer other. In other words, queerness exists in relation to straightness and vice-versa (though not even-keeled). This relationship is dominated by heteronormativity, to which homosexuality poses a significant threat. Jackson (2006) argues that hegemonic heterosexuality enables heteronormativity to thrive, in the same way that hegemonic masculinity props up patriarchy (Connell 2007; Connell and Messerschmidt 2005). To this potent social construct, in schools in particular and in society more broadly (Pascoe 2007), homosexuality once again stands as a threat. Similar to Rasmussen (2004), Short (2013) believes that queer spaces in schools have the potential to be transformative and resist heteronormativity, that they are "a place where potential resistance may find expression" (p. 120). The consequences of unchallenged heteronormativity in schools include persistent, violent, and oppressive conditions in schools and educational contexts.

Challenging Homophobia, Heteronormativity, and Homonormativity

Yep (2002) outlines the violent impact of homophobia, heterosexism, and heteronormativity on everyday life for LGBTQ+ students (and staff) in educational settings. He underscores the urgent need for more activism for LGBTQ+ people in schools. The ideological power of heteronormativity, according to Yep, is its "invisibility disguised as 'natural', 'normal', 'universal' – its 'it-goes-without-saying' character" (p. 168). He further argues that administrators and educators can and should do more than offer politically neutered antihomophobia initiatives in schools, like poster campaigns. He calls for "a more complete understanding of the oppressiveness of our current sexual hierarchy" and adds that, with this broadened understanding, "everyone can celebrate their own form of human sexual expression rather than having 'LGBT Pride Day' once a year against the backdrop of 'Everyday is Heterosexual Pride Day'" (p. 174). The suggestion Yep makes here seems to suggest that everything and anything goes. I think that is a potentially dangerous proposition because straightness certainly gets enough time in the limelight. I present Yep's idea to emphasize the importance of making space for diverse expressions of gender and queer sexualities.

Efforts have emerged in the past 20 years in schools to address rampant homophobia. For example, students often participate in Pride parades and organize their own Pride groups, such as Gay–Straight Alliances (GSAs), and unions have equity committees to encourage progressive change. While it is true that strategies need to be implemented to address the oppressive mechanisms under which queer students learn in schools, antihomophobia efforts have significant limitations. Simply being against the systematic oppression of a group of people does not address the more fundamental issue: the privileging of straight people through the fostering (conscious or otherwise) of heteronormative assumptions.

Responding to this shortcoming, some scholars call for action that goes beyond antihomophobia initiatives. Goldstein, Russell, and Daley (2007), for instance, advocate for a queering of schools that involves "pedagogical practices that trouble the official knowledge of disciplines, disrupt heteronormativity, and promote an understanding of oppression as multiple, interconnected, and ever changing" (p. 187). Similar to Bryson and de Castell (1993), Yep (2002), Rasmussen (2004), and Goldstein et al. (2007) argue that one-off Pride days are insufficient to honor, not simply tolerate, the lived experiences of LGBTQ+ youth. Some in-school campaigns do notable work in raising awareness of LGBTQ+ issues. From my vantage point as a former secondary school teacher, I have witnessed an increase in the frequency of conversations about gender and sexuality and a greater emphasis on inclusion and safety for LGBTQ+ youth. However, the primary limitation of many of these initiatives is that they do not challenge, address, or discuss straight privilege, an important factor when discussing equity issues. Privilege is a valuable part of the conversation, but it is also the elephant in the room. If straight privilege is a topic on which people remain silent, schools will continue to reinforce homophobia, heteronormativity, and heterosexism (Fischer 2013; Ingraham and Saunders 2016; Pinar 1998, 2007; Rodriguez 2007). Schools should move, instead, toward a queering model of schooling wherein the experiences of queer youth are validated by schools as institutions in similar ways as their heterosexual counterparts (Goldstein et al. 2007). Ingraham and Saunders (2016) articulate a concept they call the heterosexual imaginary to address the ways that heterosexuality seems omnipresent even if it is not overt. The heterosexual imaginary includes "ways of thinking that conceal how heterosexuality structures gender and closes off any critical analysis of heterosexuality as an institution" (p. 1). Concerned with the way that heteronormativity and compulsory heterosexuality (Butler 2004; Eyre 1993; Rich 1980) anchor critical heterosexuality studies, the authors argue that "by leaving heterosexuality unexamined we do not examine how it is learned, what keeps it in place, and the interests it serves in the way it is practiced" (Ingraham and Saunders 2016, p. 2).

Kumashiro's (2000) anti-oppressive pedagogy provides a mechanism to queer schools and classrooms. Anti-oppressive education offers a platform for educators who seek to end discrimination in all its many forms and intersections – including, but not limited to, sexism/heterosexism, racism, classism, and ableism – within their classrooms and schools. Kumashiro posits that a failure to "work against the various forms of oppression [racism, sexism, heterosexism, homophobia, classism] is to be complicit with them" (p. 29). Kumashiro reminds educators that, to work toward ending oppression, teachers must be able to name it. Naming oppression requires seeing inequity and/or relations of power playing out in a systematically disadvantageous way for individuals or groups in a school or classroom. He also emphasizes that addressing one form of marginalization (e.g. sexism) and ignoring others (e.g. racism, decolonization, ableism), is an incomplete and fragmented approach to confronting oppression. Changing oppressive dynamics rooted in these power inequities requires what he calls disruptive knowledge not as an end, but rather as "a means toward the always-shifting end/goal of learning more" (p. 34). Kumashiro's (2004) framework provides a solid foundation from which straight teachers can advocate for a queering of schools instead of engaging in reactionary, surface-level strategies that are often the limit or extent of antihomophobia efforts.

In contrast to Kumashiro (2002, 2004), Short (2014) questions whether or not combating homophobia in schools should rest on the shoulders of teachers (and by default, students). He highlights the role that the legal system can and should have in influencing heteronormative school culture. Support for GSAs, under Bill 13 in Ontario, sends a message to all students that LGBTQ+ students are welcome in schools. Furthermore, the bill emerges "out of a culture of bullying that officially recognizes that homophobic and transphobic bullying occurs in schools and that it shouldn't be considered a generic form of harassment" (p. 332). He highlights the power of such legislation, for example, in instances where administrators have been reluctant or hesitant to name and deal with homophobic and transphobic bullying and pushes for shifts in school culture (Short 2014). Like Kumashiro (2000) and Goldstein et al. (2007), Short (2014) emphasizes that "mere 'inclusive' education is inadequate. More broad-based approaches of anti-oppressive education, which place culture itself in its sights, including the privileged and the othered, are required" (p. 340). He challenges people outside schools to assume responsibility and shift heteronormative culture, emphasizing that teachers and principals alone should not be responsible for creating this change. Allies occupy space in social movements in a multiplicity of contexts: activist-minded teachers are unlikely to want to stand idly by and witness systemic forms of discrimination in schools. Like Short (2014), I think antihomophobia activism should not rest solely on the shoulders of teachers. Pressure for systemic change from within social institutions like schools, will benefit from external pressure, policy, and leadership.

For MacIntosh (2007), school-based explorations of homophobia unintentionally reinforce sameness and often fall short in their goal to include queer perspectives. Those who create safe spaces in schools often fail to clarify who it is that may need to feel safe. Too often, inclusive programming focuses on eradicating homophobia, instead of recognizing "heteronormativity as a live incendiary device – and curriculum its tripwire" (p. 36). GSAs have the potential to disrupt heteronormativity and acknowledge the lived experiences of LGBTQ+ youth, but this potential does not necessarily translate into action. Schools may go so far as to acknowledge the damage heteronormativity does to queer youth, but doing so does not necessarily result in changes to school policy. Students (and teachers) involved in GSAs, both nonhetero and straight, are often positioned in school environments as positive role models. According to MacIntosh (2007), the trouble with role models is that they create "a homogeneous and successful gay/lesbian ideal juxtaposed to which there can only be a failed queer body" (p. 39). Too often, well-intended allies depend too heavily on GSAs, perceiving them to be the sole vehicle through which work by and for sexual minority youth and allies can and should occur.

Queering School Curriculum and Pedagogical Practice

If queering school culture, rather than implementing antihomophobia efforts, is the "what" of working against heterosexual privilege and heteronormativity in schools, another important consideration is the "who." Who are the people that lead or guide the process? For Short (2013), the "who" should include people outside of the school system. Griffin and Ouellett (2002) contend that institutional leaders and policies should guide the queering of schools. Often, the leaders of social change in schools are students and staff (Kitchen and Bellini 2013; LaPointe 2014). Many LGBTQ+ youth and adults work towards greater equity in schools as part of GSAs, on administrative or policy-developing committees (Griffin and Ouellett 2002; Kitchen and Bellini 2013; Ngo 2003; Schniedewind and Cathers 2003). There are also many straight-identified staff and student allies who participate in GSAs (Eichler 2010; GLSEN 2011; Kitchen and Bellini 2013; LaPointe 2014; Russell 2011; Taylor et al. 2011, 2015). While such efforts of straight teachers as advocates yield benefits, especially for GSA members, straight peoples' participation is not entirely unproblematic (Meyer 2007; Nicholls 2013). So too are there nonhetero teachers who do not espouse a queer pedagogy. I suggest here, that identity should not be the only factor that influences the proliferation of queer pedagogies. One's identity can influence personal values and beliefs, but that does not mean that all nonhetero teachers will espouse a queer pedagogy and all straight teachers will not. The relationship between identity and pedagogy is not so clearly delineated. It is possible that one's life experiences as a nonhetero teacher may foster a queer pedagogy, but straight teachers may also be compelled on moral, ethical, and/or human rights grounds.

In order to move queer pedagogical practice from an abstraction, I will provide a few example of classroom practices that reflect the values of queer pedagogy: multiple ways of knowing and being, transgressive, contesting the notion of one dominant "norm," and ever-changing. It is noteworthy, however, that this list is by no mean exhaustive and that for queer pedagogues, a keen eye for local context and gender dynamics is critical. Because of the fluidity of the boundaries of queer pedagogies, so too must its practitioners be willing to shift and change.

Presentations of gender

In order to reenvision classroom spaces outside the heteronormative binary, queer pedagogues should look to the way gender orders their lessons (and oftentimes, their thinking) in the classroom. As a former social sciences and humanities high school teacher, I often heard my colleagues in science and math state that it was "easy" to teach gender and other concepts in social sciences, but near impossible in their subject areas because of the rigors of the curriculum. I suggest that there are a number of opportunities, regardless of one's content area, to integrate content that challenges the gender/sexuality hierarchies. One important example is using gender-neutral pronouns (they/them/their) when introducing content or problems to students. Instead of relying on the traditional gender binary, using gender-neutral pronouns shifts the foundation of discourse in the classroom. Additionally word problems and/or assignments that include same-sex couples and/or nontraditional family configurations can be introduced. Such seemingly small steps are significant to shift school culture.

Encourage creativity

Create assignments for students that enable them to present their thinking in ways that make sense to them. While this suggestion is not squarely about gender or sexuality, it reflects the fluidity that is central to queer pedagogies. Assignments should create space for students to think divergently and approach their assignments without a rigid set of format expectations. This approach also challenges educators to consider the impact their teaching has on students. This is a mechanism to teach students about their own approach to learning and representing their learning, in addition to the formal curriculum. Importantly, it also centers the learning on the students themselves and inherently values multiple and different approaches and ways of doing.

Build community

Restorative circles are lauded by many as a way to build community in a classroom. Particularly because they destabilize the teacher–student binary where the teacher stands in front of rows of desks of students and imparts knowledge. A restorative or sharing circle creates a space of equanimity where all members of the classroom can gather to discuss classroom issues, daily life, and curriculum. This also helps students dismantle their own understanding of a learning environment and makes way for new, multiple experiences and possibilities. The community built from such circles provides an opportunity to solve problems, address conflicts, and create comradery amongst students. Often circles are guided by a series of questions, depending upon the context of the circle (daily check-in, problem-solving or otherwise) the questions can be whimsical, more critically focused, or assessment-based. Whimsical questions make room for student creativity. For example, if you could have one super power what would it be and why? More critical questions could include, where do you experience social privilege in your life? How might your life be different if you didn't have that privilege?

Acknowledge privilege

Queer pedagogy should be guided by critical self-reflective thinking. Mapping individual social location – considering the way privilege and oppression play a role in the lived experiences of students – is an important starting point. Using a graphic organizer like the so-called "Power Flower," students can consider different elements of their social location, and when and where they experience privilege. This is also an excellent entry point into learning about relations of power and can be done at all levels of education (K–12; post-secondary) effectively. It is important in the facilitation of this exercise that privilege and oppression are presented as parts of a spectrum, not reinforced as a binary as this does not challenge the power structures that queer pedagogies aim to problematize.

Representations of (diverse) queer people

Educators guided by queer pedagogies should endeavor to include representation of diverse, queer people in their teaching consistently and authentically. Engagement with literature written by queer authors, films with queer actors, and media (blogs, print media) written by queer people are valuable means of creating diverse queer representations. Avoiding the "Add-Queers-and-Stir" trappings means authentically engaging with opportunities to bring queer voices and perspectives into a classroom (Rands 2009). Additionally, these representations should be intersectional, that is, this content should include racialized people, trans folks, dis/abled, fat, and otherwise queer people. As a cautionary example, in a recent course I taught whose focus was the intersection of social justice, equity, and sport culture, I noted that many of my illustrative examples of politically active athletes were straight and cisgender. Instead of covering this up and tokening queer perspectives, I led my undergraduate class in a discussion about how this exclusion might happen and how it could be rectified. The discussion revealed that my own straight, cisgender privilege played a role, but also that this was an area of greater accountability for the sporting world as there are few out queer professional athletes in North America.

This list of strategies is by no means exhaustive as queer pedagogies demand rigorous self-reflection of practitioners. In other words, there is not a recipe or one-size-fits-all approach to practicing a queer pedagogy. It is a commitment to thinking divergently, against the grain, and (re)creating new spaces from which to learn and grow for educators and students.

Future Directions

In an educational landscape that increasingly values intersectional perspectives – those that recognize the diverse experiences of marginalized peoples – queer pedagogies are situated well to gain further foothold in schooling and education. Beyond establishing queer-only schools like Harvey Milk in New York and The Triangle Project in Toronto, educators are being called upon to infuse critical perspectives including queer ones, into their classrooms and schools. For some, neoliberal educational settings, the erosion of labor unions can create a hostile environment for these values to flourish. Despite that, educators who value antiracism and antisexist teaching are also turning their gaze to the connections between queer and antihomophobia education. Put differently, equity-minded educators are focused not on being "one trick ponies," but rather on the multiplicity of ways that can create space in their classrooms and educational settings for marginalized experiences (Potvin, 2019). One such example is the work of Driskill, Finley, Gilley, and Morgensen (2011) who focus on queer indigenous experiences, including the ways that colonization regulates life for indigenous people, but also for people of all genders. Heteropatriarchy, they argue, is a key strategy of colonization. Elsewhere, Morgensen (2011) suggests the ways that settler colonialism and homophobia conflate to marginalize queer indigenous people and also white/settler queerness as normative. Intersectional scholarship such as this provides an opportunity for educators and educational scholars to deepen their understanding of the relations of power that influence and effect their activities. Decolonizing the education system – recognizing and working to dismantle a colonial past in education – can also help address inequities, such as those that exist between queer and nonqueer people.

Conclusion

I position the significance of queer pedagogies as a mechanism for social change, and have presented this chapter as an outline of queer pedagogies while also applying a critical nudge to queer pedagogues, particularly straight ones, to work against their privilege in their practice. Certainly, queer pedagogies and activism involve a messy reenvisioning of educational institutions. However, challenging the status quo in schools in the form of queer pedagogy and activism is of critical importance and educators should not abandon their efforts if they experience resistance. Like queer theory itself, queer pedagogies can be defined by what they are not: rigidity, sameness, conformity. Instead queer pedagogies are fluid, difference-seeking, space-making, critical pedagogies that encourage multiplicity. While a singular approach to queer pedagogies does not exist, I have provided some suggestions that practicing and aspiring queer pedagogues can employ to further radicalize their practice and further contest the heteronormativity that often dominates educational spaces.

Notes

1 I use LGBTQ+ as the primary acronym throughout this chapter. It is conventional to include all these identities together under one umbrella term despite their distinctions and differences, as do other scholars and activists (Taylor et al. 2011, 2015).
2 See, for example, http://www.cbc.ca/news/canada/transgender-school-policies-bathrooms-student-voices-1.3589717
3 Examples of such safe space schools include Triangle, a school for LGBTQ+ identified students in Toronto (part of the Toronto District School Board) and the Harvey Milk School in New York.

References

Battiste, Marie. 2013. *Decolonizing Education: Nourishing the Learning Spirit*. Saskatoon, SK: Purich Publishing.

Berlant, Lauren and Michael Warner. 1995. "What Does Queer Theory Teach Us About X?" *PMLA* 110(3): 343–349.

Bishop, Anne. 2002. *Becoming an Ally: Breaking the Cycle of Oppression in People*. London, UK: Zed Books.

Britzman, Deborah P. 1995. "Is There a Queer Pedagogy? Or, Stop Reading Straight." *Educational Theory* 45(2): 151–165.

Bryson, Mary and Suzanne de Castell. 1993. "Queer Pedagogy: Praxis Makes Im/Perfect." *Canadian Journal of Education / Revue Canadienne de l'éducation* 18(3): 285–305.

Butler, Judith. 1990[2011]. *Gender Trouble: Feminism and the Subversion of Identity*. New York, NY: Routledge.

Butler, Judith. 2004. *Undoing Gender*. New York, NY: Routledge.

Coloma, Roland Sintos. 2006. "Putting Queer to Work: Examining Empire and Education." *International Journal of Qualitative Studies in Education* 19(5): 639–657.

Coloma, Roland Sintos. 2013. Ladlad and Parrhesiastic Pedagogy: Unfurling LGBT Politics and Education in the Global South. *Curriculum Inquiry* 43(4): 483–511.

Connell, R.W. 2007. *Masculinities*, 2nd edn. Cambridge, UK: Polity.

Connell, R.W. and James W. Messerschmidt. 2005. "Hegemonic Masculinity: Rethinking the Concept." *Gender & Society* 19(6): 829–859. Available at: http://www.jstor.org/stable/27640853

Driskill, Qwo-Li, Chris Finley, Brian Joseph Gilley, and Scott Lauria Morgensen. 2011. "Introduction." In *Queer Indigenous Studies: Critical Interventions in Theory, Politics, and Literature*, edited by Qwo-Li Driskill, Chris Finley, Brian Joseph Gilley, and Scott Lauria Morgensen, 1–31. Tucson, AZ: University of Arizona Press.

Dworkin, Sari H. 1989. "Not in Man's Image: Lesbians and the Cultural Oppression of Body Image." *Women & Therapy* 8(1–2): 27–39.

Eichler, Matthew. 2010. "Joining the Family: Experiences of Being and Becoming Ally Activists of LGBTQ+ People." *Journal of Transformative Education* 8(2): 89–102.

Eyre, Linda. 1993. "Compulsory Heterosexuality in a University Classroom." *Canadian Journal of Education / Revue Canadienne de L'éducation* 18(3): 273–284.

Finley, Chris. 2011. "Decolonizing the Queer Native Body (and Recovering the Native Bull-Dyke): Bringing 'Sexy Back' and Out of Native Studies' Closet." In *Queer Indigenous Studies: Critical Interventions in Theory, Politics, and Literature*, edited by Qwo-Li Driskill, Chris Finley, Brian Joseph Gilley, and Scott Lauria Morgensen, 32–42. Tucson, AZ: University of Arizona Press.

Fischer, Nancy L. 2013. "Seeing "Straight," Contemporary Critical Heterosexuality Studies and Sociology: An Introduction." *The Sociological Quarterly* 54(4): 501–510.

Foucault, Michel. 1978. *The History of Sexuality, Vol.* 1. New York, NY: Random House.

Foucault, Michel and Jay Miskowiec. 1986. "Of Other Spaces." *Diacritics* 16(1): 22–27. doi 10.2307/464648.

Francis, Dennis A. 2012. "Teacher Positioning on the Teaching of Sexual Diversity in South African Schools." *Culture, Health & Sexuality* 14(6): 597–611.

Francis, Dennis and Thabo Msibi. 2011. "Teaching About Heterosexism: Challenging Homophobia in South Africa." *Journal of LGBT Youth* 8(2): 157–173.

Gay Lesbian & Straight Education Network (GLSEN). 2011. *The 2011 National School Climate Survey: The Experiences of Lesbian, Gay, Bisexual, and Transgender Youth in Our Nation's Schools.* New York, NY: GLSEN.

Goldstein, Tara, Vanessa Russell, and Andrea Daley. 2007. "Safe, Positive and Queering Moments in Teaching Education and Schooling: A Conceptual Framework." *Teaching Education* 18(3): 183–199.

Griffin, Pat and Mathew L. Ouellett. 2002. "Going Beyond Gay-Straight Alliances to Make Schools Safe for Lesbian, Gay, Bisexual, and Transgender Students." *Angles: The Policy Journal of the Institute for Gay and Lesbian Strategic Studies* 6(1): 1–7. Available at: http://www.schools-out.org.uk/research/docs/Angles_61.pdf

Halperin, David M. 1997. *Saint Foucault: Towards a Gay Hagiography.* New York, NY: Oxford University Press.

Ingraham, Chrys and Casey Saunders. 2016. "Heterosexual Imaginary." *The Wiley Blackwell Encyclopedia of Gender and Sexuality Studies*, edited by Nancy A. Naples, 1–4. Hoboken, NJ: Wiley Blackwell.

Jackson, Stevi. 2006. "Gender, Sexuality and Heterosexuality: The Complexity (and Limits) of Heteronormativity." *Feminist Theory* 7(1): 105–121.

Kitchen, Julian and Christine Bellini. 2013. "Making Schools Safe and Inclusive: Gay-Straight Alliances and School Climate in Ontario." *Canadian Journal of Educational Administration and Policy* 146(1): 1–37.

Kumashiro, Kevin K. 2000. Toward a Theory of Anti-Oppressive Education. *Review of Educational Research* 70(1): 25–53.

Kumashiro, Kevin K. 2002. *Troubling Education: "Queer" Activism and Anti-Oppressive Pedagogy.* New York, NY: Routledge.

Kumashiro, Kevin K. 2004. *Against Common Sense: Teaching and Learning Toward Social Justice.* New York, NY: Routledge.

LaPointe, Alicia A. 2014. "Gay–Straight Alliance (GSA) Members' Engagement with Sex Education in Canadian High Schools." *Sex Education* 14(6): 1–11.

Linville, Darla. 2009. "Queer Theory and Teen Sexuality: Unclear Lines." In *Theory and Educational Research: Toward Critical Social Explanation*, edited by Jean Anyon, 156–174. New York, NY: Routledge.

Luhmann, Susanne. 1998. "Queering/Querying Pedagogy? Or, Pedagogy is a Pretty Queer Thing." In *Queer Theory in Education*, edited by William F. Pinar, 141–155. Mahwah, NJ: Lawrence Erlbaum.

MacIntosh, Lori B. 2007. "Does Anyone Have a Band-Aid? Anti-Homophobia Discourses and Pedagogical Impossibilities." *Educational Studies* 39(3): 33–43.

Martino, Wayne. 1999. "'It's Okay to be Gay': Interrupting Straight Thinking in the English Classroom." In *Queering Elementary Education: Advancing the Dialogue About Sexualities and Schooling*, edited by W.J. Letts IV, J. T. Sears, 137–150. Lanham, MD: Rowman & Littlefield.

Meyer, Elizabeth J. 2007. "'But I'm Not Gay': What Straight Teachers Need to Know About Queer Theory." In *Queering Straight Teachers: Discourse and Identity in Education*, edited by Nelson M. Rodriguez and William F. Pinar, 15–29. New York, NY: Peter Lang.

Morgensen, Scott Lauria. 2011. *Spaces Between Us: Queer Settler Colonialism and Indigenous Decolonization.* Minneapolis, MN: University of Minnesota Press.

Mountian, Ilania. 2014. *A Critical Analysis of Public Policies on Education and LGBT Rights in Brazil. IDS Evidence Report 61.* Brighton: IDS. Available at: https://opendocs.ids.ac.uk/opendocs/handle/123456789/3614

Ngo, Bic. 2003. Citing Discourses: Making Sense of Homophobia and Heteronormativity at Dynamic High School. *Equity & Excellence in Education* 36(2): 115–124.

Nicholls, Rachael. 2013. Que(e)rying my Teacher Identity. *Journal of LGBT Youth* 10(4): 388–393.

Pascoe, C.J. 2007. *Dude, You're a Fag: Masculinity and Sexuality in High School*. Berkeley, CA: University of California Press.

Pinar, William F. 1998. "Introduction." In *Queer Theory in Education*, edited by William F. Pinar, 1–39. Mahwah, NJ: Lawrence Erlbaum.

Pinar, William F. 2007. "Introduction: A Queer Conversation, Toward Sustainability." In *Queering Straight Teachers: Discourse and Identity in Education*, edited by Nelson M. Rodriguez and William F. Pinar, 1–14. New York, NY: Peter Lang.

Potvin, Leigh. 2016. "Radical Heterosexuality: Straight Teacher Activism in Schools: Does Ally-Led Activism Work?" *Confero: Essays on Education, Philosophy and Politics* 4(1): 9–36.

Potvin, Leigh. 2019. Straight teacher allies: Lessons from compassionate educators. "The Compassionate Educator: Understanding Social Issues and the Ethics of Care in Canadian Schools" (pp. 73–90). In A. Jule (Ed.). Toronto, ON: Canadian Scholars Press.

Rands, Kathleen. 2009. "Mathematical Inqu[ee]ry: Beyond 'Add-Queers-and-Stir' Elementary Mathematics Education." *Sex Education* 9(2), 181–191. doi: 10.1080/14681810902829646.

Rasmussen, Mary Louise. 2004. "Safety and Subversion: The Production of Sexualities and Genders in School Spaces." In *Youth and Sexualities: Pleasure, Subversion, and Insubordination in and out of Schools*, edited by Mary Louise Rasmussen, Eric Rofes, and Susan Talburt, 131–152. New York, NY: Palgrave MacMillan.

Rich, Adrienne. 1980. "Compulsory Heterosexuality and Lesbian Existence." *Signs* 5(4): 631–660.

Rodriguez, Nelson M. 2007. "Preface: Just Queer It." In *Queering Straight Teachers: Discourse and Identity in Education*, edited by Nelson M. Rodriguez and William F. Pinar, vii–xii. New York, NY: Peter Lang.

Rodriguez, Nelson M. and William F. Pinar. 2007. *Queering Straight Teachers: Discourse and Identity in Education*. New York, NY: Peter Lang.

Russell, Glenda M. 2011. "Motives of Heterosexual Allies in Collective Action for Equality." *Journal of Social Issues* 67(2): 376–393.

Schniedewind, Nancy and Karen Cathers. 2003. "Becoming Allies for Each Other: An Inclusive Approach for Confronting Heterosexism in Schools." *Equity & Excellence in Education* 36(2): 184–193.

Sedgwick, Eve Kosofsky. 1985. *Between Men: English Literature and Male Homosocial Desire*. New York, NY: Columbia University Press.

Sedgwick, Eve Kosofsky. 1993. *Tendencies*. Durham, NC: Duke University Press.

Seidman, Steven. 1994. "Queer-ing Sociology, Sociologizing Queer Theory: An Introduction." *Sociological Theory* 12(2): 166–177.

Sensoy, Özlem and Robin DiAngelo. 2012. *Is Everyone Really Equal?: An Introduction to Key Concepts in Social Justice Education*. New York, NY: Teachers College Press.

Short, D. 2013. *Don't Be So Gay!: Queers, Bullying, and Making Schools Safe*. Vancouver, BC: UBC Press.

Short, Donn. 2014. "Queering Schools, Gay-Straight Alliances, and the Law." In *The Gay Agenda: Claiming Space, Identity, and Justice*, edited by G. Walton, 327–344. New York, NY: Peter Lang.

Taylor, Catherine and Tracey Peter, with Stacey Beldom, et al. 2011. *Every Class in Every School: Final Report on the First National Climate Survey on Homophobia, Biphobia, and Transphobia in Canadian Schools*. Full Report. Ottawa, ON: Egale Canada. Available at: http://egale.ca/wp-content/uploads/2011/05/EgaleFinalReport-web.pdf.

Taylor, Catherine, Tracey Peter, Christopher Campbell, et al. 2015. *The Every Teacher Project on LGBTQ-inclusive education in Canada's K-12 Schools*. Final Report. Winnipeg, MB: Manitoba Teachers' Society. Available at: http://news-centre.uwinnipeg.ca/wp-content/uploads/2016/01/EveryTeacher_FinalReport_v12.pdf.

Walton, Gerald. 2005. "'Bullying Widespread': A Critical Analysis Of Research On Public Discourse On Bullying." *Journal of School Violence* 4(1): 91–118.

Walton, Gerald. 2006. "H-Cubed: A Primer on Bullying and Sexuality Diversity for Educators. *Professional Development Perspectives* 6(2): 13–20.

Yep, Gust A. 2002. "From Homophobia and Heterosexism to Heteronormativity: Toward the Development of a Model of Queer Interventions in the University Classroom." *Journal of Lesbian Studies* 6(3–4): 163–176.

Part III
Health, Science, and Psychology

8

Sexuality, Science, and Technology

DONNA J. DRUCKER

Introduction

Science and technology have served multiple purposes in people's sex lives: to query, understand, and/or suppress sexual behaviors, desires, and identities; to augment and to restrict fertility; and to enhance current pleasures and to discover new ones. This chapter examines how developments in science and technology have influenced sexuality and how sexuality has influenced the direction of science and technology. It provides an overview of scholarship on these intersections from three specific perspectives: the history of the learned, academic study of human sexuality (aka sexology or sexual science); research and development regarding fertility control and its availability (in the forms of both promotion and prevention); and the intersectional history of technology with the expression of erotic desire.

New forms of knowledge about human sexuality (including identity, desire, and behavior) that multiple sciences and technologies have produced over time strongly affect everyday forms of behavior, personhood, and imagination. These forms of knowledge also inform social structures that police, punish, control, or free human sexual expression. Those sciences and technologies and their dissemination or suppression are deeply embedded in historical and political contexts. This chapter's focus is on scholarship in the three areas identified above in the United States, Western Europe, and Eastern Europe in the nineteenth and twentieth centuries. It also includes references to works on Africa, Asia, and South America. It concludes with an examination of how sexuality may intersect with science and technology in the future, specifically in the development of queer and feminist perspectives on science and technology studies.

Histories of sexuality attempting worldwide coverage tend to focus on the scientific and technological aspects in the last quarter of the nineteenth century and the early years of the twentieth century (Garton 2006; Herzog 2011). Exceptions include histories of a particular behavior or experience, such as Thomas Laqueur's history of masturbation (2003), Angus McLaren's history of impotence (2007), and Norman E. Himes's ([1936] 1970) and John M. Riddle's (1994, 1999) histories of contraception and fertility methods, which trace those behaviors and experiences back to the eighteenth century (Laqueur), the Western European Middle Ages (McLaren), and ancient Egypt (Himes and Riddle). Overarching histories of European and North American sexuality center their attention on the development of sexual science (largely in the medical and legal professions) at the turn of the last century; however, some scholars argue for dating the advent of sexual science earlier (McLaren 1999; Beccalossi and Crozier 2011; Clark 2011; Ronsin 2011; Dennis 2011; Hekma 2011; Herzog 2011). The emergence of sexual science is also closely linked to the turn-of-the-last-century historical moment when, in Michel Foucault's famous phrase, "the sodomite had been a temporary aberration, the homosexual was now a species," and a scientia sexualis emerged in Western countries (Foucault [1978] 1990, p. 43; Beccalossi and Crozier 2011; Bauer 2015). In his most famous treatise on sexuality, *History of Sexuality,* volume 1, Foucault identifies that moment as 1870, when Carl Westphal published "Die Konträre Sexualempfindung [The Contrary Sexual Feeling]" describing one man's and one woman's difficulties with their interests in becoming a member of the opposite sex (Westphal 1869–1870; Hirschfeld 1914; Bullough 1994; Beccalossi 2011; Leck 2016). However, in a series of lectures in 1974–1975, Foucault moved that date earlier, to 1844, the year Heinrich Kaan's *Psychopathia Sexualis* was published (Foucault 2003; Kaan 2016). The following discussion begins there.

Sexual Science as a Field of Academic Study

Although the science's precise origins are an ongoing subject of scholarly debate, most scholars agree that a specific science of sex developed around the last quarter of the nineteenth and beginning of the twentieth century (Bullough 1994). Academic debates about the origins of sexual science intersect with historiographies about empire-building, colonialism, imperialism, nation-building, national identity, and the role of language in expressing desire (Frühstück 2004; Tobin 2015; Willey 2016; Bauer 2017). Those debates are likewise interconnected with the advent of homosexuality as an identity category, and sexual deviance (including homosexuality) as a category of illness requiring treatment.

Scholars usually trace the origins of sexual science to German-speaking Europe, beginning as early as 1844 with the writings of Kaan, a Viennese physician whose Latin text *Psychopathia Sexualis* [*Psychopathology of Sex*] was a critical source for sexologists active in the later nineteenth century, including Iwan (aka Ivan) Bloch, Havelock Ellis, and Richard von Krafft-Ebing (Davidson 2001, Sigusch 2002, 2003; Sigusch and Grau 2008; Bauer 2015; Kaan 2016). Kaan largely focused on how masturbation impeded a healthy, reproductive sex life, and notably, if only briefly, argued that same-sex sexual desire was a psychological (as opposed to anatomic or neuroanatomic) element of human nature rooted in the imagination (Davidson 2001; Kaan 2016). In the late 1860s, Karl Maria Kertbeny and Karl Heinrich Ulrichs challenged Kaan's conceptions of same-sex human nature as pathological and needing treatment (Parkhill and Stephens 2011). They put forward concepts of same-sex selfhood that laid the foundations for a science of inquiry into conceptualizations of homosexuality (Herzer 1986; Hutter 1993; Brooks 2012; Leck 2016). Kertbeny advocated that people with "natural, fixed sexual identity deserve[d] the protection of the modern legal state," and he is best known for coining the words "homosexuality" and "homosexual" (Tobin 2015, pp. 14, 16; see also Katz 1995). Ulrichs, with whom Kertbeny corresponded, authored a series of pamphlets between 1865 and 1879 arguing that *Urnings* (men) and *Urningins* (women) had erotic drives belonging to the opposite gender; a natural, fixed sense of self that deserved equal legal protection (Beccalossi and Crozier 2011; Parkhill and Stephens 2011; Tobin 2015; Leck 2016).

Kertbeny's and Ulrichs's advocacy writing drew on depictions of same-sex relationships in classical Greco-Roman literature, the legal restructuring of sodomy codes in the German and Austro-Hungarian Empires, and considerations of sexual identity in the light of shifting empires, official languages, and nationalisms (Tobin 2015). Richard von Krafft-Ebing's popular work, also called *Psychopathia Sexualis* (first published 1886), advanced the idea that sexual behavior and desire deserved its own branch of scientific inquiry. Unlike Kertbeny and Ulrichs, Krafft-Ebing wanted to keep the professional study of sexual behavior under a specifically medical gaze. His book contained a rich catalog of detail on sex-related pathologies, some written in Latin to disguise them from noneducated readers (Oosterhuis 2000). Krafft-Ebing divided sexual deviation into four categories: paradoxia (sexual desire at the wrong time of life, i.e. childhood), anesthesia (insufficient desire), hyperesthesia (excessive desire), and paraethesia (sexual desire for the wrong goal or object, including same-sex desire) (Storr 2008; Downing 2011). Toward the end of his life, he rejected his earlier argument that same-sex desire was pathological, calling homosexuality an "anomaly" rather than a "sickness" (Krafft-Ebing 1901). However, he remained well-known for arguing that homosexuality was a perversion.

By the late nineteenth and early twentieth centuries, two strands within the study of sexual science were emerging: a medical, often psychoanalytic strand taking the perspective that sexual deviance needed correction and treatment, and an alternate strand that identified homosexuality as a possible deviance or pathology but usually avoided prescribing a cure (Herzog 2011; Beccalossi 2011). Dagmar Herzog writes that "psychoanalysis was just one of many in a welter of competing and overlapping thought-systems arising at the turn of the century to grapple with issues of gender and desire" (2017, p. 15). The first strand developed from Krafft-Ebing's thought on methodologies for categorizing sexual perversion and Freudian thought on women's sexuality and orgasm (Freud [1905] 1977). The second strand developed in different national contexts from the work of Havelock Ellis (England), Magnus Hirschfeld (Germany), and Robert Latou Dickinson (United States). However scientists decided to investigate sexuality, it is clear that "the construction of modern sexuality has deep roots in late nineteenth-century German thought" (Tobin 2015, p. 184, see also Trask 2014).

Sexual science flourished in a variety of directions in the later nineteenth and early twentieth centuries across the world. For one example, South African doctors used the term "kink" in their published case studies in this era as a catch-all metaphor for sexual problems that could potentially disturb white society (Hodes 2015).

For another, in late Tsarist and early Soviet Russia, sexual behavior was seen largely through three lenses: first, physicians treating syphilis, hermaphroditism, and victims of sexual violence; second, Russian adaptations and use of Freudian psychoanalysis; and third, increasing governmental attention to public health through regulations for urban sanitation (Engelstein 1986; Healey 2009; Mazanik 2015). Additionally, while sexological and psychoanalytic texts were widely available to physicians in German or in Russian translation, a homegrown sexual science literature did not emerge, as contemporary Russian culture placed little value on the individual sexual pleasure "which stand[s] at the heart of the Western construction of the modern subject" (Baer 2015, p. 130). Given space constraints, however, the following discussion focuses on the second strand of sexual science mentioned above.

Ellis, the English physician and prolific essayist, and Dickinson, the American physician and activist, were among the dominant figures in Anglo-American sexology. Ellis published his seven-volume study *Studies in the Psychology of Sex* between 1897 and 1910, and the first volume, *Sexual Inversion,* put forward an argument for the natural existence of homosexuality (Ellis 1897–1910). *Studies* was based largely on Ellis's (and collaborator John Addington Symonds's) personal experiences and extensive correspondence with individuals interested in their own sexual identities and patterns of desire (Ellis and Symonds [1897] 2008). The volumes were published in England, the US, and Germany at nearly the same time, and such wide distribution greatly expanded their scholarly reach and influence. The American polymath Dickinson, an obstetrician/gynecologist, birth control advocate, artist, author, and sex researcher, was active in sexual science from the 1890s until his death in 1950 (Reed 1978). In the present, he is best known for his obstetrical/gynecological drawings and sculptures, particularly of women's genitals, and for mentoring the entomologist-turned-sex-researcher Alfred Kinsey.

Hirschfeld used the tools of science and medicine to improve the lives of sexual nonconformists and "thus played an active part in the institution of sexual knowledge" (Bauer 2017, p. 3; see also Trask 2014). He published numerous books and articles on "the third sex" (a term for homosexuals that he later abandoned), "sexual intermediaries" (anyone not adhering strictly to homosexual or heterosexual behavior), transvestitism, prostitution, and hermaphroditism (Hirschfeld 1914, 1927a, 1927b; Herrn 2005). He also founded the advocacy organization Wissenschaftlich-humanitäres Komitee [Scientific Humanitarian Committee] in 1897, the Institute for Sexual Science in 1919, and the World League of Sexual Reform in 1928 – partnering with the Australian sexologist Norman Haire among others (Mancini 2010; Ronsin 2011; Wyndham 2012; Dose 2014; Leng 2017a). While Hirschfeld devoted his scientific energies to manifesting political and social reform on behalf of individuals with nonnormative sexualities, his Berlin contemporary Albert Moll's highest priority was "apolitical and impartial science" (Sigusch 2012, p. 184; see also Ronsin 2011 and Dose 2014 on Moll's and Hirschfeld's conflicts). Both Moll's contemporary Ellis and 1950s–1960s American successors William H. Masters and Virginia E. Johnson based their own explanations and research on orgasmic physiology on Moll's conception of the four phases of sexual response: arousal, plateau, orgasm, and resolution (Ellis and Symonds [1897] 2008; Masters and Johnson 1966).

The sexological works of Bloch, Moll, Hirschfeld, and Ellis, along with other synthetic texts in English and German, found receptive and interested audiences around the world (Frühstück 2003, 2004; Bauer 2015; Fuechtner, Haynes, and Jones 2017). A growing secondary literature also highlights how non-German and non-English-speaking scholars developed sciences of sexuality of their own at the turn of the last century, often through the professional fields of medicine, law, education, and criminology (Frühstück 2003; Beccalossi 2012; Fuechtner, Haynes and Jones 2017). Though these scholars were largely European men (or men of European descent), Kirsten Leng (2015, 2017b) and Britta McEwen (2016) draw attention to lesser-known women scholars and public sexual health advisors in Germany and Austria in the 1910s and 1920s. McEwen and Kristine von Soden (1998) highlight the role of women in providing scientifically based sexual advice in interwar Germany and Austria. As National Socialism and fascism gained power in Europe, however, sexual science was often shaded with arguments for eugenics and population control, as in Hungary (Kund 2016). Academic literature on German sexology is sharply divided into before, during, and after the National Socialist regime. Rainer Herrn (2005, 2013) has written on how German psychiatrists in general and sexual scientists like Hirschfeld in particular studied transsexualism and transvestitism before and during the Nazi era.

By the mid-twentieth century, sexual science in the US and Western Europe coalesced around efforts to understand sexuality as an integral element of human personhood, and scientific approaches to it naturally varied according to the researchers involved and their political and social interests. After the devastation of World War II in Europe and the dispersion, persecution, and deaths of sexual scientists and individuals with nonnormative sexualities, sexual science's professional center of gravity shifted to the US. Researchers from a variety of backgrounds continued to seek the origins of sexual desire – homosexual, heterosexual, bisexual, or otherwise (Rosario 1997; Terry 1999; Minton 2010; Ronsin 2011); to decouple stigmatizing identities from sexual behavior (Kinsey, Pomeroy, and Martin 1948, Kinsey et al. 1953); to use technology to change sexual orientation (Jagose 2012; Drucker 2014); or to investigate the basics of sexual anatomy and physiology (Masters and Johnson 1966). Some researchers, like the psychologist Harry Stack Sullivan, publicly agreed with, and upheld, the majority view that homosexuality was pathological (or at least unnatural), but maintained private hopes that society would someday change to accept them. After World War II, as Naoko Wake argues, such a split between private views and public research for sex researchers was no longer possible, as sexual minorities "began to see heteronormativity, not their own sexuality, as the ultimate problem" (2011, p. 42). After the Kinsey Reports were published, it became clear to liberal sexual scientists that attempts to modify the behavior of homosexual individuals were misguided medically as well as socially: the lives of sexual minorities would improve once heterosexually dominated society changed to accept them fully into American life. While the disseminated research of sexual scientists could have a definitive impact on American society, those scientists struggled between preserving their sense of objectivity, and producing applied scholarship that had the potential to improve the lives of sexual minorities.

In addition to pursuing more wide-ranging inquiries into homosexuality, starting in the 1930s, American sex researchers began to connect their investigations of behavior with other elements of selfhood, such as intersexuality, race and ethnicity, hormones, genetics, and sociocultural conceptions of gender as related to, but independent of, traditional markers of biological sex (Rosario 1997; Irvine [2005] 2010). To take one example, John Money established the term "gender" in 1957 as a keyword for capturing the sociocultural elements of maleness and femaleness both within and beyond elements of biological sex (Money, Hampson, and Hampson 1957). He also designed a new diagnostic vocabulary for paraphilias (in the shadow of Krafft-Ebing's four categories of perversions) that included among its "six grand paraphilic stratagems" "sacrificial/expiatory" and "stigmatic/eligibilic" (Downing 2014, p. 46). Money also suggested the term "fuckology" as an umbrella for sexual science, part of his attempt to use more true-to-life, nonacademic vocabulary in the clinical, academic study of sexuality (Money 1988; Downing, Morland, and Sullivan 2014, pp. 2–3). The term never took hold in the academic community, as its crudeness undermined the seriousness of Money's scientific claims. Nonetheless, it remains a provocative word that vividly captures the underlying radicalism of studying sexuality and the flesh-and-blood nature of sex itself, as opposed to the more genteel terms "sexology" and "sexual science."

Along with sexology's expansion into a developing field of women's studies and gender studies, and increased attention to sex-related anatomy, endocrinology, neurology, and physiology, homosexuality remained a perennial topic of scientific interest. The majority of American researchers who studied homosexuality in any capacity before and after World War II disavowed any political interests in, or motivations behind, their research on the topic, claiming that their primary interests were in pure discovery (Wake 2011; Irvine [2005] 2010; Kinsey, Pomeroy, and Martin 1948; Kinsey et al. 1953). Nevertheless, the social, legal, and medical implications of research like Kinsey's were clear to anyone reading it.

Beyond postwar sex research in Western Europe and the United States, the field of sexology in Eastern Europe flourished from the 1970s onward. State socialism deeply affected the context and goals of sexology in Central and Eastern Europe. Hadley Z. Renkin and Agnieszka Kościańska (2016), in a special issue of *Sexualities*, together point out the continuing need for more research on sexualities in this area, especially given the development of sexual science as a marker of scientific, intellectual modernity and "authentic" European identity. Kościańska (2014, 2016) shows how authors of Polish sex research and popular advice literature advocated for gender equality in public life but ongoing male dominance in heterosexual private life (see also Lišková 2016 on Czechoslovakia). The political and economic contexts of socialism and postsocialism, along with the tradition of combining medical training with philosophy and activism, is critical to understanding how sexual science developed in these countries. The narrative of sexual science as a whole demonstrates the importance of historical, social, and political contexts to what is known generally about human sexuality.

Birth Control: The Intersections of Technology and (Hetero)Sexuality

The idea that technologies outside of the body can be used to improve fertility or to avoid pregnancy predates recorded history. As Himes wrote in the 1930s, "in virtually every culture which is of historic importance the author discovers the presence of a *desire* to control fertility" (Himes [1936] 1970, p. ix, emphasis in original). Humans have attempted to prevent pregnancy by using withdrawal and having other extravaginal forms of sex, and women have tried to become pregnant by holding their legs in the air following intercourse to speed the flow of sperm into the uterus. Himes, Robert Jütte, McLaren, and Riddle have shown how, throughout recorded history, humans have also used or tried to use many kinds of nonbodily barrier methods, both male- and female-oriented; different types of food, drink, and medicine to encourage or discourage conception; and a variety of timing methods, often in concert with religious or spiritual beliefs along with family and social structures (Riddle 1994, 1999). Riddle's argument in both *Contraception and Abortion from the Ancient World to the Renaissance* and *Eve's Herbs,* that knowledge of contraceptive and abortive methods was strong in the ancient and early medieval European world but was gradually lost over time, remains provocative but unconvincing to many academic reviewers (Crellin 2012; see also Nelson 2009; McLaren 1990; Jütte [2003] 2008).

In addition to Himes's, McLaren's, Jütte's, and Riddle's wide-reaching surveys of contraception across world areas and cultures, some historians have traced the development of a particular technology over time, such as Heather Munro Prescott's study of the creation, availability, and use of the morning-after pill in recent American and Canadian history (2011); Chikako Takeshita's study of the global reach of the intrauterine device (IUD) from the 1960s through the present and how its availability and meaning changed over time and scale (2011); and Wolfgang König's examination of condom manufacture, distribution, and use in Germany from the country's unification in 1871 through the present (2016, see also Herzog 2011). Knowledge of contraceptive methods in Germany in the late nineteenth and early twentieth centuries spread both through publications, specifically the popular naturopathic Bilz guide, and through informal "Question Evenings" at Hirschfeld's Institute for Sexual Science in Berlin (Herzog 2011; Dose 2014). Additionally, sex researchers in the same era, including Hirschfeld and Marie Stopes in England, lent their scientific authority to specific brands of contraceptives to generate income (Herzog 2011; Dose 2014). Sanjam Ahluwalia, Daksha Parmar, Sanjay Srivastava, Shrikant Botre, and Douglas E. Haynes identify how ideas and practices of nationalism, law, media, and science affect how birth control access and use, sexuality, and femininity/masculinity function in both colonial and postcolonial Indian contexts (Ahluwalia 2008; Haynes 2012; Srivastava 2013; Ahluwalia and Parmar 2016; Botre and Haynes 2017). However, the following discussion focuses on the historical development of birth control technology in the early- to mid-twentieth century United States, Mexico, and Caribbean.

Scholarship on birth control technologies in the North American context is grouped around two areas. The first area concerns the activist Margaret Sanger and people who collaborated (and clashed) with her; the creation and establishment of the American Birth Control League (later Planned Parenthood) in New York City; and the founding of local clinics nationwide for the distribution of woman-controlled barrier methods (diaphragms, cervical caps, and spermicide) (Eig 2014; Hajo 2010; Holz 2014; see also McEwen 2016 for the Austrian equivalent; Cook 2005 and Fisher 2006 for the British equivalent). These barriers were imported, manufactured and sold clandestinely through local advertisements, or manufactured and distributed through physicians (Tone 2002). It is difficult to know how women users of these technologies felt about or experienced using these technologies, especially over time, except by reading through the lines of primary source literature directed to physicians from manufacturers and physicians' reports on birth control use by their users and patients (Drucker 2016). It seems clear, however, that women had mixed emotions about woman-controlled barrier methods. They often would abandon a technology or switch to another one depending on a variety of factors, such as if their partners had a religious objection; their ambivalence about pregnancy; their own or their partner's pain or discomfort; and the availability, cost, and ease of use (and replacement) of a method.

The other primary area of North American birth control scholarship is the development, testing, and use of the hormonal pill in Mexico, the United States, and the Caribbean from the 1940s through the 1960s (McLaren 1990; Watkins 2001; Marks [2001] 2010, Jütte [2003] 2008; May 2011; Eig 2014). The challenge for historians of hormonal birth control and responses to it is to balance attention to the scientists, activists, and philanthropists who were central to the development of the pill, on the one hand and to the hundreds of women (largely poor women of color in Puerto Rico) upon whom the pill was tested, often with severe health complications (including sterility), on the other. Historians like Michelle Murphy (2012) place their analysis of the pill's effect on American women's health, feminist activism, and the design and use of do-it-yourself emmenagogues (agents that promote menstruation) and abortion techniques in a broader context of population control, institutionalized sexism and racism, and health politics in the neoliberal state. While Murphy's focus is on the Feminist Women's Health Center (later part of the National Women's Health Network) in Los Angeles, California, her conclusions extend to the role of woman-oriented technologies beyond birth control in establishing or limiting cross-race, cross-class feminist solidarity around women's health.

Curiously, though heterosexual sexual behavior preconditions the need or desire for contraceptive technology in the first place, the discussion of sexual acts themselves is often limited in the above-mentioned historiographical literature on contraception. May (2011) is an exception, as she incorporates oral history interviews and online surveys from English-speaking women who have used or were currently using the pill, along with reflection on her own experience. The link between specific forms, positions, and lengths of time for sexual behavior and the efficacy of specific forms of contraception remains largely unexplored, except in a handful of little-known experiments conducted by Masters and Johnson in the early 1960s (Johnson and Masters 1962, 1963, 1965; Johnson, Masters, and Lewis 1964). Those studies found that commercially available spermicides and cervical caps worked best when women lay prone during heterosexual sex, and were less effective if the activity was rigorous, lasted more than a few minutes, or if the female partner was above the male partner. This ongoing gap between studies of contraception and what heterosexuals actually do during sex has real consequences for contraceptive efficacy, and demonstrates how manufacturer's personal ideas of how and how long sex takes place affects the physical and chemical composition of contraceptive technology.

Technologies for both supporting and suppressing fertility are continuously under development. Treatments for supporting fertility involving medical technology include intrauterine insemination and in vitro fertilization (Clarke 1998). The most widely known technologies for suppressing fertility in the past two decades are largely adjustments to existing concepts: delivering dosages of different combinations of hormones in a variety of forms (i.e. through injections or implants instead of pills); modifications of barrier methods to be used with spermicides (i.e. Lea's Shield); and hormonal and nonhormonal intrauterine devices (IUDs) that can be left in the uterus for up to 10 years (Mirena and Paraguard, respectively). None of these methods, however, is 100% effective with typical use and/or without some risk to women's health.

Regarding male-controlled methods, condom manufacturers tinker endlessly with materials, colors, sizes, and custom-made versions, and a male hormonal pill has been in development off-and-on for several decades (Oudshoorn 2003). Behavioral methods like natural family planning and withdrawal retain popularity among non-religious women who aim for "natural" lifestyles and conservative women who adhere strictly to Roman Catholic teaching on contraception (Drucker 2015; Weschler 2015). The story of birth control's technological development is far from over, and a painless, harmless, flexible-use inexpensive, simple-to-manufacture form of birth control that all sexually active individuals can agree on is still in the future.

Technology, Erotic Desire, and Sexual Expression

The presence of erotic- and sex-oriented objects from preliterate societies onwards demonstrates that the history of desire can be traced through those objects and the technologies that produce them. In literate societies, of course, histories of desires are also found in texts. Through the centuries, erotic objects, artwork, and texts have also been camouflaged or hidden, such as electromechanical vibrators marketed for muscle pain or erotic literature in books with nonerotic covers (Maines 1989). From the mid-twentieth century onward, objects more specifically designated for sexual pleasure have been available through mail-order and in storefronts (Archibald 2005, Heineman 2011; Lieberman 2017). In the present, sex-related technologies are also widely available for order on the internet and have become part of the consumer capitalist landscape. Given the great diversity of intersections between technology and sexuality, especially in the last 150 years, this section focuses on two: first, historical developments in printing and image-reproduction technologies and second, the ways that technologies have been used in sexual science.

First, the interrelated advance of pornography, technology, and subsequent regulation is visible multinationally: laws regarding the manufacture, sale, import, and distribution of obscene material followed closely the widening availability of visual images, particularly postcards, in Australia, the UK, and the US in the late nineteenth century. Ruth Ford points out that "increasing regulation, detection, and prosecution...point to the increasing concerns of the state and moral reformers regarding visual erotica from the 1860s, as new photographic technologies enabled the production and reproduction of erotic imagery for new audiences" (2011, p. 189). Kelly Dennis identifies a further development in image technologies that increased the potential for pornography production: half-tone processes, which allowed newspapers to print photographs directly instead of through engravings:

> The continued technological development in the twentieth century of photography represents perhaps the single biggest impact on visual culture generally and erotic imagery in particular. As the circulation in mass-market magazines increased, so did the market of erotic and pornographic magazines. (2011, p. 210)

The advent of moving images shifted the technological landscape once again, as pornographers quickly embraced a new media that allowed for group viewing – the first known pornographic film dates to 1896 (Ford 2011). Though censorship boards followed the establishment of movie theaters, production companies, and distribution companies, pornographers were consistently among the first users of new media technologies. Jonathan Coopersmith (1998, 2000, 2006) identifies the ways that the growth of the pornography industry in the 1980s and beyond was inseparable from the technologies in which it was embedded: videotape, home computers and software, and then the internet (see also Dennis 2011). As Gert Hekma summarizes:

> Any time a new medium was invented, especially after the sexual revolution, it was immediately used for eroticism.…Yet the more sex a new medium offers, the quicker and broader it is spread and accepted. (2011, p. 18)

Second, scientists have used technology in diverse ways to study sexuality. Many scholars identified in the first section of this chapter primarily used face-to-face interviews or clinical visits, letters, and close readings of literature. For others, electromechanical technologies such as photography, cardiographs, and electroencephalograms were integral to their findings (Drucker 2014). For example, Kinsey's analysis of more than 18,000 individual interviews would not have been possible without punched-card machines to process and to compile the data therein (Kinsey et al. 1948; Kinsey et al. 1953; Drucker 2013). Some sex researchers, famously including Wilhelm Reich and Masters and Johnson, developed their own technologies to support sexual energies and to examine physiological responses to sexual stimuli. Reich's orgone energy accumulator, or "orgone box," was designed to recharge the energy field of the person sitting inside it and improve their sexual energy, among other effects (Reich [1942] 1986). Masters and Johnson invented a dildo-camera with the assistance of a technician, which recorded still and moving images of a woman's vagina and cervix as she masturbated to orgasm (Johnson and Masters 1962, 1963, 1965; Drucker 2014). The photographic images from those studies are only available in one relatively obscure publication (Johnson, Masters, and Lewis 1964), while the researchers chose instead to use pen-and-ink charts of changes in blood pressure and sketches of tumescence and detumescence in *Human Sexual Response* (Masters and Johnson 1966). Annamarie Jagose identifies the meaning of their decision to represent orgasm so obliquely:

> Non-pictorial medico-sexological imagings of aroused and orgasmic human bodies are less obviously, but no less saliently, structured by the requirements of mechanical and

decorporealized objectivity....The authoritativeness of such images nevertheless depends on the representational distance they take from the conventionally pictorial. (2012, p. 174)

In short, technology could enhance sex research or obscure and deeroticize it, and producing images of orgasm itself – whether in pornographic film or science – remains an elusive process, given that orgasm is "a sensory event resistant to everyday perceptual capture" (Jagose 2012). However, as present-day sex researchers universally use computers, if not also additional technologies like digital cameras, voice recorders, vaginal photoplethysmographs, and magnetic resonance imaging (MRI) machines, technology is and will remain integral in the production and dissemination of sexual science.

Conclusion

The intersection of science and technology with human sexuality is fascinating and complex, and much remains to be explored in an ever-more digitalized future. To take one new strand of exploration, feminist and queer perspectives have been employed to study new developments in sex-related science and technology (Landström 2007). Over thirty years ago, Donna Haraway's "Cyborg Manifesto" identified the myriad ways that bodies and technologies interact with and produce each other ([1985] 1991). Haraway set the stage for the present-day research focus known as queer feminist science studies, using methods from science and technology studies together with those of gender, women's, and sexuality studies to interrogate and to denaturalize "natural" ideas and phenomena across time and species. A recent publication in this area is Angela Willey's *Undoing Monogamy,* which calls for "rethink[ing] the pervasive cultural privileging of sexual relationships over other types of connections" and putting forward a "dyke ethics of 'antimonogamy,' [which] through its grounding in notions of friendship, community, and social justice, decenters the sexual dyad in a way that polyamory does not" (2016, pp. 72, 97). Queer feminist science studies is just one example of how scholars are reformulating and producing new schools of thought for thinking and acting as sexual beings. Issues of power, agency, and subjectivity, not to mention the intersectionality of racial, gender, and class identities, will continue to shed light on the deep embeddedness of sciences and technologies in everyday sexual life.

References

Ahluwalia, Sanjam. 2008. *Reproductive Restraints: Birth Control in India, 1877–1947.* Urbana: University of Illinois Press.
Ahluwalia, Sanjam and Daksha Parmar. 2016. "From Gandhi to Gandhi: Contraceptive Technologies and Sexual Politics in Postcolonial India, 1947–1977." In *Reproductive States: Global Perspectives on the Invention and Implementation of Population Policy,* edited by Rickie Solinger and Mie Nakachi, 124–155. New York, NY: Oxford University Press.

Archibald, Timothy. 2005. *Sex Machines: Photographs and Interviews*. Carrboro, NC: Daniel 13.

Baer, Brian James. 2015. "Translating Sexology in Late-Tsarist and Early-Soviet Russia." In *Sexology and Translation: Cultural and Scientific Encounters across the Modern World*, edited by Heike Bauer, 115–34. Philadelphia, PA: Temple University Press.

Bauer, Heike, ed. 2015. *Sexology and Translation: Cultural and Scientific Encounters across the Modern World*. Philadelphia PA: Temple University Press.

Bauer, Heike. 2017. *The Hirschfeld Archives: Violence, Death, and Modern Queer Culture*. Philadelphia, PA: Temple University Press.

Beccalossi, Chiara. 2011. "Sex, Medicine and Disease: From Reproduction to Sexuality." In *A Cultural History of Sexuality in the Age of Empire*, edited by Chiara Beccalossi and Ivan Crozier, 101–121. Oxford: Berg.

Beccalossi, Chiara. 2012. *Female Sexual Inversion: Same-Sex Desires in Italian and British Sexology, c. 1870–1920*. Basingstoke, UK: Palgrave MacMillan.

Beccalossi, Chiara and Ivan Crozier, eds. 2011. *A Cultural History of Sexuality in the Age of Empire*. Oxford: Berg.

Botre, Shrikant and Douglas E. Haynes. 2017. "Sexual Knowledge, Sexual Anxieties: Middle-Class Males in Western India and the Correspondence in Samaj Swasthya, 1927–53." *Modern Asian Studies*. Published electronically July 18. doi: 10.1017/S0026749X16000184.

Brooks, Ross. 2012. "Transforming Sexuality: The Medical Sources of Karl Heinrich Ulrichs (1825–1895) and the Origins of the Theory of Bisexuality." *Journal of the History of Medicine and the Allied Sciences* 67: 177–216. doi: 10.1093/jhmas/jrq064.

Bullough, Vern L. 1994. *Science in the Bedroom: A History of Sex Research*. New York, NY: Basic Books.

Clark, Anna. 2011. *The History of Sexuality in Europe: A Sourcebook and Reader*. London: Routledge.

Clarke, Adele E. 1998. *Disciplining Reproduction: Modernity, American Life Sciences, and "The Problems of Sex."* Berkeley: University of California Press.

Cook, Hera. 2005. *The Long Sexual Revolution: English Women, Sex, and Contraception, 1800–1975*. Oxford: Oxford University Press.

Coopersmith, Jonathan. 1998. "Pornography, Technology, and Progress." *ICON* 4: 94–125. Available at: http://www.jstor.org/stable/23785961.

Coopersmith, Jonathan. 2000. "Pornography, Video, and the Internet." *IEEE Technology and Society Magazine* 19(1): 27–34. doi: 10.1109/44.828561.

Coopersmith, Jonathan. 2006. "Does Your Mother Know What You *Really* Do? The Changing Nature and Image of Computer-Based Pornography." *History and Technology* 22(1): 1–25.

Crellin, John K. 2012. "Revisiting Eve's Herbs: Reflections on Therapeutic Uncertainties." In *Herbs and Healers from the Ancient Mediterranean through the Medieval West: Essays in Honor of John M. Riddle*, edited by Ann Van Arsdall and Timothy Graham, 307–328. London: Routledge.

Davidson, Arnold I. 2001. "Closing Up the Corpses: Diseases of Sexuality and the Emergence of the Psychiatric Style of Reasoning." In *Homosexuality and Psychoanalysis*, edited by Tim Dean and Christopher Lane, 59–90. Chicago, IL: University of Chicago Press.

Dennis, Kelly. 2011. "Erotica." In *A Cultural History of Sexuality in the Modern Age*, edited by Gert Hekma, 203–227. Oxford: Berg.

Dose, Ralf. 2014. *Magnus Hirschfeld: The Origins of the Gay Liberation Movement*, translated by Edward H. Willis. New York, NY: Monthly Review Press.

Downing, Lisa. 2011. "Sexual Variations." In *A Cultural History of Sexuality in the Age of Empire*, edited by Chiara Beccalossi and Ivan Crozier, 63–81. Oxford: Berg.

Downing, Lisa. 2014. "A Disavowed Inheritance: Nineteenth-Century Perversion Theory and John Money's 'Paraphilia.'" In *Fuckology: Critical Essays on John Money's Diagnostic Concepts*, 41–68. Chicago, IL: University of Chicago Press.

Downing, Lisa, Ian Morland, and Nikki Sullivan. 2014. "On the 'Duke of Dysfunction.'" In *Fuckology: Critical Essays on John Money's Diagnostic Concepts*, 1–18. Chicago, IL: University of Chicago Press.

Drucker, Donna J. 2013. "Keying Desire: Alfred Kinsey's Use of Punched-Card Machines for Sex Research." *Journal of the History of Sexuality* 22(1): 105–125. doi: 10.7560/JHS22105.

Drucker, Donna J. 2014. *The Machines of Sex Research: Technology and the Politics of Identity, 1945–1985*. Dordrecht: Springer.

Drucker, Donna J. 2015. "Astrological Birth Control: Fertility Awareness and the Politics of Non-Hormonal Contraception." Notches Blog. Available at: http://notchesblog.com/2015/06/11/astrological-birth-control-fertility-awareness-and-the-politics-of-non-hormonal-contraception (accessed November 24, 2019).

Drucker, Donna J. 2016. "Materializing Gender through Contraceptive Technology in the United States." *Technology's Stories*. http://www.technologystories.org/materializing-gender-through-contraceptive-technology-in-the-united-states-1930s-1940s (accessed November 24, 2019).

Eig, Jonathan. 2014. *The Birth of the Pill: How Four Pioneers Reinvented Sex and Launched a Revolution*. New York, NY: W.W. Norton.

Ellis, Havelock. 1897–1910. *Studies in the Psychology of Sex*. 7 vols. London: Wilson and Macmillan.

Ellis, Havelock and John Addington Symonds. [1897] 2008. *Sexual Inversion: A Critical Edition*. Edited and introduced by Ivan Crozier. Basingstoke, UK: Palgrave Macmillan.

Engelstein, Laura. 1986. "Morality and the Wooden Spoon: Russian Doctors View Syphilis, Social Class, and Sexual Behavior, 1890–1905." *Representations* 14(Spring): 169–208. Available at: http://www.jstor.org/stable/2928439.

Fisher, Kate. 2006. *Birth Control, Sex, and Marriage in Britain, 1918–1960*. Oxford: Oxford University Press.

Ford, Ruth. 2011. "Erotica: Sexual Imagery, Empires, and Colonies." In *A Cultural History of Sexuality in the Age of Empire*, edited by Chiara Beccalossi, and Ivan Crozier, 171–198. Oxford: Berg.

Foucault, Michel. [1978] 1990. *The History of Sexuality: The Will to Knowledge*, vol. 1, translated by Robert Hurley. New York, NY: Vintage.

Foucault, Michel. 2003. *Abnormal: Lectures at the Collège de France, 1974–1975*. London: Verso.

Freud, Sigmund. [1905] 1977. *On Sexuality: Three Essays on the Theory of Sexuality*. New York, NY: Penguin.

Frühstück, Sabine. 2003. *Colonizing Sex: Sexology and Social Control in Modern Japan*. Berkeley: University of California Press.

Frühstück, Sabine. 2004. "Sexuality and the Nation-State." In *A Global History of Sexuality: The Modern Era*, edited by Robert M. Buffington, Eithne Luibhéid, and Donna J. Guy, 17–56. Malden, MA: Blackwell.

Fuechtner, Veronika, Douglas E. Haynes, and Ryan M. Jones, eds. 2017. *A Global History of Sexual Science, 1880–1950*. Berkeley: University of California Press.

Garton, Stephen. 2006. *Histories of Sexuality*. London: Equinox.

Hajo, Cathy Moran. 2010. *Birth Control on Main Street: Organizing Clinics in the United States, 1919–1939*. Springfield: University of Illinois Press.

Haraway, Donna J. [1985] 1991. "A Cyborg Manifesto: Science, Technology, and Socialist-Feminism in the Late Twentieth Century." In *Simians, Cyborgs and Women: The Reinvention of Nature*, 149–181. New York, NY: Routledge.

Haynes, Douglas E. 2012. "Selling Masculinity: Advertisements for Sex Tonics and the Making of Modern Conjugality in Western India, 1900–1945." *South Asia: Journal of South Asian Studies* 35(4): 787–831. doi: 10.1080/00856401.2011.647323.

Healey, Dan. 2009. *Bolshevik Sexual Forensics: Diagnosing Disorder in the Clinic and Courtroom, 1917–1939*. DeKalb: Northern Illinois University Press.

Heineman, Elizabeth. 2011. *Before Porn Was Legal: The Erotic Empire of Beate Uhse*. Chicago, IL: University of Chicago Press.

Hekma, Gert, ed. 2011. *A Cultural History of Sexuality in the Modern Age*. Oxford: Berg.

Herrn, Rainer. 2005. *Schnittmuster des Geschlechts: Transvestitismus und Transsexualität in der frühen Sexualwissenschaft* [The Pattern of Sex: Transvestitism and Transsexuality in Early Sexual Science]. Giessen: Psychosozial Verlag.

Herrn, Rainer. 2013. "Transvestitismus in der NS-Zeit: Ein Forschungsdesiderat" [Transvestitism in the Nazi Era: A Research Desideratum]. *Zeitschrift für Sexualforschung*, 26: 330–371.

Herzer, Manfred. 1986. "Kertbeny and the Nameless Love." *Journal of Homosexuality* 12(1): 1–26.

Herzog, Dagmar. 2011. *Sexuality in Europe: A Twentieth-Century History*. Cambridge: Cambridge University Press.

Herzog, Dagmar. 2017. *Cold War Freud: Psychoanalysis in an Age of Catastrophes*. Cambridge: Cambridge University Press.

Himes, Norman E. (1936) 1970. *Medical History of Contraception*. New York, NY: Schocken Books.

Hirschfeld, Magnus. 1914. *Die Homosexualität des Mannes und des Weibes: Mit einem Namen-, Länder-, Orts- und Sachregister* [The Homosexuality of Men and Women: With a Register of Names, States, Places, and Subjects]. Berlin: L. Marcus.

Hirschfeld, Magnus. 1927a. *Der erotische Verkleidungstrieb* [The Erotic Desire to Cross-Dress]. Leipzig: Verlag "Wahrheit" F. Spohr.

Hirschfeld, Magnus. 1927b. *Sexuelle Zwischenstufen: Das männliche Weib und der weibliche Mann* [Sexual Intermediaries: The Masculine Woman and the Feminine Man]. Bonn: Marcus & Weber.

Hodes, Rebecca. 2015. "Kink and the Colony: Sexual Deviance in the Medical History of South Africa, c. 1893–1939." *Journal of Southern African Studies* 41(4): 715–733.

Holz, Rose. 2014. *The Birth Control Clinic in a Marketplace World*. Rochester, NY: University of Rochester Press.

Hutter, Jörg. 1993. "The Social Constructions of Homosexuality in the Nineteenth Century: The Shift from the Sin to the Influence of Medicine in Criminalizing Sodomy in Germany." *Journal of Homosexuality* 24(3–4): 73–93.

Irvine, Janice. (2005) 2010. *Disorders of Desire: Sexuality and Gender in Modern American Sexology*. Philadelphia, PA: Temple University Press.

Johnson, Virginia E. and William H. Masters. 1962. "Intravaginal Contraceptive Study: Phase I. Anatomy." *Western Journal of Surgery, Obstetrics, and Gynecology* 70: 202–207.

Johnson, Virginia E. and William H. Masters. 1963. "Intravaginal Contraceptive Study: Phase II. Physiology (A Direct Test for Protective Potential)." *Western Journal of Surgery, Obstetrics, and Gynecology* 71: 144–153.

Johnson, Virginia E. and William H. Masters. 1965. "A Product of Dual Import: Intravaginal Infection Control and Conception Control." *Pacific Medicine and Surgery* 73: 267–275.

Johnson, Virginia E., William H. Masters, and K. Cramer Lewis. 1964. "The Physiology of Intravaginal Contraceptive Practice." In *Manual of Contraceptive Practice*, edited by Mary Steichen Calderone, 138–150. Baltimore, MD: Williams & Wilkins.

Jagose, Annamarie. 2012. *Orgasmology*. Durham, NC: Duke University Press.

Jütte, Robert. [2003] 2008. *Contraception: A History*, translated by Vicky Russell. Cambridge, UK: Polity.

Kaan, Heinrich. 2016. *Heinrich Kaan's "Psychopathia Sexualis" (1844): A Classic Text in the History of Sexuality*, edited by Benjamin Kahan, translated by Melissa Haynes. Ithaca, NY: Cornell University Press.

Katz, Jonathan. 1995. *The Invention of Heterosexuality*. New York, NY: Dutton.

Kinsey, Alfred C., Wardell B. Pomeroy, and Clyde E. Martin. 1948. *Sexual Behavior in the Human Male*. Philadelphia, PA: W.B. Saunders.

Kinsey, Alfred C., Wardell B. Pomeroy, Clyde E. Martin, and Paul H. Gebhard. 1953. *Sexual Behavior in the Human Female*. Philadelphia, PA: W.B. Saunders.

König, Wolfgang. 2016. *Das Kondom: zur Geschichte der Sexualität vom Kaiserreich bis in die Gegenwart* [The Condom: A History of Sexuality from Empire to the Present]. Stuttgart: Franz Steiner Verlag.

Kościańska, Agnieszka. 2014. "Beyond Viagra: Sex Therapy in Poland." *Sociologický časopis/ Czech Sociological Review* 50(6): 919–938.

Kościańska, Agnieszka. 2016. "Sex on Equal Terms? Polish Sexology on Women's Emancipation and 'Good Sex' from the 1970s to the Present." *Sexualities* 19(1–2): 236–256.

Krafft-Ebing, Richard von. 1901. "Neue Studium auf dem Gebiete der Homosexualität" [New Studies in the Area of Homosexuality]. In *Jahrbuch für sexuelle Zwischenstufen unter besonderer Berücksichtigung der Homosexualität, III*, edited by Magnus Hirschfeld, 1–36. Leipzig: Max Spohr.

Kund, Attila. 2016. "'Duties for Her Race and Nation': Scientific Racist Views on Sexuality and Reproduction in 1920s Hungary." *Sexualities* 19(1–2): 190–210.

Landström, Catharina. 2007. "Queering Feminist Technology Studies." *Feminist Theory* 8(1): 7–26.

Laqueur, Thomas W. 2003. *Solitary Sex: A Cultural History of Masturbation*. New York, NY: Zone Books.

Leck, Ralph M. 2016. *Vita Sexualis: Karl Ulrichs and the Origins of Sexual Science*. Urbana: University of Illinois Press.

Leng, Kirsten. 2015. "The Personal Is Scientific: Women, Gender, and the Production of Sexological Knowledge in Germany and Austria, 1900–1931." *History of Psychology* 18(3): 238–251.

Leng, Kirsten. 2017a. "Magnus Hirschfeld's Meanings: Analysing Biography and the Politics of Representation." *German History* 35(1): 96–116.

Leng, Kirsten. 2017b. *Sexual Politics and Feminist Science: Women Sexologists in Germany, 1900–1933*. Ithaca, NY: Cornell University Press.

Lieberman, Hallie. 2017. *Buzz: A Stimulating History of Sex Toys*. New York, NY: Pegasus Books.

Lišková, Kateřina. 2016. "Sex under Socialism: From Emancipation of Women to Normalized Families in Czechoslovakia." *Sexualities* 19(1–2): 211–235.

Maines, Rachel. 1989. "Socially Camouflaged Technologies: The Case of the Electromechanical Vibrator." *IEEE Technology and Society Magazine* 8(2): 3–11.

Mancini, Elena. 2010. *Magnus Hirschfeld and the Quest for Sexual Freedom: A History of the First International Sexual Freedom Movement*. New York, NY: Palgrave Macmillan.

Marks, Lara V. [2001] 2010. *Sexual Chemistry: A History of the Contraceptive Pill.* New Haven, CT: Yale University Press.

Masters, William H. and Virginia E. Johnson. 1966. *Human Sexual Response.* Boston, MA: Little, Brown.

May, Elaine Tyler. 2011. *America + the Pill: A History of Promise, Peril, and Liberation.* New York, NY: Basic Books.

Mazanik, Anna. 2015. "Sanitation, Urban Environment, and the Politics of Public Health in Late Imperial Moscow." PhD dissertation. Central European University.

McEwen, Britta. 2016. *Sexual Knowledge: Feeling, Fact, and Social Reform in Vienna, 1900–1934.* New York, NY: Berghahn.

McLaren, Angus. 1990. *A History of Contraception: From Antiquity to the Present Day.* Malden, MA: Blackwell.

McLaren, Angus. 1999. *Twentieth-Century Sexuality: A History.* Malden, MA: Blackwell.

McLaren, Angus. 2007. *Impotence: A Cultural History.* Chicago, IL: University of Chicago Press.

Minton, Henry L. 2010. *Departing from Deviance: A History of Homosexual Rights and Emancipatory Science in America.* Chicago, IL: University of Chicago Press.

Money, John. 1988. *Gay, Straight, and In-Between: The Sexology of Erotic Orientation.* Oxford: Oxford University Press.

Money, John, Joan G. Hampson, and John L. Hampson. 1957. "Imprinting and the Establishment of Gender Role." *JAMA* 77(3): 333–336.

Murphy, Michelle. 2012. *Seizing the Means of Reproduction: Entanglements of Feminism, Health, and Technoscience.* Durham, NC: Duke University Press.

Nelson, Sarah E. 2009. "Persephone's Seeds: Abortifacients and Contraceptives in Ancient Greek Medicine and Their Recent Scientific Appraisal." *Pharmacy in History* 51(2): 57–69. Available at: http://www.jstor.org/stable/41112420.

Oosterhuis, Harry. 2000. *Stepchildren of Nature: Krafft-Ebing, Psychiatry, and the Making of Sexual Identity.* Chicago, IL: University of Chicago Press.

Oudshoorn, Nelly. 2003. *The Male Pill: A Biography of a Technology in the Making.* Durham, NC: Duke University Press.

Parkhill, Chad and Elizabeth Stephens. 2011. "Heterosexuality: An Unfettered Capacity for Degeneracy." In *A Cultural History of Sexuality in the Age of Empire*, edited by Chiara Beccalossi and Ivan Crozier, 27–42. Oxford: Berg.

Prescott, Heather Munro. 2011. *The Morning After: A History of Emergency Contraception in the United States.* New Brunswick, NJ: Rutgers University Press.

Reed, James. 1978. *From Private Vice to Public Virtue: The Birth Control Movement and American Society since 1830.* New York, NY: Basic Books.

Reich, Wilhelm. [1942] 1986. *The Function of the Orgasm: Discovery of the Orgone*, vol. 1. New York, NY: Farrar, Straus, and Giroux.

Renkin, Hadley Z. and Agnieszka Kościańska. 2016. "The Science of Sex in a Space of Uncertainty: Naturalizing and Modernizing Europe's East, Past and Present." *Sexualities* 19(1–2): 159–167.

Riddle, John M. 1994. *Contraception and Abortion from the Ancient World to the Renaissance.* Cambridge: Harvard University Press.

Riddle, John M. 1999. *Eve's Herbs: A History of Abortion and Contraception in the West.* Cambridge, MA: Harvard University Press.

Ronsin, Francis. 2011. "Heterosexuality." In *A Cultural History of Sexuality in the Modern Age*, edited by Gert Hekma, 27–48. Oxford: Berg.

Rosario, Vernon A., ed. 1997. *Science and Homosexualities*. New York, NY: Routledge.
Sigusch, Volkmar. 2002. "Richard von Krafft-Ebing zwischen Kaan und Freud: Bemerkungen zur 100. Wiederkehr seines Todestages" [Richard von Krafft-Ebing between Kaan und Freud: Remarks on the 100th Anniversary of His Death]. *Zeitschrift für Sexualforschung* 15: 211–247.
Sigusch, Volkmar. 2003. "Heinrich Kaan: der Verfasser der ersten 'Psychopathia Sexualis': Eine biographische Skizze" [Heinrich Kaan: The author of the first 'Psychopathia Sexualis': A Biographical Sketch]. *Zeitschrift für Sexualforschung* 16: 116–142.
Sigusch, Volkmar. 2012. "The Sexologist Albert Moll: Between Sigmund Freud and Magnus Hirschfeld." *Medical History* 56(2): 184–200.
Sigusch, Volkmar and Günter Grau. 2008. *Geschichte der Sexualwissenschaft* [The History of Sexual Science]. Frankfurt: Campus.
Srivastava, Sanjay, ed. 2013. *Sexuality Studies*. New Delhi: Oxford University Press.
Storr, Merl. 2008. "Transformations: Subjects, Categories and Cures in Krafft-Ebing's Sexology." In *Sexology in Culture: Labelling Bodies and Desires*, edited by Lucy Bland and Laura Doan, 11–26. Cambridge, UK: Polity Press.
Takeshita, Chikako. 2011. *The Global Politics of the IUD: How Science Constructs Contraceptive Users and Women's Bodies*. Cambridge, MA: MIT Press.
Terry, Jennifer. 1999. *An American Obsession: Science, Medicine, and Homosexuality in Modern Society*. Chicago, IL: University of Chicago Press.
Tobin, Robert Deam. 2015. *Peripheral Desires: The German Discovery of Sex*. Philadelphia: University of Pennsylvania Press.
Tone, Andrea. 2002. *Devices & Desires: A History of Contraceptives in America*. New York, NY: Hill & Wang.
Trask, April Danielle. 2014. "*Remaking Men: Sexology, Homosexuality, and Social Reform in Germany, 1890–1933*." PhD dissertation. University of Irvine.
Von Soden, Kristine. 1998. *Die Sexualberatungstellen der Weimarer Republik, 1919–1933* [Sexual Advice Centers in the Weimar Republic, 1919–1933]. Berlin: Hentrich.
Wake, Naoko. 2011. *Private Practices: Harry Stack Sullivan, the Science of Homosexuality, and American Liberalism*. New Brunswick, NJ: Rutgers University Press.
Watkins, Elizabeth Siegel. 2001. *On the Pill: A Social History of Oral Contraceptives, 1950–1970*. Chicago, IL: University of Chicago Press.
Weschler, Toni. 2015. *Taking Charge of Your Fertility: The Definitive Guide to Natural Birth Control, Pregnancy Achievement, and Reproductive Health*. New York, NY: William Morrow.
Westphal, Carl. 1869–1870. "Die Konträre Sexualempfindung: Symptom eines neuropathologischen (psychopathischen) Zustandes" [The Contrary Sexual Feeling: Symptom of a Neuropathological (Psychopathic) Status]. *Archiv für Psychiatrie und Nervenkrankheiten* 2: 73–108.
Willey, Angela. 2016. *Undoing Monogamy: The Politics of Science and the Possibilities of Biology*. Durham, NC: Duke University Press.
Wyndham, Diana. 2012. *Norman Haire and the Study of Sex*. Sydney: University of Sydney Press.

9

Sexuality and Socialization

LEAH R. WARNER, EMILY A. LESKINEN, AND JANELLE LEYVA

Socialization

Sexuality is one of the many facets of human experience that is impacted by socialization processes. *Sexuality socialization* refers to the process of acquiring knowledge, norms, attitudes, cultural symbols and meanings, codes of conduct, and values about a wide range of topics concerning sex and sexuality (Janssen 2016; Shtarkshall, Santelli, and Hirsch 2007). It includes, but is not limited to, norms about sexual intercourse, scripts about romantic relationships, beliefs about sexual social identities, and information on sexually transmitted infections (STIs). This process involves incorporating messages from many different sources and occurrences over one's lifespan (Longmore 1998). Following the work done by Tolman and McClelland (2011), we use the term "sexuality"[1] over "sexual" to describe sexuality socialization. While "sexual" implies physiological processes, "sexuality" acknowledges the entwinement of physiological, psychological, and social constructionist processes that an individual undergoes to form their sexuality.

In this chapter, we approach sexuality socialization as understood by psychological science, particularly as it is informed by a feminist perspective. As defined in psychological research, sexuality is a multifaceted concept that encompasses attraction – the desire to have sexual relations or a loving sexual relationship (Savin-Williams 2006, 2011); and behavior – activity that leads to sexual arousal, and orientation, that is, the labels used to convey affiliation with social groups based on sexual preferences (Belmonte and Holmes 2016). Beyond this definition, many researchers include sexual fantasies, romantic relationships, emotional attachments, and beliefs about gender roles and identity in their conceptual framing (Klein, Sepekoff, and Wolf 1985). Finally, each of these facets of sexuality reflects and instantiates larger structures of inequality, such as sexism and heterosexism (Bowleg 2008, 2013; Diamond 2008; Valentine 2007).

Companion to Sexuality Studies, First Edition. Edited by Nancy A. Naples.
© 2020 John Wiley & Sons Ltd. Published 2020 by John Wiley & Sons Ltd.

One of the strengths of using this multifaceted definition is that it allows us to examine how focusing on different components of sexuality may lead researchers to draw different conclusions. For example, research that seeks to identify the prevalence of lesbian and gay sexual orientations finds higher rates when researchers ask participants about "same-sex attraction and behavior," but lower rates when measured by an individual's self-identification as lesbian or gay – because people may experience same-sex attraction but choose not to label themselves as lesbian or gay (Savin-Williams 2006). Thus, including multiple components affords a broader, more nuanced understanding of sexuality and related antecedents (i.e. factors that inform sexuality, such as parental perceptions of "safe" sexual practices) and outcomes (i.e. consequences related to these factors, such as adolescents' likelihood of contracting STIs).

Drawing on research from the social sciences, particularly psychology, this chapter explores factors contributing to sexuality socialization. In the first section, we highlight three overarching theories that inform feminist psychological understandings of sexuality socialization. These theories explain the processes through which sexuality is socially constructed. Next, we focus on sources of sexuality socialization. Over the course of one's life individuals acquire information on sexuality through a variety of formal and informal sources, including social relationships (e.g. parents and peers) and institutions (e.g. media, education, government and policies, and religion). We provide an overview of the content of these messages, how they are conveyed, and to what extent they occur within and across cultural contexts. We conclude with a discussion on bridging the connection between theory and sources of sexuality socialization.

Theoretical Frameworks for Sexuality Socialization

The topic of sexuality socialization is at the center of a philosophical divide amongst those who take an essentialist versus social constructionist perspective. Essentialist perspectives focus on evolutionary and genetic influences as sole drivers of sexuality, whereas social constructionist perspectives emphasize that any biological features of the human body and experience are entirely determined by social and cultural forces (see White, Bondurant, and Travis 2000 for a review of these perspectives). Challenging this dichotomy, others take an approach that integrates elements of both perspectives, arguing that neither adequately explains sexuality (e.g. Diamond 2008). Diamond views sexual feelings and experiences as embedded both in physical-biological and socialization contexts that demand "integrated biosocial research strategies" (p. 22). This approach may, for example, examine genetic predispositions, but also recognizes that such predispositions are rarely deterministic, and therefore examination of how environmental variation can modify the expression of the trait is essential for a more complete understanding. Furthermore, researchers who reject the dichotomizing of "essentialist vs. social constructionist" perspectives suggest that, in particular instances of sexual attraction or behavior, it may be impossible to separate out whether it is attributable to socialization or biological factors (Diamond 2008).

For the purpose of this chapter, we acknowledge the entwinement of physical-biological and socialization contexts; however, we focus on theoretical perspectives and empirical findings related to socialization processes that shape how sexuality is experienced, expressed via behaviors, and conceptualized through sexual identity categories. In this section, we describe three theoretical frameworks that inform feminist psychological research on sexuality socialization: symbolic interactionism, scripting theory, and intersectionality.

Symbolic interactionism

Symbolic interactionism refers to a constellation of perspectives on the use of symbols to create meaning (Stryker 1981). Within sexuality research, the dominant perspective is that sexuality is a socially constructed reality, and that the symbolic meanings attached to sexuality affect how we view ourselves and how we think about and interact with other people in sexual contexts (Longmore 1998). The physical sensation element of sexuality, for example, is not only interpreted by the symbols we associate with it, but the sexual symbolism creates the sexual experience itself by affecting what sexual responses we attend to and facilitate, and what responses we ignore (Gecas and Libby 1976). In other words, symbols are fundamentally entwined with spontaneous physiological responses. For example, in US and European cultures, heterosexual sex is symbolized as "successful" when the male ejaculates, which ignores women's pleasure and contributes to women's lower sexual satisfaction (Fine and McClelland 2006).

Within symbolic interactionist perspectives, sexuality research often focuses on face work (Longmore 1998), techniques that a person uses to portray themselves positively in the eyes of others. Derived from the colloquial term, "saving face," face work concerns engaging in behaviors that anticipate and mitigate others' negative judgments about one's self. In the context of sexuality, face work includes presenting oneself in ways that avoid negative judgments about one's sexual identity, expressions, or preferences. In sexual encounters, in particular, self-identification as a respectable person can be threatened as a result of sexual acts being construed as dirty or immoral. Therefore, individuals may engage in symbolic acts to retain this self-identification. For example, in heterosexual relationships where norms dictate that men are supposed to initiate sexual activity, women may express sexual interest indirectly through flirtation rituals. By engaging in flirtation rather than directly requesting sex, women preserve the appearance of sexual modesty (Schwartz 1994). In this example, the symbolic act is flirtation rituals, and this symbolic act functions to allow women to avoid negative judgments of them as sexually loose, a judgment they may have received if they directly admitted that they wanted to engage in sex. The primary criticism of symbolic interactionism in sexuality research is that focusing on an individual's intentional role in creating meaning undercuts the role that unconscious cognition plays in social interactions, as well as ignores the way that cultural institutions limit individual agency (Longmore 1998).

Scripting theory

Derived from symbolic interactionism (Gagnon 1990), scripting theory asserts that human behavior is experienced through schemas, or mental representations, which are then used to categorize norms regarding appropriate beliefs and behaviors. These "scripts" provide a repertoire of acts, rules for expected behavior, and expected punishments for violating the rules. According to scripting theory, sexuality is experienced through the lens of scripts that dictate how a person is expected to engage in sexual behaviors. For example, in heterosexual relationships, women are socialized to be sexually reluctant and to forestall the sexual advances of men, operating as "gatekeepers" (Byers 1996). In situations where scripts such as this are strongly enforced, girls' sexual responsiveness and interest in sexuality is lowered (Kornreich, Hearn, Rodriguez, and O'Sullivan 2003).

According to scripting theory, scripts are acquired from continual exposure to consistent communications of a script (Ahn, Brewer, and Mooney 1992), especially for those who lack knowledge about the behavior and are motivated to learn about it (Gagnon 1990). Thus, individuals who have little to no experience with sex or sexuality will seek out information, and the scripts they repeatedly encounter will eventually be integrated into memory. Simon and Gagnon (1987) identify three levels of socialization for acquiring sexual scripts: (i) intrapsychic, where individuals can construct their own scripts; (ii) interpersonal, where individuals learn scripts about sexuality from direct interactions with influential others, such as parents and peers; and (iii) cultural, where individuals learn about the scripts that are accepted by society at a widespread level, such as through mass media portrayals or laws prohibiting sexual behaviors. There are generally fewer scripts for sexualities that are marginalized (such as lesbian, gay, and bisexual (LGB) identities). For example, there are more scripts for heterosexual first dates (such as who pays and behavior rituals e.g. opening car doors) than for same-sex first dates (Eaton and Rose 2011; Klinkenberg and Rose 1994).

Although scripting theory is commonly used, scholars have critiqued the way that scripting theory has been framed as operating above culturally contextualized notions of sexuality (Stephens and Phillips 2005). In one conceptual model, Stephens and Phillips argue that the sexual scripts for adolescent African American women operate within a unique context that is specific to the intersection between their gender and race. For example, they highlight that same-race peers are found to have a high accuracy for identifying when portrayals of African Americans are stereotypical; thus, peers are one resource for navigating scripts in mass media that rely on negative stereotypes of African American women's sexuality (e.g. the "jezebel" stereotype). One way this criticism has been addressed is to use scripting theory to explain the process of conveying sexual messaging, but to pair it with other conceptual frameworks to interpret the values and meaning ascribed to the messaging, such as intersectionality (Stephens and Phillips 2005).

Intersectionality

To address the limitations of dominant sexuality socialization theories, feminist psychologists have looked to intersectionality theory (Crenshaw 1991) to address some of these limitations. As part of a larger black feminist effort (see May 2015), Kimberlé Crenshaw coined the term "intersectionality" to explain the ways that those who have multiple subordinate identities, especially women of color, often experience being caught between and/or incompletely represented by political groups representing a single identity (e.g. the women's movement or Civil Rights movement) (Crenshaw 1991).

Intersectionality theory states that sexuality, as a social structure and as an identity, has a mutually constitutive relationship with other structures/identities, such as race, class, and gender. In other words, like beads on a string, one's experience with one's sexual identity is not separable from other identities (Spelman 1988). Rather, due to their interrelation, identities create qualitatively different experiences (e.g. Anthias and Yuval-Davis 1983; Collins 1990). For example, Bowleg (2008, 2013) has found that black gay and bisexual men and women experience their race, gender, and sexuality as integrated, in navigating acceptance within black communities, microaggressions within LGBTQ communities, and gaining psychological resistance strategies navigating their outsider status within multiple contexts. In addition, intersectionality theory states that these identities are embedded within structures of power and oppression, a "matrix of domination" (Collins 1990, p. 225). The matrix of domination describes that a person's positionality results from a combination of privilege and oppression, based on the relative power a person has within the social structures of sexuality, gender, race, and so forth.

Intersectionality has contributed to the study of sexuality socialization by requiring that scholars examine social structures outside of sexuality to inform identity, attraction, and behavior. It has been particularly helpful in revealing the inadequacy of approaches that assume a homogenous population, ignoring the ways that race, class, gender, and other structures that shape identities interact to provide fundamentally different experiences of sexuality (e.g. see Lewis and Kertzner 2003). However, critiques of intersectionality (e.g. Duong 2009) contend that while an intention of intersectionality is to better represent the experiences of marginalized people (May 2015), intersectionality's approach to sexuality fails to do so. One critique is that intersectionality uses rigid categories to explain sexuality, such as "straight" or "gay," rather than recognizing the fluidity that occurs in the interplay between gender, sex, and sexuality. Furthermore, intersectionality has been critiqued as not sufficiently addressing the sociopolitical context of the categories typically used in intersectional analysis, and, as a result, fails to adequately represent multiply marginalized individuals within that category. For example, Valentine (2007) argues that the term "transgender" needs to be contextualized within the white upper-middle class activist context in which it originated, specifically in terms of how historically it had been used to exclude those outside that context. Note, however, that some scholars argue that these critiques of intersectionality are not appropriate for the theory itself, but rather only relevant to particular applications (Warner, Settles, and Shields 2018).

In sum, each theory discussed above provides a framework for understanding how sexuality is socialized in individuals. Symbolic interactionism suggests that the symbols found in a culture are used to create meaning and understanding of one's sexuality. Scripting theory states that mental representations regarding norms for appropriate beliefs and behaviors (i.e. "scripts") provide a guide for how to engage in sexuality in a society. Finally, intersectionality theory asserts that scholarship on sexuality socialization must examine how sexuality is interrelated with other social structures/identities such as race, class, and gender.

Sources of Sexuality Socialization: Social Relationships

When studying sexuality socialization, researchers have relied on a variety of theoretical perspectives to frame their research. In the section "Theoretical Frameworks for Sexuality Socialization," we described three commonly used perspectives. In this section, we review major areas of empirical research within psychological literature that has been informed, either implicitly or explicitly, by these theoretical approaches. Specifically, we examine research related to the role parental and peer relationships play in guiding individuals' understanding and development of their own sexuality.

Parents often see themselves as the primary sources of information for their children, although by the time young people become adolescents, research suggests that parental influence on children's sexuality socialization begins to wane (Tolman and McClelland 2011). Research on parental influences on sexuality socialization has tended to focus on the content, tone, and frequency of parental communication about sex, particularly in relation to risk (unprotected sex, STIs, unplanned pregnancy, etc.) (e.g. Hutchinson and Montgomery 2007; Wyckoff et al. 2008). In this section, we review the key findings from this literature.

In general, parents report discussing biological aspects of sexuality (e.g. menstruation and reproduction) and risk (specifically HIV/AIDS), while not discussing pleasure, such as wet dreams/erections and masturbation (DiIorio, Pluhar, and Belcher 2003). This is consistent with research that suggests parents emphasize sex being reserved for loving, committed relationships (Fletcher et al. 2015). However, parents tend to communicate sexuality messages differently depending on the child's gender. For example, girls tend to receive more negative messages about sex than boys (O'Sullivan et al. 1999), and these messages mirror the gendered sexual scripts that suggest women are sexual gatekeepers and men are sexual aggressors (Fletcher et al. 2015). Boys are more likely to be instructed to carry condoms (Fasula, Miller, and Weiner 2007) and cautioned against getting anyone pregnant (DiIorio et al. 2006), whereas girls are more likely to receive prohibitive messages (e.g. "boys only want one thing") (Aronowitz, et al. 2007). Some theorize that these different messages could have significant effects on engagement in sexual risk reduction behaviors (Fasula et al. 2007).

Despite consistent trends related to the information children receive about sexuality from their parents, notable differences arise when considering the intersections of gender and sexuality. For example, based on college students' retrospective reports, Calzo and Ward (2009) found that children recalled receiving most information about LGB sexualities from peers and media, with less communication coming from their parents. The communication children received from parents tended to be value laden, focusing on parental beliefs about the inherent naturalness or perverseness of LGB sexualities. However, when the parents themselves identify as LGB, emerging evidence suggests that youth receive more messages about sexual identity and positive sexuality. Cohen and Kuvalanka (2011), for example, interviewed white lesbian parents regarding messages they convey to their children, and identified four themes: "(a) diverse notions of sexual orientation and reproduction, (b) a positive sense of self, (c) the importance of safety and responsibility, and (d) that sexuality is normal/healthy" (p. 297). Another notable feature of lesbian couples' communication with their children is the attention to heterosexist incidents when they arise – a topic unmentioned in the research focusing on heterosexual parents.

The intersections of race and culture also play a defining role in the tone and content of the messages children and adolescents receive about sexuality (Kim 2009; Wang 2016). For example, in their examination of parental communication to black adolescents, Fletcher and colleagues (2015) found that the content of the conversations was more nuanced. Rather than simply discussing biology and risk, conversations included sex in the context of relationships and sex for pleasure. Additionally, in a sample of Filipino Americans, adolescents reported receiving information about sexual values from parents and grandparents, while "factual" information came from school (Chung et al. 2005).

Most parents report discussing "sex" with their children (DiIorio et al. 2003). However, research finds that some adolescents receive markedly less communication from parents about sex than others. For example, daughters receive more communication about sexuality than sons from their mothers, and mothers tend to be the primary communicators about sex and sexuality within families (DiIorio et al. 2003; Jaccard, Dittus, and Gordon 2000). Boys report markedly more communication about sexuality from their peers and media than from their parents (Epstein and Ward 2008).

Aside from parental influence, peers play a vital role in the sexuality socialization process (Calzo and Ward 2009; Epstein and Ward 2008). Children and adolescents report that peers are one of their primary sources of information about sex (Fletcher et al. 2015; Grafs and Patrick 2015). In particular, when determining who one should date or selecting a sexual partner, peers have a stronger influence than other sources; this is also true for learning how to behave in intimate relationships (Fletcher et al. 2015).

Despite the fact that adolescents frequently seek out sexuality messages from their peers, the messages are often ambiguous and contain many misperceptions (e.g. Lewis et al. 2007). Peers often provide advice before engaging in sexual experiences (Lewis et al. 2007), and this advice is pulled from diverse sources that are not adequately vetted for accuracy (Bogle 2008). Another central feature of peer-based sexuality socialization is that messages are highly gendered (Trinh and Ward 2016). For example, for young men and boys in a mainstream, predominately white US context, communicating about their sexual experiences elevates their masculinity and social dominance, as well as strengthens social ties (Trinh and Ward 2016). On the other hand, peers communicate to young women that they need to limit sexual permissiveness and confine their sexual experiences to committed relationships. These gender differences are not limited to white American contexts. Within Asian American contexts, peers communicate to young women the importance of relationships as a requirement for sexual activity (Trinh et al. 2014). African American girls are made to feel responsible for preventing sexual activity from damaging their reputations (Fletcher et al. 2015). For male Iranian university students, their sexual activity is often driven by peer pressure to engage in recreational sex (Ahmadabadi et al. 2015).

Sources of Sexuality Socialization: Institutions

While relational sources of parents and peers are important sources of sexual information, institutions are also key to sexuality socialization. Media, in particular, are identified as influential (Ward 2003). Other institutions include education, one of the few places where individuals receive formal information about sexuality (Grafs and Patrick 2015) and governments, which enact policies and laws that serve as sources of sexual information (Fine and McClelland 2006; Raifman et al. 2017). Finally, religious belief systems, which contain significant moral messages about sexuality, are central to many cultures' sexuality socialization (Regenerus 2007).

Media

Media, including traditional mass media sources such as television, movies, and magazines, online media, and explicit sexual media such as pornography, are believed to be a central contributor to sexuality socialization. For example, across many studies on youth media consumption, media ranks within the top three sources of sexual information (L'Engle, Brown, and Kenneavy 2006; Ward 2003; Wright 2009). As Ward (2003) explains, media are central to sexuality socialization for several reasons: sexual content is pervasive (Strasburger and Donnerstein 1999); they are accessible and widely consumed; media are often more explicit about sexuality and are more positive about sexuality than other sources (Brown and Keller 2000); and entertainment media are constructed to encourage consumption more so than other sources of sexuality information, such as sex education.

Despite the observed importance of media representations of sexuality, the quickly evolving nature of mass media creates difficulty in providing up-to-date assessment of sexual message content. Much of the existing literature on sexual content focuses on pornographic, network television, movie, and print media consumption, with some emerging work on internet searches and social media forums (Jones and Biddlecom 2011; Wright 2009; Ward 2003). Despite calls to classify media consumption into genres since they vary in sexualized message content (Wright 2009), the proliferation of online and social media options makes this separation a difficult task. To address the rapidly evolving nature of mass media, we first provide some general information about the characteristics of sexual messages. Then, the remainder of this section focuses on conceptual models that cut across genres to explain how media influence sexuality socialization (although, see Harris and Sanborn (2014) for a critique of models that cut across genres).

Existing research on sexualized media content focuses on a wide range of traditional media outlets that vary based on cultural context (for a particularly thorough example, see Wright 2009). Across outlets, sexuality is portrayed as recreational and nonrelational (Kunkel et al. 2007), and "good" sex is described in terms of quantity, variety, and as almost exclusively heterosexual (Ward 2003). Further, there is a widespread lack of messages about sexual risks or responsibilities (Kunkel et al. 2007). For example, Kunkel and colleagues found that responsibility messages, such as birth control and STIs, were found in 5% of sexual content scenes in shows popular with teens, although some evidence suggests that the messages of risks have increased from the 1990s to 2000s.

Consistent with intersectionality theory (Crenshaw 1991), the impact of media's sexuality messages may vary depending on intersections of social identities, both in terms of varying programming content that is marketed to or appeals to different social identities and how the programming messages are subsequently internalized. For example, Bond (2014) found that although LGB women and men seek out LGB sexual content, lack of availability means that heterosexuality is overrepresented in media popular with LGB adolescents. LGB adolescents drew messages mainly from jokes about sexuality rather than the depiction of actual sexual behaviors, which is predicted to lead to feelings of isolation and/or the tendency to disidentify from media portrayals of sexuality.

Research has found that sexualized media messages occur with high frequency, particularly on television (Ward 2003). For example, in the early 2000s two out of three programs included sexual content and 70% of shows that adolescents viewed contained one or more scenes with sexual content (Kunkel et al. 2007). More common on television is talk about sex rather than visual depictions of sexual acts (Ward 2003). Kunkel and colleagues (2007) argue that any analysis of sexualized media content should focus on the pattern of messages over time, as effects are slow and cumulative due to long-term exposure. The few studies that have assessed long-term patterns have found an increase in sexualized content over time. For example, in Kunkel et al.'s (2007) large-scale study of 2,817 television programs airing from 1997 to 2002, the percentage of shows displaying sexual intercourse doubled from 7 to 14%.

Theory and models of media message transmission

The theory most frequently applied to analysis of media sources of sexual socialization is *cultivation theory*, a derivation of symbolic interactionism theory (Gerbner et al. 2002). Cultivation theory posits that media portrayals have consistent themes that create a particular version of reality, and the more that people view this media, they "cultivate" or internalize the messages, beliefs, scripts, and other perspectives that reflect this reality. Those who apply cultivation theory to their research tend to focus on quantity of media consumption, under the premise that heavy viewers' relative greater exposure will result in more internalizing of media-constructed realities.

Research comparing light versus heavy media consumers are consistent with cultivation theory. The greater exposure to or involvement with sexualized content in media is associated with more liberal and stereotypical attitudes towards sexuality (Ward 2002) and greater sexual activity (L'Engle, Brown, and Kenneavy 2006); however, the frequency with which various media outlets depict sexual activity varies depending on media genre (Ward 2003). Additionally, individuals may begin to internalize sexual messages as exposure increases. For example, approval of sexual harassment increases with greater exposure to pop music (Strouse, Goodwin, and Roscoe 1994). Further, frequent television consumption is associated with greater endorsement of traditional gendered sexual scripts frequently depicted on television, which, in turn, predicts decreased sexual agency (Seabrook et al. 2017).

In addition to cultivation theory, a variety of cognitive models are used to explain sexuality socialization in media, such as social learning theory (Bandura 1986), social cognitive theory (2009), and cognitive susceptibility (L'Engle and Jackson 2008). These perspectives center on cognitive processes that rely on the social environment, such as the creation of mental models based on observing others and cognitive accessibility of schemas and scripts promoted by media representations. As a representative example, L'Engle and Jackson (2008) examined cognitive susceptibility, defined in this context as the internalization of cognitive models of readiness for sexual intercourse. For example, adolescents might use media portrayals of first-time sexual behaviors to determine when a person would know they are ready for sexual intercourse. Using longitudinal self-reports, L'Engle and Jackson found that cognitive susceptibility mediated the relationship between exposure to sexually permissive media norms and engagement in sexual intercourse. Rather than presenting media as if viewers passively absorb information, cognitive models suggest that viewers actively determine norms based on others' behavior and then follow suit, such as feeling pressure to engage in sexual activity once they gain the belief from viewing media that important or valued people engage in sexual activity (Bleakley et al. 2011).

Also central to understanding media message transmission is the need to acknowledge its interaction with other sources. First, viewers' media consumption is influenced by preexisting worldviews and beliefs (Harris and Sanborn 2014). Second, other sources of socialization filter the influence of media messages. For example, parental influences may filter media messages for child consumers. Vandenbosch and Eggermont (2012) found a relationship between maternal attachment and television viewing, whereby more television exposure and lower maternal attachment is associated with more liberal and stereotypical sexual attitudes. Third, media and other socialization sources influence each other to create co-constituted sexualization messages. For example, Subrahmanyam, Greenfield, and Tynes (2004) found that adolescent peers in online interactions reconstruct their offline lives by airing their concerns about sexuality and developing creative ways to construct and exchange identity information with each other. Adolescents perceived online environments to be safer for exploring their emerging sexuality than in their offline lives, suggesting that online environments both affect how peers socialize each other, and that peer socialization affects the nature of online environments.

Education

Contrary to other sources of sexuality socialization such as media, peers, and parents, sexual education is one of the most formal routes of communication about sexuality (Fine and McClelland, 2006; Grafs and Patrick 2015). For most people, sexual education in a school setting is the only formal information on sex that they will ever receive in their lifetime (Grafs and Patrick 2015).

In the US, formal sexual education is often provided to students by a health teacher or school nurse within the context of a class (Martinez, Abma, and Copen 2010). In the US, two common approaches to sexual education are: (i) comprehensive sex education and (ii) abstinence-only-until-marriage (AOUM). Comprehensive sex education may include information about sexual development and expression, contraception, prevention of STIs, pregnancy, and LGBTQ sexualities, whereas AOUM teaches students to abstain from sexual activity until marriage. Both approaches purport to reduce risky sexual behaviors providing students with information to help them make healthy sexual decisions (Grafs and Patrick 2015). These approaches are frequently at the center of ideological debates, with the AOUM approach often supported by conservative politicians and federal funding (McClelland and Fine 2008).

Advocates of AOUM express fear that teaching adolescents about contraception and STI prevention will increase sexual activity outside of a marriage context (Irvine 2004). However, research generally does not provide support for these concerns. In fact, discussion of birth control is unrelated to increased sexual activity or STIs (Kohler, Manhart, and Lafferty 2008). Further, receiving comprehensive sex education was associated with lower pregnancy risk than receiving AOUM or no sex education. The problems associated with the AOUM approach led the Society for Adolescent Medicine to describe the approach as ethically flawed due to the withholding of information (Santelli et al. 2006). Also, despite the benefits of comprehensive sex education programs, most are limited by their focus on heterosexual youth, which neglects the developmental and health concerns of LGBTQ individuals. This dearth of information specific to LGBTQ individuals is negatively correlated with psychological well-being and sexual health (Biddulph 2006).

Government and policy

Bronfenbrenner's (1979) ecological theory of development provides a framework for understanding the role laws and policies play as sources of sexuality socialization. Broadly, Bronfenbrenner argued that human development occurs as an individual interacts with their environment at various levels, from individual interactions (the microsystem) to society's overall structure, including norms, ideologies, law, and policy (the macrosystem) (Bronfenbrenner 1979). Laws and policies have the ability to expand or restrict the sexual lives of constituents. They can directly and indirectly condone or chastise individuals' sexual behaviors, limit available healthcare options, and proscribe topics within educational materials.

In the US, researchers have explored the role that policies play in sexuality socialization. For example, in 2015 the US Supreme Court ruled state-level bans against same-sex marriage unconstitutional, recognizing marriage equality at the federal level. Prior to that ruling, beginning in 2004, some individual states began recognizing same-sex marriage. Raifman and colleagues (2017) traced the gradual unfolding of marriage equality policies and examined the relationship between adolescent suicide attempts and residence in a state that adopted same-sex marriage policies. In states that adopted such policies, they found a 7% decline in adolescent suicide attempts after the passage of marriage equality legislation. This decline was greatest among sexual minority adolescents and was not seen in states that did not adopt similar policies.[2]

There is relatively less research on how state-level policies may affect sexuality socialization outside of the US. One study examining this issue in Ghana found that most people were not familiar with state laws, nor did people feel that laws pertaining to sexual regulation were (or could be) strictly enforced (Anarfi and Owusu 2011). Other research has looked at the experiences of the circumcision ritual among young Xhosa men in South Africa, a traditional practice that the government has tried to regulate (Vincent 2008).

Religion

Religious belief systems contribute to sexual socialization through texts, places of worship, religious leaders, and cultural practices. Research has found that religiosity, a multifaceted concept that reflects subjective experiences of religiousness, such as prayer frequency and spiritual connectedness (Regenerus 2007; Rew and Wong 2006), is particularly influential, more so than other aspects of religion, such as denomination and affiliation (Regenerus 2007). Religiosity has almost exclusively been examined in relation to sexual beliefs and practices that have been framed negatively, as "risky," "immoral," or in terms of health (Ritchwood et al. 2017). Rarely has religion been examined in relation to positive aspects of sexuality.

In general, religiosity is associated with decreased sexual risk among adolescents (e.g. Landor et al. 2011) as inhibiting both adolescent sexual activity (e.g. Regenerus, Smith, and Fritsch 2003), with fewer number of partners (Lammers et al. 2000), and with greater conservative attitudes about sex (e.g. Lefkowitz et al. 2004). However, religiosity affects sexual attitudes more than sexual behavior (Regenerus 2007). For example, religiosity does not predict consumption of online pornography, although it predicts perception that pornography has a negative impact on one's life (Miller, Hald, and Kidd 2017). Additionally, religiosity is better at deterring sex than promoting contraception use (Lefkowitz et al. 2004). Consistent with these findings, Rew and Wong's (2006) meta-analysis of the relationship between religiosity, spirituality, health behaviors, and health attitudes in adolescents found that 84% of the 43 studies published from 1998 to 2003 demonstrated a positive link between religiosity/spirituality and reduction of at least one sexual risk attitude/behavior or increase of at least one health promotion attitude/behavior. Rew and Wong note, however, that the wide range of measures and definitions of religiosity in the studies, as well as a pervasive absence of clear theoretical frameworks, limits the conclusions that can be made.

Central to understanding the impact of religious belief systems on sexuality socialization is to identify the interaction between religion and cultural context. Not only do religious belief systems differ from each other, but religious activities have different meanings and outcomes for individuals influenced by different cultural contexts (Elkind 1999). Importantly, many of the findings on the relationship between religiosity and sexual attitudes and behaviors are drawn from Christian populations, although some emerging research shows generalizability to Muslim populations (Sümer 2015). One example of a culturally nuanced analysis of the relationship between religion and sexuality socialization is Meldrum, Liamputtong, and Wollersheim's (2014) study examining the effects of Islam, Muslim culture, and Australian culture on young Muslim women's sexuality socialization. Meldrum and colleagues highlighted Muslim women's navigation of multiple sources of information, including diverse interpretations of Islamic doctrines that lead to, at times, contradicting messages about sexuality and a disconnect between Muslim and Australian culture. Using symbolic interactionism as a framework, Meldrum and colleagues found that the women had a fluid understanding of their sexual selves that is informed by Muslim culture and Islam, but expressed their sexuality in their own way, as influenced by Australian culture.

Conclusion

A tension is present in the sexuality socialization literature between making research conclusions that generalize across constituencies versus research conclusions that are contextualized within social and cultural contexts. Challenges arise due to the proliferation of different socialization sources, especially concerning the rapid ways that technological advances (such as hand-held devices) have fundamentally changed the way we communicate with other people and acquire information. Adding to that is a recent push in the social sciences, via theories such as intersectionality, to contextualize findings within interlocking social structures, such as culture, race, class, and gender (e.g. Collins 1990). This effort to recognize uniqueness in individuals' socialization experiences has allowed for a deeper understanding of sexuality, especially of those who have been historically underrepresented in research, such as communities of color and LGBTQ individuals. However, this presents challenges for research that attempts to make broad claims and generalize across communities and contexts, such as psychological research that seeks to determine universal patterns of human behavior. One approach to solving this tension in the literature is to rely more on larger theories and conceptual frameworks and then apply them to specific cultural and social contexts, as is suggested by Stephens and Phillips (2005).

In this chapter, we identified major theories that inform research on sexuality socialization, as well as reviewed key research on the sources of sexuality socialization. As this chapter makes clear, sexuality socialization is influenced by a variety of sources on both the micro (e.g. relational) and macro (e.g. institutional) levels. While recognizing the extensive work by researchers examining how different aspects of sexuality socialization may relate to "risky" behaviors, we join those who call for integrating positive aspects of sexuality and "normative" sexual development within this research agenda (e.g. Tolman and McClelland 2011). Prioritizing this integrated approach to studying sexuality socialization could provide new information, as well as a deeper understanding of sexuality development.

Notes

1 Holmes (2016) has added onto this by proposing that the plural form, "sexualities," should be used. Holmes describes that the term "sexuality" creates a false sense of unification, conveying that all human beings categorize their sexuality in the same way. The singular nature of this term does not include the many dimensions that sexuality encompasses, and it poses the problem of creating a line between what behaviors are seen as normative and what are defiant to this overarching idea of what sexuality should be (Holmes 2016, p. 1). In this chapter we retain "sexuality," as it is consistent with the language used in the literature we review. However, future work should consider altering language to better represent the plurality of sexualities.
2 For a thorough review of the unfolding of abstinence-only sexual education policies, parental consent laws regarding abortion, and regulation of emergency contraception, and how these policies have differentially affected marginalized groups, see Fine and McClelland (2006).

References

Ahmadabadi, Zohre, Leili Panaghi, Ali Madanipour et al. 2015. "Cultural Scripts, Reasons for Having Sex, and Regret: A Study of Iranian Male and Female University Students." *Sexuality & Culture* 19(3): 561–573.

Ahn, Woo-Kyoung, William F. Brewer, and Raymond J. Mooney. 1992. "Schema Acquisition from a Single Example." *Journal of Experimental Psychology: Learning, Memory, and Cognition* 18(2): 391–412.

Anarfi, John Kwasi and Adobea Yaa Owusu. 2011. "The Making of a Sexual Being in Ghana: The State, Religion and the Influence of Society as Agents of Sexual Socialization." *Sexuality & Culture: An Interdisciplinary Quarterly* 15(1): 1–18.

Anthias, Floya and Nira Yuval-Davis. 1983. "Contextualizing Feminism: Gender, Ethnic and Class Divisions." *Feminist Review* 15: 62–75.

Aronowitz, Teri, Erin Todd, Ethel Agbeshie, and Rachel E. Rennells. 2007. "Attitudes that Affect the Ability of African American Preadolescent Girls and their Mothers to Talk Openly about Sex." *Issues in Mental Health Nursing* 28(1): 7–20.

Bandura, Albert. 1986. *Social Foundations of Thought and Action*. New York, NY: Prentice–Hall.

Belmonte, Kimberly and Tabitha R. Holmes. 2016. "Outside the LGBTQ 'Safety Zone': Lesbian and Bisexual Women Negotiate Sexual Identity Across Multiple Ecological Contexts." *Journal of Bisexuality* 16(2): 233–269.

Biddulph, Max. 2006. "Sexualities Equality in Schools: Why Every Lesbian, Gay, Bisexual or Transgender (LGBT) Child Matters." *Pastoral Care in Education* 24(2): 15–21.

Bleakley, Amy, Michael Hennessy, Martin Fishbein, and Amy Jordan. 2011. "Using the Integrative Model to Explain How Exposure to Sexual Media Content Influences Adolescent Sexual Behavior." *Health Education & Behavior* 38(5): 530–540.

Bogle, Kathleen A. 2008. *Hooking Up: Sex, Dating, and Relationships on Campus*. New York, NY: New York University Press.

Bond, Bradley. 2014. "Sex and Sexuality in Entertainment Media Popular with Lesbian, Gay, and Bisexual Adolescents." *Mass Communication & Society* 17(1): 98–120.

Bowleg, Lisa. 2008. "When Black + Lesbian + Woman ≠ Black Lesbian Woman: The Methodological Challenges of Qualitative and Quantitative Intersectionality Research." *Sex Roles* 59(5–6): 312–325.

Bowleg, Lisa. 2013. "'Once You've Blended the Cake, You Can't Take the Parts Back to the Main Ingredients': Black Gay and Bisexual Men's Descriptions and Experiences of Intersectionality." *Sex Roles* 68(11–12): 754–767.

Bronfenbrenner, Urie. 1979. *The Ecology of Human Development: Experiments by Nature and Design*. Cambridge, MA: Harvard University Press.

Brown, Jane Delano and Sarah N. Keller. 2000. "Can the Mass Media be Healthy Sex Educators?" *Perspectives on Sexual and Reproductive Health* 32(5): 255–256.

Byers, Sandra E. 1996. "How Well Does the Traditional Sexual Script Explain Sexual Coercion? Review of a Program of Research." *Journal of Psychology & Human Sexuality* 8(1/2): 7–25.

Calzo, Jerel P. and Monique Ward. 2009. "Contributions of Parents, Peers, and Media to Attitudes toward Homosexuality: Investigating Sex and Ethnic Differences." *Journal of Homosexuality* 56(8): 1101–1116.

Chung, Paul J., Raphael J. Travis, Shelley D. Kilpatrick et al. 2007. "Acculturation and Parent-Adolescent Communication about Sex in Filipino-American Families: A Community-Based Participatory Research Study." *Journal of Adolescent Health* 40(6): 543–550.

Cohen, Rachael and Katherine A. Kuvalanka. 2011. "Sexual Socialization in Lesbian-Parent Families: An Exploratory Analysis." *American Journal of Orthopsychiatry* 81(2): 293–305.

Collins, Patricia Hill. 1990. *Black Feminist Thought: Knowledge, Consciousness, and the Politics of Empowerment*. New York, NY: Routledge.

Crenshaw, Kimberlé. 1991. "Mapping the Margins: Intersectionality, Identity Politics, and Violence Against Women of Color." *Stanford Law Review* 43: 1241–1299.

Diamond, Lisa M. 2008. *Sexual Fluidity: Understanding Women's Love and Desire*. Cambridge, MA: Harvard University Press.

DiIorio, Colleen, Sally Lehr, Jill L. Wasserman et al. 2006. "Fathers are Important People: A Study of Father-Son Sexual Communication." *Journal of HIV/AIDS Prevention in Children & Youth* 7(1): 55–72.

DiIorio, Colleen, Erika Pluhar, and Lisa Belcher. 2003. "Parent-Child Communication about Sexuality: A Review of the Literature from 1980–2002." *Journal of HIV/AIDS Prevention & Education for Adolescents & Children* 5(3–4): 7–32.

Duong, Kevin. 2012. "What Does Queer Theory Teach Us About Intersectionality?" *Politics & Gender* 8(3): 370–386.

Eaton, Asia A. and Suzanna Rose. 2011. "Has Dating Become More Egalitarian? A 35 Year Review Using Sex Roles." *Sex Roles* 64(11–12): 843–862.

Elkind, David. 1999. "Religious Development in Adolescence." *Journal of Adolescence* 22: 291–295.

Epstein, Marina and Monique Ward. 2008. "'Always Use Protection': Communication Boys Receive about Sex from Parents, Peers, and the Media." *Journal of Youth and Adolescence* 37(2): 113–126.

Fasula, Amy M., Kim S. Miller, and Jeffery Wiener. 2007. "The Sexual Double Standard in African American Adolescent Women's Sexual Risk Reduction Socialization." *Women & Health* 46(2–3): 3–21.

Fine, Michelle and Sara I. McClelland. 2006. "Sexuality Education and Desire: Still Missing after All These Years." *Harvard Educational Review* 76(3): 297–338.

Fletcher, Kyla Day, Monique Ward, Khia Thomas et al. 2015. "Will it Help? Identifying Socialization Discourses that Promote Sexual Risk and Sexual Health among African American Youth." *Journal of Sex Research* 52(2): 199–212.

Gagnon, John H. 1990. "The Explicit and Implicit Use of the Scripting Perspective in Sex Research." *Annual Review of Sex Research* 1(1): 1–43.

Gecas, Viktor and Roger Libby. 1976. "Sexual Behavior as Symbolic Interaction." *The Journal of Sex Research* 12: 33–49.

Gerbner, George, Larry Gross, Michael Morgan et al. 2002. "Growing up with Television: Cultivation Processes." In *Media Effects: Advances in Theory and Research*, edited by Jennings Bryant and Dolf Zillmann, 2nd edn., 43–67. Mahwah, NJ: Lawrence Erlbaum.

Grafs, Allyson Stella and Julie Hicks Patrick. 2015. "Foundations of Life-Long Sexual Health Literacy." *Health Education* 115(1): 56–70.

Harris, Richard Jackson and Fred W. Sanborn. 2014. *A Cognitive Psychology of Mass Communication*, 6th edn. New York, NY: Routledge/Taylor & Francis Group.

Holmes, Morgan M. 2016. "Sexualities." In *The Wiley Blackwell Encyclopedia of Gender and Sexuality Studies*, edited by Nancy A. Naples. Malden, MA: Wiley Blackwell.

Hutchinson, Katherine M. and Arlene J. Montgomery. 2007. "Parent Communication and Sexual Risk among African Americans." *Western Journal of Nursing Research* 29(6): 691–707.

Irvine, Janice M. 2004. *Talk About Sex: The Battles Over Sex Education in the United States*. Berkeley, CA: University of California Press.

Jaccard, James, Patricia J. Dittus, and Vivian V. Gordon. 2000. "Parent–Teen Communication about Premarital Sex: Factors Associated with the Extent of Communication." *Journal of Adolescent Research* 15(2): 187–208.

Janssen, Diederik F. 2016. "Socialization and Sexuality." In *The Wiley Blackwell Encyclopedia of Gender and Sexuality Studies*, 5th edn., edited by Nancy A. Naples. Malden, MA: Wiley Blackwell.

Jones, Rachel K. and Ann E. Biddlecom. 2011. "Is the Internet Filling the Sexual Health Information Gap for Teens? An Exploratory Study." *Journal of Health Communication* 16(2): 112–123.

Kim, Janna L. 2009. "Asian American Women's Retrospective Reports of their Sexual Socialization." *Psychology of Women Quarterly* 33(3): 334–350.

Klein, Fritz, Barry Sepekoff, and Timothy J. Wolf. 1985. "Sexual Orientation: A Multi-Variable Dynamic Process." *Journal of Homosexuality* 11(1–2): 35–49.

Klinkenberg, Dean and Suzanna Rose. 1994. "Dating Scripts of Gay Men and Lesbians." *Journal of Homosexuality* 26(4): 23–35.

Kohler, Pamela K., Lisa E. Manhart, and William E. Lafferty. 2008. "Abstinence-Only and Comprehensive Sex Education and the Initiation of Sexual Activity and Teen Pregnancy." *Journal of Adolescent Health* 42(4): 344–351.

Kornreich, Jennifer L., Kimberly D. Hearn, Giovanna Rodriguez, and Lucia F. O'Sullivan. 2003. "Sibling Influence, Gender Roles, and the Sexual Socialization of Urban Early Adolescent Girls." *Journal of Sex Research* 40(1): 101–110.

Kunkel, Dale, Keren Eyal, Edward Donnerstein et al. 2007. "Sexual Socialization Messages on Entertainment Television: Comparing Content Trends 1997–2002." *Media Psychology* 9(3): 595–622.

Lammers, Cristina, Marjorie Ireland, Michael Resnick, and Robert Blum. 2000. "Influences on Adolescents' Decision to Postpone Onset of Sexual Intercourse: A Survival Analysis of Virginity Among Youths Aged 13 to 18 Years." *Journal of Adolescent Health* 26(1): 42–48.

Landor, Antoinette, Leslie Gordon Simons, Ronald L. Simons et al. 2011. "The Role of Religiosity in the Relationship Between Parents, Peers, and Adolescent Risky Sexual Behavior." *Journal of Youth and Adolescence* 40(3): 296–309.

Lefkowitz, Eva S., Meghan M. Gillen, Cindy L. Shearer, and Tanya L. Boone. 2004. "Religiosity, Sexual Behaviors, and Sexual Attitudes during Emerging Adulthood." *Journal of Sex Research* 41(2): 150–159.

L'Engle, Kelly Ladin, Jane D. Brown, and Kristin Kenneavy. 2006. "The Mass Media are an Important Context for Adolescents' Sexual Behavior." *Journal of Adolescent Health* 38(3): 186–192.

L'Engle, Kelly Ladin, and Christine Jackson. 2008. "Socialization Influences on Early Adolescents' Cognitive Susceptibility and Transition to Sexual Intercourse." *Journal of Research on Adolescence* 18(2): 353–378.

Lewis, Linwood J. and Robert M. Kertzner. 2003. "Toward Improved Interpretation and Theory Building of African American Male Sexualities." *Journal of Sex Research* 40(4): 383–395.

Lewis, Marissa A., Christine M. Lee, Megan E. Patrick, and Nicole Fossos. 2007. "Gender-Specific Normative Misperceptions of Risky Sexual Behavior and Alcohol-Related Risky Sexual Behavior." *Sex Roles* 57(1–2): 81–90.

Longmore, Monica A. 1998. "Symbolic Interactionism and the Study of Sexuality." *Journal of Sex Research* 35(1): 44–57.

Martinez, Gladys, Joyce Abma, and Casey Copen. 2010. "Educating Teenagers about Sex in the United States." NCHS Data Brief, 44. US Department of Health and Human Services, CDC. Available at: https://www.cdc.gov/nchs/data/databriefs/db44.pdf.

May, Vivian M. 2015. *Pursuing Intersectionality, Unsettling Dominant Imaginaries*. New York, NY: Routledge.

McClelland, Sara I. and Michelle Fine. 2008. "Embedded Science: Critical Analysis of Abstinence-Only Evaluation Research." *Cultural Studies ↔ Critical Methodologies*, 8 (1): 50–81.

Meldrum, Rebecca, Pranee Liamputtong, and Dennis Wollersheim. 2014. "Caught Between Two Worlds: Sexuality and Young Muslim Women in Melbourne, Australia." *Sexuality & Culture* 18(1): 166–179.

Miller, Dan J., Gert Martin Hald, and Garry Kidd. 2017. "Self-Perceived Effects of Pornography Consumption Among Heterosexual Men." *Psychology of Men & Masculinity* 19(3): 469–476.

O'Sullivan, Lucia F., Beatriz M. Jaramillo, Donna Moreau, and Heino F. L. Meyer-Bahlburg. 1999. "Mother-Daughter Communication About Sexuality in a Clinical Sample of Hispanic Adolescent Girls." *Hispanic Journal of Behavioral Science* 21(4): 447–469.

Raifman, Julia, Ellen Moscoe, Bryn Austin, and Margaret McConnell. 2017. "Difference-in-Differences Analysis of the Association between State Same-Sex Marriage Policies and Adolescent Suicide Attempts." *JAMA Pediatrics* 171(4): 350–356.

Regnerus, Mark. 2007. *Forbidden Fruit: Sex & Religion in the Lives of American Teenagers*. New York, NY: Oxford University Press.

Regnerus, Mark, Christian Smith, and Melissa Fritsch. 2003. "Religion in the Lives of American Adolescents: A Review of the Literature." *A Research Report of the National Study of Youth and Religion, no. 3*. Chapel Hill, NC: NSYR. Available at: https://youthandreligion.nd.edu/assets/102506/religion_in_the_lives_of_american_adolescents_a_review_of_the_literature.pdf.

Rew, Lynn and Joel Y. Wong. 2006. "A Systematic Review of Associations Among Religiosity/Spirituality and Adolescent Health Attitudes and Behaviors." *Journal of Adolescent Health* 38(4): 433–442.

Ritchwood, Tiarney D., Terrinieka W. Powell, Isha W. Metzger et al. 2017. "Understanding the Relationship between Religiosity and Caregiver–Adolescent Communication About Sex within African-American Families." *Journal of Child and Family Studies* 26(11): 2979–2989.

Santelli, John, Mary A. Ott, Maureen Lyon et al. 2006. "Abstinence-Only Education Policies and Programs: A Position Paper of the Society for Adolescent Medicine." *Journal of Adolescent Health* 38(1): 83–87.

Savin-Williams, Ritch C. 2006. "Who's Gay? Does it Matter?" *Current Directions in Psychological Science* 15(1): 40–44.

Savin-Williams, Ritch C. 2011. "Identity Development Among Sexual-Minority Youth." In *Handbook of Identity Theory and Research, Vols. 1 and 2*, edited by Seth J. Schwartz, Koen Luyckx, and Vivian L. Vignoles, 671–689. New York, NY: Springer Science + Business Media.

Schwartz, Pepper. 1994. *How Peer Marriage Really Works: Love Between Equals*. New York, NY: Free Press.

Seabrook, Rita C., Monique L. Ward, Lilia M. Cortina et al. 2017. "Girl Power or Powerless Girl? Television, Sexual Scripts, and Sexual Agency in Sexually Active Young Women." *Psychology of Women Quarterly* 41(2): 240–253.

Shtarkshall, Ronny A., John S. Santelli, and Jennifer S. Hirsch. 2007. "Sex Education and Sexual Socialization: Roles for Educators and Parents." *Perspectives on Sexual and Reproductive Health*, 39(2): 116–119.

Simon, William and John H. Gagnon. 1987. "A Sexual Scripts Approach." In *Theories of Human Sexuality*, edited by James H. Greer and William T. O'Donohue, 363–383. New York, NY: Plenum.

Spelman, Elizabeth.(1988). *Inessential Woman*. Boston, MA: Beacon Press.

Stephens, Dionne P. and Layli Phillips. 2005. "Integrating Black Feminist Thought into Conceptual Frameworks of African American Adolescent Women's Sexual Scripting Processes." *Sexualities, Evolution & Gender* 7(1): 37–55.

Strasburger, Victor C. and Edward Donnerstein. 1999. "Children, Adolescents, and the Media: Issues and Solutions." *Pediatrics* 103(1): 129–139.

Strouse, Jeremiah S., Megan P. Goodwin, and Bruce Roscoe. 1994. "Correlates of Attitudes Toward Sexual Harassment Among Early Adolescents." *Sex Roles* 31(9): 559–577.

Stryker, Sheldon. 1981. "Symbolic Interactionism: Themes and Variations." In *Social Psychology: Sociological Perspectives*, edited by Morris Rosenberg and Ralph H. Turner, 3–29. Piscataway, NJ: Transaction.

Subrahmanyam, Kaveri, Patricia M. Greenfield, and Brendesha Tynes. 2004. "Constructing Sexuality and Identity in an Online Teen Chat Room." *Journal of Applied Developmental Psychology* 25(6): 651–666.

Sümer, Zeynep Hatipoglu. 2015. "Gender, Religiosity, Sexual Activity, Sexual Knowledge, and Attitudes Toward Controversial Aspects of Sexuality." *Journal of Religion and Health* 54(6): 2033–2044.

Tolman, Deborah L. and Sara I. McClelland. 2011. "Normative Sexuality Development in Adolescence: A Decade in Review, 2000–2009." *Journal of Research on Adolescence* 21(1): 242–255.

Trinh, Sarah L. and Monique L. Ward. 2016. "The Nature and Impact of Gendered Patterns of Peer Sexual Communications Among Heterosexual Emerging Adults." *Journal of Sex Research* 53(3): 298–308.

Trinh, Sarah L., Monique L. Ward, Kyla Day et al. 2014. "Contributions of Divergent Peer and Parent Sexual Messages to Asian American College Students' Sexual Behaviors." *Journal of Sex Research* 51(2): 208–220.

Valentine, David. 2007. *Imagining Transgender: An Ethnography of a Category*. Durham, NC: Duke University Press.

Vandenbosch, Laura and Steven Eggermont. 2012. "Maternal Attachment and Television Viewing in Adolescents' Sexual Socialization: Differential Associations Across Gender." *Sex Roles* 66(1–2): 38–52.

Vincent, Louise. 2008. "'Boys Will Be Boys': Traditional Xhosa Male Circumcision, HIV and Sexual Socialisation in Contemporary South Africa." *Culture, Health & Sexuality* 10(5): 431–446.

Wang, Ningxin. 2016. "Parent-Adolescent Communication about Sexuality in Chinese Families." *Journal of Family Communication* 16(3): 229–246.

Ward, Monique L. 2002. "Does Television Exposure Affect Emerging Adults' Attitudes and Assumptions about Sexual Relationships? Correlational and Experimental Confirmation." *Journal of Youth and Adolescence* 31(1): 1–15.

Ward, Monique L. 2003. "Understanding the Role of Entertainment Media in the Sexual Socialization of American Youth: A Review of Empirical Research." *Developmental Review* 23(3): 347–388.

Warner, Leah R., Isis R. Settles, and Stephanie A. Shields. 2018. "Intersectionality Theory in the Psychology of Women." In *APA Handbook of the Psychology of Women*, edited by

Cheryl Travis and Jacquelyn White, 521–540. Washington, DC: American Psychological Association.

White, Jacquelyn W., Barrie Bondurant, and Cheryl Brown Travis. 2000. "Social Constructions of Sexuality: Unpacking Hidden Meanings." In *Sexuality, Society, and Feminism*, edited by Cheryl Brown Travis and Jacquelyn White, 11–33. Washington, DC: American Psychological Association.

Wright, Paul J. 2009. "Sexual Socialization Messages in Mainstream Entertainment Mass Media: A Review and Synthesis." *Sexuality & Culture* 13(4): 181–200.

Wyckoff, Sarah C., Kim S. Miller, Rex Forehand et al. 2008. "Patterns of Sexuality Communication between Preadolescents and their Mothers and Fathers." *Journal of Child and Family Studies* 17(5): 649–662.

10

LGBTQ Reproduction and Parenting

KATE LUXION

Childbearing and parenting are portrayed as life's major successes. Common actors in this social narrative are played by heterosexual, cisgender couples. The cisheteronormative storyline – defining "normal" as straight and cisgender – is a limited view of family-making and parenthood. This chapter focuses on discussing a variety of family types, methods in which those families come to be, and how diverse themes in parenting and reproduction are often silenced by sociopolitical infrastructures. When family is defined in only one way, it hinders parents through the psychological burden of stigma and discrimination. Media influence can sometimes help to increase awareness and shift levels of acceptance for diverse families by making the distinctions of gender and sexual orientation evident. Acceptance of lesbian, gay, bisexual, transgender, and queer (LGBTQ+) identities as a modern phenomenon ignores historical accounts of non-cisheterosexual narratives across cultures. The complexity and exclusion go beyond gender and sexual orientation and are marked by systems reinforced by white supremacy. Discrimination in and access to health services couples with limits in availability of non-white donor gametes. Such restrictions ultimately translate into limits in research, participant diversity, and clouded lens of family-making that is narrowed to primarily white, economically stable families.

Setting the Stage: Language and the Social Narrative

Used as a stand-in for lesbian, gay, bisexual, transgender, and queer, a main societal narrative around LGBTQ+ conflates gender and sexual orientation – a casualty of the simplification. Lesbian or gay is typically used by someone sexually and/or emotionally attracted to the same gender. Bisexual has come to be used both in a binary way of "liking men and women" and as a stand-in for middle sexualities – individuals attracted to more than one gender, which may or may not correspond to genitalia.

Queer is one term that might apply to either gender or sexual orientation. For some a reclamation of the term used as a slur, a queer person feels this label is the best descriptor of their gender and/or intimate relationships.

Transgender means a gender that differs from sex assumed at birth. An umbrella term itself, a transgender person may be a transman or transwoman, gender-nonconforming, nonbinary, or may forego labels altogether. A key thing to remember is that gender is not linked to genitalia in the narrative of LGBTQ+ family-making. A parent dismantling their assumed cisgender identity by coming out may or may not decide to undergo medical procedures to aid in the gender affirmation process, since body dysphoria is not always present. Thus, using medical terminology, a transwoman can have intact penis and gonads, while a transman can carry an infant to term. This critical difference between socially defined bodies and the reality of genders and sexual orientations is erased by the cisheteronormative narrative (Davis, Dewey, and Murphy 2016). Biological essentialism supports the inaccurate idea that "productive" bodies fit into limited, binary categories further limiting roles and interactions (Moreira 2018).

While a combined single-letter abbreviation might not suggest it, these identities can coexist. A transman can be gay, allowing him and his cisgender partner to conceive through penetrative sex. Hormones as part of gender affirmation care, such as testosterone, can be adjusted for lactation or paused for gestation and birth (MacDonald et al. 2016). Breast/chestfeeding is not a gender-restricted activity or role, though it is often relegated to such by mainstream ideas (Zizzo 2009; MacDonald et al. 2016).

Everyday Limitations: The Ramifications of Cisheteronormativity

Discrimination and limitations are enacted by social, medical, and legal systems. One such additional source are people who don't agree with their LGBTQ+ peers' desires for parenthood. Intercommunity pressures often suggest LGBTQ+ family-making is reinforcing cisheteronormative ideals, leading to outsider status in general and in the LGBTQ+ community (Murphy 2013). Similar stigma is felt by parents who have children in previous heterosexual relationships prior to coming out as LGBTQ+ (Lee 2009). In these various contexts LGBTQ+ persons must petition to obtain access to parenthood.

With the conflation of gender and sex, a patient is either male or female and accessible health services are determined by the sex-as-gender listed on their records (Berger et al. 2015). Health informatics and accuracies rely on presumptions to determine services needed (i.e. cervical screenings, prostate exams, etc.). The limited lens of men's and women's health do not allocate for overlapping when bodies depart from binary assumptions conflating gender and genitalia. For intersex individuals, reproduction options are left medically and socially underexplored (Casteràs et al. 2009), labeled with unsubstantiated infertility. For transmen, gender markers present difficulties in receiving comprehensive reproductive care (Berger et al. 2015).

Conflating gender with sex/genitals often presumes fertility. Reproduction narratives, linked to fertility definitions, state acceptable parents are married, cisgender individuals. Ideals of wealth and whiteness further narrow who is expected to become a parent, shaping accessibility to parenthood. In surrogacy narratives, brown bodies are at the service of white parents; commodities instead of people (Schurr 2017). Presentation of family constellations can lead to cisheterosexual presumptions that erase bisexuality and trans individuals. The sexuality of bisexual parents is often left unexplored due to inconsistencies in employing inclusive methodologies (Ross and Dobinson 2012). Those same assumptions carry over to gender, in that sex and gender are conflated and binary options pervade research measures. Qualitative research has expanded on prior methodology to include measures on gender and sexual orientation. Carrying over to quantitative measures, the result is a more credible understanding of reproduction and parenting. As more narratives improve the understanding of family constellations, they expand accessibility to parenthood. Updated definitions of kinship go beyond genetics to reframe family and reproduction to be in tune with the diversity across history (Batza 2016; Hull and Ortyl 2018).

Seeking parenthood can vary by geographic context and is often riddled by a cascade of expenses. Infertility treatments are accessible for cisheterosexual parents, while LGBTQ+ parents are required to pay out of pocket for as many as 12 cycles in the United States before health insurance will cover costs (Carpinello et al. 2016). On top of medical expenses, legal costs accrue while determining need for donor or surrogacy contracts and adoption fees when states don't recognize co-parentage automatically (Sanabria 2013). Due to these barriers, research samples of LGBTQ+ parents are more economically stable across geographic contexts; stability being less likely due to discrimination restricting access for education and employment (Ross et al. 2008; Nebeling Petersen 2016).

Race also effects the results. Social accessibility favors white parents, prioritizing white donor gametes while placing a premium price tag for access when compared to non-white gametes (Machin 2014; Karpman, Ruppel, and Torres 2018). Because of these limitations, what is known about LGBTQ+ reproduction and parenting is centered on white, economically stable families. For the purposes of monitored reproductive services, efforts are isolated to countries with assisted medical reproduction services that are legally open to residents and/or foreigners.

Motivations for becoming a parent for LGBTQ+ parents are often stigmatized. Social narratives that remove nurturing behaviors led many of the LGBTQ+ parents interviewed to believe their sexuality and desires for parenthood were mutually exclusive (Murphy 2013; Cao et al. 2016). Desires for parenthood were more universal across research, with parents wanting to share joy-filled childhoods and raise a more tolerant generation (Goldberg, Downing, and Moyer 2012). Conscious of the double standard, LGBTQ+ parents must prove their capacity for parenting prior to conception (Wojnar and Katzenmeyer 2014). A burden of proof not imposed as stringently on cisheterosexual parents.

LGBTQ+ Rights and Parenthood on a Global Stage

The social narrative, or "what's normal," can shift from culture to culture. Prior to colonization nonbinary genders were pervasive. Contemporary examples surviving Western governing include Hijras in India, Fa'afafines and Māhū in Polynesia, and

Two-Spirit Native Americans; all terms used to honor the presence of multiple genders and sexualities. Binary colonialist narratives idealizing cisheteronormative reproduction reinforce social exclusion and erasure of LGBTQ+ parents. For histories maintained or uncovered, those identities will be interwoven into the discourse to follow. Legality of homosexuality erases identities – both for safety and exclusion – causing limited access to data for the countries listed in Table 10.1.

Definitions around success and development of countries lends itself to discourse inaccurately limiting the need for LGBTQ+ rights. Where homosexual behaviors are illegal, events of "corrective rape" can result in LGBTQ+ individuals becoming pregnant without access to abortion (Human Dignity Trust 2016). LGBTQ+ parents often cite the requirement of "compulsory heterosexuality" when attempting to navigate the legal, health, and social systems as non-cisheteronormative families (Rich 1980; Ross et al. 2008; Malmquist 2015). Removal of children from a mother found to be attracted to other women, regardless of if she acts on those attractions is not uncommon in these contexts (Human Dignity Trust 2016). Categorizing of LGBTQ+ identities as isolated to the West fails to acknowledge legal silencing of gender and sexual orientation. Global fertility monitoring provides more information about whether there is a lack of access to or a lack of desire for parenthood (Allan et al. 2016; Lo, Chan, and Chan 2016). China, which restricts access to assisted reproduction, serves as an example of how need and desire for parenthood can be hidden by stigma and access. Half of self-identified lesbians interviewed wished to become parents, but are not allowed medical access, with social channels stigmatized (Lo et. al 2016). Such approaches contribute to erasing the global need for LGBTQ+ rights and perpetuate stereotypes of LGBTQ+ identities being limited to the West.

LGBTQ+ equality is often assumed with the legality of same-gender marriage, marriage often being the precursor for family-making in cisheteronormative narratives. However, acceptance does not always extend to LGBTQ+ families or reproduction. The social order of love, marriage, family informs the legal system in a manner that limits equity. White gay men as the icon of gay marriage, coupled with the hypersexualization of lesbian couples, reduces LGBTQ+ couples to nonparenting roles (Lee 2009). These sentiments are mirrored in the removal of the ability to nurture from the narrative of fatherhood (Lynch and Morison 2016). Single parenthood by LGBTQ+ parents can be purposeful and successful but falls to the additional stigma of parenthood without marriage. Social limitations are complicated by parenthood in the context of LGBTQ+ relationships lacking support by peers for being too heteronormative an act (Cao et al. 2016). Yet, it is assumed wrongly that marriage equates to full parental rights.

Laws regarding reproductive technologies, shared in Table 10.2, are not universal either, often requiring parents to seek out-of-country reproduction for their family to be legally recognized (Van Hoof, Pennings and De Sutter 2015). The pursuit of parenthood can be punishable through stringent reproductive laws, such as in-country surrogacy regulations in Denmark (Van Hoof et al. 2015). Legal access to parenthood at times carries the prerequisite of marriage (Malmquist 2015; Mohapatra 2017). Proving genetic parenthood or marital partnership are not required for cisheterosexual couples to be recognized in the eyes of the courts. Procedures in Sweden require that the man claiming the role of father has the right to state he holds such a

Table 10.1 Countries where homosexuality is illegal

Africa	Americas	Asia	Oceania
Algeria	Antigua & Barbuda	Afghanistan	Pakistan	Cook Islands*
Angola	Barbados†	Bangladesh	Qatar	Kiribati
Botswana	Dominica	Bhutan	Saudi Arabia	Papua New Guinea
Burundi	Grenada	Brunei Darussalam	Singapore	Samoa
Cameroon	Guyana	Gaza/Occupied Palestine*	Sri Lanka	Solomon Islands
Comoros	Jamaica	India	Syria	Tonga
Egypt	St. Kitts & Nevis	Indonesia	Turkmenistan	Tuvalu
Eritrea	St. Lucia	Iran	United Arab Emirates	
Ethiopia	St. Vincent & The Grenadines	Iraq	Uzbekistan	
Gambia		Kuwait	Yemen	
Ghana		Lebanon		
Guinea		Malaysia		
Kenya		Maldives		
Liberia		Myanmar		
Libya		Oman		
Malawi				
Mauritania				
Mauritius				
Morocco				
Namibia				
Nigeria‡				
Senegal				
Sierra Leone				
Somalia				
South Sudan				
Sudan				
Swaziland				
Tanzania				
Togo				
Tunisia				
Uganda				
Zambia				
Zimbabwe				

Adapted from Carroll and Mendos (2017) and Human Rights Watch (2018).
* Self-governing with citizenship in another nation.
† In-vitro fertilization/assisted reproductive technologies (IVF/ART) accessible to single women/same-sex female couples (Allan et al. 2016).
‡ IVF/ART accessible to single women (Allan et al. 2016).

Table 10.2 Access to assisted reproductive technology, alternative insemination, and legal parent status in monitored countries

10.2a Europe

Region/Country	Automatic Co-Parent Recognition	Assisted Repro. (Couple)	Assisted Repro. (Single)
EUROPE			
Albania			
Andorra			
Armenia			●
Austria*	●†	●	
Azerbaijan			
Belarus			●‡
Belgium	●	●	●
Bosnia & Herzegovina			
Bulgaria		●‡	●‡
Croatia		●	●
Cyprus			●
Czech Republic*			
Denmark	●	●‡	●‡
Estonia		●‡	●‡
Finland	●	●‡	●‡
France*			
Georgia			●
Germany		●‡	●‡
Greece		●‡‡	●‡‡
Hungary*			●
Iceland		●	●
Ireland	●	●	●‡
Italy*			
Kosovo**			
Latvia			●
Liechtenstein			
Lithuania			
Luxembourg		●	●
Macedonia			
Malta	●		
Moldova			●
Monaco			
Montenegro			●
Netherlands	●	●	●
Norway*	●†	●	
Poland			●
Portugal*	●	●	●
Romania			●‡‡
Russia			●‡
San Marino			
Serbia			
Slovakia*			
Slovenia			
Spain	●†	●‡	●‡
Sweden*	●	●	●

Table 10.2 (Continued)

Region/Country	Automatic Co-Parent Recognition	Assisted Repro. (Couple)	Assisted Repro. (Single)
Switzerland*			
Turkey			
Ukraine			●
United Kingdom	●	●	●

10.2b Asia and Oceania; Africa and The Middle East; North And Central America, South America

Region/Country	Automatic Co-Parent Recognition	Assisted Repro. (Couple)	Assisted Repro. (Single)
ASIA AND OCEANIA			
Australia	●†		●
China*			
Japan*			
Kazakhstan*			
New Zealand*			●
Philippines*			
South Korea*			
Vietnam*			
NORTH AND CENTRAL AMERICA			
Canada		●	●
El Salvador		●‡	●
Guatemala		●‡⁂	●‡⁂
Honduras			●
Mexico	●†	●	●
Panama		●‡⁂	●‡⁂
Trinidad & Tobago		●‡	●‡
United States	●		●
AFRICA AND THE MIDDLE EAST			
Demo. Rep. of Congo*			
Israel	●†		●‡⁂
Ivory Coast*			
Jordan*			
Mali*			
South Africa	●	●‡⁂	●
SOUTH AMERICA			
Argentina	●	●‡⁂	●‡⁂
Brazil		●	●
Chile		●‡⁂	●*
Colombia			
Ecuador		●‡⁂	●‡⁂
Paraguay		●	●
Peru		●	●
Uruguay	●†	●‡⁂	●‡⁂
Venezuela		●*	●

Tables 10.2a and 10.2b adapted from IFFS Surveillance (Ory et al. 2014; Allan et al. 2016) and ILGA-Europe Annual Review (2017).
*Country requires recognized or stable heterosexual relationship.
**Under UNSCR 1244/1999.
†Limited to Same-Sex Partner(Woman).
‡Excluding single men.
⁂Excluding transgender and intersex individuals.

Table 10.3 Legal access to adoption

Region/Country	Joint Adoption	Second-Parent Adoption
AFRICA		
Niger	●	●
South Africa	●	●
AMERICAS		
Argentina	●	●
Brazil	●	
Canada*	●	●
Colombia	●	●
United States*	●	●
Uruguay	●	●
ASIA AND OCEANIA		
Australia*	●	●
Israel	●	●
New Zealand	●	●
EUROPE		
Andorra	●	●
Austria	●	●
Belgium	●	●
Denmark	●	●
Estonia		●
Finland	●	●
France	●	●
Germany		●
Iceland	●	●
Ireland	●	●
Luxembourg	●	●
Malta	●	
Netherlands	●	●
Norway	●	●
Portugal	●	●
Slovenia		●
Spain	●	●
Sweden	●	●
Switzerland		●
United Kingdom	●	●

Adapted from Carroll and Mendos 2017 and International Family Equality Day 2018.
*Varies by State, Province, and/or Territory.

position – being given the legal title in response (Malmquist 2015). For lesbian co-mothers seeking legal access for both parents, the process begins with a letter, followed by court proceedings and mandated counseling visits and approvals that can take up to a year to finalize (Malmquist 2015). Access to children at school, while seeking medical care, and even picking up drug store prescriptions are all legally inaccessible to the co-parent. Legal context and adoption laws, shown in Table 10.3, inform outcomes and access. Social exclusion and demotion to emergency contact without the power to make decisions for the well-being of the child are withheld as well. Many LGBTQ+ co-parents cite concern for access to their own child in the case of spousal death (Wojnar and Katzenmeyer 2014), the latter being something established with ease for cisheterosexual parent peers.

Questions of legality arise and shift constantly, changing access to parenthood and family-making outside of the heteronormative. Often medical tourism with less-restricted access to assisted reproductive technologies can lead to countries facilitating LGBTQ reproduction. Such an approach, however, does not remove uncertainty; often relying on a lack of laws or clearly stated exclusions for access. As an example, India was once accessible politically and economically, but now restricts access to heterosexual couples (Nebeling Petersen 2016). This cisheteronormative narrative places the act of procreation in the privacy of the home, away from the ever-present legal gaze determining suitability, while all elements of LGBTQ+ reproduction are forced into public arenas as open for debate. The global stage has seen the rise and fall of countries trying to fill the need left by India's surrogacy restrictions before soon placing their own bans to address concerns regarding race, social class, and the body as commodity (Nebeling Petersen 2016). LGBTQ+ parenthood is an intricate global dance with inconsistency in adoption, surrogacy, and parenthood laws. In the contexts of both Australia and the United States, there is a general idea of acceptability and access to surrogacy and adoption. More often, legal decisions are being made at regional and local levels which contributes to the variability (Carroll and Mendos 2017; Mohapatra 2017). Political barriers remain through limiting cisheteronormative narratives reinforcing that LGBTQ+ persons cannot be parents (Lee 2009; Lynch and Morison 2016).

Reproduction: Methods for LGBTQ+ Family-Making

Regardless of the approach taken, LGBTQ+ reproduction requires the crossing of geographic borders, making it a transnational affair requiring a delicate balance between access, facilitation, and societal navigation at all stages. For conception, sperm and ovum, or gametes, are provided by one or both parents. Gestation of the infant(s) may be done by one or both parents, or, in the cases of surrogacy, neither (Tarín, García-Pérez and Cano 2015). As for the sources of those gametes, the cisheteronormative gendering of the egg (female) and sperm (male) fails to capture procreation accurately – as two men, one with each gamete can conceive without medical assistance.

Prior to the advent of medically assisted insemination, lesbian women in the United States arranged networks of compensated donors and sperm runners (Batza 2016). Access to assisted medical reproduction opened the door for some parents, while sterilization through gender affirmation benchmarks (i.e, hysterectomies, oophorectomies, and orchiectomy) were enforced on transgender bodies to gain legal access to gender markers (von Doussa, Power, and Riggs 2015; Davis et al. 2016). Removal of these laws have enabled some access to individuals seeking parenthood, though laws have not undone providers' ability to refuse service (Chapman et al. 2012). Thus, legal access and desire are met with having to navigate social and medical exclusion from preconception onward. The myth of nature supporting inaccessibility to biological parenthood is supported through a limiting view on where

LGBTQ+ conception takes place. Non-cisheteronormative conception might be a gay couple conceiving at home and without medical assistance, since sex organs do not dictate gender. Gametes which fertilize may come from a partner/spouse, relative, or friend depending on each individual parents' situation. At-home insemination is also available to lesbian, bisexual, trans, and gender-nonconforming partners – both with and without medical assistance – meaning that there are various compositions of parents who conceive through penetrative sex alone, contrary to stereotypes used to shame and belittle LGBTQ+ families. Whether this route is taken is wholly dependent on the couple's wishes regarding which parent will carry the pregnancy in the role of gestational parent. While it is possible for trans individuals to be the gestational parents, not all transgender parents desire pregnancy themselves – instead face the emotional reconciliation of being unable to impregnate their partner (Tornello and Bos 2017). Similarly, transwomen may desire filling either pregnancy role. With technological improvements, uterine transplants may soon address this unmet need. Similarly, transmen may seek use of their own augmented gametes to fertilize a partner's gametes once the science is clinically applicable.

The process of choosing which partner will be the gestational parent can depend on factors that vary from couple to couple. The health of gametes along with health, age, and desire to carry are the primary themes that arise in the research (Hayman et al. 2014; dickey, Ducheny and Ehrbar 2016). Some fluidity to the process for lesbian and queer parents is present with the gestational carrier shifting if there are difficulties conceiving (Hayman and Wilkes 2016). Possible concurrent attempts at conception may take place, or partners may seek to change gestational parents from pregnancy to pregnancy (Carpinello et al. 2016). Each set of parents' unique circumstances dictate how they might improve their chances for conceiving.

Parents considering insemination using donor gametes are now recommended to start the process using medical services (Riggs 2008). Utilizing the institutional route to donor gametes means being met with health services that presume cisheterosexuality through standardized intake procedures (Ellis, Wojnar, and Pettinato 2014; Moreira 2018). Medical insurance considers LGBTQ+ individuals who are looking to start a family socially infertile, as defined in Table 10.4, and ineligible until biological infertility is diagnosed (Carpinello et al. 2016). Cisheterosexual couples benefit economically through insurance coverage imposing fewer clinical requirements than they do for LGBTQ+ parents (Carpinello et al. 2016). Advocates are pushing for equitable access through a reinterpretation of medical definitions (Mohapatra 2017).

On top of insurance restrictions and possible outright refusal, microaggressions are experienced during fertility and prenatal care by gestational parents. Lesbian co-mothers in Canada recall experiences in the health system that often required working through mental and emotional stresses caused by exclusion of their partner, off-hand comments by providers, and lack of culturally humble care (Ellis et al. 2014). Medical policies and procedures catering to cisheterosexual families cause preventable stress in the form of stigma and discrimination (Moreira 2018). LGBTQ+ gestational parents have shared similar experiences with office staff and care providers not trained in providing welcoming and accurate care (Ellis et al. 2014). There are exceptions, which should instead be commonplace, where providers work with their patients to ensure wants and needs are addressed, starting with method of

Table 10.4 Insemination terminology

Term	Definition
Intrauterine insemination (IUI)	Gametes mixed inside the gestational parent's uterus for fertilization and implantation.
In vitro fertilization (IVF)	When gametes are mixed outside the gestational parent or surrogate.
Cycle	For IUI, one cycle coincides with ovulation, while IVF does not require ovulation.
Reception of oocytes from partner (ROPA)	A procedure using gametes from one partner for fertilization before being implanted into their partner's uterus.
Single partner conception (SPC)	When one partner conceives and carries a pregnancy.
Double partner conception (DPC)	When both partners eventually carry a pregnancy.
Shared conception (SC)	When gametes fertilized for one partner are used for the second partner's subsequent pregnancy.
Biological infertility	When mixed gametes do not result in a live birth in an expected number of attempts.
Social infertility	Availability of only one gamete type in partnership, requiring proof of biological infertility.

Adapted from Machin 2014, Moreira 2018, Wyverkens et al. 2014, and Carpinello et al. 2016.

insemination, defined in Table 10 4. Some lesbian mothers prefer at-home intrauterine insemination (IUI), allowing the co-mother to be hands-on in the process (Somers et al. 2016). Other co-parents feel that the medical procedure and framing of "injections" better fits their ideals for queering the reproductive process (Wyverkens et al. 2014; Somers et al. 2016).

Regardless of conception method, this is where the data stops. A lack of follow-through on birth outcomes for LGBTQ+ parents – gestational and those employing surrogates – provides a half-painted picture (Tarín et al. 2015). Higher success rates are present for lesbian women who use medically assisted insemination (Tarín et al.2015) while quality of prenatal care is primarily addressed in articles calling on inclusive care practices and intake procedures. Birth outcomes for gestational parents highlight why expanding research efforts are vital. One lesbian mother recounts being kept from visiting her child in the neonatal unit by staff who told her she was "not the real mother" (Hayman and Wilkes 2016). A British study found comparable results, highlighting the process lesbian mothers must undertake not to internalize negative treatment experienced during maternal care (Lee, Taylor, and Raitt 2011). When it was assumed on a visit that they were a surrogate, the gestational parent chose to not clarify themselves as the parent to reduce the level of stigma faced during the process (Ellis et al. 2014). The current state of perinatal medicine for LGBTQ+ gestational parents is best summarized by Chapman et al. when they made clear there is "no evidence the current system does no harm" (2012).

Surrogacy

When there is a need for someone else to serve as the gestational carrier of a biological child, LGBTQ+ parents may seek to employ a surrogate. The word employ, however,

Table 10.5 Types of surrogacy

Surrogacy type	Definition
Traditional/Partial surrogacy	When a surrogate provides half of the genetic matter used to procreate, with the other half coming from the intended parent(s).
Gestational/Full surrogacy	When genetic materials implanted come from two external sources, usually connected to at least one parent.

Adapted from Sanabria 2013.

is limited in how accurately it describes the relationship between parent(s) and surrogate. For countries like Denmark, it is illegal to pay surrogates for their services, but legal for an altruistic/unpaid surrogacy to take place (Nebeling Petersen 2016). This is just one of the many reasons why the use of transnational reproduction, or crossing of geographic borders to reproduce, has sparked a contentious debate including limited diversity of donor gametes, implicitly catering to white, wealthy parents-to-be (Ryan and Moras 2016; Schurr 2017; Karpman et al. 2018). Gestational surrogacy, as defined in Table 10.5, is the most common type of surrogacy gay fathers use when seeking a biological child (Blake et al. 2016). This mode of accessing parenthood is sometimes more certain and less complicated due to the biological connection made between parent and child (Sanabria 2013).

The choice of who will be the biological parent and where the rest of the gametes come from varies from couple to couple. Gay fathers may purchase gametes from commercial resources, arrange with a biologic relation to provide a genetic connection to both parents, or have gametes donated by a friend (Blake et al. 2016; May and Tenzek 2016). Openness of the donor and the lack of contesting parentage were two other factors that influence the selection of gametes by gay fathers (Sanabria 2013). Compared with other parents using gestational surrogacy, gay fathers show higher success rates for outcomes (Tarín et al. 2015).

Whether fathers chose to inform their children of the use of a surrogate and how the surrogate is portrayed varies as well (Blake et al. 2016). In an example of two Italian fathers, both partners told their child about the "mummy tummy" that was part of their reproduction story (Carone, Baiocco, and Lingiardi 2017). As the donor and surrogate are often separate individuals, there may be gametes donated by a sibling of one partner (Blake et al. 2016) while the surrogate may go on to become a "special aunt" (Carone et al. 2017).

There is a long history of gay parents seeking surrogacy in India, using gametes fertilized by one or both partners to impregnate a local woman employed through an agency – with legally mandated anonymity of the surrogate (Blake et al. 2016). The model presented an affordability to parents while being met with global criticism due to a lack of transparency around pay and outcomes for all parties involved (Blake et al. 2016; Nebeling Petersen 2016). Communication between parents and surrogates is common with American surrogates – both Italian and Israeli gay fathers commending connections they formed during pregnancy (Ziv and Freund-Eschar 2014; Carone et al. 2017). Emotional distancing from the parents-to-be and the pregnancy has shown to be stressful for the fathers who recall using surrogacy services in India that restricted access to pregnancy updates (Ziv and Freund-Eschar

2014; Carone et al. 2017). Part of the emotional distress is feeling as if the process is procedural, caught up in charts and graphs, rather than a process of connecting through stories and experiences had by the surrogate (Ziv and Freund-Eschar 2014).

The legal status of surrogacy leaves little choice for same-sex couples. The encouraged emotional connection between parents and surrogates from the United States comes with a price tag that is not attainable to families without high income and/or resource levels (Ziv and Freund-Eschar 2014; Nebeling Petersen 2016; Carone et al. 2017). With the legal climate for parents and reproductive health service providers, surrogacy is becoming more difficult to pursue. At the time of publication, the only known location that allows for legal compensated gay surrogacy is the United States with access further restricted at the state level (Nebeling Petersen 2016; Mohapatra 2017). There are a few remaining options for altruistic surrogacy, such as Denmark and New Zealand, but not always in contexts where surrogacy contracts can be enforced by the courts (Nebeling Petersen 2016). For parents who do choose to seek surrogacy, it is important to note parents' local laws, as those often supersede the laws where surrogacy took place and can require facilitation of adoption, addressed in the next section of this chapter, for the birth certificate to contain accurate parental information (Murphy 2013).

Adoption

Having a biological connection to form a family is not always the wish or the requirement. Just as with cisheterosexual parents, there are considerations made to assess the right path to parenthood. What are the costs that might be entailed? Is our home willing or able to undergo a home study to assess fitness of parentage? Joint adoption, where parenthood is established through forming a legal connection to the child can be done through an adoption agency or after working with the foster care system. For parents who have children from a previous marriage or have conceived in a country/location without automatic parent recognition, second-parent, sometimes called step-parent, adoption would be the option to legally join the child(ren) to both parents. Depending on the context of the relationship, such as in Denmark, it may be a requirement that parents are married and undergo counseling for the adoption to be allowed by the court (Malmquist 2015). Procedural hurdles requiring levels of outness and counseling may dissuade parents from welcoming the scrutiny of the adoption process into their lives (Sanabria 2013; Nebeling Petersen 2016).

With the federal adoption ban in the United States, it was more feasible for LGBTQ+ parents to explore donor insemination rather than adoption, domestic or transnational (Goldberg and Scheib 2015). Uncertainty around legal parenthood, rights of co-parents, and legal precedents that favored grandparents and biological relations in the event of a partner's death created unfavorable spaces to seek parenthood through adoption (Goldberg et al. 2013; Goldberg and Scheib 2015). For some parents, access as a single parent enabled adoption without raising red flags, causing them to navigate the experience as closeted adults unable to recognize their partner's presence (Brown et al. 2009; Goldberg et al. 2013). LGBTQ+ parents had to put into place a legal chain of custody in hopes to ensure they would be able to co-parent with equal access to medical and school records (Goldberg et al. 2013). During pregnancy, the lack of automatic co-parent recognition met with the tragedy of maternal death during birth, a parent might lose both their partner and, in turn, legal right to their child. Clauses placed in wills aimed to make clear that the surviving parent be made legal guardian in hopes that no one contested their right to remain their child's parent (Goldberg et al. 2013). Going beyond fear of denial of legal access, couples may also navigate nonsupportive family members who might circumvent wishes to raise the child in a religious, heteronormative home (Goldberg et al. 2013).

Since the lifting of the ban, there have been some improvements in certainty through legal access to co-parentage (Goldberg et al. 2013). State level bills have begun to pass in Georgia and Oklahoma which give the court the right to deny adoption for religious and/or cultural reasons, specifically if the home is deemed to not align with the child's best interests or the agency's moral convictions (Georgia General Assembly 2018; Oklahoma 2018). Legal access to children through adoption is important to ensure the ability to bring them to school and to the doctor, as well as the ability to be recognized as a family. Due to heteronormative privilege and the expectation that parents be of differing genders, LGBTQ+ parents often cite demeaning experiences limiting co-parents to emergency contacts, rendering them unable to make decisions for their children unless they possess proof of legal parenthood (Malmquist 2015).

Expanding narratives around kinship and family

Definitions of kinship follow cisheteronormative limitations reinforced by legal systems across the life course. To some extent circumventing such limitations is made possible through chosen families. For LGBTQ+ youth and adults, disowning biological families are replaced by a network of chosen siblings and parents to ameliorate social exclusion. Redefining kinship beyond biological connections helps to address the strain of living in a cisheteronormative environment (Hull and Ortyl 2018). With the unavoidable trend of aging, a major concern is revisiting the horrors of the start of the HIV/AIDS epidemic. Partners and chosen families are left unable to access or support their households due to legal definitions of kinship (Hull and Ortyl 2018). Chosen family connections fall prey to the same systematic hurdles in place for LGBTQ+ families without the privilege of expected biological connections.

Going beyond a closed family unit, kinship can be linked through biology in a way that also reshapes family dynamics. Presumptions of two-parent households exalts a limited picture of what and who makes a family (Moreira 2018). For some, finding half-siblings of their children as a way of extending their family unit recognizes both the limited and expanded definitions of kinship (Edwards 2015). Whatever the motivations or characteristics sought when seeking a donor, the concept of kinship as sameness and genetic is outdated. There is a complexity and fluidity to the realities of kinship which varies cross-culturally (Nordqvist 2013; Edwards 2015).

In general, there is a lack of examining different family structures across research literature. Gay and lesbian households comprise the primary body of research on LGBTQ+ reproduction and parenting, leaving to the wayside transgender and nonbinary parents and LGBTQ+ partners who chose to have and/or raise children as part of polyamorous relationships. Blended families comprise the parent(s) and children from previous relationships (Costa and Bidell 2017). Missing from research are bisexual partnerships which sometimes present as heterosexual marriages while still leaving them open to discrimination (Ross and Dobinson 2012; Gato, Santos and Fontaine 2017). Biological relatedness is not necessary for family or kinship and legal connectedness is not guaranteed. Expanding the narrative of parenthood will help improve inclusion and social support.

LGBTQ+ Parenting

Often the stigma of LGBTQ+ relationships and parenthood carries assumptions that any children who are part of such relationships will suffer in that they will fail to acclimate into a heteronormative society. Prior to empirical resources, the social norms supported these assumptions as they fit with the pathologizing of gender outside the binary and sexual orientation for those who weren't heterosexual, cisgender men. Research that meets the rigors of scientific methods has found evidence to the contrary regarding the health and well-being of children of non-cisheteronormative parents. Negative sources of stress for children of LGBTQ+ parents come primarily in the form of stigma, bullying, and mistreatment of their families in health and educational systems (Kuvalanka, Leslie, and Radina 2013). Disparities in inclusive policies highlight the need for systemic changes to offset stigma carried out by discriminatory narratives of family as cisheteronormative (Nicol et al. 2013; Bennett et al. 2016).

The better adjustment outcomes seen among the 17-year-old adolescents surveyed in the US National Longitudinal Lesbian Family Study was attributed to the balance of power within the context of the lesbian homes (Gartrell and Bos 2010). Children adopted by gay fathers in the United Kingdom, when compared with peers in heterosexual families, had fewer externalizing problems despite starting with a higher level of risk (Golombok et al. 2013). Australian LGBTQ+ families have shown similar outcomes pertaining to physical health despite a negative association between health and stigma towards their family-types (Crouch et al. 2014). Foster children are often thought to be higher risk for poorer health outcomes. However, a sample adopted by LGBTQ+ parents in Los Angeles, California was found to have mental and emotional health equal to or better than their lower risk peers (Lavner, Waterman, and Peplau 2012). Children born to gay fathers via surrogacy had adjustment levels that mirrored their British peers born to lesbian mothers (Golombok et al. 2017). Research studies in Italy have shown that children of LGBTQ+ parents mirror the outcomes of their peers with cisheterosexual parents despite not having the same level of legal family support as the United States (Baiocco et al. 2015). Overall, outcomes for the children of LGBTQ+ parents show a resilience and maturity through the processes learned by navigating systems that are skewed against their families.

Positive outcomes despite daily discrimination have been attributed to the positive effects of balancing the distribution of household power, thus stepping away from gendered roles (Gartrell and Bos 2010). Discrimination of LGBTQ+ parents is cited empirically as their children's reason for leaving behind harmful gender roles (Malmquist et al. 2013). Parental successes could also be due to the level of relationship satisfaction when compared with cisheterosexual peers (Farr, Forssell, and

Patterson 2010; Borneskog et al. 2014b) as well as an understanding of social stressors and discrimination encountered by one's partner.

LGBTQ+ parent health

Mental health after birth can present complications for new parents. Often linked to biological functions of hormones, there is an adjustment period that happens when a new child is welcomed into the home. For lesbian co-parents, Canadian research has shown these changes can extend beyond the birthing parent and involve both biological processes and the social and behavioral effects of a rapid shift in schedule and social acceptance (Ross 2005). Increased isolation due to existing between and not within communities can exacerbate postpartum depression symptoms more than for heterosexual peers (Ross 2005; Cao et al. 2016). Often LGBTQ+ parents find that they are not welcome in social circles they previously belonged to when they become a parent – sometimes considered the heterosexual thing to do in social LGBTQ+ narratives (Cao et al. 2016). Unwelcomed in other public parent-centered spaces for not being heterosexual enough to meet the same standards projects on them by their peers (Cao et al. 2016), there are also positive differences as gender role dynamics mitigate parenting stress by balancing expectations in home life (Ross 2005).

A Swedish study was done questioning the level of parenting stress felt by those who used in vitro fertilization (IVF) (Borneskog et al 2014a). Comparing lesbian couples to cisheterosexual couples, the lower levels of parent stress in the Swedish study mirrored Ross's findings. The requirements of planning and psychological screenings that are prerequisite for lesbian parents seem to counteract the social pressures that typically result in levels of depression in lesbian women (Ross 2005). Gay fathers in the UK showed lower parenting stress in the cases of adoption, so the association between positive mental health outcomes is not restricted to gestational parents who are stepping outside normative gendered parenting roles – there is a clearer association with balanced responsibilities mitigating daily stresses faced by parents in ways benefiting child(ren) as well (Golombok et al. 2013). This suggests structural changes that become more inclusive and reduce discrimination will benefit mental health outcomes.

Grief and loss

Loss of a pregnancy is a difficult topic, regardless of family structure; but only some parents can receive recognition and support in their time of grief. For LGBTQ+ parents there is a delicate dance between outing themselves and their family structure in public spaces as part of the grieving process, while also seeking access to grief in a context that barely recognizes their ability to seek parenthood (Wojnar and Swanson 2006). LGBTQ+ fertility is always framed as social, erasing the experiences of biological infertility. For gestational parents who have miscarried, support groups and materials are centered for heterosexual families (Black and Fields 2014); just as is the case for gay parents who experience miscarriage while working with a surrogate.

There can be a finiteness to the loss experienced due to social and economic barriers in place for LGBTQ+ parents. To avoid loss and its emotional strain, gay fathers seeking surrogacy will structure the genetic relationship to reduce the risk of loss (Blake et al. 2017). A global online survey of lesbian and bisexual women addressed the issue that compounding loss is that it is built upon a foundation of hard-fought planning and arrangements (Peel 2009). Often alienated during the procedural aftermath of a miscarriage, nurses keeping partners from being in the same room as news of miscarriage was delivered among other methods of exclusion (Hayman and Wilkes 2016). This places LGBTQ+ parents in a position that cisheterosexual parents are not asked to achieve: navigating grief in a context of systemic homophobia, transphobia, and institutionally supported discrimination (Wojnar and Swanson 2006).

As the legal and political shifts have taken place around the topic of surrogacy, specifically for gay parents, loss can also be framed as lack of legal access to embryos. When the medical visa regulations changed in India, Klaus found himself and his partner Peter having to recover from a surrogate's miscarriage and then no longer having access to their embryos (Nebeling Petersen 2016). An unfortunate repeat of events took place for them after moving from India to Thailand – with a miscarriage right before the ban in Thailand halting their attempts to start a family (Nebeling Petersen 2016). It was no longer politically or financially feasible for them to try for children. That uncertainty of access to future attempts at conceiving is paired with a societal question of both the rights to parenthood and the potential grief along the way.

Queering lactation

Damage inflicted by upholding the gender binary goes beyond reproduction and introduces oversimplified roles in infant nutrition. Breasts are contextualized in the West as sexualized objects, disembodied from any type of functionality and gendered in all contexts (Rippey and Falconi 2016; MacDonald et al. 2016). Lactation is the primary recommended source of nutrition for infants in their first year. Despite the presence of mammary glands in bodies that have been assumed male or female at birth, the role of nutrition is presumed to fall solely to "a mother." This assumption is rooted in Western idealization of gender roles often questioned and explored through cultural anthropology (Hewlett 1987). Fluidity in sources of comfort and nutrition is more in line with cultures who have had less acculturation of Western thought. For the Aka tribe in Africa, the offering of a nipple to suckle on from the father is commonplace, along with his active care given to the infant at night (Hewlett 1987).

Western framing of fathers and men as being devoid of the capacity to nurture becomes a self-replicating outcome by limiting social access to gendered roles and responsibilities. For lesbian co-parents, it is possible for both parents to breastfeed their infant regardless of which mother carried the infant to term (Black and Fields 2014; Hayman and Wilkes 2016). This remains the case for partners of transwomen (Reisman and Goldstein 2018). Newman-Goldfarb protocols – replicating hormonal changes during pregnancy and birth along with pumping, massage, and dietary changes – can be used to induce lactation in adoptive and nongestational parents (Black and Fields 2014). For transgender and gender-nonconforming parents, there are successful cases of chestfeeding, among other verbs, after undergoing surgery as part of gender affirmation (MacDonald et al. 2016). However, there is not guaranteed access to medical services for trans individuals who wish to become breast/chestfeeding parents. Like the barriers to conception, levels of social acceptance influence willingness of physicians to aid in transitions that are healthy and logical in all ways, aside from social presumptions on roles in parenthood. Acceptance by physicians needs to be accompanied by medical knowledge to serve families, with potentially neither requirement met when LGBTQ+ parents access health services. Positive changes are evident in a recent case study sharing a protocol for hormone supplementation, which resulted in the production of enough milk for the mother to exclusively breastfeed for the first six weeks (Reisman and Goldstein 2018), which supports that there are social and not biological limitations hinged on binary gender roles.

Lesbian and transgender parents have similar fears and concerns as cisheterosexual families, but there is an abject lack of support systems. Pressures to nourish and nurture children are echoed by even narrower expectations of what that means in a cultural context (MacDonald et al. 2016). Social shaming around breast/chestfeeding is not limited to binary interpretations, leaving transgender and gender-nonconforming parents navigating systems that belittle parents for failed lactation goals while being ill-equipped to offer LGBTQ+ parents comprehensive care (MacDonald et al. 2016). Social constraints are still treated as ill-defined medical conditions that would not be questioned were the parent part of a cisheterosexual couple. Establishing good mothering, fathering, and parenting, in conjunction with lactation, is a narrative that is being written in LGBTQ+ family homes daily.

Conclusion

LGBTQ+ family-centered organization

Organizational support for families helps to mitigate the stresses of existing under oppressive social norms. The organizational websites given in Table 10.6 provide local and regional resources for LGBTQ+ parents and their families. Support is given through establishing programs and networks that advocate while providing safe spaces to gather and socialize. Larger organizations typically have listings of member organizations that are community-based, where more accessible ongoing activities are taking place. Information advocacy through the publication of equity and discrimination reports plays a vital role in combating erasure through limited cisheteronormative data collection.

Future research

LGBTQ+ parents are often stigmatized and excluded from family-oriented spaces due to cisheteronormative gender roles. As more mainstream media sources have highlighted LGBTQ+ parents, social awareness enables access to both the idea of non-cisheteronormative parents and the health services that facilitate parenthood. Regardless of whether alternative and medically assisted practices were needed, there has been an increase in legal and social protections coinciding with LGBTQ+ parenthood. Despite global tensions and ethical debates that cause political and legal

Table 10.6 LGBTQ+ family organizations

Organization	Website
International Lesbian, Gay, Bisexual, Trans, and Intersex Association (ILGA)	https://ilga.org
International Family Equality Day (IFED):	https://internationalfamilyequalityday.org
Family Equality Council (USA):	https://www.familyequality.org
Rainbow Families (AUS):	http://www.rainbowfamilies.com.au
COLAGE (USA)	https://www.colage.org

shifts, LGBTQ+ parents continue to form families and to parent to fulfill an internal desire undiminished by social constraints, with beneficial outcomes for children raised in LGBTQ+ parented homes that dismantle gendered roles and seek to improve social acceptance.

Future research should call to improve and increase access to reproductive health services for queer parents of color and parents from lower socioeconomic statuses. Needs for LGBTQ+ parents are only just starting to be made known to a larger audience as rhetoric shifts away from cisheteronormative assumptions (Lynch and Morison 2016). Addressing the limitations present in the current body of research will push for a better understanding of how laws and cultural contexts influence quality of life. Implementation of research findings needs to include shifts in the narrative-improving language use and procedures that support LGBTQ+ persons as parents. Assurances for parents experiencing grief and loss will be made by this improved access. In kind, we must expand access to nurturing roles and lactation as the primary source of nourishment to support roles that LGBTQ+ parents are already undertaking.

References

Allan, Sonia, Babak Balaban, Manish Banker, et al. 2016. "IFS Surveillane 2016." *Wolters Kluwer Health* 1(1): 1–143. Available at: https://journals.lww.com/grh/Fulltext/2016/09000/IFFS_Surveillance_2016.1.aspx.

Baiocco, Roberto, Federica Santamaria, Salvatore Ioverno, et al. 2015. "Lesbian Mother Families and Gay Father Families in Italy: Family Functioning, Dyadic Satisfaction, and Child Well-Being." *Sexuality Research and Social Policy* 12(3): 202–212.

Batza, Katie. 2016. "From Sperm Runners to Sperm Banks: Lesbians, Assisted Conception, and Challenging the Fertility Industry, 1971–1983." *Journal Of Women's History* 28(2): 82–102.

Bennett, Elaine, Karen Berry, Theophilus I Emeto, et al. 2016. "Attitudes to Lesbian, Gay, Bisexual and Transgender Parents Seeking Health Care for Their Children in Two Early Parenting Services in Australia." *Journal Of Clinical Nursing* 26(7–8): 1021–1030.

Berger, Anthony P, Elizabeth M Potter, Christina M Shutters, and Katherine L. Imborek. 2015. "Pregnant Transmen and Barriers to High Quality Healthcare." *Proceedings in Obstetrics and Gynecology* 5(2): 1–12.

Black, Beth Perry and Wendy Smith Fields. 2014. "Contexts of Reproductive Loss in Lesbian Couples." *The American Journal Of Maternal/Child Nursing* 39(3): 157–162.

Blake, Lucy, Nicola Carone, E. Raffanello, et al. 2017. "Gay Fathers'000 Motivations For and Feelings about Surrogacy as a Path to Parenthood." *Human Reproduction* 32(4): 860–886.

Blake, Lucy, Nicola Carone, Jenna Slutsky, et al. 2016. "Gay Father Surrogacy Families: Relationships with Surrogates and Egg Donors and Parental Disclosure of Children's Origins." *Fertility and Sterility* 106(6): 1503–1509.

Borneskog, Catrin, Claudia Lampic, G. Sydsjö, et al. 2014a. "How Do Lesbian Couples Compare with Heterosexual In Vitro Fertilization and Spontaneously Pregnant Couples When It Comes to Parenting Stress?" *Acta Paediatrica* 103(5): 537–545.

Borneskog, Catrin, Claudia Lampic, Gunilla Sydsjö, et al. 2014b. "Relationship Satisfaction in Lesbian and Heterosexual Couples Before and After Assisted Reproduction: A Longitudinal Follow-Up Study." *BMC Women's Health* 14(154).

Brown, Suzanne, Susan Smalling, Victor Groza, and Scott Ryan. 2009. "The Experiences of Gay Men and Lesbians in Becoming and Being Adoptive Parents." *Adoption Quarterly* 12(3–4): 229–246.

Cao, Hongjian, W. Roger Mills-Koonce, Claire Wood, and Mark A. Fine. 2016. "Identity Transformation During the Transition to Parenthood Among Same-Sex Couples: An Ecological, Stress-Strategy-Adaptation Perspective." *Journal of Family Theory & Review* 8(1): 30–59.

Carone, Nicola, Roberto Baiocco, and Vittorio Lingiardi. 2017. "Italian Gay Fathers'000 Experiences of Transnational Surrogacy and Their Relationship with the Surrogate Pre- and Post-Birth." *Reproductive Biomedicine Online* 34(2): 181–190.

Carpinello, Olivia J., Mary Casey Jacob, John Nulsen, and Claudio Benadiva. 2016. "Utilization of Fertility Treatment and Reproductive Choices by Lesbian Couples." *Fertility and Sterility* 106(7): 1709–1713.e4.

Carroll, Aengus and Lucas Ramón Mendos. 2017. "A World Survey of Sexual Orientation Laws: Criminalisation, Protection and Recognition." *State-sponsored Homophobia*. Geneva: ILGA. Available at: https://ilga.org/downloads/2017/ILGA_State_Sponsored_Homophobia_2017_WEB.pdf.

Casteràs, Anna, Purnami De Silva, Gillian Rumsby, and Gerard S. Conway. 2009. "Reassessing Fecundity in Women with Classical Congenital Adrenal Hyperplasia (CAH): Normal Pregnancy Rate but Reduced Fertility Rate." *Clinical Endocrinology* 70(6): 833–837.

Chapman, Rose, Joan Wardrop, Tess Zappia, et al. 2012. "The Experiences of Australian Lesbian Couples Becoming Parents: Deciding, Searching and Birthing." *Journal of Clinical Nursing* 21(13–14): 1878–1885.

Costa, Pedro Alexandre and Markus Bidell. 2016. "Modern Families." *Journal of Family Issues* 38(4): 500–521.

Crouch, Simon R., Elizabeth Waters, Ruth McNair, et al. 2014. "Parent-Reported Measures of Child Health and Wellbeing in Same-Sex Parent Families: A Cross-Sectional Survey." *BMC Public Health* 14(635).

Davis, Georgiann, Jodie M. Dewey, and Erin L. Murphy. 2015. "Giving Sex." *Gender & Society* 30(3): 490–514.

dickey, lore m., Kelly M. Ducheny, and Randall D. Ehrbar. 2016. "Family Creation Options for Transgender and Gender Nonconforming People." *Psychology of Sexual Orientation and Gender Diversity* 3(2): 173–179.

Edwards, Jeanette. 2015. "Donor Conception and (Dis)Closure in the UK: Siblingship, Friendship And Kinship." *Sociologus* 65(1): 101–122.

Ellis, Simon Adriane, Danuta M. Wojnar, and Maria Pettinato. 2014. "Conception, Pregnancy, and Birth Experiences of Male and Gender Variant Gestational Parents: It's How We Could Have a Family." *Journal of Midwifery & Women's Health* 60(1): 62–69.

Farr, Rachel H., Stephen L. Forssell, and Charlotte J. Patterson. 2010. "Gay, Lesbian, and Heterosexual Adoptive Parents: Couple and Relationship Issues." *Journal of GLBT Family Studies* 6(2): 199–213.

Gartrell, N. and H. Bos. 2010. "US National Longitudinal Lesbian Family Study: Psychological Adjustment Of 17-Year-Old Adolescents." *Pediatrics* 126(1): 28–36.

Gato, Jorge, Sara Santos, and Anne Marie Fontaine. 2016. "To Have or Not to Have Children? That is the Question. Factors Influencing Parental Decisions Among Lesbians and Gay Men." *Sexuality Research And Social Policy* 14(3): 310–323.

Georgia General Assembly. 2018. House Bill 159. Available at: http://www.legis.ga.gov/legislation/en-US/Display/20172018/HB/159.

Goldberg, Abbie E., Jordan B. Downing, and April M. Moyer. 2012. "Why Parenthood, and Why Now? Gay Men's Motivations for Pursuing Parenthood." *Family Relations* 61(1): 157–174.

Goldberg, Abbie E., April M. Moyer, Elizabeth R. Weber, and Julie Shapiro. 2013. "What Changed When the Gay Adoption Ban was Lifted?: Perspectives of Lesbian and Gay Parents in Florida." *Sexuality Research and Social Policy* 10(2): 110–124.

Goldberg, Abbie E. and Joanna E. Scheib. 2015. "Why Donor Insemination and Not Adoption? Narratives of Female-Partnered and Single Mothers." *Family Relations* 64(5): 726–742.

Golombok, Susan, Lucy Blake, Jenna Slutsky, et al. 2017. "Parenting and the Adjustment of Children Born to Gay Fathers Through Surrogacy." *Child Development* 89(4): 1223–1233.

Golombok, Susan, Laura Mellish, Sarah Jennings, et al. 2013. "Adoptive Gay Father Families: Parent-Child Relationships and Children's Psychological Adjustment." *Child Development* 85(2): 456–468.

Hayman, Brenda and Lesley Wilkes. 2016. "De Novo Families: Lesbian Motherhood." *Journal of Homosexuality* 64(5): 577–591.

Hayman, Brenda, Lesley Wilkes, Elizabeth Halcomb, and Debra Jackson. 2014. "Lesbian Women Choosing Motherhood: The Journey to Conception." *Journal of GLBT Family Studies* 11(4): 395–409.

Hewlett, Barry S. 1987. "Sexual Selection and Paternal Investment Among Aka Pygmies." In *Human Reproductive Behaviour: A Darwinian Perspective*. Cambridge: Cambridge University Press. Available at: http://anthro.vancouver.wsu.edu/media/PDF/Sexual_Selection_and_paternal_investment_among_Aka_pygimies.pdf.

Hull, Kathleen E. and Timothy A. Ortyl. 2018. "Conventional and Cutting-Edge: Definitions of Family in LGBT Communities." *Sexuality Research and Social Policy* 16(1): 31–43.

Human Dignity Trust. 2016. "*Breaking The Silence: Criminalisation of Lesbians and Bisexual Women and its Impacts.*" London: Human Dignity Trust. Available at: http://www.humandignitytrust.org/uploaded/Library/Other_Material/Breaking_the_Silence-Criminalisation_of_LB_Women_and_its_Impacts-FINAL.pdf.

Human Rights Watch. 2018. "Trinidad and Tobago: Court Overturns Same-Sex Intimacy Ban: Victory for LGBT Rights Activists." Available at: https://www.hrw.org/news/2018/04/13/trinidad-and-tobago-court-overturns-same-sex-intimacy-ban.

ILGA-Europe. 2017. "*Annual Review of the Human Rights Situation of Lesbian, Gay, Bisexual, Trans and Intersex People in Europe*." Brussels: ILGA-Europe. Available at: https://www.ilga-europe.org/sites/default/files/2017/full_annual_review.pdf.

International Family Equality Day. 2018. Same Sex Adoption Worldwide. Image. Available at: https://internationalfamilyequalityday.org/same-sex-adoption-worldwide/.

Karpman, Hannah E., Emily H. Ruppel, and Maria Torres. 2018. "'It Wasn't Feasible For Us': Queer Women Of Color Navigating Family Formation." *Family Relations* 67(1): 118–131.

Kuvalanka, Katherine A., Leigh A. Leslie, and Rachel Radina. 2013. "Coping with Sexual Stigma." *Journal of Adolescent Research* 29(2): 241–270.

Lavner, Justin A., Jill Waterman, and Letitia Anne Peplau. 2012. "Can Gay and Lesbian Parents Promote Healthy Development in High-Risk Children Adopted from Foster Care?" *American Journal of Orthopsychiatry* 82(4): 465–472.

Lee, Elaine, Julie Taylor, and Fiona Raitt. 2011. "'It's Not Me, It's Them': How Lesbian Women Make Sense of Negative Experiences of Maternity Care: A Hermeneutic Study." *Journal of Advanced Nursing* 67(5): 982–990.

Lee, Jordan. 2009. "'This Is Normal For Us': Resiliency And Resistance Amongst Lesbian and Gay Parents." *Gay & Lesbian Issues and Psychology Review* 5(2): 70–80.

Lo, Iris P.Y., Celia H.Y. Chan, and Timothy H.Y. Chan. 2016. "Perceived Importance of Childbearing and Attitudes Toward Assisted Reproductive Technology Among Chinese Lesbians in Hong Kong: Implications for Psychological Well-Being." *Fertility and Sterility* 106(5): 1221–1229.

Lynch, Ingrid and Tracy Morison. 2016. "Gay Men as Parents: Analysing Resistant Talk in South African Mainstream Media Accounts of Queer Families." *Feminism & Psychology* 26(2): 188–206.

MacDonald, Trevor, Joy Noel-Weiss, Diana West, et al. 2016. "Transmasculine Individuals' Experiences with Lactation, Chestfeeding, and Gender Identity: A Qualitative Study." *BMC Pregnancy and Childbirth* 16(1).

Machin, Rosana. 2014."Sharing Motherhood in Lesbian Reproductive Practices." *Biosocieties* 9(1): 42–59.

Malmquist, Anna. 2015. "A Crucial but Strenuous Process: Female Same-Sex Couples' Reflections on Second-Parent Adoption." *Journal of GLBT Family Studies* 11(4): 351–374.

Malmquist, Anna, Anna Möllerstrand, Maria Wikström, and Karin Zetterqvist Nelson. 2013. "'A Daddy is the Same as a Mummy': Swedish Children in Lesbian Households Talk About Fathers and Donors." *Childhood* 21(1): 119–133.

May, Amy and Kelly Tenzek. 2016. "'A Gift We Are Unable to Create Ourselves': Uncertainty Reduction in Online Classified Ads Posted by Gay Men Pursuing Surrogacy." *Journal of GLBT Family Studies* 12(5): 430–450.

Mohapatra, S. 2017. "Assisted Reproduction Inequality and Marriage Equality." *Chicago-Kent Law Review* 92(1). Available at: http://scholarship.kentlaw.iit.edu/cklawreview/vol92/iss1/5.

Moreira, Luciana. 2018. "Queer Motherhood: Challenging Heteronormative Rules Beyond the Assimilationist/Radical Binary." *Journal of International Women's Studies* 19(2): 14–28.

Murphy, Dean A. 2013. "The Desire for Parenthood" *Journal of Family Issues* 34(8): 1104–1124.

Nebeling Petersen, Michael. 2016. "Becoming Gay Fathers Through Transnational Commercial Surrogacy." *Journal of Family Issues* 39(3): 693–719.

Nicol, Pam, Rose Chapman, Rochelle Watkins, et al. 2013. "Tertiary Paediatric Hospital Health Professionals' Attitudes to Lesbian, Gay, Bisexual and Transgender Parents Seeking Health Care for Their Children." *Journal of Clinical Nursing* 22(23–24): 3396–3405.

Nordqvist, Petra. 2013. "Bringing Kinship into Being: Connectedness, Donor Conception and Lesbian Parenthood." *Sociology* 48(2): 268–283.

Oklahoma: Enrolled Senate of Oklahoma. 2018. Senate Bill No. 1140. Available at: http://webserver1.lsb.state.ok.us/cf_pdf/2017-18%20ENR/SB/SB1140%20ENR.PDF

Ory, Steven J., Paul Devroey, Manish Banker, et al. 2014. "International Federation of Fertility Societies Surveillance 2013: Preface And Conclusions." *Fertility and Sterility* 101(6): 1582–1583.

Peel, E. 2009. "Pregnancy Loss in Lesbian and Bisexual Women: An Online Survey of Experiences." *Human Reproduction* 25(3): 721–727.

Reisman, Tamar and Zil Goldstein. 2018. "Case Report: Induced Lactation in a Transgender Woman." *Transgender Health* 3(1): 24–26.

Rich, Adrienne. 1980. "Compulsory Heterosexuality and Lesbian Existence." *Signs* 5(4): 631–60. Available at: http://www.jstor.org/stable/3173834.

Riggs, Damien W. 2008. "Lesbian Mothers, Gay Sperm Donors, and Community: Ensuring the Well-Being of Children and Families". *Health Sociology Review* 17(3): 226–234.

Rippey, Phyllis L.F., and Laurel Falconi. 2016. "A Land of Milk and Honey? Breastfeeding and Identity in Lesbian Families." *Journal of GLBT Family Studies* 13(1): 16–39.

Ross, Lori E. 2005. "Perinatal Mental Health in Lesbian Mothers: A Review of Potential Risk and Protective Factors." *Women & Health* 41(3): 113–128.

Ross, Lori E. and Cheryl Dobinson. 2012. "Where is the "B" in LGBT Parenting? A Call for Research on Bisexual Parenting." *LGBT-Parent Families*, edited by Abbie E Goldberg and Katherine R. Allen, 87–103. New York, NY: Springer.

Ross, Lori, Rachel Epstein, Corrie Goldfinger, et al. 2008. "Lesbian and Queer Mothers Navigating the Adoption System: The Impacts on Mental Health." *Health Sociology Review* 17(3): 254–266.

Ryan, Maura and Amanda Moras. 2016. "Race Matters in Lesbian Donor Insemination: Whiteness and Heteronormativity as Co-Constituted Narratives." *Ethnic and Racial Studies* 40(4): 579–596.

Sanabria, Samuel. 2013. "When Adoption is Not an Option: Counseling Implications Related to Surrogacy." *Journal of Gay & Lesbian Social Services* 25(3): 269–286.

Schurr, Carolin. 2016. "From Biopolitics to Bioeconomies: The Art of (Re-)Producing White Futures in Mexico's Surrogacy Market." *Environment and Planning D: Society And Space* 35(2): 241–262.

Somers, Sara, Hanna Van Parys, Veerle Provoost, et al. 2017. "How yo Create a Family? Decision Making in Lesbian Couples Using Donor Sperm." *Sexual & Reproductive Healthcare* 11: 13–18.

Tarín, Juan J., Miguel A. García-Pérez, and Antonio Cano. 2015. "Deficiencies in Reporting Results of Lesbians and Gays after Donor Intrauterine Insemination and Assisted Reproductive Technology Treatments: A Review of the First Emerging Studies." *Reproductive Biology and Endocrinology* 13(52).

Tornello, Samantha L. and Henny Bos. 2017."Parenting Intentions among Transgender Individuals." *LGBT Health* 4(2): 115–120.

Van Hoof, Wannes, Guido Pennings, and Petra De Sutter. 2016. "Cross-Border Reproductive Care for Law Evasion: Should Physicians be Allowed to Help Infertility Patients Evade the Law of Their Own Country?" *European Journal of Obstetrics & Gynecology And Reproductive Biology* 202: 101–105.

von Doussa, Henry, Jennifer Power, and Damien Riggs. 2015. "Imagining Parenthood: The Possibilities and Experiences of Parenthood among Transgender People". *Culture, Health & Sexuality* 17(9): 1119–1131.

Wojnar, Danuta M. and Amy Katzenmeyer. 2014. "Experiences of Preconception, Pregnancy, and New Motherhood for Lesbian Nonbiological Mothers." *Journal of Obstetric, Gynecologic & Neonatal Nursing* 43(1): 50–60.

Wojnar, Danuta and Kristen M. Swanson. 2006. "Why Shouldn't Lesbian Women who Miscarry Receive Special Consideration?" *Journal of GLBT Family Studies* 2(1): 1–12.

Wyverkens, E., V. Provoost, A. Ravelingien, et al. 2014. "Beyond Sperm Cells: A Qualitative Study on Constructed Meanings of the Sperm Donor in Lesbian Families." *Human Reproduction* 29(6): 1248–1254.

Ziv, Ido and Yael Freund-Eschar. 2014. "The Pregnancy Experience of Gay Couples Expecting a Child Through Overseas Surrogacy." *The Family Journal* 23(2): 158–166.

Zizzo, Gabriella. 2009. "Lesbian Families and the Negotiation of Maternal Identity Through the Unconventional Use of Breast Milk." *Gay & Lesbian Issues And Psychology Review* 5(2): 96–109. Available at: https://groups.psychology.org.au/Assets/Files/GLIP-Review-Vol-5-No-2.pdf.

Part IV
Sexuality and Institutions

11

Sexuality and Religion

KELSY BURKE AND BRANDI WOODELL

Religion has been central to the social construction of sexuality across the globe. As such, scholarship in sexualities studies on religion makes up a broad and expanding field. We divide this field into four categories: (i) politics and culture; (ii) religious organizations and their messages; (iii) demographics; and (iv) identity formation and negotiation. These categories include interdisciplinary work in sexualities studies from the social science and the humanities, but we exclude theology and related scholarship that engages in feminist and queer exegesis of religious texts (some examples in these fields include Ali 2006; Cheng 2011; Isherwood 2012; Shannahan 2010). After reviewing these four major areas, we then briefly trace the conceptual and theoretical limitations we see undergirding these research areas. By noting these limitations, we identify avenues for future research.

Politics and Culture

This diverse body of literature shares a common line of inquiry: what is the relationship between religion and broader dimensions of politics and/or culture? One strand of scholarship explores how religion and sexuality are embedded within cultural knowledge as cultures shift and adapt to social change. Another strand focuses on social movement activism and organizations to show the explicit interaction between religion, sexuality, and politics.

Religion embedded in culture

Historians of diverse specializations have noted the ways in which religious practices, beliefs, and institutions influence cultural ideas about sex and sexuality across time and place (for examples, see Gordon 2002; Brintnall 2011; Cott 1978; D'Emilio and Freedman 1988; Jordan 2002; Najmabadi 2005; O'Malley 2006; Petro 2016; Roper

---

Companion to Sexuality Studies, First Edition. Edited by Nancy A. Naples.
© 2020 John Wiley & Sons Ltd. Published 2020 by John Wiley & Sons Ltd.

1994; Strub 2013; White 2015). Foucault (1978) famously argued that the history of sexuality in the modern Western world is a history of the waning influence of religion and the development of a modern, medicalized, and scientific discourse that serves to regulate sexual subjectivities. Najmabadi (2005) critiques this Euro-centric perspective, noting that it situates Europe as the home of homosexuality, making it invisible or unattainable to other places. Yet she traces a similar history of Iran and how changing interpretations of Islam and a desire to modernize the nation cemented heterosexual norms within a culture that remained highly religious (see also Bennett 2007; Davies 2010).

Under the vantage point of the largely secularized West, nation-states where religion plays a prominent formal role are often assumed to be societies that constrain sexual expression (Yip 2009). Yet in the United States, beliefs and practices associated with Protestantism have been taken for granted as normal and acceptable and are the standard by which dominant culture judges gender and sexuality (Fessenden 2007; Heath 2012). As Jakobsen and Pellegrini (2003) argue, US laws related to gendered relationships and sexual practices reveal that religion has not been disestablished from the state. Cultural practices, especially in the US South, reveal a persistent influence of Protestant Christianity. As Barton (2012) describes in her autoethnography on being gay in Kentucky, the "Bible Belt panopticon" works through symbols, language, and interactions to normalize conservative Christianity, and thus particular beliefs related to sexuality.

It is not just that religion either explicitly or implicitly influences sexual ideologies but that sexual ideologies can operation as kinds of belief systems. In his reading of Foucault's *The History of Sexuality* (1978), Jordan (2014) observes that Foucault contrasts modern definitions of sexuality with earlier religious ones in order to show the ways in which this supposed new scientific discourse, under the guise of objectivity, presents a "truth." In other words, Foucault encourages his readers to interrogate assumptions about sex, gender, and sexuality as belief systems themselves, not unlike religion. Schippert (2006) follows a similar logic in questioning whether sexual ethics can be a part of queer theory since any ethical system acts as a moral authority. And finally, cultural ideas about sex and sexuality may influence religious beliefs and practices, as recent examples of American evangelicalism showcase: the proliferation of Christian sex advice (Burke 2016; DeRogatis 2015) and dating practices (Irby 2014).

Foucault and other postmodern, feminist, and queer theorists have provided frameworks to understand religion and sexuality as intertwined systems of power. This is why, in their anthology *Queer Theory and the Jewish Question*, Boyarin, Itzkovitz, and Pellegrini (2003) draw parallels between queerness and being Jewish: both being marked as "other" according to gender and sexual prescriptions of dominant nonqueer, non-Jewish US culture. Strongman (2002) offers similar conclusions by noting the ways in which syncretic cults in Latin America are better able to incorporate nonheterosexual identities and practices than Euro-American religions and identity categories of gay and lesbian. These are examples of how religion and sexuality fashion symbolic boundaries between social groups and outsiders (see also Burke 2016; Tranby and Zulkowski 2012).

Social movements

Given the widespread and prominent religious prescriptions about sexuality across the globe, social movements that address inequities based on sexuality must engage with religion. American political debates over sex education (Williams 2011; Irvine 2004; Luker 2007), abortion and reproductive rights (Luker 1984; Munson 2009), and women's rights (Himmelstein 1986; Katzenstein 1998), illuminate this complex relationship between religious actors, institutions and organizations, and frames or discourses. In the United States, the most common example comes from the gay rights movement resisting and responding to messages of the Christian Right (Burke and Bernstein 2014; Dugan 2005; Fetner 2008; Herman 1997; Stein 2001; Stone 2016). Fetner (2008), for example, finds that the rhetoric of US social movement organizations (SMOs) in the lesbian and gay movement changed overtime as the Christian antigay movement gained prominence in the late 1970s and 1980s. The most notable shift is from claims about the similarities between homosexuals and heterosexuals to claims that gays and lesbians are victims of oppression at the hands of antigay activists and politicians.

Debates over sexuality and religion have influenced lesbian, gay, bisexual, and transgender (LGBT) organizing and conservative movements throughout the globe (Adam, Duyvendak, and Krouwel 1999; Blee and Creasap 2010; Curtis 2013; Hichy, Di Marco, and Coen 2015). A study of LGBT mobilization in Poland and Slovenia shows that the close connection between the religious and national identity of Poland enabled the success of an anti-LGBT movement, unlike Slovenia where religious and national identity were decoupled (Ayoub 2014). Similarly, Chanika Lwanda, and Muula (2013) explore Malawian political discourse that bridges together religious national identity with antigay sentiment. In Israel, gay and lesbian activists drew support from a broader population supporting "mainstream Zionism" instead of "fundamentalist Zionism" since debates over homosexuality served as a marker for broader political alignment. The influence of Western visibility of gays and lesbians alongside American Christian missionary efforts throughout the non-Western world produces competing effects, on the one hand terminology to assert LGBT identities as legitimate (Currier 2012) and on the other hand, religious justification for antigay laws and practices (Yi, Jung, and Phillips 2017).

Religion and sexuality are not always at odds within progressive social movements. Long (2005) documents how AIDS activists in the US use Christian tropes that are the same ones that can contribute to homophobia but are reframed to promote empathy and awareness of the AIDS epidemic (see also Petro 2016). O'Brien (2005) argues that queer Christians, even if inactive within social movement organizations, comprise a social movement as they take residence in Christian spaces, like churches. As the antigay movement grew in the twentieth century in the US, progressive Christians pushed for church policies and practices that welcomed gay and lesbian members and supported gay rights under the banner of Christian social justice (Kane 2013; Macke 2014; White 2015).

Religious Organizations and Messages

Another common way that scholars have studied the relationship between religion and sexuality is to examine how religious organizations (congregations, denominations, and other formal groups) engage and respond to issues related to sexuality. This section highlights how a focus on Christian denominations and homosexuality has dominated this literature. We also review scholarship on messages about premarital sex. Beyond US Christian groups, scholarly attention on religious messages about sex/sexuality often focuses on how religious practitioners make sense of these messages within their lives and relationships (a topic we cover in the following section).

Christian groups responding to homosexuality

This body of work includes how US religious leaders respond to homosexuality (Anderson 2014; Cadge et al. 2012; Olson and Cadge 2002) and how individual congregations discuss homosexuality in general and debate the inclusion of gay and lesbian congregates in particular (Cadge, Olson, and Wildeman 2008; Macke 2014; McQueeney 2009; Moon 2004). Also included in this literature is how ex-gay ministries work both within and outside of congregations to provide an avenue to manage the dissonance between allowing same-sex attracted members without condoning same-sex behavior (Bean and Martinez 2014; Cragun, Williams, and Sumerau 2015; Moon 2004).

Historians of American religion have documented mainline Protestant denominations that have been engaged in a debate about the topic of homosexuality since the 1970s (Djupe, Olson, and Gilbert 2006; White 2015). Religious congregations have a major influence on the lives of Americans (Whitehead 2013). The clergy of these congregations play an important role as they can shape the conversation of such controversial issues (Djupe et al. 2006). With many US denominations in the last two decades writing formal statements on homosexuality, scholarship has paid close attention to the individual congregational responses as it is at this level that we see variation among them and from the denomination (Anderson 2014; Cadge et al. 2008). Becker (1999) argues that local cultures develop within denominations that have an impact on members. For example, Cadge and colleagues (2008) found that some mainline congregations in the US have started identifying themselves as welcoming to gay and lesbian people (whether or not the denomination as a whole has done so) while other congregations cut ties with their denomination over such issues. Ellingson et al. (2001) and Cadge et al. (2008) find that local norms, histories, demographics, and leadership all structure and influence how congregations interact with group members leading to the conclusion that it is at this congregational level that scholars see less conflict among group members, more earnest discussion of homosexuality than the national debates and media portray, and the importance of congregational identity (instead of denomination identity) on responses to controversial issues like the inclusion of gay and lesbian members and gay rights issues like same-sex marriage.

While the debate about whether to include gay and lesbian members and whether to support gay rights issues has been the focus of mainline churches in the US for several decades, scholarship on evangelical churches and organizations traces an alternative history (White 2015). This work emphasizes the ways in which evangelical churches in the US have developed rhetoric to engage with the general societal shift that recognizes gay and lesbian rights (Erzen 2006; Fuist, Stoll, and Kniss 2012; Thomas and Whitehead 2015). While the majority are opposed to civil liberties for gay men and lesbian women and oppose marriage equality, there are two distinct strands (Reimer and Park 2001). As Bean (2014) finds, the first of these strands largely stays out of political social justice issues like gay rights by deferring to ex-gay ministries and a "hate the sin and love the sinner" mentality. By doing so they can maintain what they see to be compassion for those who are attracted to members of the same sex by calling out their sin so they can seek resolution through God. The other strand is the highly politicized religious right (Barrett-Fox 2016; Fetner 2008). Fetner (2008) argues that the religious right describes homosexuality as the single greatest threat to America (largely through its suggested change and devaluation of the traditional family form). Fetner (2008) finds that this narrative ushered in an era of antigay politics that used religious (specifically evangelical protestant Christian) language to deny legal rights to gay men and lesbian women.

Evangelical leadership in the US often disputes scientific findings that suggest an origin of homosexual behavior. For example, Thomas and Whitehead (2015) find that no matter what the believed origins of homosexuality are (including genetic, hormonal, or environmental) or whether it is something that a person can control, evangelical Christians believe it to be morally unacceptable and therefore have reason to dismiss it. In addition, Whitehead (2010) found that evangelical Christians are significantly more likely to be against same-sex marriage, a frequently used variable to measure attitudes of the acceptability of homosexuality, compared to other religious traditions including mainline Protestants, Catholics, and Jews even when controlling for the believed origin of homosexuality (controllable or not). Similarly to evangelical Christians, members of the Church of Jesus Christ of Latter-Day Saints (LDS) and Seventh-day Adventists condemn homosexuality as a violation of the natural order of the family and a rejection of appropriate gender roles which have been "divinely inspired" (Cragun et al. 2015. p. 291). Recently, US LDS and Adventist leaders have called for compassion for those who have the illness they call homosexuality and promoted the idea that, as an ailment, it can be treated (Cragun et al. 2015; Vance 2008).

Scholars have drawn from queer theory to examine religious organizations that promote the idea that God can change a person's sexual orientation. As Gerber (2011) describes, evangelical ex-gay ministries use the Western notion that gender and sexuality are linked by teaching participants to enact appropriate heterosexuality through adherence to the gender binary. The emphasis on behaviors that can be learned through gender role socialization exposes an understanding of the relationship between sex/gender/sexuality that runs counter to the conservative religious tradition from which ex-gay groups stem (Erzen 2006; Gerber 2011; Wolkomir 2006).

Other religious messages about sexuality

Religious leaders and organizations present messages about sexuality on more than the topic of homosexuality. In particular, the messages of American evangelical abstinence campaigns have received considerable scholarly attention (Diefendorf 2015; Gardner 2011; Hendershot 2004). Importantly, these messages influence broader culture, not just evangelical culture alone. These groups tend to lead the charge of "abstinence-only" education within public schools (Luker 2007; Williams 2011), and evangelical abstinence programs and events often incorporate pop culture as a way to appeal to religious and nonreligious teens alike. As Gardner (2011) argues in her analysis of the evangelical abstinence movement in the US and Africa, these programs focus on the positive outcome of marital sexuality to encourage teens to avoid premarital sex. This is similar to the findings of Bennett (2007) who shows how sex education within a Muslim community in Indonesia centers around knowledge and confidence related to sex because it was created by Allah.

The abstinence movement in the US encourages teens to make chastity pledges (written or verbal commitments to postpone sexual intercourse until marriage). Pledging does not necessarily make teens more likely to avoid sexual activities until marriage (Uecker 2008). The rhetoric of evangelical abstinence campaigns, in particular, challenge survey researchers' reliance on self-reporting to understand sexual debut. These campaigns do not assume all or most teens are sexually uninitiated, but rather emphasize the importance of choosing purity or chastity at the present moment, no matter a teen's sexual past. Using a theological framework emphasizing God's forgiveness, abstinence messages use language that symbolically restores virginity (Carpenter 2005; Gardner 2011). Just as one's soul is lost before finding the redemptive power of Jesus Christ, one can lose their virginity and find it again through religious commitment. This symbolic virginity is often referred to as second or "born again" virginity (Carpenter 2011).

Demographic Variables

Within the social sciences, there is a large body of literature that operationalizes religion and sexuality quantitatively in order to measure their effects on one another and other related variables. This scholarship takes a more positivist approach compared to the other bodies of research we analyze, treating religion and sexuality as clearly measurable phenomenon. One strand of this work examines how religiosity (or the strength of one's religious beliefs and practices) influences sexual attitudes (such as attitudes about homosexuality, abortion, or premarital sex). A second strand examines how religiosity influences reported sexual behaviors, and a third strand focuses on the relationship between religion and sexual minorities.

Sexual attitudes

Although common US stereotypes may suggest that religious people have significantly different attitudes about sex than do their nonreligious counterparts, empirical research challenges this assumption. When it comes to religion and attitudes about premarital, extramarital, and homosexual sex, an inverse relationship has been observed for what Cochran and Beeghley (1991, p. 52) refer to as "highly proscriptive religions." In other words, conservative attitudes are prevalent among select, but not all, religious traditions, and for select, but not all, sexual practices and behaviors. Still, attitudes about single issues related to sex are often connected through broader ideologies (Baunach 2012; Loftus 2001; Luker 2007), and religiosity is a strong indicator of such attitudes (Lefkowitz, Mullet, and Shafigh 2004). Accordingly, demographic researchers may rely on index measures to analyze sexual attitudes as a single variable that includes a composite score for attitudes on individual measures, such as masturbation, homosexuality, multiple sex partners, oral sex, pornography, and premarital sexuality (see Ahrold et al. 2011; Lefkowitz et al. 2004; Le Gall et al. 2002). Dillon (2014) warns, however, that researchers should be wary of combining separate issues into similar value labels given observed asynchrony within religious groups. An advantage of demographic research on the relationship between religion and sexuality is the ability to parse out these differences according to other variables like gender and race (Guittar and Pals 2014) and age (Andersen and Fetner 2008), among others.

Likely due to the significant media attention given to religious reaction and resistance to gay rights, the question of how religion influences sexual attitudes associated with homosexuality has been the focus on much scholarly research in the US. Researchers have operationalized this measure in multiple ways, including attitudes about same-sex marriage (Olson, Cadge, and Harrison 2006; Sherkat et al. 2011), the morality of homosexuality (Burdette, Ellison, and Hill 2005), the cause of homosexuality (Whitehead 2010), tolerance toward gays and lesbians (Schulte and Battle 2004), and internalized homonegativity (Meladze and Brown 2015). In the US, conservative Protestantism is a significant indicator of opposition to homosexuality, while Judaism, mainline Protestantism, and Catholicism are more accepting (Olson et al. 2006). Although there are fewer data on these groups, studies have shown that Muslims hold more conservative views of homosexuality relative to other groups (Finke and Adamczyk 2008; Yuchtman-Yaar and Alkalay 2007) and that Buddhists hold more positive views (Vilaythong T., Linder, and Nosek 2010).

While most existing studies focus on a US context, there is global variation in the influence of religion on attitudes about homosexuality (Detenber et al. 2007; Jäckle and Wenzelburger 2015). Adamczyk and Pitt (2009) theorize that, as nations shift from emphasizing "survival to self-expression," public opinion about homosexuality tends to be more tolerant. Yet at the same time, personal religious beliefs – as one mode of self-expression – becomes more influential in attitudes about homosexuality in countries like the United States and less influential in countries classified as high survival. Meladze and Brown (2015) sampled individuals living in Western and Asian countries to compare the impact of religion on internalized homonegativity (IH). They find, perhaps surprisingly, that gay men who participate in Abrahamic religions (Christianity, Judaism, and Islam) do not have higher rates of IH than gay men who participate in New Age religions. In contrast, a study on residents in Singapore finds that Christians are more likely to report negative attitudes about homosexuality than Buddhists (Detenber et al. 2007). In another study on university students in Turkey, a secular nation with a majority Muslim population, researchers found that religious attendance was more important in predicting attitudes toward abortion and homosexuality than gender, sexual activity, or sexual knowledge (Sümer 2015).

Sexual behaviors

US-focused researchers have observed that religion not only influences the sexual beliefs of individuals but also the sexual acts in which individuals choose to engage (Farmer, Trapnell, and Meston 2009). Findings suggest that religiosity has ambivalent impacts on sexual behaviors, as some studies note the role of religion in reducing the likelihood of risky sexual behaviors (Alexander et al. 1993; Burdette et al. 2005), while other studies find the reverse effect: that conservative religious beliefs are associated with lower rates of contraception use (Miller and Gur 2002) and higher rates of self-reported "addiction" to pornography (Leonhardt, Willoughby, and Young-Petersen 2017; Perry 2015). Religion also impacts how individuals experience sexual behaviors. For example, US studies find that heterosexual, married couples who are religious report greater levels of sexual pleasure than nonreligious peers (McFarland, Uecker, and Regnerus 2011; Young et al. 2000). On the other hand, Ahrold et al. (2011) find that religiosity has a negative impact on frequency and type of sexual fantasies.

Much research on sexual behavior and religion focus on adolescent (teenage and college-age) behavior (Uecker, Angotti, and Regnerus 2008), since many religious groups in the US actively promote abstinence and condemn sexual intercourse for unmarried youth. Research consistently documents the influence of religiosity on adolescent sexual behaviors (Alexander et al. 1993; Burdette and Hill 2009; McCree et al. 2003). Yet, studies also show that premarital sex is widespread for both American religious teens, including those who make abstinence pledges, and nonreligious American teens (Freitas 2008; Uecker 2008). Religious college students, on average, have more conservative views of appropriate sexual behavior (Simons, Burt, and Peterson 2009; Thornton and Camburn 1989), engage in sexual activities later than nonreligious peers (Bearman and Brückner 2001; Rostosky, Regnerus, and Wright 2003; Hull et al. 2011), and are generally less likely to engage in "hook ups" than nonreligious students (Burdette and Hill 2009).

Sexual minorities

Few scholars have studied the impact religion has on the well-being of sexual minorities in the US. Previous work suggests that being involved in a religion has positive health effects (Koenig, McCullough, and Larson 2001). In fact, higher levels of religiosity were found to be associated with lower levels of depression (Schieman, Bierman, and Ellison 2013). In addition, religious beliefs and practices were associated with many perceived benefits including comfort, strength, and social support (Siegel and Schrimshaw 2002). However, sexual minorities may experience conflict within religious contexts due to the antigay rhetoric of many Christian churches and thus have limited access to congregations (and a potential resource) (Dahl and Galliher 2010; Schuck and Liddle 2001; Whitehead 2013). On the other hand, the cognitive dissonance associated with holding conflicting identities (gay and Christian) may be exacerbated by having higher levels of religiosity (Mahaffy 1996; Ream and Savin-Williams 2005). While religion can be a form of support for some, it is unclear whether this applies to sexual minorities and, if it does, in which religions.

Questions about the relationship between religion and sexuality do not always assume religion to be an independent variable that influences sexual outcomes, but instead acknowledge that one's sexual history may impact their perception of religion. Sherkat (2002) analyzes General Social Survey data from the US to conclude that men who have sex with men and women who have sex with women are less committed to religion than their heterosexual counterparts. For instance, nonheterosexuals are less likely to report that the Bible is the inspired or absolute word of God. Yet Sherkat also finds through multivariate analysis, that men who have sex with men are actually more active in religious organizations when controlling for family factors than heterosexual men. He theorizes that gay men participate in church more willingly than straight men, who may be pressured into participating by their marriage and family arrangements.

Identity Formation and Negotiation

The final literature we review centers around collective and individual identity formation and negotiation, focusing on religious sexual minorities navigating their religious beliefs alongside their sexual identities. A smaller strand in this literature examines heterosexual believers often by focusing on women (sexual agency) or men (the practice of masculinity).

Religious sexual minorities

Around the world, most previous work addressing issues of same-sex sexuality and religion have focused on the identity negotiations of gay men and lesbian women (Schnoor 2006; Siraj 2012; van Klinken 2015; Walton 2006). Transgressing norms related to sexual and gender identity is typically considered to be incompatible with religiosity within the Abrahamic religions (Erzen 2006; Meladze and Brown 2015; O'Brien 2004; Sumerau, Cragun, and Mathers 2015; Wilcox 2003). Therefore, holding a sexual minority identity is considered to be in direct violation of tenets within Judaism, Christianity, and Islam which contributes to what scholars have termed an "identity dilemma" (Barton 2012; Thumma 1991; Wolkomir 2006). Given that 70% of Americans consider themselves to be Christian (Pew Research Center 2014), it is no surprise that much US-focused research examines the identity negotiations of gay and lesbian Christians (Barton 2012; Bradshaw et al. 2015; Crapo 2005; Drumm 2005; Radojci 2016; Vance 2015; Wolkomir 2006). Outside of Christianity and the US, scholars have studied how gay men and lesbian women negotiate these often-conflicting identities within Judaism (Schnoor 2006) and Islam (Siraj 2006, 2012). These studies provide an important insight into the religious and sexual lives of these groups as they negotiate their potentially conflicting identities.

Research on sexual identity formation for practitioners of religions other than Abrahamic traditions draw significantly different conclusions. For example, Vance (2015) finds that the Wiccan religion promotes gender and LGBT equality, and therefore participants do not experience such conflict with integrating their religious and sexual identities. Walters and colleagues (2006) finds that American Native Two-Spirit identified individuals discuss this sexual minority identity as a part of their cultural and spiritual heritage by rejecting the Eurocentric binaries of man/woman and heterosexual/homosexual. Other scholarship suggests that "more philosophical religions" like Paganism, Buddhism, and New Age movements in the US do not condemn same-sex relationships so they would not pose the same identity conflicts that Abrahamic religions (Judaism, Christianity, and Islam) do for sexual minorities (de Visser et al 2007; Meladze and Brown 2015, p. 1953; Szymanski, Kashubeck-West, and Meyer 2008).

Although not all LGBT Christians experience identity conflict (Rodriques and Ouellette 2000), previous research spanning several countries has consistently shown that gay Christians, Jews, and Muslims do experience varying levels of cognitive dissonance due to trying to maintain these two identities (Mahaffy 1996; Schnoor 2006; Siraj 2012; Woodell, Kazyak, and Compton 2015). Few studies include bisexual, transgender, or queer identified people within their sample as distinct categories for analysis. One study that focused on bisexual Christian identity negotiation in the UK finds that bisexuals have similar obstacles as gay and lesbian members of Christian churches with the added obstacle of being openly told their sexuality is a choice and that they are only encouraged to bring an "opposite-sex" partner into the church (Toft 2012). In their study of US transgender Mormons and ex-Mormons, Sumerau et al. (2015) argue that religious communities engage in practices of "cisgendering," or assuming a natural and inevitable relationship between the sex assigned at birth and one's gender identity, to exclude transgender participants.

Existing studies have suggested a multistep process of integrating identities (Schnoor 2006; Siraj 2006). First, sexual minorities must understand that their religious beliefs can be changed. Second, they must then change their beliefs into what is termed a gay-positive theology. This step is usually accomplished through a guided reinterpretation of scripture. The last step requires that they apply this new theology to their lives (Wolkomir 2006). This idea of rebuilding your faith into one that does not conflict with your gay identity is one of the most important steps in integrating identities (Thumma 1991; Yip 1997, 2002).

Empirical examples of identity integration suggest that individuals often focus on finding religious communities that interpret scripture to affirm nonheterosexual identities. Wolkomir (2006) found that the Metropolitan Community Church (MCC), which is a US Christian and gay-friendly denomination, emphasizes that Bible verses that are believed to condemn homosexuality have been misinterpreted in the King James Bible Version from their original intent that focused on prostitution and immoral sexual activity with young boys. Through groups like these, gay Christians established a new theology that centered on Jesus's love and compassion and the belief that all people are part of God's plan (White 2015; Wolkomir 2006). Muslim gay men focused on rereading the Qur'an and passages of love and compassion within it to help integrate their identities (Siraj 2006). In a study focused on Muslim lesbian women in England, Siraj (2012) found that a Muslim LGBT group called Imaan helped them integrate their identities through affirmation of a positive relationship between Islam and sexuality. Similarly, Schnoor (2006) found that Jewish gay men in Canada who maintained a religious identity of Judaism (as opposed to only an ethnic-based Jewish identity) focused on reinterpreting the Torah for more inclusive language. It is through these means that religious sexual minorities reconcile their identities even in the face of unaccepting churches, synagogues, mosques, and communities (Minwalla et al. 2005; Thumma 1991; Yip 1997, 2002).

The finding that sexual minorities adapt and change their religious beliefs is common to literature on identity negotiation (Mahaffy 1996; Peterfeso 2011; Ponticelli 1999; Wilcox 2003, 2009). This has been well documented in research on individuals who choose to join religious communities that are visibly accepting of LGBT members (e.g. Christian churches that are "open and affirming"). Gay-friendly synagogues also exist to give Jewish gay men and lesbian women a place to worship; however, we can find no mention in previous literature of places of worship for gay and lesbian Muslims. In fact, Yip (2007, p. 212) states that Muslims do not currently have the "theological capital" to have gay-affirming mosques. Given the limited availability of open and affirming worship centers, a significant proportion of religious sexual minorities must find other ways to deal with the intersection of these identities.

Another strand in this literature suggests that an alternative to finding theological support for nonheterosexual identities is individuals who choose to adapt their sexual practices according to their existing religious beliefs. Researchers of the US evangelical ex-gay movement, for example, find that the movement does not demonize same-sex attraction although it discourages same-sex sexual behavior. This research finds that ex-gay support groups encourage participants to talk openly about their desires and attempt to reconcile the conflict between those desires and their religious beliefs. In fact, scholars have pointed out this movement's "queerness": Erzen (2006) describes ex-gay therapy as a "queer conversion" and Gerber (2008) calls aspects of the movement "queer-ish." This is because evangelical ex-gays believe in sexual fluidity, that sexual change is possible, and that there is space beyond the narrow identity categories of homosexual or heterosexual. This allows individuals who fail to meet normative heterosexual standards to be accepted within a Christian framework.

Heterosexual sexual identity in religious context

Instead of taking for granted heterosexuality as a natural, assumed identity for religious people, some scholarship has drawn from critical heterosexual studies and queer studies to problematize and investigate experiences of heterosexuality within religion. A common finding from this body of work is that heterosexuality, like nonheterosexual sexualities, is regulated by religious communities, rules, and practices, but that individuals exhibit agency as they navigate these religious prescriptions (Avishai and Burke 2016; Burke 2016).

Because religions are highly gendered (Avishai, Jafar, and Rinaldo 2015), scholarship finds that men and women may have differing experiences when it comes to sex and sexuality. As Burke and Moff Hudec (2015) note, US Christian and Latter-Day Saint men must navigate their beliefs about masculinity alongside their sexual experiences (see also Burke 2016). This is why some men who challenge sexual stereotypes about men presented within their religious communities – such as that men have stronger sex drives than women – rely on their status as men to maintain their respected positions as Christian patriarchs. Similarly, Diefendorf (2015) finds that US evangelical men who pledged abstinence before marriage find ways to express masculinity in ways other than sexual prowess. These findings are similar to the ones presented by Sumerau (2012) in a study of a US LGBT congregation where gay men emphasize normative masculinity to reject homophobia.

There is a large body of literature examining women's agency in gender traditional religions (see Burke 2012 for a review), and some of this scholarship centers on women's sexual experiences and identities. For instance, Avishai (2012) finds that some Orthodox Jewish women use their religious beliefs to affirm women's sexuality. One marriage counselor Avishai interviewed encouraged women to use the seven days following menstruation when Jewish women do not engage in sexual intercourse with a spouse to explore their own bodies. Similarly, Burke (2016) examines American evangelical women who use the internet for sex advice and finds that these online communities validate women's sexual experiences and empower women to assert their sexual desires and feelings within their marriages. Yet at the same time, these women must situate their experiences according to their relationships with God and their husbands, two male figures in their lives. This is similar to studies of Muslim women in South Africa and Iran who use their sexual practices to express devotion to their husbands, and thus a form of religious devotion as well (Hoel and Shaikh 2013; Khoei, Whelan, and Cohen 2008).

Conclusion

Scholars addressing the relationship between sexualities and religion have used multiple theoretical frames, methodological approaches, and assumptions based on disciplinary knowledge. Even in this broad literature, we note three themes that are limitations and may be areas of future scholarship. First, we observe a heavy emphasis on the Christian tradition (specifically Protestantism) and the United States context. This skews research to ask questions in relation to Christian dogma related to sexuality. Second, we observe a reliance on a sexual binary (heterosexual or homosexual), with specific emphasis on homosexuality as a measure of sexual tolerance and sexual debates. This makes invisible variation within sexual minority communities (like queer or bisexuality) and may make religious traditions appear progressive when it comes to gays and lesbians, when they are not actually sexually inclusive. Third, we find sexuality largely missing from analysis of topics in religion that relate to sex, including family life, fertility, and gender (primarily religious women). This means that researchers may miss important findings and theoretical opportunities that could be gleaned from sexuality studies. As this review showcases, the field of religion and sexuality is expanding and ripe for future avenues of research.

References

Adam, Barry D., Jan Willem Duyvendak, and André Krouwel, eds. 1999. *The Global Emergence of Gay and Lesbian Politics*. Philadelphia, PA: Temple University Press.

Adamczyk, Amy and Cassady Pitt. 2009. "Shaping Attitudes About Homosexuality: The Role of Religion and Cultural Context." *Social Science Research* 38(2): 338–351.

Ahrold, Tierney K., Melissa Farmer, Paul D. Trapnell, and Cindy M. Meston. 2011. "The Relationship Among Sexual Attitudes, Sexual Fantasy, and Religiosity." *Archives of Sexual Behavior* 40(3): 619–630.

Alexander, Cheryl S., Mark R. Somerfield, and Margaret E. Ensminger. 1993. "Consistency of Adolescents' Self-Report of Sexual Behavior in a Longitudinal Study." *Journal of Youth & Adolescence* 22(5): 455–471.

Ali, Kecia. 2006. *Sexual Ethics and Islam; Feminist Reflections on Qur'an, Hadith, and Jurisprudence*. Oxford: Oneworld Publications.

Andersen, Robert and Tina Fetner. 2008. "Economic Inequality and Intolerance: Attitudes toward Homosexuality in 35 Democracies." *American Journal of Political Science* 52(4): 942–58.

Anderson, John J. 2014. "Coming Out under Prohibition.: Ordination and Queer identity in Mainline Protestantism." In *Queering Religion, Religious Queers*, edited by Y. Taylor and R. Snowdon, 211–228. New York, NY: Routledge.

Avishai, Orit and Kelsy Burke. 2016. "God's Case for Sex." *Contexts* 15(4): 30–35.

Avishai, Orit, Afshan Jafar, and Rachel Rinaldo. 2015. "A Gender Lens on Religion." *Gender & Society* 29(1): 5–25.

Avishai, Orit. 2012. "What to do with the Problem of the Flesh?: Negotiating Orthodox Jewish Sexual Anxieties." *Fieldwork in Religion* 7(2): 148–162.

Ayoub, Phillip M. 2014. "With Arms Wide Shut: Threat Perception, Norm Reception, and Mobilized Resistance to LGBT Rights." *Journal of Human Rights* 13(3): 337–362.

Barrett-Fox, Rebecca. 2016. *God Hates: Westboro Baptist Church, American Nationalism, and the Religious Right*. Lawrence, KS: University Press of Kansas.

Barton, Bernadette. 2012. *Pray the Gay Away: The Extraordinary Lives of Bible Belt Gays*. New York, NY: New York University Press.

Baunach, Dawn Michelle. 2012. "Changing Same-Sex Marriage Attitudes in America from 1988 through 2010." *Public Opinion Quarterly* 76(2): 364–378.

Bean, Lydia. 2014. *The Politics of Evangelical Identity: Local Churches and Partisan Divides in the United States and Canada*. Princeton, NJ: Princeton University Press.

Bean, Lydia and Brandon C. Martinez. 2014. "Evangelical Ambivalence toward Gays and Lesbians." *Sociology of Religion* 75(3): 1–23.

Bearman, Peter S. and Hannah Brückner. 2001. "Promising the Future: Virginity Pledges and First Intercourse." *American Journal of Sociology* 106(4): 859–912.

Becker, Penny Edgell. 1999. *Congregations in Conflict: Cultural Models of Local Religious Life*. Cambridge University Press.

Bennett, Linda Rae. 2007. "Zina and the Enigma of Sex Education for Indonesian Muslim Youth." *Sex Education* 7(4): 371–386.

Blee, Kathleen M. and Kimberly A. Creasap. 2010. "Conservative and Right-Wing Movements." *Annual Review of Sociology* 36(1): 269–286.

Boyarin, Daniel, Daniel Itzkovitz, and Ann Pellegrini, eds. 2003. *Queer Theory and the Jewish Question*. New York, NY: Columbia University Press.

Bradshaw, William S., Tim B. Heaten, Ellen Decoo, et al. 2015. "Religious Experiences of GBTQ Mormon Males." *Journal for the Scientific Study of Religion* 54(2): 311–329.

Brintnall, Kent. 2011. *Ecce Homo: The Male-Body-in-Pain as Redemptive Figure*. Chicago, IL: University of Chicago Press.

Burdette, Amy M., Christopher G. Ellison, and Terrence D. Hill. 2005. "Conservative Protestantism and Tolerance toward Homosexuals: An Examination of Potential Mechanisms." *Sociological Inquiry* 75(2): 177–196.

Burdette, Amy M. and Terrence D. Hill. 2009. "Religious Involvement and Transitions into Adolescent Sexual Activities." *Sociology of Religion* 70(1): 28–48.

Burke, Kelsy. 2012. "Women's Agency in Gender-Traditional Religions: A Review of Four Approaches." *Sociology Compass* 6(2): 122–133.

Burke, Kelsy. 2016. *Christians Under Covers: Evangelicals and Sexual Pleasure on the Internet*. Berkeley, CA: University of California Press.

Burke, Kelsy and Amy Moff Hudec. 2015. "Sexual Encounters and Manhood Acts: Evangelicals, Latter-Day Saints, and Religious Masculinities." *Journal for the Scientific Study of Religion* 54(2): 330–344.

Burke, Mary C. and Mary Bernstein. 2014. "How the Right Usurped the Queer Agenda: Frame Co-optation in Political Discourse." *Sociological Forum* 29 (4): 830–850.

Cadge, Wendy, Jennifer Girouard, Laura R. Olson, and Madison Lylerohr. 2012. "Uncertainty in Clergy's Perspectives on Homosexuality: A Research Note." *Review of Religious Research* 54(3): 371–387.

Cadge, Wendy, Laura R. Olson, and Christopher Wildeman. 2008. "How Denominational Resources Influence Debate about Homosexuality in Mainline Protestant Congregations." *Sociology of Religion* 69(2): 187–207.

Carpenter, Laura. 2005. *Virginity Lost: An Intimate Portrait of First Sexual Experiences*. New York, NY: New York University Press.

Carpenter, Laura. 2011. "Like a Virgin…Again?: Secondary Virginity as an Ongoing Gendered Social Construction." *Sexuality & Culture* 15(2): 115–140.

Chanika, Emmie, John L. Lwanda, and Adamson S. Muula. 2013. "Gender, Gays and Gain: The Sexualised Politics of Donor Aid in Malawi." *Africa Spectrum* 48(1): 89–105.

Cheng, Patrick S. 2011. *Radical Love: An Introduction to Queer Theology*. New York, NY: Church Publishing.

Cochran, John K. and Leonard Beeghley. 1991. "The Influence of Religion on Attitudes toward Nonmarital Sexuality: A Preliminary Assessment of Reference Group Therapy." *Journal for the Scientific Study of Religion* 30(1): 45–62.

Cott, Nancy F. 1978. "Passionlessness: An Interpretation of Victorian Sexual Ideology, 1790–1850." *Signs* 4(2): 219–236.

Cragun, Ryan T., Emily Williams, and J. E. Sumerau. 2015. "From Sodomy to Sympathy: LDS Elites' Discursive Construction of Homosexuality over Time." *Journal for the Scientific Study of Religion* 54(2): 291–310.

Crapo, Righley H. 2005. "Latter-Day Saint Lesbian, Gay, Bisexual, and Transgendered Spirituality." In *Gay Religion*, edited by S. Thumma and E.R. Gray, 99–114. Walnut Creek, CA: Altamira Press.

Currier, Ashley. 2012. *Out in Africa: LGBT Organizing in Namibia and South Africa*. Minneapolis, MN: University of Minnesota Press.

Curtis, Jennifer. 2013. "Pride and Prejudice: Gay Rights and Religious Moderation in Belfast." *Sociological Review* 61: 141–159.

Dahl, Angie and Renee Galliher. 2010. "Sexual Minority Young Adult Religiosity, Sexual Orientation Conflict, Self-Esteem and Depressive Symptoms." *Journal of Gay & Lesbian Mental Health* 14(4): 271–90.

Davies, Sharyn Graham. 2010. *Gender Diversity in Indonesia: Sexuality, Islam and Queer Selves*. London: Routledge.

D'Emilio, John and Estelle B. Freedman. 1988. *Intimate Matters: A History of Sexuality in America*. Chicago, IL: University of Chicago Press.

de Visser, Richard O., Anthony M. A. Smith, Juliet Richter, and Chris E. Rissel. 2007. "Associations Between Religiosity and Sexuality in a Representative Sample of Australian Adults." *Archives of Sexual Behavior* 36(1): 33–46.

DeRogatis, Amy. 2015. *Saving Sex: Sexuality and Salvation in American Evangelicalism*. New York, NY: Oxford University Press.

Detenber, Benjamin H., Mark Cenite, Moses K.Y. Ku, et al. 2007. "Singaporeans' Attitudes toward Lesbians and Gay Men and Their Tolerance of Media Portrayals of Homosexuality." *International Journal of Public Opinion Research* 19(3): 367–379.

Diefendorf, Sarah. 2015. "After the Wedding Night: Sexual Abstinence and Masculinities over the Life Course." *Gender & Society* 29(5): 647–669.

Dillon, Michele. 2014. "Asynchrony in Attitudes toward Abortion and Gay Rights: The Challenge to Values Alignment." *Journal for the Scientific Study of Religion* 53(1): 1–16.

Djupe, Paul A., Laura R. Olson, and Christopher P. Gilbert. 2006. "Whether to Adopt Statements on Homosexuality in Two Denominations: A Research Note." *Journal for the Scientific Study of Religion* 45(4): 609–621.

Drumm, Rene. 2005. "No Longer an Oxymoron: Integrating Gay and Lesbian Seventh-Day Adventist Identities" In *Gay Religion*, edited by S. Thumma, and E.R. Gray, 47–66. Walnut Creek, CA: Altamira Press.

Dugan, Kimberly B. 2005. *The Struggle over Gay, Lesbian, and Bisexual Rights: Facing Off in Cincinnati*. New York, NY: Routledge.

Ellingson, Stephen, Nelson Tebbe, Martha Van Haitsma, and Edward Laumann. 2001. "Religion and the Politics of Sexuality." *Journal of Contemporary Ethnography* 30(l): 3–55.

Erzen, Tanya. 2006. *Straight to Jesus: Sexual and Christian Conversions in the Ex-Gay Movement*. Berkeley, CA: University of California Press.

Farmer, Melissa A., Paul D. Trapnell, and Cindy M. Meston. 2009. "The Relation between Sexual Behavior and Religiosity Subtypes: A Test of the Secularization Hypothesis." *Archives of Sexual Behavior* 38(5): 852–865.

Fessenden, Tracy. 2007. *Culture and Redemption: Religion, the Secular, and American Literature*. Princeton, NJ: Princeton University Press.

Fetner, Tina. 2008. *How the Religious Right Shaped Lesbian and Gay Activism*. Minneapolis, St. Paul: University of Minnesota Press.

Finke, Roger and Amy Adamczyk. 2008. "Cross-National Moral Beliefs: The Influence of National Religious Context." *Sociological Quarterly* 49(4): 617–652.

Foucault, Michel. 1978. *The History of Sexuality: An Introduction, Vol. 1*. New York, NY: Vintage publishing.

Freitas, Donna. 2008. *Sex and the Soul: America's College Students Speak Out about Hookups, Romance, and Religion on Campus*. New York, NY: Oxford University Press.

Fuist, Todd Nicholas, Laurie Cooper Stoll, and Fred Kniss. 2012. "Beyond the Liberal-Conservative Divide: Assessing the Relationship between Religious Denominations and Their Associated LGBT Organizations." *Qualitative Sociology* 35(1): 65–87.

Gardner, Christine J. 2011. *Making Chastity Sexy: The Rhetoric of Evangelical Abstinence Campaigns*. Berkeley, CA: University of California Press.

Gerber, Lynne. 2008. "The Opposite of Gay: Nature, Creation, and Queerish Ex-Gay Experiments." *Nova Religio: The Journal of Alternative and Emergent Religions* 11(4): 8–30.

Gerber, Lynne. 2011. *Seeking the Straight and Narrow: Weight Loss and Sexual Reorientation in Evangelical America*. Chicago, IL: University of Chicago Press.

Gordon, Sarah Barringer. 2002. "Mormon Question: Polygamy and Constitutional Conflict in Nineteenth Century America." *Journal of Supreme Court History* 28(1): 14–29.

Guittar, Nicholas A. and Heili Pals. 2014. "Intersecting Gender with Race and Religiosity: Do Unique Social Categories Explain Attitudes Toward Homosexuality?" *Current Sociology*, 62(1): 41–62.

Heath, Melanie. 2012. *One Marriage under God: The Campaign to Promote Marriage in America*. New York, NY: New York University Press.

Hendershot, Heather. 2004. *Shaking the World for Jesus: Media and Conservative Evangelical Culture*. Chicago, IL: University of Chicago Press.

Herman, Didi. 1997. *The Antigay Agenda: Orthodox Vision and the Christian Right*. Chicago, IL: University of Chicago Press.

Hichy, Zira, Graziella Di Marco, and Sharon Coen. 2015. "The Interplay between Religious Orientations, State Secularism, and Gay Rights Issues." *Journal of GLBT Family Studies* 11(1): 82–101.

Himmelstein, Jerome L. 1986. "The Social Basis of Antifeminism: Religious Networks and Culture." *Journal for the Scientific Study of Religion* 25(1): 1–15.

Hoel, Nina and Sa'diyya Shaikh. 2013. "Sex as Ibadah: Religion, Gender, and Subjectivity among South African Muslim Women" *Journal of Feminist Studies in Religion* 29(1): 69–91.

Hull, Shawnika J., Michael Hennessy, Amy Bleakley, et al. 2011. "Identifying the Causal Pathways from Religiosity to Delayed Adolescent Sexual Behavior." *Journal of Sex Research* 48(6): 543–553.

Irby, Courtney Ann. 2014. "Dating in Light of Christ: Young Evangelicals Negotiating Gender in the Context of Religious and Secular American Culture." *Sociology of Religion* 75(2): 260–283.

Irvine, Janice M. 2004. *Talk about Sex: The Battles over Sex Education in the United States*. Berkeley, CA: University of California Press.

Isherwood, Lisa. 2012. "Feminist Critique of Sexuality and Religion." In *Ashgate Research Companion to Contemporary Religion and Sexuality*, edited by S.J. Hunt and A.K.T. Yip, 31–44. Burlington, VT: Ashgate.

Jäckle, Sebastian and Georg Wenzelburger. 2015. "Religion, Religiosity, and the Attitudes toward Homosexuality – A Multilevel Analysis of 79 Countries." *Journal of Homosexuality* 62(2): 207–241.

Jakobsen, Janet R. and Ann Pellegrini. 2003. *Love the Sin: Sexual Regulation and the Limits of Religious Tolerance*. New York, NY: New York University Press.

Jordan, Mark D. 2002. *The Ethics of Sex*. Oxford: Blackwell Publishing.

Jordan, Mark D. 2014. *Convulsing Bodies: Religion and Resistance in Foucault*. Stanford, CA: Stanford University Press.

Kane, Melinda D. 2013. "LGBT Religious Activism: Predicting State Variations in the Number of Metropolitan Community Churches, 1974–2000." *Sociological Forum* 28(1): 135–158.

Katzenstein, Mary. 1998. *Faithful and Fearless: Moving Feminist Protest inside the Church and Military*. Princeton, NJ: Princeton University Press

Khoei, Effat Merghati, Anna Whelan, and Jeffrey Cohen. 2008. "Sharing Beliefs: What Sexuality Means to Muslim Iranian Women Living in Australia." *Culture, Health & Sexuality* 10(3): 237–248.

Koenig, Harold G., Michael E. McCullough, and Dana B. Larson. 2001. *Handbook of Religion and Health*. New York, NY: Oxford University Press.

Lefkowitz, Eva S., Meghan M. Gillen, Cindy L. Shearer, and Tanya L. Boone. 2004. "Religiosity, Sexual Behaviors, and Sexual Attitudes During Emerging Adulthood." *Journal of Sex Research* 41(2): 150–59.

Le Gall, Armelle, Etienne Mullet, and Sheila Rivière Shafighi. 2002. "Age, Religious Beliefs, and Sexual Attitudes." *Journal of Sex Research* 39(3): 207–216.

Leonhardt, Nathan D., Brian J. Willoughby, and Bonnie Young-Petersen. 2017. "Damaged Goods: Perception of Pornography Addiction as a Mediator between Religiosity and Relationship Anxiety Surrounding Pornography Use." *The Journal of Sex Research* 1–12.

Loftus, Jeni. 2001. "America's Liberalization in Attitudes toward Homosexuality, 1973 to 1998." *American Sociological Review* 66(5): 762–782.

Long, Thomas L. 2005. *AIDS and American Apocalypticism: The Cultural Semiotics of an Epidemic*. Albany, NY: State University of New York Press.

Luker, Kristin. 1984. *Abortion and the Politics of Motherhood*. Berkeley: University of California Press.

Luker, Kristin. 2007, *When Sex goes to School: Warring views on Sex – and Sex education – Since the Sixties*. New York, NY: W.W. Norton.

Macke, Karen. 2014. "Que(e)rying Methodology to Study Church-Based Activism: Conversations in Culture, Power, and Change" In *Queering Religion, Religious Queers*, edited by Y. Taylor and R. Snowdon, vol. 38, 13–31. New York, NY: Routledge.

Mahaffy, Kimberly. 1996. "Cognitive Dissonance and Its Resolution: A Study of Lesbian Christians." *Journal for the Scientific Study of Religion* 35(4): 392–402.

McCree, Donna Hubbard, Gina M. Wingood, Ralph DiClemente, et al. 2003. "Religiosity and Risky Sexual Behavior in African-American Adolescent Females." *Journal of Adolescent Health* 33(1): 2–8.

McFarland, Michael J., Jeremy E. Uecker, and Mark D. Regnerus. 2011. "The Role of Religion in Shaping Sexual Frequency and Satisfaction: Evidence from Married and Unmarried Older Adults." *Journal of Sex Research* 48(2/3): 297–308.

McQueeney, Krista. 2009. "'We are God's Children, Y'all:' Race, Gender, and Sexuality in Lesbian- and Gay-affirming Congregations." *Social Problems* 56(1): 151–173.

Meladze, Pikria and Jac Brown. 2015. "Religion, Sexuality, and Internalized Homonegativity: Confronting Cognitive Dissonance in the Abrahamic Religions." *Journal of Religion & Health* 54(5): 1950–1962.

Miller, Lisa and Merav Gur. 2002. "Religiousness and Sexual Responsibility in Adolescent Girls." *Journal of Adolescent Health* 31(5): 401–406.

Minwalla, Omar, B.R. Simson Rosser, Jamie Feldman, and Christine Varga. 2005. "Identity Experience among Progressive Gay Muslims in North America: A Qualitative Study within Al-Fatiha." *Culture, Health & Sexuality* 7(2): 113–128.

Moon, Dawne. 2004. *God, Sex, and Politics: Homosexuality and Everyday Theologies*. Chicago, IL: University of Chicago Press.

Munson, Ziad W. 2009. *The Making of Pro-life Activists: How Social Movement Mobilization Works*. Chicago, IL: University of Chicago Press.

Najmabadi, Afsaneh. 2005. *Women with Mustaches and Men without Beard: Gender and Sexual Anxieties of Iranian Modernity*. Berkeley: University of California Press.

O'Brien, Jodi. 2004. "Wrestling the Angel of Contradiction: Queer Christian Identities." *Culture and Religion* 5(2): 179–201.

O'Brien, Jodi. 2005. "How Big is Your God? Queer Christian Social Movements." In *Interdisciplinary Readings on Sex and Sexuality*, edited by Margaret Sönser Breen and Fiona Peters, 237–261. Amsterdam: Rodopi.

Olson, Laura R. and Wendy Cadge. 2002. "Talking about Homosexuality: The Views of Mainline Protestant Clergy." *Journal for the Scientific Study of Religion* 41(1): 153–167.

Olson, Laura R., Wendy Cadge, and James T. Harrison. 2006. "Religion and Public Opinion About Same-Sex Marriage." *Social Science Quarterly* 87(2): 340–360.

O'Malley, Patrick R. 2006. *Catholicism, Sexual Deviance, and Victorian Gothic Culture*. Cambridge: Cambridge University Press.

Perry, Samuel L. 2015. "Pornography Consumption as a Threat to Religious Socialization." *Sociology of Religion* 76(4): 436–458.

Peterfeso, Jill. 2011. "From Testimony to Seximony, from Script to Scripture: Revealing Mormon Women's Sexuality through the Mormon Vagina Monologues." *Journal of Feminist Studies in Religion* 27(2): 31–49.

Petro, Anthony. 2016. "After the Wrath of God: AIDS, Sexuality, and American Religion." *Journal of Church and State* 58(3): 582–584.

Pew Research Center. 2014. "Religious Landscape Study." *Pew Research Center's Religion & Public Life Project*. Available at: http://www.pewforum.org/religious-landscape-study/ (accessed October 5, 2017).

Ponticelli, Christy. 1999. "Crafting Stories of Sexual Identity Reconstruction." *Social Psychology Quarterly* 62(2): 157–172.

Radojcic, Natasha. 2016. "Building a Dignified Identity: An Ethnographic Case Study of LGBT Catholics." *Journal of Homosexuality* 63(10): 1297–1313.

Ream, Geoffrey L. and Ritch C. Savin-Williams. 2005. "Reconciling Christianity and Positive Non-Heterosexual Identity in Adolescence, with Implications for Psychological Well-Being." *Journal of Gay & Lesbian Issues in Education* 2(3): 19–36.

Reimer, Sam and Jerry Z. Park. 2001. "Tolerant(in) Civility? A Longitudinal Analysis of White Conservative Protestants' Willingness to Grant Civil Liberties." *Journal for the Scientific Study of Religion* 40(4): 735–745.

Rodriques, Eric and Suzanne Ouellette. 2000. "Gay and Lesbian Christians: Homosexual and Religious Identity Integration in the Members and Participants of a Gay Positive Church." *Journal for the Scientific Study in Religion* 39(3): 333–347.

Roper, Lyndal. 1994. *Oedipus and the Devil: Witchcraft, Religion and Sexuality in Early Modern Europe*. London: Routledge.

Rostosky, Sharon S., Mark D. Regnerus, and Margaret Laurie Comer Wright. 2003. "Coital Debut: The Role of Religiosity and Sex Attitudes in the Add Health Survey." *Journal of Sex Research* 40(4): 358–367.

Schieman, Scott, Alex Bierman, and Christopher G. Ellison. 2013. "Religion and Mental Health." In *Handbook of the Sociology of Mental Health*, edited by Carol S. Aneshensel, Jo C. Phelan, and Alex Bierman, 2nd edn., 457–478. New York, NY: Springer.

Schippert, Claudia. 2006. "Containing Uncertainty: Sexual Values and Citizenship." *Journal of Homosexuality* 52(1/2): 285–307.

Schnoor, Randal F. 2006. "Being Gay and Jewish: Negotiating Intersecting Identities." *Sociology of Religion* 67(1): 43–60.

Schuck, Kelly D. and Becky J. Liddle. 2001. "Religious Conflicts Experienced by Lesbian, Gay, and Bisexual Individuals." *Journal of Gay & Lesbian Psychotherapy* 5(2): 63–82.

Schulte, Lisa J. and Juan Battle. 2004. "The Relative Importance of Ethnicity and Religion in Predicting Attitudes Towards Gays and Lesbians." *Journal of Homosexuality* 47(2): 127–142.

Shannahan, Dervla Sara. 2010. "Some Queer Questions from a Muslim Faith Perspective." *Sexualities* 13(6): 671–684.

Sherkat, Darren E. 2002. "Sexuality and Religious Commitment in the United States: An Empirical Examination." *Journal for the Scientific Study of Religion* 41(2): 313–323.

Sherkat, Darren E, Melissa Powell-Williams, Gregory Maddox, and Kylan Mattias de Vries. 2011. "Religion, Politics, and Support for Same-Sex Marriage in the United States, 1988–2008." *Social Science Research* 40(1): 167–180.

Siegel, Karolynn and Eric W. Schrimshaw. 2002. "The Perceived Benefits of Religious and Spiritual Coping Among Older Adults Living with HIV/AIDS." *Journal for the Scientific Study of Religion* 41(1): 91–102.

Simons, Leslie Gordon, Callie Harbin Burt, and F. Ryan Peterson. 2009. "The Effect of Religion on Risky Sexual Behavior among College Students." *Deviant Behavior* 30(5): 467–485.

Siraj, Asifa. 2006. "On Being Homosexual and Muslim: Conflicts and Challenges" In *Islamic Masculinities*, edited by L. Ouzgane, 202–216. London: Zed Books.

Siraj, Asifa. 2012. "'I Don't Want to Taint the Name of Islam': The Influence of Religion on the Lives of Muslim Lesbians." *Journal of Lesbian Studies* 16(4): 449–467.

Stein, Arlene. 2001. *A Stranger Next Door: The Story of a Small Community's Battle over Sex, Faith, and Civil Rights*. Boston, MA: Beacon Press.

Stone, Amy, L. 2016. "The Impact of Anti-Gay Politics on the LGBTQ Movement." *Sociology Compass* 10(6): 459–467.

Strongman, Roberto. 2002. "10 Syncretic Religion and Dissident Sexualities." In *Queer Globalizations: Citizenship and the Afterlife of Colonialism*, edited by A. Cruz-Malave and M.F. Manalansan, 176–192. New York, NY: New York University Press.

Strub, Whitney. 2013. *The Politics of Pornography and the Rise of the New Right*. New York, NY: Columbia University Press.

Sümer, Zeynep. 2015. "Gender, Religiosity, Sexual Activity, Sexual Knowledge, and Attitudes Toward Controversial Aspects of Sexuality." *Journal of Religion & Health* 54(6): 2033–2044.

Sumerau, J.E. 2012. "That's What a Man is Supposed to Do: Compensatory Manhood Acts in an LGBT Christian Church." *Gender & Society* 26(3): 461–487.

Sumerau, J.E., Ryan T. Cragun, and Lain A.B. Mathers. 2015. "Contemporary Religion and the Cisgendering of Reality." *Social Currents* 3(3): 293–311.

Szymanski, Dawn M., Susan Kashubeck-West, and Jill Meyer. (2008). "Internalized Heterosexism: Measurement, Psychosocial Correlates, and Research Directions." *The Counseling Psychologist* 36(4): 525–574.

Thomas, Jeremy N. and Andrew L. Whitehead. 2015. "Evangelical Elites' Anti-Homosexuality Narratives as a Resistance Strategy Against Attribution Effects." *Journal for the Scientific Study of Religion* 54(2): 345–362.

Thornton, Arland and Donald Camburn. 1989. "Religious Participation and Adolescent Sexual Behavior and Attitudes." *Journal of Marriage & Family* 51(3): 641–653.

Thumma, Scott. 1991. "Negotiating a Religious Identity: The Case of the Gay Evangelical." *Sociological Analysis* 52(4): 333–347.

Toft, Alex, 2012, "Bisexuality and Christianity: Negotiating Disparate Identities in Church Life." In *The Ashgate Research Companion to Contemporary Religion and Sexuality*, edited by S.J. Hunt and A.K.T. Yip, 189–203. New York, NY: Routledge.

Tranby, Eric and Samantha E. Zulkowski. 2012. "Religion as Cultural Power: The Role of Religion in Influencing Americans' Symbolic Boundaries Around Gender and Sexuality." *Sociology Compass* 6(11): 870–882.

Uecker, Jeremy E. 2008. "Religion, Pledging, and the Premarital Sexual Behavior of Married Young Adults." *Journal of Marriage & Family* 70(3): 728–744.

Uecker, Jeremy E., Nicole Angotti, and Mark D. Regnerus. 2008. "Going Most of the Way: 'Technical Virginity' among American Adolescents." *Social Science Research* 37(4): 1200–1215.

van Klinken, Adriaan. 2015. "Queer Love in a 'Christian Nation': Zambian Gay Men Negotiating Sexual and Religious Identities." *Journal of The American Academy Of Religion* 83(4): 947–964.

Vance, Laura. 2008. "Converging on the Heterosexual Dyad: Changing Mormon and Adventist Sexual Norms and Implications for Gay and Lesbian Adherents." *Nova Religio* 11(4): 56–76.

Vance, Laura. 2015. *Women in New Religions*. New York, NY: New York University Press.

Vilaythong T. Oth, Nicole M. Lindner, and Brian A. Nosek. 2010. "'Do Unto Others': Effects of Priming the Golden Rule on Buddhists' and Christians' Attitudes toward Gay People." *Journal for the Scientific Study of Religion* 49(3): 494–506.

Walters, Karina L., Teresa Evans-Campbell, Jane M. Simoni, et al. 2006. "'My Spirit in My Heart': Identity Experiences and Challenges Among American Indian Two-Spirit Women." *Journal of Lesbian Studies* 10(1/2): 125–149.

Walton, Gerald. 2006. "Fag Church: Men who Integrate Gay and Christian Identities." *Journal of Homosexuality* 51(2): 1–17.

White, Heather R. 2015. *Reforming Sodom: Protestants and the Rise of Gay Rights*. Chapel Hill, NC: UNC Press Books.

Whitehead, Andrew L. 2010. "Sacred Rites and Civil Rights: Religion's Effect on Attitudes Toward Same-Sex Unions and the Perceived Cause of Homosexuality." *Social Science Quarterly* 91(1): 63–79.

Whitehead, Andrew L. 2013. "Religious Organizations and Homosexuality: The Acceptance of Gays and Lesbians in American Congregations." *Review of Religious Research* 55(2): 297–317.

Wilcox, Melissa M. 2003. *Coming Out in Christianity: Religion, Identity, and Community*. Bloomington, IN: Indiana University Press.

Wilcox, Melissa M. 2009. *Queer Women and Religious Individualism*. Bloomington, IN: Indiana University Press.

Williams, Jean Calterone. 2011. "Battling a 'Sex-Saturated Society': The Abstinence Movement and the Politics of Sex Education." *Sexualities* 14(4): 416–443.

Wolkomir, Michelle. 2006. "'*Be not Deceived:' The Sacred and Sexual Struggles of Gay and Ex-Gay Christian Men*." Piscataway, NJ: Rutgers University Press.

Woodell, Brandi, Emily Kazyak, and D'Lane Compton. 2015. "Reconciling LGB and Christian Identities in the Rural South." *Social Sciences* 4(3): 859–878.

Yi, Joseph, Gowoon Jung, and Joe Phillips. 2017. "Evangelical Christian Discourse in South Korea on the LGBT: The Politics of Cross-Border Learning." *Society* 54(1): 29–33.

Yip, Andrew Kam-Tuck. 1997. "Attacking the Attacker: Gay Christians Talk Back." *British Journal of Sociology* 48(1): 113–127.

Yip, Andrew Kam-Tuck. 2002. "The Persistence of Faith Among Nonheterosexual Christians: Evidence for the Neosecularization Thesis of Religious Transformation." *Journal for the Scientific Study of Religion* 41(2): 199–212.

Yip, Andrew Kam-Tuck. 2007. "Sexual Orientation Discrimination in Religious Communities." In *Sexual Orientation Discrimination: An International Perspective*, edited by L. Badgett and J. Frank, 209–223. London: Routledge.

Yip, Andrew Kam-Tuck. 2009. "Islam and Sexuality: Orthodoxy and Contestations." *Contemporary Islam* 3(1): 1–5.

Young, Michael, George Denny, Tamera Young, and Raffy Lucquis. 2000. "Sexual Satisfaction among Married Women." *American Journal of Health Studies* 16(2): 73–85.

Yuchtman-Yaar, Ephraim and Yasmin Alkalay. 2007. "Religious Zones, Economic Development and Modern Value Orientations: Individual Versus Contextual Effects." *Social Science Research* 36(2): 789–807.

12

Sexuality Education

Louisa Allen

Mapping the Global Landscape of School-Based Research

This chapter is concerned with conceptualizing school-based sexuality education research undertaken around the world in the last ten years. It takes place in a moment characterized within the social sciences as an "ontological turn" where the nature of things, including the nature of sexuality education, is being questioned (Coole and Frost 2010). Such questioning is less about the legitimacy of sexuality education's presence in schools – an issue which has historically plagued this subject – and instead, influenced by ideas from quantum physics and new materialist thinkers like Karen Barad (2007), it entails a more fundamental engagement with the nature of reality as we currently understand it. This ontological shift has in part been prompted by a recognition of crises of thought and practice (Deleuze and Guattari 1987), around issues like global warming and conflict, which remain intellectually unresolved. In pausing to take account of the issues which have occupied sexuality education researchers in recent years, this chapter marks a crisis of thought and practice in the field of school-based sexuality education. It argues that, while the international research landscape is rich and diverse, it simultaneously grapples with underpinning questions which are predictable and repetitive. For example, should sexuality education be taught, who should teach it, and what should be taught? Despite researchers expending considerable time and effort on them, these questions remain unresolved.

What is presented here is not a traditional review of the global literature on school-based sexuality education. It does not profess to document and survey most of the international research in the area. This task is impossible given the world's geographical diversity and the constant generation of studies which inevitably mean some will be overlooked. Given the current critique of representational forms of methodology that promise an impossible "god's eye view," this approach is also somewhat redundant (for more on this argument see MacLure 2013). This chapter maps the conceptual contours of the research landscape from my own engagement in the field of school-based sexuality education research for the past 24 years. This engagement has occurred as a researcher, conference attendee, journal reviewer and editor, undergraduate teacher, and postgraduate supervisor. It has also involved recently reading almost 1,000 abstracts traversing the last 10 years of two leading international journals in the field of sexuality education. The first of these, *Sex Education: Sexuality, Society and Learning* is a British-based journal publishing sexuality education research from across the globe directed at academics and practitioners. The other, the *American Journal of Sexuality Education* is oriented to the professional needs of sexuality educators and trainers and was formerly known as *The Journal of Sex Education and Therapy*, established in 1975. This exercise in reading journal abstracts was undertaken as part of an unrelated project for a recently completed book (Allen 2018).

The conceptualization of existing literature presented here is not offered as a systematic survey or analysis, but rather a sharing of impressions. Via this practice, I seek to open space for others to join the conversation about what matters to school-based sexuality education researchers and how this has influenced the contours of the field. This discussion is shaped by two questions: What kind of sexuality education research has predominantly been undertaken in the world in the last 10 years? And, how might it be characterized in terms of where its emphases lie and where it has yet to travel? This chapter is concerned less with the findings of studies, and more with the shape of questions and interests which have guided them. The purpose of undertaking this work is to think "the project of school-based sexuality education research" in its entirety. Sexuality education researchers often undertake discrete projects in specific global locations and social contexts, which, while articulating with international literature, do not conceptualize it. Such conceptualization is important for developing this field of research globally and delineating its existing im/possibilities. That is, those structures of thought which regulate and make possible what we understand as the nature of sexuality education and configurations of school-based practice.

The chapter begins by identifying some of the existing literature's foundational threads. These constitute enduring questions around sexuality education which weave and surface through this literature landscape. Next, I note areas of coagulation which mark particular foci and perspectives which frequently appear in sexuality education research. In the chapter's final section, I offer a conceptualization of these general research emphases, to ascertain the limits of the field's exploration and provoke possibilities for thinking it differently.

Enduring Questions for School-Based Sexuality Education Research

The field of sexuality education research is much wider than school-based literature and incorporates the teaching of sexuality in a myriad settings outside the classroom (e.g. community contexts, prisons, digital media, television, radio, literature, popular culture) (Allen and Rasmussen 2017). It is important to note, however, that due to confines of space, sexuality education in this chapter references education in school-based settings only, but it is likely that the enduring questions which underpin school-based programs also hold currency for wider forms of sexuality education.

Sexuality education research coagulates around particular perspectives such as those of young people, parents and teachers. It also concentrates in areas such as program evaluation, and issues like pleasure and sexual diversity. As outlined below, a series of enduring and repetitive questions thread through these areas, intersecting with concerns about whether sexuality education is *effective*. The question of sexuality education's effectiveness is foundational in the literature because it is the premise upon which the legitimacy of school-based programs rest. Without demonstrating their value in effectively reducing perceived negative outcomes of sexual activity, the need for sexuality education at school is fragile. Subsequently, at the heart of the global literature lies a permanent tension between those who believe this subject should be taught at school, and those who oppose this phenomenon. Controversy and debate have shaped thought about sexuality education since the discussions that have preceded its inception in schools (Irvine 2002). Questions about sexuality education's effectiveness therefore constitute one of the unresolved "crises" of this field of research and practice.

To answer the question of whether sexuality education is effective, other related questions are necessary and subsequently run through the literature. The first of these coheres around what should be taught, as the content of sexuality education is perceived to be related to its effectiveness. For sexuality education to be effective, its proponents contend that particular content about, for example, safer sex and condom use must be taught. Opponents of sexuality education often argue that such content exhibits a morality that can offend particular modes of thinking and being. Examples of this discord feature in tabloid stories where parents express anger when information about oral and anal sex is taught (Warth 2017). This content is often deemed graphic and inappropriate and in the case of anal sex, invoking homosexuality. Debates about '"appropriate" and "inappropriate" content often ultimately circle back to the necessity of this subject's presence in school.

Also aligned with concerns about sexuality education's effectiveness are questions around the best pedagogy and teachers for this subject. When sexuality education fails to deliver on its promises of reducing sexually transmissible infections and unplanned pregnancies, this is often attributed to poor program design and educators. Subsequently, much literature seeks to ascertain *who* sexuality education's stakeholders (for instance, parents and young people), think make the best sexuality educators. Interestingly, both proponents and opponents of sexuality education mobilize similar arguments about perceived inadequacies of program design and educators to bolster their positions. Proponents of sexuality education argue that program ineffectiveness can be attributed to poor pedagogy and educators. For instance, in the case of abstinence-only education which they perceive fails to address young people's lived realities and whose educators are deemed "moralistic." Similarly, opponents of sexuality education argue that its school-based version fails because parents are the rightful educators of young people's sexuality and can deliver information in accordance with family culture and values. As such, teachers and program pedagogy constitute the reasons for both program failure and program success.

Another persistent question threading through the literature is what is missing from sexuality education? In an endeavor to deliver sexuality education which effectively meets all students' and their associated communities' needs, much literature is preoccupied with the question of which identities and issues does sexuality education leave out? Answers cohere around those who are "lesbian, gay, bisexual, trans, queer/, intersex and asexual" (LGBTQIA+) (DePalma and Francis 2014) from minority cultures (Coleman 2007), religious communities (Kam-Tuck Yip, Keenan, and Page 2011), live in developing nations (Vanwesenbeeck et al. 2015), and people with disabilities (Rogers 2016). Missing issues have been identified as pleasure (McGeeney 2017), homophobia (O'Higgins-Norman, 2009), transphobia (DePalma and Jennett 2012), pornography (Albury 2014), digital sexual citizenship (Renold and Ringrose 2016), sexual ethics (Carmody 2009), violence (Cameron Lewis and Allen 2012), and gender inequities (Ferfolja and Ullman 2017). While identifying what is missing, sexuality researchers also often attempt to determine how these identities and issues might be successfully included. Their successful inclusion addresses the tension around which this field pivots, that of sexuality education's effectiveness and subsequently, legitimate place in schools.

Areas of Coagulation in Sexuality Education Research

Canvassing young people's perspectives of sexuality education is a feature of the international literature. These studies seek to understand what young people think of programs, how they experience them, and how the programs might be improved (Van der Geugten et al. 2014; Newby et al. 2011). Acknowledging and exploring young people's perspectives is connected to the field's enduring preoccupation with program effectiveness. To be effective, sexuality education must meet the needs and interests of a diversity of young people. Subsequently, researchers have sought to include the opinions of young people who are LGBTI (Formby 2011), ethnically diverse (Coleman 2007), and marginalized or at risk (Brown, Sorenson and Hildebrand 2012). The desire to gather and listen to young people's voices forms part of a wider movement within child and youth research endeavoring to recognize young people as able to think, speak, and act independently of adults (Kehily 2007).

Research that centers young people's perspectives has also sought to understand their experience of sexual relationships (Waszak Geary et al. 2013). These studies have typically focused on sexual intercourse because of its connection with unplanned pregnancy and higher risk of contracting sexually transmissible infections (STIs). Understanding why young people have sex and recording details such as age of first sexual initiation are deemed valuable for designing programs relevant to young people's lives (Holland et al. 2010). A related focus here has been exploring young people's intention to use, and then subsequent application of, contraception (Suvivuo, Tossavainen, and Kontula 2009). Such insights highlight why young people do not always translate the safer sex knowledge they acquire from sexuality education into practice (McKee 2014). These contextual features of young people's sexual relationships can be incorporated into program design to increase the likelihood of sexuality education's messages being operationalized.

Understanding young people's levels of sexual knowledge has been another emphasis in this literature. In parts of the world where sexuality education is not mandatory (for instance, some African, Asian, and East European nations) it has been identified that young people do not have access to adequate knowledge to look after their sexual health (Kamal 2012). In other global locations where sexuality education is taught, but its coverage is haphazard, students receive limited, inadequate or inaccurate information (Njue, Voeten, and Maina Ahlberg 2011). Determining what sexual knowledge young people possess and where information is missing, is deemed valuable for increasing program effectiveness in reducing unplanned pregnancies and STIs. The logic which underpins this research, is that the first step toward practicing safer sex and contraception is acquiring the information necessary to do so.

The gendered nature of sexual experiences and sexuality education also predominates in the literature featuring young people's voices. How gendered discourses of sexuality restrict young people's ability to refuse or practice safer sex are frequently examined (Austrian and Anderson 2015). The identification of economic factors as a barrier to health and behavior change, have provided insights into challenges faced by young women in practicing safer sex and experiencing sexuality positively. Research about young men and sexuality education has examined the relationship between masculinities and sexualities and how performance of masculinity may inhibit the achievement of sexual health (Hilton 2007). This literature assumes there are gendered differences in the way sexual health and sexuality education are experienced and that if programs are to be effective, content and pedagogy must take these into account.

Parents

Another area of coagulation in the international literature is parents' perspectives of sexuality education. Parental support is identified as key to program success and so ascertaining if parents approve of sexuality education and their views about what should be covered is important (Thi Thu Ha and Fisher 2011). In some countries like the United States, parents are typically highly supportive of sex education (Fisher et al. 2015) while in others, such as Greece, they are not (Gerouki 2007). In global regions such as Tanzania, parents are generally supportive of school-based programs but may object to specific topics such as homosexuality and masturbation (Mkumbo and Ingham 2010). There are also some parents who perceive sexuality education as primarily their responsibility and view learning that occurs at school as merely an important adjunct (Dyson and Smith 2012).

A substantial body of literature explores parental communication around sexual issues with young people. It traverses issues parents cover with their children (Trinh et al. 2009), the main messages they offer (Rouvier et al. 2011), and which parent, children are more likely to talk with (Sneed et al. 2013). Some of these studies explore why some parents may be reluctant to talk to their children about sexual issues (Malacone and Beckmeyer 2016). While parents believe such communication is important for the sexual health of their children, they can feel embarrassed or uncomfortable, or lack knowledge to conduct such conversations confidently (Morawska et al. 2015). Subsequently, studies find the messages some parents offer are limited, or that these discussions do not occur at all (Meschke and Dettmer 2012). For parents who are reluctant to engage in these conversations, school-based programs provide a welcome relief from the perceived responsibility of educating their children about sexuality.

Studies around parent–child communication often extend to investigate how these discussions mediate young people's romantic and sexual practice (Wisnieski, Sieving, and Garwick 2015). Some studies find that young people with high levels of general communication with their mothers or fathers are more likely to talk with partners about pregnancy and STI prevention (Schonfeld Hicks, McRee and Eisenberg 2013). These studies provide evidence of how discussion with parents can influence children's sexual behavior. An important caveat here is that the quality of these discussions can vary and sometimes provide no value, or may be detrimental to young people's sexual practice (Bay-Cheng 2013). To improve parent–child communication around sexual issues and engender parental support for school-based programs, another feature of this literature is discussion around sexuality education programs for parents. The design of these programs and how they might encourage parents to talk with their teenagers about sexuality issues are often a focus (Kesterton and Coleman 2010).

The body of work on parental perspectives is substantial, and its volume indicative of how this literature intersects with debate about whether programs should exist. Parental opposition to school-based programs generates significant workload for teachers and can be publicly damaging to a school's reputation. Parents are much more likely to support programs they understand and are invested in, and so research that engages their perspectives and preferences is beneficial for developing programs that they approve of. Studies also reveal the importance of encouraging parents to talk to children about sexuality to supplement program information and thus increase the chances of meeting goals around preventing unplanned pregnancies and STIs. In this way, the literature on parental perspectives endeavors to make sexuality education more effective.

Teachers

Quality teachers are perceived as central to effective sexuality education and therefore examining teachers' attitudes to this subject, how they teach it, and what support they require is a critical undertaking (Smith and Harrison 2013). This body of literature investigates teachers' willingness to provide sexuality education and factors which might affect this. Studies reveal that fear of complaints about what they teach and how they are teaching it mean educators are often reluctant to teach this subject (Cohen, Byers, and Sears 2012). Some also express a lack of confidence about this topic due to inadequate professional development and school management support. The low priority often accorded to sexuality education by schools relative to other curriculum subjects, means that funding and opportunities for teacher professional development can be scarce. Outsourcing the teaching of sexuality education (Duffy et al. 2013) or use of guest speakers (McRee, Madsen, and Eisenberg 2014) is often seen as a solution in situations where teachers are underprepared or unwilling to teach it. Literature on teachers also links teacher levels of sexual knowledge with sexuality education's effectiveness. These studies assess teachers' sexual health knowledge to determine if they are adequately prepared to teach this area. The logic of this literature rests on the idea that to successfully practice safer sex, young people need to be given accurate knowledge from a teacher, who in turn holds correct knowledge on this subject.

Teachers' attitudes toward sexuality issues and student sexuality is also a feature of this literature (Preston 2016). When specific topics are missing from the curriculum despite policy provision for their inclusion, teacher reluctance to incorporate them is often blamed. One example here is teacher practices regarding coverage of lesbian, gay, bisexual, and transgender issues in the curriculum. While studies reveal that, in principle, teachers can demonstrate support for LGBTQIA+-inclusive education, this may not be borne out in practice due to queer sexualities being perceived as inherently "controversial" (Meyer, Taylor, and Peter 2015). Research reveals many teachers do not implement gay themes in their teaching because of fear of criticism from parents and administrators, along with a lack of professional training and their own negative attitudes towards these topics (Flores 2014).

Teachers' experience of teaching sexuality education and the challenges they confront is also highlighted in this literature. Research reveals teachers' capacity to provide quality education is often hampered or enhanced by factors such as organizational change levels, support of administrators, district policy, and structural factors like time, financial resources, and the diversity of the student body (Eisenberg et al. 2012). Teachers also describe the way conservative attitudes to young people's sexual activity and social adherence to gender stereotypes can limit their work (Iyer and Aggleton 2013). Such studies address the central concern with sexuality education's effectiveness running throughout the school-based sexuality education literature. When teachers' experiences and the challenges they face are known, then improved support might be garnered to bolster program's effectiveness.

Sexuality Education Evaluation and Effectiveness

Studies that evaluate school-based programs to determine their effectiveness are another point of coagulation in the literature. This research is demarcated from that which seeks to uncover findings to improve sexuality education's effectiveness, by directing attention to whether sexuality education is achieving its desired aims. One of the motivations for program evaluation is to ascertain the characteristics of effective programs in order to replicate them (Rocha, Leal, and Duarte 2016). The identification of program shortcomings and obstacles is also sought so changes may be implemented to avoid or overcome them. Evaluation is a staple element of sexuality education research and, depending on whether it uncovers significant flaws or successes, is utilized to justify programs or call for their abolishment.

Literature in this area often takes the form of evaluating a program's effectiveness by testing the knowledge of students exposed to a program, compared to a control group who were not (Smylie, Maticka-Tyndale, and Boyd 2008). A variation here is discerning intention to use condoms or contraception at next intercourse or the delay of sexual involvement (Koo et al. 2011). While many studies reveal improvement in sexual knowledge acquisition and behavioral change (Milhausen et al. 2008), some programs reveal no change or variable results (Raj et al. 2008). These discrepancies continue to fuel debate about the presence of sexuality education at school. They also propel the continuation of research which seeks to identify "the best" content, teachers and pedagogy to quell sexuality education's critics. However, the search for "the-silver-bullet-of-sexuality-education" program design, which is unremittingly effective, remains elusive.

Pedagogy

Program pedagogy is tied to debates about sexuality education's effectiveness in that literature in this area focuses on whether certain pedagogies increase its benefits. This thinking has been generated by the way program failure has been attributed to poorly designed and executed pedagogies. Traditional forms of sexuality education pedagogy for instance, such as pen and paper methods or watching videos, have been identified as failing to adequately engage students or address their interests and lived experiences. These shortcomings have engendered creative ideas around new methods of teaching and learning. The last 10 years have witnessed an increased focus on theater-based pedagogy as a means of educating about sexuality inspired by a larger movement toward arts-based methods in education (Ponzetti 2009). The prominence of digital media in young people's lives has driven experimentation with digital forms of pedagogy. This exploration has included use of mobile technology to promote young people's sexual health and the creation of digital reality games to encourage responsible sexual decision making (Gilliam et al. 2016).

Missing Elements of Sexuality Education

Sexual diversity

Evaluations of program effectiveness and studies of teacher and student perspectives have highlighted the heteronormative nature of schooling and the sexuality education curriculum. This critique has been fueled by the activism of LGBTIA+ movements and the wider academic work of queer studies and queer theory scholars. The literature makes this critique in terms of two schooling arenas: its general sexual culture (Allan et al. 2008), and the official curriculum which includes sexuality education (Elia and Eliason 2010). These areas are not discrete, in that improvements in queer students' experiences of wider schooling culture can filter into the content and pedagogy of the sexuality education curriculum. Young LGBTIQA students are often consulted in these studies to determine their experiences of school culture and sexuality education with findings typically highlighting how queer issues and identities are missing in these contexts (Gowen and Winges-Yanez 2014).

The presence of homophobia at school is a strong theme in this literature. Explorations of this issue reveal how students, teachers, and senior management understand and experience homosexuality and homophobic bullying (Neary 2013; O'Higgins-Norman 2009). Other studies look at specific aspects of the sexuality curriculum such as the extent to which heterosexism and heteronormativity are present in text books (Wilmot and Naidoo 2014). Associated with this literature is a series of studies that examine strategies and pedagogic practices to combat homophobia and heteronormativity at school (Marston 2015). Their findings reveal how schools might better align their strategies to address homophobia and bullying with pupil's own values and understandings of these issues (Warwick and Aggleton 2014).

There is a general acknowledgement that homophobia and heteronormativity are difficult practices to eradicate because of the complexity of their operation and diverse configuration in multiple contexts.

Subsequently, the literature contains a collection of studies which consider the effectiveness of different approaches for combating heteronormativity. Some focus on the utility of strategies such as gay–straight alliances, claiming that straight allies can use their heterosexual privilege to address LGBTIQA+ issues with their peers (Lapointe 2015). Others reflect on particular pedagogies such as performance-based arts engagement for expanding queer youth subjectivities beyond "victim" and "at-risk" narratives (Harris and Farrington 2014). The tendency within these studies is for such practices to produce mixed results. Main barriers to their success include, some students' and teachers' mutual discomfort in discussing sexuality, insufficient professional training for teachers, the low priority accorded to homophobic bullying and negative parental views on homosexuality (Formby 2015).

Gender diversity is a relatively recent addition to the literature compared with a much longer history of the invisibility of LGBT issues in sexuality education. Surfacing with some density in the last 5 years, it explores experiences of transgender and gender-diverse students paying attention to binary understandings of gender identity in these students' experiences of sexuality education, as well as treatment by staff (Jones et al. 2016). What this burgeoning research area signals, is that sexuality education generally negates these students in curriculum content, and this deficit necessitates a need for sexuality educators, policy designers, and school management to make transgender issues a focus.

Pleasure

Fine's (1988) early work around the missing discourse of desire not only identified desire as absent in sexuality education, but hinted at the potential benefits of its inclusion. Her seminal paper generated a spate of studies which have continued within the last ten years to identify whether desire and pleasure are still missing from curricula in diverse global locations. This body of literature advocates for the inclusion of pleasure on grounds of a myriad potential positive outcomes around sexual health, rights, equality, and safeguarding against coercion and harm (Beasley 2008). Feminists particularly, have been drawn to researching this area in relation to expanding possibilities for understanding young women's sexual subjectivities as desiring and agentic (Lamb 2010a).

Despite a few exceptions, the literature reveals that sexuality education that recognizes pleasure and desire for young people remains absent in many global contexts (McGeeney and Kehily 2016). This continued absence is partly attributable to the controversy attached to associating sex with pleasure, rather than reproduction. Where programs do include pleasure, research has cohered around the challenges around teaching this issue. Studies have critically reflected on how, for instance, pre-service teachers were reluctant to include pleasure in their classes (Ollis 2016). Other authors have detailed strong opposition from community members to resources supporting educators to teach about pleasure (Hirst 2014). Cumulatively, these studies highlight that the inclusion of pleasure in sexuality education has been more complex and challenging than first imagined.

As part of this ongoing conversation there has been a move to problematize conceptualizations of pleasure and examine the politics of its emergence and implementation (Allen, Rasmussen, and Quinlivan 2014). This dialogue reveals how pleasure has been incorporated into some programs, in ways and with effects that were not originally envisioned by its proponents (Allen and Carmody 2012). Pleasure in some of its permutations has become an imperative, a marker of healthy sexuality and way of configuring "superior" sexual subjects (i.e. those who can give, and those who can experience pleasure) compared with those who are deemed "deficit" in these terms (Allen 2012). Other research signals the individualized way in which pleasure is conceptualized in sexuality programs and as devoid of issues of social ethics (Lamb 2010b). This work calls for a shift from individualistic moral or health implications of one's individual sexual decision-making and toward the broad ethics of living in, and belonging to, communities.

Within this coagulation of pleasure research, concerns surface around the content of programs and their appropriateness. Inherent in the pleasure literature lie disagreements over the purpose of this subject in terms of teaching young people to avoid sexual risk and danger and encouraging notions of sexual health in which pleasurable sexual activity might be a possibility. This pleasure/danger binary has structured thought about sexuality since Vance's (1989) identification of it in her work around women's sexuality and debates about pornography. It seeps into sexuality education research seeking to polarize opponents of pleasure's inclusion as sex-negative and conservative, and pleasure's proponents as sex-positive and progressive. This false polarization, which also designates progressive and conservative positions on sexuality education, is the subject of critique in newly emerging discussions around religious and secular accounts of sexuality education (see Rasmussen 2016). Literature on pleasure also intersects with debates around sexuality education's effectiveness, as pleasure's proponents imply its inclusion will have positive effects. Questions about pedagogy also thread through this discussion around the best way to teach about pleasure and who are the most appropriate and capable educators to do this.

Conceptual Contours of the Literature

An overriding feature of this literature landscape is an emphasis on how to improve sexuality education in relation to reducing unwanted or negative effects of sexual behavior and making young people's experience of sexuality more positive. The latter is a more recent aim, particularly in countries where school-based sexuality education has an entrenched history and epidemics like HIV/AIDS have subsided. The importance and necessity of these objectives are taken for granted, with few philosophical discussions challenging sexuality education's current purpose or how it addresses young people as sexual subjects. While there are some important exceptions (see for example Illes 2012; Jones 2011; Greteman 2013; Rasmussen 2016), this work does not appear in the same density as research on how to make sexuality education more effective in terms of conventional objectives.

When discussions about the purpose of sexuality education do occur, they are often limited to specific foci. For instance, concern with improving young people's health or making curricular more inclusive of marginalized groups such as queer students and those who are religiously and/or culturally diverse. A fundamental questioning of the nature and epistemology of sexuality education is absent. The idea that sexuality education is something which should offer young people knowledge or practical skills (such as correct condom usage) and addresses them as individual and autonomous agents is largely unquestioned. Neither is there any challenge that notions of pedagogy (teaching and knowledge) may have limited value as indicated by variable results around the effectiveness of educating about sexuality (by parents or school).

Implicit within the literature are enduring disagreements over sexuality education's presence and configuration in schools. For some countries where sexuality education is not a mandatory element of the national curriculum, this issue is paramount (e.g Turkey, Russia, Greece). Yet, even in locations where school-based programs are entrenched, studies constantly argue for the importance of sexuality education in schools. These arguments rest on grounds of improving young people's sexual health, keeping them sexually safe or providing them with knowledge and agency to make their own (responsible and respectful) sexual decisions. It appears that school-based sexuality education exists in constant fear of its controversial position and research is subsequently poised to justify its seemingly precarious existence in schools.

This discord around sexuality education is organized within the literature as a binary between those who are for, or against, particular programs, content, and pedagogy. At least this is the way in which the debate has unfolded in countries where school-based programs are well established. This polarization is stark in literature around abstinence-only education (Gilbert 2010). Its supporters herald its effectiveness while those who oppose its stance of "no sex before marriage," argue this incurs damage to young people and that comprehensive sexuality education is superior. Lesko (2010) draws attention to an interesting phenomenon in this dispute between supporters of either abstinence-only or comprehensive programs. She identifies how both curricula promise similar things by directing knowers to feel sure, optimistic, and free and both types of program harbor a desire for stable knowledge and guaranteed meanings. Yet, neither curriculum has indisputable evidence that *its* approach, irrefutably works.

At the centre of all the literature on school-based sexuality education sits the human subject. This centering occurs in several ways. Firstly, the focus of this education which is sexuality, is perceived as housed in the bodies of humans as its locus and site of expression. This understanding of sexuality is apparent in the curriculum emphasis on teaching about human bodily functions such as menstruation, reproduction, and puberty. Secondly, programs are taught by (educator) humans to other (student) humans conveying a recognition that sexuality is a human capacity and concern. Lastly, all of sexuality education's messages harbor the idea of human agency to direct behavior through knowledge acquisition. The directive to practice safer sex for instance, assumes that young people have agency to do this, and when they don't, it is the failure of an individual to act responsibly. The idea that sexuality might be more-than human as is now being proposed within new materialist thought, is yet to be fully explored (Allen and Rasmussen 2017).

Another major conceptual premise underpinning the literature is the power of education to change things. This assumption is seen in an understanding of sexuality education's capacity to increase students' knowledge, change their attitudes (about for example homophobia), and influence their behavior (in relation to practicing safer sex). This is an implicit assumption of the value of sexuality education, in fact all education, that knowledge can change the world. This presumption is now being questioned with the emergence of new thought about the role of education and an increased recognition of the complex materiality of the planet (see Snaza et al. 2016). The endurance of particular foci in sexuality education, such as whether it is effective or how to reduce homophobia, implies that it continues to "fail" at these aims. Sexuality education's major issues do not seem to disappear, but morph into contemporary permutations. For example, moral panic around the sexualization of young people (i.e. sexualized media makes young people precociously sexual and these dangers should be talked about in sexuality education) contain residues of the idea that offering young people knowledge about sexuality will encourage their sexual behavior.

Sexuality education literature is simultaneously as diverse and rich as it is predictable and repetitive. Its diversity lies in its global coverage, methodological approaches, and the range of issues it explores. However, researchers are caught with unsolvable questions and issues that have been circulating since the inception of this subject in schools. For example, how to encourage young people to practice the knowledge sexuality education offers, how to overcome gender and sexual inequities, and how to attend to cultural and religious diversity. These are universal, enduring issues that are still unsolvable despite endless explorations to determine how to make efforts in these areas more successful. What if these dilemmas are beyond the power of the individual to orchestrate? Where does that leave sexuality education?

The reader might be forgiven for thinking that I am a not an advocate of school-based sexuality education. I raise these provocations as a means of thinking the current state of the field anew. With the advent of new materialist thought, sexuality researchers in some parts of the world are poised at what Barad (2007) coins an "agential cut" – a moment of ontological and epistemological possibility for the field. It is important to acknowledge that this is a position of specific power and perspective – not unrelated to privilege that is cultural and institutional as found for instance, in universities rather than community groups and developing nations. This moment makes possible the conceptualization of sexuality education research, and philosophical questions about its ontology and epistemology raised here. It promises new ways of thinking the im/possibilities of sexuality education research at the same time as history (and nature/materiality) predicts changes to this field will be minimal.

References

Albury, Kath. 2014. "Porn *and* Sex Education, Porn *as* Sex Education." *Porn Studies* 1(1–2): 172–181.

Allan, Alexandra, Elizabeth Atkinson, Elizabeth Brace, et al. 2008. "Speaking the Unspeakable in Forbidden Places: Addressing Lesbian, Gay, Bisexual and Transgender Equality in the Primary School." *Sex Education* 8(3): 315–329.

Allen, Louisa. 2012. "Pleasure's Perils? Critically Reflecting on Pleasure's Inclusion in Sexuality Education." *Sexualities* 15(3/4): 455–471.

Allen, Louisa. (in 2018). *Sexuality Education and New Materialism: Queer Things*. New York: Palgrave.
Allen, Louisa and Moira Carmody. 2012. "Pleasure has No Passport: Re-visiting the Potential of Pleasure in Sexuality Education." *Sex Education* 12(4): 455–468.
Allen, Louisa and Mary Lou Rasmussen, eds. 2017. *The Palgrave Handbook of Education*. London: Springer Nature.
Allen, Louisa, Mary Lou Rasmussen, and Kathleen Quinlivan. 2014. *The Politics of Pleasure in Sexuality Education: Pleasure Bound*. New York, NY: Routledge.
Austrian, Karen and Althea Anderson. 2015. "Barriers and Facilitators To Health Behaviour Change and Economic Activity among Slum-Dwelling Adolescent Girls and Young Women in Nairobi, Kenya: The Role of Social, Health and Economic Assets." *Sex Education* 15(1): 64–77.
Barad, Karen. 2007. *Meeting the Universe Halfway: Quantum Physics and the Entanglement of Matter and Meaning*. Durhman, NC: Duke University Press.
Bay-Cheng, Laina. 2013. "Ethical Parenting of Sexually Active Youth: Ensuring Safety While Enabling Development." *Sex Education* 13(2): 133–145.
Beasley, Chris. 2008. "The Challenge of Pleasure: Re-imagining Sexuality and Sexual Health." *Health Sociology Review* 17(2): 151–163.
Brown, Graham, Anne Sorenson, and Janina Hildebrand. 2012. "How They Got It and How They Wanted It: Marginalised Young People's Perspectives on Their Experiences of Sexual Health Education." *Sex Education: Sexuality, Society and Learning* 12(5): 599–612.
Cameron Lewis, Vanessa and Louisa Allen. 2012. "Teaching Pleasure *and* Danger in Sexuality Education." *Sex Education* 13(2):121–132. doi: 10.1080/14681811.2012.697440.
Carmody, Moria. 2009. *Sex and Ethics: Young People and Ethical Sex*. Houndmills: Palgrave Macmillan.
Cohen, Jacqueline, Sandra Byers, and Heather Sears. 2012. "Factors Affecting Canadian Teachers' Willingness to Teach Sexual Health Education." *Sex Education* 12(3): 299–316.
Coleman, Lester. 2007. "Preferences Towards Sex Education and Information from an Ethnically Diverse Sample of Young People." *Sex Education* 7(3): 293–307.
Coole, Diana and Samantha Frost, eds. 2010. *New Materialisms: Ontology, Agency, and Politics*. London: Duke University Press.
Deleuze, Gilles and Félix Guattari. 1987. *A Thousand Plateaus: Capitalism and Sschizophrenia*, translated by B. Massumi. Minneapolis: University of Minnesota Press.
DePalma, Renée and Dennis Francis. 2014. "South African Life Orientation Teachers: (Not) Teaching About Sexuality Diversity." *Journal of Homosexuality* 16(12): 1687–1711.
DePalma, Renée and Mark Jennett. 2012. "Homophobia, Transphobia and Culture: Deconstructing Heteronormativity in English Primary Schools." *Intercultural Education* 21(1): 15–26.
Duffy, Bernadette, Nina Fotinatos, Amanda Smith, and Jenene Burke. 2013. "Puberty, Health and Sexual Education in Australian Regional Primary Schools: Year 5 and 6 Teacher Perceptions." *Sex Education* 13(2): 186–203.
Dyson, Suzanne and Elizabeth Smith. 2012. "'There are Lots of Different Kinds of Normal': Families and Sex Education – Styles, Approaches and Concerns." *Sex Education* 12(2): 219–229.
Eisenberg, Marla, Nikki Madsen, Jennifer Oliphant, and Michael Resnick. 2012. "Policies, Principals and Parents: Multilevel Challenges and Supports in Teaching Sexuality Education." *Sex Education* 12(3): 317–329.
Elia, John and Mickey Eliason. 2010. "Discourses of Exclusion: Sexuality Education's Silencing of Sexual Others." *Journal of LGBT Youth* 7(1): 29–48.

Ferfolja, Tania and Jacqueline Ullman. 2017. "Gender and Sexuality in Education and Health: Voices Advocating for Equity and Social Justice." *Sex Education* 17(3): 235–241.

Fine, Michelle. 1988. "Sexuality, Schooling and Adolescent Females: The Missing Discourse of Desire." *Harvard Educational Review* 58(1): 29–53.

Fisher, Christine, Susan Telljohann, James Price, et al. 2015. "Perceptions of Elementary School Children's Parents Regarding Sexuality Education." *American Journal of Sexuality Education* 10(1): 1–20.

Flores, Gabriel. 2014. "Teachers Working Cooperatively with Parents and Caregivers when Implementing LGBT Themes in the Elementary Classroom." *American Journal of Sexuality Education* 9(1): 114–120.

Formby, Eleanor. 2011. "Sex and Relationships Education, Sexual Health, and Lesbian, Gay and Bisexual Sexual Cultures: Views from Young People." *Sex Education* 11(3): 255–266.

Formby, Eleanor. 2015. "Limitations of Focussing on Homophobic, Biphobic and Transphobic 'Bullying' to Understand and Address LGBT Young People's Experiences Within and Beyond School." *Sex Education* 15(6): 626–640.

Gerouki, Margarita. 2007. "Sexuality and Relationships Education in the Greek Primary Schools – See No Evil, Hear No Evil, Speak No Evil." *Sex Education* 7(1): 81–100.

Gilbert, Jen. 2010. "Ambivalence Only? Sex Education in the Age of Abstinence." *Sexuality, Society and Learning* 10(3): 233–237.

Gilliam, Melissa, Patrick Jagoda, Erin Jaworski, et al. 2016. "'Because if We Don't Talk About It, How Are We Going To Prevent It?': *Lucidity*, A Narrative-Based Game About Sexual Violence." *Sex Education* 16(4): 391–404.

Gowen, Kris and Nick Winges-Yanez. 2014. "Lesbian, Gay, Bisexual, Transgender, Queer and Questioning Youths' Perspectives of Inclusive School-Based Sexuality Education." *The Journal of Sex Research* 51(7): 788–800.

Greteman, Adam. 2013. "Fashioning a Bareback Pedagogy: Towards a Theory of Risky (Sex) Education." *Sex Education* 13(1): S20–S31.

Harris, Anne and David Farrington. 2014. "'It Gets Narrower': Creative Strategies for Re-Broadening Queer Peer Education." *Sex Education* 14(2): 144–158.

Hilton, Gillian. 2007. "Listening to the Boys Again: An Exploration of What Boys Want to Learn in Sex Education Classes and How They Want to be Taught." *Sex Education* 7(2): 161–174.

Hirst, Julia. 2014. "'Get Some Rhythm Round the Clitoris': Addressing Sexual Pleasure in Sexuality Education in Schools and other Youth Settings." In *The Politics of Pleasure in Sexuality Education: Pleasure Bound*, edited by Louisa Allen, Mary Lou Rasmussen, and Kathleen Quinlivan, 35–56. New York, NY: Routledge.

Holland, Janet, Caroline Ramazanoglu, Sue Sharpe, and Rachel Thomson. 2010. "Deconstructing Virginity: Young People's Accounts of First Sex." *Sexual and Relationship Therapy* 25(3): 351–362.

Illes, Judit. 2012. "Young Sexual Citizens: Reimagining Sex Education as an Essential Form of Civic Engagement." *Sex Education* 12(5): 613–624. doi:10.1080/14681811.2011.634152.

Irvine, Janice. 2002. *Talk about Sex: The Battles over Sex Education in the United States*. Berkeley: University of California Press.

Iyer, Padmini and Peter Aggleton. 2013. "'Sex Education Should be Taught, Fine….But We Make Sure They Control Themselves': Teachers' Beliefs and Attitudes Towards Young People's Sexual and Reproductive Health in a Ugandan Secondary School." *Sex Education* 13(1): 40–53.

Jones, Tiffany Mary. 2011. "Saving Rhetorical Children: Sexuality Education Discourses from Conservative to Post-Modern." *Sex Education* 11(4): 369–387.

Jones, Tiffany, Elizabeth Smith, Roz Ward, et al. 2016. "School Experiences of Transgender and Gender Diverse Students in Australia." *Sex Education* 16(2): 156–171.

Kamal, S.M. Mostafa. 2012. "Vulnerable Sexuality and HIV/AIDS Prevention Knowledge among Ethnic Tribal Male Youth in Bangladesh." *Sex Education* 12(2): 127–145.

Kam-Tuck Yip, Andrew, Michael Keenan, and Sarah-Jane Page. 2011. *Religion, Youth and Sexuality: Selected Key Findings from a Multi-faith Exploration*. Nottingham: University of Nottingham.

Kehily, Mary Jane. 2007. "A Cultural Perspective." In *Understanding Youth: Perspectives, Identities and Practices*, edited by Mary Jane Kehily, 11–44. London: Sage in Association with The Open University.

Kesterton, David and Lester Coleman. 2010. "Speakeasy: A UK-wide Initiative Raising Parents' Confidence and Ability to Talk about Sex and Relationships with Their Children." *Sex Education* 10(4): 437–448.

Koo, Helen, Allison Rose, M. Nabil El-Khorazaty, et al. 2011. "Evaluation of a Randomized Intervention to Delay Sexual Initiation among Fifth-Graders Followed Through the Sixth Grade." *Sex Education* 11(1): 27–46.

Lamb, Sharon. 2010a. "Feminist Ideals for a Healthy Female Adolescent Sexuality: A Critique." *Feminist Forum* 62(5): 294–306.

Lamb, Sharon. 2010b. "Toward a Sexual Ethics Curriculum: Bringing Philosophy and Society to Bear on Individual Development." *Harvard Educational Review* 80(1): 81–141.

Lapointe, Alicia Anne. 2015. "Standing 'Straight' Up to Homophobia: Straight Allies' Involvement in GSAs." *Journal of LGBT Youth* 12(2): 144–169.

Lesko, Nancy. 2010. "Feeling abstinent? Feeling comprehensive? Touching the affects of sexuality curricula." *Sex Education* 10(3): 281–297.

MacLure, Maggie. 2013. "Researching Without Representation? Language and Materiality in Post-Qualitative Methodology." *International Journal of Qualitative Studies in Education* 26(6): 658–667.

Malacane, Mona and Jonathon J Beckmeyer. 2016. "A Review of Parent-Based Barriers to Parent-Adolescent Communications about Sex and Sexuality: Implications for Sex and Family Educators." *American Journal of Sexuality Education* 11(1): 27–40.

Marston, Kate. 2015. "Beyond Bullying: The Limitations of Homophobic and Transphobic Bullying Interventions for Affirming Lesbian, Gay, Bisexual and Trans (LGBT) Equality in Education." *Pastoral Care Education* 33(3): 161–168.

McGeeney, Esther. 2017. "Possibilities for Pleasure: A Creative Approach to Including Pleasure in Sexuality Education." In *The Palgrave Handbook of Sexuality Education*, edited by Louisa Allen and Mary Lou Rasmussen, 571–590. London: Springer Nature.

McGeeney, Esther and Mary Jane Kehily. 2016. "Editorial Introduction: Young People and Sexual Pleasure – Where Are We Now?" *Sex Education* 16(3): 235–239.

McKee, Alan. 2014. "'It's All Scientific To Me': Focus Group Insights into Why Young People Do Not Apply Safe-Sex Knowledge." *Sex Education* 14(6): 652–665.

McRee, Annie-Laurie, Nikki Madsen, and Marla E. Eisenberg. 2014. "Guest Speakers in School-Based Sexuality Education." *Sex Education* 9(2): 205–218.

Meschke, Laurie L. and Kim Dettmer. 2012. "'Don't Cross a Man's Feet': Hmong Parent-Daughter Communication about Sexual Health." *Sex Education* 12(1): 109–123.

Meyer, Elizabeth J., Catherine Taylor, and Tracey Peter. 2015. "Perspectives on Gender and Sexual Diversity (GSD)-inclusive Education: Comparisons Between Gay/Lesbian/Bisexual And Straight Educators." *Sex Education* 15(3): 221–234.

Milhausen, Robin, Ralph J. DiClemente, Delia L. Lang, et al. 2008. "Frequency of Sex after an Intervention to Decrease Sexual Risk-Taking among African American Adolescent Girls: Results of a Randomized, Controlled Clinical Trial." *Sex Education* 8(1): 47–57.

Mkumbo, Kitila A.K. and Roger Ingham. 2010. "What Tanzanian Parents Want (and Do Not Want) Covered in School-Based Sex and Relationships Education." *Sex Education* 10(1): 67–78.

Morawska, Alina, Anthony Walsh, Melanie Grabski, and Renee Fletcher. 2015. "Parental Confidence and Preferences for Communicating with their Child about Sexuality." *Sex Education* 15(3): 235–248.

Neary, Aoife. 2013. "Lesbian and Gay Teachers' Experiences of 'Coming Out' in Irish Schools." *British Journal of Sociology of Education* 34(4): 583–602.

Newby, Katie, Louise M. Wallace, Orla Dunn, and Katherine E. Brown. 2011. "A Survey of English Teenagers' Sexual Experience and Preferences for School-Based Sex Education." *Sex Education: Sexuality, Society and Learning* 12(2): 231–251.

Njue, Carolyne, Helene Voeten, and Beth Maina Ahlberg. 2011. "'Youth in a Void': Sexuality, HIV/AIDS and Communication in Kenyan Schools." *Sex Education* 11(4): 459–470.

O'Higgins-Norman, James. 2009. "Straight Talking: Explorations on Homosexuality and Homophobia in Secondary Schools in Ireland." *Sex Education* 9(4): 381–393.

Ollis, Debbie. 2016. "'I Felt Like I Was Watching Porn': The Reality Of Preparing Pre-Service Teachers To Teach About Sexual Pleasure." *Sex Education* 16(3): 308–323.

Ponzetti, James. 2009. "The Effectiveness of Participatory Theatre with Early Adolescents in School-Based Sexuality Education." *Sex Education* 9(1): 93–103.

Preston, Marilyn J. 2016. "'They're Just Not Mature Right Now': Teachers' Complicated Perceptions of Gender and Anti-Queer Bullying." *Sex Education* 16(1): 22–34.

Raj, Anita, Michele Decker, Jessica Murray, and Jay G. Silverman. 2008. "Gender Differences in Associations Between Exposure to School HIV Education and Protective Sexual Behaviors and Sexually Transmitted Disease/HIV Diagnosis among High School Students." *Sex Education* 7(2): 191–199.

Rasmussen, Mary Lou. 2016. *Progressive Sexuality Education: The Conceits of Secularism*. New York, NY: Routledge.

Renold, Emma and Jessica Ringrose. 2016. "Selfies, Relfies and Phallic Tagging: Posthuman Part-Icipants in Teen Digital Sexuality Assemblages." *Educational Philosophy and Theory* 49: 1066–1079.

Rocha, Ana Cristina, Cláudia Leal, and Cidália Duarte. 2016. "School-Based Sexuality Education in Portugal: Strengths and Weaknesses." *Sex Education* 16(2): 172–183.

Rogers, Chrissie. 2016. "Intellectual Disability and Sexuality: On the Agenda?" *Sexualities* 19(5–6): 617–622.

Rouvier, Mariel, Lourdes Campero, Dilys Walker, and Marta Caballero. 2011. "Factors that Influence Communication about Sexuality Between Parents and Adolescents in the Cultural Context of Mexican Families." *Sex Education* 11(2): 175–191.

Schonfeld Hicks, Meredith, Annie-Laurie McRee, and Marla E. Eisenberg. 2013. "Teens Talking with Their Parents about Sex: The Role of Parent Communication." *American Journal of Sexuality Education* 8(1–2): 1–17.

Smith, Kelley Alison and Abigail Harrison. 2013. "Teachers' Attitudes Towards Adolescent Sexuality and Life Skills Education in Rural South Africa." *Sex Education* 13(1): 68–81.

Smylie, Lisa, Eleanor Maticka-Tyndale, and Dana Boyd. 2008. "Evaluation of a School-Based Sex Education Programme Delivered to Grade Nine Students in Canada." *Sex Education* 8(1): 25–46.

Snaza, Nathan, Debbie Sonu, Sarah E. Truman, and Zofia Zaliwska, eds. 2016. *Pedagogical Matters: New Materialisms and Curriculum Studies*. New York, NY: Peter Lang.

Sneed, Carl, Christian G. Somoza, Taurean Jones, and Sandra Alfaro. 2013. "Topics Discussed with Mothers and Fathers for Parent-Child Sex Communication among African-American Adolescents." *Sex Education* 13(4): 450–458.

Suvivuo, Pia, Kerttu Tossavainen, and Osmo Kontula. 2009. "Contraceptive Use and Non-Use among Teenage Girls in a Sexually Motivated Situation." *Sex Education* 9(4): 355–353.

Thi Thu Ha, Tran and Jane R.W. Fisher. 2011. "The Provision of Sexual and Reproductive Health Education to Children in a Remote Mountainous Commune in Rural Vietnam: An Exploratory Study of Parents' Views." *Sex Education* 11(1): 47–59.

Trinh, Thang, Allan Steckler, Anh Ngo, and E. Ratliff. 2009. "Parent Communication about Sexual Issues with Adolescents in Vietnam: Content, Contexts and Barriers." *Sex Education* 9(4): 371–380.

Vance, Carole. 1989. *Pleasure and Danger: Exploring Female Sexuality*. London: Pandora.

Van der Geugten, Jolien, Marlies Dijkstra, Berno van Meijel, Marion den Uyl, and Nanne K. de Vries. 2014. "Sexual and Reproductive Health Education: Opinions of Students and Educators in Bolgatanga Municipality, Northern Ghana." *Sex Education* 15(2): 113–128.

Vanwesenbeeck, Ine, Judith Westeneng, Thilly de Boer, et al. 2015. "Lessons Learned from a Decade Implementing Comprehensive Sexuality Education in Resource Poor Settings: *The World Starts with Me*." *Sex Education* 16(2): 471–486.

Warth, Gary. 2017. "Complaints about Sex Education Classes Escalate." *The San Diego Union-Tribune*, May 18.

Warwick, Ian and Peter Aggleton. 2014. "Bullying, 'Cussing', and 'Mucking About': Complexities in Tackling Homophobia in Three Secondary Schools In South London, UK." *Sex Education* 14(2): 159–173.

Waszak Geary, Cynthia, Joy Noel Baumgartner, Maxine Wedderburn, et al. 2013. "Sexual Agency and Ambivalence in the Narratives of First Time Sexual Experiences of Adolescent Girls in Jamaica: Implications for Sex Education." *Sex Education* 13(4): 437–449.

Wilmot, Mark and Devika Naidoo. 2014. "'Keeping Things Straight': The Representation of Sexualities in Life Orientation Textbooks." *Sex Education* 14(3): 323–337.

Wisnieski, Deborah, Renee Sieving, and Ann Garwick. 2015. "Parent and Family Influences on Young Women's Romantic and Sexual Decisions." *Sex Education* 15(2): 144–157.

13

Sexuality, Employment, and Discrimination

PATTI GIUFFRE AND COURTNEY CAVINESS

The workplace is not sex neutral; rather, it is a sexualized site because humans are sexualized beings (Colgan and Rumens 2014; Connell 2015; Williams and Giuffre 2011). Workplaces, governments, and individual workers contribute to beliefs about "proper" sexual behavior in work settings. Earliest work on sexualities in workplaces, particularly in the United States, focused on unwanted forms of sexual behaviors and sexual harassment. Early research also documented homophobia, and sexual discrimination and orientation biases experienced by gay men and lesbians. The theoretical perspective of sexuality in organizations, written by British scholars Jeff Hearn, Wendy Parkin and their colleagues, emerged in the late 1980s (Hearn et al. 1989; Hearn and Parkin 1987). This work argued that sexuality is embedded in all organizations, and demonstrated that workplace sexualities are highly contextualized, varying by industry, occupation, region, and country, among other factors. Contemporary feminist approaches to research on sexualities in workplaces, influenced by the contributions of critical race theorists such as Kimberlé Crenshaw (1991) and Patricia Hill Collins (1990), have also highlighted the need to consider workplace sexualities in relation to other intersecting identities such as race, class, gender, and ethnicity.

Our chapter examines contemporary cross-cultural research on sexualities in workplaces. We discuss studies of experiences and perceptions of lesbian, gay, bisexual, transgender, and queer (LGTBQ) workers. Some of the studies in this chapter focus on LG workers, while others explore experiences and perceptions of LGB, LGBT, or LGBTQ workers. Thus, our terminology changes throughout the chapter depending on the particular study. We review research on laws and policies related to sexualities at work, sexual orientation discrimination, organizational cultures, coming out at work in different countries, and sexuality under neoliberalism. We also describe scholars' calls to challenge heteronormativity in workplaces and to queer work and organizations. The conclusion discusses compelling areas for future research.

Laws and Policies

Antidiscrimination laws and policies vary by country, state, province, and business. Current research on sexual inequalities in the workplace is predominantly focused on North American and European contexts, highlighting a considerable gap in scholarly knowledge on African, Asian, and the Middle Eastern workplaces (Ozturk 2011). The International Labour Organization (ILO) is a United Nations agency established in 1919 to facilitate alliances among government, employers, and workers. One of its emphases is to document and raise awareness about sexual inequalities in economies. It has found, for example, that the absence of legal protections for sexual orientation and gender identity in Indonesia hinders access to job opportunities for LGBT workers – workers who fear retribution for, and thus, avoid disclosure of, sexual orientation or gender identity in their respective workplaces. Interestingly, the same research also finds that LGBT workers still believe in the notion of meritocracy: that work ethic, education, and soft skills are the keys to others' acceptance of their gender and sexual identities at work (International Labour Office 2016).

According to the International Lesbian, Gay, Bisexual, Trans, and Intersex Association (ILGA), employment protections in the United States have consistently lagged 72 other countries such as Australia, Botswana, Canada, Mexico, New Zealand, and Peru, that have implemented extensive legal protections for LGBTQ workers (ILGA: Carroll and Mendos 2017). This represents a modest increase from a previous count of 61 countries that have sexual orientation as part of their federal or national antidiscrimination law (Lloren and Parini 2017; see also Lee and Ostergard 2017). Formal government support for LGBTQ rights has generally increased in a number of countries. For example, the US Supreme Court legalized same-sex marriage in 2015, and Australians voted in 2017 to legalize same-sex marriage (Baidawi and Cave 2017). Yet, as evidenced in the case of Australia legalizing same-sex marriage four years after instituting employment protections for LGBTQ people, formal policy change often reflects a mismatch between *employment* protections and *marriage* rights. Five countries – Bolivia, Ecuador, Fiji, Malta, and the United Kingdom – have constitutions that guarantee equal rights on the basis of sexual orientation *and* gender identity (Raub et al. 2017). Other countries have maintained, bolstered, or increased enforcement of homophobic laws (e.g. Russia) (Lloren and Parini 2017). As an example, Russia's passage and enforcement of an antigay propaganda law has contributed to increased homophobic harassment and extreme violence towards LGBTQ Russians (Buyantueva 2018).

The most progressive employment laws and policies exist in Australia, Mexico, Greenland, Greece, Portugal, Scandinavia, Iceland, Thailand, Germany, Netherlands, United Kingdom, France, South Africa, Philippines, and New Zealand among others. Most of these nations have employment protections for both sexual orientation and gender identity. The least progressive nations comprise many Middle Eastern nations such as Saudi Arabia, Sudan, Iran, Afghanistan, and Syria. In some countries, homosexuality is illegal and is punishable by life imprisonment, or death (Equaldex 2017; McGoldrick 2016). In the case of Indonesia, for example, the law prohibits employment discrimination based on anything other than that which is required to do one's job. In theory, this would protect LGBT workers from discrimination, yet the ambiguity in some laws offers no explicit protections for sexual orientation, gender identity, or gender nonconformity (Badgett et al. 2017; McGoldrick 2016). Indonesia is a nation in which popular opinions view homosexuality as morally unacceptable (Badgett et al. 2017; Pew Research Center 2013). Thus, it would be surprising if the ambiguity in Indonesian employment nondiscrimination law were interpreted as protecting LGBT workers from sexual orientation and gender identity-based discrimination.

The United States, like China, and Russia, does not offer federal legal protections based on sexual orientation or identity. In the US, Title VII of the Civil Rights Act of 1964 includes protected statuses, such as sex (male or female), race, and religion (Dixon, Kane, and DiGrazia 2017; Williams and Giuffre 2011). However, some states, cities, municipalities, and businesses have opted to have sexual orientation or identity as part of their antidiscrimination policies. In the US, computer corporations were the first to voluntarily include sexual orientation as part of their antidiscrimination policies, starting in the 1970s (Raeburn 2004).

In contrast, some countries have provided extensive legal protections for LGBTQ employees. In these countries (e.g. New Zealand), employee discrimination protections are defined as basic human rights (McGoldrick 2016). In the US context, Title VII of the Civil Rights Act of 1964 specifically prohibits discrimination on the bases of race, religion, national origin, and sex (US Equal Employment Opportunity Commission [EEOC] n.d.). To date, provisions categorizing sexual orientation and gender identity as protected statuses alongside race, religion, national origin and sex, are noticeably absent. The official stance by the EEOC is that sexual orientation and gender identity discrimination represents a form of gender stereotyping, which is in turn protected under the umbrella of sex discrimination. The EEOC's interpretation of Title VII is significant, because in addition to extending legal protections to lesbian, gay, and bisexual employees, it also views discrimination of transgender employees as a form of sex discrimination and thus federally protected. Even so, the scope of these EEOC protections is quite narrow, as they apply to federal employment and do not extend into the private sector. As of July 10, 2017, only 20 US states plus the District of Columbia have employment nondiscrimination laws that provide workplace protections for gender identity and sexual orientation (Movement Advancement Project 2017).

United States-based LGBT groups and allies have pushed for explicit federal protections against sexual orientation discrimination in the workplace since the 1970s (Vitulli 2010). Even significant moments in US LGBTQ history, for example as evidenced by the landmark 2003 Supreme Court ruling *Lawrence v. Texas* that decriminalized sodomy, are in the collective national memory. Touted as a major victory for LGBTQ rights in the US, this decision helped pave the way for future proposed policies such as the (not-yet-passed) Employment Non-Discrimination Act (ENDA) and the repeal of Don't Ask Don't Tell (DADT). However, legislation such as ENDA has consistently failed to gain the bicameral approval necessary to name sexual orientation and gender identity as protected statuses under Title VII of the Civil Rights Act of 1964 (Thompson 2015).

In another step toward greater workplace protection, President Obama issued an executive order on July 21, 2014 that prohibited gender identity discrimination in federal workplaces as well as prohibiting sexual orientation or gender identity discrimination in the hiring of federal contractors. Importantly, both the 2013 ENDA and President Obama's 2014 executive decision allowed exemption based on religious belief (Gates and Rodgers 2014; Gates and Saunders 2016). Though many hold out hope for the passage of a future version of the ENDA bill, others such as Vitulli (2010) draw attention to ENDA's complicated relationship with issues of gender inclusivity under the broader umbrella of sexual orientation discrimination protections.

In addition to laws, workplaces have utilized other policies to attempt to eradicate sexual inequality at work. Various employer initiatives have been implemented to address bias and discrimination directed toward LGBTQ workers (e.g. domestic partner benefits, diversity initiatives, and implicit bias training). Lloren and Parini (2017) conducted a quantitative analysis about the effects of LGB-supportive workplace policies in Switzerland. Switzerland's Constitution does not prohibit discrimination based on sexual orientation. The authors analyzed how policies affect LGB workers' perceptions of discrimination, and their own well-being, and psychological health. Forty-two percent of the respondents were out to all coworkers (with 40% of lesbians, 49% of gay men, and 19% of bisexual people surveyed stating that they were out to all coworkers). The rest of the respondents surveyed reported that they were out only to certain people at work. Lloren and Parini found that the presence of LGB-supportive policies decreased rates of perceived discrimination although lesbians perceived more discrimination than gay men. Respondents who worked for companies that had LGB-supportive policies reported feeling better about their work, but the effects of policies on psychological health were less clear.

Of course, discussions about "most" or "least" progressive policies should be placed in larger historical and political contexts (Franzway and Fonow 2011b). Scholars who conduct research on sexualities at work should consider how other policies or lack thereof indirectly contribute to employment inequality on the basis of sexual orientation. For example, while considered progressive in many ways, France has no housing protections for LGBTQ individuals. Examining sexual inequalities in different countries should incorporate attention to the larger context of these nations (e.g. demographics, citizenship, social, cultural, and political climates, union and/or nongovernmental support, and the history of colonialism and war).

Sexual Orientation Discrimination: Wages and Hiring

Numerous studies have examined sexual orientation discrimination in workplaces in several countries. One stream of research on discrimination compares earnings between heterosexual and/or different groups of LGBTQ workers. Nationally representative datasets measuring the relationship between sexual orientation and earnings did not exist until the 1990s. Since then, countries such as Australia, Canada, France, Greece, Netherlands, Sweden, United Kingdom, and the US have incorporated sexual orientation questions in their surveys (Klawitter 2015). Several studies find that gay men earn less than heterosexual men in most countries (for a study of Sweden, see Hammarstedt, Ahmed, and Andersson 2015; for a study of Germany, see Humpert

2016; for a study of Australia, see Smith, Oades, and McCarthy 2013). Research that compares the earning of lesbians and heterosexual women have produced contradictory results: studies find that lesbians earn more than heterosexual women, while others also find that lesbians experience more wage inequality than straight women (Hammarstedt et al. 2015). Some research suggests supply-side explanations for these differences may be due to the self-sorting of gay and lesbian workers into public and nonprofit sectors or their greater concentration in particular careers and occupations (Anteby and Anderson 2014; Klawitter 2015; Lewis and Ng 2013). While demand-side explanations suggest that lesbians experience a slight wage premium due, in part, to employers' heterosexist assumptions that they are precluded from possible demands of family life and parenthood and are thus likely to be more devoted and productive employees (Elmslie and Tibaldi 2007).

A study of a random sample of workers across the US found that LGB workers experience wage discrimination compared to heterosexual workers and that discrimination toward bisexual workers was even more pronounced (Mize 2016). Cech and Pham (2017) conducted a survey analysis of over 37,000 LGBT and "non-LGBT" workers employed in six federal agencies in the US. Although there was variation among workers in different agencies, LGBT respondents were much more likely than non-LGBT workers to report less support for their career success, fewer work resources available, and a lack of transparent evaluations by supervisors, and they were more likely to report lower job satisfaction. In contrast to studies that find that lesbian or queer women report less inequality than heterosexual women, Cech and Pham found similar rates of sexual inequalities for men and women in the sample. They argue that the rates of LGBT discrimination are likely higher in the private (vs. public/federal) workplace. Large-scale quantitative studies demonstrate the pervasiveness of workplace disadvantages based on sexual orientation and gender identity (see also Baumle and Poston 2011; Waite and Denier 2015; Yoder and Mattheis 2016).

Another line of research examines sexual orientation discrimination at the hiring juncture. In quantitative experimental or audit studies, respondents are asked to evaluate fictitious employee resumes to determine whether they might hire them. Currently, audit study research has been conducted in the US and Greek context. Researchers have used this "audit method" or similar models based on the experimental method to ask respondents to evaluate the resumes. The resumes are identical with regards to skills, training, and other forms of human capital except for one mention of involvement in a gay and/or lesbian organization. This methodology has permitted researchers to examine regional differences in sexual orientation discrimination and the effects of laws and policies in respondents' attitudes towards "hiring" gay men and lesbians. In an audit study of fictitious US job "applicants" (Tilcsik 2011), men applicants who were perceived as gay were less likely to be called back for interviews by employers. Tilscik also compared results between states that did and did not have sexual orientation as part of their antidiscrimination polices. Employers in states that had sexual orientation as part of their antidiscrimination policies engaged in hiring-discrimination less frequently. In a similar experimental study of Greek employers in the private sector, Drydakis (2009) found that employers were less likely to call back applicants who were perceived to be gay. However, the applicants who *did* receive call backs (i.e. researchers passing as applicants in phone calls) were offered the same salary regardless of their presumed "gay" or "straight" orientations (see also Drydakis 2011, 2015).

Mishel (2016) utilized an audit study to examine the prevalence of direct hiring-discrimination toward queer women (referred to in this study as women of any LGBT identity) in the US. In part, this study sought to empirically contend with previously suggested demand-side explanations that queer women may experience less wage discrimination than heterosexual women (see Elmslie and Tibaldi 2007). Mishel found that queer-perceived women in her sample were less likely to receive a call back compared to straight women. Like Tilcsik, there was variation by state: queer-perceived women were more likely to get a call back in states that offered legal protections based on sexual orientation.

Few studies that use experimental methods to assess hiring-discrimination have examined the intersection between race and sexual orientation. One exception is Pedulla's (2014) experimental internet-based survey study. Respondents from a national probability sample in the US evaluated one of four resumes, all of which described the same skills but varied in terms of name and whether the "applicant" was involved in a college advisory council for gay students, or an advisory council for students. Men applicants that were perceived to be black and heterosexual received less recommended salary than straight white men. White gay men received less recommended salary than white straight men, and gay black men earned more than straight black men. Pedulla argues that stereotypes about race, gender, and sexuality interact to produce biases among the respondents. He maintains that gay black men are perceived as less threatening than straight black men.

These experimental and audit method studies show how employers single out perceived sexual orientation to determine whether they will call an applicant for an interview, and how hiring discrimination varies by state and country. Moreover, human capital is controlled for in this line of research; the "applicants" have the same skills. The only difference is an indicator of sexual orientation (typically, that the applicant is or is not involved in a gay or lesbian organization). While these findings prove the importance of laws and policies, it is much more difficult to enforce antidiscrimination laws at hiring than among employees (Tilscik 2011).

Workplace Context and Culture

The type and frequency of sexual biases and discrimination varies depending upon the work context (e.g. public or private, male- or female-dominated, and type of industry or work). Organizational context and organizational cultures vary dramatically around the world and even within a culture. Laws and policies (or the lack thereof) help to define workplace contexts and cultures along a continuum of hostility to inclusivity. Researchers have characterized workplaces as homophobic, gay-tolerant, gay-friendly, heteronormative, homonormative, and/or queer. Queer workplaces "actively challenge heteronormativity and serve the interests of diverse queers" (Williams and Giuffre 2011, p. 558). In queer work contexts, "heteronormativity is questioned, and workers openly express and endorse queer sexuality," (p. 559) without employment penalties. Workplaces range in tolerance for LGBTQ workers due in part to informal, less overt, workplace practices and norms that naturalize and reward particularly gendered and sexualized behaviors, dispositions, and identities while marginalizing others. Within these different contexts, LGBTQ workers might remain closeted, come out to certain people at certain times, or be out with all workers and clients. A number of studies explore the process of coming out at work, and how this process varies not only by the context and culture of the workplace, but also by the intersection of other salient identities (e.g. race, ethnicity, nationality, gender).

Qualitative research (most of which is based on worker experiences in Western countries) reveals LGBTQ workers' everyday experiences, emotions, perceptions, and feelings. These studies allow us to understand workplace cultures and subcultures. Early research on experiences of LGBT workers (typically, LG workers in the early studies) focused on discrimination faced by out-of-closet men and women. Over the last few years, studies have begun to examine the conditions under which LGB workers come out, as well as contexts in which heteronormativity can be challenged and even potentially dismantled. Research by Giuffre, Dellinger, and Williams (2008) explores experiences of LGB workers in the US who are out and perceive their workplaces to be gay friendly. They find that even in workplaces that are subjectively defined by LGB workers as gay friendly, respondents downplayed their sexual identity in different ways, or they emphasized that they are "normal." In this "gay friendly closet" (Williams, Giuffre, and Dellinger 2009), out LGB workers must still follow certain sexual and gender norms in line with heteronormativity. Similar to Rumens's research on gay men workers in the United Kingdom (Rumens 2016), respondents emphasized that they must be "respectable," "normal," and not like "flag waving" gay workers (see also Ward 2008). American legal scholar Kenji Yoshino (2006) refers to downplaying essential parts of our identity as "covering." Instead of attempting to pass as straight (Woods and Lucas 1993), LGBTQ workers (as well as workers of color, workers of particular religions and other groups) try to assimilate in order to be accepted, be successful, and get promoted.

LGBTQ workers' use of normalization rhetoric is also evident in studies of how they negotiate coming out at work. Several studies examine workers' experiences of coming out, and how the process of coming out varies according to the workplace context (McKenna-Buchanan 2017; see also Orne 2011). Benozzo and his colleagues (2015) interviewed white gay men employed in the UK. While focusing on the benefits and disadvantages of coming out at work, the authors identified three main ways that these men described coming out at work. First, respondents discussed being gay as a central part of their identity, which was coupled with a discourse of "guilt" about their revealing their sexual identity. Second, workers came out by talking about their partner, which was a way to disclose without the "emotional charge" of saying, "I'm gay." Men in the study said they talked about their boyfriend or partner but not about their sex, romance, or love for one another. They emphasized that they are "normal" gay men, and not promiscuous gay men. Third, respondents came out by emphasizing that they are "different" from other gay men, and/or that they are "normal" gay men (see also Williams, Giuffre, and Dellinger 2009). Using a poststructuralist framework, the authors maintain that coming out in a heteronormative society always presumes two binary categories, with one (homo) that is lesser than the other (hetero).

In some work environments, homophobia and heteronormativity are overt, extreme, and even dangerous. Although there is variation, religious-based organizations, jobs and careers that involve children, and highly masculinized work environments (e.g. police work, jobs in science, technology, engineering, and science) tend to be more homophobic, making it difficult for LGBTQ workers to come out, or else face rampant biases and unequal treatment if "choosing" to come out (see Cech and Pham 2017; Connell 2015). Connell (2015) explores the experiences of gay and lesbian teachers in California and Texas. She notes that the US has a history of preferring to hire heterosexual teachers, particularly for teachers of children. The teachers she interviewed struggled with their public, professional, teaching identity, finding it difficult to be professional (which means in this setting, downplaying sexual identity) *or* being out and proud. Queer sexuality is seen as unprofessional in a teaching context where teachers are supposed to present themselves as asexual. Respondents described an emphasis on needing to be seen as "normal," what Connell refers to as a passive form of homonormativity.

In a study of LGB teachers in Ireland, teachers faced even more overt forms of discrimination compared to the teachers interviewed in Connell's study (Fahie 2016). Ireland offers fewer legal protections for LGB workers. Fahie argues that Ireland's policies represent a contradiction between the EU law (Employment Equality Directive 2000/78/EC – European Union 2000) and the power of religion (in this case, the Catholic Church) in deciding on equality for only particular groups of workers. The LGB teachers she interviewed described being fearful, angry, and frustrated as they tried to navigate ideas about equality "in theory" but not for them as teachers. (For a similar study of LGTBQ teachers in Australia, see Gray, Harris, and Jones 2016).

Another area of research on workplace context examines the differences between inequalities experienced in public sector vs. private sector work. Evidence suggests LGBT people are more likely than their heterosexual counterparts to favor employment in the public and nonprofit sectors because, in part, they anticipate they will encounter fewer challenges on the basis of their sexual orientations (Lewis and Ng 2013). Several researchers argue that LGB employees in public sector organizations will experience fewer disadvantages compared to LGB workers in private sector work, particularly in countries that offer federal work protections based on sexual orientation. Priola and her colleagues (2014) interviewed heterosexual and LGBT workers in order to explore discrimination towards LGBT workers in "inclusive" organizations in Italy. Inclusive organizations are committed to equality in the workplace. Italian law offers a directive against sexual orientation discrimination except when "characteristics 'affect the performance of work or constitute decisive requisites for its carrying out', still thus constructing homosexuality as a potential force for disrupting work functioning" (2014, p. 492). The Italian government has said that it is committed to equality in the workplace and seeks remedies for those who are marginalized. Cooperatives in Italy are linked to government services; hence, the authors explored whether and to what extent LGBT workers were included, and whether they experienced biases. They found that even in these inclusive organizations that seek to decrease work inequalities, heterosexual workers used discriminatory language when talking about LGBT workers and created what the authors refer to as a culture of silence around sexual orientation. In a study of public sector LGB employees in the UK, Colgan and Wright (2011) found that respondents were encouraged by support from trade unions and the application and enforcement of Employment Equality regulations. However, most also reported that their managers were not comfortable discussing the regulations in trainings, and that sexual orientation discrimination seemed to be on a lower rung compared to other forms of discrimination. Additionally, despite their promising possibilities of the regulations, only half of the women and three quarters of the respondents said they were out about their sexuality at work.

Homonormativity

Homonormativity is the enveloping of LGBTQ identities and bodies that are most palatable to, or fall most closely in line with, white masculine heteronormativity (Collins 2009; Orzechowicz 2016). In other words, homonormativity is the extension of historically heteronormative privileges to a narrow subset of "normative" gay and lesbian individuals. In some workplaces, gay sexuality is celebrated; yet, even in these settings we see evidence of homonormativity. Fashion, particularly fashion design, is considered to be welcoming to gay men in many Western countries such as the US and Canada (Stokes 2015). The fashion industry has a history of not only welcoming but prioritizing the work of gay men (and, there are stereotypes that most men fashion designers are gay). Stokes conducted a content analysis of fashion articles and found that gay men received more awards, accolades, and praise compared to women in the industry. Stokes refers to the advantages that gay men receive in fashion as "the glass runway." Stokes argues that "reliant on cultural conflations of femininity and homosexuality, the framing of a gay aesthetic portrays gay men as well-suited to a career concerned with aesthetics and appearance, traditionally seen as feminine pursuits" (2015, p. 235). Despite the accolades and praise received, Stokes finds that gay men are also depicted using a homophobic discourse. She maintains that gay men receive gender-based advantages as men in part because they pose no threat to masculinity. Likewise, the performing arts are considered gay-friendly work sites (Rumens and Broomfield 2014). In a qualitative study of gay men in the performing arts in the UK, (Rumens and Broomfield 2014), respondents reported a sense of sexual freedom and openness about sexuality but they also said that they learned in drama school not to engage in overtly or exaggerated feminine behaviors ("camp") as performers. Gay male sexuality was accepted but the authors argue that heteronormativity shaped the type of gay male sexuality that was allowed. Men were careful about their presentation of gender and sexuality in school and as they considered and applied for roles in performances.

Given that gay-friendly workplaces and industries still show evidence of gendered and sexual inequalities, do *any* work settings demonstrate a "post closet" culture? In his observational study, Orzechowicz (2016) explored the possibilities of dismantling of the closet at work (see also Orzechowicz 2010). In contrast to a "gay friendly closet" (Williams, Giuffre, and Dellinger 2009), Orzechowicz examines experiences of workers in a homonormative culture that offers post-closeted contexts within it. Wonderland is a theme park in the US in which mostly gay men work in certain areas of the park. Orzechowicz conducted a participant observation in the Entertainment section of the park, a work subculture in which gay men and gay masculinity are elevated, not marginalized. Here, workers are "gay until proven straight." While this setting challenged heteronormative practices, gay workers were told to be more masculine-presenting outside the Entertainment part of the park. To move up they could not "act too gay." Camp –exaggerated sexual and gendered performances – was only encouraged and permitted in one limited, less public, and "unseen" area of the park. Orzechowicz argues that the setting is not truly post-closet because it marginalizes certain groups of men, certain expressions of sexuality, excludes queer women, and requires gay men to downplay their sexual performances. Queering the workplace would mean that binaries would be deconstructed and not used as a basis for inequality (Pullen et al. 2016); in particular, sexual and gender performances would not be confined to particular spaces at work.

Neoliberalism and LGBTQ Worker Rights

As employers have begun to consider the economic implications for investing in LGBTQ-inclusive policies and initiatives (see Badgett et al. 2013), a body of literature ties the acceptance and increased formal inclusion of LGBTQ persons in historically marginalizing contexts into larger narratives of neoliberalism (David 2015; Duggan 2012; Montegary 2015; Puar 2007; Spade 2013; Tiemeyer 2013). Duggan (2012) and other queer studies scholars see this as just another example of homonormativity. Normativity, in this case, is constituted by an alignment with the primacy of traditional nuclear family structures, essentialized gender roles, and the accumulation of property and wealth. While homonormativity does, in fact, expand the bounds of what constitutes acceptable gender and sexuality, it also reinforces white supremacy by situating gay and lesbian acceptability exclusively in terms of middle-class whiteness (Puar 2007; Vitulli 2010). This enveloping serves the interests of whiteness, heterosexuality, and nationalism most, effectively exploiting the very individuals to whom the formal gates of inclusion are now open.

Further exploring the relationships among neoliberalism, globalization, and homonormativity, David (2015) conducted interviews with 41 transgender call center employees in the Philippines, a country that is often considered to be gay-friendly (Collins 2009). David found evidence of "purple-collar labor." David develops this concept and uses it as a theoretical frame to examine how transgender workers in the Philippines are incorporated into, rather than excluded from, hegemonic patterns of global accumulation of capital. Not unsurprisingly, David found that transgender workers were often occupationally segregated and experienced limited upward mobility in their call center occupations. Yet, surprisingly, he found that instead of experiencing overt discrimination and exclusion by their employers, transgender workers at these call centers were embraced, in part because they produced what Wesling (2012) calls "queer value" by engaging in unique forms of affective labor characterized by their easing of coworker anxieties, fostering productivity, and boosting employee morale. More specifically, David found that many such call center workers served as "emotional shock absorbers," shouldering more than their fair share of emotional labor in their respective workplaces. Further, David's interviews reveal how core neoliberal ideals of competitive individualism and entrepreneurship help cultivate a hierarchy among transgender subjects and their cisgender peers in which some trans workers are viewed as more valuable, respectable, and appropriate in the workplace because they performed these values in their interactions with coworkers and customers. These performances generally coincided with conduct and dress viewed within the bounds of what is deemed suitable for their genders. As similarly reflected by Orzechowicz (2016), queerness and respectability are bounded by deeply entrenched assumptions and expectations of what constitutes normative genders and sexualities.

Conclusion and Implications for Future Research

Current research on sexualities in workplaces demonstrates the challenges of coming out in heteronormative workplaces, countries, and/or states. It shows how the closet is being dismantled but that LGBTQ workers often come out with a cost: LGBTQ workers feel the need to downplay, emphasize that they are normal, deemphasize their romance and eroticism, and assimilate (through to varying degrees) into different aspects of heteronormative cultures. Research has moved from simply acknowledging that workplaces are, in fact, sexualized to varying degrees, to studying biases and discrimination against LGBTQ workers to raising questions about queering the workplace. Yet, the move toward greater workplace inclusion of historically marginalized workers presents opportunities to shape new institutional and interactional workplace arrangements (David 2015, 2016). Future researchers should take intersectional approaches when possible. Studies of workers who are marginalized in terms of gender and sexuality must incorporate more voices from LGBTQ workers of color, who often experience racism and homophobia simultaneously (Ghabrial 2017; Majied 2015).

We argue that scholars who conduct research on sexualities in workplaces must take up the questions of what it means to be a "good/bad sexual citizen" at work (Orzechowicz 2016), theoretically and in everyday lived experiences of workers (Pullen et al. 2016: 2; see also Rumens and Broomfield 2014; Tiemeyer 2013). More research is needed on the roles of straight allies in queering workplaces (Rumens 2016), and the importance of labor movements for transforming workplaces (Kelly and Lubitow 2014; Tiemeyer 2013). As Blum (2012) writes, antidiscrimination laws are not enough in a heteronormative society to eradicate sexual inequalities, and according to Duggan (2012), certainly not enough in a neoliberal global economy. In some countries, same-sex marriage is legal but gay men and lesbians may still be fired at work (Dixon et al. 2017). Marginalized workers who are essentially required to downplay, or engage in particular gendered and sexualized performances are not truly equal. Resisting and challenging heteronormativity and homophobia in workplaces should be defined as human rights issues. According to legal scholar Kerstin Braun (2014), the United Nations has yet to address the fact that "homosexual acts" are illegal in over 78 countries, and that in a few countries, homosexuality is punishable by the death penalty. Additionally, most of the current research on sexualities in workplaces is concentrated in the Global North context. Emphasizing this larger global context and incorporating research on global queer labor activism (Franzway and Fonow 2011a, 2011b) can encourage governments and workplaces to identity and develop laws and policies that will help to eradicate sexual inequalities at work.

The move toward increased public support for LGBTQ rights in some countries and, in turn, the (albeit slow) adoption of formally inclusive laws and employment policies affording explicit workplace protections for sexual orientation and to a lesser extent, gender identity, requires new directions in researching sexual and gender inequalities in the workplace. Continued research on laws and policies explicitly focused on eradicating the overt discrimination of LGBTQ individuals in the workplace with a focus on human rights is necessary (Lee and Ostergard 2017; McGoldrick 2016). Future research must move beyond the purview of overt discrimination to examine the explicit and implicit implications of workplace policies that are oft-touted as gender and sexual orientation neutral – for example, parental and family leave policies, health benefits, networking and mentorship practices and initiatives, and recruitment and hiring practices. In many cases, these policies and initiatives operate in tandem with explicit forms of discrimination, yet their effects are perhaps less easily identifiable without systematic empirical studies.

References

Anteby, Michel and Caitlin Anderson. 2014. "The Shifting Landscape of LGBT Organizational Research." *Research in Organizational Behavior* 34: 3–25.

Badgett, M.V. Lee, Laura Durso, Christy Mallory, and Angeliki Kastanis. 2013. "The Business Impact of LGBT-Supportive Workplace Policies." The Williams Institute. Available at: https://williamsinstitute.law.ucla.edu/wp-content/uploads/Business-Impact-of-LGBT-Policies-May-2013.pdf

Badgett, M.V. Lee, Amira Hasenbush, and Winston Ekaprasetia Luhur. 2017. "LGBT Exclusion in Indonesia and its Economic Effects." The Williams Institute. Available at: https://williamsinstitute.law.ucla.edu/wp-content/uploads/LGBT-Exclusion-in-Indonesia-and-Its-Economic-Effects-March-2017.pdf.

Baidawi, Adam and Damien Cave. 2017. "Australia Votes for Gay Marriage, Clearing Path to Legalization." *New York Times*. Available at: https://www.nytimes.com/2017/11/14/world/australia/yes-same-sex-marriage-gay.html (accessed February 12, 2018).

Baumle, Amanda K. and Dudley L. Poston Jr. 2011. "The Economic Cost of Homosexuality: Multilevel Analyses." *Social Forces* 89(3): 1005–1031.

Benozzo, Angelo, Maria Chiara Pizzorno, Huw Bell, and Mirka Koro-Ljungberg. 2015. "Coming Out, but into What? Problematizing Discursive Variations of Revealing the Gay Self in the Workplace." *Gender, Work & Organization* 22(3): 292–306.

Blum, Richard. 2012. "Equality with Power: Fighting for Economic Justice at Work." *Scholar & Feminist Online* 11/12 (10.1–10.2).

Braun, Kerstin. 2013. "Do Ask, Do Tell: Where is the Protection Against Sexual Orientation Discrimination in International Human Rights Law." *American University International Law Review* 29(4): 871–903.

Buyantueva, Radzhana. 2018. "LGBT Rights Activism and Homophobia in Russia." *Journal of Homosexuality* 65(4): 456–483.

Cech, Erin A. and Michelle V. Pham. 2017. "Queer in STEM Organizations: Workplace Disadvantages for LGBT Employees in STEM Related Federal Agencies." *Social Sciences* 6(12): 1–22.

Colgan, Fiona and Nick Rumens. 2014. *Sexual Orientation at Work: Contemporary Issues and Perspectives*. London: Routledge.

Colgan, Fiona and Tessa Wright. 2011. "Lesbian, Gay and Bisexual Equality in a Modernizing Public Sector 1997–2010: Opportunities and Threats." *Gender, Work & Organization* 18(5): 548–570.

Collins, Dana. 2009. "'We're There and We're Queer': Homonormative Mobility and Lived Experience among Gay Expatriates in Manila." *Gender & Society* 23(4): 465–493.

Collins, Patricia Hill. 1990. *Black Feminist Thought: Knowledge, Consciousness, and the Politics of Empowerment*. Boston, MA: Unwin Hyman.

Connell, Catherine. 2015. *School's Out: Gay and Lesbian Teachers in the Classroom*. Berkeley, CA: University of California Press.

Crenshaw, Kimberlé. 1991. "Mapping the Margins: Intersectionality, Identity Politics, and Violence Against Women of Color." *Stanford Law Review* 43(6): 1241–1299.

David, Emmanuel. 2015. "Purple-Collar Labor: Transgender Workers and Queer Value at Global Call Centers in the Philippines." *Gender & Society* 29(2): 169–194.

David, Emmanuel. 2016. "Outsourced Heroes and Queer Incorporations Labor Brokerage and the Politics of Inclusion in the Philippine Call Center Industry." *GLQ: A Journal of Lesbian and Gay Studies* 22(3): 381–408.

Dixon, Marc, Melinda Kane, and Joseph DiGrazia. 2017. "Organization, Opportunity, and the Shifting Politics of Employment Discrimination." *Social Currents* 4(2): 111–127.

Drydakis, Nick. 2009. "Sexual Orientation Discrimination in the Labour Market." *Labour Economics* 16(4): 364–372.

Drydakis, Nick. 2011. "Women's Sexual Orientation and Labor Market Outcomes in Greece." *Feminist Economics* 17(1): 89–117.

Drydakis, Nick. 2015. "Sexual Orientation Discrimination in the United Kingdom's Labour Market: A Field Experiment." *Human Relations* 68(11): 1769–1796.

Duggan, Lisa. 2012. "After Neoliberalism? From Crisis to Organizing for Queer Economic Justice." *Scholar & Feminist Online* 11/12 (10.1–10.2).

Elmslie, Bruce and Edinaldo Tibaldi. 2007. "Sexual Orientation and Labor Market Discrimination." *Journal of Labor Research* 28(3): 436–53.

Equaldex. 2017. Homepage. Available at: www.equaldex.com (accessed November 1, 2017).

Fahie, Declan. 2016. "'Spectacularly Exposed and Vulnerable' – How Irish Equality Legislation Subverted the Personal and Professional Security of Lesbian, Gay and Bisexual Teachers." *Sexualities* 19(4): 393–411.

Franzway, Suzanne and Mary Margaret Fonow. 2011a. "Demanding their Rights: LGBT Transnational Labor Activism." In *Making Globalization Work for Women: The Role of Social Rights and Trade Union Leadership*, edited by Valentine M. Moghadam, Suzanne Franzway, and Mary Margaret Fonow, 289–308. Albany, NY: State University of New York Press.

Franzway, Suzanne and Mary Margaret Fonow. 2011b. *Making Feminist Politics: Transnational Alliances between Women and Labor*. Champaign, IL: University of Illinois Press.

Gates, Trevor and Colleen Rodgers. 2014. "Repeal of Don't Ask Don't Tell as 'Policy Window': A Case for the Passage of the Employment Non-Discrimination Act." *International Journal of Discrimination and the Law* 14(1): 5–18.

Gates, Trevor and Margery Saunders. 2016. "Executive Orders for Human Rights: The Case of Obama's LGBT Nondiscrimination Order." *International Journal of Discrimination and the Law* 16(1): 24–36.

Ghabrial, Monica A. 2017. "'Trying to Figure Out Where We Belong': Narratives of Racialized Sexual Minorities on Community, Identity, Discrimination, and Health." *Sexuality Research and Social Policy* 14(1): 42–55.

Giuffre, Patti, Kirsten Dellinger, and Christine Williams. 2008. "'No Retribution for Being Gay'?: Inequality in Gay-Friendly Workplaces." *Sociological Spectrum* 28: 254–277.

Gray, Emily M., Anne Harris, and Tiffany Jones. 2016. "Australian LGBTQ Teachers, Exclusionary Spaces and Points of Interruption." *Sexualities* 19(3): 286–303.

Hammarstedt, Mats, Ali M. Ahmed, and Lina Andersson. 2015. "Sexual Prejudice and Labor Market Outcomes for Gays and Lesbians: Evidence from Sweden." *Feminist Economics* 21(1): 90–109.

Hearn, Jeff, Deborah L. Sheppard, Peta Tancred-Sherriff, and Gibson Burrell, eds. 1989. *The Sexuality of Organization*. London: Sage.

Hearn, Jeff and Wendy Parkin. 1987. *"Sex at Work": The Power and Paradox of Organization Sexuality*. New York, NY: St. Martin's Press.

Humpert, Stephan. 2016. "Somewhere over the Rainbow: Sexual Orientation and Earnings in Germany." *International Journal of Manpower* 37(1): 69–98.

International Labour Office. 2016. "PRIDE at Work: A Study on Discrimination at Work on the Basis of Sexual Orientation and Gender Identity in Indonesia." Working Paper No. 3. Gender, Equality, and Diversity Branch. Available at: http://www.ilo.org/wcmsp5/groups/public/---dgreports/---gender/documents/publication/wcms_481580.pdf.

International Lesbian, Gay, Bisexual, Trans and Intersex Association: Carroll, A. and L.R. Mendos. 2017. *State Sponsored Homophobia 2017: A World Survey of Sexual Orientation Laws: Criminalisation, Protection and Recognition*. Geneva: ILGA.

Kelly, Maura and Amy Lubitow. 2014. "Pride at Work Organizing at the Intersection of the Labor and LGBT Movements." *Labor Studies Journal* 39(4): 257 -277.

Klawitter, Marieka. 2015. "Meta-Analysis of the Effects of Sexual Orientation on Earnings." *Industrial Relations* 54(1): 4–32.

Lee, Chelsea and Robert L. Ostergard Jr. 2017. "Measuring Discrimination against LGBTQ People: A Cross-National Analysis." *Human Rights Quarterly* 39(1): 37–72.

Lewis, Gregory B. and Eddy Ng. 2013. "Sexual Orientation, Work Values, Pay, and Preference for Public and Nonprofit Employment: Evidence from Canadian Postsecondary Students." *Canadian Public Administration/Administration Publique du Canada* 56(4): 542–564.

Lloren, Anouk and Lorena Parini. 2017. "How LGBT-Supportive Workplace Policies Shape the Experience of Lesbian, Gay Men, and Bisexual Employees." *Sexuality Research and Social Policy* 14(3): 289–299.

Majied, Kamilah F. 2015. "Racism and Homophobia in Cuba: A Historical and Contemporary Overview." *Journal of Human Behavior in the Social Environment* 25(1): 26–34.

McGoldrick, Dominic. 2016. "The Development and Status of Sexual Orientation Discrimination under International Human Rights Law." *Human Rights Law Review* 16: 613–668.

McKenna-Buchanan, Tim. 2017. "It's Not All 'One Story': A Narrative Exploration of Heteronormativity at Work." *Departures in Critical Qualitative Research* 6(1):11–29.

Mishel, Emma. 2016. "Discrimination against Queer Women in the US Workforce: A Résumé Audit Study." *Socius: Sociological Research for a Dynamic World* 2: 1–16.

Mize, Trenton D. 2016. "Sexual Orientation in the Labor Market." *American Sociological Review* 81(6): 1132–1160.

Montegary, Liz. 2015. "Militarizing US Homonormativities: The Making of 'Ready, Willing, and Able' Gay Citizens." *Signs* 40(4): 891–915.

Movement Advancement Project. 2017. "Non-Discrimination Laws." Available at: http://www.lgbtmap.org/equality-maps/non_discrimination_laws (accessed July 1, 2017).

Orne, Jason. 2011. "'You Will Always Have to 'Out' Yourself': "Reconsidering Coming Out through Strategic Outness." *Sexualities* 14(6): 681–703.

Orzechowicz, David. 2010. "Fierce Bitches on Tranny Lane: Gender, Sexuality, Culture, and the Closet in Theme Park Parades." *Research in the Sociology of Work* 20: 227–252.

Orzechowicz, David. 2016: "The Walk-In Closet: Between 'Gay-Friendly' and 'Post-Closeted' Work." *Research in the Sociology of Work* 29: 187–213.

Ozturk, Mustafa Bilgehan. 2011. "Sexual Orientation Discrimination: Exploring the Experiences of Lesbian, Gay, and Bisexual Employees in Turkey." *Human Relations* 64(8): 1099–1118.

Pedulla, David S. 2014. "The Positive Consequences of Negative Stereotypes: Race, Sexual Orientation, and the Job Application Process." *Social Psychology Quarterly* 77(1): 75–94.

Pew Research Center. 2013. "Global Views on Morality." Washington, DC. Available at: http://www.pewglobal.org/2014/04/15/global-morality/country/indonesia/ (accessed November 1, 2017).

Priola, Vincenza, Diego Lasio, Silvia De Simone, and Francesco Serri. 2014. "The Sound of Silence: Lesbian, Gay, Bisexual and Transgender Discrimination in 'Inclusive Organizations'." *British Journal of Management* 25(3): 488–502.

Puar, Jasbir K. 2007. *Terrorist Assemblages: Homonationalism in Queer Times*. Durham, NC: Duke University Press.

Pullen, Alison, Torkild Thanem, Melissa Tyler, and Louise Wallenberg. 2016. "Sexual Politics, Organizational Practices: Interrogating Queer Theory, Work and Organization." *Gender, Work & Organization* 23(1): 1–6.

Raeburn, Nicole. 2004. *Changing Corporate America from the Inside Out: Lesbian and Gay Workplace Rights*. Minneapolis: University of Minnesota Press.

Raub, Amy, Adele Cassola, Isabel Latz, and Jody Heymann. 2017. "Protections of Equal Rights across Sexual Orientation and Gender Identity: An Analysis of 193 National Constitutions." *Yale Journal of Law & Feminism* 28(1): 149–169.

Rumens, Nick. 2016. "Towards Queering the Business School: A Research Agenda for Advancing Lesbian, Gay, Bisexual and Trans Perspectives and Issues." *Gender, Work & Organization* 23(1): 36–51.

Rumens, Nick and John Broomfield. 2014. "Gay Men in the Performing Arts: Performing Sexualities within 'Gay-friendly' Work Contexts." *Organization* 21(3): 365–382.

Smith, Ian Patrick, Lindsay Oades, and Grace McCarthy. 2013. "The Australian Corporate Closet, Why It's Still So Full: A Review of Incidence Rates for Sexual Orientation Discrimination and Gender Identity Discrimination in the Workplace." *Gay and Lesbian Issues and Psychology Review* 9(1): 51–63.

Spade, Dean. 2013. "Intersectional Resistance and Law Reform." *Signs*: 38(4):1031–1055.

Stokes, Allyson. 2015. "The Glass Runway: How Gender and Sexuality Shape the Spotlight in Fashion Design." *Gender & Society* 29(2): 219–243.

Thompson, Erik. 2015. "Compromising Equality: An Analysis of the Religious Exemption of in the Employment Non-Discrimination Act and its Impact on LGBT Workers." *Boston College Journal of Law & Social Justice* 35: 285–318.

Tiemeyer, Phil. 2013. *Plane Queer: Labor, Sexuality, and AIDS in the History of Male Flight Attendants. Berkeley, CA*: University of California Press.

Tilcsik, András. 2011. "Pride and Prejudice: Employment Discrimination against Openly Gay Men in the United States." *American Journal of Sociology* 117(2): 586–626.

US Equal Employment Opportunity Commission. n.d. "What You Should Know About EEOC and the Enforcement Protections for LGBT Workers." Available at: https://www.eeoc.gov/eeoc/newsroom/wysk/enforcement_protections_lgbt_workers.cfm (accessed July 1, 2017).

Vitulli, Elias. 2010. "A Defining Moment in Civil Rights History? The Employment Non-Discrimination Act, Trans-Inclusion, and Homonormativity." *Sexuality Research & Social Policy* 7: 155–167.

Waite, Sean and Nicole Denier. 2015. "Gay Pay for Straight Work: Mechanisms Generating Disadvantage." *Gender & Society* 29(4): 561–588.

Ward, Jane. 2008. *Respectably Queer: Diversity Culture in LGBT Activist Organizations*. Nashville, TN: Vanderbilt University Press.

Wesling, Meg. 2012. "Queer Value." *GLQ: A Journal of Lesbian and Gay Studies* 18:107–125.

Williams, Christine and Patti Giuffre. 2011. "From Organizational Sexuality to Queer Organizations: Research on Homosexuality and the Workplace." *Sociology Compass* 5(7): 551–563.

Williams, Christine, Patti Giuffre, and Kirsten Dellinger. 2009. "The Gay-Friendly Closet." *Sexuality Research & Social Policy* 6: 29–45.

Woods, James D. and Jay H. Lucas. 1993. *The Corporate Closet: The Professional Lives of Gay Men in America*. New York, NY: The Free Press.

Yoder, Jeremy B. and Allison Mattheis. 2016. "Queer in STEM: Workplace Experiences Reported in a National Survey of LGBTQA individuals in Science, Technology, Engineering, and Mathematics Careers." *Journal of Homosexuality* 63(1): 1–27.

Yoshino, Kenji. 2006. *Covering: The Hidden Assault on our Civil Rights*. New York, NY: Random House.

14

Commodification of Intimacy and Sexuality

Julia Meszaros

This chapter examines the growing global market for commodities that include some form of intimate exchange for payment, with a particular focus on intimate labor performed by migrant women. Intimacy is the state of having a close or personal relationship. Common narratives in Western societies mark clear boundaries between personal relationships, particularly those of a romantic or sexual nature, and economic transactions. While narratives of "gold diggers" are often used to frame intimate romantic relationships for money in contemporary society, many societies have recognized the importance of economic considerations within marriages and sexual relationships (Coontz 2004). In fact, marriage was viewed as a business transaction for most of recorded human history, demonstrating that economic considerations are often an important component of long-term intimate relationships.

Viviana Zelizer (2005) theorizes that society often presents the intersection of economic and intimate relationships as contaminating the purity of relationships, based on the false dichotomy that separates public from private realms. Her research on court cases demonstrates that people utilize differentiated ties and forms of payment in their various relationships with one another. All intimate relationships are some form of negotiated exchange. Thus, this chapter examines the intimacy for sale in domestic labor, sexual labor, and international marriage. Some scholars of economic processes ignore the blurred lines between the public realm of the economy and the intimate, but gender scholars are bringing to the forefront the importance of micro-level relationships of intimacy to larger macro-level economic processes. Feminist geographers term this interdependent relationship the "global intimate" (Mountz and Hyndman 2006; Pratt and Rosner 2006).

Building upon theories of the global intimate and Zelizer's work regarding the relationship between intimacy and payment, Boris and Parreñas (2010) define intimate labor as work that centers on the daily practice of intimacy, both emotional and bodily labor that is centered within what is perceived of as the private realm. For instance, donating sperm is considered a form of intimate labor, as it is private, genetic material that one is exchanging for payment, but this labor does not involve interactions with customers per se. Intimate labor builds upon Hochschild's (1983) definition of emotional labor, which refers to face-to-face encounters in which a worker displays certain emotions to induce feelings in clients or customers. By joining the terms intimate and labor, Boris and Parreñas (2010) are problematizing the separation of home from work, work from labor, and productive from nonproductive forms of labor that have characterized capitalist globalization.

The growing global industries commodifying intimate labor are intimate industries, which Parreñas, Thai, and Silvey (2016) define as transnational market processes of commercial intimacy that are increasingly becoming formalized within the larger global economy. Intimate industries commodify the labor of intimacy on a global scale, and include surrogacy, sexual labor, international marriage, domestic labor, call centers, hostesses, etc. While the commodification of intimate labor is not new in the economy, the scope and scale of the global commodification of intimacy is new (Parreñas et al. 2016). Social practices are increasingly moving into the marketplace, creating a new "commodity frontier" (Hochschild 2003) where elements of intimate life are sold and valued lower than other forms of labor. Hochschild (2002) calls the international transfer of love and care the new emotional imperialism, as emotional resources are being drained from the Global South and shifting to the Global North through women's intimate labor.

Boris, Gilmore, and Parreñas (2010) elaborate upon notions of intimate labor by redefining sex work as sexual labor, in order to expand the discussion surrounding commercial sex as an economic and labor enterprise that can be exploitative for workers. This is a departure from the terms prostitution and sex work, which originate in the debates concerning whether this labor is sexual slavery or a legitimate form of labor (Alexander 1998; Clement 2006; Kempadoo 2004). The concept of sexual labor moves past the moral acceptance of "sex work" and instead allows scholars to focus on the race, class, gender, and sexuality struggles of workers without the need to justify the legitimacy of their occupation.

Considering the gendered nature of intimate labor and sexual labor, I will be adopting a transnational feminist framework that connects intimate, microprocesses of relationships to the larger transnational processes of migration, globalization, and economic development. Alexander and Mohanty (1997) argue that feminist theorists also need to explore the role of states across the globe in erasing certain women's experiences, such as sexual laborers, out of their respective national memories in both the Global North and Global South. They further contend that transnational feminist scholarship should examine the most marginalized populations of society in order to highlight the ways in which nationality, race, gender, class, and sexuality influence systems of imperialism and capitalism within an increasingly transnational framework. Examining commodified intimate labor allows scholars to highlight the global economic importance of marginalized women's labor within the current neoliberal capitalist manifestation of globalization. Intimate labor is typically performed by women, and in particular, women on the margins of society: women of color, migrant women, and poor women.

The majority of scholarly debate surrounding intimate labor regards how much agency women who participate in intimate industries exercise, with most feminist scholarship highlighting the different forms of agency that marginalized women exercise in order to challenge perceptions that paint them as victims of trafficking. Grewal (2005) points out that while feminist scholars often highlight marginalized women's ability to have agency and choice in selling their intimate labor, individual choice is the main framework for neoliberal consumer practices. Choice is a key discourse in neoliberal thought, since choice is necessary to participate in both democracy and consumption. The feminist struggle is against, but often dependent upon, neoliberalism. "Having choices" is the opposite of "being oppressed" and thus, choice is increasingly portrayed as feminist agency (Grewal 2005).

However, this chapter moves beyond the common framing of intimacy and economy as an issue of women's agency and instead focuses on the importance of the global market for commodified intimacies as a transference of labor across borders. By recognizing the legitimacy of the intimate labor performed in various intimate industries, I am challenging narratives that consider various forms of intimate labor to be examples of involuntary labor trafficking, particularly domestic labor, sexual labor, and marriage migration. The human rights issues of human labor trafficking, in addition to sex trafficking, have increasingly been in the US national policy spotlight. Numerous governments have imposed laws aimed at protecting victims of trafficking, but these laws often do not consider intimate forms of labor to be legitimate choices (Bernstein and Shih 2014; Hoang and Parreñas 2013). By studying the growing global economy of intimacy, feminist scholars are shining light on the various forms of invisible intimate labor that are increasingly valuable in the global market and challenging perceptions of intimate laborers as victims of human trafficking.

The debate around human sex trafficking centers on ideas that identify the Global North as a place of progress that protects innocent women, while identifying the countries of the Global South as backward spaces that victimize vulnerable women and facilitate the global sex trade. Policy debates surrounding sex trafficking between countries portray all sexual laborers as women duped into sexual slavery through coercive measures, such as taking their passports upon arrival in a new country (Hughes 2004). The supposed inaccessibility of trafficked victims to researchers justifies many unsubstantiated claims that human trafficking is occurring within intimate industries that employ predominantly women migrants from poorer countries, like domestic labor and sexual labor. However, Parreñas (2011) did access Filipina migrant hostess laborers working in a Japanese club, challenging the perception that vulnerable migrant populations are inaccessible slaves. Thus, Parreñas (2011, p. 8) instead argues for adopting the more nuanced framework of indentured mobility, which acknowledges migrant workers' vulnerability to human rights violations but also simultaneously rejects the prevailing discourses that portray migrant workers as helpless victims in need of rescue. The movements against human trafficking in the Global North often revive rescue narratives that portray intimate laborers as victims of coercion, echoing colonial narratives of white slavery, to characterize migrant women sexual laborers (Doezema 2010). Therefore, Bernstein (2012) demonstrates that the antitrafficking movement in the United States is an example of the transnationalization of carceral politics and the reincorporation of these policies into domestic politics under the guise of benevolent feminist activism.

A number of societies, including the US, the Philippines, and China, have regulated women's mobility by passing various forms of antitrafficking measures that limit women's abilities to participate in various forms of intimate industries, from international dating agencies to sexual labor. While antitrafficking laws gain a lot of popular media and political support, these laws often victimize intimate laborers. Despite the government policies surrounding human trafficking, many intimate industries are still largely dependent upon marginalized populations' labor and find ways to circumvent navigation that limits migrant women's mobility. These populations include migrant women from the Global South, and women of color and poor women within the Global North.

Trafficking

The United Nations defines human trafficking as the recruitment, transportation, transfer, harboring, or receipt of persons by improper means (such as force, abduction, fraud, or coercion) for an improper purpose including forced labor or sexual exploitation. As intimate relationships become increasingly commodified, people's anxieties regarding the distinction between the world of the intimate and the world of the economy become pronounced within government policies. For example, Congress passed the International Marriage Broker Regulation Act (IMBRA) in response to the murders of marriage migrants, women commonly referred to as "mail-order brides"' since they gain citizenship by marrying someone from the Global North, and this law identifies women marriage migrants as potential victims of sexual trafficking (Constable 2012). In addition to the US, both the Philippines and China have strict laws regulating the matchmaking industry. The US Congress also passed the Stop Enabling Online Sex Trafficking Act (SESTA) in early 2018, which is a law that holds websites legally accountable for third-party posts on their websites. Many sexual laborers claim that this law dramatically puts them in more danger, as it closes their access to attracting and vetting potential clients. Organizations of sexual laborers opposed the bill, arguing that it would not help prevent human trafficking in any significant way, and also took resources away from consensual sexual laborers (Arnold 2018).

Antitrafficking legislation impacts the operation of the entire industry that has developed to serve migrant laborers. The migration industry (Hernández León 2008) is an ensemble of entrepreneurs, firms, and services, mainly motivated by financial gain, that facilitate international migration. While some migrants are able to secure their own employment (Hwang 2017), many migrants use agencies or middlemen brokers for labor placement and often lose half of their earnings in the process (Chin 2013). Parreñas (2011) argues that no one monitors the middleman brokers, and they often double dip on both the migrant and the client for various fees. Legislation that monitors migrant women's mobility, as an attempt to stop human trafficking, makes vulnerable migrants more dependent upon third-party brokers, which actually increases the likelihood of exploitative labor situations (Parreñas 2011). The moral disciplining of women's bodies occurs in many intimate industries, as policies created to end trafficking create new forms of vulnerability.

Parreñas (2011) argues that migrant hostess workers' increasing dependence upon third-party migration agents, which are part of the larger migration industry, puts laborers into more vulnerable positions. Based on laws regarding trafficking in the Philippines and Japan, Parreñas (2011) demonstrates that hostess migrants face a form of indentured mobility. While migrant hostesses are increasing their social mobility and earning potentials as migrants, they are also in a state of servitude with migration agents and other third-party brokers. The notion of indentured mobility captures the state's role in creating policies that monitor migrant bodies and increase their vulnerabilities to third parties. Moving beyond the case of migrant women hostesses, many women involved within the realm of intimate industries are victimized by state policies that are in fact created to help or "rescue" them.

Sexual laborers, or willing participants in the selling of their sexual labor, are most often described as victims of human trafficking in the media. However, numbers of scholars have challenged the notion that sexual laborers are victims of trafficking (Brennan 2004; Kempadoo 1999, 2004; Hoang 2015). These scholars do still highlight the fact that many sexual laborers are nevertheless a vulnerable population, especially migrant sexual laborers, but that they have agency in choosing to perform sexual labor. In addition to sexual laborers, women who participate in intimate industries such as surrogacy, domestic labor, and marriage migration are also portrayed as potential victims of human trafficking, based on the ideological separation of intimacy from the world of the economy.

Many societies and governments adopt a viewpoint regarding the commodification of intimacy that places the realms of intimacy and economy into separate and hostile worlds from one another (Zelizer 2005). This view also posits that commodified relationships are morally contaminated, which ultimately devalues intimate labor and questions in its legitimacy as economic activity. Laws such as IMBRA and the Anti Mail-Order Bride Law in the Philippines regarding the international marriage industry demonstrate that many people in various societies view the commodification of intimacy as morally contaminated, even when consensual. Current organizations committed to ending sexual trafficking portray women who participate in intimate industries as "victim-subjects" and do not allow women agency in their decision to enter into sexual labor as a viable economic choice (Bernstein 2007a). In narratives of sex trafficking created in the US, the victim narrative is especially prevalent when discussing poor women and women of color's intimate labor domestically, as well as in the Global South. The antitrafficking movements ultimately "coalesced around the notion of violence against women, concentrating particularly on abuses suffered by third-world women" (Soderlund 2005, p. 69). The antitrafficking movement within US foreign policy garnered more attention and resources during the George W. Bush presidency because of his increasing use of faith-based organizations to carry out both domestic and foreign policies (Bernstein 2007a; Constable 2012; Weitzer 2007).

Antitrafficking campaigns focus most on sexual labor, as it is often considered the most morally contaminated form of intimate exchange. Moralistic views condemning sexual labor do not recognize the influence of corporate capitalism and the state in promoting sexual labor, since both benefit from the billions of tourism dollars spent every year on sex. As Bernstein (2007a, p. 144) argues,

> In this way, the masculinist institutions of big business, the state, and the police are reconfigured as allies and saviors, rather than enemies, of unskilled migrant workers, and the responsibility for slavery is shifted from structural factors and dominant

institutions onto individual, deviant men: foreign brown men (as in the White Slave trade of centuries past) or even more remarkably, African American men living in the inner city.

Therefore, while many women take advantage of being "freed" by prostitution raids conducted by the masculinist state, many other women perceive rehabilitation programs themselves as a different form of slavery. Scholars examining antitrafficking campaigns have noted that contemporary antitrafficking campaigns are often interwoven with moral agendas surrounding sexual labor, particularly from religious-based institutions (Agustín 2007; Bernstein 2007a, 2012; Cheng 2011). During a sex trafficking tour in Thailand, Bernstein and Shih (2014) noted that tour guides repeated the prevalent media narrative that equates sexual labor with poverty and human trafficking and often did not distinguish commercial sexual labor from human trafficking. Thus, dominant policy and media narratives surrounding sexual labor within the US simply reduce all sexual labor to forms of human trafficking (Hoang and Parreñas 2013). According to the organization Rights4Girls, women of color in the US are more likely to be imprisoned for their sexual labor, demonstrating the carceral undertone to antitrafficking enforcement both on transnational and domestic levels that Bernstein (2012) observed.

The international dating and marriage industry is commonly linked to human trafficking (Hughes 2004). Common media discourse in the US characterizes international introduction and dating agencies as facilitating human trafficking, which is the reason that Congressional bipartisan support existed to pass the International Marriage Broker Regulation Act in 2005 (Constable 2012). In fact, the Philippines government began to heavily regulate the international marriage and dating industry in 1990, but many bride agencies circumvent the laws by basing their offices abroad. Hwang and Parreñas (2018) argue that both sexual laborers and brides are types of intimate migrants, as both categories of women fulfill both emotional and sexual desires. They find that intimate migrants are more often viewed with moral suspicion than other types of migrants, based on the notion that the intimate realm is separate from the realm of economics. Therefore, narratives of transnational human trafficking often focus on intimate migrants.

In addition to intimate forms of migration, commodified intimacy in the realms of domestic labor and commercial surrogacy are continually contested spaces as well, with stories of trafficking common in both industries. Domestic labor brings migrants and women of color into the intimate realm of the home, the supposed sanctuary from the market. Commercialized surrogacy commodifies the mother–child relationship and the process of pregnancy. Thus, the media often portray domestics and surrogates as victims of exploitative practices, but the increasing market for commodified intimate relationships continues to expand beyond geographic and moral boundaries. Since societies typically separate intimate labor from the realm of the market, oftentimes intimate labor is not recognized as real labor that should be paid. Thus, in the history of the US, women of color have largely been regulated to backstage reproductive labor, such as laundering and cleaning, and paid very little for their labor, if they were paid at all (Nakano Glenn 1992). In the contemporary market of commodified intimate labor, most lower-paid intimate labor, such as elder care, continues to be performed by women of color, poor women, and migrant women. There are examples of intimate labor that can be lucrative, but Bernstein's (2007b) study of middle-class sex workers in the San Francisco area demonstrates that intimate labor pays better than entry-level work for college-educated white women. Therefore, the commodification of intimate labor has always reflected the hierarchies of race, ethnicity, class, and nationality (Dodson and Zincavage 2007; Duffy 2005).

Throughout history, women have been relegated within the labor market to performing intimate labor. For example, in the early 1900s, many poor white women and women of color in the US worked within wealthy households as maids, laundresses, or cooks, as intimate labor performed within the household was considered more appropriate work for women than work outside of the home. The hierarchies of race, class, and gender remain within the domestic labor market to this day, as most domestic laborers are still poor women, women of color, or migrant women in the Global North (Nakano Glenn 1992). Domestic labor, which includes cooking, cleaning, and laundering, is considered low-skilled reproductive labor. Due to domestic labor's association with unskilled labor, most jobs in the industry do not pay high wages. Yet, domestic labor is an important form of intimate labor, as domestic workers are brought inside the home to work. Thus, they experience the family's intimate life by taking care of the home, particularly those working as live-in domestic workers.

Domestic Labor

Domestic labor, both paid and unpaid, is inherently a form of interchange between the realm of the intimate and the economy, challenging the notion of separate and hostile spheres (Lan 2003). Migrant and working-class women's domestic service allows class-privileged women in the Global North to use the labor of another class of women in order to escape the gendered demands of the household, as most men have not taken on their share of the reproductive labor (Duffy 2005; Parreñas 2001). This produces an international transfer of care, where class and racially privileged women hire migrants to do their "dirty" work (Parreñas 2001). Beyond performing the reproductive labor of the home, domestic workers provide love and care to the families they work for. Thus, domestic work is an intimate industry that has existed for thousands of years and still remains largely unregulated by states. Historically, domestic work has been performed by ethnic and racial minorities, and issues of citizenship status, ethnicity, and race formed the domestic worker into an "other" who does not deserve better pay or working conditions (Browne and Misra 2003).

Domestic labor brings intimate labor into people's homes with little oversight and regulation by the government, as this labor is hidden from the view of the public and considered invisible since this labor does not occur in a public work space environment, is largely unregulated by labor laws and is not formally recognized as part of the labor market (Ehrenreich and Hochschild 2003). Since their labor is unregulated by most governments and the work conditions are often informal, domestic workers' experiences vary considerably, based on the family that they are placed with. Migrant women, particularly from Latin America, Southeast Asia and the Caribbean, form the large reserve army of low-wage labor for both domestic service and institutional service work (Nakano Glenn 1992). Regardless of their citizenship status, many migrant women continue to be constructed as lesser citizens, based upon their employment in low-level intimate industries (Bakan and Stasiulus 1995).

Hochschild (2002) identifies both love and care as the new gold in the global economy. In addition to resources and gold, European imperial countries extracted both natural resources and intimate resources from countries in Africa, Asia, and Latin America through systems of indentured and enslaved labor. The contemporary extraction of love and care continues to move resources from the Global South to the North. Media often present countries outside of the North as more traditional, communal, and loving. Thus, many employers in the Global North believe that their domestic laborers belong to a more loving culture, where warm family ties and a long of tradition of patient maternal love for children still dominate instead of the individualistic culture dominant in the US and Europe. By hiring migrant women, people are hoping to replenish their own country's depleted culture of care (Hochschild 2002). Hochschild (2002) considers this a new form of emotional imperialism, where care resources are taken from poor migrant families and placed at the disposal of families in wealthy countries. This new imperialism is evidenced by the fact that most migrant workers receive only partial citizenship and their movements are highly regulated by receiving countries (Ong 2006; Yuval-Davis 1999).

Transnational Mothering

Much like class-privileged women in wealthy countries, most migrant workers must rely on their grandmothers, sisters, aunts, and other women kin to care for their children, while some even hire nannies, creating a global chain of outsourced reproductive labor (Parreñas 2008; Lan 2003). Studies of transnational mothering by migrant women highlight the importance of technology, remittances, gifts, and family members in maintaining familial ties transnationally (Parreñas 2008). However, the maintenance of close relationships can be difficult, as migrant domestic workers' daily emotional labor is focused on their employers. In addition, most migrant-receiving countries do not allow family unification or the children of migrants to join their family members (Lan 2003). Children left behind by migrant mothers often struggle with the emotional strains of long-distance mothering (Hondagneu-Sotelo and Avila 1997), particularly since women are often charged with the nurturing role within the family, based upon traditional understandings of gender roles (Parreñas 2001). Based on these gender roles, domestic workers remain the main source of emotional labor and care within the family, thus creating a care deficit (Parreñas 2001).

Domestic labor migrants are rejected as full citizens by their destination countries, but are still accepted as cheap temporary labor (Parreñas 2001). Thus, migrant domestic workers face a form of contradictory mobility, as they receive increased wages but a decrease in social status and state protections (Parreñas 2001). Migrant domestic workers' partial citizenship places them in much more vulnerable positions, since in addition to often not being allowed to bring their families, they also are often not allowed to apply for permanent residence. Thus, many governments place domestic migrants into vulnerable positions by only allowing them partial citizenship and placing stringent limitations on their mobility. Government policies intended to stop human trafficking and labor abuses create increased risks for many migrant domestic workers instead of alleviating them, in what Parreñas (2008) terms the "moral disciplining" of migrant women.

Sexual Labor

Sexual labor is also an important form of intimate labor that often goes unrecognized as actual labor since it is not part of the formal recognized labor market in most countries (Cabezas 1998, 2009; Enloe 1990; Kempadoo 1999, 2001, 2004; Law 1997) While common discourses surrounding sexual labor and prostitution posit that male clients are seeking a physical experience centered upon emotionless sexual release (Bernstein 2007b), many men are often seeking some form of emotional connection beyond an orgasm. The rise of sexual tourism in the Global South and the popularity of the "girlfriend experience" (GFE) demonstrate that men often seek bounded forms of authentic intimate connections in which the intimacy they pay for is authentic, but recognize that the exchange is temporarily and emotionally bounded, or what Bernstein (2007b) terms "bounded authenticity." The stereotype of men is that they pay sexual laborers to "go away" and maintain emotional distance. However, Bernstein's (2007b) study, as well as other scholars' studies (Brennan 2004; Kempadoo 2004; Padilla 2007), demonstrate the importance of both intimate and emotional labor to men that purchase sexual services. In Brennan's (2004) study of sex tourism in the Dominican Republic, she noted that Dominican women's intimate labor was the main draw for many men to purchase their services, as they can purchase short-term sexual encounters anywhere.

Sexual exchanges that are premised on bounded authenticity (Bernstein 2007b) often include intimate and emotional interactions that resemble typical heterosexual courtship scripts, despite the exchange of payment (Hoang 2015; Guidroz and Rich 2010; Lucas 2005; Milrod and Monto 2012), which supports Zelizer's argument that all intimate relationships contain complex negotiations of payment. Sharp and Earle (2003) conducted a study of male customers' online entries and found that most men valued the GFE or sexual laborers' personalities versus their physical appearances, demonstrating that men are often seeking meaningful, personal connections in their commercialized intimate relationships (Lucas 2005; Sanders 2008) Sexual laborers, as well as strippers and phone sex operators (Frank 2002), are at times engaging in a form of counterfeit intimacy, which is based upon a manufactured emotional connection (Milrod and Weitzer 2012). The GFE moves beyond transactional sexual labor and includes commercialized forms of bounded, but authentic, intimate connections. Many men that purchase access to women's bounded intimate and sexual labor are searching for the fantasy of a mutually desired, special encounter, even within a commercialized setting (Holzman and Pines 1982), that Plumridge (2001) terms the "myth of mutuality."

Intimate labor within the sex industry exists upon a continuum that includes hostess labor, erotic dancing, massage parlors, webcam work, the GFE, and phone sex operators, in addition to transactional sex. The sexual labor that strippers and hostesses provide does not necessarily include sexual intercourse, but instead is predicated upon providing their clients with the fantasy of mutually desired flirtations and the potential of sexual contact (Choi 2017; Frank 2002; Parreñas 2011). Allison (2009) argues that hostesses in Japan make men "feel like men" and Parreñas (2011) argues that migrant karaoke bar hostesses in Japan work to buttress men's masculinity by performing femininity through such things as aesthetic labor, emotional labor, storytelling, and acting. Much like the hostess bars, the space of the strip club is also a place where men "feel like men", as women's erotic dancing and emotional labor reinforce their masculinity, even without sexual intercourse (Frank 2002).

Many workers in the transnational sex industry perform poverty (Hoang 2014; Padilla 2007; Parreñas 2011) in order to gain sympathy from their clients and thus garner larger tips, and to engender feelings of chivalry in the men participating. Male purchasers of sexual services feel a boost in their own masculinity when interacting with sexual laborers who evoke their sympathy. The emotional capital of sympathy (Parreñas 2011) builds upon customers' heightened masculinity, and many workers within intimate industries utilize structural global inequalities to secure material gains. In addition to increasing men's feelings of desirability and masculinity, women within various intimate economies must also cultivate their physical appearances in order to attract men who can provide them with financial opportunities.

Moving beyond the commercial flirtations found in strip clubs and hostess bars is the practice of commercial dating in Hong Kong and Japan, which is a mutually agreed-upon contract between a young woman and a relatively older man that involves the exchange of intimate labor for payment. The woman provides emotional labor, companionship, and potentially sexual favors to the older man, who in turn provides some form of monetary benefit that can include cash, tuition, dinner, temporary shelter, vacations, drugs, or luxury goods (Chu 2014). The practice of commercial dating started in Japan during the early 1990s, and has since spread to Korea, Taiwan, Hong Kong, Macau, and parts of mainland China (Kong 2003). Much like the practice of commercial dating, male sexual laborers' intimate labor often follows the same heterosexual courtship scripts.

Male sexual laborers

The sex tourists that have received the majority of scholarly attention (Enloe 1990; Fusco 1998; Kempadoo 2001; Manderson 1997) have been male sex tourists in the Global South. However, increasing numbers of scholars are focusing on the phenomenon of wealthy, most often white, women traveling to the Caribbean, the Sinai, and Africa in search of sexual relationships. Pruitt and LaFont (1994) term this phenomenon in the Caribbean context "romance tourism" in order to differentiate women's experiences from the sex tourism engaged in by men, which is often portrayed as entirely transactional. Women participating in forms of sexual tourism engage in "relationships" with local men and buy them gifts, dinners, and airfare tickets. A large number of these women do not accept their participation in the sexual economy, but instead view their relationships as based on mutual affection and "helping" local men out of impoverished situations (Pruitt and LaFont 1994). Due to this gendered power dynamic, early scholars studying this phenomenon portrayed the women as the "victims" of opportunistic men (Pruitt and Lafont 1994), by highlighting local men's dependence on the economic component of their relationship with foreign women. However, other scholars have demonstrated that women sexual tourists are exploiting men's sexual labor and, therefore, are not just innocent victims of romance schemes (Sanchez Taylor 2001).

Despite scholars early portrayal of women's participation in commodified intimate relationships as different than men's participation in global sex tourism, Sanchez Taylor (2006) argues that deeming women's adventures to be "romantic" denies the fact that they engage in the same types of exoticization and exploitation that men on sexual tours do. Kempadoo (1999) additionally argues that male sexual laborers call themselves players, hustlers, beach boys, or gigolos, demonstrating that men benefit from the patriarchal assumption that having sex with many women enhances their masculinity, whereas women are considered damaged if they engage in similar sexual labor practices. Many women tourists interviewed in the Gambia believe that their relationships are based upon emotions of "true love" (Heinskou 2013). Thus, these relationships trouble clear boundaries between the realm of the intimate and the realm of the economy.

Women who feel ignored in their local dating markets go abroad as sex tourists to feel sexually empowered, as a result of being considered desirable by local men (de Albuquerque 1998; O'Connell Davidson, and Sanchez Taylor 1999). Therefore, many white women who engage in sexual tourism in the Caribbean and Africa act as "ethno-sexual adventurers" (Nagel 2003) who engage in liminal sex acts while abroad (Meszaros and Bazzaroni 2014). Therefore, empowerment is an important component of sex tourism's appeal for both male and female tourists while the potential of cultivating long-term relationships and potential migration provides an incentive for many workers to get into the industry.

International Marriage

In the current transnational configuration of citizenship and migration, marriage is often the easiest route for migrants from Latin American, Southeast Asia, and countries from the former USSR to access the Global North. For this reason, migration through marriage is seen as a tool of both social and economic mobility. The line between migration for marriage or migration for employment is blurred, since oftentimes marriage decisions are made based upon economic security (Piper and Roces 2004). Marriage provides security for families through cultural traditions surrounding family obligations and remittances (Mix and Piper 2003). Thus, many contract workers utilized marriage as a strategy towards establishing secure citizenship and employment status (Piper and Roces 2004). Marriage to a local man provides migrant women with a potential means of escaping stereotypes, segregation, and labor deskilling (McKay 2003). Most of the Filipina women migrant domestic workers in McKay's (2003) sample married Canadian husbands shortly after their arrival, since many felt insecure about their legal status. Many Taiwanese employers propose marriage to their domestic workers, but the women know that if they accept, they will do the same work for no pay, as it will become a familial obligation (Lan 2003). For these reasons, scholars have argued that the marriage migration system is an example of the larger outsourcing of care and reproductive labor to migrant women. The boundaries between paid labor in domestic service and the economic relations of marriage are difficult to draw (McKay 2003).

Domestic work is commonly viewed as a "labor of love" within the confines of marriage (Kojima, 2001). Kojima (2001) argues that the state promotes the gendered division of labor by creating policies that promote certain heteronormative ideals of family. Therefore, women's role in domestic work is naturalized and provides the state a means of externalizing the reproductive costs of maintaining the labor force (Oishi 2005). Despite the second-wave feminist movement's successful gains in the workplace, the economic system is still dependent upon unpaid, and often gendered, labor for social and human reproduction (Nakano Glenn 1992).

In addition to domestic workers, many migrant sexual laborers utilize romancing and marriage to secure citizenship status. For many sexual laborers working to service foreign clientele in "sexscapes" (Brennan 2004), marriage with a foreigner is the goal, since many women fantasize about a financially stable man who will take care of them (Cabezas 1998). Many sexual laborers opt to marry foreign men in order to avoid becoming long-term sexual laborers (Ehrenreich and Hochschild 2003). In one study, most women who had migrated as sexual laborers expressed the desire to get married to a foreigner in order to secure residency status (Hilsdon and Giridharan 2008). Thus, sexual laborers and domestic migrants' insecure statuses often encourage them to search for secure citizenship through marriage to a foreign man. While marriage is a desire for many marginalized migrant populations to secure their statuses, most of these populations still want to marry for love as well (Brennan 2004). Thus, considerations of love and legal status both play an important role in migrant women's marriage choices, demonstrating the constant interaction between intimate and economic realms within people's intimate relationships.

O'Rourke (2002) argues that economic factors in the Global South encourage women to seek migration through marriage by joining introduction agencies that charge men to correspond online with women in foreign countries. Although this industry is often referred to as the mail-order bride industry, numerous studies have demonstrated that women involved in this industry are not bought and sold commodities and that they in fact are choosing to search for potential foreign husbands (Constable 2003; Johnson 2007; Schaeffer 2013). Those participating in Constable's (2005) research on the online cyberdating industry argued that, while their images may be commodified online, they do not consider themselves to be commodities. Constable (2005) further argues that matchmaking is a deceptive name for some of the larger international introduction agencies, as they only provide contact information for correspondence and romance tours.

While many large introduction and correspondence agencies do not engage in matchmaking, they often provide a litany of services to prospective husbands, such as sending gifts, offering tours, providing housing, and teaching women English through hiring tutors. Many agencies offer romance tours, which are packages that include airfare, hotel accommodation, and arranged meetings with individual women or groups of women at social events. Tours often also include legal assistance for couples navigating the legal marriage migration process. Many men spend years researching romance tours before embarking upon them by discussing various topics related to the process online in forums such as planetlove.com (Schaeffer-Grabiel 2006).

Schaefer (2013) found that American men in online forums dedicated to international dating explain their use of international introduction agencies to find a more "traditional" wife, based upon the belief that women in the Global South will proudly provide reproductive labor to her husband, unlike American women who have allegedly been ruined by feminism. Studies of men participating in international dating demonstrate that they characterize American women as materialistic, spoiled, masculine, and too career-oriented (Meszaros 2018; Schaefer 2013; Taraban 2007). On the other hand, international dating agencies and men using them define women abroad as more feminine, family-oriented and traditional (Constable 2003; Taraban 2007). Both Schaeffer (2013) and Constable (2003) found that many of the American men participating in correspondence relationships and romance tours with foreign women are older than 40 years old, and are middle-class white men who are frustrated with feminist demands for egalitarian relationships. Constable (2003) claims that international marriages provide a complimentary life, where women do the domestic work of the home and men provide the economic support. Her interviews with Filipina and Chinese women demonstrated that many of her interviewees would prefer performing the reproductive labor of the home as a stay-at-home wife rather than laboring in factories (Constable 2012). Meszaros (2017) found that men desire the emotional labor of selflessness, which includes women's maintenance of a feminine and sexy appearance, as well as staying home to provide support and quality time in addition to reproductive labor.

Filipina and Chinese women view correspondence marriages as a means of increasing freedom and opportunities, as well as providing economic assistance to their families and helping their children emigrate (Constable 2005). Mexican women perceive men from the US as more equitable marriage partners who can potentially offer a stable, middle-class lifestyle (Schaeffer 2013). For women involved in the industry, meeting an American husband is desirable for many practical reasons, but these considerations do not necessarily preclude feelings of love (Constable 2003). Constable (2003) further argues that correspondence relationships are often based on ideals of romantic love, or at least reflect an attempt to define themselves in such terms.

Schaeffer (2013) contends that many women's pronouncements of love are colored by the surveillance and repression of American immigration laws. In this way, the state relies upon heteronormative ideals of the family (Bernstein and Naples 2010) to enforce its system of determining the "realness" of marriages involving a migrant and US citizen. Men are very concerned about the legitimacy of cross-border marriages, applying different assessments of agency to women in different racial groups (Meszaros 2018). Early scholarship on cross-border marriages focused on women from the economically developing countries who marry men from the US, Canada, and Western Europe, but other recent scholarship has focused on cross-border marriages within Asia. For instance, scholars have noted increased cross-border marriages between Vietnamese women and Viet Kieu migrants abroad (Thai 2008), rural South Korean men who look for Filipina brides (Choo 2016; Kim 2014), Japanese men who marry Filipina women (Piper 1997), Vietnamese women who marry Taiwanese men (Bélanger 2010) and men in Singapore (Yeoh et al 2005), and mainland Chinese women who marry men in Taiwan (Friedman 2006). In addition to for-profit introduction and matchmaking agencies, potential cross-border spouses meet through migrant networks established by migrant pioneers (Bélanger and Tran 2011). Most people assume that cross-border marriages are hypergamous, and that marriage is a strategy that women use to increase their social and geographic mobility. However, a number of scholars have found that female marriage migrants to the US often decline in class positioning upon migration (Constable 2005; Hoang 2013; Liu 2018), experiencing what Kimberly Kay Hoang (2013) refers to as a form of "gender vertigo."

The term "mail-order bride" itself implies a level of commodification within the introduction industry that does not exist; one cannot simply pay and "order" a bride to one's home. However, the term contributes to common media perceptions that women involved in the introduction industry are more likely to be victims of human trafficking and domestic violence. The perception that marriage migrants are actual commodities sold and trafficked has influenced numerous governments to pass legislation regulating the industry, such as in China and the Philippines. Much like sexual laborers and migrant domestic workers, migrant brides are portrayed in popular media as a victimized population, exploited and abused. Many scholars recognize the vulnerability of these populations to exploitation, but recognize that nuances exist within various intimate industries. The sale of intimate labor is much more complex, as it challenges the artificial moral boundaries set in place by separate and hostile theories regarding the intersection of the economy and intimacy.

Conclusion

The increasing commodification of intimate labor across global spaces demonstrates that the realm of the intimate, of the human body and family, are inherently interconnected to the realms of the economy and the nation-state. Despite the fact that most economists have viewed these scales as separate and hostile to one another (Zelizer 2005), historians such as Cole and Durham (2007) demonstrate that intimate relationships played an important role in shaping modernity and capitalism. Contrary to the hostile worlds viewpoint, many feminist theorists argue that intimate relationships between individuals are the building blocks of social, economic, and political worlds (Ahmed 2004; Freeman 2001). Therefore, many transnational feminist scholars encourage one another to be attentive to micro-level politics of context and subjectivity, in addition to macro-level analyses of global economic and political processes, thereby connecting intimate and global processes across borders (Alexander 2005; Grewal and Kaplan 1994; Mohanty 1988; Silvey 2004). Feminist geographers employ the concept of the global intimate (Mountz and Hyndman 2006; Pratt and Rosner 2006) to theoretically analyze the ways in which intimate and global processes are in a constant process of shaping one another.

States often monitor participants of intimate industries closely, especially industries that include sexual, reproductive, or domestic services. However, states create vulnerable intimate migration populations through their policies that restrict and limit noncitizens' mobility and access to citizenship. The narratives of human trafficking that are often applied to intimate migrants (Hwang and Parreñas 2018) allow the state to regulate the movement of migrant women in order to "protect" them from exploitation. Andrijasevic and Mai (2016) argue that tougher state actions aimed at combating human trafficking, developed after major public outcries against sexual slavery, are in fact creating more stringent anti-immigration measures and shifting migration patterns towards irregular channels managed by third parties and agencies. The strict laws passed against human trafficking make migrants more vulnerable. These laws make migrants dependent on third parties to cross borders, allowing ample space for abuse and profiteering from low wage and irregular work.

Thus, populations performing commodified intimate labor often overlap with other vulnerable populations, including women, migrants, poor people and people of color. Due to intimate labor's association with women's work, it is often considered a form of unskilled labor, if it is even recognized as labor at all. Processes of economic globalization have increased the demand for intimate labor and formalized this labor within the global economy, yet this labor is often performed by marginalized populations for low pay.

Despite the vulnerability that many women intimate laborers face in the domestic, sexual labor, and marriage industries, participants are often denied agency in making economic choices to better their lives. Intimate laborers are often judged through the lens of Zelizer's hostile and separate worlds view, which posits that intimate relationships are polluted by economic considerations. Many people feel anxious about the increasingly blurry line that exists between the intimate and economic realms within intimate industries and turn to the state to regulate intimate labor and workers. While the state presents its antitrafficking policies as a means of protecting vulnerable populations, these policies often place women and migrants in more vulnerable positions, as their dependence upon third-party actors increases.

References

Agustín, Laura María. 2007. *Sex at the Margins: Migration, Labour Markets and the Rescue Industry*. London: Zed Books.

Ahmed, Sarah. 2004. *The Cultural Politics of Emotion*. Edinburgh: Edinburgh University Press.

Alexander, M. Jacqui. 2005. *Pedagogies of Crossing: Meditations on Feminism, Second Politics, Memory and the Sacred*. Durham, NC: Duke University Press.

Alexander, M. Jacqui and Chaundra Talpade Mohanty. 1997. "Introduction: Genealogies, Legacies, Movements." In Feminist Genealogies, Colonial Legacies, Democratic Futures, edited by *M. Jacqui Alexander and Chaundra Talpade Mohanty, xiii–1*. New York, NY: Routledge.

Alexander, Priscilla. 1998. "Prostitution: Still a Difficult Issue for Feminists." In *Sex Work: Writings by Women in the Industry*, edited by Frederique Delacoste and Priscilla Alexander, 184–230. San Francisco, CA: Cleis Press.

Allison, Anne. 2009. *Nightwork: Sexuality, Pleasure and Corporate Masculinity in a Tokyo Hostess Club*. Chicago, IL: University of Chicago Press.

Andrijasevic, Rutvica and Nicola Mai. 2016. "Trafficking (in) Representations: Understanding the Recurring Appeal of Victimhood and Slavery in Neoliberal Times." *Anti-Trafficking Review* 7: 1–10.

Arnold, Amanda. 2018. "Here's What's Wrong with the So-Called Anti-Sex Trafficking Bill." *The Cut*. https://www.thecut.com/2018/03/sesta-anti-sex-trafficking-bill-fosta.html (accessed June 22, 2018).

Bakan, Abigail and Dalva Stasiulis. 1995. "Making the Match: Domestic Placement Agencies and the Racialization of Women's Household Work." *Signs* 20(2): 881–891.

Bélanger, Daniele. 2010. "Marriages with Foreign Women in East Asia: Bride Trafficking Or Voluntary Migration?" *Population & Societies* 469: 1–4.

Bélanger, Danièle and Tran Giang Linh. 2011. "The Impact of Transnational Migration on Gender and Marriage in Sending Communities of Vietnam." *Current Sociology* 59(1): 59–77.

Bernstein, Elizabeth. 2007a. "The Sexual Politics of the New Abolitionism." *differences: A Journal of Feminist Cultural Studies* 18(3): 128–151.

Bernstein, Elizabeth. 2007b. *Temporarily Yours: Intimacy, Authenticity, and the Commerce of Sex Work (Worlds of Desire: The Chicago Series on Sexuality, Gender and Culture*. Chicago, IL: University of Chicago Press.

Bernstein, Elizabeth. 2012. "Carceral Politics as Gender Justice? The "Traffic in Women" and Neoliberal Circuits of Crime, Sex, and Rights." *Theory and Society* 41(3): 233–259.

Bernstein, Elizabeth and Elena Shih. 2014. "The Erotics of Authenticity: Sex Trafficking and 'Reality Tourism' in Thailand." *Social Politics* 21(3): 430–460.

Bernstein, Mary and Nancy Naples. 2010. "Sexual Citizenship and the Pursuit of Relationship-Recognition Policies in Australia and United States." *Women's Studies Quarterly* 38(1/2): 132–156.

Boris, Eileen, Stephanie Gilmore, and Rhacel Salazar Parreñas. 2010. "Sexual Labors: Interdisciplinary Perspectives Towards Sex as Work." *Sexualities* 13(2): 131–137.

Boris, Eileen and Rhacel Salazar Parreñas. 2010. "Introduction." In *Intimate Labors: Cultures, Technologies and the Politics of Care*, edited by Eilieen Boris and Rhacel Salazar Parreñas, 1–12. East Palo Alto, CA: Stanford University Press.

Brennan, Denise. 2004. *What's Love Got to Do with It? Transnational Desires and Sex Tourism in the Dominican Republic*. Durham, NC: Duke University Press.

Browne, Irene and Joya Misra. 2003. "The Intersection of Gender and Race in the Labor Market." *Annual Review of Sociology* 29(1): 487–513.

Cabezas, Amalia. 1998. "Discourses of Prostitution: The Case of Cuba." In *Global Sex Workers: Rights, Resistance, and Redefinition*, edited by Kamala Kempadoo and Jo Doezema, 79–86. New York, NY: Routledge.

Cabezas, Amalia. 2009. *Economies of Desire: Sex and Tourism in Cuba and the Dominican Republic*. Philadelphia, PA: Temple University Press.

Cheng, Sealing. 2011. *On the Move for Love: Migrant Entertainers and the US Military in South Korea*. Philadelphia, PA: University of Pennsylvania Press.

Cheng, Shu-Ju Ada. 2003. "Rethinking the Globalization of Domestic Service: Foreign Domestics, State Control, and the Politics of Identity in Taiwan." *Gender and Society* 17(2): 166–186.

Chin, Christine B.N. 2013. *Cosmopolitan Sex Work: Women and Migration in a Global City*. Oxford: Oxford University Press.

Choi, Carolyn. 2017. "Moonlighting in the Nightlife: From Indentured to Precarious Labor in Los Angeles Koreatown's Hostess Industry." *Sexualities* 20(4): 446–462.

Choo, Hae Yeon. 2016. "Selling Fantasies of Rescue: Intimate Labor, Filipina Migrant Hostesses, and US GIs in a Shifting Global Order." *Positions* 24(1): 179–203.

Chu, Sai-kwan. 2014. "Compensated Dating in Hong Kong." *HKU Theses Online* (HKUTO)

Clement, Elizabeth. 2006. *Love for Sale*. Chapel Hill, NC: University of North Carolina Press.

Cole, Jennifer and Deborah Lynn Durham, eds. 2007. *Generations and Globalization: Youth, Age, and Family in the New World Economy*, vol. 3. Bloomington, IN: Indiana University Press.

Constable, Nicole. 2003. *Romance on a Global Stage: Pen Pals, Virtual Ethnography, and Mail Order Marriages*. Berkeley, CA: University of California Press.

Constable, Nicole. 2005. "A Tale of Two Marriages: International Matchmaking and Gendered Mobility." In *Cross-Border Marriages: Gender and Mobility in Transnational Asia*, edited by Nicole Constable, 167–186. Philadelphia, PA: University of Pennsylvania Press.

Constable, Nicole. 2012. "International Marriage Brokers, Cross-Border Marriages and the US Anti-Trafficking Campaign." *Journal of Ethnic and Migration Studies*: 38(7): 1137–1154.

Coontz, S. 2004. "The World Historical Transformation of Marriage." *Journal of Marriage and Family* 66(4): 974–979.

de Albuquerque, Klaus. 1998. "In Search of the Big Bamboo." *Transitions* 77: 48–57.

Dodson, Lisa and Rebekah M. Zincavage. 2007. "'It's Like a Family' Caring Labor, Exploitation, and Race in Nursing Homes." *Gender & Society* 21(6): 905–928.

Doezema, Jo. 2010. *Sex Slaves and Discourse Matters: The Construction of Trafficking*. New York, NY: Zed Press.

Duffy, Mignon. 2005. "Reproducing Labor Inequalities: Challenges for Feminist Conceptualizing Care at the Intersections of Gender, Race, and Class." *Gender and Society* 19(1): 66–82.

Ehrenreich, Barbara and Arlie Russell Hochschild. 2003. "Introduction." In *Global Woman: Nannies, Maids, and Sexual Workers in the New Economy*, edited by Barbara Ehrenreich and Arlie Russell Hochschild, 1–14: Macmillan.

Enloe, Cynthia. 1990. *Bananas, Beaches and Bases: Making Feminist Sense of International Politics*. Berkeley: University of California Press.

Frank, Katherine. 2002. *G-Strings and Sympathy: Strip Club Regulars and Male Desire*. Durham, NC: Duke University Press.

Freeman, Carla. 2001. "Is Local:Global as Feminine:Masculine? Rethinking the Gender of Globalization." *Signs* 26(4): 1007–1037.

Friedman, Sara L. 2006. "Determining 'truth' at the Border: Immigration Interviews, Chinese Marital Migrants, and Taiwan's Sovereignty Dilemmas." *Citizenship Studies* 14(2): 167–183.

Fusco, Coco. 1998. "Hustling for Dollars: Jiniterismo in Cuba." In *Global Sexual Workers: Rights, Resistance, and Redefinition*, edited by Kamala Kempadoo and Jo Doezema, 151–166. New York, NY: Routledge.

Grewal, Inderpal. 2005. *Transnational America: Feminisms, Diasporas, Neoliberalisms*. Durham, NC: Duke University Press.

Grewal, Inderpal and Caren Kaplan. 1994. "Introduction." *In Scattered Hegemonies: Postmodernity and Transnational Feminist Practices*, edited by Inderpal Grewal and Caren Kaplan. Minneapolis: University of Minnesota Press.

Guidroz, Kathleen and Grant J. Rich. 2010. "Commercial Telephone Sex: Fantasy and Reality." In *Sex for Sale: Prostitution, Pornography, and the Sex Industry*, edited by Ronald Weitzer, 139–162. New York, NY: Routledge.

Heinskou, Marie Bruvik. 2013. "'Our Love is Not Like all the Others, our Love is True Love': Social Constructions of Intimate Encounters between Women from the Global North and Men from the Global South." Presented at the Intimate Migration Conference, Copenhagen, Denmar (April 2–5, 2013).

Hernández-León, Rubén. 2008. *Metropolitan Migrants: The Migration of Urban Mexicans to the United States*. Berkeley, CA: University of California Press.

Hilsdon, Anne-Marie and Beena Giridharan. 2008. "Racialised Sexualities: The Case of Filipina Migrant Workers in East Malaysia." *Gender, Place and Culture* 15(6): 611–628.

Hoang, Kimberly Kay. 2013. "Transnational Gender Vertigo." *Contexts* 12(2): 22–26.

Hoang, Kimberly Kay. 2014. "Competing Technologies of Embodiment: Pan Asian Modernity and Third World Dependency in Vietnam's Contemporary Sex Industry." *Gender and Society* 28(4): 513–536.

Hoang, Kimberly Kay. 2015. *Dealing in Desire: Asian Ascendancy, Western Decline, and the Hidden Currencies of Global Sex Work*. Berkeley, CA: University of California Press.

Hoang, Kimberly Kay and Rhacel Salazar Parreñas. 2013. "Introduction." In *Human Trafficking Reconsidered: Rethinking the Problem, Envisioning New Solutions*, edited by Kimberly Kay Hoang and Rhacel Salazar Parreñas, 1–18. New York, NY: The International Debate Education Association.

Hochschild, Arlie 1983. *The Managed Heart: Commercialization of Human Feeling*. Berkeley: University of California Press.

Hochschild, Arlie 2002. "Love and Gold." In *Global Woman: Nannies, Maids and Sex Workers in the New Economy*, edited by Barbara Ehrenreich and Arlie Hochschild, 15–30. New York, NY: Holt.

Hochschild, Arlie. 2003. "The Commodity Frontier." In *The Commercialization of Intimate Life: Notes from Home and Work*, edited by Arlie Hochschild, 30–44. Berkeley, CA: University of California Press.

Holzman, Harold R. and Sharon Pines. 1982. "Buying Sex: The Phenomenology of being a John." *Deviant Behavior* 4(1): 89–116.

Hondagneu-Sotelo, Pierrette and Ernestine Avila. 1997. "'I'm here, but I'm there' the Meanings of Latina Transnational Motherhood." *Gender & Society* 11(5): 548–571.

Hughes, Donna M. 2004. "The Role of 'Marriage Agencies' in the Sexual Exploitation and Trafficking of Women from the Former Soviet Union." *International Review of Victimology* 11: 49–71.

Hwang, Maria Cecilia. 2017. "Offloaded: Women's Sex Work, Migration across the South China Sea and the Gendered Antitrafficking Emigration Policy of the Philippines." *Women's Studies Quarterly* 45(1): 131–147.

Hwang, Maria Cecilia and Rhacel Salazar Parreñas. 2018. "Intimate Migrations: The Case of Marriage Migrants and Sex Workers in Asia." In *Routledge Handbook of Asian Migrations*, edited by Gracia Liu-Farrer and Brenda S.A. Yeoh, 78–88. London: Routledge.

Johnson, Ericka. 2007. *Dreaming of a Mail Order Husband*. Durham, NC: Duke University Press.

Kempadoo, Kamala. 1999. "Freelancers, Temporary Wives and Beach-Boys: Researching Sex work in the Caribbean." *Feminist Review* 67(Sex Work Reassessed): 39–62.

Kempadoo, Kamala. 2001. "Women of Color and the Global Sex Trade: Transnational Feminist Perspectives." *Meridians: Feminism, Race, Transnationalism* 1(2): 28–51.

Kempadoo, Kamala. 2004. *Sexing the Caribbean: Gender, Race and Sexual Labor*. New York, NY: Routledge.

Kim, Mijeong. 2014. "South Korean Rural Husbands, Compensatory Masculinity, and International Marriage." *Journal of Korean Studies* 19(2): 291–325.

Kojima, Yu. 2001. "In the Business of Cultural Reproduction: Theoretical Implications of the Mail-Order Bride Phenomenon." *Women's Studies International Forum* 24(2): 199–210.

Kong, Mee-Hae. 2003. "Material Girls: Sexual Perceptions of Korean Teenage Girls Who have Experienced 'Compensated Dates.'" *Asian Journal of Women's Studies* 9(2): 67–94.

Lan, Pei-Chia. 2003. "Maid Or Madam?: Filipina Migrant Workers and the Continuity of Domestic Labor." *Gender and Society* 17(2): 187–208.

Law, Lisa. 1997. "A Matter of 'Choice": Discourses on Prostitution in the Philippines." In *Sites of Desire, Economies of Pleasure: Sexualities in Asia and the Pacific*, edited by Margaret Jolly and Lenore Manderson, 233–261. Chicago, IL: University of Chicago Press.

Liu, Monica. 2018. "Devoted, Caring, and Home Loving: A Chinese Portrayal of Western Masculinity in Transnational Cyberspace Romance." *Men and Masculinities* 22(2).

Lucas, Ann M. 2005. "The Work of Sex Work: Elite Prostitutes' Vocational Orientations and Experiences." *Deviant Behavior* 26(6): 513–546.

Manderson, Lenore. 1997. "Parables of Imperialism and Fantasies of the Exotic: Western Representations of Thailand-Place and Sex." In *Sites of Desire, Economies of Pleasure*, edited by Lenore Manderson and Margaret Jolly, 123–144. Chicago, IL: University of Chicago Press.

McKay, Deirdre. 2003. "Filipinas in Canada – De-Skilling as a Push Toward Marriage." In *Wife Or Worker?: Asian Women and Migration*, edited by Nicola Piper and Mina Roces, 23–52. Oxford: Rowman & Littlefield.

Meszaros, Julia. 2017. "American Men and Romance Tourism: Searching for Traditional Trophy Wives as Status Symbols of Masculinity." *Women's Studies Quarterly* 45(1): 225–242.

Meszaros, Julia. 2018. "Race, Space, and Agency in the International Introduction Industry: How American Men Perceive Women's Agency in Colombia, Ukraine and the Philippines." *Gender, Place and Culture* 25(2): 268–287.

Meszaros, Julia and Christina Bazzaroni. 2014. "From Taboo to Tourist Industry: The Construction of Interracial Intimacies between Black Men and White Women in Colonial and Contemporary Times." *Sociology Compass* 8(11): 1256–1268.

Milrod, Christine and Martin A. Monto. 2012. "The Hobbyist and the Girlfriend Experience: Behaviors and Preferences of Male Customers of Internet Sexual Service Providers." *Deviant Behavior* 33(10): 792–810.

Milrod, Christine and Ronald Weitzer. 2012. "The Intimacy Prism: Emotion Management among the Clients of Escorts." *Men and Masculinities* 15(5), 447–467.

Mix, Prapairat R. and Nicola Piper. 2003. "Does Marriage 'liberate' Women from Sex Work? Thai Women in Germany." In *Wife or Worker? Asian Women and Migration*, edited by Nicola Piper and Mina Roces, 53–71. Lanham, MD: Rowman & Littlefield.

Mohanty, Chandra Talpade. 1988. "Under Western Eyes." *Feminist Review* 30(Summer): 51–80.

Mountz, Alison and Jennifer Hyndman. 2006. "Feminist Approaches to the Global Intimate." *Women's Studies Quarterly* 34(1–2): 613–632.

Nagel, Joane. 2003. *Race, Ethnicity, and Sexuality: Intimate Intersections, Forbidden Frontiers*. Oxford: Oxford University Press.

Nakano Glenn, Evelyn. 1992. "From Servitude to Service Work: Historical Continuities in the Racial Division of Paid Reproductive Labor." *Signs* 18(1): 1–43.

O'Connell Davidson, Julia and Jacqueline Sanchez Taylor. 1999. "Fantasy Islands: Exploring the Demand for Sex Tourism." In *Sex, Sex and Gold: Tourism and Sex work in the Caribbean*, edited by Kamala Kempadoo, 37–54. Lanham, MD: Rowman & Littlefield.

O'Rourke, Kate. 2002. "To Have and to Hold: A Postmodern Feminist Response to the Mail Order Bride Industry." *Denver Journal of International Law and Policy* 30(4): 476–497.

Oishi, Nana. 2005. *Women in Motion: Globalization, State Policies, and Labor Migration in Asia*. Palo Alto, CA: Stanford University Press.

Ong, Aihwa. 2006. *Neoliberalism as Exception: Mutations in Citizenship and Sovereignty*. Durham, NC: Duke University Press.

Padilla, Mark. 2007. "'Western Union Daddies' and their Quest for Authenticity: An Ethnographic Study of the Dominican Gay Sex Tourism Industry." *Journal of Homosexuality* 53(1–2): 241–275.

Parreñas, Rhacel Salazar. 2008. *The Force of Domesticity: Filipina Migrants and Globalization* New York, NY: New York University Press.

Parreñas, Rhacel Salazar. 2011. *Illicit Flirtations: Labor, Migration, and Sex Trafficking in Tokyo*. Palo Alto, CA: Stanford University Press.

Parreñas, Rhacel Salazar. 2001. *Servants of Globalization: Women, Migration and Domestic Work*. Palo Alto, CA: Stanford University Press.

Parreñas, Rhacel Salazar, Hung Cam Thai, and Rachel Silvey. 2016. "Guest Editors' Introduction Intimate Industries: Restructuring (Im)Material Labor in Asia." *Positions: East Asia Cultures Critique* 24(1): 1–15.

Piper, Nicola. 1997. "International Marriage in Japan: 'Race' and 'Gender' Perspectives." *Gender, Place and Culture* 4(3): 321–338.

Piper, Nicola and Mina Roces. 2004. *Wife or Worker?: Asian Women and Migration*. New York, NY: Rowman & Littlefield.

Plumridge, Abel. 2001. "A Segmented Sex Industry in New Zealand: Sexual and Personal Safety of Female Sex Workers." *Australia and New Zealand Journal of Public Health* 25(1): 78–83.

Pratt, Geraldine and Valerie Rosner. 2006. "Introduction: The Global and the Intimate." *Women's Studies Quarterly* 34(1–2): 13–24.

Pruitt, Deborah and Suzanne LaFont. 1995. "For Love and Money: Romance Tourism in Jamaica." *Annals of Tourism* 22(2): 422–440.

Sanchez Taylor, Jacqueline. 2001. "Dollars are a Girl's Best Friend? Female Tourists' Sexual Behaviour in the Caribbean." *Sociology* 35(3): 749–764.

Sanchez Taylor, Jacqueline. 2006. "Female Sex Tourism: A Contradiction in Terms." *Feminist Review* 83(1): 42–59.

Sanders, Teela. 2008. *Paying for Pleasure: Men Who Buy Sex*. Cullompton, UK: Willan.

Schaeffer, Felicity. 2013. *Love and Empire: Cybermarriage and Citizenship across the Americas*. New York, NY: New York University Press.

Schaeffer-Grabiel, Felicity. 2006. "Planet-Love.Com: Cyberbrides in the Americas and the Transational Routes of US Masculinity." *Signs* 31(2): 331–356.

Sharp, Keith and Sarah Earle. 2003. "Cyberpunters and Cyberwhores: Prostitution on the Internet." In *Dot.Cons: Crime, Deviance and Identity on the Internet*, edited by Yvonne Jewkes, 36–52. Cullompton, UK: Willan.

Silvey, Rachel. 2004. "Transnational Migration and the Gender Politics of Scale: Indonesian Domestic Workers in Saudi Arabia." *Singapore Journal of Tropical Geography* 25(2): 141–155.

Soderlund, Gretchen. 2005. "Running from the Rescuers: New US Crusades Against Sex Trafficking and the Rhetoric of Abolition." *NWSA Journal*: 64–87.

Taraban, Svitlana. 2007. "Birthday Girls, Russian Dolls and Others: Internet Bride as the Emerging Global Identity of Post-Soviet Women." In *Living Gender After Communism*, edited by Janet E. Johnson and Jean C. Robinson, 105–127. Bloomington, IN: University of Indiana Press.

Thai, Hung Cam. 2008. *For Better or for Worse: Vietnamese International Marriages in the New Global Economy. New Brunswick, NJ: Rutgers* University Press.

Weitzer, Ronald. 2007. "The Social Construction of Sex Trafficking: Ideology and Institutionalization of a Moral Crusade." *Politics and Society* 35(3): 447–475.

Yeoh, Brenda S.A., Shirlena Huang, and Theodora Lam. 2005. "Transnationalizing the 'Asian' Family: Imaginaries, Intimacies and Strategic Intents." *Global Networks* 5(4): 307–315.

Yuval-Davis, Nira. 1999. "The 'Multi-Layered Citizen.'" *International Feminist Journal of Politics* 1(1): 119–136.

Zelizer, Viviana. 2005. *The Purchase of Intimacy*. Princeton, NJ: Princeton University Press.

Part V
Popular Culture

15

Sexuality and Popular Culture

Diane Grossman

Over the last 30 or so years, scholarly attention to the subject of sexuality has burgeoned. More than 50 academic journals now exist that focus on sexuality and related subjects like sexual aggression, impotence, and sex education; the *Journal of the History of Sexuality* (originally published in 1990), *Law and Sexuality* (originally published in 1991), the *Journal of Lesbian Studies* (originally published in 1996), and *Studies in Gender and Sexuality* (first published in 2000), are among those peer-reviewed journals whose central concern is sexuality. Where once the subject of sexuality, if addressed at all seriously, was reserved for the fields of biology and possibly psychology, more recently fields like history, sociology, education, law, philosophy, and literary theory have all taken up the subject. A Google search for "scholarly books on sexuality" yields 5,500,000 hits.

This growth in academic interest in sexuality parallels the dramatic growth of work in feminist theory, gay and lesbian studies, and queer theory, whose influence on our understanding of sex and sexuality cannot be overestimated. Though often treated as interchangeable, there are important differences among these perspectives, and those differences have led to an array of theoretically rich arguments and analyses.

But where scholarly work has only recently arrived at its fascination with sexuality, for the field of popular culture, sexuality has always been a mainstay, perhaps the "bread and butter" of popular culture. Whether it be romantic films, gothic novels, soap operas, Harlequin romances, country and western music, or television comedies, popular media have long found ways to present and exploit the powerful pull of sex and sexuality. This chapter explores the relationship between popular culture and sexuality, and the ways that depictions of sexuality have evolved. In addition, the chapter examines the ways that feminist theory, LGBT studies, and queer theory have enabled new readings of popular culture. To do so, a brief summary of how these theoretical perspectives shape the ways that we think about sexuality introduces the subject.

Introductory Theoretical Considerations

A brief summary article cannot adequately address the complex and contested terrains of feminist theory, LGBT theory, and queer theory. But this chapter examines four major theoretical interventions with significant implications for popular culture analysis: the distinction between sex and gender; the concept of gender as performative; the critique of the institution of heterosexuality and heteronormativity; and the de-essentializing of sexuality.

The distinction between sex and gender

Since Simone de Beauvoir (1952) declared that "one is not born a woman," feminist theory has challenged both essentialist understandings of gender and the conflation of sex with gender. Early analyses of the sex/gender distinction tended to consider "gender" the mutable category, and "sex" fixed and biological. Feminists and theorists of transsexuality like psychologist Robert Stoller found it useful to separate sex from gender, often for the purpose of explaining a mismatch between the two. Where theorists like Stoller aimed to explain inter sexuality and transsexuality, feminist theory and activism of the 1960s sought not only to challenge gender discrimination in legal, economic, and educational policy but also to critique the ways that gender socialization taught biological boys and girls how to be, respectively, "masculine" and "feminine."

Separating sex and gender allowed feminists like Gayle Rubin to posit a sex/gender system as "a set of arrangements by which the biological raw material of human sex and procreation is shaped by human, social intervention" (1975, p. 165). Now labeled "social constructionism," such views posited gender as a kind of ideological interpretation of sex, where sex is immutable but gender is fluid. Social constructionists saw gender not only as binary but also as hierarchical, where so-called masculine traits were always more valued than so-called feminine traits. Kate Millett, for example, views gender differences as culturally based, resulting from how boys and girls are treated; for her, gender is "the sum total of the parents', the peers', and the culture's notions of what is appropriate to each gender by way of temperament, character, interests, status, worth, gesture, and expression" (1971, p. 31). Borrowing from de Beauvoir, Monique Wittig adds a layer to that analysis, arguing, like de Beauvoir, that women are not a "natural group" (1993, p. 103) and that sex and gender are political categories; but, unlike de Beauvoir, for Wittig, the lesbian is "beyond the categories of sex" because "what makes a woman is a specific social relation to a man" (p. 108), namely heterosexuality. Catherine Mackinnon's (1989) analysis notes how *gender* and *sexuality* are imbricated; for her, gender theory becomes a theory of sexuality where being feminine means nothing other than being an object for men, being sexually submissive.

Yet these views all presume the fixed, biological nature of sex. In contrast, biologist Ann Fausto-Sterling offers a radical rethinking of how bodies, genitals,, and gender are related. In her essay, "Should there be only Two Sexes?" (2000a), she rethinks an earlier (1993) essay in which she defended five (rather than two) sexes. Her later view rejects assigning any particular number to the sexes; for

Fausto-Sterling, "our bodies are too complex to provide clear-cut answers about sexual difference" (2000b, p. 4). Likewise, philosopher Judith Butler has argued that feminists have been mistaken even in assuming that we can meaningfully theorize about *a* gender identity. Rather, gender, as feminists of color like bell hooks, Patricia Hill Collins, and others have argued, is raced. To assume a universal notion of gender is to ignore the ways that gender is inflected not only by race but also by other aspects of identity, including class, age, and so forth. For Butler, sexed bodies are not "factic" entities waiting patiently to be awakened by a gendered expression. For Butler, bodies are discursively constructed within social meanings. The "physical features" that seem to mark the body as both unified and sexual "gain social meaning and unification through their articulation within the category of sex" (1990, p. 114).

The concept of gender as performative

In a small but groundbreaking article, sociologist Erving Goffman described gender as a form of "expressive behavior" (1976, p. 71), and, despite his emphasis on the "optionality" of gender, he laid the groundwork for viewing gender as a kind of performance or, in his term, a "portrayal." As he puts it: "One might just as well say there is no gender identity. There is only a schedule for the portrayal of gender" (p. 76). Sociologists Candace West and Don H. Zimmerman later argued that gender is a kind of situated doing: "Doing gender involves a complex of socially guided perceptual, interactional, and micropolitical activities that cast particular pursuits as expressions of masculine and feminine 'natures'" (1987, p. 126). Our gendered acts have a personal as well as an institutional context, and they are intelligible when they follow gender norms, and unintelligible (and possibly punishable) when they do not:

> If we do gender appropriately, we simultaneously sustain, reproduce, and render legitimate the institutional arrangements that are based on sex category. If we fail to do gender appropriately, we as individuals – not the institutional arrangements – may be called to account [for our character, motives, and predispositions].
> (West and Zimmerman 1987, p. 146)

It was not uncommon for feminists implicitly or explicitly to consider gender "artificial," accomplished through, for example, clothing, make-up, and "feminine" manners (e.g. Bartky, 1982, 1988); Butler (1988), however, sees gender as *performative* (not simply performed), where our acts and not our "being" create the illusion of gender as stable and foundational. Though it is commonplace to think of gender as a way people *are*, for Butler, gender is a set of activities repetitively performed. Echoing Nietzsche, Butler insists that there is no stable "doer behind the deed" (1990, p, 142); rather, the deed constructs the doer. Through the acts that define gender, we mime an unrealizable ideal. Drag performance, perhaps, most obviously reveals the performative nature of gender, but every expression of gender is a kind of drag performance. The fact that gender must be performed repetitively and obsessively suggests to Butler the anxiety that underlies heterosexuality; it is, according to Butler, "tenuously constituted in time" (1988, p. 519). Butler has been mistakenly understood to be claiming that we can easily slip in and out of gender, but that is not the claim; as Butler notes in an interview 24 years after the publication of *Gender Trouble,* "I did not mean to argue that gender is fluid and changeable," or that it is a "fiction" (Williams 2014). Rather, for Butler, seeing gender as performative allows for multiple, nearly infinite, expressions of gender and for the deconstruction of gender, sex, *and* sexuality.

The critique of the institution of heterosexuality and heteronormativity

Radical lesbian feminist Adrienne Rich's (1980) essay "Compulsory Heterosexuality and Lesbian Existence" challenged not only the cultural presumption that women are "naturally" heterosexual but also the invisibility of lesbians in feminist theory and literature. Rich deploys the concept of a "lesbian continuum" to acknowledge "women-identified experience" to "embrace many more forms of primary intensity between and among women" (p. 27) that is neither clinical nor necessarily sexual. Rich's essay has come under fire for its essentializing of women and for its unabashed attacks on gay male sexuality, but her essay is a powerful indictment of psychoanalytic theory, traditional medicine, and cultural norms that see lesbians as defective women, man-haters, and/or sexually immature. For Rich, heterosexuality is neither natural nor universal, and she cites a number of mostly unacknowledged resistance strategies that women have adopted to challenge heterosexuality and its norms. If one sees heterosexuality as an institution, then what becomes immediately clear are the ways that cultures reward adherence to the norm, and punish offenders. A "cluster of forces" from "physical brutality to control of consciousness" (p. 20) join to discipline women, suggesting that a liberal emphasis on equality will not be enough to liberate women; likewise, mere tolerance of alternative "lifestyles" is inadequate to address the deep societal forces that limit women's sexual and emotional expression. Like Mackinnon (mentioned above in the section "The distinction between sex and gender"), Rich links women's subordination with "daily 'eroticization'" (p. 22), with an ideology that sees women as "expendable as long as the sexual and emotional needs of the male can be satisfied" (p. 23).

Rich's perspective offered an important corrective to mainstream, heterosexual feminism and paved the way for new historical, literary, and sociological research that aimed to foreground lesbian experience. Butler offers a more theoretically sophisticated analysis of heterosexuality, interrogating the notion that homosexuality is somehow derivative from, or a (poor) copy of heterosexuality. Rather, she hypothesizes, analogous to her argument about gender, that "heterosexuality ... presupposes homosexuality," because "if it were not for the notion of the homosexual *as* copy, there would be no construct of heterosexuality *as* origin" (Butler 1993, p. 313). Butler's antifoundationalist approach differs radically from Rich's; for Butler, sexuality operates at the level of signifying practices, and, as with gender, heterosexuality is phantasmatic – an impossible imitation of itself where its compulsion to repeat exposes "an incessant and *panicked* imitation of its own naturalized idealization" (1993, p. 314). Further, Butler sees the ways that gender and sexuality are imbricated; she asks "what happens to the subject and to the stability of gender categories when the epistemic regime of presumptive heterosexuality is unmasked as that which produces and reifies those ostensible categories of ontology?" (1990, p. viii).

The de-essentializing of sexuality

Michel Foucault's seminal work, *The History of Sexuality*, rejects the notion of sexuality as a "natural given" which is either repressed by or celebrated in cultural norms. Rather, for Foucault, sex "is the name that can be given to a historical construct: not a furtive reality that is difficult to grasp, but a great surface network" tied to a variety of strategies of knowledge and power (1990, pp. 105–106). Foucault maintains that there is no concept of sex "in itself": "Is 'sex' really the anchorage point that supports the manifestations of sexuality, or is it not rather a complex idea that was formed inside the deployment of sexuality?" (p. 52). *The History of Sexuality* points to the ways that sex and sexuality are put into discourse, even as hegemonic cultural norms seek to efface it discursively and punish it juridically. Laws prohibiting sodomy, the trial of Oscar Wilde, raids on so-called "Molly Houses," and the McCarthy hearings all functioned not only as warnings about sexually nonnormative behavior; they also served to name sexual identities and thereby help to create transgressive communities.

Libertarian feminist Gayle Rubin insists on the "urgent need to develop radical perspectives on sexuality" (1975), part of which includes the abandonment of what she terms "sexual essentialism,.... the idea that sex is a natural force that exists prior to social life." Like Foucault, who offers a "genealogy" of sexuality, Rubin maintains that "we never encounter the body unmediated by the meanings that cultures give to it." Unlike Foucault, however, Rubin's normative agenda is clear: both sex negativity – the view that sex is destructive and dangerous – and the Western "hierarchical system of sexual value" (privileging heterosexual, monogamous, "vanilla" sex) ought to be replaced with the repeal of all sexually repressive laws and an ethically neutral approach to sexual differences. Rubin links her radical critique to feminist critiques of gender and "gender hierarchy," but seeks an "autonomous theory and politics specific to sexuality." Though the "sex negativity" of some second-wave radical feminist theory has no doubt been exaggerated, there is no question that Rubin's completely libertarian approach to sexuality and sexual practices aligns her less with traditional feminism and more with queer theory.

Eve Sedgwick, often referred to as the "mother of queer theory," refuses to enter the nature/nurture debate about sexuality, and instead prefers the language of "minoritizing" and "universalizing" approaches to nonnormative sexualities. Like Rubin, Sedgwick wants to emphasize as well as destigmatize the wide variety of practices that people may or may not find erotic. For Sedgwick, the truism "people are different from each other" is analytically richer than one might assume at first glance. And she notes, "It is astonishing how few respectable conceptual tools we have for dealing with this self-evident fact" (1990, p. 22). Seeing ourselves and each other in this new light allows for a move away from a rigid gay or straight identity to a "more active potential pluralism on the heavily contested maps of sexual definition" (p. 26). Such a move effectively destabilizes binary (or even trinary, if one includes bisexuality) understandings of sexuality and opens up a space to "queer" sex.

Sexuality and Popular Culture

Popular culture might be simply defined as the "vernacular, everyday culture of the people, as opposed to the narrow elitist culture which artificially constitutes some ten percent of a national's lifestyle" (Browne 1988, p. i). More neutrally, "popular culture refers to the beliefs and practices, and the objects through which they are organized, that are widely shared among a population" (Mukerji and Schudson 1991, p. 3). Popular culture – unlike folk culture, for example – is a product of twentieth-century technologies that have allowed the easy proliferation and reproduction of a variety of cultural products – film, television, radio, books, and music, for example. In the late twentieth and early twenty-first centuries, new digital technologies rendered popular culture far more diverse, more individualized, and more ephemeral; the omnipresence of personalized blogs, individual and group Facebook accounts, tweets, Instagram, and Pinterest means that popular culture is not only personal, mass, *and* global but also decentralized. Though some laud popular culture as a site that nurtures democratic, progressive values, others condemn what is seen as popular culture's inherent predictability, conservatism, and aesthetic worthlessness. Regardless of one's normative stance, however, no one doubts the power and influence of the products of popular culture, particularly their impact on identity construction. Philosopher and cultural studies theorist Douglas Kellner even notes that "media images and celebrities" are so powerful that they have replaced "families, schools, and churches as arbiters of taste, value, and thought" (1995, p. 17).

As mentioned, sex has never been absent from popular culture. In 1896, *The Kiss* was screened, featuring a four-second sequence of a kiss. The act drew near-riots in the theater that had to be quelled by the police, but soon such images became familiar to audiences, and "filmmakers were also discovering… that sex was a sure-fire sell" (Bronski 1984, p. 94). Even early radio programming leveraged the power of sex with serials about, for example, cynical private detectives and the femme fatales who tempted them to stray. Radio's auditory nature might have required sexy on-air voices and dramatic music in place of visual images, but audiences didn't miss the allusions to sex and sexuality. Popular films, even of the silent era, unabashedly exploited sex and sexuality; *The Sheik* (1921) made Rudolph Valentino an international sex symbol, and the plot of *Sunrise* (1927) concerned a husband so torn between his country wife and an alluring woman from the city that he even plans his wife's murder. In *Morocco* (1930), Marlene Dietrich is a cabaret singer who famously sang dressed in a man's tailcoat and kisses another woman at the song's end. Advertisers knew even nearly 100 years ago how to promote the sexual content of films; for example, *BoxOffice Magazine* of 1936 suggested the following ad for the film *Camille*: "Her love was like a great flame burning … scorching … withering…and when the flame died she no longer cared to live." It was not unusual for films in the 1920s and early 1930s to include references to homosexuality, miscegenation, drug and alcohol use, abortion, and infidelity. *Queen Christina* (1933), for example, did not shy from portraying the bisexuality widely acknowledged of the historical queen. In a famous scene from the musical *Wonder Bar* (1934), a man cuts in on a dancing heterosexual couple only to end up dancing with the other man.

That early sexual openness was soon to end, however, with the 1930 passage of the Hays Code. Strictly enforced as of 1934, the Hays Code forbade any expression of sexuality ("sex perversion or any inference thereof"), including even partial or suggested (as in a silhouette) nudity. No kiss was allowed to last for more than three seconds, though creative directors like Alfred Hitchcock circumvented the rule in films like *Notorious* where he broke up a two-and-a-half-minute kissing scene every three seconds in order to adhere to the code. Vito Russo (1987) uncovered material in the production history of the classic film *Singin' in the Rain* that revealed that censors cut out lines that suggested a homosocial erotic connection between two men. The Code mandated that depictions of criminal acts had to include punishment for those acts, profanity was banned, any "necessary" violence had to be off-screen, and traditional values had to emerge victorious at film's end. Film critic Andrew Sarris (1998) points out that the Hays Code had near-disastrous plot implications for women in film: they could not leave their husbands, find fulfillment in work outside the home, or demonstrate "passionate" feelings, even *within* marriage. Sarris also conjectures that the "screwball comedy" emerged as a means to deal with sexual frustration, a "sex comedy without the sex." A Foucauldian perspective on the Hays Code era would, however, point to the many ways that the panic over sexual content and the ongoing need for rulings on contested content resulted in the proliferation of "discourse" about sex – what could and could not be done, what topics were permissible and which were not, and which values win the day.

Starting in the 1950s and gaining headway in the 1960s, a number of factors coalesced to undermine the power of the Hays Code: competition from television and foreign films; significant Supreme Court decisions like *Joseph Burstyn, Inc. v. Wilson* (1952), which held that movies were entitled to first amendment protections; changing social mores regarding sex and sexuality, resulting at least in part from the women's movement and radical student activism; and the increasing popularity, despite the absence of a Production Code Seal, of films featuring controversial topics, including drug use, adultery, and prostitution. Sexually suggestive language and conduct were increasingly permitted for one reason or another, and by 1966 the Code was abandoned. The legacy of that Code, however, endures in movie ratings like PG-13 and R. For Rubin and other sexual libertarians, the conflation of sex and violence implicit in those codes makes clear that dominant social norms continue to problematize sex and to demonize marginal sexual identities and practices.

As sexual content and imagery became more explicit in popular media, second-wave feminism in both its popular and academic versions launched attacks on the hypersexualizing of women's images, particularly in relation to television, film, magazines like *Playboy*, and advertising. Such criticism focused on the objectification of women, on the absence of depictions of women with agency, and the emphasis on women's appearance. For traditional second-wave theory, including radical feminism, liberal feminism, and Marxist-feminism, femininity itself, including beauty norms, was deeply complicit with patriarchy and gender inequality. In addition, the period's psychoanalyticallyoriented perspectives on gender and popular culture constructed femininity as passivity and submission. As Jackie Stacey points out, psychoanalytically and poststructurallyinclined feminists have indicted television and film for "its passive positioning of the woman as sexual spectacle, as there 'to be looked at,' and at the active positioning of the male protagonist as bearer of the look"

(2000, p. 109). Such critical perspectives share four key premises: that women can be treated as a homogeneous group with shared interests and shared experiences under capitalism/patriarchy; that the male gaze is universal, active, and monolithic; that popular culture itself is static, top-down, and univocal; and that "the spectator is … an already fully constituted subject and is fixed by the text to a predetermined gender identification" (Stacey 2000, p. 111).

But a large body of scholarship in the 1980s and 1990s challenged those premises; in particular, critics charged psychoanalytic theories of gender as sexual difference with essentialism and overdetermination. As such challenges emerged, feminists began to question whether the gaze is inherently male and whether gender is as overdetermined as many had argued. Teresa de Lauretis (1987, 1991), for example, challenged feminist analyses of gender as sexual difference. Doing so, she argues, not only positions men in opposition to women; it also undermines the "radical epistemological potential of feminist thought" to posit a "subject … not unified but rather multiple, and not so much divided as contradicted" (1987, p. 2). Gender, then, becomes an effect produced *in* bodies, but is not any sort of property *of* bodies. De Lauretis thinks of gender "as the product of various social technologies, such as cinema, and of institutionalized discourses, epistemologies, and critical practices, as well as practices of daily life" (1987, p. 2). Stacey urges feminist critics to consider the ways that subjectivity is more fluid than earlier theory had implied; what would feminist popular culture criticism look like if we were to assume that "object choice" and "identification" are "shifting, contradictory or precarious" (Stacey 2000, p. 111)?

Further, in contrast to earlier theorizing that assumed audiences to be monolithic and homogeneous, theorists, influenced by poststructuralist and queer theory, saw audiences as "fragmented, polymorphous, contradictory, and 'nomadic'" (Doty 1993, p. 1). With such a view as a given, feminists of color and lesbian critics questioned what bell hooks describes as the "totalizing agenda" (1992, p. 124) of white feminism and of feminist film criticism in particular. Like de Lauretis, theorists of color such as hooks, Jacqueline Bobo (1995), and Jane Gaines (1986) challenge feminist cultural criticism's emphasis on gender as *sexual* difference, but they add that doing so confines feminist theory to a single-lensed focus that ultimately erases differences of race, class, and sexuality. For theorists of color, women of color have always been "oppositional" readers of popular culture; they have rejected both the phallocentric gaze *and* the alleged passivity of the white female spectator to offer readings "against the grain" (hooks 2000, p. 126). Black women in particular, as spectators, "have had to develop looking relations within a cinematic context that constructs our presence as absence" (hooks 2000, p. 126). Gaines, for example, argues that the focus on sexual difference has meant that such theory is "unequipped to deal with a film which is about race difference and sexuality" (1986, p. 12). Such critical approaches maintain that gender cannot be teased apart from other aspects of identity, including race, sexuality, and social class, and that women's lived experiences cannot be analyzed from a gendered perspective alone. Stacey notes the ways that feminist film criticism has failed to consider the pleasure (and agency) of female viewers; as she puts it, "the specifically homosexual pleasures of female spectatorship have been ignored completely" (Stacey 2000, p. 109). For such theorists, *gender itself* is transformed through its imbrication with other aspects of identity.

Communications theorist George Gerbner shifted his cultural criticism from film to television. For Gerbner (Gerbner and Gross 1976), television is far more powerful than any other aspect of U.S. society:

> We begin with the assertion that television is the central cultural arm of American society. It is an agency of the established order and as such serves primarily to extend and maintain rather than to alter, threaten, or weaken conventional conceptions, beliefs, and behaviors. Its chief cultural function is to spread and stabilize social patterns, to cultivate not change but resistance to change. Television is a medium of the socialization of most people into standardized roles and behaviors. Its function is, in a word, enculturation.
>
> (p. 175)

Gerbner coined the term "symbolic annihilation" to capture the myriad ways that women (and other members of marginalized groups, including gays and lesbians) are either missing in popular culture or portrayed in highly negative and/or stereotypical ways. Sociologist Gaye Tuchman (1978) takes Gerbner's notion of "symbolic annihilation" and divides it into three strategies: omission, trivialization, and condemnation. Analyses like those of Gerbner and Tuchman lead naturally to a focus on content analysis of films, television programs, and advertising. For example, in 1970, Jan Sinott reviewed 34 hours of Saturday morning cartoons for the journal *Off Our Backs*. She created a scale of 1 through 5 for the "chauvinism" of the programming, where a "1" meant a "liberated female character." Sinott found no 1s and only one 2, and the majority of the shows earned 4s or 5s (Blakemore 2015). Such second-wave projects continue in more popular tools like the Bechdel Test, which first appeared in Alison Bechdel's comic strip "Dykes to Watch Out For" (1985), as a "rule" articulated by one of the characters who boycotts any film that doesn't have at least two female characters[1] who talk to each other about something other than a man. Likewise, the Geena David Institute on Gender in Media, begun in 2004, tracks female characters in popular media to draw attention to gender disparities and gender stereotyping (https://seejane.org/).

The Geena Davis Institute's focus is on girls under 11 years of age, and popular and scholarly considerations of sex and sexuality in mass media have often focused on explicit sexual content and its impact on younger viewers. Typically, these studies use quantitative analyses to look at correlations between, for example, teenagers with high rates of television viewing and/or social media activity and their rates of sexual intercourse, use of contraception, and pregnancy rates. Pediatrician Dr. Victor C. Strasburger (2012), for example, notes that the US has the highest rates of teenage pregnancy as well as high rates of social media use. Using studies previously conducted, he notes the pervasive nature of sexual messaging (he calls them "scripts") in popular media: 37% of the most popular songs included sexual references, including some that were misogynistic (p. 20); reality television shows (like *Temptation Island*), which now number more than 30, often have explicit sexual content (p. 20); mainstream advertising typically uses sexual messaging to sell products (p. 21); and, as revealed by a 2005 study, 75% of all prime time television content includes sexual content (p. 18). Though such analyses often advocate sex education and more accessible contraception, the proliferation of sexual imagery and content cannot be assumed to represent a move away from heterosexist norms.

Queer Theory

There is not sufficient space here to analyze either the myriad understandings of 'queer' and queer theory or to consider its contested status within the Academy. But there seems to be general agreement that queer theory is a "body of work which does not represent a specific kind of thing as much as it does a number of interdisciplinary texts which emphasize the constructedness of sexuality" (Beemyn and Eliason, 1996). One of the first mentions of the term "queer" occurred in Teresa de Lauretis's 1991 essay in the journal *differences*. There she sets up a series of oppositional frames, where queer is both "interactive and resistant," "participatory and yet distinct," "claiming at once equality and difference," and "demanding political representation while insisting on its material and historical specificity" (p. iii). For both Butler and Sue Ellen Case (1991), queer allows us to move theoretically beyond binaries, including gender binaries. Beemyn and Eliason, while acknowledging many of the shortcomings of queer theory, also note that it "allows us to view the world from perspectives other than those which are generally validated by the dominant society" (1996, p. 165) and that it "leaves room for all people who are attracted to others of the same sex or whose bodies or sexual desires do not fit dominant standards of gender and/or sexuality" (p. 5). Whereas lesbian, gay, and bisexual (LGB) studies has traditionally operated to document and theorize past and current manifestations of nonnormative sexualities, a queer theoretical approach, as mentioned above in the discussions of Sedgwick and Butler in particular, argues the ways that the normative is conceptually *dependent* on the non-normative. Though critics worry that "queer" may efface real differences of class, race, gender, and even sex, defenders maintain that queer theory allows everyone to "articulate their own queerness" (Daumer 1992, p. 100). Unlike liberal theory which tends to see gay sexuality as a "lifestyle" choice or preference, a queer sensibility is more radical, unapologetic, and antiassimilationist.

Queer theory, like poststructuralist theory, rejects both the idea of audiences as monolithic and passive and the notion that seeing is a neutral activity. Relying on reception theory, queer theory acknowledges the variety of ways that "readers" (used here globally to refer to any viewer of popular media) can interpret a text. Reading is always a site of struggle, but it is also potentially liberating "because it allows the possibility that meanings can be changed and challenged" (Thomas 2001, p. 8). For these reasons, Gerbner and Tuchman's notion of "symbolic annihilation" might be overly simplistic for queer readers. For example, the 1980 film *Cruising* was seen by many as explicitly homophobic, and some LGBT groups picketed the film. But, as Kellner points out, *Cruising* also "shows the sexual ambivalence of the male cop ... and, indirectly, the excitement of the gay scene in some of the cinematic representations" (1995, p. 113).

Queer Readings and Popular Culture

Though modern Western societies are now far more accepting of nonnormative sexualities, for years (if not centuries) LGBT peoples had to hide their identities and lived in fear of being physically and/or psychologically terrorized. Given that the world of film is a world of unreality, LGBT people could find, in the words of film critic Michael Bronski, "an alternative world that offers solace and understanding": "for many gay men, the movies became a place to experience strong feelings and sexuality with others in a socially acceptable environment," a place where "the imagination could flourish" (1984, p. 93). With this context in mind, it is not surprising that the film *The Wizard of Oz* would be a gay classic – the film itself sets up two worlds, one literally gray and real, the other colorful, fantastic, and "over the rainbow."[2]

Cultural studies theorist Alexander Doty (1993) identifies three ways that "queerness" develops in mass culture: through queer influences in production (e.g. authors, directors, actors, etc.); through the ways "self-identified gays, lesbians, bisexuals … and queers" (p. xi) read texts; and queer "reception positions" that "stand outside the relatively clear-cut and essentializing categories of sexual identity" (p. 15) and "result in the recognition and articulation of the complex ranges of queerness that has been in popular texts and their audiences all along" (p. 16). Noticeably absent in this list, as Doty acknowledges, is the text itself; but, Doty, like other recent cultural theorists, rejects the idea that there is some "real" meaning waiting to be discovered in a text. Though popular media increasingly incorporate queer content and characters, Doty is more interested in outing what he calls "ghosts" – the queer connotations of a "shadowy realm" (p. xi) that for so long allowed LGBT people to identify with even the most putatively mainstream popular texts like buddy films (*Thelma and Louise*, *Lethal Weapon*, etc.), the homoerotics of a film like *Top Gun*, television programs (*Cagney and Lacey*, *Laverne and Shirley*), and "straight gay men" like Jack Benny and Gene Kelly. In fact, Doty points out in a footnote that denotatively queer or gay texts like *Silence of the Lambs*, *Cruising*, or *Boys in the Band* might not be queer texts at all because they "oppress the queer" (1993, p. 105).

Many queer cultural theorists like Doty, Michael Warner, Eve Sedgwick, and Michael Bronski argue that homophobia and heteronormativity limit viewers' ability to "see" how pervasive queer influences are in mass culture, and how the pleasures even heterosexual viewers derive from texts may be described as queer. Communications theorist Marye C. Tharp (1991) coined the term "gay vague" to refer to advertisements that could be "read" as queer by a LGBT audience but whose gay subtext would likely be missed by majority group members. As Janice Radway has argued about romance novels, there is nothing in the text itself that forces readers to interpret that text based on the author's intention; viewers, in her words, are "actively productive readers" (1984, p. 52), not passive receivers of media. And texts themselves are "multivocal or riddled with contradictions" (Mukerji and Schudson 1991, p. 47). And if there is no "essential" or true meaning lying in wait in a text, then a queer reading isn't a "willful misreading" or an oppositional reading (Doty 1993, p. 16). In another essay, Doty and co-author Corey Creekmur describe such readings as "negotiated" (1995, p. 1), and Stuart Hall suggests the notion of a "preferred reading" which always permits oppositional or alternative reading (2010, p. 483). Likewise, media studies scholar Maria Pramaggiore notes that, for bisexual viewers, "bisexual reading practices may be invited by recent mainstream films that depict fluid eroticisms and nonheterosexual desire" (2004, p. 485).

There have always been depictions of nonnormative sexualities in popular culture, but their earliest iterations were often intended as cautionary, as a contrast to the "real" or as stereotypical foils for the other characters. For example, in *Rebel without a Cause* (1955), the homosexual subtext is clear: Sal Mineo keeps a picture of Alan Ladd in his school locker; and there is no question that the film challenges patriarchal norms of masculinity. But, by the end of the film, the main character has found heterosexual love and the closeted friend has been shot and killed. A later film, *The Killing of Sister George* (1968), offered viewers one of the first films explicitly about lesbians, but the main character, an aging soap opera star, losers her lover, has a nervous breakdown, assaults two nuns, and ends up being written off the show. In the mid-1960s, however, "homosexuality" came to be recognized as "an important social problem" (Capsuto 2000, p. 46), at first with television talk shows and soon after as more television programming featured gay-themed topics. But, even with these more explicit themes, the shows tended to do without "openly gay characters" (Capsuto 2000, p. 47).

On the other hand, a number of mainstream films of the 1960s and 1970s included gay men and lesbians, including *Boys in the Band*, *Dog Day Afternoon*, and *Midnight Cowboy*. In the 1980s, the AIDS epidemic led to a number of major films (e.g. *Philadelphia*, *It's My Party*, etc.) and made-for-television dramas (e.g. *Early Frost*, 1985) featuring gay, though virtually completely asexual, characters. Hollywood experimented in the 1980s with lesbian love stories: *Personal Best* (1982), *Lianna* (1983), and *Desert Hearts* (1986) were all box office successes, though critics complained that only femme lesbians were portrayed and that the lesbians were all cisgender.

On television, MTV was one of the first cable stations to embrace gay and queer identities, featuring drag queens like Ru Paul and Public Service Announcements like the "Free Your Mind" campaign. MTV's debut of its *Real World* series featured a bisexual male artist. And, in 1994, Pedro Zamora became the first *Real World* character (*Real World: San Francisco*) whose story line included his being gay, his dating life, and his HIV-positive status. Much was made of the "lesbian kiss" on the *Roseanne* show in 1994; three years earlier, *L.A. Law* had aired an episode where a bisexual character kisses another woman.[3] MTV videos likewise pushed sexual boundaries, and videos like Madonna's *Like a Virgin* and *This is not a Love Story* mocked heterosexual anxiety and played with sexual boundaries. Androgynous performers like Michael Jackson and Boy George similarly challenged norms for masculinity, and the coming out of stars like Elton John and Boy George in the 1980s signaled a new kind of openness to gays and lesbians. In the 1990s, *Xena the Warrior Princess* (1995–2001) excited lesbian and bisexual fans with the homoerotic undertones between Xena and her "traveling companion" Gabrielle; off screen, star Lucy Lawless did not hesitate to acknowledge the chemistry between the two characters.[4]

Toto, We're Not in Kansas Anymore

Recalling Doty's 1993 reading of the "ghosts" of queerness in popular film and television cannot help but strike one as a nostalgic and unnecessary reading strategy in the twenty-first century. LGBT themes and characters have proliferated far beyond what theorists imagined less than 30 years ago, in part no doubt a result of the radically changed legal landscape: *Lawrence v. Texas* (2003) ruled that laws criminalizing sodomy were unconstitutional; the Clinton-era military policy of "Don't Ask, Don't Tell" was struck down; and same-sex marriage became legal in *Obergefell v. Hodges* (2015). A 2008 Brookings Institute paper credited *The Real World* with shifting attitudes toward "Don't Ask, Don't Tell" (Singer 2008). Whether popular media leads the way in changing social norms or whether media react to those changing social norms is indeterminate; but there is no doubt that the more sympathetic treatment of LGBT people on mainstream hit shows like *The Real World*, *Will and Grace*, and Bravo's *Queer Eye for the Straight Guy*, helped to normalize marginal sexualities. Popular culture has seemed to move, almost at lightning speed, well beyond Tuchman's triad of omission, trivialization, and condemnation. It is unusual for any film or television series not to feature at least one LGBT person, and many shows (e.g. *Modern Family, Orange is the New Black*) have LGBT characters central to the ongoing narrative. Though it is impossible to identify all of these examples, an overview of some of the more significant ones follows.

In 2004, the Showtime soap opera *Queer as Folk* was one of the most popular television shows for that network. On the popular show, *Glee*, Curt's coming out experience is woven into the narrative of high school life. The HBO show *Six Feet Under* featured a central character who, though he struggles to come out to his family in the first season, is unabashedly gay and eventually in a long-term relationship. The characters in the popular Netflix hit *Orange is the New Black* include lesbians, bisexuals, and a trans character played by Laverne Cox; several of the show's actors have come out, and Taylor Schilling, who plays the lead role, has admitted that she's had relationships with both men and women. Reality television, in particular, because it is so inexpensive to produce, has offered dating shows like *Next*, *Queer Eye for the Straight Guy*, and soaps like *Undressed* that include LGBT characters. *Saturday Night Live* teased viewers with the androgynous character Pat, the "Ambiguously Gay Duo" (which appeared in 12 episodes), and sketches like Cheri Oteri's 1990s "Mickey the Dyke" and Aidy Bryant and Kate McKinnon's "Fats and Dyke."[5]

Suzanna Walters juxtaposes two defining moments in the "new [gay] visibility" (2001, p. xvi): the coming out of Ellen DeGeneres in 1997, and the 1998 murder of Matthew Shepard. Ellen DeGeneres's enormous popularity is a testament to the broader culture's willingness to accept (tolerate?) lesbianism, but many critics accuse her of "selling out to the feel-good milieu of middlebrow daytime television" (Miejewsky 2014, p. 192). The *Ellen* show is replete with product placements as Ellen surprises her viewers and her audience with often-lavish gifts. Others criticize the ways that popular media depictions of LGBT people have been depoliticized and policed; rarely does one see butch lesbians, for example, and LGBT people of color are rare in popular culture. If not invisible, then people of color are often stereotyped; for example, Madonna's video *Bye Bye Baby* (1993) features six dancers, three of whom are women dressed in men's tuxedos, with the remaining three "femmes" scantily clad in bustiers; the "femmes" are all Asian women, reinscribing the stereotype of Asian women as passive and docile.

Other critics argue that "MTV and its viewers are more concerned with the styling of identities" rather than with how those identities operate in daily life. As a result, these sorts of programming "will work as a closeted space in which queer style is divested of its queer politics" (Goldstein 1996, p. 276). Rosemary Hennessy notes that popular culture production "goes where the money is," and that 'gay' is becoming a warmer if not a hot commodity" (2004, p. 742). Cohan maintains that *Queer Eye*'s gay male cast are effectively desexualized in their mission to save heterosexual masculinity and to sell commodities; indeed, episodes of *Queer Eye* "encouraged more males to go shopping with a buddy the day afterward than at any other time during the week" (2007, p. 178). On the other hand, a reboot of *Queer Eye* (which started in 2017) seems to promise a more diverse cast and the show's first female and trans makeover; one sympathetic critic (Jones 2018) notes that *Queer Eye* has "struck a chord" with its charm and "overriding tone of kindness and acceptance."

The explosion in queer representations in popular culture may lead one to infer that earlier scholarly strategies of "reading against the grain" or finding alternative readings to mainstream texts have been abandoned. But such is not the case, and the wide availability of vintage film and television programs made possible by channels specializing in these genres and by digitizing technology have allowed scholars to return to and reconsider earlier popular culture texts. McGill (2018), for example, analyzes the queer sensibility of the villains in Disney animated films like *Aladdin*, *The Little Mermaid*, and *Beauty and the Beast*. McDonald reconsiders the MTV hit show *Daria* and the ways that its eponymous "misanthropic teenager" (2018, p. 52) calls out to misfits – queers – of all types. *Buffy the Vampire Slayer* continues to invite queer readings.

Given today's far more open political and cultural climate, it's hard to imagine a time when popular movie stars like Rock Hudson were forced by studios to marry women in order to quell any gossip about their sexuality; it's perhaps even harder to imagine a time when mainstream audiences did not immediately recognize the queerness of the "flamboyant" Liberace. Hudson only came out in 1985, when he was dying of AIDS, and Liberace, a devout Catholic and political conservative, denied that he was gay even in the face of palimony suits and up to the day he died of AIDS in 1987. Where once "playing gay" might have been career suicide, mainstream stars Tom Hanks, Robin Williams, Will Smith, Hillary Swank, Charlize Theron, Jared Leto, Heath Ledger, and Sean Penn, among others, have all played gay, bisexual, or trans characters in successful films. Likewise, openly gay actors like David Hyde Pierce, Jim Parsons, and Neil Patrick Harris have all starred in major television programs (*Frasier*, *The Big Bang Theory*, and *How I Met Your Mother*, respectively) and played heterosexuals. A small sample of popular culture figures who have come out include comedian Rosie O'Donnell who came out in 2002, Neil Patrick Harris in 2006, CNN anchor Anderson Cooper in 2012, singer Ricky Martin in 2010, *Good Morning America* co-anchor Robin Roberts in 2013, Jim Parsons in 2012, and comedian Wanda Sykes in 2008.

While a return to the earlier days of the closet seems unlikely, troubling signs appear on the cultural and political horizon and must be acknowledged. A conservative presidency and a more conservative Supreme Court have, according to GLAAD (originally an acronym for Gay & Lesbian Alliance Against Defamation) President Sarah Kate Ellis, represented a "permission slip for discrimination" (Miller 2018). Title IX protections have been lifted for trans students, and President Trump has rescinded the order to allow trans people to serve in the military. Surveys report increases in violence against LGBT people. A 2017 GLAAD report shows that 79%

of non-LGBT Americans support equal rights for the LGBT community, but only 49% stated that they were "very" or "somewhat" comfortable around LGBT people, down from 53% in 2016. Whether this trend will continue and what might be its repercussions cannot be predicted at this time.

If we return to Eve Sedgwick's distinction between "minoritizing" and "universalizing" discourse, then it would seem that the proliferation of popular cultural representations of LGBT people have allowed for a broader, more diverse vision of the LGBT community. LGBT people have been integrated ("universalizing") into films, television programming, and advertising with little fanfare; in other cases, popular culture programming features LGBT people ("minoritizing") as a unique and marginal social group. Though there is no doubt that it is still unusual to find gender-nonconforming (e.g. butch lesbians) LGBT people, that portrayals of the queer community are still not as diverse as they could be[6], and that the political nature of queer activism is typically invisible, today's "readers" of popular culture, particularly in the Western industrialized world, are exposed to a dizzying array of images of the queer community. And, despite conservatizing moves from the religious right, it does seem that that progress is inexorable.

Notes

1 At times, the test adds that the female characters must be *named*.
2 It is also often the case that the queer sources of popular culture are effaced by mainstream norms. For example, the phenomenon of disco originated in black gay clubs, but its popularity is usually attributed to films like *Saturday Night Fever*.
3 Later, the show's writers would admit that the kiss was a ploy to get ratings and that they had never intended to develop a story line around the two women (Kennedy 1997).
4 Rumor has it that there may be a reboot of the series, with the lesbian subtext explicit.
5 On the other hand, many critics argue that *Saturday Night Live* has had only two out LGBT cast members in its more than 40-year history.
6 Racial diversity is obviously one issue. But, in addition, class is typically effaced, as lesbians and gay men seem to be portrayed mostly as comfortable members of the middle- or upper-class.

References

Bartky, Sandra Lee. 1982. "Narcissism, Femininity and Alienation." *Social Theory and Practice* 8(2): 127–143.
Bartky, Sandra Lee. 1988. "Foucault, Femininity, and the Modernization of Patriarchal Power." In *Feminism and Foucault: Reflections on Resistance*, edited by Irene Diamond and Lee Quimby. 61–86. Boston, MA: Northeastern University Press.
Beeman, Brett and Mickey Eliason, eds. 1996. *Queer Studies: A Lesbian, Gay, Bisexual, and Transgender Anthology*. New York, NY: New York University Press.
Blakemore, Erin. 2015. "How Second-Wave Feminists Saw Saturday Morning Cartoons." *JStor Daily*, July 8. Available at: https://daily.jstor.org/second-wave-feminists-saw-saturday-morning-cartoons/.
Bobo, Jaqueline. 1995. *Black Women as Cultural Readers*. New York, NY: Columbia University Press.

Bronski, Michael. 1984. *Culture Clash: The Making of Gay Sensibility*. Boston, MA: South End Press.

Browne, Ray B. 1988. "Preface.". In *Symbiosis: Popular Culture and Other Fields*, edited by Ray B. Browne and Marshall W. Fishwick, i–vii. Bowling Green, OH: Bowling Green University Press.

Butler, Judith. 1988. "Performative Acts and Gender Constitution: An Essay in Phenomenology and Feminist Theory." *Theatre Journal* 40(4): 519–531.

Butler, Judith. 1990. *Gender Trouble: Feminism and the Subversion of Identity*. New York, NY: Routledge.

Butler, Judith. 1993. "Imitation and Gender Insubordination." In *The Lesbian and Gay Studies Reader*, edited by Henry Abelove, Michele Aina Barale, and David M. Halperin, 307–320. New York, NY: Routledge.

Case, Sue Ellen. 1991. "Tracking the Vampire." *differences: A Journal of Feminist Cultural Studies* 3(2): 1–20.

Capsuto, Steven. 2000. *Alternate Channels: The Uncensored Story of Gay and Lesbian Images on Radio and Television, 1930s to the Present*. New York, NY: Ballantine Books.

Cohan, Steven. 2007. "Queer Eye for the Straight Guise: Camp, Postfeminism, and the Fab Five's Makeovers of Masculinity." In *Interrogating Postfeminism: Gender and the Politics of Popular Culture*, edited by Yvonne Tasker and Diane Negra, 153–175. Durham: Duke University Press.

Creekmur, Corey K. and Alexander Doty. 1995. "Introduction." In *Out in Culture*, edited by Corey K. Creekmur and Alexander Doty, 1–11. Durham, NC: Duke University Press.

Daumer, Elisabeth. 1992. "Queer Ethics, or the Challenge of Bisexuality to Lesbian Ethics." *Hypatia* 7: 91–105.

de Beauvoir, Simone. 1952. *The Second Sex*, translated by H.M. Parshley. New York, NY: Vintage Books.

De Lauretis, Teresa. 1987. *Technologies of Gender: Essays on Theory, Film, and Fiction*. Bloomington, IN: Indiana University Press.

De Lauretis, Teresa. 1991. "Queer Theory: Lesbian and Gay Sexualities: An Introduction." *differences: A Journal of Feminist Cultural Studies* 3(2): iii–xviii.

Doty, Alexander. 1993. *Making Things Perfectly Queer*. Minneapolis: University of Minnesota Press.

Fausto-Sterling, Anne. 2000a. "Should there be only Two Sexes?" In *Sexing the Body: Gender Politics and the Construction of Sexuality*, 78–114. New York, NY: Basic Books.

Fausto-Sterling, Anne. 2000b. *Sexing the Body: Gender Politics and the Construction of Sexuality*. New York, NY: Basic Books.

Foucault, Michel. 1990. *The History of Sexuality*, translated by Robert Hurley. New York, NY: Vintage Books.

Gaines, Jane. 1986. "White Privilege and Looking Relations: Race and Gender in Feminist Film Theory." *Screen* 29(4): 12–27.

Gerbner, George and Larry Gross. 1976. "Living with Television: The Violence Project." *Journal of Communication* 26(2): 172–199. Available at: http://web.asc.upenn.edu/gerbner/Asset.aspx?assetID=276

Goffman, Erving. 1976. "Gender Display." *Studies in the Anthropology of Visual Communication* 3(2): 69–77.

Goldstein, Lynda. 1996. "Revamping MTV: Passing for Queer Culture in the Video Closet." In, *Queer Studies: A Lesbian, Gay, Bisexual, and Trangender Anthology*, edited by Brett Beeman and Mickey Eliason, 262–279. New York, NY: New York University Press.

Hall, Stuart. 2010. "Encoding, Decoding." In *The Cultural Studies Reader, edited by Simon During*, 3rd edn, 477–487. New York, NY: Routledge.

Hennessy, Rosemary. 2004. "Queer Visibility in Commodity Culture." In Queer Cultures, edited by *Deborah Carlin and Jennifer DiGrazia*, 720–757. Upper Saddle River, NJ: Pearson.

hooks, bell. 1992. *Black Looks: Race and Representation*. Boston, MA: South End Press.

hooks, bell. 2000. "The Oppositional Gaze: Black Female Spectators." In *Reading Images*, edited by Julia Thomas, 123–137. New York, NY: Palgrave.

Jones, Henrietta. 2018. "Why America ceeds Queer Eye season 2." *Metro*, June 13. Available at: https://www.metro.us/entertainment/tv/why-america-needs-queer-eye-season-2.

Kellner, Douglas. 1995. *Media Culture: Cultural Studies, Identity and Politics between the Modern and the Postmodern*. London: Routledge.

Kennedy, Roseanne. 1997. "The Gorgeous Lesbian in *L.A. Law*: The Present Absence?" In Feminist Television *Criticism: A Reader, edited by Charlotte Brunsdon, Julie D'Acci, and Lynn Spigel*, 318–324. New York, NY: Oxford University Press.

MacKinnon, Catherine. 1989. *Toward a Feminist Theory of State*. Cambridge, MA: Harvard University Press.

McDonald, R.A. 2018. "'You're Standing on My Neck': Feminist Cynicism and Queer Antisociality in MTV's *Daria*." *Queer Studies in Media & Popular Culture* 3(1): 51–65.

McGill, Craig M. 2018. "'This Burning Desire is Turning Me to Sin': The Intrapersonal Sexual Struggles of Two Disney Singing Villains." *Queer Studies in Media & Popular Culture* 3(1): 27–49.

Miller, Sarah. 2018. "Tolerance Takes a Hit: Americans Less Accepting of LGBT people in 2017, Survey Shows." *USA Today*, January 25. Available at: https://www.usatoday.com/story/news/nation/2018/01/25/tolerance-takes-hit-americans-less-accepting-lgbt-people-2017-survey-shows/1062188001/.

Millett, Kate. 1971. *Sexual Politics*. London: Granada.

Mizejewski, Linda. 2014. *Pretty/Funny: Women Comedians and Body Politics*. Austin: University of Texas Press.

Mukerji, Chandra and Michael Schudson, eds. 1991. *Rethinking Popular Culture: Contemporary Perspectives in Cultural Studies*. Berkeley: University of California Press.

Pramaggiore, Maria. 2004. "Straddling the Screen: Bisexual Spectatorship and Contemporary Narrative Film." In Queer Cultures, edited by *Deborah Carlin and Jennifer DiGrazia*, 483–507. Upper Saddle River, NJ: Pearson.

Radway, Janice. 1984. "Interpretive Communities and Variable Literacies: The Functions of Romance Reading." *Daedalus* 113(3): 49–73.

Rich, Adrienne. 1980. "Compulsory Heterosexuality and Lesbian Existence." *Journal of Women's History* 15(3): 11–48.

Rubin, Gayle. 1975. "The Traffic in Women: Notes on the 'Political Economy' of Sex." In *Toward an Anthropology of Women*, edited by R. Reiter, 157–210. New York, NY: Monthly Review Press.

Russo, Vito. 1987. *The Celluloid Closet: Homosexuality in the Movies*. New York, NY: Harper and Row.

Sarris, Andrew. 1998. "*You Ain't Heard Nothin' Yet: The American Talking Film, History and Memory, 1927–1949*." New York, NY: Oxford University Press.

Sedgwick, Eve Kosofsky. 1990. "Introduction: Axiomatic." In *Epistemology of the Closet by Eve Ksofsky Sedgwick*, 1–65. Berkeley: University of California Press.

Singer, P.W. 2008. "How *The Real World* Ended 'Don't Ask, Don't Tell.'" Brookings Institute Policy Paper 6, 2–14. Available at: https://www.brookings.edu/wp-content/uploads/2016/06/08_military_singer.pdf

Stacey, Jackie. 2000. "Desperately Seeking Difference: Jackie Stacey Considers Desire between Women in Narrative Cinema." In *Reading Images*, edited by Julia Thomas, 109–122. New York, NY: Palgrave.

Strasburger, Victor C. 2012. "Adolescents, Sex, and the Media." *Adolescent Medicine* 23: 15–33.

Tharp, Marye C. 2001. *Marketing and Consumer Identity in Multicultural America*. Thousaand Oaks, CA: Sage.

Thomas, Julia. 2001. *Reading Images*. New York, NY: Palgrave.

Tuchman, Gaye. 1978. "The Symbolic Annihilation of Women by the Mass Media." In *Hearth and Home: Images of Women in the Mass Media*, edited by Gaye Tuchman, Arlene Kaplan Daniels, and James Benet, 3–38. New York, NY: Oxford University Press.

Walters, Suzanna Danuta. 2001. *All the Rage: The Story of Gay Visibility in America*. Chicago, IL: University of Chicago Press.

West, Candace and Don H. Zimmerman. 1987. "Doing Gender." *Gender and Society* 1(2): 125–151.

Williams, Cristan. 2014. "Gender Performance: The TransAdvocate interviews Judith Butler." *The TransAdvocate,* May 1. Available at: http://www.transadvocate.com/gender-performance-the-transadvocate-interviews-judith-butler_n_13652.htm

Wittig, Monique. 1993. "One is not Born a Woman." In *The Lesbian and Gay Studies Reader*, edited by Henry Abelove, Michele Aina Barale, and David M. Halperin, 103–109. New York, NY: Routledge.

16

LGBT Literature

JULIE BEAULIEU

In 2014, British-Somali writer Diriye Osman, author of *Fairytales for Lost Children*, a short-story collection on the lesbian, gay, bisexual, and trans (LGBT) Somali experience, described his drive to represent LGBT Somali lives in literature. Osman writes, "I write because I want to give a long-overdue voice to a community that has experienced a tremendous array of challenges but who constantly face these challenges with the most wicked sense of humour, humility and dignity" (2014). Twenty years earlier and from the southern US, Dorothy Allison expressed a similar sentiment: "I have wanted our lives taken seriously and represented fully – with power and honesty and sympathy – to be hated or loved, or to terrify and obsess, but to be real, to have the power of the whole and the complex" (1994, p. 165). For Osman, to "tell our own stories" is to challenge reductive and clichéd media representations, portrayals that reduce the Somali diaspora experience to images of "pirates, warlords, terrorists, passive women and girls" (2014).

Allison and Osman share this feeling – the experience of being written about by others and being written about in ways that obscure and appropriate the meanings and truths of the lived experience; Allison writes, "We are the ones they make fiction of – we queer and disenfranchised and female – and we have the right to demand our full, nasty, complicated lives, if only to justify all the times our reality has been stolen, mismade, and dishonored" (1994, p.166). French-Moroccan gay writer and film-maker Abdellah Taïa, author of *Salvation Army* (2009a) and *An Arab Melancholia* (2012), expresses a similar sentiment in "Homosexuality Explained to My Mother": "I exist in writing. That's to say I have a certain responsibility towards myself and towards the society I come from" (2009b). Like Taïa, in an interview with *Lambda Literary*, author and scholar Cameron Awkward-Rich explains that they took up writing to make space for different ways of being; they explain, "initially, I wrote in order to alleviate that sense of strangeness: writing allowed me to invent worlds that matched my internal landscape, to invent characters who I could imagine myself as or with" (2016).

These authors share a desire to capture LGBT stories with texture and complexity, but other social and material aspects of their lives equally mark their work – where they call home, their relationship to this location, structural oppressions, strategies for freedom or liberation from oppression, and tools for living with and resisting injustice. LGBT experiences, as captured in literature, are always enmeshed in other structures of power and systems of meaning that collectively shape our individual experiences in the world we share. On the other hand, world systems of sexual organization foster shared experiences and familiar narratives – including religious persecution, systemic homophobia, coming out, and rejection from family and/or kin – that become common themes across texts in different parts of the world and at different times in history.

In the following five sections, I will introduce a set of considerations for scholars and/or readers of LGBT literature: first, an introduction to disciplinary debates in and around LGBT, LGBT studies, and the history of sexuality; second, sexuality in literature in a historical context; third, twentieth-century LGBT literature in context; fourth, central themes in LGBT literature; and lastly, I will conclude with new trends and new considerations for reading and researching LGBT literature.

LGBT, LGBT Studies, and the History of Sexuality

In this section, I introduce a range of different global, theoretical, and historical concerns to develop a critical frame for thinking about what counts as LGBT, and thus what might be included in the genre LGBT literature. To do this, I begin with a brief analysis of LGBT as a concept in global and historical context. From there, I turn to LGBT studies as a field (and more specifically, LGBT studies as it relates to queer studies). Next, I turn to Foucault's well-known classic, *The History of Sexuality, Volume I*, which fundamentally challenged and transformed how we approached sexual identity, representation, and literature. Finally, I introduce a set of key thinkers in both the history of Western formations of sexuality and LGBT and/or queer literary studies, who provide insight for developing a foundation for theorizing and historicizing LGBT literature.

LGBT in global and historical context

Thinking critically about LGBT literature requires readers and scholars to be attentive to what connects a range of texts from different parts of the world, all under the name of LGBT; it also requires a close look at the boundaries and obstacles that disrupt shared experiences among LGBT writers, and an analysis of which narratives of LGBT experience will be accepted as real, true, or universal. This requires a critical global approach to LGBT literature. The use of LGBT to refer to all nonnormative forms of sexual and gender identity across the globe assumes that we all share, or ultimately should share, the same sexual and gender system; even further, the sexual and gender system that is most commonly understood as universal is, in fact, a Western construct. Such assumptions about the global and universal applicability of LGBT do two things: they naturalize hegemonic US hetero sexualities and genders by assuming a universal, natural, and ahistorical heterosexuality unshaped by time and culture, and they erase indigenous, non-Western, and counterhegemonic genders and sexualities, many of which do not fit into Western understandings of LGBT neatly, or at all. Scholarship on global sexualities highlights how the habit of universalizing LGBT should be recognized as both imperial and neocolonial as it accedes to the power of Western thinkers to define the terms of gender and sexuality for all (see Luibhéid and Cantú 2005; Puar 2007; Rupp 2009; Currier 2012; Barker 2017).

As a concept that emerged around the late 1990s and early 2000s, LGBT responded to the shared struggle of lesbian, gay, bisexual, and trans people. As Zein Murib explains, "The ubiquitous use of the LGBT initialism across various social, academic, and political discursive contexts in the United States suggests that the constitutive categories of lesbian, gay, bisexual, and transgender are equivalent, informed by similar experiences, and, as such, appropriate to collapse into a single category: LGBT" (2014, p. 118). Indeed, lesbian, gay, bisexual, and trans individuals do share a commitment to challenging hegemonic ideas that link sex category (or sex assignment at birth) to both sexuality and gender, which produce prescriptive norms for both gender and desire that ultimately lead to the stigmatization and oppression of LGBT people; yet, on the other hand, the initialism glosses over a social and political history of differences within this group, which includes political attempts to distance gay and lesbian from gender transgression more broadly in efforts to gain rights, privileges, and respectability.

Beyond the imperial and neocolonial implications of using Western constructs to speak for all, the foundation of LGBT relies on taxonomies of gender and desire that are shaped by social and cultural context; and yet, there is an abundance of research on LGBT lives and experiences that recognize the categories lesbian, gay, bi, and trans as distinct, knowable, and stable identities across time and place. Early LGBT movements borrowed heavily from other social justice movements that focus on what many see as immutable identities, like race or gender – including civil rights and women's rights – and this shaped how individuals conceptualized sexuality and gender identity more broadly. Even as biological and/or natural theories of LGBT are critiqued, "born this way" theories of sexuality continue to shape public consciousness; of note, this trend continues in the absence of evidence to prove the biology of LGBT identity.

LGBT studies

From its emergence in the 1970s to the present, gay and lesbian studies has engaged directly with the question of identity: what causes it (nature vs. nurture), how does our understanding of it recapitulate or challenge the status quo, and how do we explain and narrate histories of desire that do not neatly fit into existing sexual categories (see Bullough 1976; Katz 1976; Foucault 1978; Rich 1980; Bray 1982; Weeks 1985; D'Emilio and Freedman 1988; Duberman, Vicinus, & Chauncey 1989; Halperin 1990; Faderman 1991; Castle 1993; Duberman 1993; Goldberg 1994; Bravmann 1997; Moore 1997; Rupp 2009; Lanser 2014). Historical inquiries into the nature of sexuality challenge popular framings of sexuality as natural and inborn, otherwise known as essentialist models of sexual difference, a way of thinking about sexuality that also has deep roots in a longer history of sexual biological essentialism in medicine, history, and theory (see Foucault 1978; Somerville 1994; Irvine 2005).

The essentialist position is also critiqued in sociological, anthropological, feminist, queer, and trans studies from the 1980s to the present (see Rubin 1984; Butler 1990; Jagose 1997; Lyons and Lyons 2004; Seidman 2010; Weeks 2011; Stryker 2008). More broadly, critical sexuality studies complicates the notion of sexual identity and sexual categorization by introducing theories of sexuality that mark desire as a profoundly social, mutable, and historical attribute of the self (see Rubin 1984; Plummer 2012). The history of academic inquiries into LGBT identities, lives, and experiences provides a critical backdrop that shapes the LGBT literary canon as well as the analysis of LGBT representation in literature.

Historical questions routinely lead to key challenges for researchers, theorists, and activists. Modernist LGBT studies might mark any text that explores same-gender sexual contact or intimacy, or any text with so-called gender-nonconforming practice or expression as LGBT, including literature from antiquity to the present. Postmodern LGBT studies and queer studies begin with a challenge to the imagined community of LGBT as such. Postmodern and queer theories have characterized LGBT studies as woefully undertheorized and steeped in a history of discourse and politics that ultimately prolongs the myth of sexual subjectivity (the myth that creates, in part, the conditions for oppression); LGBT studies has critiqued queer theory for its lack of analysis of lived, material conditions of LGBT people (see Jagose 1997).

The division between LGBT and queer approaches to literary criticism tends to typify LGBT literary history as largely governed by recovery politics – the desire to discover and properly anthologize LGBT writers across time and location. In much of LGBT studies, recovery is political. As noted in the 1995 introduction to *The Gay and Lesbian Literary Heritage: A Reader's Companion to the Writer's and their Works, from Antiquity to the Present*, "Given the nature of homosexuality – both historically and currently – as a controversial subject, this book cannot help partaking of a specific cultural (and political) agenda, the recovery and consolidation of a perpetually threatened legacy of same-sex love in literature and life" (Summers 1995, p. ix). In queer readings, "documentation and reclamation" are characterized as part of the wider system of sexuality; and significantly, this system (which defines the language and the logic of sexuality) is a necessary part of the widespread production and regulation of sex. In other words, queer theories recognize LGBT claims to identity as part of the same network of power that controls, defines, and regulates sexuality. Internal debates within LGBT and queer scholarship reflect the diverse and complex ways that we experience gender and sexuality.

LGBT and the history of sexuality

Late twentieth-century analysis of LGBT literature is intensely influenced by one key thinker: the French philosopher, Michel Foucault. In 1976, Foucault published the first volume of his multivolume text entitled, *The History of Sexuality*. In this first volume, Foucault outlines the historical processes that have guided us to understand and organize ourselves around a presumed sexual interiority – what is commonly referred to as a sexual identity (heterosexual, bisexual, gay, lesbian, etc.). Foucault's work explores the genealogy of the sexual self, a history of the present that helps us to see LGBT identities from a different angle, which might, in turn, create a new politics of sexuality.

For readers and/or researchers of LGBT literature, Foucault provides new ways of reading LGBT representation in literature. An awareness of social, historical, and political shifts in understanding LGBT allows readers and researchers to trace different patterns and politics of representation across time and location. In practice, this means reading representations of sexuality and gender as more than mere representations; literature plays a central role in representing, defining, and restricting what counts as LGBT. This allows us to recognize that the meaning of LGBT – and gender and sexuality more broadly – is always in process and contested.

After Foucault, a set of historical-conceptual questions and debates created new terms and conditions for the question of periodization. What are the historical processes that made it possible for us to have a literary cultural heritage based on how people seek sexual pleasure and/or how they experience gender? Can we call literature LGBT if it was published 100 years before the invention of LGBT? What about global LGBT literature, particularly if and when indigenous understandings do not follow the same systems of logic that define Western ideas about LGBT? Technically speaking, LGBT literature is a relatively young genre (if we accept the late 1990s as its inception), and yet anthologies routinely include literary works that are written well before the invention of sexual identities or works that have forms of gender and sexuality that are not identical to LGBT. This practice is critiqued in the introduction to *The Gay and Lesbian Literary Heritage*:

> Too often, however, attempts to document the gay and lesbian cultural legacy paid little attention to historical differences and tended to make few distinctions between different kinds of homosexualities, equating the emergent homosexual of the nineteenth century with the Greek pederast, the medieval sodomite, and the North American *berdache*, for example, as though all four phenomena were merely minor variations on the same pattern.
> (quoted in Summers 1995, p. x)

In both cases – using historical or cross-cultural approaches – we risk universalizing LGBT experience if we are not attuned to the specific conditions of sexual practice, identity, and community in space and time.

Global LGBT

Just as historical approaches require a willingness to suspend contemporary understandings of sexuality, gender, and LGBT, cross-cultural approaches to LGBT identity and representation involve careful considerations of individuals in context. Scholars in critical global sexuality studies have noted several key considerations when looking at sexuality and the politics of location. Leila Rupp's essay "Toward a Global History of Same-Sex Sexuality" (2001) explores the limits of using "same-sex" to refer to what might look like similar forms of sexual acts across the globe. Rupp writes, "There are various ways that sexual acts involving two genitally alike bodies may in fact not be best conceptualized as 'same-sex'" (2001, p. 287). First, Rupp explains, some other form of difference might trump sex category as the most central factor of sexual orientation and sex/gender systems (such as age or status). The ancient Athenian sex/gender system is a commonly cited example of this cultural difference. Second, sex category is an insufficient lens because of a wide range of different systems for understanding, experiencing, and structuring sex/gender systems. For Two-Spirit people, who are found in many different tribes among indigenous peoples of the Americas, as an example, what might be interpreted as "same-sex" might be better captured as "different gender." Last, the definition and boundaries of what counts as a sexual act are cultural and thus vary from location to location (consider, as an example, the act of holding hands, or exposed breasts in public, from a global perspective).

On global perspectives, Evan Towle and Lynn Morgan discuss the use of transgender and third gender from a critical global standpoint in "Romancing the Transgender Native: Rethinking the 'Third Gender' Concept" (2002). They argue that "third gender" is treated as "exotica" in much of Western writing on global nonbinary gender practices (2002, p. 667). More recently, trans scholars have used the existence of "third gender" practices in a global context to "buttress the argument that Western binary gender systems are neither universal nor innate" (2002, p. 667).

For Towle and Morgan, uncritical use of "third gender" reproduces imperial and colonial national imaginaries that routinely mark third gender in non-Western cultures as evidence of the "primordial" and thus natural state of gender-nonconforming behavior; this, in turn, marks the West as more civilized (with less proximity to a natural state) (2002, p. 672). Even further, as Towle and Morgan note, the practice of selecting "queer" behaviors among other cultures to promote LGBT as natural at home is a flawed tactic: "An argument that relies on cross-cultural evidence of gender variation elsewhere to support the possibility of radical change at home is illogical: if gender is determined by culture elsewhere, then it must be determined by culture at home, too" (2002, p. 678). A critical global approach focuses on context without erasing complexities via systemic ways of thinking about what shapes LGBT literary production across the globe.

Perhaps in most cases readers and scholars of LGBT literature have a basic, everyday familiarity with the challenges and contradictions that sexual and gender categorization entail in both cross-cultural and historical perspectives. Martha Vicinus explores this in "'They Wonder to Which Sex I Belong': The Historical Roots of the Modern Lesbian Identity." Vicinus writes, "Virtually every historian of sexuality has argued that the present-day sexual identity of both homosexuals and heterosexuals is socially constructed and historically specific. Yet same-sex erotic attraction appears to be transhistorical and transcultural and to appear repeatedly in a limited range of behaviors" (1992, p. 433). In our everyday experiences, Vicinus notes, we experience contradictory ideas about sex and gender; studies in LGBT literature bring these contradictions into analysis, to demonstrate how literature – and the humanities more broadly – helps us to imagine the self as historical and cultural production. Moreover, Vicinus, together with numerous other scholars in early and early-modern sexuality studies, helps us to see how history shapes sexual identity. Yet equally key, historians of sexuality invite us to recognize how sexuality (much of which is represented in literature) shapes history.

This is to say that thinking about sexuality and historicity allows readers of LGBT literature in the present to have a broader and more theoretical understanding of the multiple meanings of LGBT literature in the present; it also means having an awareness of how LGBT literature has shaped history. In *The Sexuality of History: Modernity and the Sapphic, 1565–1830*, Susan Lanser writes, "I hope to show not only that sexuality has a history but that sexuality is history: that just as the historical constructs the sexual, so too does the sexual construct the historical, shaping the social imaginary and providing a site for reading it" (2014, p. 3). Lanser's motive in reversing the order of impact is in part underpinned by a desire to universalize sexuality studies: to increase "the relevance of sexuality to 'mainstream' scholarship" (2014, p. 4). I will return to this universalizing approach in the conclusion, when I note some more recent trends (notably, the LGBT bestseller). Lanser continues, "Not least among the implications of my inversion of terms is the possibility, largely ignored outside sexuality studies proper, that sexuality might be not only an effect but a stimulus" (2014, pp. 3–4). With Lanser's approach we can reimagine the impact of LGBT writers in the present. They are not merely speaking long-suppressed words; they are responsible for creating the conditions of being, possibility, *and* change.

In the next section, I look more specifically at historical periods, texts, and research in LGBT literary studies. Far from a comprehensive survey, instead I provide a set of examples to reflect on historical change as it relates to LGBT literature and the study of sexuality in literature more broadly. In many cases, by including writers in this list that by far precede the invention of homosexuality, as noted, I participate in the ongoing politics of recovery – the naming and claiming of literature for the canon of LGBT. Be that as it may, I also include scholars who continue to advance deconstructive approaches to sexuality, identity, and literature; all together, I provide tools for thinking about the long history of LGBT literature rather than a coherent history of LGBT literature per se.

Sexuality in Literature in Historical Context: What Counts as LGBT Literature?

Among the earliest icons of LGBT literature is Sappho; "To lesbians around the world today, she is the archetypal lesbian and their symbolic mother" (George, quoted in Summer 1995, p. 630). A prolific poet in ancient Greece, Sappho has been widely historicized in LGBT literature, routinely with little attention to historicity. Susan Cavin, author of *Lesbian Origins*, explains, "It is ironic that heterosexuals omit lesbians from discussions of early society, since the earliest recorded history, art, and literature of western society documents the existence of lesbians," including, "Sappho's poetry on Lesbos (c. 600 BC)" (1985, p. 43). Cavin continues, "Lesbianism has been reported in Athens (450 BC), and in Rome (AD 100). Plato, a homosexual himself, invents an origin myth of homosexuality in the *Symposium*, but speaks through Aristophanes" (1985, p. 43). To the question of history, Cavin notes, "I am aware of the fact that many scholars of patri-classics heatedly attempt to refute even Sappho's lesbianism, even as Sappho writes, 'Afraid of losing you/I ran fluttering/like a little girl/after her mother'" (1985, p. 243).

In *The Gay and Lesbian Literary Heritage*, Anita George notes, "it is hard to believe that scholars continue to argue that Sappho was not a lesbian in the modern sense of the word" (quoted in Summers 1995, p. 632). George argues that such claims are part of the larger denial of lesbian existence. George writes, "attempts range from deliberately mistranslating words that indicate that the beloved is female to forcing a heterosexual context on poems depicting lesbian desire" (quoted in Summers 1995, p. 632).

Cavin and George's comments add critical context to LGBT as recovery project; denial is one form of erasure that prevents the formation of LGBT literary archives (LGBT writing is also subject to censorship via pornography laws, and low institutional value and circulation). Academic work that accedes to the hetero-hegemonic common sense of heterosexual as women's natural state – which leads to a higher standard of evidence required to prove a writer's lesbianism – is part of a broader network of knowledge and power relations that attempt to code lesbian as impossible (or highly unlikely); when present, lesbianism is characterized as playful, or subordinate to heterosexuality. Certainly, "lesbian impossibility" in literary history can be a deeply historicized standpoint (uttered in the spirit of thinking critically about history, subjectivity, and desire, not in the service of hetero-patriarchy), yet we see here how that particular interpretation could be read (or used) to mark intimate relations between and among women as trivial, or impossible (see Faderman 1991; Castle 1993; Moore 1997; Wahl 1999; Dave 2012).

As Adrienne Rich has argued in "Compulsory Heterosexuality and Lesbian Existence," withholding information via erasure is one of eight forms of power that restrict and obscure lesbian existence. Rich writes, "The denial of reality and visibility to women's passion for women, women's choice of women as allies, life companions, and community, the forcing of such relationships into dissimulation and their disintegration under intense pressure have meant an incalculable loss to the power of all women *to change the social relations of the sexes, to liberate ourselves and each other*" (1980, p. 139). LGBT literature more broadly fits into this narrative of absence and recovery since it provides detailed representations of other ways of being, ways of being that are suppressed in the public sphere. LGBT representation in literature opens up possibilities for LGBT people – new terms, new standards, and new practices.

On the topic of LGBT historiography, it seems significant to note that Sappho is one of two authors with a name that defines a specific (and specifically lesbian) form of contact: the Sapphic and Platonic Love. As Leila Rupp writes in her introduction to *Sapphistries: A Global History of Love Between Women*, "The lesbian poet Sappho, whatever her erotic history, bequeathed both her name and her place of residence to the phenomenon of desire, love, and sex between women. Her iconic image as a lover of women has transcended the boundaries of history and geography, bestowing on women who desire women the labels *Sapphic* and *lesbian*" (2009, p. 1). Platonic love, defined in the writings of Plato, holds a dramatically different meaning today than it did in antiquity. Louis Crompton writes, "Among Greek writers on homosexual themes, Plato is preeminent not only as a major philosopher but also as the greatest master of Greek prose. The *Symposium* and the *Phaedrus*, dialogues that deal directly with the subject of male love, stand among Plato's finest literary achievements" (quoted in Summers 1995, p. 548). And yet, this homosexuality is routinely erased from the record; in fact, the effort to "obliterate any homosexual details" from Plato's work, together with the effort to transform Platonic love into heterosexual practice, begins with the rediscovery of Plato's erotic dialogues in Renaissance literature (p. 551). Crompton writes, "Castiglione's *The Courtier* (1518), a highly influential work, completely 'heterosexualized' Platonic love, thus obscuring its real origins" (quoted in Summers 1995, p. 551). Todd Reeser's *Setting Plato Straight: Translating Ancient Sexuality in the Renaissance* (2015), which explores the effort to cleanse ancient texts of same-sex Eros and sexuality during the Renaissance, provides an expansive summary of how the meaning of literary works is transformed across time and location. Given this connection – the cleansing of both lesbian and gay prehistories – it seems key to note Gayle Rubin's critical intervention in sexuality studies, the essay, "Thinking Sex" (1984). As Rubin argued, feminist theory was an insufficient lens for studying the theory and regulation of sex; though impacted by gender, Rubin argued, sex has its own logic. We see this here in the censorship of homosexual content in literature across gender categories.

David Halperin's work is also useful for readers and scholars interested in what some might call ancient homosexuality. Halperin's historical approach to sex and sexuality, heavily guided by Foucault, presents an alternative way to think about LGBT literature in a long historical perspective. Most key, as Halperin explains in "Is There a History of Sexuality," sex, for the ancients, does not create sexual identity; sexual identity "implies that human beings are individuated at the level of their sexuality, that they differ from one another in their sexuality and, indeed, belong to different types or kinds of being by virtue of their sexuality" (1989, p. 417). Assessing ancient texts as "homosexual" or LGBT literature obscures key historical differences in the absence of a critical historical approach.

Scholars in queer Renaissance studies encounter similar questions on the topic of LGBT literature (and sexuality in literature more broadly). On Foucault's influence on queer Renaissance studies, Jonathan Goldberg writes, "the aim is not to 'find' gays and lesbians hidden from history, which is to say that the assumption of a transhistorical homosexual identity is not the motivation behind this work" (2009, p. 4). He continues, "to follow Foucault à la lettre, the Renaissance comes before the regimes of sexuality, and to speak of sexuality in the period is a misnomer" (2009, p. 5). In light of this, we might want to consider early modern literature that represents and/or is crafted by what we might now call LGBT people as prehistory, or as the historical and critical context through which we read LGBT literary production today.

In "Homosexuality and the Signs of Male Friendship in Elizabethan England," Alan Bray explores how Elizabethan literature, including dramatic works, was central to the discursive division between friendship and sodomy (1994). Far from obscure, subcultural pastime or concern, as the expressions "sexual minority" and "LGBT" may lead us to believe, Bray discovers that the sodomitical was absolutely central to social life and literary production. This, Bray proposes, is linked to the marked absence of a distinct, identifiable, sexual minority – the homosexual. Bray writes,

> The intimacy between men in Europe and in North America today is protected to a large extent by the notion of a quite distinct homosexual minority for whom alone homosexual desire is a possibility. This was a shield Elizabeth England did not have and we might well wonder if this cultural difference is the reason why later historians have been so blind to the fearsome weapon its absence provided.
>
> (1994, p. 56)

As Bray notes, "perhaps there is always a potential ambiguity about intimacy between men" (1994, p. 57). Historical context allows us to consider the function of such ambiguity; for men in Elizabethan England, fuzzy boundaries provided the conditions whereby any man could find himself accused of sodomy, thus weaponizing sexual practice. Literature became one of many public spaces to define the boundaries of sexual desire and identity, and it continues to exist as a space where questions about the sexual self in society are worked out in the present.

In *Between Men: English Literature and Male Homosocial Desire* (1985), Eve Kosofsky Sedgwick takes a similar approach by showcasing how canonical literary texts – texts not typically read as LGBT – show a marked preoccupation with the public use and definitional boundaries of men's relationships with other men. Sedgwick promoted queer reading practices, which, for Sedgwick, meant believing "an obstinate intuition that the loose ends and crossed ends of identity are more fecund than the places where identity, desire, analysis, and need can all be aligned and centered" (1985, p. viii).

Like women's studies or women's literature, LGBT literary studies encounters similar field-specific, historical-political questions. As Sedgwick explains, her work in feminist literary scholarship, and the intellectual and institutional ways that women's literature is imagined in these spaces, informed her approach in *Between Men*. As we can see, before and after Foucault, the exact meaning, canonization, and interpretation of what we might now call LGBT literature raises a set of key questions about the nature of the self, the political use of sexual identities, the relationship between desire and history, and the very effects of our ways of reading sex in time and location. Whether readers and scholars of LGBT literature are more concerned with erasure (and thus committed to recovering our LGBT literary history) or reification (and thus challenging what counts as LGBT literature), questions about what counts as LGBT literature echo a common concern: our readings, as much as homophobic readings, have the potential to construct a false "coherence, cohesion, and stability against the multiply fractured subject positions that constitute the lives of lesbian and gay individuals" (Bravmann 1997, p. 5).

By the late-nineteenth and early-twentieth century, Western medical-therapeutic discourse on sexuality begins to shape Western understandings of sexual identity. Early medical terms, like "invert" and "homosexual" mark a key shift; what was once an act or feeling becomes constitutive of identity (see Foucault 1978; Wilchins 2004; Doan and Prosser 2001). These medical terms pave the way for self-identification. In terms of LGBT literature, the possibility of self-identification lessens the historical-conceptual questions about historicity; namely, can we call something LGBT if it precedes the emergence of LGBT? With that said, LGBT literature in the twentieth century deserves our continued curiosity about the representation of identity and desire in historical, cultural, and political context. In the next section, "LGBT Literature in the Twentieth Century," I survey a set of noteworthy authors and themes to provide a brief overview of LGBT literature (from the late-nineteenth to the mid- to late-twentieth century).

LGBT Literature in the Twentieth Century: Politics, Trends, and Challenges

The intellectual and political project of countering the dominant narratives of hetero-hegemonic culture becomes one of the hallmarks of the twentieth century LGBT movement. LGBT literary production becomes a central vehicle for this project. Even before the twentieth century, as I will discuss with the case of Oscar

Wilde, artists used a range of literary forms to question the implications of sexual restrictions and prohibitions. However, in *The History of Sexuality, Volume I*, Foucault encourages us to consider not simply sexual restrictions and prohibitions, but any discourse on sex, and more specifically, the context under which any discourse on sex is produced. We bear witness to the truths expressed in LGBT writing, much of which takes the form of the autobiography or memoir; we are asked to attend to the ideological logics of such truths with the same level of scrutiny that we apply to outwardly regulatory or disciplinary forms of discourse (like religious, criminal, or medical "laws").

The canon of LGBT literature, even when (and some might say *especially when*) penned by LGBT authors, creates sexuality as much as more transparently prescriptive texts do and thus has the potential and power to shape how we think about desire, intimacy, and sex more broadly. Even further, we must consider the conditions that make some voices more able to speak and to tell their own stories. Class oppression is a central cause of the significant lack of diverse stories in early twentieth-century LGBT literature; even further, the vast majority of LGBT literature from the first half of the twentieth-century comes from white, Western authors. It is not until the mid- to late-twentieth century that we see a diversity of voices in the broader canon of LGBT literature.

Oscar Wilde and the history of LGBT literature

Among the more infamous of LGBT writers to influence twentieth-century thinking on sexuality is Oscar Wilde. Although technically Wilde's writing is commonly understood as late nineteenth-century literature (Wilde having passed in the year 1900), his work is noteworthy here as it showcases a striking and iconic encounter – the queer artist and the critique of society. With the following words, quoted in Frank Harris's classic, *Oscar Wilde: His Life and Confessions*, we can see a range of historical and epistemological questions, mirrored in later LGBT politics; consider, as an example, the significance of this question posed by Wilde: "What difference is there between one form of sexual indulgence and another?" (1974, p. 492). As well, we see Wilde using these questions to move away from a shame and/or deviancy model of sexuality toward a more political understanding of how knowledge and power structure experience via the capacity to define the boundaries of sin and/or deviancy. Harris, quoting Wilde in conversation on homosexual vice, writes,

> What you call vice, Frank, is not vice: it is as good to me as it was to Caesar, Alexander, Michelangelo and Shakespeare. It was first of all made a sin by monasticism, and it has been made a crime in recent times, by the Goths – the Germans and English – who have done little or nothing since to refine or exalt the ideals of humanity. They all damn the sins they have no mind to, and that's their morality. A brutal race; they overeat and overdrink and condemn the lusts of the flesh, while reveling in all the vilest sins of the spirit. If they would read the 23rd chapter of St. Matthew and apply it to themselves, they would learn more than by condemning a pleasure they don't understand.
>
> (1974, p. 493)

In Harris's retelling of this exchange, Wilde challenges the epistemological basis of religious conviction (and its uneven application); he uses historical figures (who are widely celebrated in Western culture) as evidence to contradict theories of "vice" and so-called degeneracy; and he does all of this critical work with an eye to the paradoxical, which will later become one of the central methods of gender and sexual criticism in feminist, queer, and trans studies (exposing the illogic of hetero systems of truth and domination through queer reading, a long historical perspective, and cross-cultural comparison).

Born in the 1850s in Ireland, Wilde is perhaps most well-known for his literary work, and more specifically, *The Picture of Dorian Gray* (1890). Wilde's other writing, including *The Soul of a Man under Socialism* (1891), showcases some of his deeply antiauthoritarian attitudes. With Wilde, we see a strong link back in time to the libertines of the Restoration period, whose writings advocated for an ethics of pleasure seeking, together with deep resonances with a queer future, where new queer politics deconstruct the logic of vice more broadly, rather than focusing on the rights of those who identify as LGBT. He is, in other words, a pivotal figure – writing, no less, at the same time that Foucault and many other scholars argue that the homosexual and the heterosexual (and endless other typologies from sexology and the pseudo-scientific search for sexual taxonomies and laws) are invented. On Wilde, Harriette Andreadis writes, "He is one of the most accomplished writers of his generation, but quite apart from his actual literary achievement, he is significant as a symbolic figure who exemplified a way of being homosexual at a pivotal moment in the emergence of gay consciousness, the crucial final decade of the nineteenth century" (quoted in Summers 1995, p. 742). Readers can read Wilde's words for access to this landscape – a historically distinct yet familiar way of thinking about sex, desire, and politics.

Early- and mid-twentieth century voices to late-twentieth century activism

By the turn of the twentieth century, LGBT writers and artists are gradually speaking for themselves, marking a strong break in the twentieth century from the past; we see an increasingly diverse set of first-person accounts of the LGBT experience in literature (even if the majority of early twentieth-century writing is still not written by self-identified LGBT authors and the majority are writing from the West). Over the course of 100 years, LGBT authors engage with topics as varied as law, health, science, love, family, religion, spirituality, rejection, shame, grief, oppression, nationalism, exile, racism, and more. I will turn to some of the more common themes in LGBT literature in critical global perspective in the next section, "Central Themes in LGBT Literature." In this section I hope to mark a few key writers and historical moments to provide a brief analysis of some points of entry for readers and scholars of twentieth-century Western LGBT literature.

Much like Wilde, Radclyffe "John" Hall, who is most well-known for the lesbian classic, *The Well of Loneliness* (1928), experienced the phenomenon of the LGBT artist; both Wilde and Hall were recognizable as much for their sartorial as their literary choices, in both cases for gender nonconforming dress and behavior. Hall's *The Well* reflects a deep identification with, and political hopefulness in, medical-therapeutic texts on the nature and origin of sexuality, including the works of Dr. Havelock Ellis, who endorsed Hall's novel. Hall's depiction of Stephen Gordon in *The Well* reflects an indisputable familiarity with theories of inversion in sexology, which read homosexual desires as evidence of gender inversion. Such theories, steeped as they were in heteroreproductive biological essentialism, allowed LGBT people to identify nonnormative sexualities as natural – a diagnosable, medical condition or state – which some viewed as a pathway to decriminalization and discrimination more broadly. Hall's call for acceptance marks an early iteration of the "born this way" theory of sexual etiology that dominates much of LGBT politics in the present (see Doan and Prosser 2001).

It seems key to note the tremendous amount of economic privilege that Hall experienced in spite of living outside of social, historical, and cultural expectations. At the age of 21, Hall became a multimillionaire (by today's equivalent) through inheritance. This allowed Hall to travel (notably, to Italy, Paris, and London), socialize with other writers, write, and live independently and/or with women (or independent of men) (see Doan and Prosser). Also of note, since the 1990s, trans studies has challenged lesbian and gay historiography, noting that some historical figures who we have declared lesbian or gay might in fact be best understood as trans (see Stryker 2008; Gill-Peterson 2018). Hall certainly opens up this possibility, given the archive we have (see Doan and Prosser 2001). Critical inquiries into LGBT history attune us to the various politics of epistemologies of sexuality and gender; most notably, who gets to define the boundaries of our conceptual categories.

This question of definitional power is particularly key in regards to considerations of the intersection of race and sexuality. As Hall is writing in England, contemporaneously in the US we are in the midst of what is now known as the Harlem Renaissance. Throughout the 1920s in particular, African American literary production flourished. More recently, numbers of authors from this period have been recognized as LGBT (see Garber 1983; Schwarz 2003). As A.B. Christa Schwarz argues in *Gay Voices of the Harlem Renaissance*, although the Harlem Renaissance was deeply shaped by men who loved men, including Langston Hughes, Claude McKay, Richard Bruce Nugent, and Countée Cullen, this period is only recently acknowledged as a part of gay literary history (see Garber 1983). On the topic of categorization, similar to Radclyffe's Hall's work, which does not fit neatly into lesbian or trans fiction, literature from the Harlem Renaissance displays a more fluid and at times coded representation of sexual desire than the categories of LGBT suggest. That the Harlem Renaissance is both left out of LGBT literary history and recognized as breaking the mold of the universalized notions of LGBT speaks to the broader issues of white hegemony within LGBT studies which privileges, centers, and attempts to universalize the white experience (see Johnson 2016; Schwarz 2003; Ferguson 2004; McCune 2014; Snorton 2017).

Another noteworthy period in twentieth century LGBT literature is mid-century pulp fiction. As Susan Stryker notes in *Queer Pulp: Perverted Passions from the Golden Age*, "before the sexual revolution of the 1960s and the explosion of soft- and hard-core pornographic magazines that came in its wake, paperback books were pretty much the only game in town when it came to explicit portrayals of sexuality in the mass media" (2001, p. 8). Stryker continues, "Mid-twentieth century paperbacks mapped a world of loose women and lost men who wandered in a moral twilight, a world of sin and sex and drugs and booze and every ugly thing human beings could conspire to do to one another" (2001, p. 8). Stryker's characterization of this genre showcases the conditions of visibility that structured mid-century representations of LGBT lives. As with pre-twentieth century representations of LGBT in literature, pulp fiction provides a historically specific example of how time and location shape the representation of LGBT lives in literature.

The late 1950s, 1960s, and 1970s brought a new spirit of sexual revolution in US LGBT literature. Key texts from this generation of writers include Patricia Highsmith's *The Price of Salt* (1952), an early US LGBT novel with a happy ending; James Baldwin's *Giovanni's Room* (1956), which explored both bisexuality and homosexuality; and John Rechy's *City of Night* (1963), a frank portrayal of gay male sex workers. In the 1980s and 1990s, LGBT literature focused heavily on the AIDS crisis. Notable works during this time, primarily from the U.S., include Samuel Delaney's *Flight from Nevèrÿon* (1985), Randy Shilts's *And the Band Played On* (1987), Sarah Schulman's *People in Trouble* (1990), Tony Kushner's *Angels in America* (1991), David Wojnarowicz's *Close to the Knives* (1991), Dale Peck's *Martin and John* (1993), and Patricia Powell's *A Small Gathering of Bones* (1993). There is an abundance of available research and writing on the AIDS epidemic that can provide historical, political, and social context for this period of LGBT literature (see Sontag 1989; Kramer 1989; Cohen 1999; Gould 2009; France 2016).

Central Themes in LGBT Literature

In an interview with Abdellah Taïa, the author responds to American readers who tend to see his novel, *A Salvation Army*, as a coming-out narrative. Taïa writes, "I understand that many American readers considered it a coming-out story. I actually don't mind that. Every reader is free to interpret my work the way he prefers. But, I repeat again, my intention with this novel was to talk about the idea of transformation. The fragmented transformation of a Moroccan 'I' who happens to be gay" (2016). This documents one of the many different ways that white, Western narratives (and the literary practices and tropes that are routinely present in this literature) dominate discussions of LGBT literature; literary works are read in and through coming out. The presumed universality of the coming-out narrative, among the most familiar topics in white US LGBT literature, ties liberation to the speech act (consider, as example, the queer slogan "silence=death"). Because of this, being out is used as an index, not only of liberation but also of pride or shame, and of one's proximity to the good life. The closet is understood as unlivable, never a worthwhile sacrifice; the narrative of being out as liberation makes it impossible to read silence in other ways, least of all, to read silence (or withholding/refusing) in a positive or even neutral way. On silence, in "Watering the Imagination," the opening story in Osman's *Fairytales for Lost Children*, Osman describes a mother's response to her daughter's love interests. Osman writes,

> In Somali culture many things go unsaid: how we love, who we love and why we love that way. I don't know why Suldana loves the way she does. I don't know why she loves who she does. But I do know that by respecting her privacy I am letting her dream in a way that my generation was not capable of. I'm letting her reach for something neither of us can articulate. So we take our voices and our stories to the sea.
>
> (2013, pp. 3–4)

The layers of possible meaning here are complex: Osman's notes on the epistemology of subjugation (Suldana's mother's ability to give the gift of freedom, which she did not receive), the recoding of silence (as an act that creates, rather than withholds), and the relationship between love and dreaming (and our attachment to the utopia of sexual freedom more broadly). Osman's challenge to the silence=death formula provides a different context for reading the politics and poetics of silence.

In addition to coming out, coming of age is a central theme in the LGBT novel. Numerous authors have explored this topic, including Shyam Selvadurai (*Funny Boy*, 1996), Jacqueline Woodson (*The House You Pass on the Way*, 1997), Mariko and Jillian Tamaki (*Skim*, 2008), Audre Lorde (*Zami*, 1982), Rita Mae Brown (*Rubyfruit Jungle*, 1973), Reinaldo Arenas (*Before Night Falls*, 1994), Staceyann Chin (*The Other Side of Paradise*, 2010), and Abha Dawesar (*Babyji*, 2005). In all of these cases, childhood and coming of age are presented as complex processes that are dramatically shaped by historical moment, location, and access to knowledge and privilege. In many cases, sexuality is not the central or sole issue that shapes childhood or coming of age in LGBT literature; instead, war, political unrest, poverty, racism, or sexism are more central or equally at play.

Familial rejection is a persistent theme in LGBT literature across the globe. In *Ties That Bind*, Sarah Schulman explores the hallmarks of familial homophobia, including shunning, differential treatment, rejection, and violence; for Schulman, this process is amplified by the fact that the family is supposed to be a safe space, "a refuge from the cruelties of culture" (2009, p. 14). LGBT literature on familial homophobia frequently intersects with religious persecution as parental figures reject their children based on their spiritual and community beliefs. This theme is highly common in cross-cultural perspective, which highlights the shared experiences among LGBT people in different times and locations. Some noteworthy texts that explore LGBT experience, family, and/or religion include Audre Lorde's *Zami: A New Spelling of My Name* (1982), Jeanette Winterson's *Oranges Are Not the Only Fruit* (1985), Sara Farizan's *If You Could Be Mine* (2013), and Chinelo Okparanta's *Under the Udala Tress* (2015). The global LGBT novel provides key insight into the ways in which location shapes our experiences of sexual and/or gender identity.

Lastly, attention to gender is a central theme in LGBT literature. Classic and widely read works like Leslie Feinberg's *Stone Butch Blues* (1993), which tells the story of a young character, Jess Goldberg, a working-class butch who lives and works in upstate New York during the 1940s and 1950s, showcase the enduring value of representing trans experiences in literature. Feinberg's text provides an early representation of gender outside of the binary; it has been immensely influential in the field of LGBT studies and in gender and sexuality studies more broadly. Jennifer Finney Boylan's memoir, entitled *She's Not There: A Life in Two Genders* (2003), represents one woman's experience navigating trans experience and family life. Both Boylan and Feinberg showcase how an individual's gender identity can impact those they love, shifting and in some cases ending relationships simply for expressing a long-felt desire to represent the self authentically. Research in trans studies is useful for contextualizing trans representation in literature (see Stryker 2008; Halberstam 2018; Stein 2018).

Conclusion: New Trends, New Considerations

More recently, LGBT writers have experienced increased readership well beyond LGBT audiences. It is now possible to speak of an era of the LGBT bestseller. Even further, we find heterosexual writers turning to LGBT topics in literature, not out of a desire to ridicule, punish, sensationalize, or defame (as we have seen in the past), but to capture the next great love story, or to open the hearts of readers to the lives and dreams of LGBT people.

The mainstreaming of LGBT literature showcases a growing interest in LGBT literature among diverse readers and audiences. The popularity of LGBT literature, including the Pulitzer Prize winning novel *Middlesex* (2002) by Jeffrey Eugenides and the novel-turned-film *Call Me By Your Name* (2007) by André Aciman, provide clear examples of the mainstreaming of LGBT content. These mainstream examples of LGBT representation raise a set of political, conceptual, and historical questions: Who should represent LGBT lives in literature? How do histories of privilege within the LGBT community shape our understandings of LGBT in the present? Who is left out of LGBT literature?

Literature provides an ideal medium for tracing a range of different experiences with gender and sexuality, which we have broadly defined as LGBT. What I have focused on in this chapter – the diverse definitions of LGBT, the significance of history, and the relationship between sexuality and culture – is all central to our understanding of LGBT literature in the present and the future. The diverse range of authors and scholars named here provide a rich archive, demonstrating just a fraction of the tremendous contributions from LGBT authors.

References

Aciman, André. 2007. *Call Me By Your Name*. New York, NY: Farrar, Straus, Giroux.
Allison, Dorothy. 1994. *Skin: Talking About Sex, Class, and Literature*. Ithaca, NY: Firebrand Books.
Arenas, Reinaldo. 1994. *Before Night Falls*. London: Penguin.
Awkward-Rich, Cameron. 2016. "On Engaging with Trans Literary Tropes and Writing for the Future." *Lambda Literary* June 8. Available at: https://www.lambdaliterary.org/interviews/06/08/cameron-awkward-rich-on-engaging-with-trans-literary-tropes-and-writing-for-the-future/.
Baldwin, James. 1956. *Giovanni's Room*. New York, NY: Dial Press.
Barker, Joanna, ed. 2017. *Critically Sovereign: Indigenous Gender, Sexuality, and Feminist Studies*. Durham, NC: Duke University Press.
Boylan, Jennifer Finney. 2003. *She's Not There: A Life in Two Genders*. New York, NY: Random House.
Bravmann, Scott. 1997. *Queer Fictions of the Past: History, Culture, and Difference*. Cambridge: Cambridge University Press.
Bray, Alan. 1982. *Homosexuality in Renaissance England*. New York, NY: Columbia University Press.
Bray, Alan. 1994. "Homosexuality and the Signs of Male Friendship in Elizabethan England." In *Queering the Renaissance*, edited by Jonathan Goldberg, 40–61. Durham, NC: Duke University Press.

Brown, Rita Mae. 1973. *Rubyfruit Jungle*. Plainfield, VT: Daughters.
Bullough, Vern. 1976. *Sexual Variance in Society and History*. Chicago, IL: University of Chicago Press.
Butler, Judith. 1990. *Gender Trouble: Feminism and the Subversion of Identity*. New York, NY: Routledge.
Cavin, Susan. 1985. *Lesbian Origins*. San Francisco, CA: Ism Press.
Castle, Terry. 1993. *The Apparitional Lesbian: Female Homosexuality and Modern Culture*. New York, NY: Columbia University Press.
Chin, Staceyann. 2010. *The Other Side of Paradise*. New York, NY: Scribner.
Cohen, Cathy. 1999. *The Boundaries of Blackness: AIDS and the Breakdown of Black Politics*. Chicago, IL: University of Chicago Press.
Currier, Ashley. 2012. *Out in Africa: LGBT Organizing in Namibia and South Africa*. Minneapolis, MN: University of Minnesota Press.
Dave, Naisargi. 2012. *Queer Activism in India: A Story in the Anthropology of Ethics*. Durham, NC: Duke University Press.
Dawesar, Abha. 2005. *Babyji*. New York, NY: Anchor Books.
Delaney, Samuel. 1985. *Flight from Nevèrÿon*. New York, NY: Bantam Books.
D'Emilio, John and Estelle Freedman. 1988. *Intimate Matters: A History of Sexuality in America*. Chicago, IL: University of Chicago Press.
Doan, Laura and Jay Prosser, eds. 2001. *Palatable Passion : Critical Perspectives on The Well of Loneliness*. New York, NY: Columbia University Press.
Duberman, Martin. 1993. *Stonewall*. New York, NY: Penguin Books.
Duberman, Martin, Martha Vicinus, and George Chauncey, Jr., eds. 1989. *Hidden from History: Reclaiming the Gay and Lesbian Past*. New York, NY: Penguin Books.
Eugenides, Jeffrey. 2002. *Middlesex*. New York, NY: Farrar, Straus, Giroux.
Faderman, Lillian. 1991. *Odd Girls and Twilight Lovers: A History of Lesbian Life in Twentieth-Century America*. New York, NY: Penguin.
Farizan, Sara. 2013. *If You Could Be Mine*. Chapel Hill, NC: Algonquin Young Readers.
Ferguson, Roderick. 2004. *Aberrations in Black: Toward a Queer of Color Critique*. Minneapolis, MN: University of Minnesota Press.
Feinberg, Leslie. 1993. *Stone Butch Blues*. Ithaca, NY: Firebrand Books.
Foucault, Michel. 1978. *The History of Sexuality: An Introduction, Vol.* I. New York, NY: Random House.
France, David. 2016. *How to Survive a Plague: The Inside Story of How Citizens and Science Tamed AIDS*. New York, NY: Knopf.
Garber, Eric. 1983. "T'Aint Nobody's Bizness: Homosexuality in 1920s Harlem." In *Black Men White Men: Afro-American Gay Life and Culture*, edited by Michael Smith. San Francisco, CA: Gay Sunshine Press.
Gill-Peterson, Julian. 2018. *Histories of the Transgender Child*. Minneapolis, MN: University of Minnesota Press.
Goldberg, Jonathan, ed. 1994. *Queering the Renaissance*. Durham, NC: Duke University Press.
Gould, Deborah. 2009. *Moving Politics: Emotion and ACT UP's Fight against AIDS*. Chicago, IL: University of Chicago Press.
Halberstam, Jack. 2018. *Trans*: A Quick and Quirky Account of Gender Variability*. Oakland, CA: University of California Press.
Hall, Radclyffe. 1928. *The Well of Loneliness*. Garden City, NY: Sun Dial Press.
Halperin, David. 1989. "Is There a History of Sexuality?" *History and Theory* 28(3): 257–274.

Halperin, David. 1990. *One Hundred Years of Homosexuality and Other Essays on Greek Love*. New York, NY: Routledge.

Harris, Frank. 1974. *Oscar Wilde: His Life and Confessions*. New York, NY: Horizon Press.

Highsmith, Patricia. 1952. *The Price of Salt*. New York NY: W.W. Norton.

Irvine, Janice. 2005. *Disorders of Desire: Sexuality and Gender in Modern American Sexology*. Philadelphia, PA: Temple University Press.

Jagose, Annamarie. 1997. *Queer Theory: An Introduction*. New York, NY: New York University Press.

Johnson, E. Patrick, ed. 2016. *No Tea, No Shade: New Writings in Black Queer Studies*. Durham, NC: Duke University Press.

Katz, Jonathan Ned. 1976. Gay American History: Lesbians and Gay Men in the U.S.A. New York City, NY: T.Y. Crowell.

Kramer, Larry. 1989. *Reports from the Holocaust: The Making of an AIDS Activist*. New York, NY: St. Martin's Press.

Kushner, Tony. 1991. *Angels in America: A Gay Fantasia on National Themes*. New York, NY: Theatre Communications Group.

Lanser, Susan. 2014. *The Sexuality of History: Modernity and the Sapphic, 1565–1830*. Chicago, IL: University of Chicago Press.

Lorde, Audre. 1982. *Zami: A New Spelling of My Name*. Freedom, CA: The Crossing Press.

Luibhéid, Eithne and Lionel Cantú, Jr., eds. 2005. *Queer Migrations: Sexuality, U.S. Citizenship, and Border Crossings*. Minneapolis, MN: University of Minnesota Press.

Lyons, Andrew and Harriet Lyons. 2004. *Irregular Connections: A History of Anthropology and Sexuality*. Lincoln, NE: University of Nebraska Press.

McCune, Jeffrey. 2014. *Sexual Discretion: Black Masculinity and the Politics of Passing*. Chicago, IL: University of Chicago Press.

Moore, Lisa. 1997. *Dangerous Intimacies: Toward a Sapphic History of the British Novel*. Durham, NC: Duke University Press.

Murib, Zein. 2014. "LGBT." *Transgender Studies Quarterly* 1(1–2): 118–120.

Okparanta, Chinelo. 2015. *Under the Udala Tress*. Boston, MA: Houghton Mifflin Harcourt.

Osman, Diriye. 2013. *Fairytales for Lost Children*. London: Team Angelica.

Osman, Diriye. 2014. "Why We Must Tell Our Own Stories." Huffpost Gay Voices. June 18.

Peck, Dale. 1993. *Martin and John*. New York, NY: Harper Perennial.

Plummer, Ken. 2012. "Critical Sexuality Studies." In *The Wiley Blackwell Companion to Sociology*, edited by George Ritzer, 243–268. Hoboken, NJ: Blackwell.

Powell, Patricia. 1993. *A Small Gathering of Bones*. Portsmouth, NH: Oxford.

Puar, Jasbir. 2007. *Terrorist Assemblages: Homonationalism in Queer Times*. Durham, NC: Duke University Press.

Rechy, John. 1963. *City of Night*. New York, NY: Grove Press.

Reeser, Todd. 2015. *Setting Plato Straight: Translating Ancient Sexuality in the Renaissance*. Chicago, IL: The University of Chicago Press.

Rich, Adrienne. 1980. "Compulsory Heterosexuality and Lesbian Existence." *Signs* 5(4): 631–660.

Rubin, Gayle. 1984. "Thinking Sex: Notes for a Radical Theory of the Politics of Sexuality." In *Pleasure and Danger*, edited by Carole S. Vance, 267–319. Boston, MA: Routledge and K. Paul.

Rupp, Leila. 2001. "Toward a Global History of Same-Sex Sexuality." *Journal of the History of Sexuality* 10(2): 287–302.

Rupp, Leila. 2009. *Sapphistries: A Global History of Love Between Women*. New York, NY: New York University Press.

Schulman, Sarah. 1990. *People in Trouble*. New York, NY: Dutton.
Schulman, Sarah. 2009. *Ties That Bind: Familial Homophobia and its Consequences*. New York, NY: The New Press.
Schwarz, A.B. Christa. 2003. *Gay Voices of the Harlem Renaissance*. Bloomington, IN: Indiana University Press.
Sedgwick, Eve Kosofsky. 1985. *Between Men: English Literature and Male Homosocial Desire*. New York, NY: Columbia University Press.
Seidman, Steven. 2010. *The Social Construction of Sexuality*. New York, NY: W.W. Norton.
Selvadurai, Shyam. 1996. *Funny Boy*. New York, NY: W. Morrow.
Shilts, Randy. 1987. *And the Band Played On*. New York, NY: St. Martin's Press.
Snorton, Riley. 2017. *Black on Both Sides: A Racial History of Trans Identity*. Minneapolis, MN: University of Minnesota Press.
Somerville, Siobhan. 1994. "Scientific Racism and the Emergence of the Homosexual Body." *Journal of the History of Sexuality* 5(2): 243–266.
Sontag, Susan. 1989. *AIDS and its Metaphors*. New York, NY: Farrar, Straus, Giroux.
Stein, Arlene. 2018. *Unbound: Transgender Men and the Remaking of Identity*. New York, NY: Pantheon Books.
Stryker, Susan. 2001. *Queer Pulp: Perverted Passions from the Golden Age of the Paperback*. San Francisco, CA: Chronicle Books.
Stryker, Susan. 2008. *Transgender History*. Berkeley, CA: Seal Press.
Summers, Claude, ed. 1995. *The Gay and Lesbian Literary Heritage: A Reader's Companion to the Writer's and their Works, from Antiquity to the Present*. New York, NY: Henry Holt.
Taïa, Abdellah. 2009a. *Salvation Army*. Los Angeles, CA: Semiotext(e).
Taïa, Abdellah. 2009b. "Homosexuality Explained to My Mother." *Asymptote Journal*. Available at: https://www.asymptotejournal.com/nonfiction/abdellah-taia-homosexuality-explained-to-my-mother/.
Taïa, Abdellah. 2012. *An Arab Melancholia*. Los Angeles, CA: Semiotext(e).
Taïa, Abdellah. 2016. "Abdellah Taïa Discusses His Novels and Why He Uses the Language that He Does." *Lambda Literary*, March 27. Available at: https://www.lambdaliterary.org/features/03/27/french-arabic-english-abdellah-taia-discusses-his-novels-and-why-he-uses-the-language-that-he-does/.
Tamaki, Mariko and Jillian Tamaki. 2008. *Skim*. Berkeley, CA: Groundwood Books.
Towle, Evan and Lynn Morgan. 2002. "Romancing the Transgender Native: Rethinking the 'Third Gender' Concept." *GLQ* 8(4): 469–497.
Vicinus, Martha. 1992. "'They Wonder to Which Sex I Belong': The Historical Roots of the Modern Lesbian Identity." *Feminist Studies* 18(3): 467–497.
Wahl, Elizabeth Susan. 1999. *Invisible Relations: Representations of Female Intimacy in the Age of Enlightenment*. Stanford, CA: Stanford University Press.
Weeks, Jeffrey. 1985. *Sexuality and its Discontents: Meanings, Myths, and Modern Sexualities*. New York, NY: Routledge.
Weeks, Jeffrey. 2011. *The Languages of Sexuality*. New York, NY: Routledge.
Wilchins, Riki. 2004. *Queer Theory, Gender Theory: An Instant Primer*. Los Angeles, CA: Alyson Books.
Wilde, Oscar. 1890. The Picture of Dorian Gray. *Lippincott's Monthly Magazine*.
Wilde, Oscar. 1891. *The Soul of a Man under Socialism*. New York, NY: Humbolt.
Winterson, Jeanette. 1985. *Oranges Are Not the Only Fruit*. New York, NY: Grove Press.
Wojnarowicz, David. 1991. *Close to the Knives: A Memoir of Disintegration*. New York, NY: Vintage Books.
Woodson, Jacqueline. 1997. *The House You Pass on the Way*. London: Puffin.

17

Queer Comics and LGBT in Comparative Perspective

HELIS SIKK

Introduction

Queer comics were once an illicit art form, circulating from person to person through underground networks. Although comics have always been a little queer (Batman and Robin, anyone?), not all superheroes wear capes. When censorship began to loosen in the late 1960s and especially in the 1970s, comics emerged as a powerful medium in lesbian, gay, bisexual, trans, and queer/questioning (LGBTQ) meaning-making and provided another window into a world that to this day tends to remain hidden. This chapter offers a comparative analysis of comics in two different national contexts to demonstrate how comics function as practical communication that is historically specific and produced under particular social, economic, and political conditions. Often mistakenly dismissed as not serious or too simplistic, the work of artists such as Tom of Finland to Alison Bechdel in the United States, and Gengoroh Tagame to Minami Ozaki in Japan, has extended beyond the panels and reshaped the world outside of comics.

In Japan, queer comics are a subgenre of the vast manga scene. Queer comics are known as gei komi (gay comics), sometimes called bara (rose), bara manga, and yaoi or boys' love. All these terms refer to different genres within the broad category of queer manga or comics. Translating terms that are culturally specific is an impossible task. Even the use of broad categories such as yaoi or bara eliminates the nuances and subgenres that exist within these most well-known genres. Writing in English is a limitation that I am very much aware of, especially when it comes to contrasting two very different queer cultures – the United States and Japan. Hence, this chapter is not an all-comprehensive discussion of queer art in those two countries. The purpose of this chapter is to provide a brief overview of queer manga in Japan and queer comics in the United States since the 1950s and to challenge some of the commonly held understandings of (trans)national identity politics.

Few academic works exist in Japanese or English that focus on the topic of queer manga. The most comprehensive overview of erotic art can be found in Gengoroh Tagame's *Gay Erotic Art in Japan (vol. 1): Artists from the Time of the Birth of Gay Magazines* (2003) and the postwar gay publishing scene in Mark McLelland's *Queer Japan from the Pacific War to the Internet Age* (2005). Since the 1990s, there has been more academic writing on the less hardcore yaoi or boys' love comics, but the hardcore gei komi/bara has not received the scholarly attention it deserves (McLelland et. al. 2015). Similarly, although comics studies has emerged as a serious scholarly inquiry since the 2000s, there are not that many comprehensive studies on queer comics in the United States. American journalist Justin Hall's *No Straight Lines: Four Decades of Queer Comics* (2012) and artist Robert Triptow's edited anthology *Gay Comics* (1989) are the two comprehensive collections on the topic. What is missing is more critical scholarly writing on queer comics in transnational context. German journalist Markus Pfalzgraf's *Stripped: A Story of Gay Comics* (2012) is a bilingual attempt in this direction, but more academically rigorous writing is sorely needed on this topic.

Historically, in the United States, queer comics as well as other popular media have lacked racial and ethnic diversity, and underground artists have been mostly white with a few exceptions such as Larry Fuller (McCabe 2016). Japan has a complicated history of race and ethnic diversity and, since World War II, has maintained an official image of a monocultural and monoethnic country. However, in reality, the Japanese population consists of a significant number of minority groups such as North and South Koreans, Chinese, Brazilians, and Filipinos (Arudou 2010; Howell 1996; Tsuda 1998; Graburn, Ertl, and Tierney 2010). To this day, the Japanese government does not collect data on ethnicity, but conflates it with nationality (Arudou 2010). Hence, the world of queer manga in Japan is predominantly occupied by artists who identify as Japanese.

Another important shortcoming of comics in Japan and the United States is how much of a male-dominated medium it has been in both countries. There have been interventions from women since the 1970s, but as I will discuss later, this has not been without major controversy. Due to the gender bias, this overview of queer comics in the United States and Japan will mostly include depictions of male-on-male intimacy. Nevertheless, queer comics tell us a lot about queer culture and activism in post-1950s Japan and the United States. Increased internationalization of communication, relaxation of censorship laws and social pressures made the latter half of the twentieth century a crucial time in the development of LGBTQ culture as we understand it today in both countries (D'Emilio 1989; McLelland 2005). The intent of this chapter is to explore the significance of comics as a queer activist strategy by identifying queer comics and considering the importance of audiences in the United States and Japan since the 1950s. I will begin by first unpacking the term "queer comics" itself by providing a working definition of the word "queer" and look at some of the defining characteristics of comics.

"Queer" and "Comics" in Queer Comics

"Queer comics" is a very broad and ambiguous term. Both "queer" and "comics" have been notoriously difficult to define. You may use these words in your everyday life without considering their full weight and the academic debate around them. The word queer was a pejorative, used to refer to LGBT people until it was reclaimed by activists in the 1980s and 1990s. Today we can use it as a noun, verb, and an adjective, less seldom perhaps as an adverb. Queer theorist David M. Halperin (1995) notes that "queer is by definition *whatever* is at odds with the normal, the legitimate, the dominant. There is nothing in particular to which it necessarily refers. It is an identity without an essence" (p. 62). In other words, queer marks a resistance to the norm and cannot be pinned down. Queer theory studies the social and political dimensions of sexuality and gender identity. Gender studies scholar Siobhan B. Somerville (2007) points out that queer is often used in contradictory contexts: sometimes it refers to the identities "gay" and "lesbian" in popular context while in political and theoretical writing it seeks to challenge the existence of these identity categories. Queer is used as an umbrella term for nonnormative sexualities and genders, but it also challenges this very umbrella that includes the normative definitions of these identities. For this current chapter, it is important to keep in mind that queer is political and forms of expression marked as queer involve resistance to oppressive social norms.

The word "comics" has been equally difficult to define. The debates concern when an image and its interaction with words combine in a way that can be considered a comic and whether words are even necessary. Visual studies scholar Will Eisner (1985) provides a very liberal definition of comics and sees them as "the arrangement of pictures or images and words to narrate a story or dramatize an idea" (p. 5). As Eisner points out, the main goal of comics is to adapt a story and/or exaggerate the main points. Comics theorist Scott McCloud (2005) emphasizes one of the key characteristics of comics – they are a monosensory medium that intend to embrace all the senses (sound, smell, touch, and even taste). The more abstract an image is, the more universal and easily relatable it is for the audience. The drawing of a round shape and two dots and a half circle below the dots is a relatively abstract representation of a face that most of us could identify with. The more specific in terms of age, race, and gender we make this drawing of the face, the less abstract it gets and, hence, less people can directly identify with it. These are a few of the key characteristics of comics to keep in mind as we look more closely at specific examples of queer comics in the following sections.

Censorship in the United States and Japan

Comics need a readership to function. According to Scott McCloud (1993), producing an aesthetic response in the reader is one of the main goals of comics. For queer artists, the idea of a reader has been precarious, as not all aesthetic responses have been publicly accepted. In this section, I will consider artistic expression under censorship in the United States and Japan.

In the United States, the 1873 Comstock Act permitted postal authorities to exclude homosexual publications from the mail (Gurstein 1996). Hollywood's Motion Picture Production Code (also known as the Hays Code), adopted in 1934, prohibited the depiction of gay characters or open discussion of homosexuality in film (Couvares 2006). Until 1974, the American Psychiatric Association's diagnostic manual defined homosexuality as a psychopathology (D'Emilio 1989). The 1950s lavender scare fueled by Joseph McCarthy's witch-hunt on communism, deemed homosexuals as "moral perverts" and security risks (D'Emilio 1989; Johnson 2004; Cuordileone 2000). As a result, the government adopted rules explicitly excluding homosexuals from federal jobs and military service ((D'Emilio 1989; Johnson 2004; Cuordileone 2000). Industry group, the Comics Code Authority (formed in the early 1950s), was part of this restrictive censorship culture and directly restricted the content of comic books (Hajdu 2008; Costello 2009). The fear was that any kind of content deemed disturbing – for instance, vampires, zombies, certain kinds of crime, rape, seduction, and homosexuality – would corrupt the young who made up the majority of the readers (Hajdu 2008; Costello 2009). Publishers could not be directly restricted, but most distributors refused to sell comics that did not carry the Comics Code Authority seal. These strict censorship laws created an underground market for comics with explicit content, and they were often distributed from person to person.

While in the United States the Comics Code Authority (CCA) influence started to wane in the 1970s, Japan to this day prohibits all drawn or photographic depictions of genitals in books (Pfalzgraf 2012). Publishers who do not follow the law face the risk of being charged with distributing obscene materials. Bara artist Gengoroh Tagame explains that there are no direct guidelines as to how to avoid this (Pfalzgraf 2012). Tagame himself started to whiten out penises and use black bars to cover up genitals as a way to avoid being censored (Pfalzgraf 2012). These techniques allow for the reader to still see the size and shape of the penis, although with less detail. Of course, similar to United States, the censorship rules in Japan were ignored by underground publishing.

1950s: Perverse Press and Physique Magazines

Unlike the United States, Japan witnessed explicit homoerotic images in the underground publishing of the 1950s. Homoerotic comics similar to the later hardcore bara can be found in the 1950s' "perverse press." McLelland (2005) argues that while the United States was cracking down on "deviant" sexualities, Japan experienced a sexual renaissance evidenced by the publication of a number of magazines devoted to nonnormative sexualities and genders. Significantly, these early magazines did not segregate the material into heterosexual or homosexual themed issues, as became increasingly common in the 1970s, but presented a wide range of "perverse desires." According to McLelland (2005), the press was organized around "a perverse paradigm based on an all-encompassing interest in queer desire and its diverse manifestations" (p. 11). The earliest site for male-on-male desire was in *Adonis* – one of the first magazines to feature gay art and content (established in 1952). A little bit later, the magazine *Fū zoku zō shi* (Sex Customs Storybook, 1953–1955) included a correspondence column for homosexual men alongside general discussions of "perverse sexuality," including the sudden postwar popularity of fellatio and kissing (McLelland 2005). These publications can be seen as an example of the prepolitical sexual subcultures that existed before the 1970s and 1980s.

However, depictions of male homosexual desire in Japan go back much further than the perverse press of the 1950s. When we think about queer manga in contemporary context, we cannot overlook this long history of artistic expression that includes images of same-sex desire and continues to influence artists today. "Shunga" or erotic art depicting male-on-male eroticism can be traced back to at least mid-eighteenth century and to the work of Suzuki Harunobu. "Danshoku-shunga" or "male erotic art" directly depicts homosexual desire and sex. Harunobu's art includes pederasty and mostly depicts sex between an older and a younger male. The dichotomy of submissive and dominant or junior and senior (sempai/kohai) plays an important part in Japanese society even today and hence can be found throughout the history of queer manga (Reichert 2006; Lunsing 2001). This system involves an hierarchical relationship between an older and younger person and is observed in most social interactions in Japanese society even today (Reichert 2006; Lunsing 2001). The younger person (kohai) performs menial tasks for the older person (sempai) in return for mentorship.

Harunobu's art influenced artists who followed a less sexually explicit style and published for a more ambiguous readership. Most notably, Harunobu's influence can be seen in the work of Kasho Takahata and later in the more explicit work of Tatsuji Okawa. Kasho Takahata was an early twentieth century illustrator whose work included book illustrations and drawings for fashion magazines (Milner 2008). Takahata's imagery, although not explicitly erotic, can be seen as an inspiration for the cool manga of the late twentieth century. The pictures are very graceful and often capture both women and men in motion or mid-air in the middle of a fight. Takahata art also includes "otoko-e" or male pictures that illustrate "the charms of men." Earlier the term referred to a more rudimentary style of drawing that was meant to be viewed only by men. In the twentieth century context, these were drawings of slender and very beautiful Japanese men, often dressed as samurais or soldiers.

There are similarities between the milder otoko-e and the images in physique magazines in the 1950s United States. Due to the oppressive cultural climate and restrictions placed by censorship laws in the United States, the work of one of the most influential artists, Tom of Finland, was first published in 1957 in the Los Angeles based *Physique Pictorial*, a magazine intended for men who enjoyed working out and spending time outdoors. Tom of Finland did over 200 scenes of attractive and fit young men engaged in outdoor activities for the *Physique Pictorial* (Triptow 1989). Although mainstream understanding of the magazine's readership included young men who were interested in bodybuilding and fitness, the actual audience was much more complex since access to gay male erotica was very limited at the time.

Tom of Finland is one of the most influential artists to shape gay culture and fashion in the United States and beyond. Born Touko Laaksonen in a small Finnish village in 1920, the artist got his penname from the publisher of *Physique Pictorial*, Bob Mizer (Hanson 2014). His work has shaped generations of comic book artists across the world. Dom Orjeudos (known under the pennames Stephen and Etienne) and British artists Bill Ward, Sean, Mike Kuchar, and Jerry Mills have all been influenced by Tom's work (Triptow 1989). Laaksonen's work became very quickly popular first among gay underground, then gay mainstream publishing and eventually extended beyond the world of comics to shape public perception of gay men in the United States.

When Laaksonen began producing his work, the effeminate "sissy" stereotype of gay men prevailed. The sissy had been a common trope in the 1920s and 1930s

Hollywood that relied on this image of an effeminate and sexually ambiguous male figure for comic relief (Russo 1981; Benshoff and Griffin 2005). The sissy remained a common character even during the time of the previously mentioned Hays Code, but the image shifted from humorous to villainous and dark (Russo 1981; Benshoff and Griffin 2005). The sissy represented everything that was "unnatural" and not "normal," and hence greatly influenced mainstream culture and gay men's perception of themselves in the first half of the twentieth century.

Micha Ramakers, who wrote Tom of Finland's principal biography, saw his "great achievement … as having liberated gay men from the shackles of femininity and unnaturalness" (Ramakers 2000). Tom of Finland's characters were mostly hypermasculine and hypersexual white men with bulging muscles and exaggerated penises. After serving as a lieutenant in World War II, Laaksonen started to draw erotic pictures inspired by soldiers (Hanson 2014). The characters prominently feature figures in traditionally masculine spaces and professions and show the main character having sex with police officers and military personnel in both dominant and passive positions.

In the 1950s Japan, somewhat similarly, the initial association of gay men was with the effeminate "gei bōi" (gay boys), who worked at Tokyo's "gei bā" (gay bars) (McLelland 2005). Mainstream media wrote about the bars often and the term "gei" became known and used among the Japanese much earlier than in the United States. McLelland (2005) describes the gei bōi as a hybrid category that combined premodern practices of transgender entertainment with modern European ideals of androgyny. The term "lezu," derived from the English "lesbian" was used from the mid-1960s to refer to a genre of pornography for heterosexual males (McLelland 2005). Hence, the terms "gay" and "lesbian" were part of Japanese vocabulary many decades before the 1980s, which is when some earlier histories claim gay and lesbian emerged in Japan as a Western export (Summerhawk, McMahill, and McDonald 1998; Conlan 2001). Imagining gay and lesbian as Western exports eliminates the long history of nonnormative genders and sexualities in Japan that thrived independently from the West and plays into the false image of "backwardness" often associated with non-Western cultures.

The terms gei and lezu were not used to refer to politicized identities that demanded recognition by the state, as we understand gay and lesbian in the United States context. These terms emerged due to the unique historical conditions of the postwar period, and as McLelland (2005) states, are "not some copy of a western original" (p. 111). The particular rights-based connotation of these terms was mixed with the earlier meanings that were already in use decades before and, hence, the culture that surrounds them is specific to Japan.

The queer artwork in Japan challenges normative Western progressive narratives and Eurocentric notions of identity that tend to focus on the idea of a journey from oppression to liberation. When it comes to the movement of people, this development is often seen as not just psychological, but also geographical from rural to urban, from East to West. In Japan, nonnormative sexualities and genders contested Confucianist morality in their own unique way, which does not mean that homosexuality as we understand it today was accepted by Japan's mainstream society. The story of queer artistic expression and societal oppression is as complex and multilayered in Japan as it is in the United States.

1960s: Hypermasculinity, Sadomasochism, and Bara

In the United States, the underground comics scene began to take shape as baby boomers became part of the counterculture (Hall 2012). Feminist, gay liberation, and the Civil Rights movements opened up the space for more offstream publishing. Censorship began to crumble court case by court case in the United States, which opened up the market for a diverse range of openly homosexual and erotic magazines. In the 1960s through the 1980s, artists were not confined only to a few illustrations or the comic strip at the end of the magazine, but often illustrated the entire publication.

Tom of Finland started to work for *The Advocate* and moved to more sequential narrative imagery with an ongoing character Kake he had developed by the late-1960s (Hanson 2014). Kake has dark gelled hair, a square jaw, prominent chest and arm hair, well-defined abs and biceps, and a seductive, yet sweet smile. He is usually dressed head-to-toe in leather, except for a tight white shirt, sometimes with 'Fucker' written across it. The development of Kake as a character shows a shift in United States' gay culture. The image of gay men as effeminate and desexualized sissies was taken over by the hypersexual and over-the-top masculine Kake.

The masculine aesthetic of Tom of Finland became known in the gay community as the "clone look," which was very popular in the 1960s and 1970s (Filiault and Drummond 2007). Clones exhibited a sculptured physique (bugling pectorals, large biceps, body and facial hair) and working-class aesthetic (leather jackets, denim, flannel shirts, and work boots) (Filiault and Drummond 2007). Gay men's obsession with the physical body was part of a larger cultural trend that included the opening of the first Gold's Gym, the creation of the Chippendales, and men's fitness magazines (Snaith 2003). Tom of Finland's hypermasculine images helped the previously effeminized gay men to fit in with this newly emerging fitness culture.

Japan also experienced a gay publishing boom, which allowed for gay erotic art to become more widely accessible to interested readers. In Japan, a specific style that developed during the 1960s was bara. Bara can vary in visual style and plot, but typically features masculine men with considerable muscle and body hair, similar to what in the United States could be seen as representative of the bear culture. Bear culture is a gay male subculture that consists of larger and hairier men with beards (Kampf 2000; Wright 2001). Unlike the more polished clones, gay men who identify as bears display a more rugged masculinity.

In the 1960s, a key theme found in queer manga was sadomasochism, which is related to the sempai/kohai dynamic developed in earlier homoerotic works. While bara usually features adult content and violent or exploitative sex, it also often includes autobiographical themes that are less likely to be found in the lighthearted and playful art of Tom of Finland. Similar to Tom of Finland's work, Japanese comics drew inspiration from homosocial professions, featuring samurais, soldiers, or Japanese gangsters. However, unlike the Tom of Finland work, which included men who appear expressionless or sport a modest naïve smile, the men in Japanese drawings look serious and often pained. The reasons for this difference are varied. Some scholars have argued that the pained expressions are a response to the official Japanese culture that was still sexually very oppressive and attached considerable shame to homosexuality and sex outside the bounds of heterosexual marriage

(Tagame 2003). It is also important to consider the cultural differences in interpersonal communication between Japan and the United States – the latter places considerable emphasis on smiling, especially in photographs.

Photography was a major influence in shaping queer visual culture and the bara scene in Japan. *Bara kei* (*Ordeal by Roses*, published in 1961) was a collection of seminude photographs of writer Yukio Mishima taken by Eikoh Hosoe (Tagame 2003). The photos show Mishima's muscular body in bondage while wearing fundoshi, a traditional Japanese loincloth. Other photographic visual influences that shaped the bara scene include the work of Yato Tamotsu and Haga Kuro. Both men published picture books that featured male nudity and homoerotic content. The work of these visual artists had a major influence in shaping gay bara artists in the 1960s and later years. Tatsuji Okawa was one of the earliest bara artists influenced by the Hosoe's photographs. His graceful drawings of young muscular men feature bondage and torture. Okawa's work appeared first in *Fuzokukitan* (1960–1974), an erotic magazine that featured the work of some of the most well-known bara artists.

One such artist was Sanshi Funayama. Funayama's obsession was mostly with policemen. Hence, Funayama's work, similar to that of Tom of Finland in the United States, speaks to a major theme in Japanese queer comics: a focus on traditionally masculine and homosocial professions. However, in Japan, the sadomasochistic fantasy gets pushed to the extreme and often the main character dies. The stories feature a young and muscular police officer who gets kidnapped and tortured by cannibals who eventually cut him up and eat his flesh. Funayama was a police officer himself and used to draw the images during his night shift (Tagame 2003). His work challenges a traditionally masculine institution, yet only to a degree, as the sexual transgression always means death for the police officer.

Two other artists who started out in *Fuzokukitan* were Hirano Go and Mishima Go. Both men represent a more traditionally Japanese aesthetic in bara, which was influenced by Hosoe's photographs of Mishima in the traditional Japanese loincloth. Their work includes men with tattoos and Japanese swords, wearing loincloths and hachimaki (Japanese headbands that signify courage or perseverance). The main topic of Hirano Go and Mishima Go's work is the sexual act itself, which includes explicit depictions of oral and anal sex without an apparent storyline. The focus on traditionally Japanese themes was a way to make a statement against Western influence that was becoming more prominent in the late 1960s and especially in early 1970s with the publication of the first commercial gay magazine *Barazoku* (*The Rose Tribe*; established in 1971) (Tagame 2003).

The post-1960s focus on hypermasculinity has been controversial both in the United States and Japan. Some herald the work of Tom of Finland as progressive because his inclusion of excessive masculinity defied stereotypes of gay men as effeminate and subverted masculine occupations and spaces (Lahti 1998; Snaith 2003). His work eroticizes and fetishizes traditional symbols of masculinity by showing gay men in traditionally masculine and historically homophobic professions such as the military and law enforcement. His work has also been seen as subversive through exaggeration and parody (Snaith 2003). At the same time, a counterargument can be made that Tom of Finland's work is not radical, but complicit in supporting the system that oppresses women and more effeminate gay men. As mentioned in the beginning of this chapter, the word queer signifies radical politics that seek to question normalizing institutions, such as the police or the military. Tom of Finland's work, however, only seems to subvert traditionally masculine professions with gay sex acts, but does not challenge the state institutions themselves.

Japanese bara art has also been critiqued for not challenging the normative mainstream culture beyond the overt sexual content (McLelland 2005). Although later artists acknowledge the varied reactions to homosexuality in modern Japan, bara does not have a public political agenda (McLelland 2005). Similar to gay male culture in United States, there was little interaction between gay men and lesbians or the gender-nonconforming gei bōi (McLelland 2005). As the next section shows, women created their own unique space in both queer comics and queer manga in the late 1970s, although this was not done without controversy.

1970s: Women in Comix and Boys' Love

As the previous discussion shows, queer comics in the United States and Japan have been very much a male-dominated world, which replicates the gender bias evident in the mainstream comic book industry. Yet in the 1970s, queer comics, especially with an "x" emerged as a medium where more and more female artists would find opportunities to share their work. The letter "x" marked comics that were part of the underground scene, which included works that were not endorsed by the Comics Code Authority. Underground comix – especially the controversial works of Robert Crumb and S. Clay Wilson – tended to be homophobic and misogynist. In an attempt to counter these trends, women artists in the United States created their own publications and collectives. The earliest feminist and lesbian publications included the anthology *It Ain't Me, Babe* (1970), the series *Tits and Clits* (1972) and the *Wimmen's Comix* (1972) collective. These publications and collectives were the home for female creators whose art focused more on social justice issues and community building rather than sexual escapades and power play.

The first lesbian character appeared in "Sandy Comes Out" in 1972, which was created by Trina Robbins and published in *Wimmen's Comix* #1. As Hall (2012) and Triptow (1989) have stated, the controversy around "Sandy Comes Out" involved Trina Robbins's identity. She was a feminist and close with the gay and lesbian community, but did not identify as a lesbian herself. Sandy's character was based on Robbins's friend who moved into the Bay Area after her divorce and eventually came out as a lesbian. In response to Robbins's work, cartoonist Mary Wings created *Dyke Shorts* because she felt that "Sandy Comes Out" was superficial, too reliant on stereotypes, and did not have emotional depth (Hall 2012). More lesbian characters appeared in Roberta Gregory's self-published semi-autobiographical comic book *Dynamite Damsels* in 1976. The main character is Frieda Phelps, a young idealistic woman who navigates the feminist circles of the 1970s. Besides social issues, the book also includes fantasy and science fiction stories about lesbian superheroines ("Superdyke") and women-only lands ("Liberatia").

A number of female artists relied on personal experiences to address social issues such as sex discrimination in the workplace or violence towards women. Cartoonist

Lee Mars explored sexuality and beauty standards in *The Further Fattening Adventures of Pudge, Girl Blimp* ([1973–1978] 2016). The main character, Pudge, is a chubby teenager who has run away to San Francisco from Normal, IL. Pudge is on a mission to lose her virginity, yet every attempt to have sex fails terribly. Marrs's work is a milestone for women in comics: she created a female character who is unabashedly horny, likes to eat junk food without feeling bad about it, and is not conventionally feminine in her interactions with the world. Pudge inspired other artists to create characters that would draw attention to the double standard of societal gender norms. Most of the underground comix created by women in the 1970s and early 1980s are nearly all unavailable now. Yet, the 1970s marked the start of a strong community of female artists whose focus on social issues influenced male artists to take on political themes in their work as well.

In Japan, by the 1970s the "perverse" subculture began to splinter into ever more specialized identity categories, which opened up queer manga for women artists. In the late 1970s, a major queer manga genre emerged in Japan – yaoi. Yaoi or boys' love (BL) features romantic love stories between young, slender, effeminate men. In terms of style, the characters are more minimalist and less realistic that the ones found in bara. The men have very narrow jawlines, long flowing hair, pointy noses, and large eyes. Their bodies are lanky and hairless rather than muscular and hirsute as the men in bara. One of the most well-known BL artists is Minami Ozaki. Her work *Zetsuai 1989* tells the story of Kouji Nanjo, a self-destructive rock singer who falls in love with a talented soccer player, Takuto Izumi. The two have a tumultuous romance that is strained by secrets and complicated family relationships.

When queer manga became a subject of academic inquiry in the 1990s, more critique emerged from feminist and queer activists that addressed the identity politics involved in the production of BL. BL is mostly created by heterosexual women for heterosexual women. Ishida Hitoshi (2015) writes about the 1990s discursive clash between BL writers and gay men, what is known as the yaoi ronsô (yaoi wars). Gay men's stance was that BL is a misrepresentation and misappropriation of gay realities and artists who do not identify as male and gay should not contribute to representations of gay culture. However, recent scholarship has found that young gay men today find BL more realistic because it focuses on romance and allows them to be more vulnerable and passive (Baudinette 2015; Nagaike 2015). The BL genre has also provided women with an outlet to express themselves and explore their sexuality outside traditional societal gender norms.

The extreme ends of the genres – BL and bara – speak to the two sides inherent to gay culture: romantic on the one end and explicitly sexual on the other end. According to Tagame (2003), bara is the representation of "real" and "hard" gay masculinity. Bara drawings have heavy line work and shading, which makes the images appear more realistic. BL leaves more space for background elements and landscape, whereas in bara the bodies of muscular men fill the entire frame. Today, the milder BL is more widespread in Japan than bara (McLelland et al. 2015). This is partially due to a commonly held misconception about BL: the audience is presumed to be young heterosexual women, which negates the homoerotic content and allows it to be distributed with less constraints. However, as with the earlier, less-explicit homoerotic images, the readership of BL is more complicated than that and includes people who identify in numerous ways.

1980s: Aids, Politics, and Sex

The first cases of HIV/AIDS in the United States appeared in 1983. The AIDS epidemic spread quickly and devastated the LGBTQ community. Queer cartoonists in the United States responded in numerous ways to express their anger and despair, but also courage and hopefulness. Visual artist David Wojanarowicz wrote an angry and raw autobiographical *7 Miles a Second*; Ivan Velez, Jr. and Jennifer Camper provided an insight into the crisis by showing the devastating effects it had on the community on a very intimate, everyday level. Carl Vaughn Frick used allegory and sarcasm to address the challenges of the AIDS epidemic. In 1988, Trina Robbins, Robert Triptow, and Bill Sienkiewicz created *Strip AIDS USA*, a comics anthology that aimed to educate and raise money.

Publications and artists in Japan did not address AIDS as a concern until the 1990s, and even then it remained on the periphery of LGBTQ media (McLelland 2005). 1980s' publications and art continued to focus on sex, fantasy, and entertainment. A major artist to emerge in the 1980s was Gengoroh Tagame. Gengoroh Tagame is arguably Japan's most well-known queer manga artist. His work was first published in 1982 while he was still a student at Tama Art University (Tagame 2018a). All of his work until recent years can be considered part of the bara genre. Tagame's fantasy themes focus on uniform fetish, bondage, sadomasochism, and a variety of representations of sexual agony and pleasure. Tagame lists hardcore British artist Tom Ward and United States based The Hun and Etienne as some of his main influences (Pfalzgraf 2012). The work of these men is part of what can be considered bear gay culture that, as mentioned earlier, includes larger and hairier men.

One of Tagame's most known series is *Naburi-Mono* ("laughing stock"; 2017a), published in the 1990s in various gay magazines (Pfalzgraf 2012). The series narrates a love story between a mobster and a kidnapped wrestler who end up committing suicide to restore their honor. Although Tagame's work could be categorized as hardcore pornography, his drawings are not impulsive, but drawn out very methodologically (Pfalzgraf 2012). He first writes out the story and then draws the sketches and colors the drawings. In the 2000s, a few of Tagame's comics were translated into French, Italian, and Spanish, and in the 2010s into English.

Tagame's work shows that it has become more and more difficult to draw clear boundaries between the two major styles: BL and bara. Both are part of the broad category of queer manga, which leaves room for blending and mixing of themes, topics, and styles. Not all bara involves hardcore pornography without a romantic storyline or humor. For instance, the work of Seizo Ebisubashi employs humor and stands out by being more purely gachi-muchi ("muscly-chubby") – a subgenre that features big-boy-next-door characters, rather than the more heroically built men found in Tagame's art. Ebisubashi stories are a mixture of BL and bara that often include a romantic, at times even domestic, setting and explicitly sexual content. This blending of genres also speaks to the dynamic and multilayered nature of queer manga readership.

Although the AIDS epidemic stigmatized the LGBTQ community, queer comics were becoming more popular among the mainstream audience in the United States (Triptow 1989). Some of the most prolific and influential artists who launched their career in the 1980s were Howard Cruse and Alison Bechdel. Cruse was the first editor of *Gay Comix*, a series published by Kitchen Sink Press in the 1980 that marked a step toward the mainstream for queer comics (Triptow 1989). Cruse's remarkable ability to always make the reader both laugh and think allowed him to connect with a wide range of audiences and influence the next generation of queer comic book artists.

Born in small-town Alabama to a preacher's family, Cruse's work often reflected on his own upbringing. Growing up in segregated and conservative South, Cruse became an advocate for social justice, and his comics unabashedly addressed issues concerning sexism, racism, and homophobia. Cruse published the series *Barefootz* and *Wendel* for *The Advocate* (Triptow 1989) – both comics illustrate his ability to depict humanity in the most empathetic ways.

Alison Bechdel's work is quintessential to the repoliticized queer culture and identity politics of 1980s. Her comic strip, *Dykes to Watch Out For* (1983–2008) was first published in New York's *Womennews* (Triptow 1989). Other lesbian newsletters and newspapers followed and *Dykes to Watch Out For* ended up running for 25 years. The focus of the series is on a tight-knit group of friends and lovers living in a midsize American city. The main character Mo is a lesbian feminist activist with a habit of constantly complaining about politics and critiquing everything and everyone around her. Mo, the sex-positive drag king Lois, and Thea, a Jewish lesbian with multiple sclerosis, all at some point work at the lesbian Madwimmin Bookstore owned by a black lesbian activist Jezanna. Other characters include Toni, a business manager and Clarice, a workaholic environmental lawyer.

The lives of characters in *Dykes to Watch Out For* are played out against the backdrop of current political and cultural events. On these pages, Bechdel comments on the Michigan Womyn's Music Festival (Odahl-Ruan et. al. 2015) and lesbian pregnancy; pokes fun atidentity politics; reflects on the sad effects of neoliberalism when Jezanna's bookstore is closed down; and critiques same-sex marriage when Toni and Clarice get married (and divorced later in the series). Bechdel's *Dykes to Watch Out For* packs a lot in one comic strip. It is a lesbian sit-com drama, but also a rigorous social and political commentary. With her free-flowing and seemingly casual style, Bechdel, similar to Howard Cruse, always manages to make the reader laugh, think, and at times also cry.

Japan and the United States had very different LGBTQ publishing cultures in the 1980s. While AIDS and politics dominated the pages in the United States, artists in Japan continued focus on the sexual aspect of the LGBTQ culture. In the United States, erotic images that were part of the magazines in the 1960s and 1970s did not last beyond the 1980s. Media scholar Michael Schudson (1995) has argued that publications that had moved leftward in the 1970s shifted to the right in the 1980s, following the Reagan administration and the influence of the conservative movement. This shift toward the conservative coincided with the AIDS epidemic, which further relegated the sexual aspect of LGBTQ culture to the private realm (Baim 2012; Stein 2014).

1990s and 2000s: Memoirs, Young Adults, and Trans Creators

Despite the very different approaches in Japan and the United States in the 1980s, as artists matured in the 1990s and 2000s, surprisingly similar themes have emerged in both countries. The last 15 years have witnessed a renaissance of queer comics, which is evidenced by the increase in graphic novels and graphic memoirs, web comics, and trans and queer writers of color. The memoirs mark a big change in queer comics and activist strategies: the focus has shifted from depictions of explicit sex to family and children.

Howard Cruse pioneered the memoir trend when he published his incredible semi-autobiographical graphic novel, *Stuck Rubber Baby* in 1995. The book tells the story of a young gay man growing up in segregated South in the 1950s–1960s. Following her success with *Dykes to Watch Out For,* Bechdel also went on to publish her very popular graphic memoirs *Fun Home: A Family Tragicomic* (2006) and *Are You My Mother?: A Comic Drama* (2012). Similar to the success of Tom of Finland, Bechdel's work had expanded beyond the panels of the comic book page. *Fun Home* was adapted into a Broadway musical in 2013.

In Japan, Tagame's topics and style have also extended beyond the hardcore bara aesthetics of the 1980s, which has made his work more transnationally available. In 2014–2017, Tagame published the family focused gay-themed manga series, *My Brother's Husband* (*Otouto no Otto*). *My Brother's Husband* tells the story of Yaichi, a divorcee and a single father to his only daughter Kana. Their lives get complicated when Yaichi's deceased brother's Canadian husband Mike comes to Japan to pay his respects to the family. Yaichi became estranged from his brother Ryōji after he came out to him as gay and now has an opportunity to get to know him again through Mike. The story takes a deep look into how bias and homophobia shape communities and relationships beyond those who are directly affected. The reader can still detect Tagame's familiar stylistic elements even in this very family-oriented work. Although the story does not include explicit displays of gay eroticism, Mike is still a bear – a large and rugged gay man with a beard. The series has received very positive reviews from queer comic book artists across the world, including Alison Bechdel. Pantheon books published the first volume of the *My Brother's Husband* in English in May 2017 (2017b); volume 2 was released in September 2018 (2018b). In spring 2018, NHK, Japan's only public broadcaster, released *My Brother's Husband* as a television series.

Children and family have also been the focus of queer comics artists in the United States. *The Princess*, a web comic by Christine Smith, serves as an example of some of recent trends in queer comics coming together in web comics: family, memoir, children, and transgender rights. *The Princess* is a semi-autobiographical coming of age story about a trans girl named Sarah. Smith's comic strip is very different from earlier works by Tom of Finland or Bechdel in terms of tone, coloring, themes, and characters. Sarah's main concerns involve bullying and parental acceptance. Having elementary school children as the main characters shows how much the discourse on LGBTQ rights and identities has shifted – from muscular men with tight jeans and exaggerated penises to young children exploring their gender identity and sexuality while navigating their relationships with parents, peers, and teachers. Even when such issues came up in earlier comics, the representation was much more visceral and crude. Bullying meant that someone was beaten up and navigating relationships with parents meant moving to the big city.

A key characteristic of *The Princess* is its accessibility as an educational tool. The internet has revolutionized the world of queer comics and activism in a number of ways. It allows for artists to distribute comics at less cost and to reach wide transnational audiences. More than ever, trans writers and queer writers of color have started to take up space with their work. Jamie Cortez's bilingual *Sexilio/Sexile* (2004), published by the AIDS Project Los Angeles, is a visionary intervention into prevention literature. *Sexilio* is narrated by Adela Vázquez – an immigrant trans woman from Cuba who shares her life story and arrival in the United States in the 1980s. *Sexilio* has been valued for its empathetic and nonpreachy approach toward sexual health and has been widely distributed in prisons, libraries, and clinics.

The internet also allows for queer comics to travel transnationally with relative ease. This means that boundaries between genres specific to Japan get blurred when artists in Indonesia, who have been influenced both by BL and bara culture, start to produce their own work. For instance, the work of the Indonesia- and Philippines-based group of artists, Black Monkey Pro, features youthful boys with very muscular and hairless bodies, strong romantic storylines, and explicit sex.

Conclusion

Queer comics are extremely diverse in motivation, style, and themes. They can be sexually explicit, angry, educative, political, sad, and funny. In the United States, the development of themes in queer comics reflects the changes in LGBTQ activist tactics since the 1960s. The late 1960s and 1970s were a unique moment in LGBTQ culture when one among several movement-building strategies included consciously combining eroticism with serious news stories. Tom of Finland's work became popular at a time when gay liberation (in contrast to the earlier homophile movement) used explicit sexuality as an integral part of their activism.

Queer manga in Japan emerged out of a long history of homoerotic imagery and the underground "perverse press" of the 1950s. In the 1960s, male-on-male eroticism and sadomasochism dominated the queer manga scene. This male-focused hypermasculine culture was challenged by women in the late 1970s with the creation of boys' love comics that focused more on romantic storylines. In the United States, women artists of the 1970s also led the way in expanding the topics beyond the sexually explicit. Their focus was more on social justice and community building. During the 1980s' AIDS crisis, queer comics in the United States continued to become more desexualized and politicized. In Japan, however, artists maintained explicit sexuality and fantasy as key parts of their repertoire.

Today, queer comics as activism mostly function to educate young adults and their parents. This could be seen as a reaction to the disproportionally high rate of suicides among trans and gender-nonconforming youth in the 2010s. Contemporary queer comics focus on the personal and emotional struggles of young people rather than radical politics or explicit sex. Politics are expressed implicitly through affective personal narratives, and less as direct political commentary on the evening news as Bechdel did in the 1980s. This affective turn can be detected in the work of Jamie Cortez, the memoirs of Alison Bechdel, and the graphic novels of Gengoroh Tagame. In both countries, since the 1990s and 2000s, the sexual aspect of LGBTQ culture has been pushed even more into the private as queer comics have entered the mainstream media market.

References

Arudou, Devito. 2010. "Census Blind to Japan's True Diversity." *The Japan Times*. Available at: https://www.japantimes.co.jp/community/2010/10/05/issues/census-blind-to-japans-true-diversity/#.WzKJMRJKjOQ (accessed June 25, 2018).

Baim, Tracy. 2012. *Gay Press, Gay Power: The Growth of LGBT Newspapers in America*. Chicago, IL: Prairie Avenue Productions and Windy City Media Group.

Baudinette, Thomas. 2015. "'Gay manga' in Japanese Gay Men's Life Stories: Bara, BL and the Problem of Genre." Available at: https://www.academia.edu/11591779/_Gay_manga_in_Japanese_Gay_Men_s_Life_Stories_Bara_BL_and_the_Problem_of_Genre (accessed May, 31, 2018).

Bechdel, Alison. 2006. *Fun Home: A Family Tragicomic*. Boston, MA: Mariner Books.

Bechdel, Alison. 2008. *The Essential Dykes to Watch Out For*. Boston, MA: Houghton Mifflin Harcourt.

Bechdel, Alison. 2012. *Are You My Mother?: A Comic Drama*. Boston, MA: Mariner Books.

Benshoff Harry M. and Sean Griffin. 2005. *Queer Images: A History of Gay and Lesbian Film in America (Genre and Beyond: A Film Studies Series)*. Lanham, MD: Rowman & Littlefield.

Camper, Jennifer. 1993. "Bearing Angry Witness." In *No Straight Lines: Four Decades of Queer Comics* edited by Justin Hall (2012), 104. Seattle, WA: Fantagraphics Books.

Conlan, Francis. 2001. "Introduction." In *Coming Out in Japan: The Story of Satoru and Ryuta* by Ito Satoru and Yanase Ryuta. Melbourne: Trans Pacific Press.

Cortez, Jaime. 2004. *Sexilio/Sexile*. Los Angeles, CA and New York, NY: The Institute for Gay Men's Health.

Costello, Matthew J. 2009. *Secret Identity Crisis: Comic Books and the Unmasking of Cold War America*. New York, NY: Continuum.

Couvares, Francis G. 2006. *Movie Censorship and American Culture*. Amherst, MA: University of Massachusetts Press.

Cruse, Howard. 1995. *Stuck Rubber Baby*. New York, NY: Paradox Press.

Cuordileone, Kyle A. 2000. "'Politics in an Age of Anxiety': Cold War Political Culture and the Crisis in American Masculinity, 1949–1960." *The Journal of American History* 87(2): 515–545.

D'Emilio, John. 1989. *Sexual Politics, Sexual Communities: The Making of a Homosexual Minority in the United States, 1940–1970*. Chicago, IL: University of Chicago Press.

Eisner, Will. 1985. *Comics and Sequential Art*. New York, NY: W.W. Norton.

Filiault, Shaun, Murray Drummond. 2007. "The Hegemonic Aesthetic." *Gay and Lesbian Issues and Psychology Review* 3(3): 175–184.

Frick, Carl Vaughn. 1986. *Watch Out Comix #1*. San Francisco, CA: Last Gasp.

Graburn, Nelson H.H., John Ertl, and R. Kenji Tierney, eds. 2010. *Multiculturalism in the New Japan: Crossing the Boundaries Within*. New York, NY and Oxford: Berghahn Books.

Gregory, Roberta. 1976. *Dynamite Damsels*. Self-Published.

Gurstein, Rochelle. 1996. *The Repeal of Reticence: A History of America's Cultural and Legal Struggles over Free Speech, Obscenity, Sexual Liberation, and Modern Art*. New York, NY: Hill & Wang.

Hajdu, David. 2008. *The Ten-Cent Plague: The Great Comic-Book Scare and How It Changed America*. New York, NY: Farrar, Straus and Giroux.

Hall, Justin. 2012. *No Straight Lines: Four Decades of Queer Comics*. Seattle, WA: Fantagraphics Books.

Halperin, David M. 1995. *Saint Foucault: Towards a Gay Hagiography.* Oxford: Oxford University Press.

Hanson, Dian. 2014. *Tom of Finland: The Complete Kake Comics.* Cologne: Taschen.

Hitoshi, Ishida. 2015. "Representational Appropriation and the Autonomy of Desire in *Yaoi/BL.*" In *Boys Love Manga and Beyond: History, Culture, and Community in Japan* edited by Mark McLelland, Kazumi Nagaike, Katsuhiko Suganuma, and James Welker, 210–233. Jackson, MS: University Press of Mississippi.

Hosoe, Eikoh. *Bara kei.* 1961 (Reprinted in 1985). New York, NY: Aperture.

Howell, David L. 1996. "Ethnicity and Culture in Contemporary Japan." *Journal of Contemporary History* 31(1): 171–190.

Johnson, David K. 2004. *The Lavender Scare: The Cold War Persecution of Gays and Lesbians in the Federal Government.* Chicago, IL: University of Chicago Press.

Kampf, Ray, ed. 2000. *The Bear Handbook: A Comprehensive Guide for Those Who Are Husky, Hairy and Homosexual, and Those Who Love 'Em.* New York, NY: Harrington Park Press.

Lahti, Martti. 1998. "Dressing Up in Power." *Journal of Homosexuality* 35(3–4): 185–205.

Lunsing, Wim. 2001. *Beyond Common Sense: Sexuality And Gender In Contemporary Japan.* New York, NY: Routledge.

Marrs, Lee. 1973–1978. 2016. *The Further Fattening Adventures of Pudge, Girl Blimp.* Berkeley CA: Marrs Books.

McCabe, Caitlin. 2016. "Profiles in Black Cartooning: Larry Fuller." *Comic Book Legal Defense Fund.* Available at: http://cbldf.org/2016/02/profiles-in-black-cartooning-larry-fuller/ (accessed June 25, 2018).

McCloud, Scott. 1993. *Understanding Comic.* Northampton, MA: Tundra.

McCloud, Scott. 2005. "The Visual Magic of Comics." Conference presentation, Technology, Entertainment, Design (TED), February.

McLelland, Mark. 2005. *Queer Japan from the Pacific War to the Internet Age.* Lanham, MD.: Rowman and Littlefield.

McLelland, Mark, Kazumi Nagaike, Katsuhiko Suganuma, and James Welker, eds. 2015. *Boys Love Manga and Beyond: History, Culture, and Community in Japan.* Jackson, MS: University Press of Mississippi.

Milner, Rebecca. 2008. "The Demure and the Moody: Kasho Takahata." *Tokyo Art Beat.* Available at: http://www.tokyoartbeat.com/tablog/entries.en/2008/03/the-demure-and-the-moody-kasho-takahata.html (accessed June 25, 2018).

Nagaike, Kazumi. 2015. "Do Heterosexual Men Dream of Homosexual Men? BL *Fundashi* and Discourse on Male Feminization." In Boys Love *Manga and Beyond: History, Culture, and Community in Japan* edited by Mark McLelland, Kazumi Nagaike, Katsuhiko Suganuma, and James Welker, 189–210. Jackson, MS: University Press of Mississippi.

Odahl-Ruan, Charlynn, Elizabeth McConnell, Mona Shattell, and Christine Kozlowski. 2015. "Empowering Women through Alternative Settings: Michigan Womyn's Music Festival." *Global Journal of Community Psychology Practice* 6(1): 1–12.

Ozaki, Minami. 1989. *Zetsuai 1989.* Tokyo: Shueisha.

Pfalzgraf, Markus. 2012. *Stripped: A Story of Gay Comics.* Berlin: Bruno Gmunder Verlag.

Physique Pictorial. 1957. *Volume 7(3).* Los Angeles, CA: AMG.

Ramakers, Micha. 2000. *Dirty Pictures: Tom of Finland, Masculinity, and Homosexuality.* New York, NY: St. Martin's Press.

Reichert, James. 2006. *In the Company of Men: Representations of Male-Male Sexuality in Meiji Literature.* Palo Alto, CA: Stanford University Press.

Reichert, Jim. 2009. *In the Company of Men: Representations of Male–Male Sexuality in Meiji Literature*. Stanford, CA: Stanford University Press.

Robbins, Trina. 1972. "Sandy Comes Out." *Wimmen's Comix #1*. San Francisco, CA: Last Gasp.

Robbins, Trina, Robert Triptow, and Bill Sienkiewicz. 1988. *Strip AIDS USA*. San Francisco, CA: Last Gasp.

Russo, Vito. 1981. *The Celluloid Closet: Homosexuality in the Movies*. New York, NY: Harper & Row.

Schudson, Michael. 1995. *The Power of News*. Cambridge, MA: Harvard University Press.

Smith, Christine. 2011. The Princess. Available at: http://www.theprincesscomic.com/ (accessed May 31, 2018).

Snaith, G. 2003. "Tom's Men: The Masculinization of Homosexuality and the Homosexualization of Masculinity at the end of the Twentieth Century." *Paragraph*, 26(1–2): 77–88.

Somerville, Siobhan B. 2007. "Queer." In *Keywords for American Cultural Studies*, edited by Bruce Burgett and Glenn Hendler, 203–207. New York, NY: New York University Press.

Stein, Marc. 2014. "Heterosexuality in America: Fifty Years and Counting." Notches: (Re)marks on the History of Sexuality. Available at: http://notchesblog.com/2014/07/22/heterosexuality-in-america-fifty-years-and-counting/ (accessed June 25, 2018).

Summerhawk, Barbara, Cheiron McMahill, and Darren McDonald. 1998. *Queer Japan: Personal Stories of Japanese Lesbians, Gays, Bisexuals and Transsexuals*. Norwich, VT: New Victoria Publishers.

Tagame, Gengoroh. 2003. *Gay Erotic Art in Japan (vol. 1): Artists from the Time of the Birth of Gay Magazines*. Tokyo: Potto Shuppan.

Tagame, Gengoroh. 2017a. *Naburi-Mono*. Tokyo: Pot Publishing Plus.

Tagame, Gengoroh. 2017b. *My Brother's Husband, Vol. 1 translated by Anne Ishii*. New York, NY: Pantheon Books.

Tagame, Gengoroh. 2018a. "About Me." Gay Erotic Art of Gengoroh Tagame. Available at: http://www.tagame.org/aboutme/index.html (accessed June 25, 2018).

Tagame, Gengoroh. 2018b. *My Brother's Husband, Vol. 2*, translated by Anne Ishii. New York, NY: Pantheon Books.

Triptow, Robert. 1989. *Gay Comics*. New York, NY: Plume Publishing.

Tsuda, Takeyuki. 1998. "The Stigma of Ethnic Difference: The Structure of Prejudice and 'Discrimination toward Japan's New Immigrant Minority." *The Journal of Japanese Studies* 24(2): 317–359.

Velez, Jr., Ivan. "Untitled." 1991. In *No Straight Lines: Four Decades of Queer Comics* edited by Justin Hall (2012), 94. Seattle, WA: Fantagraphics Books.

Wings, Mary. 1978. *Dyke Shorts*. Self-Published.

Wojanarowicz, David. 1996. *7 Miles a Second*. New York, NY: Vertigo Comics.

Wright, Les. 2001. *The Bear Book II: Further Readings in the History and Evolution of a Gay Male Subculture*. New York, NY: Routledge.

Part VI
Citizenship, Policy, and Law

18

Sexual Citizenship in Comparative Perspective

CAROL JOHNSON AND VERA MACKIE

In its broadest sense, the concept of sexual citizenship refers to the ways in which conceptions of citizen identity, practices, relationships, rights, and entitlements are constructed in ways which presuppose, reflect, shape, influence, and reproduce the sexual. The concept of sexual citizenship can therefore be used to interrogate diverse questions such as: Does the traditional construction of welfare or taxation benefits in a particular society assume the citizen is part of a heterosexual family structure? What rights and entitlements do same-sex couples have? How is abortion regulated? How is sex-work regulated? Are there laws against sex-trafficking? Are particular forms of sexual relationships between citizens being privileged over others? Sexual citizenship is a concept which is commonly applied to the public sphere of government and law. It can also, however, be used to interrogate the nature of cultural representation, the economy, and power relations within the politics of personal life.

The discussion in this chapter will begin with an account of the broad conception of citizenship, going beyond issues of nationality and passports, from which the concept of sexual citizenship originally grew. It will draw attention to some of the gaps which the concept of sexual citizenship filled in regard to previous conceptions of citizenship, as well as some of the problems that have been identified with the concept of sexual citizenship. The extent to which the concepts of sexual citizenship from the Anglophone capitalist liberal democracies are relevant to analyses of diverse societies will be discussed. The chapter will conclude with an assessment of sexual citizenship issues in a wide range of countries and the insights which the concept has been able to offer as well as some of the problems that arise with the concept in a comparative perspective. The chapter will conclude by arguing for the need for a broad and flexible conception of sexual citizenship that can make it a useful tool for analysis in a range of contexts and countries.

Sexual Citizenship: The Background

In order to understand the origins of the concept of sexual citizenship it is necessary to provide some background regarding the broad conception of citizenship that the concept grew out of. In the second half of the twentieth century, conceptions of citizenship moved far beyond the narrow considerations of nationality and passports to include consideration of the social entitlements that one becomes eligible for as the citizen of a nation-state. As exemplified by T.H. Marshall's (1950) work, the broader conception of social citizenship was related to a welfare state view whereby governments had a major responsibility for ensuring a citizen's well-being and opportunities in life. Consequently, issues from welfare benefits to state provision of education and health benefits were seen as part and parcel of one's legitimate entitlements as a citizen (see also Vandenberg 2000).

The concept of sexual citizenship (Evans 1993) had its origins in that broader conception of the nature of citizenship but developed aspects that had previously been neglected (Richardson 2018, pp. 7–19). Much of the original literature on sexual citizenship was developed during the 1990s and early 2000s, predominantly in the Anglophone capitalist liberal democracies of the United Kingdom, the USA, Canada, Australia, and New Zealand, and drew on a number of disciplines including sociology, law, gender studies, and political science (Richardson 2018, p.27). While conceptions of social citizenship such as Marshall's expanded citizenship beyond issues of passports and nationality they were still very much confined to the public sphere, with little direct consideration of the private sphere of family and intimate life. Yet, as many feminist critics have pointed out (Pateman 1996), particular conceptions of private life were already shaping the nature of public provision in both theory and practice. Conceptions of citizenship such as Marshall's were not neutral. Rather, citizenship was being constructed in highly gendered ways that privileged conceptions of the citizen as a male breadwinner and head of household. The citizenship benefits and entitlements of the male head of household were then intended to flow on to his wife and children. Women were constructed as both subordinate to their husbands and as second-class citizens on the periphery of public policy.

Feminist struggles have been successful in improving the rights and entitlements of women in many countries. Nonetheless, despite its ostensible focus on public life, the state is still deeply involved in the regulation of personal life. Taxation and welfare benefits reward particular types of familial relationships. Governments commonly regulate marriage, divorce, reproduction, and access to reproductive control. Constructions of citizenship are thus implicated in the construction of particular types of personal life, which Ken Plummer (2003) has termed "intimate citizenship."

They are also often forms of "sexual citizenship." The traditional privileging of the male head of household as the archetypal citizen was not just about gender; it was just as much about conceptions of heterosexuality (Rich 1980). In this respect, as Bell and Binnie (2000, p. 10), amongst others, have noted, all citizenship is a form of sexual citizenship based on particular conceptions of the sexual identity of individual citizens and the familial citizenship unit related to that identity. As Bell and Binnie remind us, however, we are not all "*equal* sexual citizens" (2000, p. 142). Traditional conceptions of citizenship were heteronormative (Johnson 2002), assuming a family based on a heterosexual married couple and their children.

Nonheterosexuals were constructed, in Shane Phelan's (2001) words, as "sexual strangers," passport citizens of countries but lacking some of the broader citizenship rights, entitlements, and privileges associated with heterosexuality. Even in countries where homosexuality was decriminalized, same-sex couples could find themselves discriminated against compared with heterosexual couples in terms of benefits and entitlements in areas ranging from health and welfare to superannuation and taxation. Furthermore, state policies in a diverse range of fields, from immigration and military service to health and welfare (Canaday 2009) played a role in constructing forms of both a privileged heterosexual and a subordinated homosexual identity. Such gendered and heteronormative constructions of citizenship entitlements have been increasingly challenged by the feminist and lesbian, gay, bisexual, trans, intersex, and queer/questioning LGBTIQ+ movements, with varying degrees of success in specific countries, as we shall see later in this chapter. As we shall also see, some residual heteronormative influences arguably remain in conceptions of rights and entitlements, even in those countries where same-sex couples have been able to achieve access to them.

Much of the sexual citizenship literature has been about same-sex rights. From the beginning, however, conceptions of sexual citizenship also covered other issues related to sexuality – including bisexual, intersex, transgender, and transsexual rights, as well as issues of reproductive control, pornography, and sex work (Evans 1993; Richardson 2000; Hearn 2006). Nonetheless, contributors to these debates argue that there is still much work to be done in many of these areas. Richardson and Monro (2012, pp. 175–176, 69) argue that conceptions of sexual citizenship have neglected bisexual issues and have still not incorporated an adequate analysis of trans issues. Monro and Warren (2004, p. 357) have cautioned, however, about simply reducing trans issues to issues of *sexual* citizenship given that, despite historical alliances between the trans and gay and lesbian movements, and intersections in their struggles, transgender issues need to retain a major focus on the component of gender identity.

The Trajectory of Sexual Citizenship and Same-Sex Rights

Academic analysis developed alongside actual political struggles as issues of sexual citizenship entitlements became increasingly contested in debates over same-sex rights. Sexual citizenship also involved a politics of identity. The heteronormative majority identity that underlay traditional constructions of citizenship met increasing resistance from those whose identity had been marginalized and discriminated against. The development of a politics around gay identity often led initially to struggles over the decriminalization of male homosexuality and related discriminatory social attitudes. These struggles are partly over issues of misrecognition (Richardson and Monro 2012), such as challenging conceptions of male homosexuality as deviant or disgusting. Once steps such as decriminalization were won, political action then frequently proceeded to struggles over recognition of same-sex relationships, as in claims that same-sex couples should be eligible for the same government benefits as heterosexual couples via recognition of de facto relationships (in countries such as Australia where these are recognized) or arguments in relation to same-sex marriage.

Similarly, conceptions of sexual citizenship embraced issues of same-sex family rights, including issues of access to adoption, assisted reproduction, and surrogacy.

Such sexual citizenship issues have very practical, and often material, consequences. They can influence access to government welfare benefits, taxation requirements, healthcare entitlements, immigration matters, and whether one can visit or make decisions regarding an ill partner in hospital. As such, sexual citizenship claims often involve a transformed relationship with the state, especially in those countries where male homosexuality had previously been illegal, as the state moves from repressing homosexuality to recognizing same-sex rights and entitlements (Tremblay, Paternotte, and Johnson 2011). Nonetheless, many commentators have stressed the importance of having conceptions of sexual citizenship that stretch beyond the sphere of government to include the economy, society, and the cultural rights of minority sexual groups to be represented symbolically as legitimate in popular culture (Bell and Binnie 2000, p. 20). In such views, the state is seen as just one of many political, cultural, and economic institutions that shape forms of sexual citizenship, albeit a "very important one" (Bernstein and Naples 2010, p. 133).

For all of the above reasons, analyzing citizenship became, in Richardson's words (2018, p. 1), "the new black," in other words highly fashionable, as well as the common language "of political activism around sexual inequality and discrimination."

Problematic Aspects of Sexual Citizenship

Nonetheless, even in the early Anglophone literature, struggling for sexual citizenship rights was often seen as a somewhat problematic, even if an absolutely necessary, part of addressing the second-class citizenship of gays and lesbians (Bell and Binnie 2000, p. 2). One problem was that the model of citizenship that gays and lesbians were arguing for inclusion within was not necessarily the model that the earlier, liberationist, gay and lesbian movement would have chosen (Seidman 2002, p. 184). There were arguments (Evans 1993; Duggan 2003, pp. 65–66) that the model of citizenship being utilized was one that was unduly influenced by neoliberal ideas of individual choice, consumerism, and privatized self-reliance as members of couples became financially responsible for each other. There were concerns that gays and lesbians were being incorporated into conceptions of citizenship that still privileged a white, male, able-bodied, and straight ideal (Seidman 2002, p. 204). Richardson (2018, p. 2) expressed concern that the focus on citizenship might be contributing to an unduly restrictive conception of politics around issues of sexuality. Constructing sexual politics largely in terms of formal rights granted by the state potentially downplays earlier feminist and gay liberationist conceptions of the importance of personal politics in ensuring equitable and rewarding relationships. It also overlooks the need to counter gender inequality and to adequately recognize caregiving in existing family units. Josephson (2017, p. 12) has argued that in order to change "hegemonic, heteronormative sexual citizenship," to produce a more equitable conception of citizenship, it would be necessary to create "basic changes in the organization of work, the nature of the economy, and the structure of social benefits."

Furthermore, precisely because struggles over sexual citizenship are also related to struggles over the politics of identity, those struggles can themselves be implicated in forms of inclusion and exclusion. Some people can be constructed as belonging while some can be constructed as "others" (Stychin 1998, pp. 14–15). Citizens can be constructed as "good" or "bad" homosexuals. For example, the "good" homosexual during the Thatcher period (1975–1990) in Britain was one who kept their identity a private matter and did not ask for sexual citizenship rights and entitlements (Anna Marie Smith 1994). In more recent periods, the "good" homosexual might be part of a long-term married couple in a stable, monogamous same-sex relationship (Valverde 2006).

Miriam Smith (2018) has explained the strategy behind a focus on "marriage equality" in countries such as the US (and Australia). Equating same-sex marriage with majority rights counters socially conservative arguments that same-sex rights are "special interests." Similarly, the focus on "love" encourages empathy and helps to counter arguments that homosexuality is unnatural or disgusting. Nonetheless, such a framing does have a down side. Richardson argues that this "represents a significant shift: it is no longer whom we love but that we love that is central to normative (sexual) citizenship, or perhaps, more appropriately to intimate citizenship, to the extent that it might even be better to speak of love citizens rather than sexual citizens" (2018, p. 86). Judith Butler (2002, pp. 14–34) has long criticized the normalizing aspects of such conceptions, pointing out the potential to exclude those who are not in long-term, monogamous relationships. In Richardson's (2018, p. 88) view, such exclusions are already happening. Richardson (2018, p. 93) argues that citizenship has become overly associated with coupledom and "it is the sexual couple, within a particular domestic setting, that has become the rights-bearing subject of lesbian and gay claims to citizenship" (Richardson 2018, p. 93). Gay culture is seen to be disappearing (Richardson 2018, p. 90) as same-sex relationships mimic heterosexual ones. Rather than "challenging political structures and institutions" gays and lesbians are now arguing for rights within them in a way that has "depoliticized conflict and division" (Richardson 2018, p. 105), instead of making broader calls for sexual and economic justice (2018, p. 173). On the other hand, one would not want to take such critiques too far. Whatever the limitations in regards to issues of rights or coupledom, as many of the critics would agree, addressing issues of sexual citizenship has contributed to major discriminatory policies being removed in many countries. Furthermore, the socially conservative opposition to "normalizing" same-sex relationships suggests that there might be more subversion of heteronormativity occurring than critics such as Valverde or Butler recognize (Johnson 2013, pp. 249–250).

The concept of sexual citizenship is therefore not considered to be an unproblematic one, even in the Euro-American capitalist liberal democracies. Constructing same-sex issues as issues of citizenship rights and entitlements can result in a restrictive view of politics as involving the state and detract from the need, for example, to improve the politics of interpersonal relationships and to engage in changing a range of cultural attitudes. It can result in patterns of inclusion and exclusion.

Nonetheless, the concept of sexual citizenship is a useful concept that throws considerable light on the measures obtained by the gay and lesbian movement in parts of Europe, North America, South America, and countries such as South Africa. It does help to explain a trajectory in countries such as Britain, Canada, Australia and the US in which issues of decriminalization are followed by a further expansion of sexual citizenship rights. Even this pattern is not as clear as it may seem, though. After all, the Anglophone world was very slow to decriminalize homosexuality compared with countries such as France, which decriminalized sodomy in the eighteenth century. Povencher (2016, pp. 11–12) has emphasized the need to analyze French gay and lesbian identity and the resulting forms of sexual citizenship rather than uncritically apply a US-influenced model. The influence of Napoleonic law on Spanish law (Pablo 2010, p. 34) had implications for the trajectory of some Latin American countries which had not criminalized homosexuality in the way that US law did (and indeed some US states were exceedingly slow to decriminalize homosexuality). By contrast British colonial law criminalizing homosexuality spread throughout the former British Empire (and now the Commonwealth) and is still on the statute books in countries such as Malaysia and Singapore. Nor should one assume forms of teleological progress on sexual citizenship given, for example, that the Trump administration in the US wound back some antidiscrimination measures established under the Obama administration, including for transgendered members of the military.

Before moving beyond the Anglophone sphere, it is also necessary to recognize the specificities of each of the abovementioned Anglophone systems. For this purpose, a brief mention of recent campaigns on equal marriage is instructive. The discourse of rights is strongest in the US, with its Constitutional Bill of Rights. Activists for equal marriage in the US have been successful in using the Constitution to extend some rights to same-sex partnerships or marriages, and the US Supreme Court on 27 June 2015 ruled that it was un-Constitutional to deny marriage to same-sex couples. This was both aided and constrained by the Federal system, with different outcomes in each of the states where marriage rights were contested before the Supreme Court decision.[1] The need to argue for equal marriage has also been shaped by the specificities of, for example, the provision of medical benefits in the US. Without a universal medical insurance scheme, until recently, individuals were reliant on private medical insurance or employer contributions to insurance schemes. If such schemes were applicable to spouses and family members, then this could be an incentive to enter into a recognized partnership or marriage. Failures to extend medical insurance and other benefits to those outside the heterosexual marriage system have real material effects on individuals (Richardson 2000, p. 127; Treat 2013, pp. 265–281).[2]

Canada was the fourth country in the world to legalize same-sex marriage in 2005. Some Canadian provinces and territories had brought down decisions in favour of same-sex marriages from 2003 on; and same-sex cohabiting partners had been treated similarly to married partners for most purposes since 1999. In Australia and New Zealand, the prevalence of de facto marriage among heterosexuals, the provision of most rights and benefits to legally married partners as well as de facto partners, and the extension of most benefits to those in nonheterosexual partnerships meant that the demand for equal marriage had less urgency (Johnson 2017; Dreher 2017). Nevertheless, due to the vagaries of party politics, there have been different trajectories in these two neighboring countries. New Zealand recognized equal marriage in 2013 with the passing of the Marriage (Definition of Marriage) Amendment Bill on 17 April 2013, which came into effect on 19 August 2013. In Australia, until recently, marriage was defined as occurring between a "man and a woman." Marriage equality was only achieved in Australia in 2017 after a divisive debate and public opinion survey. Regulation of marriage is devolved in the United Kingdom, so that there are differences between England, Wales, and Scotland, which passed same-sex marriage legislation in 2014 and Northern Ireland, where same-sex marriage was legalized in January 2020. Needless to say, legal recognition of marriage and partnerships is just one aspect of sexual citizenship. Furthermore, as we have seen above, many queer thinkers and activists resist being assimilated into normative forms of family and relationships (Cadwallader and Riggs 2012, unpaginated; Pendleton and Serisier 2012, unpaginated).

So, if the concept of sexual citizenship is problematic and has diverse implications when applied to the Euro-American liberal democracies, how appropriate is it when examining a range of other countries? This is an issue that a significant body of academic literature has engaged with. In considering conceptions of sexual citizenship outside the Euro-American capitalist liberal democracies, it is necessary to be sensitive to the particular form the state takes in each local site and thus the particular relationship between individual and state. That is the case in areas ranging from Eastern Europe to Central Asia and Africa. Given that it is not possible to discuss all of these regions in a chapter of this length, the following discussion will use examples mainly from the Asia-Pacific region to illustrate broader issues about the need to take cultural and national specificity into account.

Sexual Citizenship: Comparative Perspectives

The Asia-Pacific region includes both socialist states and liberal democracies. Mackie and McLelland posit an East Asian geocultural sphere which draws on aspects of Chinese-influenced culture and vocabulary and the influence of Confucianism, neo-Confucianism and Buddhism (2015, pp. 1–14). Peter Jackson (2015, p. 11) argues for a Hindu and Buddhist-influenced cultural sphere which draws on vocabulary from the Indian languages of Sanskrit and Pali in parts of Southeast Asia. These writers then move to "provincialize" (cf. Chakrabarty 2000) European notions of sexuality which draw on Judeo-Christian ideas. That is, what is seen as "unmarked" to the Anglophone observer, can now be seen as very culturally specific:

> While now an international field of comparative research, sexuality studies has in fact emerged from reflections on those societies that have been deeply impacted by Christianity and which use Latin and Greek as the bases of their technical vocabularies...[M]any of the terminologies of Western analyses of sexuality, which often misrepresent themselves as general or universal, are in fact based on Latin and Greek and bear the implicit imprint of this history of Christian moral doctrine even when they are presented in an ostensibly secular frame.
>
> (Jackson 2015, p. 11)

When we discuss sexual citizenship in the Anglophone capitalist liberal democracies we are thus often referencing worldviews derived from this Eurocentric Judeo-Christian influence. By provincializing this worldview we can open up the discussion to other ways of thinking about sexuality and sexual citizenship, as we discuss below. Precisely because many critics are aware of the limitations of forms of sexual citizenship in the capitalist liberal democracies, they are also well aware of the need to take international perspectives into account (Bell and Binnie 2006; Richardson 2018, pp. 103–125; Mackie 2017).

This is not to suggest that broader conceptions of sexual citizenship cannot be of use. Clearly issues of sexual citizenship, broadly understood, are highly relevant to the situation in many countries, and are not confined to same-sex or broader LGBTIQ+ issues. The right to live free from sexual harassment, and the legal and cultural changes required to address this are issues that face heterosexual women in all countries. Some other issues, though, may be more country-specific. These include the right of people of different castes to marry in India and Nepal, the right to avoid arranged marriages if they so wish, and the rights of those coerced into sex work (Richardson 2018, pp. 56–57, 112). There are countries, such as the United Arab Emirates, where it is illegal for unmarried men and women to have sex or even share hotel rooms and where adultery is severely punished.[3] Adultery, broadly defined, also remains on the statute books of some US states (Rhode 2016).

There are also, as Altman and Symons (2017, p. 256) point out, around 75 countries where homosexuality is illegal and "even in states which support rights in international forums, there is considerable hostility, violence and persecution directed at people perceived as transgressing hegemonic norms of sex and gender." Debates over issues of sexual citizenship are therefore often now global ones, including at the level of the United Nations (Ban 2012) as Altman and Symons (2016) have documented in their book *Queer Wars*. Some participants in the resulting queer wars debates have acknowledged that international human rights arguments, particularly when articulated with key input from local groups, can bring about beneficial forms of change that improve sexual citizenship rights. They also, however, raise queer critiques of equal rights campaigns which, they argue, can result in a normalization of LGBTI issues, assimilating them into existing conceptions of rights and existing political institutions (Langlois 2017, pp. 244–245). As Weber has pointed out, one must be particularly careful about discourses which contrast liberal Western LGBTQI+ rights with those in many repressive non-Western states, given not only that this may be experienced as a neo-imperialist discourse but that it also neglects the extent to which some rights have still to be won in such places as the US (Weber 2017, pp. 232–234; see also Sabsay 2012). Indeed, under the Trump administration, the US voted against a broad United Nations resolution which included condemnation of the death penalty for homosexuality. Wilkinson points out that "globally there can be little doubt that LGBT activism" has been the winner in terms of increasing decriminalization of same-sex relationships and acceptance of same-sex marriage in a number of countries (Wilkinson 2017, p. 237). Wilkinson also cautions that even in those countries, there is a pressure to be "queer in a way that mainstream society finds at least tolerable, if not completely acceptable" with exclusion and possible violence still the price to be paid by those who are not deemed acceptable (Wilkinson 2017, pp. 237–238). Similarly, Jasbir Puar has coined the concept of "homonationalism," whereby those in some first world countries see themselves as superior to countries where homosexuality is stigmatized or punished (Puar 2007; Puar 2013: pp. 336–339; see also Dreher 2017, pp. 176–195). Miriam Smith (2017, pp. 467, 474), however, suggests that Puar neglects the extent to which LGBTQI+ rights are opposed by homophobic forces, both domestically and internationally. Sexual citizenship remains a highly contested site.

Sexual Citizenship beyond the Anglosphere

When we move outside the Anglosphere and outside the Euro-American centers, there are distinctive political systems, social systems, understandings of rights and citizenship, configurations of public and private, understandings of the place of sexuality in culture and society, and different taxonomies of sexes, genders, and sexualities. In many countries, for example, religious courts rather than the state might determine issues of sexual and intimate citizenship (Benedicto 2014; Boelstorff 2005, 2007; Chalmers 2002; Jackson 1997, pp. 166–190; Jackson 2011; Mackie and McLelland 2015, pp. 1–17; Manalansan 1994, pp. 73–90; Martin et al. 2008; McLelland 2005; Morris 1994, pp. 15–43; Offord 2013, pp. 335–349; Yue and Zubillaga-Pow 2012).

As we have discussed at the beginning of this chapter, the concept of citizenship originally had the narrow meaning of a legal status involving nationality, the right to vote, the right to stand for public office, and concomitant duties. In its broader sense, citizenship has come to refer to legitimacy to participate in politics, the ability to contribute to debate in the public sphere, legitimacy to occupy public space, and a sense of national belonging. Citizenship, in its narrow and its broad senses, is shaped in the intersections of age, gender, class, caste, ethnicity, racialized positioning, indigeneity, religion, ability/disability, and sexuality (Mackie 2002, pp. 245–257).

Citizenship has historically been connected with military service, originally expected of males only. Most militaries, until recently, prevented the participation of women or openly gay or transgender service personnel (Mackie and Tanji 2015: 60–73; Mackie 2019). The LGBT Military Index was created by the Hague Centre for Strategic Studies. It ranks countries according to the inclusion of LGBT service personnel in the armed forces and related policies and best practice. Currently several dozen countries in Europe, North and South America, and South Africa allow openly gay and lesbian individuals to serve, while several others have no explicit prohibition. Taiwan removed prohibitions in 2002, Thailand in 2005, and the Philippines in 2010 (Polchar et al. 2014). In Vietnam, men must do military service and women may do military service. There are no explicit laws against homosexuality in Vietnam, but in the past it has been dealt with in campaigns against so-called "social evils" (Newton 2015). Homosexuality is, however, classified as a mental disease for the purposes of determining suitability for military service (Nguyen Thi Huyen Linh, personal communication; UNDP, USAID 2014a, Annex 3). In 2007, two soldiers in the Nepal army were accused of having a lesbian relationship and were discharged. UNDP reports, however, that gays and lesbians can now serve openly in Nepal (UNDP, USAID 2014b, Annex 2). As recently as May 2017, a soldier in South Korea was punished under the Military Criminal Act 92 (6), which prohibits members of the military from engaging in sexual activity with members of the same sex (Amnesty International 2017). North Korea reportedly mandates celibacy for the first 10 years of military service (Hassig and Oh 2009).

In liberal democracies, there is a particular view of the relationship between individual and state, where voting and standing for office are seen as the quintessential ways of exercising citizenship. This, in turn, shapes understandings of the place of sexuality in discourses of citizenship. Many countries historically prevented women from voting or standing for public office, or failed to extend the franchise to slaves, indigenous peoples, colonial subjects, or other subordinated groups. Sexual orientation was rarely explicitly mentioned in terms of qualifications for voting or standing for public office. Nevertheless, the legitimacy of those of nonnormative sexual orientation could be affected by laws which criminalized nonprocreative sexual behavior. Where nonnormative sexualities are stigmatized, this also affects an individual's legitimacy as an actor in the public sphere. It is only relatively recently that openly gay, lesbian, or transgender individuals have been elected to public office. New Zealand had one of the first ever openly transgender members of Parliament; Australia has a few openly gay and lesbian members of national and state parliaments and local governments, including an openly lesbian former Cabinet minister. Japan has had a few openly gay, lesbian, or transgender members of parliament or local government assemblies, while India has had some *hijra* members of local assemblies. Johanna Sigurðardóttir in Iceland in 2009 was the first openly lesbian head of state, and she has been followed by several other openly gay or lesbian national leaders (Beyer and Casey 1999; Mackie 2001, p. 185–192; Baird 2004, pp. 67–84; McLelland and Suganuma 2009, pp. 329–343).

There are distinctive conceptions of citizenship in the People's Republic of China, Singapore, Malaysia, Vietnam, Thailand, and the Special Administrative Regions of Hong Kong and Macao. In places where democracy is circumscribed, discourses of citizenship may focus on broader senses of social participation and national belonging. It has been argued that, in places like Thailand, Singapore, and Hong Kong, commercial spaces provide important sites of belonging for those of nonnormative sexual orientation. Bars, cafés, dance parties, and film festivals are spaces where queer identities may be affirmed and distinctive forms of sociality practiced. Taking to the streets, whether in celebrations, demonstrations, or pride parades, is a way of claiming citizenship. Pride parades and festivals may now be observed in diverse sites in the Asia-Pacific region (Suganuma 2005, 2012; Jackson 2009, pp. 357–395; Yue and Zubillaga-Pow 2012; Kong, Lau, and Li 2015, pp. 188–201; Maree 2015, pp. 230–243; Tang 2015, pp. 218–229; Newton 2015). Gay and lesbian military personnel regularly participate in the pride parade at the Gay and Lesbian Mardi Gras in Sydney, since 2013 in uniform (Riseman 2017, pp. 43–50; Riseman et al. 2018, pp. 176–178).

In Sinophone cultures, gays and lesbians have appropriated the language of comradeship. In the People's Republic of China, individuals were constructed as comrades (*tongzhi*). Gays and lesbians in Hong Kong started to describe themselves as *tongzhi* in the late 1980s. The term, which in its original sense referred to a specific construction of comradely relationships in Communist China, has been adopted in several Sinophone cultures and the Chinese diaspora (Martin 2015, p. 43; Bao 2018).

In Japan, debates around the use of public space crystallized around a lesbian couple who wished to undertake a wedding ceremony at Tokyo Disneyland, something which was unremarkable for heterosexual couples. Although the ceremony would have no legal force, as same-sex marriage is not recognized in Japan, the couple still wanted to make a public affirmation of their commitment. Tokyo Disneyland at first demurred, but eventually agreed to host the ceremony (Maree 2017). In Vietnam, too, gay and lesbian couples often wish to celebrate their commitment with a ceremony. The Vietnamese government banned such ceremonies for a time. This ban on ceremonies has been lifted, but the government still does not recognize same-sex marriage.

As noted above, several former British colonies inherited laws which made sodomy a crime (Kirby 2011; Sanders 2015, pp. 127–149). Such laws have now been overturned in Australia and New Zealand, but still exist in Singapore and Malaysia. The law in India was only successfully challenged and removed in 2018. In Malaysia, the antisodomy law was used in the past to discredit and imprison then opposition politician Anwar Ibrahim, who is now active in mainstream politics again. In 2014, Singapore's High Court ruled against a suit seeking to prove that the antisodomy law was unconstitutional. Further challenges were due to be heard in late 2019 (Yi 2019, unpaginated). In some places, like China and Vietnam, laws and policies concerning so-called "social evils" have been used against those who do not conform to expectations of heteronormativity (Newton 2015, pp. 255–267). In China, until 1997, laws on "hooliganism" were used against members of sexual minorities (Kam 2015, p. 83). Japan has no prohibition of nonheterosexual sexual practices, but also has no national legislation prohibiting discrimination on the grounds of sexual orientation (although there is some case law on the topic). Taiwan has specific laws prohibiting discrimination on the grounds of sexual orientation in employment and education. Taiwan embarked on a trajectory to become the first country in Asia to recognize same-sex marriage when the Constitutional Court ruled on May 24, 2017 that the Constitutional right to equality and freedom of marriage also applied to same-sex couples (Sanders 2015, p. 127; Haas 2017). There was a conservative backlash in the form of several referendum questions related to same-sex marriage (AFP-Jiji 2018), but eventually the Constitutional decision to reccognize same-sex marriage was implemented when the Enforcement Act of Judicial Yuan Interpretation 748 came into force on May 24, 2019 (Chiang 2019). Hong Kong has recently recognized same-sex partnerships for visa purposes (Cheng 2018). In the People's Republic of China it is now possible for same-sex partners to become each other's legal guardian, although only small numbers have taken up this opportunity (Zhang 2019). Even in places where there are no laws concerning sexual behavior, however, the nuclear family centered on the heteronormative couple is privileged in various ways in the law, social policy, welfare policy, and social institutions. The family is also intimately concerned with discourses of nationalism (Mackie 2009, pp. 139–163).

In several jurisdictions, it is now possible for someone diagnosed with gender identity disorder to undergo gender reassignment, to change their gender on official documents, and to marry someone of the opposite sex to their new identity. In Japan, a trans father who has undergone gender reassignment and married is now able to be recognized as the father of a child born to his wife through artificial insemination by donor. Such recognition, however, depends on conformity to mainstream gender norms and heteronormative family forms (Aizura 2006, pp. 289–309; Mackie 2001, pp. 185–192; 2008, pp. 411–423; 2010, pp. 111–128; 2013, pp. 1–18; 2014, pp. 203–220; Sanders 2015, pp. 127–149). At the time of writing, "X" gender (indeterminate, unspecified, or intersex) is not officially recognized in Japan, but has been in Australia and New Zealand. Nepal has recognized a third gender since 2007; Pakistan since 2009; and the Supreme Court of India recognized a third gender in April 2014. In some other jurisdictions, this is only available for intersex people. Such designations on official documents are an important aspect of citizenship. Where there is a gap between the official designation and an individual's preferred name and gender identity, this can affect access to employment and the ability to travel across national borders.

In Japan, same-sex partnerships are not legally recognized at national level, but several local government areas are now willing to recognize same-sex partnerships for some purposes ("Time to Discuss Same-Sex Marriage" 2019). In the absence of recognition of same-sex marriage, some couples use the adult adoption system to create family-like relationships.[4] The adoption of one adult by another is an accepted way of making a familial relationship in Japan. Only legally married couples, however, can adopt a child; and assisted reproduction is generally only provided to married couples. This limits the kinds of alternative family forms available to gays and lesbians, although there is evidence that some are finding ways to bypass these restrictions (Mackie 2009, pp. 139–163; 2013, pp. 1–18; 2014, pp. 203–220; Maree 2004, pp. 541–549; Maree 2015, pp. 187–202; Maree 2017; Higashi and Masuhara 2013; Ringler 2016). In South Korea, it is reported that gay males and lesbians enter into "contract marriages" with each other in order to secure some social legitimacy and evade scrutiny of unconventional lifestyles (Cho 2009: 401–22). Similar strategies have been observed in Hong Kong (Kam 2015, pp. 89–104).

Much of the discussion of sexuality and citizenship focuses on the distinction between public and private. The International Council on Human Rights Policy argues that "sexuality and therefore sexual rights arise at the point where public and private domains – the private body and the body politic – meet" (2009, p. 2). Each society, however, has a different configuration of "public" and "private," different degrees of state intervention in so-called private matters, different degrees of protection of privacy, and distinctive configurations of state, market, civil society, and family. For this reason alone, it is just not possible to create a one-size-fits-all conception of sexual citizenship.

Global Governance and Sexual Citizenship

Although issues concerning citizenship in general, and sexual citizenship in particular, are necessarily played out with reference to the government of a specific nation-state, there are also transnational dimensions to these discussions (Mackie and Pendleton 2010; Pendleton 2015, pp. 21–34). Questions of sexual citizenship are particularly acute when individuals travel across national borders, sometimes as migrant workers or international students, sometimes seeking asylum, sometimes hoping to be (re)united with their partners. In such cases, individuals move from one regime of sexual rights to another. If an individual's claim for asylum on the grounds that they would suffer persecution because of their sexuality is denied then the individual may be stranded between different rights regimes, without the "right to have rights" (Mackie 2009, pp. 139–163; Offord 2013, pp. 335–349; Seuffert 2013, pp. 752–784; Yue 2012, pp. 269–287; on the "right to have rights," see Arendt 1951, p. 290). Most governments give preferential treatment to family members or marriage partners in immigration matters. If a state does not recognize same-sex partnerships, marriages, or civil unions, then those in same-sex partnerships can be disadvantaged in immigration matters. In the Asia-Pacific region, until recently, only Australia and New Zealand officially recognized same-sex partners for immigration purposes (Mackie 2009, pp. 139–163). As noted above, there has been some recent case law on this matter in Hong Kong.[5]

Questions of sexual citizenship also have a transnational dimension in the context of engagements with the institutions of global governance. The United Nations Human Rights Committee ruled in 1994 in the Toonen case that a Tasmanian law which criminalized homosexual acts was in violation of the International Covenant on Civil and Political Rights (Sanders 2015: 129). There is no United Nations Convention on sexuality, but some reports of the Committee on the Elimination of all form of Discrimination Against Women (CEDAW) do mention the issue of discrimination against *women* due to sexual preference/ sexual orientation. In other cases, sexuality is often subsumed under other categories to do with family, marriage, reproduction, and health. In 2004, however, a United Nations Special Rapporteur, Paul Hunt, affirmed that,

> sexual rights include the right of all persons to express their sexual orientation, with due regard for the well-being and rights of others, without fear of persecution, denial of liberty or social interference... The contents of sexual rights, the right to sexual health and the right to reproductive health need further attention, as do the relationships between them.
> (United Nations Economic and Social Council 2004)

In 2006, a group of human rights activists met at Gadjah Mada University in Indonesia and issued a declaration on sexual orientation and gender identity known as the "Yogyakarta Principles." The group included the International Commission of Jurists and the International Service for Human Rights. The document comprises 29 principles along with recommendations to governments, regional intergovernmental institutions, civil society, and the United Nations.

Since 2008, there have been attempts to have the UN General Assembly pass a declaration on sexual orientation and gender identity (Human Rights Watch 2008). In June 2011, South Africa led a motion for the UN Human Rights Council (UNHRC, Resolution 17/19) to investigate the situation of lesbian, gay, bisexual, and transgender citizens worldwide, and the report of the United Nations High Commissioner for Human Rights (UNHRC) was released in December 2011 (UN Human Rights Council 2011; see also United Nations Secretary General 2012). In 2012, UN Secretary General Ban Ki-Moon issued a message to the UN Human Rights Council condemning violence based on sexual orientation and gender identity.

There are also transnational dimensions to political campaigns on LGBTIQ+ rights. Local non-governmental organizations (NGOs) learn from practices in neighboring countries, while some local campaigns may be funded by international aid agencies. The influence of aid agencies sometimes leads to a certain homogeneity in the way that questions of sexual citizenship are framed, as seen by the increasing use of terms like "sexual orientation and gender identity" (SOGI) (Newton 2015). Nevertheless, NGOs necessarily engage with local configurations of state, communities, societies, and individuals in developing strategies for change.

Conclusion

The concept of sexual citizenship was developed in the Anglophone liberal democracies in the late twentieth century, with discussion continuing into the twenty-first century. This chapter has explained how the concept both drew attention to the sexual nature of all citizenship and the need to extend citizenship rights and entitlements to previously excluded and marginalized minorities. It has also, however, drawn attention to critiques of those conceptions of sexual citizenship that confine political struggles over issues of sexuality to issues of individual rights, or the state, or that commodify sexuality, instead arguing for a broader conception that can also address a range of sexual power relationships. In that light, the chapter has identified a number of areas where further analyses are needed, including in regard to bisexual and trans issues and in regard to developing flexible conceptions of sexual citizenship that go beyond the Euro-American capitalist liberal democracies. In considering how this concept might be translated into other contexts, we need to be sensitive to the specificities of the state in each local site and the specificities of relationships between individuals, communities, society, and the state. As long as one is sensitive to such differences, and does not attempt to develop a universalizing one-size-fits-all construction of sexual citizenship, the concept remains a useful one. Issues of sexual citizenship remain central to struggles for LGBTIQ+ rights in diverse locations.

Notes

1. At the time of the Supreme Court decision, 36 states in the USA had legalized same-sex marriage, while 14 states still prohibited it. Information available at: http://gaymarriage.procon.org/view.resource.php?resourceID=004857 (accessed 5 September 2015). Nevertheless, there was still some resistance to same-sex marriage, with a County Clerk in Kentucky refusing to issue licenses for same-sex marriages for some months after the decision (Bittenbender 2015).
2. Some have also pointed out that the recognition of same-sex marriage might also mean that companies which had earlier been flexible about extending benefits to same-sex partners might now require them to be legally married in order to gain these benefits.
3. Consequently, foreign governments have regularly issued warnings to their citizens travelling through the United Arab Emirates. See, for example, Department of Foreign Affairs and Trade Australia, United Arab Emirates, Laws. Information available at: http://smartraveller.gov.au/countries/middle-east/pages/united_arab_emirates.aspx#laws (accessed 29 July 2018).
4. The strategy of creating family-like relationships through adoption of an adult partner is not unknown in other jurisdictions. See Mackie (2009, p. 156, n. 45) and Pavano (1986–1987: pp. 251–277).
5. In immigration matters in Australia, same-sex partners, de facto partners, and marriage partners are treated the same. New Zealand also recognizes same-sex partners for immigration purposes. A recent newspaper article reported that, although the Japanese government does not officially recognize same-sex partnerships, some discretion has been exercised in granting visas to same-sex partners of holders of Japanese working visas, with the partner being listed as a "dependent" (Buckton 2015)

References

Altman, Dennis and Jonathan Symons. 2016. *Queer Wars*. Cambridge: Polity Press.
Altman, Dennis and Jonathan Symons. 2017. "Response to *Queer Wars* Special Commentary Section," *Australian Journal of International Affairs* 71: 255–258.

Aizura, Aren. 2006. "Of Borders and Homes: The Imaginary Community of (Trans)Sexual Citizenship." *Inter-Asia Cultural Studies* 7(2): 289–309.

Amnesty International. 2017. "South Korea: Soldier Convicted in Outrageous Military Gay Witch-Hunt." Available at: https://www.amnesty.org/en/latest/news/2017/05/south-korea-soldier-convicted-in-outrageous-military-gay-witch-hunt/ (accessed May 24, 2017).

APF-Jiji. 2018. "Taiwan to Enact Separate Law on Same-Sex Marriage, Raising Fears about LGBT Equality after Referendum Backlash." *Japan Times*, November 30.

Arendt, Hannah. 1951. *The Origins of Totalitarianism*. New York, NY: Schocken Books.

Baird, Barbara. 2004. "Contexts for Lesbian Citizenship across Australian Public Spheres." *Social Semiotics* 14(1): 67–84.

Ban Ki-moon. 2012. "Message to Human Rights Council meeting on Violence and Discrimination Based on Sexual Orientation or Gender Identity, Secretary-General Ban Ki-moon," Geneva (Switzerland), March 7. Available at: https://www.un.org/sg/en/content/sg/speeches/2012-03-07/message-human-rights-council-meeting-violence-and-discrimination (accessed November 30, 2019).

Bao, Hongwei. 2018. *Queer Comrades: Gay Identity and Tongzhi Activism in Post-Socialist China*. Copenhagen: Nordic Institute of Asian Studies.

Bell, David and Jon Binnie. 2000. *The Sexual Citizen: Queer Politics and Beyond*. Cambridge: Polity.

Bell David and Jon Binnie. 2006. "Geographies of Sexual Citizenship." *Political Geography* 25: 869–873.

Benedicto, Bobby. 2014. *Under Bright Lights: Gay Manila and the Global Scene*. Minneapolis: University of Minnesota Press.

Bernstein, Mary and Nancy Naples. 2010. "Sexual Citizenship and the Pursuit of Relationship-Recognition Policies in Australia and the United States." *Women's Studies Quarterly* 38(1): 132–156.

Beyer, Georgina and Cathy Casey. 1999. *Change for the Better: The Story of Georgina Beyer as Told to Cathy Casey*. Auckland: Random House.

Bittenbender, Steve. 2015. "Kentucky Clerk's Office Ends Ban on Same-Sex Marriage Licenses." *Reuters*, September 4. Available at https://www.reuters.com/article/us-usa-gaymarriage-kentucky/kentucky-clerks-office-ends-ban-on-same-sex-marriage-licenses-idUSKCN0R13S220150904

Boellstorff, Tom. 2005. *The Gay Archipelago: Sexuality and Nation in Indonesia*. Princeton, NJ: Princeton University Press.

Boellstorff, T. 2007. *A Coincidence of Desires: Anthropology, Queer Studies, Indonesia*. Durham, NC: Duke University Press.

Buckton, Mark. 2015. "Foreign Same-Sex Couples Here Enjoy Rights that Japanese Don't." Japan Times, January 10. Available at: https://www.japantimes.co.jp/community/2015/06/10/issues/foreign-sex-couples-enjoy-rights-japanese-dont/#.XfD7pr97lqw (accessed December 11, 2019).

Butler Judith. 2002. "Is Kinship Always Already Heterosexual?" *differences* 13: 14–34.

Cadwallader J.R. and Damien Riggs. 2012. "The State of the Union: Towards a Biopolitics of Marriage." *M/C Journal* 15 (6): unpaginated. Available at http://journal.media-culture.org.au/index.php/mcjournal/article/viewArticle/585 (accessed November 13, 2014).

Canaday Margot. 2009. *The Straight State: Sexuality and Citizenship in Twentieth-Century America*. Princeton, NJ: Princeton University Press.

Chakrabarty, Dipesh. 2000. *Provincializing Europe: Postcolonial Thought and Historical Difference*, Princeton, NJ: Princeton University Press.

Chalmers Sharon. 2002 *Emerging Lesbian Voices from Japan*. London: RoutledgeCurzon.

Cheng, Kris. 2018. "'Love Wins': Hong Kong Changes Same-Sex Spouse Visa Policy after Historical Ruling." *Hong Kong Free Press*, September 18. Available at: https://www.hongkongfp.com/2018/09/18/love-wins-hong-kong-changes-sex-spouse-visa-policy-historic-ruling/ (accessed January 13, 2018).

Chiang, Howard. 2019. "Perspective: Gay Marriage in Taiwan and the Struggle for Recognition." *Current History: A Journal of Contemporary World Affairs* 118(809): 241.

Cho, John Song Pae. 2009. "The Wedding Banquet Revisited: 'Contract Marriages' between Korean Gays and Lesbians," *Anthropological Quarterly* 82(2): 401–422.

Dreher, Tanja. 2017. "The Uncanny Doubles of Queer Politics: Sexual Citizenship in the Era of Same Sex Marriage Victories." *Sexualities* 20(1–2): 176–195.

Duggan, Lisa. 2003. *The Twilight of Equality? Neoliberalism, Cultural Politics and the Attack on Democracy*. Boston, MA: Beacon Press.

Evans, David T. 1993. *Sexual Citizenship: The Material Construction of Sexualities*. London: Routledge.

Haas, Benjamin. 2017. "Taiwan's Top Court Rules in Favour of Same-Sex Marriage." *The Guardian*, May 24. Available at: https://www.theguardian.com/world/2017/may/24/taiwans-top-court-rules-in-favour-of-same-sex-marriage (accessed April 29, 2018).

Hassig, Ralph and Kongdan Oh. 2009. *The Hidden People of North Korea: Everyday Life in the Hermit Kingdom*, Lanham, MD: Rowman & Littlefield.

Hearn, Jeff. 2006. "The Implications of Information and Communication Technologies for Sexualities and Sexualized Violence: Contradictions of Sexual Citizenships." *Political Geography* 25: 944–963.

Higashi, Koyuki and Hiroko Masuhara, 2013. *Futari no Mama kara Kimitachi e (From your Two Mothers to You)*. Tokyo: Īsuto Puresu.

Human Rights Watch. 2008. "UN: General Assembly Statement Affirms Rights for All: 66 States Condemn Violations Based on Sexual Orientation and Gender Identity." Available at: https://www.hrw.org/news/2008/12/18/un-general-assembly-statement-affirms-rights-all (accessed December 11, 2019).

International Council on Human Rights Policy. 2009. "*Sexuality and Human Rights*." Geneva: International Council on Human Rights Policy.

Jackson, Peter. 1997. "Kathoey > < Gay > < Man: The Historical Emergence of Gay Male Identity in Thailand." In *Sites of Desire/Economies of Pleasure, Sexualities in Asia and the Pacific*, edited by Margaret Jolly and Lenore Manderson, 166–190. Chicago, IL: University of Chicago Press.

Jackson, Peter. 2009. "Capitalism and Global Queering: National Markets, Parallels among Sexual Cultures and Mutiple Queer Modernities." *GLQ: A Journal of Lesbian and Gay Studies* 15(3): 357–395.

Jackson, Peter, ed. 2011. *Queer Bangkok: Twenty-First-Century Markets, Media, and Rights*. Hong Kong: Hong Kong University Press.

Jackson, Peter. 2015. *Spatialities of Knowledge in the Neoliberal World Academy: Theory, Practice and 21st Legacies of Area Studies*, Bonn: Crossroads Asia Working Paper Series.

Johnson, Carol. 2002. "Heteronormative Citizenship and the Politics of Passing." *Sexualities* 5(3): 316–336.

Johnson, Carol. 2013. "Fixing the Meaning of Marriage: Political Symbolism and Citizen Identity in the Same-Sex Marriage Debate." *Continuum* 27(2): 242–253.

Johnson, Carol. 2017. "Sexual Citizenship in a Comparative Perspective: Dilemmas and Insights." *Sexualities* 20(1–2): 159–175.

Josephson, Jyl J. 2017. *Rethinking Sexual Citizenship*, New York, NY: SUNY Press.
Kam, Lucetta. 2015. "The Demand for a Normal Life: Marriage and its Discontents in Contemporary China." In *The Routledge Handbook of Sexuality Studies in East Asia*, edited by Mark McLelland and Vera Mackie, 77–86. Oxford: Routledge.
Kirby, Michael. 2011. "The Sodomy Offence: England's Least Lovely Criminal Law Export?" *Journal of Commonwealth Criminal Law* 1: 22–43.
Kong, Travis S.K., Hoi Leung Lau, and Cheuk Yin Li. 2015. "The Fourth Wave: A Critical Reflection on the Tongzhi Movement in Hong Kong." In *The Routledge Handbook of Sexuality Studies in East Asia*, edited by Mark McLelland and Vera Mackie, 188–201. Oxford: Routledge.
Langlois, Anthony J. 2017. "Queer Rights?" *Australian Journal of International Affairs* 71(3): 241–246.
Mackie Vera. 2001. "The Trans-sexual Citizen: Queering Sameness and Difference." *Australian Feminist Studies* 16(35): 185–192.
Mackie, Vera. 2002. "Embodiment, Citizenship, and Social Policy in Contemporary Japan." In *Family and Social Policy in Japan*, edited by Roger Goodman, 200–229. Cambridge: Cambridge University Press.
Mackie, Vera. 2008. "How to be a Girl: Mainstream Media Portrayals of Transgendered Lives in Japan." *Asian Studies Review* 32(3): 411–423.
Mackie, Vera. 2009. "Family Law and its Others." In Japanese Family *Law in Comparative Perspective*, edited by Harry Scheiber and Laurent Mayali, 139–163. Berkeley, CA: The Robbins Collection.
Mackie, Vera. 2010. "Necktie Nightmare: Narrating Gender in Contemporary Japan." *Humanities Research* XVI(1): 111–128. Available at: https://press.anu.edu.au/node/1237/download.
Mackie, Vera. 2013. "Genders and Genetics: The Medical and Legal Regulation of Family Forms in Japan." *Australian Journal of Asian Law* 14(1): 1–18. Available at: https://ssrn.com/abstract=2297156.
Mackie Vera. 2014. "Birth Registration and the Right to Have Rights: The Changing Family and the Unchanging *Koseki*." In *Citizenship and Japan's Household Registration System: The State and Social Control*, edited by David Chapman and Karl J Krogness, 203–220. Oxford: Routledge.
Mackie, Vera. 2017. "Rethinking Sexual Citizenship: Asia-Pacific Perspectives." *Sexualities* 10(1–2): 143–158.
Mackie, Vera. 2019. "Militarism and Sexualities in the Asia-Pacific Region." In *Global Encyclopedia of Gay, Lesbian, Bisexual, Transgender, and Queer History*, edited by Howard Chiang, 1054–1057. Farmington Hills, MI: Scribner.
Mackie, Vera and Mark McLelland. 2015. "Introduction: Framing Sexuality Studies in East Asia." In *The Routledge Handbook of Sexuality Studies in East Asia*, edited by Mark McLelland and Vera Mackie, 1–17. Oxford: Routledge.
Mackie, Vera and Mark Pendleton. 2010. "On the Move: Globalisation and Culture in the Asia-Pacific Region." *Intersections: Gender and Sexuality in Asia and the Pacific* 23: unpaginated. Available at: http://intersections.anu.edu.au/issue23/mackie_pendleton.htm (accessed September 28, 2014).
Mackie, Vera and Miyume Tanji. 2015. "Militarised Sexualities in East Asia. In *The Routledge Handbook of Sexuality Studies in East Asia*, edited by Mark McLelland and Vera Mackie, 60–73. Oxford: Routledge.
Manalansan M. F. 1994. "(Dis)Orienting the Body: Locating Symbolic Resistance among Filipino Gay Men." *positions: east asia cultures critique* 2(1): 73–90.

Maree, Claire. 2004. "Same-Sex Partnerships in Japan: Bypasses and other Alternatives." *Women's Studies* 33(4): 541–549.

Maree, Claire. 2015. "Queer Women's Culture and History in Japan." In *The Routledge Handbook of Sexuality Studies in East Asia*, edited by Mark McLelland and Vera Mackie, 230–243. Oxford: Routledge.

Maree, Claire. 2017. "Weddings and White Dresses: Media and Sexual Citizenship in Japan." *Sexualities* 20(1–2): 212–233.

Marshall, Thomas H. 1950. *Citizenship and Social Class and Other Essays*. Cambridge: Cambridge University Press.

Martin, Fran. 2015. "Transnational Queer Sinophone Cultures." In *The Routledge Handbook of Sexuality Studies in East Asia*, edited by Mark McLelland and Vera Mackie, 35–48. Oxford: Routledge.

Martin, Fran, Peter A. Jackson, Mark McLelland, and Audrey Yue, eds. 2008. *AsiaPacifiQueer: Rethinking Gender and Sexuality*. *Champaign*: University of Illinois Press.

McLelland, Mark. 2005. *Queer Japan from the Pacific War to the Internet Age*. Lanham, MD: Rowman and Littlefield.

McLelland, Mark and Katsuhiko Suganuma. 2009. "Sexual Minorities and Human Rights in Japan: An Historical Perspective." *The International Journal of Human Rights* 13(2–3): 329–343.

Monro, S. and L. Warren. 2004. "Transgendering Citizenship." *Sexualities* 7(3): 345–362. doi: 10.1177/1363460704044805.

Newton, Natalie. 2015. "Homosexuality and Transgenderism in Vietnam." In *The Routledge Handbook of Sexuality Studies in East Asia*, edited by Mark McLelland and Vera Mackie, 255–267. Oxford: Routledge.

Offord, Baden. 2013. "Queer Activist Intersections in Southeast Asia: Human Rights and Cultural Studies." *Asian Studies Review* 37(3): 335–349.

Pablo, Ben. 2010. "Male Same-Sex Sexuality and the Argentinian State, 1880–1930." In *The Politics of Sexuality in Latin America: A Reader on Lesbian, Gay and Bisexual and Transgender Rights*, edited by Javier Corrales and Mario Pecheny, 33–43. Pittsburgh, PA: University of Pittsburgh Press.

Pateman, Carole. 1996. Democratization and Citizenship in the 1990s: The Legacy of T.H. Marshall. Vilhelm Aubert Memorial Lecture 1996. Oslo: Institute for Social Research and Department of Sociology, University of Oslo.

Pavano, Thomas Adolph. 1986–1987. "Gay and Lesbian Rights: Adults Adopting Adults." *Connecticut Probate Law Journal* 38: 251–277.

Pendleton, Mark. 2015. "Transnational Sexual Politics in East Asia." In *The Routledge Handbook of Sexuality Studies in East Asia*, edited by Mark McLelland and Vera Mackie, 21–34. Oxford: Routledge.

Pendleton, Mark and Tanya Serisier. 2012. "Some Gays and the Queers." *M/C Journal* 15(6): unpaginated. Available at http://journal.media-culture.org.au/index.php/mcjournal/article/viewArticle/569 (accessed November 13, 2014).

Phelan, Shane. 2001. *Sexual Strangers: Gays, Lesbians and Dilemmas of Citizenship*. Philadelphia, PA: Temple University Press.

Plummer, Ken. 2003. *Intimate Citizenship. Private Decisions and Public Dialogues*. Seattle: University of Washington Press.

Polchar, Joshua, Tim Sweijs, Philipp Marten, and Jan Hendrik Galdiga. 2014. *LGBT Military Index*. The Hague: The Hague Centre for Strategic Studies. Available at: http://projects.hcss.nl/monitor/88/.

Povencher, Denis. 2016. *Queer French: Globalization, Language and Sexual Citizenship in France*. Oxford: Routledge.
Puar, Jasbir. 2007. *Terrorist Assemblages: Homonationalism in Queer Times*. Durham, NC: Duke University Press.
Puar, Jasbir. 2013. "Rethinking Homonationalism." *International Journal of Middle East Studies* 45(2): 336–339. doi: 10.1017/S002074381300007X.
Rhode, Deborah L. 2016. *Adultery, Infidelity and the Law*. Cambridge: Harvard University Press.
Rich, Adrienne. 1980. "Compulsory Heterosexuality and Lesbian Existence." *Signs* 5(4): 631–660.
Richardson Diane. 2000. "Constructing Sexual Citizenship: Theorizing Sexual Rights." *Critical Social Policy* 20(1): 105–135.
Richardson, Diane. 2018. *Sexuality and Citizenship*. Cambridge: Polity.
Richardson, Diane and Monro, Surya. 2012. *Sexuality, Equality and Diversity*. Basingstoke: Palgrave Macmillan.
Ringler, Guy. 2016. "A California Doctor is Helping Build Gay Families in Japan." Advocate, January 6. Available at https://www.advocate.com/commentary/2016/1/06/california-doctor-helping-build-gay-families-japan (accessed May 6, 2018).
Riseman, Noah. 2017. "'Just another start to the denigration of Anzac Day': Evolving Commemorations of LGBTI Military Service." *Australian Historical Studies* 48(1): 43–50.
Riseman, Noah, Shirleene Robinson, and Graham Willett. 2018. *Serving in Silence? Australian LGBT Servicemen and Women*, Sydney: New South.
Sabsay Leticia. 2011. "The Emergence of the Other Sexual Citizen: Orientalism and the Modernisation of Sexuality." *Citizenship Studies* 16(5–5): 605–623.
Sanders, Douglas. 2015. "'What's Law got to Do with It? Sex and Gender Diversity in East Asia." In *The Routledge Handbook of Sexuality Studies in East Asia*, edited by Mark McLelland and Vera Mackie, 127–149. Oxford: Routledge.
Seidman, Steven. 2002. *Beyond the Closet The Transformation of Gay and Lesbian Life*. New York and London: Routledge.
Seuffert, Nan. 2013. "Haunting National Boundaries: LGBTI Asylum Seekers." *Griffith Law Review* 22(3): 752–784.
Smith, Anna Marie. 1994. *New Right Discourse on Race and Sexuality: Britain, 1968–1990*. Cambridge: Cambridge University Press.
Smith. Miriam. 2017. "Homonationalism and the Comparative Politics of LGBTQ Rights." In *LGBTQ Politics: A Critical Reader*, edited by Marla Brettschneider, Susan Burgess, and Christine Keating, 458–476. New York, NY: New York University Press.
Smith, Miriam. 2018. "Historical Institutionalism and Same-Sex Marriage: A Comparative Analysis of the U.S. and Canada." In *Global Perspectives on Same-Sex Marriage: A Neo-Institutionalist Approach*, edited by Bronwyn Winter, Maxime Forest, and Réjane Sénac, 61–79. Cham: Palgrave Macmillan.
Stychin, Carl F. 1988. *A Nation by Rights: National Cultures, Sexual Identity Politics, and the Discourse of Rights*. Philadelphia, PA: Temple University Press.
Suganuma, Katsuhiko. 2005. "Festival of Sexual Minorities in Japan: A Revival of the Tokyo Lesbian and Gay Parade in 2005." *Intersections: Gender, History and Culture in the Asian Context* 12: unpaginated. Available at http://intersections.anu.edu.au/issue12/katsuhiko.html (accessed October 29, 2014).
Suganuma, Katsuhiko. 2012. *Contact Moments: The Politics of Intercultural Desire in Japanese Male-Queer Cultures*. Hong Kong: Hong Kong University Press.

Tang, Denise Tse-Shang. 2015. "Lesbian Spaces in Hong Kong." In *The Routledge Handbook of Sexuality Studies in East Asia*, edited by Mark McLelland and Vera Mackie, 218–229. Oxford: Routledge.

"Time to Discuss Same-Sex Marriage." 2019. *Japan Times*. Available at: https://www.japantimes.co.jp/opinion/2019/09/28/editorials/time-discuss-sex-marriage/#.XfDtVr97lqw (accessed December 11, 2019).

Treat, John Whittier. 2013. "Returning to Altman: Same-Sex Marriage and the Apparitional Child." In *After Homosexual: The Legacies of Gay Liberation*, edited by Carolyn D'Cruz and Mark Pendleton, 265–281. Crawley: UWA.

Tremblay, Manon, David Paternotte, and Carol Johnson, eds. 2011. *The Lesbian and Gay Movement and the State: Comparative Insights into a Transformed Relationship*. Farnham: Ashgate.

UNDP, USAID, 2014a. *Being LGBT in Asia: Vietnam Country Report*. Bangkok: UNDP.

UNDP, USAID, 2014b. *Being LGBT in Asia: Nepal Country Report*. Bangkok: UNDP.

United Nations Economic and Social Council. 2004. *Report of the Special Rapporteur on the Right to Health*. United Nations.

United Nations Secretary General. 2012. "Message to Human Rights Council Meeting on Violence and Discrimination Based on Sexual Orientation or Gender Identity," March 7. Available at: https://www.un.org/sg/en/content/sg/speeches/2012-03-07/message-human-rights-council-meeting-violence-and-discrimination (accessed December 11, 2019).

"UN Human Rights Council: First Resolution against Discrimination Based on Sexual Orientation." 2011. Global Legal Monitor, June 28. Available at: https://www.loc.gov/law/foreign-news/article/u-n-human-rights-council-first-resolution-against-discrimination-based-on-sexual-orientation/ (accessed December 11, 2019).

Valverde, Mariana. 2006. "A New Entity in the History of Sexuality: The Respectable Same-Sex Couple." *Feminist Studies* 32: 155–162.

Vandenberg, Andrew, ed. 2000. *Democracy and Citizenship in a Global Era*. London: Macmillan.

Weber, Cynthia. 2017. "Thinking about Queer Wars: 'International Polarization' and Beyond." *Australian Journal of International Affairs* 71: 231–235.

Wilkinson, Cai. 2017. "Are We Winning? A Strategic Analysis of Queer Wars." *Australian Journal of International Affairs* 71(3): 236–240.

Yi, Beh Lih. 2019. "Singapore Court to Hear Legal Challenges on Gay Sex Ban." *Reuters*. Available at: https://www.reuters.com/article/us-singapore-lgbt-rights/singapore-court-to-hear-legal-challenges-on-gay-sex-ban-idUSKBN1XM15 (accessed December 10, 2019).

Yue, Audrey. 2012. "Queer Asian Mobilities and Homonational Modernity: Marriage Equality, Indian Students in Australian and Malaysian Transgender Refugees in the Media." *Global Media and Communication* 8(3): 269–287.

Yue, Audrey and Zubillaga-Pow J., eds. 2012. *Queer Singapore: Illiberal Citizenship and Mediated Cultures*. Hong Kong: Hong Kong University Press.

Zhang, Phoebe. 2019. "Why are so Few LGBT Chinese Couples Taking Advantage of Laws that could Protect their Rights?" *South China Morning Post*, September 8. Available at https://www.scmp.com/news/china/society/article/3026104/why-are-so-few-lgbt-chinese-couples-taking-advantage-laws-could (accessed September 8, 2019).

19

Sexuality and Migration

SHWETA M. ADUR

Introduction

How does sexuality inform migration and, in turn, how has migration shaped sexuality? This meaningful question has catalyzed a growing body of literature at the nexus of migration, sexuality, and queer studies in the last couple of decades (Luibhéid 2004, 2008a, 2008b; Luibhéid and Cantú 2005; Manalanson 2006; Cantú, Naples, and Vidal-Ortiz 2009; Lewis and Naples 2014). Prior to this, sexuality had been confined to and conflated with the study of gender, or subsumed under an overarching framework of crime, deviance, morality, or public health concerns. Migration scholarship, too, either neglected the importance of sexuality or obscured it in its heterosexist leanings (Luibhéid and Cantú 2005; Manalanson 2006; Luibhéid 2004, 2008a). While the scholarly inquiry maybe recent, there is nothing new about the actual interface between the two phenomena. The link is ubiquitous and has structured societies since the beginning of time.

Sexuality impels migration as much as migration reshapes and shifts meanings surrounding sexuality; both are critical to the survival and regeneration of the human population. Intricate proscriptions regarding who can "acceptably" reproduce with whom and what kinds of kinship units are deemed legitimate and preferred are endemic to every society. On the other hand, a similar impetus – the threat of miscegenation (and of mixed race babies) – makes the regulation of migration a necessity to forestall the racial/ethnic dilution and demise of a society. Borders, therefore, become important sites where "biopower" is manifested and is exercised; regulating migration and sexuality become central to regulating social life itself, regardless of whether the agent of regulation is a tribal chief or an array of sophisticated administrative apparatus of a modern nation-state (Foucault 1978).

This chapter provides a bird's eye view of the scholarship that demonstrates the interlinkages between sexuality and migration and its most salient themes.

The chapter takes on an intersectional framework and situates itself within a temporal frame that spans the colonial era to the contemporary processes of globalization. This is not to imply that sexuality and migration were not linked in important ways in the precolonial times. However, as I elaborate here, the decision to begin with the colonial era is deliberate. First, it is not possible to understand the current global sexual order and the contentious relationship between the Global North and Global South without first locating the discourse in the period of colonialism. The colonial period served as a blueprint that remade the world economic and social order. During the colonial era, not only did migration pick up pace in unprecedented ways, but the discursive legacies that frame sexuality and migration extend into the ways in which contemporary societies regulate sexuality in the context of migration. Furthermore, prior links between countries of origin and destination are significant predictors of migration, and colonial networks are very important in that regard.

Before proceeding further, in order to explicate the usage of sexuality and migration, I will provide a concise definition of the two terms. It is also important to highlight here that given the breadth of the issue, the cases described in this chapter are merely illustrative and not exhaustive.

Sexuality

Sexuality refers to the myriad ways in which we identify, experience, enact, and express our emotions, desires, and relationships. It includes the many ways in which we come to know, understand, and manifest our deepest selves in juxtaposition with the social systems that influence us. For an individual, sexuality is as much inborn and instinctive as it is a product of socialization and culture. At the societal level, the meanings and legitimacy we impute to sexualities vary across spatial and temporal dimensions and an individual's ability to live their "authentic" sexual selves depend on the historical moment and the sociopolitical climate. As Foucault (1978) has said, there is not just *a history* of sexuality but *histories* of sexuality. What is considered a sexual act in one era or one culture is not so in another. Similarly, the notion of what is moral, acceptable and normal is *manufactured* in direct contrast to that which is named immoral, abnormal. and exceptional. In the late nineteenth century, "heterosexuality" was used to define a person who engaged in sex for pleasure without the procreative desire. As a result, at the time, heterosexuality was deemed as immoral and perverse. Heterosexuality emerged as a sign of normatively sanctified sex over a period of time and in direct opposition to "homosexuality" (Katz 2007). Similarly, identity and behavior are not necessarily linked and sexual object-choice does not necessarily signal sexual orientation. In fact, as many scholars of sexuality have already documented, the concern with identity is a modern-western preoccupation and has become globalized in this era (Altman 2002). Rupp (2001) reasoned that adult male citizens of Athens could penetrate social inferiors, including women, boys, foreigners, and slaves, and the act itself was more about power and domination than about homosexuality. In Basotho society of Lesotho, Rupp (2001, p. 296) notes that women can act sexually, fall in love, and form a marriage-like union with other women without defining any of this as sexual, as "sex" in this context "requires a penis and marriage means sex with a man, so there is no such concept as lesbian sex or lesbian relationships." In the contemporary era, Ward (2015) finds that straight white men may engage in overtly sexual acts while continuing to think of themselves as "not gay." As stated concisely by Weeks (2013, p. 19) sexuality

> is a result of diverse social practices that give meaning to human activities, of social definitions and self-definitions, of struggles between those who have power to define and regulate, and those who resist. Sexuality is not a given, it is a product of negotiation, struggle and human agency.

In summary then, the private realm of sexuality is definitively tied with its public realm. The imperative of controlling and managing the population and shaping the demographic contours of the modern nation-state makes sexuality a locus of power and a site of contentious politics; its ties to governmentality are therefore vital (Foucault 1978). Discursively, sexuality has been deployed to make and mark boundaries in order to separate the "desirable and good" subjects – citizens and denizens – from the "undesirable and bad" ones (Luibhéid 2008b). It has operated in conjunction with other axes of power such as class, gender, race, and nationality to empower and disempower groups of people, within and across national borders (Foucault 1978; Rubin 1993; Weeks 2013, Rupp 2001). The rise of the modern-western states and modern colonial empires reinforced the importance of sexuality as a regulatory force (Foucault 1978).

Migration

Migration refers to the movement of people from one place to another. Based on the parameters of nation-states whose geopolitical borders enforce belonging, migration can be internal or external. Internal migration signifies the movement within geopolitical borders while external migration takes place outside of these borders. The International Organization of Migration (IOM) estimated that in 2017, 3.4% of the world's population consisted of international migrants, that is, roughly 258 million persons. Counting internal migration is more elusive given that internal mobility takes place without the use of official paperwork such as visas and passports.

The scholarship broadly differentiates between two types of migrants – voluntary and involuntary. Voluntary migrants, alternatively called "economic migrants," are those who have moved from one place to another out of volition. They typically move in pursuit of better conditions of life and their mobility or the direction of movement lack any type of coercion. On the other hand, involuntary or forced migrants consist of populations/individuals who have been displaced due to political (wars, genocide, conflict), economic (development projects), or environmental (epidemics, floods, earthquakes, fires) crises in their place of origin and have typically had little say over their movement. Refugees, asylum seekers, displaced persons, and victims of trafficking are considered involuntary migrants. Going beyond the standard material motivations for migration, contemporary scholars of sexuality introduce a third category, namely sexual migration. According to Carillo (2004, p. 59) the term

> refers to international migration that is motivated, fully or partially, by the sexuality of those who migrate, including motivations connected to sexual desires and pleasures, the pursuit of romantic relations with foreign partners, the exploration of new self-definitions

of sexual identity, the need to distance oneself from experiences of discrimination or oppression caused by sexual difference, or the search for greater sexual equality and rights.

International migrants are also distinguished on the basis of legality; those with requisite paperwork and visas authorizing their immigration status in countries of destination are considered "documented," while those without adequate authorization are known as "undocumented." Contrary to popular wisdom, these categories are not stable. A documented migrant who arrives lawfully but overstays their visa may become undocumented and an undocumented migrant can become documented, especially with favorable political shifts. For example, the Immigration Reform and Control Act of 1986 granted a path to citizenship to approximately 2.7 million undocumented immigrants who could establish their stay in the US before the first day of 1982 (Badger 2014). Instead, as Luibhéid (2008b, p. 292) suggests, illegality like legality is a "process" that is mediated by "by empire, racism, sexism – and, …heterosexism – this means that undocumented people are not just one unified mass but exist in heterogeneous relationships to the possibility of legality. Equally, holders of legal status exist in heterogeneous relationship to the possibility of becoming undocumented (or being deported, which is, effectively, expulsion)".

Making of the World Sexual Order: The Colonial Encounters and the Colonial Empire

During the nineteenth and early twentieth centuries, international migration consisted largely of settler colonizers, missionaries, and wage earners. Typically, migration from the metropolis to the colony was initiated by men, women followed later once the men settled in. Using the word "migration" to describe colonial expansion euphemistically attenuates the violence – physical, sexual, mental, and moral – pervasive to conquest. Yet, this *was* a time of unprecedented international migration as people moved across countries to found new territories, to serve in military and administrative installations in colonies, for missionary activity, and under duress through the coolie system, transatlantic slavery, and convict transportation. Unlike medieval conquests, the modern-Western colonial empires were expansive, with vast swathes of land being taken over by a handful of European countries. The British Empire was arguably the most formidable; not only did Britain create a host of dependent colonies, but it populated the majority of settler colonies such as Australia, South Africa, and North America. Hammerton (2007) estimated that during the eighteenth century the largest emigration flow from Britain was to colonial America.

As European/white men and women came into contact with non-white populations around the world, sex became a significant site of colonial anxieties and the regulation of sexuality became crucial to imperial policy. Laws against promiscuity, buggery, sodomy, fornication, bastardy, and prostitution were made to control sexuality and intimacy, especially the sexuality of women and the specter of interracial intimacy. These laws were concurrently a colonial attempt to "set standards of behavior, both to reform the colonized and to protect the colonizers against moral lapses" (Human Rights Watch 2008). The regulatory bulwark of the period set the tone for contemporary global sexual order; as the "Europeanization" of the newly conquered territories led to (i) the superiority of the West in matters of sexual importance, and (ii) the standardization and global diffusion of modern-western values steeped in Victorian conservatism. Until this day "much of the sex law currently on the books also dates from the nineteenth-century morality crusades" wherein sexual agency and autonomy outside of the procreative imperative was frowned upon (Rubin 1993, p. 144). As noted earlier, this is why it becomes important to examine the temporal continuum between colonial era and contemporary times to comprehensively understand the relationship between sexuality and migration.

The reform and modernization of the colonized "savage" was realized and enforced through gendered, racialized, and sexualized boundaries and metaphors of morality. White colonial masculinity was at the apex, constructed as noble and virile, while the masculinity of the colonized (the brown and the black) was deemed perverse, excessive, barbarous, and deficit (Connell 1998; Collins 2004; Levine 2007). White men saw themselves as the protectors of white women's chastity and sexuality and positioned themselves as the "saviors" of the brown women. In colonial India, a slew of acts was passed to ban Sati (1829), institutionalize widow remarriage (1856), and raise the age of consent (1892) in the name of modernization. Yet in reality, the benevolent paternalism was only half the story. Tambe (2009, p. 32) writes:

> Interestingly, these reformed practices were often related to widely circulating conceptions about female sexuality: early marriage, for instance, was increasingly seen to fuel sexual precocity among girls, and remarriage for widows was believed to channel their potentially untrammeled sexuality in appropriate directions.

Indigenous women were seen simultaneously as helpless but sexually exotic and licentious. The stereotype of the unbridled libido of the brown women justified the colonizer's pogrom of sexual assault and violence.

During the early settlement phases of the empire, concubinage between white male and "native" women was not only accepted but also encouraged in order to gain intimate knowledge about the native (Levine 2007). This was partially on account of the uneven sex ratio, as white men far outnumbered white women in the colonies. Over time, as the sex ratio evened out, the practice of concubinage became stigmatized for fear of racial dilution through the birth of mixed-race babies. For example, the East Indian Company in colonial India forbade the marriage of senior officials with local women (Levine 2007). While sexual relationships between white men and native women were tolerated, sex between white women and non-white men was always troubling; the idea that white women would consent to these relationships was considered unthinkable. Levine (2007, p. 140) writes that in 1903, colonists in Southern Rhodesia prohibited illicit affairs between non-white males and white women. In rare circumstances, where non-white men partnered with white women, the latter were immediately ostracized. In colonial America, during Jim Crow, the "one-drop rule" ensured that a single drop of black blood, i.e. even one black ancestor, made a person black, therefore consigning them to a lower racial status (Collins 2004).

Beyond concubinage and interracial intimate relationships, prostitution was another "vice" that was rigorously managed. There was widespread fear that excessive sex would emasculate the colonists. Prostitution was regulated under the pretext that sex workers were immoral and a threat to public health as vectors of sexually transmitted diseases (STDs). In India, the Contagious Diseases Act of 1868 was passed to protect British soldiers from contracting STDs, and the imperial government did not hesitate to detain women who identified as sex workers in hospitals, where they were subjected to indignities of invasive medical examinations under the pretext of treatment (Tambe 2009). Brothels during colonial era were heavily regulated and racially segregated; women working for white clients were prohibited from taking non-white clients. Eventually, in many colonies European women were trafficked in to discourage interracial sex without compromising a soldier's access to "rest and leisure." In 1902, a law was passed in Cape Colony that forbade European sex workers from accepting black clients (Levine 2007). In colonial Bombay, European women were trafficked to serve British soldiers. The imperial government, however, made sure that these women were not Britons lest it reflect poorly on British womanhood (Tambe 2009, p. 56). In the US – a settler colony – the Page Act of 1875 was written with the aim of preventing the traffic of "immoral women" yet in its enforcement it disproportionately targeted Asian, particularly Chinese, women (Luibhéid 2002). The underlying motives of these acts were classist as much as they were sexist and racist. They overwhelmingly targeted poor women by limiting their sexual agency and controlling their mobility.

Bastardy laws around the world punished women whose children were born out of wedlock. In effect, it firmly established patriliny in societies where it wasn't necessarily the custom. Before the arrival of Europeans, Native American writer and feminist Paula Gunn Allen (2009, p. 21) mused that "no child is ever considered illegitimate among the Indians....If a girl gets pregnant, the baby is still part of the family, and the mother is too." Colonial advent not only stigmatized out-of-wedlock pregnancies but also created laws to criminalize it. It wasn't until 1986, that the Parliament of Antigua and Barbuda got rid of the colonial bastardy laws making "illegitimacy" legitimate (Lazarus-Black 1992).

Nonnormative sexualities and genders also fell within the perception of 'vices against nature.' In the US, the McCarren-Walter Act barred the entry of non-heterosexuals on the grounds that homosexuality was psychopathological and the Immigration and Naturalization Act of 1965 classified it as sexual deviance (Luibhéid 2005). Sodomy laws of the colonial era criminalized sex between mutually consenting same-sex adults in both dependent and settler colonies (Human Rights Watch 2008; Shah 2011). As the Human Rights Watch report "This Alien Legacy" (2008) notes:

> Section 377 was, and is, a model law in more ways than one. It was also the first colonial "sodomy law" integrated into a penal code – and it became a model anti-sodomy law for countries far beyond India, Malaysia, and Uganda. Its influence stretched across Asia, the Pacific islands, and Africa, almost everywhere the British imperial flag flew.

Section 377, a British imperial anti-sodomy law that was enacted in approximately 80 of the British colonies continues to exist on the legal books of many of these countries even after independence, making the discourse more complicated than a simple story of transplantation.

Though the indigenous gender and sexual order was subverted to the modern-Western heteronormative, heteropatriarchal, and homophobic discourse of the colonizer, many of the laws were ultimately retained by the local/nationalist/male elite because it was the perfect discursive "tool kit" to uphold the dominance of the straight male elite. Hence, though Britain decriminalized consensual homosexual sex in 1967, the majority of its colonies continue to grapple with the archaic law. In fact, at the time this chapter is being written, Kenya's high court upheld the colonial law criminalizing same-sex act (CNN 2019). In an ironic move, the Kenyan president, President Uhuru Kenyatta, defending the colonial relic, disavowed homosexuality as "un-African" and said "it is not human rights issue as you would want to put it, this is an issue of society; our own culture as a people irregardless (sic) of which community you come from…This is not acceptable, this is not agreeable." (CNN 2019). That homosexuality is a western import has been echoed by a number of African and Asian leaders and it is also repeated by immigrant communities who settle in the Western nations. Parents of South Asians in the US often claim homosexuality is a Western evil (Prashad 2001, Adur 2018). The repudiation of the Two-Spirit in Native American traditions, the Hijras in India, and the travesti in Brazil can also be attributed to the colonial encounter. The colonial government in India associated nomadism with sexual immorality and considered the women immoral (Human Rights Watch 2008). In a curious move, it clubbed "eunuchs" with "criminal" tribes (nomadic tribes) and vagrancy with sexual immorality. Human Rights Watch (2008, p. 30) illustrates:

> The 1897 amendment – subtitled "An Act for the Registration of Criminal Tribes and Eunuchs" – linked "eunuch" identity to Section 377. It showed how the vagrancy and sodomy provisions stemmed from the same motive: to place not just behaviors, but classes of people, under surveillance and control…. The categories of the vagrant catamite and criminal eunuch allowed the state to arrest people on the presumption of sodomy, without proof of an actual act.

To sum up, all of these laws buffered the colonist's masculinity and heteropatriarchal arrangements of intimacy, kinship, and family. Even though the local male elites were construed as deficient in comparison to white masculinity, the colonial state was cautious about not antagonizing them excessively. The brunt of these laws regulating sexuality and migration were borne disproportionately by women and sexual minorities. In the next section, "Post-Colonialism and the Processes of Globalization," the chapter discusses the paradigmatic shifts and the continuing legacy of colonial laws in the contemporary era of globalization.

Post-Colonialism and the Processes of Globalization: Continuity and Change

As shown in the foregoing paragraphs, the colonial encounters reinforced the importance of sexuality in defining and policing mobility and the boundaries of belonging, nationality, and citizenship. Even after independence, many of the previously colonized countries retained the laws enacted by the colonizers to buttress the authority of the straight male elite by disempowering women and sexual minorities.

On the scholarly front, the scholarship on migration and sexuality received a boost on account of three interrelated processes – globalization, the AIDs pandemic, and the ascent of queer theory in the 1990s (Manalanson 2006). First, processes of globalization – enhanced air transport, the growing interconnectedness of the world through global capitalism, the growth of a transnational state apparatus such as the UN, World Bank etc., and the transnational justice networks – have all led to the intensification of migration across borders. Second, the AIDs epidemic of the 1980s made it necessary for nation-states to once again focus on controlling sex and quarantining the border against "sexual threats." For example, in 1987, the US made it compulsory for all prospective legal permanent residents to show that they are HIV-negative (Luibhéid 2005). Sex workers and gay men became suspects and the targets of public health policing and criminalization. Finally, the combination – the AIDS pandemic and globalization – influenced queer theory and sexuality research to study sexuality from a global and transnational perspective. Sexuality became "unmoored from a static geographic frame to a mobile one" (Manlanson 2006, p. 229). Consequently, in this era, sexual migration reified the border(s) that globalization sought to eliminate, and the seismic shifts recalibrated scholarly interest.

Scholarship confirms that repercussions of globalization on sexuality – identity, behavior, and practices – are not always linear; in fact, the interaction between the Global North/West and the Global South/ non-West has been messy, uneven, and sometimes circuitous. Consider, for an example, the international gay and lesbian liberation movement. That (internal) migration from rural to urban areas was generic to the movement is uncontested, but its spillover from the Global North to the Global South is not necessarily unidimensional. Altman (2002, p. 416) describes this connection by noting that the "growing scientific awareness of homosexuality owed a great deal to the growth of European colonialism, and the accompanying interest in other ways of organizing sexuality and gender in non-European societies." Thus, while Western colonial migration reorganized sexual and gender order in its colonies to mirror Victorian conservatism, the lesbian, gay, bisexual, transgender, and queer (LGBTQ) movement that took off in the West and spilled over to the rest of the world was inspired, in part, by the precolonial non-West that exposed the "unnaturalness" of modern-western binaries of sex, gender, and sexuality. Paradoxically, also, the incursion of global/Western culture has led to the growth of conservative/oppositional nationalist cultures in the Global South, which has hardened in its stance against what is seen as the West's lax sexual values and norms. (As noted in the section "Making of the World Sexual Order," political leaders of erstwhile colonies have often claimed that homosexuality is a Western import exported by the West to systematically corrode the traditional nation culture). In some places, such as Uganda, reactionary Western conservatives (US Christian Right missionaries) migrate to work in tandem with the African clergy to persecute LGBT communities (Kaoma 2013).

The circuitous route described above has resulted in the West repositioning itself as the beacon of civilization, gender equality, and sexual liberation. The impact on migration and sexual politics around the world is definitive. The contemporary stance of the West as a liberal sexual haven creates a pull factor for queer migrants from the world over who imagine a life free of persecution (Carrillo 2004; Vogel 2009; Adur 2018). On the ground, it has set into motion the contradictory yet simultaneous processes of *standardization* and *differentiation*, i.e. the emergence of hybrid forms of sexual identities that interact with Western sexual ideologies. While the usage of "gay" and "lesbian" identities is globally widespread (Altman 2002), immigrants have not always subscribed to a homogenous understanding of same-sex desire. Thing (2010) shows that for some Mexican gay immigrants the object-choice gay paradigms (central to Western homosexuality) and *activo/pasivo* coexist with each other. Decena (2008) points to the ways in which Dominican men in the US resist the confessional politics of coming out associated with authentic gayness in the US, and instead see themselves as "tacit" subjects. At an everyday interpersonal level, economic benefits of migration provide some bargaining power to negotiate sexual and gender identities and practices with families in transnational contexts. Venezuelan *transformistas*, who travel to Europe for transgender sex work find acceptance within their families by sending remittances (Vogel 2009).

In recent years, many countries primarily in the Global North, have adopted schemes for queer asylum. In the 1990s, the US overturned laws that previously prohibited "sexual deviants" from migrating into the country and later, in 1994, created refugee and asylum policies to admit LGBTI identified persons who experienced a "well-founded fear of persecution" in their home countries. Australia, Belgium, Canada, Denmark, Finland, France, Germany, Ireland, Italy, the Netherlands, New Zealand, Thailand, and the United Kingdom are other countries that recognize sexual orientation and gender identity as grounds for petitioning asylum. Despite the rhetoric of freedom, the reality that greets many of the queer immigrants is different (Acosta 2013; Adur 2018). The majority of the cases are rejected, Lewis (2014, p. 960) citing the UK Lesbian and Gay Immigration Group notes "in the year 2009–2010, between 98% and 99% of all lesbian and gay asylum cases were rejected at the initial interview stage, compared with a 73% rejection rate for other asylum claims." Proving "well-founded fear" tantamount to persecution is often onerous and the costs of adjudication are prohibitive (Randazzo 2005; Lewis 2014). Proving that one is homosexual is equally burdensome, to the extent that some couples have resorted to videotaping themselves having sex to provide credible evidence of their homosexuality for their asylum petitions. Yet the benefits of these tactics are not equally distributed and as Lewis (2014) finds, queer female migrants of color are at a disadvantage since they are less likely to use such means. Amidst the growing anti-immigrant sentiments and policy in the US, the undocumented and the asylum seekers have also found themselves in immigration detentions centers where abuse and violence is amply recorded (Human Rights Watch 2016; Adur 2018). Mobility, especially international relocation, has been shown to be particularly onerous for transgender individuals who face further harassment if and when travel documents do not align seamlessly with the appearance. While some countries recognize third gender, others continue to institutionalize the binary, forcing people to choose one or the other on their passports.

The contemporary era of globalization is also known for having "feminized" migration. Approximately half of the world's international migrants are women. Female migrants outnumber male migrants in Europe and Northern America, while in Africa and Asia, particularly Western Asia, migrants are predominantly men (United Nations 2015). Women, today, move not only for reasons of family reunification but also independently to work as nannies, nurses, maids, internet brides, and sex workers in the global economy. Countries like Sri Lanka and Philippines have created bureaus to promote overseas employment of women. Sri Lanka offers women predeparture training in performing domestic chores such as cleaning, cooking, and handling appliances (Maymon 2017). Yet, several other countries actively limit women's movement in the name of protection.

There is a veritable amount of scholarship that analyzes the nexus between gendered care work and migration in this era of globalization; however, as Manalanson (2006) has alleged, issues of sexuality and intimacy are often overlooked and the majority operate from a heteronormative orientation. Sex work, in the context of feminized migration, is intensely scrutinized. It is not a coincidence that the majority of the discourse on the interface of migration, gender, and sexuality has been dominated by the discourse on sex work, sex trafficking, and sex tourism. Though a significant number of women are trafficked for sex work in appalling conditions, scholars have also pointed to machinations used to throttle all forms of voluntary sex work in the name of trafficking. In this regard, the contemporary states are not very different from the feverishness with which the imperial government regulated sex work (Tambe 2009). Bernstein (2018), based on her ethnographic work in Thailand, shows that the dramatic refashioning of all commercial sex work as "slavery" is borne of the expedient alliances between evangelical activists and secular feminist groups. The moralizing discourse ignores that women, both in developed and developing countries, may engage in sex work out of their own volition (Kempadoo and Doezema 1998). The moralizing discourse provides the perfect alibi to securitize and militarize the border and enhance the repressive police crackdown of sex workers (Bernstein 2018). For example, the contemporary Indian law that regulates sex work, the Immoral Traffic (Prevention) Act, 1956, conflates trafficking and sex work. Women's bodies, particularly women unbound by ties of matrimony, are scrutinized as either victims of trafficking or as sexual threats even though in the context of global tourism, states have gained from revenue generated from sex tourism (Kempadoo and Doezema, 1998). "Savior discourses" used in the past continue to flourish as tourists travel to "exotic" lands for sexual pleasure. Writing about the commercial sex industry in Vietnam, Hoang (2015) shows that a number of affluent males visit developing countries for sex tourism, not only to feed their carnal desires but also to concoct feel-good narratives by describing their behavior as one of helping the "helpless" women.

Apart from a handful of countries that extend immigration benefits to same-sex spouses, for the most part, legal admission in most countries depends on fitting the (hetero)normative image of marriage and family. Family-based visas are the primary means for relocation. As Thai (2008) finds, in 2005about 58% of those who migrated to the US arrived through various routes of family sponsorship. Amongst this group, about half came directly through the means of marriage. Spouses and children are most favored in these categories. However, immigrant family size matters as sexual stereotypes of the immigrant's unbridled fecundity is often used to limit migration. As Luibhéid (2008a, p. 174) has argued, "unwelcome migrants are often characterized as engaging in 'unrestrained' childbearing, which is seen to reflect their deviation from or imperfect mastery over mainstream heterosexual norms, resulting in the birth of 'undesirable' children." The alleged fertility of Mexican immigrants in the US is often used to limit migration, particularly chain migration. Simultaneously, immigrants may also be framed as upholders of family values and filial piety, a stereotype which then is deployed to remoralize citizenry or other communities of color.

The model minority stereotype used to describe Asian Americans has also been used to denigrate other communities of color in the US (Prashad 2001). Thus heteronormativity is deployed as much for anti-immigrant purposes as it is for pro-immigrant purposes, depending on the political climate.

An interesting stream of migration scholars has examine the transformation of sexual norms and values in response to assimilative compulsions in the countries of destination. Garcia (2012) finds young Latinas enact their sexual subjectivity by negotiating external stereotypes (Latina teens being viewed as high risk for pregnancy or repressed) and internal pressures (parental disapproval). They claim "respectability" based on the practice of safe sex and by constructing white women's sexual behavior as promiscuous and shameless. The strategy of counterracializing and denigrating the dominant group's sexuality is not unique to Latina teens; Espiritu (2001) points to a similar trend among Filipinas, and Manohar (2008) among South Asian Americans. Acosta (2013) shows how lesbian Latinas gain a certain degree of autonomy from their families upon their migration. These sexualized processes become boundaries through which us/them, citizen/migrant, moral/immoral are enacted and grappled with.

While the scholarship about immigrants making their journey from the Global South to the Global North abounds, the reverse is not necessarily true. A comparatively newer, relatively smaller, stream of scholarship examines the question. Farrer and Dale (2014) show the "downward sexual mobility" of white women in Shanghai's sex scene, who are seen as undesirable and less feminine. Their marginalization, in some ways, goes in tandem with their decision to exclude Chinese men as potential partners. More recently, scholars such as Brainer (2019) have written critically about negotiating their whiteness and queerness in Taiwan.

Conclusion

As shown in this chapter, sexuality, race, class, and gender have been integral to the work of disciplining populations, policing borders, and nation-building. Migrant exceptionalism – sifting between desirable and undesirable immigrants – depends on a range of criteria that include race, class, gender, and nationality and as this chapter demonstrates, sexuality is an important, though comparatively undertheorized, dimension. At the individual level, sexuality is at times a precursor to migration and sexual practices. Identity and behavior undergo shifts during processes of migration and assimilation. At the macrostructural level, this chapter additionally examines the interrelationship between the Global North/West and Global South/non-West. Examining the temporal continuity between the colonial era and contemporary era, this chapter shows that many of the changes introduced during the colonial period continue to resonate through the contemporary era of globalization. First, the proscriptive laws regarding sexuality and migration from the colonial period continue to influence jurisprudence around the world. Western hegemony remains intact in the name of "progress" although in an ironically circuitous way. While progress for the colonist meant a slew of conservative and homophobic laws that marginalized alternative arrangements of gender and sexuality and heavily curtailed the mobility of women, nonnormative genders, and sexualities, today many of the stances have been reversed in the name of progressiveness. The Global South has not been a tabular rasa; instead the interface has been contentious, yielding both expected and unexpected outcomes. Finally, straight white male elites have enjoyed the most privileges and least obstacles when crossing borders whereas the rest – "others," i.e. males of color, women, and sexual minorities – have encountered varying degrees of scrutiny along the way. Borders are not just sexualized but (hetero)sexualized and heteronormative; conversely migrants who do not fit the heteronormative definition of family are either denied entry or are believed to present a sexual threat (as immoral women, carriers of disease, or sexual deviants and perverts). Women, their bodies, and reproductive capacity have been heavily scrutinized and directly implicated in securitizing the border. Though, some countries have become more open to the admission of queer immigrants, the policies have been criticized for being homonormative. In sum, sexuality in association with race, gender, and nationality has always informed processes of migration and nation-building whether it be clandestine or open.

References

Acosta, Katie. 2013. *Amigas y amantes: Sexually Nonconforming Latinas Negotiate Family (Families in Focus)*. Brunswick, NJ: Rutgers University Press.

Adur, Shweta M. 2018. "In Pursuit Of Love: 'Safe Passages', Migration and Queer South Asians in the US. *Current Sociology* 66(2): 320–334.

Altman, Dennis. 2002. "Globalization and the International Gay/Lesbian Movement." In *Handbook of Lesbian and Gay Studies*, edited by Diane Richardson and Steven Seidman, 415–424. Thousand Oaks, CA: Sage.

Badger, Emily. 2014. "What Happened to the Millions of Immigrants Granted Legal Status Under Ronald Reagan?" The Washington Post, November 26. Available at: https://www.washingtonpost.com/news/wonk/wp/2014/11/26/what-happened-to-the-millions-of-immigrants-granted-legal-status-under-ronald-reagan/?utm_term=.f04abffd12fc (accessed April 14, 2019).

Bernstein, Elizabeth. 2018. *Brokered Subjects. Sex Trafficking and the Politics of Freedom.* Chicago, IL: University of Chicago Press.

Brainer, Amy. 2019. *Queer Kinship and Family Change in Taiwan.* Brunswick NJ: Rutgers University Press.

Cantú, Lionel, Nancy Naples, and Salvador Vidal-Ortiz. 2009. *The Sexuality of Migration: Border Crossings and Mexican Immigrant Men.* New York, NY: New York University Press.

Carrillo, Héctor. 2004. "Sexual Migration, Cross-Cultural Sexual Encounters, and Sexual Health." *Sexuality Research & Social Policy* 1(3): 58–70.

Collins, Patricia, H.2004. *Black Sexual Politics: African Americans, Gender, and the New Racism.* New York, NY: Routledge.

CNN 2019. "Kenyan Court Upholds Law Making Gay Sex Illegal." Available at: https://m.cnn.com/en/article/h_6f19efb4ae1d8abd276ffaf5ad1bec8d (accessed May 25, 2019).

Connell, R.W. 1998. Masculinities and Globalization. *Men and Masculinities* 1(1): 3–23.

Decena, Carlos. 2008. "Tacit Subjects." *GLQ: A Journal of Lesbian and Gay Studies* 14(2/3): 339–359.

Espiritu, Yen Le. 2001. "We Don't Sleep around like White Girls Do': Family, Culture, and Gender in Filipina American Lives." *Signs* 26(2): 415–440.

Farrer, James and Sonja Dale. 2013. "Sexless in Shanghai: Gendered Mobility Strategies in a Transnational Sexual Field." In *Sexual Fields: Toward a Sociology of Collective Sexual Life*. edited by Adam Isaiah Green, 143–170. Chicago, IL: University of Chicago Press.

Foucault, Michel. 1978. *The History of Sexuality, vol.* 1, An Introduction, translated by Robert Hurley. London: Allen Lane.

Garcia, Lorena. 2012. *Respect Yourself, Protect Yourself: Latina girls and Sexual Identity*. New York, NY: New York University Press.

Gunn Allen, Paula. 2009. "Where I Come from is Like This." In *Feminist Frontiers*, edited by Taylor, Verta, Nancy Whittier, and Leila Rupp, 8th edn., 31–35. Boston, MA: McGraw-HIll.

Hammerton. James, A. 2007. "Gender and Migration." In *Gender and Empire*, edited by Phillipa Levine, 156–180. Oxford: Oxford University Press.

Hoang, Kimberly, Kay. 2015. *Dealing in Desire Asian Ascendancy, Western Decline, and the Hidden Currencies of Global Sex Work*. Oakland, CA: University of California Press.

Human Rights Watch. 2008. "This Alien Legacy: The Origins of 'Sodomy' Laws in British Colonialism." Available at: Error! Bookmark not defined. (accessed May 30, 2019).

Human Rights Watch. 2016. "'Do You See How Much I'm Suffering Here?' Abuse Against Transgender Women in US Immigration Detention." Available at: https://www.hrw.org/sites/default/files/report_pdf/us0316_web.pdf (accessed May 30, 2019).

Kaoma, Kapya J. 2013. "The Marriage of Convenience: The U.S. Christian Right, African Christianity, and Postcolonial Politics of Sexual Identity." In *Global Homophobia: States, Movements, and the Politics of Oppression*, edited by Meredith L.Weiss and Michael J. Bosia, 75–102, Champaign: University of Illinois Press.

Katz, Jonathan N. 2005. *The Invention of Heterosexuality*. Chicago, IL: The University of Chicago Press.

Kempadoo, Kamala and Jo Doezema. 1998. *Global Sex Workers*. New York, NY: Routledge.

Lazarus-Black, M., 1992. "Bastardy, Gender Hierarchy, and the State: The Politics of Family Law Reform in Antigua and Barbuda." *Law and Society Review* 26(4): 863–899.

Levine, Phillipa, 2007. "Sexuality, Gender and Empire". In *Gender and Empire*, edited by Phillipa Levine, 134–155. Oxford: Oxford University Press.

Lewis, Rachel. A. 2014. "'Gay? Prove it': The Politics of Queer Anti-Deportation Activism." *Sexualities* 17(8): 958–975.

Lewis, Rachel A. and Nancy A. Naples. 2014. "Introduction: Queer Migration, Asylum, and Displacement." *Sexualities* 17(8): 911–918.

Luibhéid, Eithne. 2002. *Entry Denied: Controlling Sexuality at the Border*. Minneapolis, MN: University of Minnesota Press.

Luibhéid, Eithne, 2005. "Introduction." In *Queer Migrations: Sexuality, U.S. Citizenship, and Border Crossings*, edited by Eithne Luibhéid and Lionel Cantú, Jr., .ix – xlvi. Minneapolis: University of Minnesota Press.

Luibhéid, Eithne. 2008a. Queer/Migration: An Unruly Body of Scholarship. *GLQ: A Journal of Lesbian and Gay Studies* 14(2–3): 169–190.

Luibhéid, Eithne. 2008b. Sexuality, Migration, and the Shifting Line between Legal and Illegal Status. *GLQ: A Journal of Lesbian and Gay Studies* 14(2): 289–315.

Luibhéid, Eithne and Lionel Cantú, Jr., ed. 2005. *Queer Migrations: Sexuality, U.S. Citizenship and Border Crossing*. Minneapolis, MN: University of Minnesota.

Manalanson M. 2006. "Queer Intersections: Sexuality and Gender in Migration Studies." *International Migration Review* 40(1): 224–249.

Manohar, Namita. 2008. "'Sshh …!! Don't Tell My Parents': Dating among Second-Generation Patels in Florida. (Report)." *Journal of Comparative Family Studies* 39(4) 571–588.

Maymon 2017. "The Feminization of Migration: Why are Women Moving More?" *Cornell Policy Review*. Available at: http://www.cornellpolicyreview.com/the-feminization-of-migration-why-are-women-moving-more/. (accessed May 30, 2019).

Prashad, Vijay. 2001. *The Karma of the Brown Folk*. Minneapolis, MN: University of Minnesota Press.

Randazzo, Timothy. 2005. "Social and Legal Barriers: Sexual Orientation and Asylum in the United States." In *Queer Migrations: Sexuality, U.S. Citizenship and Border Crossing*, edited by Eithne Luibhéid and Lionel Cantú, Jr., 30–60. Minneapolis, MN: University of Minnesota.

Rubin, Gayle. 1993. "Thinking Sex: Notes for a Radical Theory of the Politics of Sexuality." In *The Lesbian and Gay Studies Reader*, edited by Henry Abelove, Michael Aina Barale, and David M. Halperin, 3–44. New York, NY: Routledge.

Rupp, Leila. J. 2001. "Toward a Global History of Same-Sex Sexuality." *Journal of History of Sexuality* 10(2): 287–302.

Shah, Nayan. 2011. *Stranger Intimacy: Contesting Race, Sexuality, and the Law in the North American West*. Berkeley, CA: University of California Press.

Tambe, Ashwini. 2009. *Codes of Misconduct: Regulating Prostitution in Late Colonial Bombay*. Minneapolis, MN: University of Minnesota Press.

Thai, Hung, C. 2008. *For Better or for Worse: Vietnamese International Marriages in the New Global Economy*. Piscataway, NJ: Rutgers University Press.

Thing, James. 2010. "Gay, Mexican and Immigrant: Intersecting Identities among Gay Men in Los Angeles." *Social Identities* 16(6): 809–831.

United Nations. 2015. International Migration Report 2015. Available at: https://www.un.org/en/development/desa/population/migration/publications/migrationreport/docs/MigrationReport2015_Highlights.pdf (accessed June 1, 2019.

Vogel, Katrin. 2009. "The Mother, the Daughter, and the Cow: Venezuelan 'Transformistas' Migration to Europe." *Mobilities* 4(3): 367–387.

Ward, Jane. 2015. *Not Gay: Sex Between Straight White Men*. New York, NY: New York University Press.

Weeks, Jeffrey. 2013. *Sexuality*, 2nd edn. Hoboken, NJ: Taylor and Francis.

20

Sexuality and Criminal Justice

SHARON HAYES AND CRISTINA KHAN

Introduction: Moral and Legal Space

Sex and sexualities are governed by space. Geographical space in most contemporary societies is dominated by heteronormative discourses and practices, which are hostile to nontraditional sexualities and what becomes classified as "nontraditional sexual behavior." In this context, public space is characterized as areas in which people do not have a choice about what they are exposed to – in other words, they are reliant on the discretion of others in determining what visible, tactile, and audible experiences they will encounter. Because of the heteronormative nature of public morality, which privileges traditional institutions such as families and heterosexual marriage, public spaces are governed by legislation preventing individuals from engaging in acts considered as offensive to those ideals (Halberstam 2005). This chapter examines the nature and sociohistorical development of those ideals and how they relate to the criminalization of sexual behaviors. We center criminalization, space and place, and different forms of sexual labor to show how the governance of sexualities is specific to context and varies over time and space.

One of the most entrenched attitudes surrounding public space is the fear of public nudity. Public nudity generally is considered to be inappropriate or wrong, and in many cases is also illegal. Nudity is acceptable under certain circumstances, in certain spaces (mostly private), and with prior notice. The notion of public nudity is therefore linked to the notion of consent. Geographies of sex appear to be dyadically delineated into public and private. This dualism also extends to sexuality – public spaces must, for the most part, be heterosexual spaces. There are very limited public spaces for nontraditional sexualities, and those that exist are often hidden, or if occupying visible public space, tend to be subcultural and/or rendered nonthreatening by heteronormative laws and conventions. For example, the practice of "cottaging" – where sex between men occurs in public lavatories and similar spaces – is commonly frowned

---

Companion to Sexuality Studies, First Edition. Edited by Nancy A. Naples.
© 2020 John Wiley & Sons Ltd. Published 2020 by John Wiley & Sons Ltd.

upon, and known "beats" are usually patrolled by police. Similarly, nonheterosexual displays of love and affection, even where participants are fully clothed, often are considered offensive and policed under public obscenity or public nuisance laws (Feinberg 1988). Heterosexual partners who engage in such public displays are more often tolerated, depending on the extent of the display. However, irrespective of sexual preference, public sex is illegal and members of the general public are affronted when faced with such displays. This policing of sex and nudity in public spaces is far-reaching across cultures and ethnic boundaries, and doubly discriminates against nonheterosexuals and those who deviate from sexual and/or gender norms.

Significantly, sexual practice is not neutral but is embodied in heteronormative interpretations of gender and sexuality, as well as the proper constitution of a relationship and what that stands for. This is most obvious in how children's sexuality is governed in terms of spaces. Recent ethnographic research has found, for example, that parents, in relaying messages about sexual threats while also trying to maintain children's innocence, give out the erroneous message that public space is dangerous while private space is safe (Massey 2004, p. 12). Where children were able to roam the streets and play freely with each other in times past, they are now more often locked behind closed doors, and both play and school time are closely regulated to ensure they are protected from anything sexual – including but not limited to naked bodies, sexual intercourse, and the display of erotic images and scenes. This moral governance of the risk of sex for children in large part determines where and when nudity and sexual practices may occur.

Such moral governance also determines the timeframe for sex – sex has become associated with the night, and so where public spaces are allocated to "adult entertainment," they are temporally confined to darkness. Needham comments that daylight is always associated with and reserved for families, because children, in particular, have access to the realm of the public during the day (Needham 2008). Thus we find television content regulated so that shows which offer content over and above a PG rating, must be held back until the relevant watershed time – usually 8:30 or 9pm, when all children are safely tucked into bed. Similarly, adult entertainment must not only be confined to spaces where families are unlikely to congregate, but also temporally to the night time, following the television watershed or even later. This ensures that not only will the unsavory activities conducted in these venues occur outside of family time, but also that they are covered by darkness, rendering them less visible, and thereby less threatening to wholesome heteronormative values.

Foucault comments on the regulation of public spaces in his work on madness and prisons. Prisons discipline populations within confined spaces through an interweaving of medical, policed, urban, and national spaces (Philo 2005). This facilitates the "careful organisation of time, space, bodies and action" (p. 329) and "condones particular associations but not others between different classes of people, specific forms of sexual encounter, and certain spaces and times for the 'doing' of the sex acts in question" (p. 330). Similarly, Philo argues that there is a "collision of population, sex and space – an interest in the spaces of sex acts, sex work, sex workers, sexual diseases, sexual health and sexual policies…" that govern the way in which sex is enacted in society (p. 330).

The way in which sex is regulated, then, speaks to a fear of embodied sex in real life and real situations, which in turn creates an artificial moral category of sexual deviance focused (for the most part) on indecency and offense. The following sections explore particular categories of sexual offense, and the ways in which they are governed by social mores and criminal justice systems.

Sex, Sexuality, and Crime

At the beginning of the eighteenth century, to be called a whore "brought into question one's honesty, probity and personal ability as much as ones sexual behaviour" (Hitchcock 1997, p. 99). Attempts to regulate morally inappropriate sexual behavior, however, were made many centuries prior to this. In the tenth century, for example, those to be banished for their crimes included "wizards, sorcerers, perjurers, conspirators to murder and horewenan, which included whores, fornicators and adulterers" (Mayhew, cited in Agustin 1988, p. 99). Nine hundred years later, the Vagrancy Act of 1822 classified vagrants, professional beggars, cheats, and thieves as well as "any woman who yields to her passions and loses her virtue" as prostitutes (Mayhew, cited in Agustin 1988, p. 99). The difficulty of accurately identifying whores was partly due to the way in which such behavior was understood as a moral failure. "It was not their participation in illegal sex which put them beyond the pale of normal society, but that their circumstances proved their own lack of moral worth" (Hitchcock 1997, p. 99).

However, over the course of the eighteenth century, the imaginary of the prostitute was revised from one of individual moral failure to that of a victim of seduction. Due in large part to the enlightened understandings of male and female sexuality that emerged during this time, specifically, women's capacity to conceive was not linked to their sexual pleasure. Men were given the active part, naturally speaking, in sex. "The stereotype of seduction placed new onus on male activity and female passivity." (Hitchcock 1997, p. 100) In the space of a century, women went from being lustful and full of a barely controlled desire to being sexually numb and passive. In contrast, men, who had begun the century thinking that they could easily control their sexual desires, "due to their greater rationality and mental strength," and that they had a duty to do so, "ended the period being told that their sexual desires were largely beyond their control" (Hitchcock 1997, 100).

In such a context, the crime of rape was also revised. In the eighteenth century, rape went from being seen as equivalent to other forms of violent crime, to a uniquely horrific event. The events that led to this change are related to the shift in how prostitution was understood. As Hitchcock notes, sexually explicit accounts of rape and sodomy in the Old Bailey Sessions Papers, for example, formed a prominent site for the discussion of sex in eighteenth-century public culture. Moreover, the vast majority of men and women would have felt it appropriate to read this material, with the brutal details which it inevitably included considered to be the "common coin of everyday conversation for both sexes" (Hitchcock 1997, p. 15). However, by the end of the eighteenth century, by arguing that women in public were potential victims of rape, due in part to the new understanding that male sexuality was "out of control," women were encouraged to be fearful of rape and to keep off the streets for their own protection (Hitchcock 1997, p. 101).

The Figure of the Dangerous Sex Offender

Thus the context of sex and sexuality prior to the nineteenth century offers very different ways of thinking about appropriate sexual behavior, defining deviant sex as danger. Over the course of the last two centuries, sex crimes have become increasingly associated with extreme dangerousness.

In 2003, the Dangerous Prisoners (Sexual Offenders) Act (Queensland, Australia) enabled criminal justice authorities for the first time to indefinitely detain sex offenders who are assessed to be manifestly and continually dangerous. This is not uncommon legislation. In the United States, for example, a prediction of "future dangerousness" is the basis for indefinite treatment and detainment in specialized treatment facilities, such as the Wisconsin Sex Offender Treatment Facility, where dangerous sex offenders are moved once they have completed their prison sentences. Such civil commitment laws are now operating in 39 states across the country. Similarly, in the UK, the 2003 Criminal Justice Act enables those assessed with future dangerousness to be detained after completing the sentence for their initial sexual crime (Thomas 2005). These various pieces of legislation, some civil and some criminal, predict the future dangerousness of a convicted sex offender via an individual clinical diagnosis of paraphilia, personality disorder, or other mental abnormality (Petrunik 2003).

In contrast, The Sex Offenders Bill, passed in the UK in 1997, and then subsumed under the Sexual Offences Act of 2003, required all those convicted of Schedule 1 sex offenses, upon release from prison, to notify the police in person of any change in address within 14 days. Those convicted of serious sex offenses of more than 30 months' imprisonment meant a lifetime requirement to notify the police, while lesser sentences required decreased periods of time on the register. By 2003, there were more than 15,000 individuals recorded on the register (Thomas 2005). In this second example, there is no clinical diagnosis of dangerousness. In fact, these prisoners were released precisely because they were not perceived to be dangerous in the future. They are, however, a population deemed "at risk."

Thus while selective incapacitation ensures that dangerous offenders are expunged from public space in ways reminiscent of what Foucault calls "the great confinement" (Foucault 1961, p. 55), sex offenders who complete their sentences but are not predicted to be dangerous still face a range of restrictions on their movements in public space. Depending on jurisdiction, sex offenders can be subject to a range of techniques which mark their bodies as sites of governance in public spaces. This is enabled via community notification statutes that employ strategies such as leaflet drops, community meetings, media reporting of addresses, and telephone hotlines, to name just a few (Thomas 2005).

All of these approaches have been trialed in various parts of the Western world, and are a clear attempt at managing the risk of the sex offender by making them visible in public space. Such visibility becomes a powerful regulatory mechanism that oversees the spaces sex offenders inhabit in their local communities. Indeed, in some approaches, the general public becomes a form of moral police, ensuring that sex offenders are kept at an appropriate distance from (morally) respectable society. Interestingly, community notification techniques like these have been found to be ineffective (Australian Institute of Criminology 2007; Vasquez, Madden, and Walker

2008), while more telling is research demonstrating how the stigma of community notification processes "may inadvertently increase the likelihood of recidivism among some sex offenders…by making it more difficult to achieve meaningful stability in important areas of their lives and facilitate positive relationships" (Meoy, Saleh, and Wolff 2007, p. 438). Gaining and maintaining employment is also seriously hampered by employer attitudes to known sex offenders (Brown, Spencer, and Deakin 2007). Moreover, the moral panic underpinning community notification has been found to increase the probability of recidivism because these laws make it "more difficult for them to achieve meaningful stability in important areas of their lives and facilitate positive relationships. Both of these factors are associated with criminal desistance" (Meloy et al. 2007, p. 438).

The rise of risk did not supplant the older idea of dangerousness but rather widened its ambit to a larger population. With sex offender registers in their various guises, we have a form of regulation of an at-risk population which sits easily with religious ideas of moral worth and fear of dangerous individuals. Perhaps more interestingly, in the exponential rise of sex offender legislation we also see a shift to passive female sexuality and active male sexuality. It will not be surprising to note, for example, that it is men who are the most likely to be identified as either dangerous sex offenders requiring of indeterminate incapacitation and/or at-risk sex offenders placed on public registers, while women and female children are most likely identified as victims of such offenses (Petrunik 2003, p. 44).

Much more than property offenses, or even physical assaults, "sex offences against persons are considered to be violations that damage the very core of victims." (Petrunik 2003, p. 43). The more sacred, pure, or innocent the victim, the more profane the violation and the offender. Children are the most innocent group in contemporary society and because of this are also perceived as the most vulnerable, out of all proportion to reality. For example, at the end of the twentieth century, the number of sex offenses against adults in the UK was reported at 37,492, of which 6,000 were rapes and the remainder indecent assaults. In contrast, indecent assaults against girls under 16 was 2116 and against boys, 476 (Thomas 2005).

Despite these low numbers, much of the impetus for the increased public surveillance of sex offenders is motivated by calls for public safety, especially of children. Residency restrictions exemplify how governmental authorities maintain moral and spatial distance between children and sex offenders by legislating the physical distances sex offenders may reside from spaces where children congregate. This may include proximity to schools, childcare centers, shopping centers, playgrounds, skating rinks, neighborhood centers, gymnasiums, and youth centers. However, if we consider for a moment the number of childcare centers alone in a local community, we begin to understand how residency restrictions work to further isolate and exclude sex offenders from society. An American study by Zandbergen and Hart (cited in Levenson 2008, 155) used geographical information system data to calculate how much housing would be unavailable to sex offenders in the area of Orange County, Florida, due to residence restrictions. They found "23% of the 137,944 properties zoned for residential use were located within 1000 feet of schools and 64% fell within 2500 feet, reducing the number of available residences to 106,888 and 50,108 respectively."

Other studies have noted the continuum of negative outcomes for the lives of sex offenders, from lack of access to housing to living homeless long term (Levensen,

Zgoba, and Tewksbury 2007). Perhaps the most powerful element of residency restriction legislation, though, is that it can apply for between 10 and 15 years after the sex offender has been released from prison. Moreover, given that many people are defined as sex offenders for very minor crimes, including public exposure, or conducting a consensual sexual relationship with a person who is only just under the age of consent, such management techniques seem harsh in the extreme. This has been exacerbated through the use of global positioning systems (GPSs), which ensure perpetual surveillance of sex offenders (Gies, Gainey, and Healy 2016). Such mechanisms have been implemented in various parts of the United States, Britain, and Australia, for example, through electronic monitoring anklets and bracelets. These have already proved useful in serving breach notices related to this legislation and in having sex offenders re-incarcerated. More importantly though, these forms of regulation restrict free movement to the point where regulation becomes "punishment in the absence of any evidence of wrongdoing" (Gies et al. 2016).

Child Sexual Abuse

Since the media "discovery" of the pedophile in the 1990s, sex abuse against children has dominated the press (Thomas 2005) and the popular imagination. What is most important, however, is the overwhelmingly popular belief that the sex offender is exclusively male. Indeed, given that the majority of research fails to even contemplate the female sex offender (Landor 2009), it is reasonable to conclude that in the public psyche, as well as in the knowledge domains of academia, the sex offender is male. However, there is an emerging body of international research that challenges this perception, particularly with respect to child sexual abuse.

Research to date indicates that it is difficult to determine prevalence of sexual abuse due to high levels of underreporting (Hayes and Carpenter 2013; Denov 2003; Eastwood 2003; Neame and Heenan 2003), and this necessarily impacts what we know about the gender of sex offenders. Nevertheless, "official statistics" do exist and generally indicate the majority of sex offenders are male, and most victims female (Gavin 2005). As a result, most sex offending research has focused on male perpetrators and female victims (Landor 2009; Thomas 2005, Denov 2003, Vandiver and Walker 2002). Recent statistics, however, show an increase in numbers of both convicted female sex offenders and male victims under 16. Boroughs (2004), for example, reports that in the United States in the late 1990s, official statistics show that women made up 25% of convicted sex abusers of children under 16. In the United Kingdom, The Lucy Faithful Foundation reported in 2009 that up to 30% of sexual abusers of children under 16 are women (Cited in Townsend and Syal, 2009). However, Gelb (2007, 16) reports that of the 853 sex offenders adjudicated in Magistrates Courts across Australia in 2004–2005, only 12 were women, although these statistics were not broken down according to age of victim, and there are no statistics to date reporting the numbers of female perpetrators in Australia. Again in the Australian arena, MAKO, a website devoted to identifying sex offenders in Australia, reports that out of "over 1,500" identified offenders, only 29 are female. However, the methodology for arriving at these figures is unclear. Nathan and Ward (2002) report that the official rate for Australia is 5% of all sexual offenses against children, but that the true number is thought to be considerably higher. The fact that Australian statistics tend to be far lower than those reported in the United States and United Kingdom suggests there are some anomalies in the way official statistics are kept in this country, or that female sexual abuse is highly underreported, or both.

Factors impacting the underreporting of sexual offenses include embarrassment, self-blame, fear of further victimization by legal processes, lack of confidence in the criminal justice system, disruption to the family unit, perceptions of low impact of damage, and the fact that for some young people (especially males), sexual precocity is seen as a rite of passage (Deering and Mellor 2011, Denov 2003). What little research there is on female sex offenders suggests that victims of sexual abuse – especially child victims – may be more reluctant to report being accosted by a female than by a male (Davidson 2008). Nevertheless, while the official picture of the ratio of male to female sex offenders suggests that women offend less, there is considerable speculation in the media and amongst those working in the field that numbers of female offenders are increasing (e.g. Young 2017; Darling 2017; Kernsmith, Comartin, and Kubiak 2019; Knight 2019). To date, there has been little other research comparing sex offenders or victims based on gender, age, or sexuality, or exploring discrepancies in sentencing. Additionally, in spite of the flawed nature of official statistics, these same statistics inform current policy and practice, which therefore remains largely ignorant of, and blind to, the impact of female sexual offenses against children.

Sex Work

There is no doubt that over the past 30 years, the demand for commercially available sexual services has massively increased and diversified along technological, spatial, and social lines. Leaving aside the pornographic part of the sex industry, sexual commerce now encompasses live sex shows, fetish clubs, adult entertainment clubs, escort agencies, telephone and cybersex contacts, drive-through striptease venues, and organized sex tours of developing countries. Sexual commerce has become a large, complex, multibillion dollar industry, producing and supporting a global economy in sectors as diverse as tourist resorts and hotel chains, mobile telephone companies, paid television networks, and information technology (Bernstein 2007).

According to Agustin (2005), any accurate depiction of the modern sex industry must include all commercial goods and services of an erotic and sexual kind. This would necessarily widen the gaze beyond sex work to erotic phone lines, escort services, films and videos, souvenirs, toys, clothes, equipment, and live and virtual performances via web cameras. Sites are similarly expanded to take into account bars, restaurants, cabarets, clubs, brothels, discotheques, saunas, massage parlors, sex shops with private booths, hotels, flats, internet sites, cinemas, and anywhere else that sex is offered for sale on an occasional basis including stag and hen nights, shipboard festivities, and modelling parties. Finally, the actors involved would multiply beyond direct buyers and sellers of sex, to business owners and investors, nonsexual employees (waiters, cashiers, guards, drivers, accountants, lawyers, doctors), and middlemen and women who facilitate business processes (travel agents, travel guides, estate agents, newspaper and magazine editors, internet entrepreneurs). However, our reaction to commercial sex – moral revulsion and/or resigned tolerance – has changed very little over the past 150 years, and as a consequence the identified harms have also remained the same.

The sex industry challenges the sanctity of the family and monogamous intimate relations between husbands and wives. Within such a conceptualization of harm and understanding of the sex industry through a lens of deviance, the exchange of money is largely irrelevant, although it may be seen to encourage the seller and diminish the guilt of the buyer and thus to enable promiscuity and adultery. Access to commercial sex is positioned at the forefront of marriage and family breakdowns by increasing the capacity for cheating and infidelity. This harm speaks to an idealized and heterosexist form of intimate sexual relations, a quest for the return to traditional relations between sex, romantic love, and family (Cowper, cited in Weitzer 2009, p. 7). As the idea of noncommercial sexual relations outside of marriage has become more acceptable, conceptualizations of the harm of the sex industry has shifted from promiscuity and adultery, to the harm of impersonal and unemotional sexual acts. Commercial sex becomes the exemplar of a society in which traditional values associated with sex are debased and commodified.

The second harm, and that which is argued to have most salience in contemporary society, is the harm of commercial sex to women. Here the capacity of the buyer (usually a man) to purchase sexual access to the seller (usually a woman) exemplifies the inherent inequality of both gender relations and the class structure. This harm is intrinsic to sexual commerce and is due to the exchange itself, which, for some, exemplifies the exploitation and victimization of all women. This is based on the argument that the sex industry commodifies and objectifies women as sex objects for male pleasure. The commercial transaction exemplifies the unequal power relations between men and women in society since the capacity to purchase gives ownership over property. In this way of thinking, men purchase women's bodies for their own sexual gratification. Central to this harm is the assertion that there is an intrinsic property of sex that makes its commodification wrong. As a consequence, women involved in sexual entertainment are oppressed by a system that privileges male pleasure over female pleasure and safety. Such a transaction objectifies women's bodies for men who use them as commodities for pleasure. Oppressed women are thus victims of a system which forces them to commodify very private, intimate sexual behaviors, and therefore sexually objectify themselves through their involvement in the industry (Raymond 2003). The sex industry represents women as sexual servants to men, as they are a class of women who exist to service men's sexual needs. This contributes directly to the inequality of women in society because it helps to shape notions of female subordination. Commercial sex becomes one of the more extreme examples of harm in a patriarchal society, where women have little to no access to power and great earning potential through the use of their sexualized bodies. Finally, the sex industry is positioned as violence against women, akin to rape and sexual abuse. Violence is intrinsic and endemic to the sex industry. In this way of thinking, commercial sex is not wrong because it causes harm; rather, it constitutes a harm in and of itself. Any distinction between forced and voluntary sex work, for example, is a myth, since in this view, coercion is always involved, even if the worker is unaware of it. Moreover, differentiating street work from escort work or sex trafficking is illusory since the simple act of purchase or money exchange is viewed as the harm (Farley 2005).

There is of course, a growing critique of such findings, especially in methodological terms, with research supporting a more nuanced understanding of the range of activities now included within sexual commerce. There are a number of critical feminist interventions that speak to agency within the realm of erotic labor, specifically in terms of black and Latina women's participation in the exotic dance, webcam, and pornography industries (Nash 2014; Jones 2016; Miller-Young 2014; Brooks 2012). These works argue that it is possible for women to retain agency within erotic industries and pose a critique of universalizing women's experiences in such industries as inherently exploitative and demeaning. Brooks (2012) notes the structural discrimination contended with by black participants in erotic labor, as does Jones (2016), which cause black women to earn less than their white counterparts across a number of sexual industries. Miller-Young (2014) asserts in her coinage of *illicit eroticism* that hypersexuality is attributed to black women who participate in pornography. She finds room for empowerment by claiming that hypersexuality can be employed by black women seeking to assert autonomy and power over the conditions of their labor and achieve mobility. Nash (2014) also explores expressions of agency through the performance of racial fictions, which she argues possess potential as a source of pleasure for black women.

Despite individual-level expressions of agency, the sex industry is conceptualized as posing a harm to society. It is perceived to be integral to the perpetuation of organized crime, especially drug and people trafficking, the spread of sexually transmitted disease, and an increase in sexual violence. Research does support some of these claims, especially with regard to sex work. Here, relationships have been discovered across the world between the initial motivation to enter the industry and sex abuse as children or drug use as adults. Similarly, sexual abuse by clients, and exploitation from police, pimps, and managers has been found to be part of the life of some sex workers, and evidence of coerced entry into sex work via trafficking and organized crime has also been found. Finally, there is a pervasive fear of infection from sex workers, in both a physical and moral sense (Vanwessenbeeck 2001).

However, there are variations dependent on the type of sex work. Those who engage in sex work due to a history of sexual victimization are generally young homeless women. Sexual victimization and exploitation is also related to the type of sex work performed, with indoor sex workers reporting much lower levels than street workers, the latter more vulnerable to legal intervention and police arrest as well as experiences of violence (Weitzer 2009). Importantly, most research on the harm of commercial sex continues to focus on the most vulnerable groups in the industry – predominantly street workers and those in prison – and those with the additional problems of economic hardship, histories of sexual victimization, homelessness, and drug addictions. These then get presented as a feature of sex work per se, and sexual commerce retains its relationship with misery, harm, and victimization. And while a relationship between sex work, organized crime, and trafficking can be seen to exist, media claims that it has intensified over the last decade is virtually impossible to demonstrate with certainty. Rather, while sex work across national boundaries has always existed, it may be that certain patterns of migration have changed (from non-Western to the Western world) or become more visible, "resulting in an exaggeration of its increasing magnitude worldwide" (Vanwessenbeeck 2001, p. 263).

Sex Trafficking

Concern over the phenomenon of sex trafficking has been steadily growing over the last 30 years, but the twenty-first century has seen sex trafficking reach new heights of national and international attention. The clandestine gains made from trafficking in women and girls is estimated by some to exceed those made from the underground trade of arms and narcotics (Sanghera 2005). In the media, sex trafficking is now proclaimed as a multimillion dollar underground industry, and along with terrorism and drug trafficking, one of three major concerns for governments internationally (Kempadoo 2005).

This was borne out between 2000 and 2003, when the United Nations (UN) Convention Against Organised Transnational Crime was accompanied by the Protocol to Prevent, Suppress and Punish Trafficking in Persons with Special Reference to Women and Children. Here trafficking was defined as:

> The recruitment, transportation, transfer, harboring or receipt of persons, by means of the threat or use of force or other forms of coercion, of abduction, of fraud, of deception, of the abuse of power or of a position of vulnerability or of the giving or receiving of payments or benefits to achieve the consent of a person having control over another person, for the purpose of exploitation.

For sex trafficking in particular, exploitation includes, at a minimum, the exploitation of the prostitution of others and herein lies the problem, when is sex work exploitation and when is it emancipation or at least independence? When is sex work forced and when is it voluntary? When is one person's "rescue from exploitation" another person's "interrupted employment contract" (David 2008, p. 3). If you are of the opinion that all sex work is violence against women, there can be no voluntary prostitution because consent is meaningless. In this view all sex work is exploitation. Since all sex work is coerced, all migration, both within and between borders for the purposes of sex work, comes under the definition of trafficking. Internationally, this position is supported by the Coalition Against Trafficking in Women (CATW).

If, on the other hand, you believe that sex work can be a valid and rational occupational choice for women, then there is a clear difference between adult women who migrate or are smuggled into a country for the purposes of sex work, and those who are forced, coerced, or deceived into migrating for the same purpose. In such cases, the distinction between forced and voluntary sex work is a valid one, and only the former includes trafficking. This position is supported at an international level by the Global Alliance Against Traffic in Women (GAATW). This is also the current position of the UN.

Obviously, such definitional differences have a major impact on how trafficking is identified; especially as the data on sex trafficking varies widely. For example, in the same year (2001) that the FBI estimated 700,000 women and children were trafficked worldwide, UNICEF estimated 1.75 million, and the International Organization on Migration (IOM) 500,000. Also in 2001, the UN drastically changed its own estimate of trafficked people – from 4,000,000 to 1,000,000, and again in 2010, to between 600,000 and 800,000 (Touzenis 2010). Victims of sexual exploitation in Germany range from 2,000 to 20,000 while in Russia, estimates are from 10,000 to 100,000 (Putt 2007). In Australia, numbers of sexually trafficked persons range from 10 to 1,000 (David 2008), and in the US the number of sexually trafficked persons is estimated to be from 14,500 to 50,000 (Makkai 2004). The most cited statistics on sex trafficking come from the US State Department's Annual Reports on Trafficking in Persons. According to the 2006 Report, 600,000 to 800,000 people are trafficked across international borders each year, 80% of these are believed to be female and up to 50% children. In 2016, the International Labor Organization reported that there currently exist around 20 million victims of trafficking globally (Polaris 2016). It is argued that the majority of these persons are trafficked for the purposes of sexual exploitation (Putt 2007).

The variation in these figures has partly to do with the definition of trafficking, especially the conflation of figures for sex trafficking, with those for human smuggling and illegally migrating for the purposes of sexual labor. Thus "in some accounts, all undocumented migrants assisted in their transit across national borders are counted as having been trafficked. In others, all migrant sex workers are defined as trafficking victims regardless of consent and conditions of labour" (Chapkis 2005, p. 54). These variable statistics are also related to the population under scrutiny – undocumented, transient people. Victims may be hesitant to provide information or cooperate with authorities out of fear of reprisals for themselves or their families. There is also a blurring between smuggling and trafficking for many people, especially where large undocumented irregular labor migration is a common occurrence, as in for example, South East Asia (Putt 2007). In such cases, "victims" may not perceive themselves as part of a trafficking problem.

Even the methodology used by the US State Department to access their annual figures remains unclear according to the US Government Accountability Office (2006). "Rough estimates" of people trafficked into the sex industry thus tend to rely on extrapolations from secondary sources, "including non-government organisation surveys, estimates by police, sex workers and journalists as well as information from diplomatic agencies and key informants" (Carrington and Hearn 2003). As such, all statistics on sex trafficking should be treated with caution.

When official statistics are available they identify very small numbers. In Australia, 105 trafficking cases were officially investigated in 2016 (US Department of State 2017). In the US in the same year there were 1029 documented cases of human trafficking (US Department of State 2017). These low official numbers have not deterred governments from legislating against trafficking and/or resourcing the fight. Since 2003, Australia has enacted new federal offenses to criminalize trafficking, and committed AUS$46.3 million to support initiatives to combat trafficking in persons (David 2008). The US passed the Victims of Trafficking and Violence Protection Act in 2000; in 2001 the Economic Community of West African States (ECOWAS) passed their Declaration and Action Plan on Human Trafficking; in 2002 the South Asian Association for Regional Cooperation (SAARC) enacted the Convention on Preventing and Combating Trafficking in Women and Children for Prostitution; in 2002 the European Union Council proclaimed the Directive on Short Term Residency Permits for Victims of Trafficking; and the Philippines Anti-Trafficking in Persons Act was passed in 2003 (Kempadoo 2005, p. xiii). All support the UN Protocol on Trafficking and thus emphasize a growing concern about trafficking in general, and sex trafficking in particular.

Pornography

The word "pornography" was not to be found in the Oxford English Dictionary before 1864 and derives from the Greek word *pornographos*, which literally means "whore's story" (Hitchcock 1997, p. 17). The distinctiveness of pornography, in comparison to sexual material in general at that time, "was its explicitness and its intent to arouse a sexual response." While such material existed prior to this time, the mid-nineteenth century saw a major increase in the market and supply of pornography (Weeks 1989). Moreover, while the control of these printed works in Europe between the 1500s and the 1800s was undertaken primarily in the name of religion and politics (Hunt 1993), by the mid-1800s it was the issue of decency which motivated regulation. In 1857, the Obscene Publications Act was passed in England, while in 1868 the Hicklin test entered English common law. These two changes have been identified as key to the identification of pornography as a specific social harm threatening the moral health of the population (Sullivan 1997). Pornography in the sense that we understand it today as a distinct category of written or visual representation, began to exist significantly from the middle of the nineteenth century (Weeks 1989).

The creation of a modern engagement with sexually explicit material also charts the creation of the category of erotic, lewd, and obscene materials which were identified for the first time as having a specific immorality, related to their function in sexual arousal. This new way of thinking about the erotic came at the same time as an expanding print culture, which put the written and visual word into the hands of a large proportion of the population, as well as raising concerns over children and the working class and their involvement in sexual activity outside of middle-class norms of appropriate behavior. These concerns over sex, children, and the working class required, among other things, controlling access to pornography through regulation.

The point of such regulations is twofold. First, adults were regarded as entitled to read and view what they wished in private or in public; second, members of the community were entitled to protection (extending both to themselves and those in their care) from exposure to unsolicited material that they found offensive (Sullivan 1997).

At the time of writing, concerns about pornography in terms of the content categories of children, and of violence, are escalating globally. While a number of government inquiries in Australia have concluded that "there was no convincing criminological or psychological evidence that exposure to such material produced measurable harm to society" (Wilson and Nugent 1992, p. 139), they have specifically excluded child pornography and violent pornography from their conclusions. Commissions established in Canada and the United States to specifically investigate sexually violent pornography found inconclusive evidence on any direct relationship between viewing, attitudes and acting (Wilson and Nugent 1992). In terms of censorship, "explicit or gratuitous depictions of sexual violence against non-consenting persons" remains illegal in many countries while materials which include "explicit depictions of sexual acts involving adults, but does not include any depiction suggesting coercion or non-consent of any kind" is rated as restricted (X) and is illegal in many jurisdictions (Wilson and Nugent 1992, p. 140). Interestingly, "depictions of sexual violence only to the extent that they are discreet, not gratuitous and not exploitative" are rated R, which gives them wide circulation in society. In fact, the classification system is more focused on sex than violence and enables the most violent content in the least restricted sexual category. With regard to child pornography there is no grey area – it remains illegal.

Criminalizing Nonheterosexualities

The governing of nonheterosexualities has always tended to focus on specific sexual acts – in particular, sodomy – although such governance has also extended to oral sex between men, the banning of same-sex marriage, and public displays of affection between same-sex couples. USLegal (2010) defines sodomy as a "crime against nature," suggesting that what is natural is heterosexual, despite the fact that sodomy may also be committed upon women by men and vice versa. The overarching meaning of a crime against nature is that it is not committed for the purposes of procreation or male–female marital bonding. It is defined in one US state law as "Any act of sexual gratification between persons not married to each other involving the sex organs of one person and the mouth or anus of another."

Western laws are based on Judeo-Christian principles derived from the Old Testament book of Leviticus, the King James version (18:22) of which states "Thou shalt not lie with mankind, as with womankind, it is abomination." In England, Henry VIII passed the Buggery Act of 1533, making sodomy an offense; it was punishable by hanging until 1861. Sir William Blackstone's eighteenth-century *Commentaries on the Laws of England*, described the crime of sodomy as an "abominable and detestable crime against nature," though nowhere were the details of what actually constituted the act of sodomy clearly outlined (Morrison 2001). Although the death penalty was eventually dropped, sodomy continued to be a crime against nature in the United Kingdom until 1957 when the *Wolfenden Report* argued that "homosexual behavior between consenting adults should no longer be a criminal offence" (Menninger 1964). However, while many Western governments proceeded to decriminalize "homosexual behavior" in general, many retained their laws against the act of sodomy itself.

Australia inherited Britain's laws in 1788 and operated under similar legislation until 1972 when the Dunstan Labor government introduced a "consenting adults in private" defense in South Australia (*Toonan v Australia* 1972). The state's sodomy law was duly repealed in 1975, triggering a spate of similar reforms throughout the other states, with Tasmania being the last state to conform. In the United States, however, it wasn't until 2003 that sodomy was finally decriminalized after the Supreme Court case of *Lawrence v Texas* ruled that "state laws criminalizing private, non-commercial sexual activity between consenting adults at home on the grounds of morality are unconstitutional since there is insufficient justification for intruding into people's liberty and privacy." Thus, while states such as Alabama and Mississippi continue to list sodomy laws on their books, it is doubtful that any challenge to them would be defeated in a court of law. Nevertheless, recent news footage from Uganda covering a campaign to bring in the death penalty for sodomy highlights the very precarious status of homosexuality and acts of sodomy on the world stage (Smith 2010). Where the Western world has appeared to move forward with respect to recognizing nonheterosexualities, at least some other nations remain seemingly fixed in their view of homosexual acts as crimes against nature and humankind.

As we can see from this brief legislative history, sexuality has largely been regulated through the criminalization of certain acts. Interestingly, such legislation was always directed at acts involving penal penetration and consequently, lesbianism has never been formally regulated or criminalized.

Although discriminatory attitudes towards homosexuality have received some much-needed attention in recent years, and sodomy has been largely decriminalized throughout the Western world, there still remain many laws that exclude and/or discriminate against same-sex couples, and transgender and intersex individuals. Indeed, in spite of these decriminalizations, nonheterosexual individuals still remain othered in society.

Recent research suggests that even in largely tolerant societies where nonheterosexualities are more or less accepted, a large number of people are still what can be called "homo-queasy" if not outright homophobic. "Homo-queasy" is the term employed by the Gay and Lesbian Alliance Against Defamation (GLAAD) to describe attitudes that poke fun at homosexuality, albeit often good-naturedly. Research by Hayes and Ball (2009) applied this conceptualization to research on attitudes toward gay and lesbian peers amongst a group of Australian university students and discovered that, while most students expressed support for queer issues and individuals, they "wouldn't want to be one."

This homo-queasiness appears to pervade Western society in general, even in the face of campaigns supporting equal rights. Certainly, the rights of same-sex couples are becoming more of an issue. The UK Civil Partnership Act 2004, for example, allows same-sex couples to register their partnership and thereby obtain similar rights to heterosexual married couples. That same year the UK also passed the Gender Recognition ACT 2004, allowing "transsexual" individuals to change their legal gender. Same-sex marriage was subsequently legalized in England and Wales in June 2013. In New Zealand, both same-sex and heterosexual couples can choose to register a civil union, and also have the choice of traditional marriage. And in the US, same-sex marriage has been legal in all states since the US Supreme Court ruled in 2015 in *Obergefell v Hodges* that bans against same-sex marriage were unconstitutional. Prior to that date, some states – Alaska, Alabama, Florida, and Indiana, among others, for example – had passed laws specifically banning same-sex marriage, although one state, Massachusetts, has passed legislation that prohibits the banning of marriage between same-sex couples.

Most recently, Australia legalized marriage equality in 2017, albeit at the expense of a public plebiscite which gave rise to much homophobic debate. Prior to the 2017 legislation, the Commonwealth Marriage Act 1961 was amended to specifically prohibit recognition of same-sex marriage. In addition, same-sex couples are now recognized to the same degree as heterosexual de facto couples, often described as "unregistered cohabitation," and a recent Human Rights Commission report, *Same Sex, Same Entitlements* (Human Rights Commission 2007), has resulted in the amendment of 84 Commonwealth laws "to eliminate discriminations against same-sex couples and their children." Specific laws amended include those affecting taxation, superannuation, social security and family assistance, aged care, child support, and immigration. In addition, formal domestic partnership registries exist in Tasmania, Victoria, and the Australian Capital Territory.

When we add all this legislative reform occurring in Western nations to our previous observations about public discourses on sex and sexuality, one would think that attitudes towards "deviant" sexualities and same-sex couples would have taken a turn for the better. But if deviant sexualities have really made it into "real" (as opposed to marginalized) public spaces, then how do we account for the still high numbers of hate crimes perpetrated against gay, lesbian, and transgender people? Clearly, there is no little discrepancy between the public discourses that allow some people to be transgressive of heterosexual norms in public spaces, and the other discourses we hear that condemn, discriminate against, and threaten the queers and deviants who are objects of street bashings and public ridicule because of their sexuality.

Conclusion

In this chapter, we have provided a cross-cultural overview of historical government intervention on sex and sexualities. By tracing the governance of sex and sexuality over time and space, we have explored the political, moral, and religious milieus in reference to what constitutes a "sex crime." We explored child sex abuse, sex work, sex trafficking, the criminalization of homosexuality, and pornography as sites in which the governmentality of sex and sexuality are made particularly evident. The intersectional understandings regarding the impact of criminal justice on sex and sexualities is central to this chapter, as we have elucidated how race, nationhood, class, and gender come together to situate how criminality is defined and which bodies experience persecution based on sex and sexuality.

References

Agustin, Laura María. 1988. 2007. *Sex at the Margins*. London: Zed Books.
Agustin, Laura María. 2005. "New Research Directions: The Cultural Study of Commercial Sex." *Sexualities* 8(5): 618–631.
Australian Institute of Criminology. 2007. *Is Notification of Sex Offenders in Local Communities Effective?* Canberra: AIC.
Bernstein, Elizabeth. 2007. *Temporarily Yours: Intimacy, Authenticity and the Commerce of Sex*. Chicago IL: University of Chicago Press.
Boroughs, Deborah S. 2004. "Female Sexual Abusers of Children." *Children and Youth Services Review* 26(5): 481–487.
Brooks, Siobhan. 2012. *Unequal Desires: Race and Erotic Capital in the Stripping Industry*. Albany, NY: State University of New York.
Brown, Kevin J. Spencer and Jo Deakin. 2007. "The Reintegration of Sex Offenders: Barriers and Opportunities for Employment." *Howard Journal of Criminal Justice* 46(1): 32–42.
Carrington, Kerry and Jane Hearn. 2003. "*Trafficking and the Sex Industry, From Impunity to Protection*." Current Issues Brief no. 28. Canberra, Information and Research Services, Department of the Parliamentary Library.
Chapkis, Wendy. 2005. "Soft Glove, Punishing Fist: The Trafficking Victims Protection Act of 2000." In *Regulating Sex: The Politics of Intimacy and Identity*, edited by Elizabeth Bernstein and Laurie Schaffner, 51–66. New York, NY: Routledge.
Darling, Andrea. 2017. "The Truth About Female Sex Offenders." *The Telegraph*, March 7. Available at: https://www.telegraph.co.uk/women/life/truth-female-sex-offenders/.
David, Fiona. 2008. "Trafficking of Women for Sexual Purposes." *Research and Public Policy Series, No 95*. Canberra: Australian Institute of Criminology.

Davidson, Julia. 2008. *Child Sexual Abuse: Media Representations and Government Reactions*. Abingdon: Routledge-Cavendish.

Deering, Rebecca and David Mellor. 2011. "An Exploratory Qualitative Study of the Self-Reported Impact of Female-Perpetrated Child Sexual Abuse." *Journal of Child Sexual Abuse* 20(1): 58–76.

Denov, Myriam S. 2003. "To a Safer Place? Victims of Sexual Abuse by Females and Their Disclosures to Professionals." *Child Abuse and Neglect* 27(1): 47–61.

Eastwood, Christine. 2003. The Experiences of Child Complainants of Sexual Abuse in the Criminal Justice System. *Trends and Issues in Crime and Criminal Justice*, no. 250. Canberra: Australian Institute of Criminology.

Farley, Melissa. 2005. "Prostitution Harms Women even if Indoors." *Violence Against Women* 11(7): 950–964.

Feinberg, Joel. 1988. *The Moral Limits of the Criminal Law*, vol. 2. Cambridge, Cambridge University Press.

Foucault, Michel. 1961. *Madness and Civilization: A History of Insanity in the Age of Reason*. London: Routledge.

Gavin, Helen. 2005. "The Social Construction of the Child Sex Offender Explored by Narrative." *The Qualitative Report* 10(3): 395–415.

Gies, Stephen, Randy Gainey, and Eoin Healy. 2016. "Monitoring High-Risk Sex Offenders with GPS." *Criminal Justice Studies* 29(1): 1–20. doi: 10.1080/1478601X.2015.1129088.

Gelb, Karen. 2007. "*Recidivism of Sex Offenders: A Research Paper*." Melbourne, Australia: Sentencing Advisory Council, Victoria. Available at: https://www.sentencingcouncil.vic.gov.au/publications/recidivism-of-sex-offenders-research-paper.

Halberstam, Judith. 2005. *In a Queer Time and Place: Transgender Bodies, Subcultural Lives*. New York, NY: New York University Press.

Hayes, Sharon L. and Matthew J. Ball. 2009. "Queering Cyberspace: Fan Fiction Communities as Spaces for Expressing and Exploring Sexuality." In *Queering Paradigms*, edited by Burkhard Scherer, 219–239. Oxford: Peter Lang.

Hayes, Sharon and Belinda Carpenter. 2013. "Social Moralities and Discursive Constructions of Female Sex Offenders." *Sexualities* 16(1–2): 147–157.

Hitchcock, Tim. 1997. *English Sexualities, 1700–1800*. London: Macmillan.

Human Rights Commission. 2007. *Same Sex, Same Entitlements*, Canberra: HRC.

Hunt, Lynn. 1993. "Introduction: Obscenity and the Origins of Modernity, 1500–1800." In *The Invention of Pornography*, edited by Lynn Hunt, 9–48. New York, NY: Zone Books.

Jones, Angela. 2016. "'I Get Paid to Have Orgasms.' Adult Webcam Models Negotiation of Pleasure and Danger." *Signs* 42(1): 227–256.

Kempadoo, Kamala. 2005. "From Moral Panic to Global Justice, Changing Perspectives on Trafficking." In *Trafficking and Prostitution Reconsidered: New Perspectives on Migration, Sex Work and Human Rights*, edited by Kamala Kempadoo, vii–xxxiv. London: Paradigm.

Kernsmith, Poco, Erin B. Comartin, and Sheryl Kubiak. 2019. "What the Jeffrey Epstein Case Reveals About Female Sex Offenders." *The Conversation*, September 24. Available at: https://theconversation.com/what-the-jeffrey-epstein-case-reveals-about-female-sex-offenders-123423.

Knight, Kathryn. 2019. "Predator Women: How Deviant Babysitters Abusing Toddlers and Twisted Paedo 'Mistresses' are Fuelling the Rise of Female Sex Offenders." *The Sun*, January 29. Available at: https://www.thesun.co.uk/news/5867301/female-sex-offenders-paedo-mistress-babysitter/.

Landor, Roland V. 2009. "Double Standards? Representation of Male vs Female Sex Offenders in the Australian Media." *Griffith Working Papers in Pragmatics and Intercultural Communication* 2(2): 84–93.

Levenson, Jill. 2008. "Collateral Consequences of Sex Offender Residence Restrictions." *Criminal Justice Studies* 21(2): 153–166.

Levenson, Jill, Kristen Zgoba, and Richard Tewksbury. 2007. "Sex Offender Registry Restrictions: Sensible Crime Policy or Flawed Logic?" *Federal Probation* 71(3): 2–9.

Makkai, Toni. 2004. "What Do We Need to Know? Improving the Evidence Base on Trafficking in Human Beings in the Asia-Pacific Region." *Development Bulletin (Canberra)* 66: 36–42.

Massey, Doreen. 2004. "Geographies of Responsibility." *Geografiker Anneler* 86B(1): 5–18.

Meloy, Michelle L., Yustina Saleh, and Nancy Wolff. 2007. "Sex Offender Laws in America: Can panic-Driven Legislation Ever Create Safer Societies?" *Criminal Justice Studies* 20(4): 423–443.

Menninger, Karl. 1964. *The Wolfenden Report*. London: Her Majesty's Stationery Office.

Miller-Young, Mireille. 2014. *A Taste for Brown Sugar, Black Women in Pornography*. Durham, NC: Duke University Press.

Morrison, Wayne, ed. 2001. *Commentaries on the Laws of England*. London: Cavendish Publishing.

Nash, Christine J. 2014. *The Black Body in Ecstasy: Reading Race, Reading Pornography*. Durham, NC: Duke University Press.

Nathan, Pamela and Tony Ward. 2002. "Female Child Sex Offenders: Clinical and Demographic Features." *Journal of Sexual Aggression* 8(1): 5–21.

Neame, Alexandra and M. Colleen Heenan. 2003. "What Lies Behind the Hidden Figure of Sexual Assault? Issues of Prevalence and Disclosure." Briefing Paper, No. 1. Australian Centre for the Study of Sexual Assault.

Needham, Gary. 2008. "Scheduling Normality: Television, the Family and Queer Temporality." In *Queer TV: Theories, Histories, Politics*, edited by Gary Needham and Glyn Davis, 143–158. New York, NY: Routledge.

Petrunik, Michael. 2003. The Hare and the Tortoise: Dangerousness and Sex Offender Policy in the United States and Canada. *Canadian Journal of Criminology and Criminal Justice* 45(1): 43–72.

Philo, Chris. 2005. "Sex, Life, Death, Geography: Fragmentary Remarks Inspired by Foucault's Population Geographies." *Population, Space and Place* 11(4): 326–333.

Polaris. 2016. "The Facts." Available at: http://polarisproject.org/human-trafficking/facts.

Putt, Judy. 2007. "Human Trafficking to Australia: A Research Challenge." *Trends and Issues in Crime and Criminal Justice*, no. 338. Canberra: Australian Institute of Criminology.

Raymond, Janice G. 2003. "Ten Reasons for Not Legalizing Prostitution and a Legal Response to the Demand for Prostitution." *Journal of Trauma Practice* 2(3–4): 315–332.

Sanghera, Jyoti. 2005. "Unpacking the Trafficking Discourse." In *Trafficking and Prostitution Reconsidered: New Perspectives on Migration, Sex Work and Human Rights*, edited by Kamala Kempadoo, 3–24. London: Paradigm.

Smith, David. 2010. "UN's Human Rights Chief Urges Uganda to Scrap Anti-Gay Legislation." *Guardian*, January 15. Available at: http://www.guardian.co.uk/world/2010/jan/15/un-human-rights-uganda-gay-legislation (accessed January 17, 2018).

Sullivan, Barbara Ann. 1997. *The Politics of Sex: Prostitution and Pornography in Australia since 1945*. Cambridge: Cambridge University Press.

Thomas, Terry. 2005. *Sex Crime: Sex Offending and Society*. London: Willan.

Toonen v Australia. 1972. Communication No. 488/1992, UN Doc CCPR/C/50/D/488/1992 1994). Available at: http://hrlibrary.umn.edu/undocs/html/vws488.htm.

Touzenis, Kristina. 2010. *Trafficking in Human Beings, Human Rights and Transnational Criminal Law, Developments in Law and Practices*. Paris: UNESCO.

Townsend, Mark and Rajeev Syal. 2009. "Up to 64,000 Women in UK 'Are Child Sex Offenders.'" *The Observer*, October 4. Available at: https://www.theguardian.com/society/2009/oct/04/uk-female-child-sex-offenders.

US Department of State. "2017 Trafficking in Persons Report." Available at: https://www.state.gov/j/tip/rls/tiprpt/2017/index.htm (accessed January 17, 2018).

US Government Accountability Office (GAO). 2006. "Human Trafficking: Better Data, Strategy, and Reporting Needed to Enhance U.S. Antitrafficking Efforts Abroad." Available at: https://www.gao.gov/new.items/d06825.pdf (accessed January 17, 2017).

USLegal. 2010. Homepage. Available at http://www.uslegal.com/ (accessed January 17, 2018).

Vandiver, Donna M. and Jeffrey T. Walker. 2002. "Female Sex Offenders: An Overview and Analysis of 40 Cases." *Criminal Justice Review* 27(2): 284–300.

Vanwesenbeeck, Ine. 2001. "Another Decade of Social Scientific Work on Sex Work: A Review of Research 1990–2000." *Annual Review of Sex Research* 12(1): 242–289.

Weeks, Jeffrey. 1989. *Sex, Politics and Society: The Regulation of Sexuality Since 1800*. London: Longman.

Weitzer, Ronald. 2009, "Legalizing Prostitution: Morality Politics in Western Australia." *British Journal of Criminology* 48(1): 88–105.

Wilson, Paul R. and Stephen Nugent. 1992. "Sexually Explicit and Violent Media Material: Research and Policy Implications." In *Issues in Crime, Morality and Justice*, edited by Paul R. Wilson, 139–140. Canberra, Australian Institute of Criminology.

Young, Sarah. 2017. "Female Sex Offenders are More Common Than You Think, Reveals Study." *The Independent*, July 13. Available at: https://www.independent.co.uk/life-style/female-sex-offenders-more-common-gender-bias-statistics-rape-abuse-a7839361.html.

21

Sexual Harassment Policy in the US and Comparative Perspective

JENNIFER ANN DROBAC

Introduction

Most people know the #MeToo movement that started in the United States of America (US) in October 2017. A quick Google search of the phrase produces "about 50,400,000 results [in] (0.54 seconds)" (Google 2019). For those who do not know the movement, the hashtag symbolizes that the social media user has experienced or is discussing sex-based harassment or sexual assault (Chuck 2017). By the end of its first year, this movement had spread all over the world. "From Stockholm to Seoul, from Toronto to Tokyo, a torrent of accusations has poured forth. Survivors spoke out, and many were taken seriously. Powerful men lost their jobs" (Adam and Booth 2018).

This chapter explores sexual harassment law. The first section introduces the subject by detailing its statistical prevalence and exactly what constitutes sex-based harassment. It looks at the nature and extent of the problem, primarily in the US but also elsewhere. The second section reviews the passage and implementation of civil laws that proscribe sex-based harassment. It focuses, in particular, on US employment law and the early governmental agency and theorist interpretations of sex-based harassment. It also notes legal proscriptions in educational institutions and housing. This section examines how the #MeToo movement began and how it highlights the failures of current legal antidiscrimination laws.

The remainder of the chapter takes a closer look at the operation of US law but also explores sexual harassment law, or the lack thereof, worldwide. Specifically, the third section delves into federal US court interpretation and enforcement of antidiscrimination law to address sexual harassment. The cases demonstrate how narrow interpretation of legal protections shaped the case requirements for complainants who want to prosecute their claims. This section sets forth the five requirements: membership in a protected class; harassment based on sex; unwelcome conduct that has an effect on the term, condition, or privilege (of employment); (employer) liability; and a brief consideration of extralegal initiatives that supplement law to foster cultural change for the protection of harassed people who face systemic discrimination.

The fourth section considers other proscriptions against sex-based harassment. Clearly, a comprehensive review of the variety of global approaches to the eradication of sex-based harassment and discrimination is beyond the scope of this chapter, which, therefore, briefly introduces an Israeli law passed to address the problem. The Israeli response serves as a useful example because the Israeli law relies not on notions of equality, but on the dignity of all people, to justify protections against sexual harassment. The fourth section of this chapter also scans which countries have yet to implement protections against sex-based discrimination and harassment. Finally, the section reports how UN Women recommends that countries address sex/gender-based discrimination and harassment.

While sexual harassment is first and foremost an abuse of power, people should not ignore that the mechanism for oppression is the exploitation of culturally defined sex, gender, and sexuality. Therefore, a study of discriminatory sexual harassment and laws designed to eradicate it complements any study of sexuality.

Prevalence and the Conduct Studied

Prevalence

The #MeToo movement highlights that sexual harassment of women, and some men, is probably epidemic in parts of the US, and perhaps throughout the world. No one really knows how prevalent it is, however, because no national statistics regularly measure it (J.M.F. 2017). Stop Street Harassment commissioned one private study by Growth from Knowledge in January 2018. It conducted a nationally representative survey of 2,000 persons in the US regarding sexual harassment and assault. It found that nationwide, "81% of women and 43% of men reported experiencing some form of sexual harassment and/or assault in their lifetime" (Kearl 2018). A YouGov study of women in Britain, France, Germany, and the US determined that 50% had experienced some form of sexual harassment. Of those, 64% experienced the harassment at work (Frankovic 2017).

UN Women monitors statistics worldwide, in addition to those for the US and Europe. "In a South African study, 77% of women reported experiencing sexual harassment at some point during their working lives" (UN Women 2018). "In Australia, approximately one in two women (53% or 5 million) had experienced sexual harassment by a male or female perpetrator during their lifetime" (UN Women 2018). These are sobering statistics and highlight the need for regular, worldwide monitoring.

A number of governmental and private organizations have tracked the prevalence of sex-based harassment in specific contexts. For example, in 2015, several studies found that large numbers of college and university students, mostly female, had experienced sexual assault. *The Washington Post*/Kaiser Family Foundation poll reported that 20% of women in college had said that they had been violated

(Anderson and Clement 2015; DiJulio et al. 2015). The American Association of University Women (AAUW) surveyed 150,000 students at 27 colleges and universities across the country and published that 27.2% of female college seniors recounted that they had experienced an unwanted sexual contact since entering college (Cantor et al. 2017).

In another context, Professor Rigel Oliveri recently conducted a pilot study of sexual harassment in housing, which sought information about the victims, perpetrators, and the type of housing. She conducted detailed interviews with 100 randomly selected low-income women. Of those, 10% had experienced actionable sexual harassment by their landlords (Oliveri 2018).

When people also consider offensive sexualized content in advertising and music, church and sport sex scandals, and prisons and military sexual abuses, they realize just how pervasive sex-based discrimination and abuse is. But, what does the label sexual harassment describe? What behaviors constitute sexual harassment?

The conduct studied

Sexual harassment encompasses a wide variety of behaviors. Working outside of strict legal definitions, Psychology Professor Louise Fitzgerald offered an excellent classification system that allows investigators to identify sexually harassing behavior. She first highlighted the exploitation of power: "Sexual harassment consists of the sexualization of an instrumental relationship through the introduction or imposition of sexist or sexual remarks, requests or requirements, in the context of a formal power differential." She acknowledged, however, "Harassment can also occur where no such formal differential exists, if the behavior is unwanted by or offensive to the woman" (Fitzgerald 1996).

Fitzgerald divided sex-based harassment into three general categories. The most common form, gender harassment, involves sexist behavior and remarks. It can include: sex-based hostility, such as misogynistic jokes; sexual hostility, through which the harasser degrades women with language and behavior; or gender policing, which penalizes women who are not stereotypically feminine. Studies suggest that 15–20% of US women experience gender harassment annually (J.M.F. 2017). The second category, unwanted sexual attention "includes the making of sexual advances that are unwelcome and unreciprocated." Researchers believe that about 10% of women experience this conduct annually. "Finally, sexual coercion combines unwanted sexual attention with job-related pressures, such as bribes or threats, in an attempt to force acquiescence." Sexual coercion happens to 2–4% of women in the US. (J.M.F. 2017).

One might think that #MeToo would have raised consciousness about sexual harassment and seen a resulting decline in its prevalence. However, one study suggests otherwise. It found that young men have grown more (not less) accepting of offensive behavior. For example, the percentage "of men under 30 who think that a stranger flashing his genitals at a woman constitutes sexual harassment" declined "from 97% to 79% in Britain, and from 91% to 78%" in the US. YouGov's data reflect a parallel drop in young men concerning requests for sexual favors and the telling of sexual jokes ("Young Men are Changing Their Definitions of Sexual Harassment" 2019).

The fact that millions of women and men endure sex-based abuse and exploitation, reinforces the worth of exploring this phenomenon as part of a broader study of sex-based relations and sexuality. As noted, a study of this topic considers exactly what the law recognizes as sexual harassment, which laws address it, both in the US and elsewhere, and how remedial approaches differ throughout the world.

Again, the brevity of this chapter precludes a comprehensive discussion of US antiharassment law and sister legislation worldwide. Therefore, the second section of this chapter briefly explores legal definitions of sex-based harassment and describes the #MeToo movement. The following section reviews Title VII of the Civil Rights Act (CRA) of 1964, the US federal law that addresses systemic, sex-based discrimination in the workplace (42 U.S.C. § 2000e et seq. (1964)). It also discusses case law interpretation of Title VII and the developing jurisprudence. The fourth section explores how Title VII has inspired or differs from other nations' laws in its approach to sex-based harassment and discrimination.

Sex-Based Harassment and #MeToo

Nothing in the US Constitution or the US Code specifically defines, or for that matter, even explicitly prohibits sexual harassment in civilian contexts. Neither specific criminal charges nor individual personal injury claims adequately address systemic discrimination and the subordination of women and other target populations. Criminal charges and personal injury complaints fail to deal with pernicious but subtle stereotypes and particular class harms.

Twentieth-century feminist attempts to secure protection for US women through the Equal Rights Amendment failed. However, piecemeal antidiscrimination legislation, including Title VII (employment), Title VIII of the Civil Rights Act of 1968 (housing), and Title IX of the 1972 Education Amendments (education), was passed to protect workers, tenants, and students, respectively, from sex-based abuse and discrimination (42 U.S.C. § 2000e et seq. (1964); 42 U.S.C. § 3601 et seq. (1968); 20 U.S.C.A. §§ 1681–1688 (1972)). Courts ultimately interpreted all of these laws to proscribe sex-based harassment.

While courts borrow from tort law in the interpretation of Title VII, Professor Catharine MacKinnon argued against treating sexual harassment as a tort. She explained that such treatment "rips injuries to women's sexuality out of the context of women's social circumstances as a whole." She suggested that sexual harassment "is a group-defined injury which occurs to many different individuals regardless of unique qualities or circumstances. ... Such an injury is *in essence* a group injury" (MacKinnon 1979).

Today, most legislators understand the systemic nature of sex-based harassment. State fair employment and practice statutes (FEPS) and parallel state antidiscrimination statutes for educational institutions and housing also address sex-based harassment. A review of all of these state laws is also beyond the scope of this chapter. Therefore as noted, it focuses on Title VII with reference to important differences in the other contexts.

Defining sexual harassment

The original draft of the bill that would become Title VII addressed only race discrimination, not sex discrimination. In the final hours of debate on the floor of the House of Representatives, when the passage of the bill appeared imminent, conservative Representative Howard W. Smith (R-VA), who opposed the bill, proposed adding "sex" as a prohibited ground for discrimination. Smith expressed concern that white women would be disadvantaged in comparison to African Americans if the bill did not include a prohibition of sex discrimination.

Liberal male members of the House spoke against the amendment, which they feared would endanger the underlying legislation. However, several female supporters of women's rights spoke in favor of Smith's proposal. The amendment passed, as did the bill, without Smith's support. The Senate approved the bill with little discussion of the sex provision (Drobac, Baker, and Oliveri 2020).

Thus, limited history of congressional intent as to the meaning of "sex" remains to guide jurists. The law, which applies to employers with 15 or more employees, states:

> It shall be an unlawful employment practice for an employer –
> 1) to fail or refuse to hire or to discharge any individual, or otherwise to discriminate against any individual with respect to his compensation, terms, conditions, or privileges of employment, because of such individual's race, color, religion, sex, or national origin; or
> 2) to limit, segregate, or classify his employees or applicants for employment in any way which would deprive or tend to deprive any individual of employment opportunities or otherwise adversely affect his status as an employee, because of such individual's race, color, religion, sex, or national origin.
>
> (42 U.S.C. § 2000e-2 (1964))

Sex in this statute seemingly refers to chromosomal sex, female or male. That constructed polarity, however, ignores the diversity of human nature and particularly intersex and trans persons. Similar limitations apply to a definition of sex that refers to socially constructed gender expression: masculinity and femininity. A third meaning of sex relates to intimate sexual activity (Drobac et al. 2020). Because this statute did not specify that harassment was a subset of discrimination because of sex, this question went to the lower courts.

In 1979, Professor MacKinnon defined sexual harassment as:

> the unwanted imposition of sexual requirements in the context of a relationship of unequal power. Central to the concept is the use of power derived from one social sphere to lever benefits or impose deprivations in another.
>
> (MacKinnon 1979, p. 1)

This definition explicitly included sexual behavior. It clarified that sexual harassment was sex discrimination.

In 1980, the Equal Employment Opportunity Commission (EEOC), the agency charged with Title VII's enforcement, issued guidance which confirmed that Title VII prohibits sexual harassment. It defined sexual harassment as "unwelcome sexual advances, requests for sexual favors, and other verbal or physical conduct of a sexual nature" (29 C.F.R. § 1604.11(a) (1980)). For example, a supervisor harasses a subordinate employee when he makes offensive conduct a term or condition of employment or the basis for employment decisions involving that individual. Workplace sexual harassment includes unwelcome sexual behavior that targets anyone (even customers) when this behavior unreasonably interferes with a worker's performance or creates an intimidating, hostile, or offensive work environment (29 C.F.R. § 1604.11(a) (1980)).

This EEOC description of sexual harassment also explicitly identifies exploitative sexual activity. A request for a date by itself does not constitute sexual harassment. Under Title VII and most state FEPS, the conduct must be not only unwelcome, but also either severe or pervasive to qualify as actionable sexual harassment for which the target can file a lawsuit. A jury or judge decides what conduct qualifies as severe or pervasive in light of the totality of the circumstances (*Meritor Savings Bank v. Vinson*, 477 U.S. 57, 67 (1986)). Severity is inversely related to frequency, so one incident of rape constitutes actionable sexual harassment. The conduct must be offensive to not only the target (subjectively offensive) but also to the reasonable person (objectively offensive) (*Harris v. Forklift Sys., Inc.* 510 U.S. 17, 21–22 (1993)).

Since the early days of Title VII's implementation, courts and the EEOC have acknowledged a broadened definition of sexual harassment. EEOC guidance from 1990 confirms that

> harassment not involving sexual activity or language – may also give rise to Title VII liability (just as in the case of harassment based on race, national origin or religion) if it is "sufficiently patterned or pervasive" and directed at employees because of their sex.
> (EEOC 1990)

Thus, Title VII prohibits gender and sex-based hostility.

Title IX's definition of sexual harassment in federally funded schools is similar to Title VII's. The US Department of Education (ED)'s Office for Civil Rights (OCR) states, "Sexual harassment is unwelcome conduct of a sexual nature[,]… unwelcome sexual advances, requests for sexual favors, and other verbal, nonverbal, or physical conduct." The definition continues, "Title IX also prohibits gender-based harassment, which is unwelcome conduct based on a student's sex, harassing conduct based on a student's failure to conform to sex stereotypes" (US Department of Education 2017). One important distinction between these two laws is that the Supreme Court requires harassment to be "severe, pervasive, and objectively offensive" under Title IX, but only "severe or pervasive" under Title VII (*Davis v. Monroe Co. Bd. Ed.* 526 U.S. 629, 633, 651 (1999); *Meritor*, 477 U.S. at 67). Neither law explicitly prohibits discrimination based on sexual orientation, or on transgender or other sexual minority status.

Because the Title VII and Title IX definitions leave out so much conduct that arguably constitutes sex-based harassment, I offer the following definition: "To sexually harass is to dominate another person physically or psychologically by annoying, frightening, demeaning, or taking unfair advantage of that person through the exploitation of human sexuality or gender stereotypes" (Drobac 2016). This definition includes many behaviors that would not meet the threshold levels for a lawsuit.

The point, however, is to end discriminatory and harassing conduct. If the goal is to create harmonious environments for everyone, society needs a broad definition of sex-based harassment.

Sexual harassment law did not receive major national attention until the Senate confirmation hearings for Supreme Court nominee, Clarence Thomas. In 1991, Anita Hill's testimony that Clarence Thomas had harassed her at the ED sparked much debate. That discussion, however, focused more on whether Anita Hill was credible than on the application of Title VII and the nature of the problem more generally (Drobac et al. 2020).

A confluence of events in late 2017 prompted a paradigm shift in some attitudes about sex-based harassment and sexual assault. Sexual assault and harassment allegations against Harvey Weinstein (Farrow 2017) and others led to a discussion of the applicable state and federal antidiscrimination law.

#MeToo

In October 2017, media reports regarding egregious sexual assault and misconduct by movie producer, Harvey Weinstein, outraged the public (Ashbrook 2017). *The New York Times* reported, "previously undisclosed allegations against Mr. Weinstein stretching over nearly three decades …" (Kantor and Twohey 2017). Americans had earlier watched the downfalls of former President of Fox News, Roger Ailes, and political commentator, Bill O'Reilly, because of sexual misconduct (Paul and LaMagna 2018). However, Weinstein allegedly abused many more women, including Ashley Judd, Ambra Battilana, and Emily Nestor, to name just three discussed in *The New York Times* article (Kandor and Twohey 2017).

As these women evidenced, many of Weinstein's accusers were not employees of the Weinstein Company. They were independent actresses or temporary employees, who may have received their pay checks from contract worker agencies. Such workers do not have the same civil rights as regular company employees, as will be reviewed below (Horowitz and O'Brien 2017).

Events that followed the Weinstein stories in October 2017 created a new understanding concerning the scope and breadth of sex-based discrimination in the US. The Weinstein accusations acted as a catalyst for activism. Other women revealed their stories of abuse at the hands of additional famous and powerful men (Akin 2017). Erica Werner explained:

> As reports pile up of harassment or worse by men in entertainment, business and the media, one current and three former female lawmakers tell The Associated Press that they, too, have been harassed or subjected to hostile sexual comments – by fellow members of Congress.
>
> (Werner and Linderman 2017)

Misconduct allegations surfaced against Matt Lauer, Al Franken, Louis C.K., and many others. These revelations demonstrated the prevalence and magnitude of this problem (Akin 2017; Donnelly and Boucher 2017; Farrow 2017; Levenson and Guerra 2017; Paul and LaMagna; Schwartz and Calderone 2017; Stolberg, Alcindor, and Fandos 2017; Werner and Linderman 2017).

In response to these high-profile cases, actress Alyssa Milano encouraged women in a tweet on October 15, 2017 to use the #MeToo marker. She wanted to highlight further the pervasiveness of systemic discrimination, assault, and harassment (Sayej 2017). Tarana Burke had created the "Me Too" campaign in 2006 when she founded "Just Be Inc., a nonprofit organization that helps victims of sexual harassment and assault" (Garcia 2017).

Milano suggested that the #MeToo movement erupted after her tweet only because of the ascendency of Donald Trump, a politician accused by at least 24 women of inappropriate sexual conduct. He was elected US President, despite these charges. Milano said:

> This man in office is an admitter of "grabbing pussy[.]" It not only horrified sexual assault survivors, but all women, as he's trying to roll back our rights .... I don't know if this movement would have turned into what it has if this president wasn't in office."
>
> (Sayej 2017)

The idea is that many women at first feared and then were appalled by Trump's victory on November 7, 2017. They have had enough exploitation, sexual assault, and harassment and are speaking out about it.

The #MeToo campaign went viral, with more than 500,000 uses on Twitter by October 16 and 12 million Facebook posts during the first 24 hours (Smartt 2017). This campaign became part of a national discussion of sexual misconduct and exploitation that has continued to the present day. The debate has also included an evaluation of the efficacy of antidiscrimination laws. Laws and legal guidance, drafted to elucidate the law and policy in this area, have proven grossly dated, confusing, or inadequate.

US Court Interpretation of Title VII

The evolution of sexual harassment law provides a clue as to why many current provisions are problematic. Many of the early courts that considered sexual harassment claims in the context of Title VII ruled against the plaintiffs (Drobac et al. 2020). The district court judges who decided these early cases focused on whether the complained of conduct was workplace discrimination or a *private* matter.

This latter approach was reminiscent of the separate spheres doctrine of the post-Civil War era. This view assigned women to the sphere of the private family, beyond purview, and men to the public market place. During that period, society cast sexually active working women alternately as "the unfeeling vamp," "the vulnerable victim," or "a new kind of woman, a moral and strong-minded individual" (Berebitsky 2012, p. 23). In parallel roles, a man was alternately "the victim of his base desires, a sexual predator ... or a gentleman who had failed in his role as protector of female innocence" (Berebitsky 2012, pp. 22–23).

In the sexual harassment cases of the 1970s, the plaintiffs argued that sexual coercion in the workplace was an economic issue that impaired women's participation in the workplace. The defendants contended that the conduct was personal, not a violation of corporate policy, and that employers were not responsible. In all but Dianne

Williams's case, the judges concluded that sexual workplace misconduct was a private matter, not related to employment or based on sex. They opined that employers were not liable for this behavior under Title VII.[1]

Meritor Savings Bank v. Vinson and the prima facie (plaintiff's) case

Twenty-two years after Title VII's passage, the US Supreme Court confirmed that Title VII prohibited sexual harassment as part of its protective force. In *Meritor Savings Bank v. Vinson*, the Court held that severe or pervasive sexual harassment violates Title VII when it alters the worker's conditions of employment and creates an abusive working environment (*Meritor*, 447 U.S. at 67). Courts should assess the working environment by

> "looking at all of the circumstances" including the "frequency of the discriminatory conduct; its severity; whether it is physically threatening or humiliating, or a mere offensive utterance; and whether it unreasonably interferes with an employee's work performance"
> (Faragher v. City of Boca Raton, 524 U.S. 775, 787–88 (1998)
> (quoting *Harris*, 510 U.S. at 23))

The Court reversed the precedents established in the lower courts but it could not change opinions quickly.

The *Meritor* Court also affirmed the decision in *Henson v. City of Dundee* (*Meritor*, 477 U.S. at 66–67, 76). *Henson* had confirmed that in order to bring a case of sexual harassment against an employer under Title VII, a plaintiff must show: (i) membership in a protected class; (ii) unwelcome sexual harassment; (iii) harassment based on sex; (iv) an effect on the terms or conditions of employment; and (v) direct or indirect employer liability (*Henson v. City of Dundee*, 682 F.2d 897, 903-05 (11th Cir. 1982)).

Employer liability does not include individual liability. No claim against individual perpetrators exists under Title VII (*Miller v. Maxwell's Int'l, Inc.*, 991 F.2d 583, 588 (9th Cir. 1993). However, some state FEPS permit sexual harassment damage claims against individual harassers Cal. Gov't Code § 12940 (1992); *Matthews v. Superior Court*, 40 Cal. Rptr. 2d 350, 351 (1995); *Page v. Superior Court*, 37 Cal. Rptr. 2d 529, 532 (1995)).

Class membership and harassment based on sex

Because Mechelle Vinson was female and her supervisor Sydney Taylor was male, protected class membership was not an issue in the *Meritor* decision. For years, courts acknowledged only male-perpetrated harassment of females. They ignored same-sex harassment.

In *Oncale v. Sundowner Offshore Services, Inc.*, 523 U.S. 75 (1998), however, the US Supreme Court ruled that members of one biological sex can sue members of the same sex for sexual harassment under Title VII. While appearing to confirm an expansive reading of Title VII, the Court's reasoning relied on a strict chromosomal interpretation of discrimination based on sex. The Court also introduced the notion, however, that "common sense" and "social context" play a role in the objective analysis of harassing behaviors (*Oncale*, 523 U.S. at 81–82).

The hypothetical Justice Scalia crafted to clarify the Court's point regarding the influence of context in *Oncale* aptly demonstrates *Oncale*'s flaws, and invites further exploration of the case from a pansexual perspective. In 1999, the term "pansexuality" was new to formal legal analysis. With respect to the *Oncale* decision, I suggested:

> Pansexuality encompasses all kinds of sexuality. It differs, however, from pansexualism, a perspective that declares "all desire and interest are derived from the sex instinct." Pansexuality includes heterosexuality, homosexuality, bisexuality, and sexual behavior that does not necessarily involve a coupling. It includes, for example, masturbation, celibacy, fetishism, and fantasy. Moreover, pansexuality includes heteroerotic and homoerotic play and sexual aggression, sometimes mislabeled as "horseplay."
> (Drobac 1999a, pp. 300–301)

I also noted that pansexuality provides a useful tool for understanding *Oncale* because, as a concept, pansexuality deconstructs the stereotypical interrelation of biological sex and sexual behavior prevalent in American society. The pansexual perspective helps to identify stereotypical assumptions made in *Oncale* (Drobac 1999b).

Taking a narrow perspective in *Oncale*, Justice Scalia reasoned:

> A professional football player's working environment is not severely or pervasively abusive, for example, if the coach smacks him on the buttocks as he heads onto the field – even if the same behavior would reasonably be experienced as abusive by the coach's secretary (male or female) back at the office" (*Oncale*, 523 U.S. at 81)

In this hypothetical, Justice Scalia assumes that: (i) the football coach is male; (ii) the male football coach is heterosexual; (iii) the football player is male; and (iv) buttsmacking on a football field is not sexual whereas it is either sexual or hostile at the office.

Taking a pansexual, gender-neutral approach, we would acknowledge that: (i) male coaches are sometimes homosexual (in addition to being pansexual); (ii) coaches are occasionally female; (iii) women play professional sports; and (iv) on-field butt-smacking may be sexual (or hostile) (Drobac 1999b). In sum, a strict interconnection between chromosomal sex, gender, and sexuality fails to contemplate all social contexts and even defies "common sense." Thus, a broad view of sex, gender, and sexuality, may promote the fair resolution of a case.

Unwelcome harassment that affects a term, condition, or privilege of employment

First in *Harris v. Forklift Sys., Inc.* and then in *Faragher v. City of Boca Raton*, the Court emphasized that the "objectionable environment must be both objectively and subjectively offensive, one that a reasonable person would find hostile or abusive, and one that the victim in fact did perceive to be so" (*Harris*, 510 U.S. at 21–22; *Faragher*, 524 U.S. at 787). Jurists refer to the objective component as the "reasonableness" standard and to the subjective element as the unwelcomeness requirement.

Every state FEPS – including, for example, the California Fair Employment and Housing Act – that similarly prohibits sex discrimination and sexual harassment also makes "unwelcomeness" an element of the prima facie case (Cal. Gov't Code § 12940).

The *Meritor* Court had specifically addressed the issue of volition in its discussion of unwelcomeness:

> While the question whether particular conduct was indeed unwelcome presents difficult problems of proof and turns largely on credibility determinations committed to the trier of fact, the District Court in this case erroneously focused on the "voluntariness" of respondent's participation in the claimed sexual episodes. The correct inquiry is whether respondent by her conduct indicated that the alleged sexual advances were unwelcome, not whether her actual participation in sexual intercourse was voluntary.
>
> (*Meritor*, 477 U.S. at 68)

Thus, acquiescence to sex is not consent. The plaintiff must prove only that she somehow indicated that the sexual behavior was unwelcome.

One can see how the unwelcomeness requirement invites a trial of the aggrieved target's conduct. Federal Rule of Evidence Rule 412, amended after *Meritor*, prohibits introduction of the target's prior sexual history with anyone other than the respondent into evidence in civil cases. It restricts, "(1) Evidence offered to prove that any alleged victim engaged in other sexual behavior. (2) Evidence offered to prove any alleged victim's sexual predisposition" (28 U.S.C. §412 (1994)). Limited exceptions to these evidentiary rules exist and require that parties who wish to offer such evidence satisfy certain procedural requirements. Legislators meant Rule 412 to counter the harassing litigation practices in criminal rape trials and post-*Meritor* civil cases (O'Neill 1989).

A judge might allow introduction of prior sexual conduct and history if she deems that the probative value of the evidence, concerning whether the target found the alleged conduct unwelcome, outweighs any prejudice to the plaintiff. During pretrial discovery, however, attorneys have great latitude to explore topics that might lead to admissible evidence. Professor Deborah Rhode explains:

> [Pretrial,] attorneys ... can often grill victims about their sex lives, birth control practices, and counseling histories. If a plaintiff alleges physical or psychological damage resulting from harassment, opposing attorneys can explore possible alternative causes for her distress – everything from closeted lesbian experiences to intimate marital difficulties. As a result, defendants' lawyers can discredit or deter a harassment complaint with harassing tactics of their own.
>
> (Rhode 1997, p. 102)

Some lawyers and judges declare how easily plaintiffs can bring sexual harassment claims and how difficult those claims are to defend. These jurists ignore the realities summarized by Professor Rhode. They also ignore the robust social science statistics which indicate that only 2–10% of assault cases are falsely reported, while 60% of sexual assaults are not reported to police ("Measuring the #MeToo backlash" 2018).

Employer liability

According to *Meritor*, employers are strictly liable for harassment by a supervisor that results in a tangible economic penalty for an employee. Thus, liability depends on the identity of the harasser, the status of the target, *and* the nature of the behavior. With respect to the harasser, the Court distinguishes between an employer's agent, a supervisor, and an employer's proxy. The Court has confirmed that Title VII fixes strict liability on an employer when a proxy for the organization, such as an owner or president – someone who clearly speaks for the company – engages in abusive conduct. In such a case, liability attaches whether or not the misconduct results in an economic penalty (*Faragher*, 524 U.S. at 789). For coworker harassment, the employer is liable only if it knew or should have known of the harassment and failed to take immediate and appropriate corrective action (Meritor, 477 U.S. at 63). This standard tracks the basic standard of care in common negligence claims brought under tort law.

With respect to the target, the code defines "employee" as "an individual employed by an employer" (42 U.S.C. § 2000e (f)). Typically, an individual must receive a salary or regular financial compensation in order to qualify as an employee within the meaning of Title VII (*Juino v. Livingston Parish Fire Dist. No. 5*, 717 F.3d 431 (5th Cir. 2013)). Additionally, the employer must control the work of the paid employee (*Covington v. International Ass'n of Approved Basketball Officials*, 710 F.3d 114 (3rd Cir. 2013)).

Therefore, most independent contractors, clients, unpaid volunteers, and unpaid student interns do not qualify as employees and do not enjoy Title VII protections. These omissions make clear that court interpretation of sexual harassment laws is very important. Newly proposed legislation, "Bringing an End to Harassment by Enhancing Accountability and Rejecting Discrimination" (BE HEARD) would fill many of these gaps to expand the application of antidiscrimination protections. BE HEARD would also implement other needed changes concerning restrictive nondisclosure agreements, mandatory binding arbitration (that favors employers), and tipped wage minimums (that make women vulnerable to exploitation). This legislation, however, is not likely to make it past the Republican-controlled Senate or White House (North 2019).

In addition to the rank or status of the parties, the nature of the conduct also influences employer liability. In *Sexual Harassment of Working Women*, MacKinnon distinguished between two types of sexual harassment: "quid pro quo" sexual harassment (a phrase she coins) and what she calls "condition of work" harassment (later called "hostile work environment" harassment). Quid pro quo harassment she defined as a situation where a "woman must comply sexually or forfeit an employment benefit." The second category, condition of work sexual harassment, includes less direct sexual behavior where the woman is "never promised or denied anything explicitly connected with her job" but which makes her work environment unbearable (MacKinnon 1979, pp. 32, 40).

Courts adopted MacKinnon's characterizations and distinguish quid pro quo harassment from hostile work harassment when sex-based abuse by supervisors results in a tangible economic detriment for the target. Thus, if a boss retracts a salary increase because the worker refuses sexual advances, the principal is strictly liable. If the worker refuses the sexual advance but no tangible economic consequence results, modern case law provides for employer liability, subject to an affirmative defense.

In 1998 the US Supreme Court added an affirmative defense to a Title VII claim. In *Faragher v. City of Boca Raton* and *Burlington Industries, Inc. v. Ellerth*, the Court examined a victim's unreasonable failure to avail herself of an employer's preventive or corrective procedures. The Court determined that, unless the sexual harassment results in a tangible employment detriment, such a failure insulates the employer from liability for supervisor harassment. The *Ellerth* Court explained, "The defense comprises two necessary elements: (a) that the employer exercised reasonable care to prevent and correct promptly any sexually harassing behavior, and (b) that the plaintiff employee unreasonably failed to take advantage of any preventive or corrective opportunities provided by the employer or to avoid harm otherwise" (*Burlington Indus., Inc. v. Ellerth*, 524 U.S. 742, 765 (1998); *Faragher*, 524 U.S. at 807–808).

Thus, if the employer adopts a complaint procedure that a target "unreasonably" fails to follow, the *Faragher* and *Ellerth* decisions effectively bar her from pursuing a sexual harassment claim for a supervisor's conduct. This affirmative defense finds no application in coworker harassment cases because the negligence standard applies in those.

The rationale behind the new affirmative defense centers on motivating employers to adopt preventive and corrective procedures regarding their agents' conduct (*Faragher*, 524 U.S. at 805–806; *Ellerth*, 524 U.S. at 764). The Court's *Faragher* and *Ellerth* decisions encourage targets to complain and employers to cure hostile work environments. However, a complaint procedure and corrective action cannot remedy the damage already done by a harasser. Moreover, by completely insulating the employer from liability for past harassment by a supervisor, the Court has ultimately charged the cost of this incentive system to the injured victim. For example, in *Ashton ex rel. Ashton v. Okosun*, 266 F. Supp. 2d 399 (D. Md. 2003), a juvenile worker complained the day after she left work because her manager allegedly touched her on her buttocks and attempted to hug her. The court found that she had unreasonably failed to avail herself of all complaint procedures. She had refused to return to work after an investigating manager declared her allegations unfounded but offered to transfer her to another shift to avoid the accused.

Beyond the law

This brief review of Title VII and its evolution provides just a glimpse of the efforts to curb sex-based harassment in the US. All the laws and legal victories combined, however, will not serve to eradicate this problem completely. Cultures and traditions must evolve to recognize and protect the rights and dignity of all persons. People must be willing to share power and help their neighbors in order for the world to progress beyond habits of oppressive subordination and exploitation. As a 2014 Obama task force organization explains:

> It's On Us asks everyone – students, community leaders, parents, organizations, and companies – to step up and realize that the conversation changes with us. It's a rallying

cry to be a part of the solution. The campaign combines innovative creative content and grassroots organizing techniques to spark conversation on a national and local level.

(It's On Us 2014)

This organization makes clear that there are many ways to prevent and remediate sex-based harassment. Legal prohibitions and sanctions are only two.

International Laws and Approaches

US sexual harassment law has undeniably influenced responses to sex-based harassment throughout the world. A 1992 international survey of sexual harassment law by Robert Husbands focuses on 23, mostly European, nations. This study confirms the US as the first nation to interpret law to prohibit sex-based harassment. It also acknowledges MacKinnon's role in disseminating the term "sexual harassment" and clarifying foundational concepts. While dated, this article offers a useful glimpse of the legal landscape of the time (Husbands 1992).

The article concludes, "Four types of laws have been found to be potentially applicable to sexual harassment: equal opportunity law, labour law, tort law, and criminal law." Husbands suggests that the last three types have "a much broader approach to the issue, frequently addressing the issue in terms of an unacceptable affront to the dignity and privacy of the individual." In those countries where women are not yet fully regarded as equal to men, a dignity- or privacy-based approach allows jurists to condemn offensive and harmful conduct.

Israeli Sexual Harassment Law

An example of such dignity-based legislation is the Israeli Prevention of Sexual Harassment Law, 5758-1998, which prohibits broadly defined sexually harassing behavior. It covers not only workplace harassment but proscribes sexual harassment in every other social setting (Prevention of Sexual Harassment Law 1998). Orit Kamir, who facilitated the passage of this legislation, explains:

> Due to the significant political influence of Jewish Orthodox parties in the Knesset and the lack of a formal constitution, equality is not a fully recognized constitutional right in Israel.... But whereas equality has not been legislated as a fundamental legal right, the combined concept of "right to human dignity, respect, honor and liberty" has recently been defined as a fundamental human right.... In light of these developments, a new approach to sexual harassment law seemed feasible as well as warranted – an approach defining sexually harassing behaviors as violations of human dignity, liberty, and the basic right to respect.
>
> (Kamir 2003, pp. 567–568)

The Israeli example confirms that even in countries which lack formal recognition of women's equality, sexual harassment prohibitions are possible.

Additionally, Kamir emphasizes that a multitheorized legal protection scheme is not only possible, but preferable. She stresses:

I should make it clear that conceptualizing sexual harassment in terms of dignity, respect, and liberty does not require its separation from notions of equality. Dignity, respect, liberty, and equality need not be posed as competing or exclusionary values; on the contrary, in the context of sexual harassment law, they should rather be read as complementary. Sexual harassment discriminates against women by not respecting them as women and as human beings, by violating their dignity, and by restricting their liberty to determine themselves and to lead lives free of fear and restriction. It disrespects women and violates their dignity by mirroring and perpetuating a social reality that does not treat them as equal. The more commonsense notions of dignity, respect, and liberty can be useful in conveying the harm caused by sexual harassment, and in illuminating its sex-discriminatory harm.

(Kamir 2003, p. 568)

This passage highlights how notions of dignity, respect, and liberty provide the foundational basis for some sexual harassment laws. Note that Professor Kamir also relied on common sense in the interpretation of concepts. One can doubt whether, in 2003, her notion of commonsense would have borne any relation to Justice Scalia's, reflected in *Oncale*. Twenty years later, Israel celebrates what at the time was considered a revolutionary law (Mualam 2018).

Sex-based protections (or lack thereof) around the world

Robert Husbands concluded in the International Labour Office report, "Perhaps more important than the type of law upon which the prohibition of sexual harassment is based is the fundamental recognition of sexual harassment as a distinct legal wrong" (Husbands 1992, p. 558). While many nations recognize sexual harassment as a distinct legal wrong, not all do.

The University of California at Los Angeles (UCLA) World Policy Analysis Center (WORLD) tracks worldwide efforts to address sexual harassment. According to Dr. Jody Heymann, founding director of WORLD:

"And while progress has been made, hundreds of millions of women face discrimination with no recourse, and women in underrepresented groups have the least protections. There are 152 countries that have prohibited discrimination in promotions and/or demotions based on gender, but only 126 countries guarantee protections from discrimination based on both gender and race/ethnicity."

("Nearly 235 Million Women Worldwide Lack Legal Protections From Sexual Harassment at Work" 2017)

The same study reported "that nearly 82 million working women live in 24 countries that do not have any legal protections against gender-based discrimination in compensation, promotions and/or demotions, or vocational training at work." A list of those nations without protections includes (to name just a few): Afghanistan, Chad, Cuba, Guatemala, Indonesia, Iran, Myanmar, Nigeria, the Russian Federation, Saudi Arabia, Sudan, and the United Arab Emirates. Among those nations that prohibit sexual harassment of only women China, Egypt, and India do not protect men ("Nearly 235 Million Women Worldwide Lack Legal Protections From Sexual Harassment at Work" 2017; Drobac 2017).

The WORLD report aptly illustrates that consciousness regarding the problems associated with sexual harassment is spreading. #MeToo is similar to many other movements, however, in that for every two steps forward, a step backward may occur. It remains to be seen whether President Donald Trump ever faces significant consequences for his alleged sexual abuse of numerous women. Commenting on recent events in the US, Dr. Heymann noted "that even with laws in place, we will only make enough progress when all people and all institutions contribute to changing norms and practices" ("Nearly 235 Million Women Worldwide Lack Legal Protections From Sexual Harassment at Work" 2017).

The future

UN Women is actively monitoring the problem of sexual harassment worldwide and offers some useful guidelines for establishing antiharassment policies and procedures. First, it recommends that organizations (or countries) have a policy with a clear definition of sex-based harassment, which classifies it as "gender-based discrimination…in a context of unequal power relations." It also emphasizes that consent is not relevant to the dynamic because of the unequal power. It promotes the unwelcomeness standard (UN Women 2018).

Second, UN Women suggests a reporting procedure that is "victim-friendly," "equitable," and "extends over everyone who can be sexually harassed or who can sexually harass within the system." It advances clear, enumerated recommendations to assist drafters. Its protocols address topics such as data collection, retaliation, statutes of limitations, confidentiality, training for experts and adjudicators, settlements, and nondisclosure agreements (UN Women 2018). Finally, the UN Women publication emphasizes the need for cultural change, as part of a tripartite scheme to prevent and cure sex-based discrimination and harassment. It focused on "leadership buy-in," "advance[ment] of women to high positions of power," and "transparent accountability."

The UN Women's compelling presentation of facts from countries around the world, as well as its prescription for how nations and organizations can combat sex-based harassment, create a powerful tool. Resources like UN Women offer hope that humankind can make progress to secure the rights and dignity of all persons.

Conclusion

This summary review of sexual harassment law highlights the need for reform, not only in the US, but also around the world. The #MeToo movement further confirms that this problem mandates additional eradication efforts. New initiatives that rely on extralegal methods, such as education and training, to address the problem are increasingly prevalent. Without legal reforms, however, narrow definitions of sex-based harassment and traditional laws such as Title VII, will continue to prove inadequate in the response. The developing jurisprudence that has established the requirements for a plaintiff's case must take new understanding regarding this phenomenon into account. Other nations have taken innovative steps to deal with sex-based discrimination but too many countries have yet to act or provide adequate protections for women and other oppressed groups. This survey suggests that we all can make a difference by understanding the problem and speaking out against sex-based harassment and discrimination. Consciousness regarding systemic discrimination is the first step to effective eradication.

Note

1 See e.g. *Barnes v. Train*, 13 Fed. Empl. Prac. Cas. 123 (D.D.C. 1974), *rev'd sub nom. Barnes v. Costle*, 561 F. 2d 983 (D.C. Cir. 1977); *Corne v. Bausch & Lomb, Inc.*, 390 F. Supp. 161 (D. Ariz. 1975), *vacated and remanded*, 562 F.2d 55 (9th Cir. 1977); *Garber v. Saxon Bus. Products, Inc.*, 14 Empl. Prac. Deci. ¶7586 (E.D. Va. 1976), *rev'd and remanded*, 552 F.2d 1032 (4th Cir. 1977); *Williams v. Saxbe*, 413 F. Supp. 654 (D.D.C. 1976), *rev'd in part and vacated in part sub nom. Williams v. Bell*, 587 F.2d 1240 (D.C. Cir. 1978); *Miller v. Bank of Am.*, 418 F. Supp. 233 (N.D. Cal. 1976), *rev'd*, 600 F.2d 211 (9th Cir. 1979); *Tomkins v. Pub. Serv. Elec. and Gas Co.*, 422 F. Supp. 553 (D.N.J. 1976), *rev'd*, 568 F.2d 1044 (3rd Cir. 1977). See Carrie N. Baker, *The Women's Movement Against Sexual Harassment* 16–17 (2008) for detailed descriptions of the facts of these cases. African American women brought all of the early precedent-setting cases.

References

Adam, Karla and William Booth. 2018. "A Year After It Began, Has #MeToo Become a Global Movement?" *Washington Post*, October 5. Available at: https://www.washingtonpost.com/world/a-year-after-it-began-has-metoo-become-a-global-movement/2018/10/05/1fc0929e-c71a-11e8-9c0f-2ffaf6d422aa_story.html.

Akin, Stephanie. 2017. "Congress Took Three Decades to Come This Far, Sexual Harassment Victim Says." *Roll Call*, November 11. Available at: https://www.rollcall.com/news/politics/congress-took-three-decades-come-far-sexual-harassment-victim-says.

Anderson, Nick, and Scott Clement. 2015. "1 in 5 College Women Say They Were Violated." *Washington Post*, June 12. Available at: https://www.washingtonpost.com/sf/local/2015/06/12/1-in-5-women-say-they-were-violated/.

Ashbrook, Tom. 2017. "Harvey Weinstein and Sexual Harassment in the Workplace." *On Point*, October 11. Available at: http://www.wbur.org/onpoint/2017/10/11/harvey-weinstein-harassment.

Baker, Carrie N. 2008. *The Women's Movement Against Sexual Harassment*. New York, NY: Cambridge University Press.

Berebitsky, Julie. 2012. *Sex and the Office: A History of Gender, Power, and Desire*. New Haven, CT: Yale University Press.

Cantor, David, Bonnie Fisher, Susan Chibnall, et al. 2017. Report on the AAU Campus Climate Survey on Sexual Assault and Sexual Misconduct. Available at: https://www.aau.edu/sites/default/files/AAU-Files/Key-Issues/Campus-Safety/AAU-Campus-Climate-Survey-FINAL-10-20-17.pdf.

Chuck, Elizabeth. 2017. "#MeToo Hashtag Becomes Anti-Sexual Harassment and Assault Rallying Cry." *NBC News*, October 16. Available at: https://www.nbcnews.com/storyline/sexual-misconduct/metoo-hashtag-becomes-anti-sexual-harassment-assault-rallying-cry-n810986.

Civil Rights Act of 1964, 42 U.S.C. § 2000e.

Civil Rights Act of 1968, 42 U.S.C. § 3601.

DiJulio, Bianca, Mira Norton, Peyton Craighill, et al. 2015. "Survey of Current and Recent College Students on Sexual Assault." *Kaiser Family Foundation*, June 12. Available at: https://www.kff.org/other/poll-finding/survey-of-current-and-recent-college-students-on-sexual-assault/.

Donnelly, Matt and Ashley Boucher. 2017. "Masturbation as Harassment: Experts Try to Understand Bizarre Secret Behavior." *SFGate*, November 9. Available at: https://www.thewrap.com/masturbation-harassment-experts-try-understand-bizarre-secret-behavior/.

Drobac, Jennifer A. 1999a. "Pansexuality and the Law." *William & Mary Journal of Women and the Law* 5: 297–308.

Drobac, Jennifer A. 1999b. "The Oncale Opinion: A Pansexual Response." *McGeorge Law Review* 30: 1272–1291.

Drobac, Jennifer A. 2016. *Sexual Exploitation of Teenagers: Adolescent Development, Discrimination & Consent Law*. Chicago, IL: University of Chicago Press.

Drobac, Jennifer A. 2017. "Equality, Dignity & Privacy: Indian & US 'Pansexual' Human Rights." *Indian Const. L.R.* 2: 1–38. Available at: http://www.iclrq.in/editions/apr/4.pdf.

Drobac, Jennifer A., Carrie N. Baker, and Rigel C. Oliveri. 2020. *Sexual Harassment Law: History, Cases, and Practice*. Durham, North Carolina; Carolina Academic Press.

Education Amendments of 1972, 20 U.S.C. 1681.

US Equal Employment Opportunity Commission (EEOC). 1990. Policy Guidance on Current Issues of Sexual Harassment, March 19. Available at: https://www.eeoc.gov/policy/docs/currentissues.html.

Farrow, Ronan. 2017. "Harvey Weinstein's Accusers Tell Their Stories." *The New Yorker*, October 10. Available at: https://www.newyorker.com/news/news-desk/from-aggressive-overtures-to-sexual-assault-harvey-weinsteins-accusers-tell-their-stories.

Fitzgerald, Louise F. 1996. "Sexual Harassment: The Definition and Measurement of a Construct." In *Sexual Harassment on College Campuses: Abusing the Ivory Power*, edited by Michele A. Paludi, 25–47. Albany, NY: State University of New York Press.

Frankovic, Kathy. 2017. "Sexual Harassment Reports May Just Be the Tip of the Iceberg." *Economist/YouGov Poll*, November 17. Available at: https://today.yougov.com/topics/politics/articles-reports/2017/11/17/sexual-harassment-reports-may-just-be-tip-iceberg.

Garcia, Sandra E. 2017. "The Woman Who Created #MeToo Long Before Hashtags." *New York Times*, October 20. Available at: https://www.nytimes.com/2017/10/20/us/me-too-movement-tarana-burke.html.

Google. 2019. Search for "#Metoo Movement." Available at: https://imgur.com/a/NdcmAHr? (accessed April 9, 2019).

Horowitz, Julia and Sara Ashley O'Brien. 2017. "How Do You Report Sexual Harassment When There's No HR?" *CNNMoney*, October 13. Available at: http://money.cnn.com/2017/10/13/news/harvey-weinstein-sexual-harassment-reporting/index.html (accessed April 9, 2019).

Husbands, Robert. 1992. "Sexual Harassment Law in Employment: An International Perspective." *International Labour Review* 131(6): 535–559.

Israel Ministry of Foreign Affairs Prevention of Sexual Harassment Law, 5758-1998. 1998. March 10. Available at: https://mfa.gov.il/MFA/AboutIsrael/State/Law/Pages/Prevention_of_Sexual_Harassment_Law_5758-1998.aspx.

It's On Us. 2014. The Story of Our Movement. Available at: https://www.itsonus.org/our-story/.

J.M.F. [pseud]. 2017. "What is Sexual Harassment and How Prevalent is It?" *Economist*, November 24. Available at: https://www.economist.com/the-economist-explains/2017/11/24/what-is-sexual-harassment-and-how-prevalent-is-it.

Kamir, Orit. 2003. "Dignity, Respect, and Equality in Sexual Harassment Law: Israel's New Legislation." In *New Directions in Sexual Harassment Law*, edited by Catharine A. MacKinnon and Reva B. Siegel, 561–581. New Haven, CT: Yale University Press.

Kantor, Jodi and Megan Twohey. 2017. "Harvey Weinstein Paid Off Sexual Harassment Accusers For Decades." *New York Times*, October 5. Available at: https://www.nytimes.com/2017/10/05/us/harvey-weinstein-harassment-allegations.html.

Kearl, Holly. 2018. *The Facts Behind the ##MeToo Movement: A National Study on Sexual Harassment and Assault*. Reston, VA: Stop Street Harassment. Available at: http://www.stopstreetharassment.org/wp-content/uploads/2018/01/Full-Report-2018-National-Study-on-Sexual-Harassment-and-Assault.pdf.

Levenson, Michael and Cristela Guerra. 2017. "Sexual Harassment Allegations Lead Millions of Women to Say #Metoo." *Boston Globe*, October 16. Available at: https://www.bostonglobe.com/metro/2017/10/16/metoo-campaign-highlights-prevalence-harassment/NH4hDAFk6F7XXKgETSo0jI/story.html.

MacKinnon, Catharine A. 1979. *Sexual Harassment of Working Women*. New Haven, Connecticut: Yale University Press.

"Measuring the #MeToo Backlash." 2018. Economist, October 10. Available at: https://www.economist.com/united-states/2018/10/20/measuring-the-metoo-backlash.

Mualem, Mazal. 2018. "Israel's Revolutionary Sexual Harassment Law." *Al-Monitor*, February 28. Available at: https://www.al-monitor.com/pulse/originals/2018/02/israel-law-sexual-harassment-knesset-gender-equality.html.

"Nearly 235 Million Women Worldwide Lack Legal Protections From Sexual Harassment at Work." 2017. UCLA Newsroom, October 25. Available at: https://www.socialworktoday.com/news/dn_111317.shtml.

North, Anna. 2019. "Democrats' Sweeping New Anti-Harassment Bill, Explained." *Vox*, April 9. Available at: https://www.vox.com/2019/4/9/18300478/sexual-harassment-me-too-be-heard-democrats.

Oliveri, Rigel C. 2018. "The Sexual Harassment of Low-Income Women in Housing: Pilot Study Results." *Missouri Law Review* 83: 597–639.

O'Neill, Catherine A. 1989. "Sexual Harassment Cases and the Law of Evidence: A Proposed Rule." *University of Chicago Legal Forum* 1989(11): 219–250. Available at: https://chicagounbound.uchicago.edu/uclf/vol1989/iss1/11/.

Paul, Kari and Maria LaMagna. 2018. "The Damaging, Incalculable Price of Sexual Harassment." *MarketWatch*, January 9. Available at: https://www.marketwatch.com/story/as-harvey-weinstein-takes-a-leave-of-absence-heres-how-much-sexual-harassment-costs-companies-and-victims-2017-10-07.

Rhode, Deborah. 1997. *Speaking of Sex*. Cambridge, MA: Harvard University Press.

Sayej, Nadja. 2017. "Alyssa Milano on the #MeToo Movement: 'We're Not Going to Stand for It Any More.'" *Guardian*, December 1. Available at: https://www.theguardian.com/culture/2017/dec/01/alyssa-milano-mee-too-sexual-harassment-abuse.

Schwartz, Jason and Michael Calderone. 2017. "NBC's Shifting Statements on Lauer Draw Scrutiny." *Politico*, November 30. Available at: https://www.politico.com/story/2017/11/30/matt-lauer-nbc-management-complaints-272954.

Smartt, Nicole. 2017. "Sexual Harassment in the Workplace in a #MeToo World." *Forbes*, December 20. Available at: https://www.forbes.com/sites/forbeshumanresourcescouncil/2017/12/20/sexual-harassment-in-the-workplace-in-a-metoo-world/#149254ac5a42.

Stolberg, Sheryl Gay, Yamiche Alcindor, and Nicholas Fandos. 2017. "Al Franken to Resign From Senate Amid Harassment Allegations." *New York Times*, December 7. Available at: https://www.nytimes.com/2017/12/07/us/politics/al-franken-senate-sexual-harassment.html.

UN Women. 2018. *Towards An End To Sexual Harassment: The Urgency And Nature Of Change In The Era Of #Metoo*. New York, NY: UN Women. Available at: http://www.unwomen.org/-/media/headquarters/attachments/sections/library/publications/2018/towards-an-end-to-sexual-harassment-en.pdf?la=en&vs=4236.

US Department of Education, Office of Civil Rights (OCR). 2017. Sex-based Harassment, September 22. Available at: https://www2.ed.gov/about/offices/list/ocr/frontpage/pro-students/issues/sex-issue01.html.

Werner, Erica and Juliet Linderman. 2017. "Female lawmakers Allege Harassment by Colleagues in House." *AP News*, November 3. Available at: https://www.apnews.com/ca32653c458c4a3e9ef07d31700c14e6/Female-lawmakers-allege-harassment-by-colleagues-in-House.

"Young Men are Changing Their Definitions of Sexual Harassment." 2019. *Economist*, January 4. Available at: https://www.economist.com/graphic-detail/2019/01/04/young-men-are-changing-their-definitions-of-sexual-harassment.

22

Sex Work and Sex Trafficking

KAMALA KEMPADOO AND ELYA M. DURISIN

Introduction

Sex work and sex trafficking are two concepts that are often confused and sometimes conflated. In this chapter we trace the genealogy of both terms separately and discuss the ways in which they converge, coalesce, and diverge. This review and discussion draws from the most widely circulated ideas arising from social movements and studies that address sex work and sex trafficking globally, and, as such, it is a representation of hegemonic trends, which we recognize might overlook important local or regional nuances. It is written from the authors' location in Canada and informed by our long-standing engagement with global movements and sex work and with human trafficking debates.

Sex Work

"Sex work" emerged from activism and feminist theory as a term to speak about prostitution and other sexual services as a form of labor, a job, or employment. Two key trends are identifiable over the years on the subject, which we distinguish here as "materialist feminist" and "sexual libertarian," yet which in practice are often indiscernible or negligibly different.[1]

Understandings developed by materialist feminist scholars see sexual labor as a type of productive labor that "produces human life, satisfies human needs, and reproduces the laboring population" (van der Meulen, Durisin, and Love 2013, p. 17; see also van der Veen 2001; Zatz 1997). The notion of sexual labor is useful for thinking through the emergence of sex work as a labor category because it describes productive labor that is directly related to the sexualized elements and energies of the body and differs from, for instance, the reproductive (biological and

---

Companion to Sexuality Studies, First Edition. Edited by Nancy A. Naples.
© 2020 John Wiley & Sons Ltd. Published 2020 by John Wiley & Sons Ltd.

social) labor involved in childbirth and work such as cleaning and caregiving. Disaggregating sexual labor from other forms of labor relating to the reproduction of human beings is the subject of much debate in feminist thought. Drawing on earlier feminist theorizing, Thanh Dam Truong (1990) argues that there is a human need for sexual and psychological nurturance and sexual satisfaction that exceeds the specific needs expressed in biological and social reproduction. Thus, while difficult to delineate sexualized forms of labor that comprise sexual and reproductive labor, it is understood that there is a specific, historically contingent, form of labor relating to sexualized elements and energies of the body. The provision of such labor occurs in various forms and through differing social arrangements and is essential for sustaining humankind. Truong deepens the understanding that the organization, including exchange, of sexual labor takes no universal form, but is a result of historical human activity, and is intertwined with economics, politics, and meanings associated with sexuality.[2]

Sex work as a category of labor in this approach is deeply connected to the political economy of women's work and is heavily influenced by Marxist and socialist ideas and struggles surrounding social and economic inequalities and the rights to decent work, wages, and living conditions (see, for example, Kotiswaran 2011; van der Veen 2001). The extreme economic exploitation and social dispossession in Global South countries in the context of colonialism, development strategies, and globalization is also seen to have given rise to vibrant social movements, and to demands for social and economic justice for marginalized women workers, including sex workers (Kempadoo and Doezema 1998).

The second trend here is the sexual libertarian formulation of sex work that has predominantly developed in North American contexts, often expressing demands for rights in relation to liberal notions of individual choice and identity. Borrowing key concepts from liberal feminist theory, the emphasis in this approach has been on rational choice and agency, viewing sex and sexuality as sites of self-determination (Jaggar 1997). Sex workers, from this perspective, are sometimes described as sexual rebels, sex-radicals, or sex-positive feminists who transgressively deploy their sexuality. Sex worker rights groups emerging in the 1970s and 1980s emphasized concerns relating to occupational choice and sexual autonomy taken up through discourses on individual rights, and were represented through the politics of the early organizations such as COYOTE (Call Off Your Old Tired Ethics) in the United States; CORP (Canadian Organization for the Rights of Prostitutes) in Canada, and the ICPR (International Committee for Prostitutes' Rights) in Western Europe. Sex worker rights organizations and scholars consider questions of control of women's sexuality and sexual subjectivity, abuse of sex workers by police and other state actors, and the need for legal reform (see Pheterson 1989; Bell 1994; Chapkis 1997; Grant 2014).

However, discourses of sex work do not have neat and exclusive genealogies or theoretical legacies that can be easily disentangled. Differing feminist approaches to theorizing sex work show points of convergence and divergence; for example, both liberal and socialist feminist perspectives liken sex workers to waged laborers (Jaggar 1997) yet the latter show ambivalence toward the notion of sex work as legitimate labor, despite its productive dimensions (Kotiswaran 2011). Further, it would be inaccurate to assume that the idea of rights for sex workers is the legacy of Western feminist thought. Because of the importance of sex work to the economies of many countries in Asia, Africa, the Caribbean, and Latin America, the discourses emerging from Global South locations guide and shape those in the Western context as well as the aims and discourse of the global sex workers movement. Likewise, the struggle for sex worker visibility that emanates from the North through a sexual libertarian politics greatly influences self-representation and mobilization in the Global South and East.

Moreover, there is agreement in this discourse that a variety of transnational factors have given rise to sex work as a labor category and, for some, an identity category as well. Licia Brussa (1991) was one of the earlier feminists to locate the migration of women from South America, Asia, and Africa to work in prostitution markets in Europe as early as the mid-1970s, as significant. This was linked to development strategies in Asia evolving after the Vietnam War that relied heavily on women's reproductive and sexual labor, such as the export of female sex and domestic workers abroad and the rise of the international tourism industry where sex tourism comprised a central element (see also Enloe 1989; Mies 1986). The deep intertwining of sexualized bodies and labor in the process of globalization and development thus alerted feminist scholars to the importance of theorizing the economic contributions of (migrant) women's sexual labor to capital and the state (Lim 1998; Truong 1990).

With the collapse of state socialist projects that began in 1989, women from former socialist states in Eastern Europe likewise started to migrate into sex sectors globally (see Andrijasevic 2010; Durisin and Heynen 2015; Suchland 2015), triggering a new international legal response about trafficking, which, until that point, was limited to concern about women in the context of development projects in Asia (Kempadoo 2001). Gülçür and İlkkaracan (2002) connected Eastern European women's involvement in sex sectors to the "suitcase industry" that emerged after the fall of socialism, where women would migrate between countries carrying goods for trade in their suitcases. Sex work, then, was another aspect of trade that emerged as women migrated from their home countries and sought out economic opportunities abroad. While poverty and need for income were seen to influence women's migration, women were found to be also searching out economically and personally beneficial relationships, including finding male partners and recreating their lives with income earned through sex work (Davies 2009).

In the latter part of the twentieth century, profound social and economic shifts began to unfold with the turn toward neoliberalism, leading North America and Western Europe to a reconceptualization of urban space, which had disastrous effects on sex workers, and which was taken up in the ongoing scholarship on sex work. As cities gentrified, it was noted that sex workers and sex-related businesses found themselves unwelcome in their neighborhoods as middle-class residents displaced existing communities (Brock 1998; Sanchez 2004; Schulman 2013). Sex workers became the targets of exclusionary public policies, policing, and new forms of legal repression. In these "revanchist" (Papayanis 2000) urban environments that sought to "cleanse" and remake social space in a manner appealing to new bourgeois residents, violence against sex workers was seen to increase, as sex work moved to less safe environments and a discourse of sex work as social contagion ensued (see Lowman 2000).

Out of this pathologization of sex work, a push to end the demand for commercial sex resulted in the introduction of new legislation, beginning in Sweden in 1999. The Swedish approach to prostitution law reform was a nation-state project to defend a national morality and sexuality from perceived threats emerging from shifting migration patterns and globalization (Kulick 2005; Mattson 2016). Clients of sex workers were defined as the problem and the purchases of sexual services criminalized. While laws against the selling of sexual labor were lifted, laws and policies continued to directly disrupt the lives of sex workers through eviction, deportation, child apprehension, and lack of harm-reduction services such as condoms, clean drug-use supplies, and information on how to safely sell sex (Levy and Jakobsson 2014; see also Amnesty International 2016). Sex workers themselves were no longer defined as criminals, yet remained mired in a system where prostitution was criminalized, and they were stigmatized for their engagement in what was deemed a socially unacceptable activity. Similar legislative changes have been made in Norway, France, and Canada. In the US, recent measures targeting online classified ads for sex work, perceived to facilitate sex trafficking, called FOSTA (Fight Online Sex Trafficking Act) and SESTA (Stop Enabling Sex Traffickers Act), have allowed authorities to take legal action against web sites hosting sex workers' advertisements. Electronic communication is a ubiquitous feature of contemporary sex sectors, yet, in a context where street-based sex work is already heavily criminalized, such repressive measures aimed at indoor markets for sexual labor through the internet hold consequences in particular for those sex workers who are racialized, non-middle class, or undocumented, and who are likely to experience intensified exclusions and marginalization as a result.

In the few places where prostitution was legalized, such as in the Netherlands in 2000, this led to a certain legitimacy and normalization of sex work and the sex worker. It also, however, gave rise to greater control over and containment of the sex sector, forcing many workers and establishments out of older red-light areas and streets and into more hidden and underground work spaces and places (Goodyear and Weitzer 2011). The increasing flexibilization of work, diversification of sexual demands, products, and services, and widespread digital connectivity under neoliberalism, also blurred lines between public and private spaces, enabling growing numbers of sex workers to work from private homes, hotels, through the internet and on cellphones (Bernstein 2007a). Increasing border control in the name of crime control and national security, moreover, moved non-European and non-North American sex workers in the Global North into greater invisibility as well as greater insecurity and vulnerability.

In the Global South, neoliberalism brought with it International Monetary Fund (IMF) and World Bank policies for national debt-repayment, and international free trade negotiations and agreements. These policies and agreements squeezed national economies, causing further displacement from rural agricultural communities, rising unemployment in urban centers, drops in real wages, and greater dependency on labor migration and remittances. The establishment of Free Trade and Special Economic Zones for offshore and export-oriented production, cuts by governments in national expenditures in social, educational, and health sectors, and removals of trade restrictions, local food subsidies, and price controls, accompanied these measures and agreements, imposing even further hardships on working people.

The transnational corporate drive to increase profit margins through increasing consumption also led to a proliferation of new products, goods, and services and the cultivation of new desires and needs, but also to more precarious employment options including sex work, and a greater reliance on labor migration (Kempadoo and Doezema 1998). With larger populations in the Global North as well as transnational and local elites having access to greater amounts of disposable income, advances in technology and international connections – both physical and virtual – boomed, enabling a greater integration of sexual labor into the tourism and entertainment sectors. But despite the increasing significance of sexual labor to the globalized neoliberal economy and to the well-being of local communities, sex workers continued to be marginalized by laws and stigmas against prostitution.

In addition to migration, neoliberal globalization, and renewed feminist attention for sex work, a number of factors contributed to the emergence of a global sex worker movement and the adoption of "sex work" as both a labor and identity category. Beginning in the 1970s and 1980s, sex worker organizations and networks were forming in North America, Asia, Europe, and Latin America and sex workers' self-representation began to take form in earnest (Kempadoo and Doezema 1998). It was during these early years that the first and second World Whores' Conferences were held in Europe and the World Charter for Prostitutes' Rights was formulated, which at the time primarily reflected Global North perspectives and experiences (see Pheterson 1989). Carol Leigh, an American sex worker-activist, is credited with coining the term "sex work" in 1979, which sex workers used to challenge dominant feminist understandings that positioned them as victims of patriarchal oppression (Leigh 1997; see also Delacoste and Alexander 1988). In South and Central America, Brazilian and Ecuadorian sex workers took the lead in the 1980s to organize strikes, mobilize, and "build a new discourse of prostitution," (De Lisio 2017; see also Blanchette and Murray 2016; Koné 2016), while in Asia, the movement was led by EMPOWER (Education Means Protection of Women Engaged in Recreation) in Thailand and by the DMSC (Durbar Mahila Samanwaya Committee) in India.

It was, arguably, the emergence of the HIV and AIDS pandemic and the scapegoating of sex workers as vectors of contagion alongside oppressive legal environments that increased sex workers' risks of acquiring the infection and of violence, which were galvanizing forces in the global sex worker movement. The global movement grew solidly in the early 1990s as sex workers responded to stigmatization and demanded access to prevention and treatment grounded in the language of international law surrounding human rights. It is this sex worker self-representation and expression of their concerns as workers in relation to their lack of access to health, human, and labor rights that resulted in significant reconceptualizations that reshaped feminist theorizing on sex work and prostitution. It was also in this movement around health rights that male and transgender sex workers became most visible, including leading activists such as Paolo Longo and Andrew Hunter, who helped found the Global Network of Sex Work Projects (NSWP). Such action and representation mirrored the wider shift in some feminist circles from a focus on "women" to "gender" and the inclusion of lesbian, gay, bisexual, and transgender (LGBT) subjectivities and rights in gender studies and feminist movements.

The above shifts in understanding were complemented and encouraged by developments outside the sex workers movement that were usefully applied to theorizations of sex work. Research in the field of the sociology of emotion identified emotional labor as labor that involves the activating, creating, and invoking of emotion. Arlie Russell Hochschild's landmark study examining the work of flight attendants defined emotional labor as labor that "requires one to induce or suppress feeling in order to sustain the outward countenance that produces the proper state of mind in others" (1983, p. 7). Researchers saw clear connections between the emotional labor involved in service work and that involved in sex work and used this to further develop notions of sex work as labor. Wendy Chapkis (1997) took up the concept of emotional labor to show parallels in boundary maintenance, the creation of a work persona, and the mobilization of feelings and emotions in the context of work between sex work and nonsex work occupations, effectively challenging antiprostitution theorizations that see the commodification of intimacy as inherently harmful.

Feminist researchers in many fields have built upon this earlier theorizing on emotional labor and expanded it to explore intersections between emotional, intimate, affective, caring, and sexual labor. Eileen Boris and Rhacel Salazar Parreñas (2010) explore how commodification of intimacy is suffused in daily life in the context of global capitalism. This scholarship challenges the deeply held separation between intimacy and economics in Western thought that refutes any connection between love and money (see also Zelizer 2005) and sees domestic, care, and sex work on a continuum. Boris and Parreñas define intimate labor as "work that involves embodied and affective interactions in the service of social reproduction" (2010, p. 7), with social reproduction being the maintenance of self and others on a daily and generational basis. In this vein, Miliann Kang (2010), explores the intimate labor involved in Asian women's work in nail salons in the United States, and examines the complex relationship between manicurists and their (largely) female customers. She argues that the intimacy involved in this type of body service work benefits customers and owners and acts as an impediment to workers' labor organizing. Nail salon work is an interesting counterpoint to feminist concerns with sex work as the customer base is largely women, yet there are similarities between labor rights concerns for sex and nail salon workers.

In a similar manner, academic research on sex work itself has become increasingly actor-centered, nuanced, and attentive to a multiplicity of experiences of selling sexual labor (Agustín 2007; Bernstein 2005; Davies 2009; Miller-Young 2014). Contemporary research on sex work challenges orthodoxies seeing sex workers as either victims or liberated sexual subjects. This marks a shift from both antiprostitution and sexual libertarian feminisms, theoretical traditions that shaped debates in the early years of the sex worker rights movement, to understandings that see complex interactions between structure and agency and the variety of sex workers' perceptions of their work and subjectivity. In Global South countries, where sexual labor was primarily identified and conceptualized as a survival strategy or tactic, in the last decade, there has been a move on the one hand, toward articulating a sex-positive identity politics such as "puta feminism," "whore feminism," and "sex worker feminism" (Blanchette and Murray 2016; Seshu and Murthy 2013), and on the other hand, to explore the transactional character of sexual labor, highlighting its instability as a category of work, the deep and intricate entanglements with affect, desire, and economics, and its continuing imbrication with racialized desires and embodiments (see, for example, Piscitelli 2017; Cabezas and Campos 2016; Groes-Groen 2013). In this second line of inquiry, the notion of "sex work" is almost abandoned, as it is argued that the concept tends to flatten and homogenize those social relations that involve some form of sexual labor yet are not seen or experienced as a job or a form of employment, or as integral to one's identity as a worker or sexual subject.

Gender and race in sex work

Even while there has been a persistent positioning of and focus on the categories of "women" and "the feminine" as key providers of sexual labor in both the movements and studies, men and trans have been continuously involved, servicing both male and female clients, and are to some extent recognized in sex work studies (see, for example, de Alburquerque 1999; Slamah 1998; Longo 1998; Aggleton 1999; Padilla 2007; Mitchell 2011). Masculine, male, and trans presence in sex work is, for a great part, exploratory, as scholars grapple with how to conceptualize and understand this labor beyond notions of individual choice and matters of homosociality and identity formation. However, in looking globally at male sex work, Peter Aggleton and Richard G. Parker (2015) identify key factors within a broader set of political, economic, and structural transformations that reshape male sex work in the twenty-first century, namely, an increase in informal income-generating strategies including men's participation in sex work, global migration by men who sell sex that is underpinned by accelerated global flows including population movement, and the reorganization of sex work identities, subjectivities, and practices with the expansion of the internet. This analysis places the upsurge of male sex work firmly in the context of neoliberal global hegemony, with sex work conceptualized as informal, marginalized, strategic labor, and as an area for nonnormative expressions of sexuality. Nicola Mai (2012) seems to agree with this conceptualization of men and hegemonic masculinity in sex work, proposing that the global sex industry is a place or "zone" where nonnormative/queer sexualities are expressed, which challenge and reinscribe both hetero- and homonormativity. This "fractally queer zone" he argues, must be understood as being produced through neoliberal globalization with its attending international flows of labor, people and technology.

Gendered sex work is also at times analyzed as entangled with constructions of race and the eroticization of black and brown sexualities, especially in tourism sectors in the Global South (see, for example, Cabezas 2009; Williams 2013), but also within Global North contexts where racism is institutionally structured (Brooks 2010; Miller-Young 2014; Maynard 2017). In these antiracist and postcolonial readings of sex work, hierarchies of race and the privileging of whiteness are taken to have worked both to benefit from and to disadvantage the sexual labor of people of color, especially black and indigenous women, and to reinscribe racist paradigms. Indeed, racialized sexual labor has long been recognized as primary source for exploitation, development, and wealth globally, and as a constituent part of national economies and transnational industries. In the Americas, for example, the intertwining of the enslavement of Africans with the hypersexualization of the black body under European rule produced situations where black sexual energies and labor were deliberately engaged to grow the laboring populations on plantations, to serve as wet-nurses and surrogate mothers for children of the elite, or to sexually service plantation workers, managers and slave-owners (Kempadoo 1999, 2004). Yet, the historical legacy of racialized sexual relations that are now cemented in tourism or entertainment industries is also identified as a strategy for black women, men, and trans to mitigate the hostilities and injustices of global uneven exchange (Cabezas 2009).

And while blackness in the Americas is imbued with notions of hypersexuality, specific histories of racialization locate certain bodies as more erotic and desirable than others, structuring sex industries in particular ways and configuring a person's erotic capital. Dark-skinned black bodies that may be highly desirable in tourist locations in Brazil, might not be valued the same in the porn industry in the US or in sex sectors in Cuba or Curacao (Williams 2013; Kempadoo 2004; Miller-Young 2014). Indigenous sex work is not highly valued in sex sectors as a result of colonial violence and the historical construct of the sexually available/rapable, promiscuous indigenous woman who inhabits degenerate spaces (Hunt 2015; Kaye 2017). Globally, it is whiteness that dictates, for women, the value of sexual labor, with white women tending to have access to the most highly paid work, the better working conditions, and the most secure and rewarding types of employment. However, whiteness too is hierarchized. Taking whiteness to reference an "insider" status within the global neoliberal economy and society, where poorer, working class and "unruly" groups are positioned as outsiders – as threats and contaminants – the postsocialist sex worker within Western contexts comes to be located on the outside, due to her presumed association with postsocialist criminality and "backwardness." The postsocialist sex worker then is often excluded from the privileges of whiteness (Durisin 2017).

Sex Trafficking

Unlike the concept of sex work, which is grounded in the perspectives, accounts and struggles of women, men and trans engaged in sexual labor, "sex trafficking" emerged through feminist antiprostitution theorizing and movements. Beginning in the early 1980s, a tremendous amount of feminist activism was directed toward advancing women's human rights within the United Nations (UN) (Wijers and Lap-Chew 1997), with a radical feminists' understanding of prostitution as a form of sexual violence against women coming to dominate within the UN arena (see, for example, Barry 1981). The critical analysis centering the political economy of women's sexual labor, especially that which was emerging from the Global South, was undercut by one that emphasized sexual harm (Suchland 2015). Moreover, changes in women's migratory movements as well as discourses about transnational crime and modern-day slavery provided the background for renewed international concerns over human trafficking.

The term "sex trafficking" was first established when the UN and US began to formulate the Palermo Protocol on human trafficking and the US Trafficking in Persons Act (later TVPA (Trafficking Victims Protection Act)) in the late 1990s. The concept was from the outset wedded to a radical feminist approach that defines all prostitution as constituting female sexual slavery (Barry 1984), which that builds upon a much older feminist tradition around the subject, dating back to social purity and social reform movements in the nineteenth century. This conceptualization has been carried forward in the work of a number of feminist scholars who are, at times, (self-) identified as abolitionist feminists[3] (see, for example, Raymond and Hughes 2001; Jeffreys 1997; D'Cunha 2011; Bindel 2017). Here, the notions of sex work and sexual labor are rejected, and terms such as "prostituted woman," "sexually exploited person," "or child used in prostitution" are advocated (CATW 2011). Prostitution, then, is a male-created, patriarchal institution for the terrorization, control and exploitation of women, seen as similar to the patriarchal institutions of marriage, the family, and the veil (Barry 1984; Jeffreys 1997) and women and femininity in the sex trade are located as inherently forced or trafficked. Prostitution is unconditionally defined as violence against women and, it is argued, needs to be abolished for women and the feminine to be free. Antisex trafficking studies and interventions tend to emphasize sexual exploitation, physical violence that occurs in the sex trade, lack of self-esteem, trauma, and alternative work opportunities, representing the global sex industry as a "uniformly dismal, violent and oppressive institution" (O'Connell Davidson 2015). "Survivors of prostitution" is a preferred term in this perspective to refer to victims who are helped to exit the sex industry by former/nonsex workers or other survivors.

The idea of sex trafficking has strong foundations in Global North concerns about cross-border migrations by women. This also has roots in the nineteenth century, when the mobility and trade of Western European and North American women's labor and bodies were linked to the emergence on the global stage of migrant women in prostitution (see, for example, Guy 1991), and is coupled to notions of "loose" sexual relations, degraded feminine sexuality, and the immorality of migrant men. Scholars such as Jo Doezema (2010), Ronald Weitzer (2005), and Elizabeth Bernstein (2007b) have written about this as producing a racialized social panic about a "White Slave Trade" that was concerned primarily with what was believed to be the entrapment and enslavement of predominantly white women in prostitution. The panic led to campaigns, laws, and international conventions to abolish the morally defined "social evil" of prostitution through control of women's migration, and in effect, exercised control over women's sexuality and mobility.

The contemporary idea of sex trafficking builds upon these antimigration, antiprostitution legacies and is fully established in the US Trafficking and Victims Protection Act, where sex trafficking is defined as the key severe form of trafficking of persons. As Melissa Ditmore (2005) observes about the negotiations around the initial UN Protocol on human trafficking, a group of feminists fought hard to insert an antiprostitution framework into the international arena; although they were only partially successful at the UN level, they succeeded at the US national level due to the conservative political climate under the Bush administration backed up by a media monopoly, and as Bernstein (2007b) carefully documents, through an unusual, but powerful alliance with the Christian Right. This feminism, then, "helped to transform the campaign against sex trafficking into an official government campaign against prostitution" (Weitzer and Ditmore 2009, p. 327). The criminalization of prostitution in the US legal context is enforced globally through its annual antitrafficking (TIP) reporting system, as well through its international aid and development policies (Ditmore 2005). Countries are ranked by the US State Department according to how well they comply with its notions of human trafficking and antitrafficking, and to avoid economic sanctions, strive to produce evidence to fit the bill (Chuang 2006). This submission of policies and laws around the globe, especially in countries whose economies and trade are heavily dependent upon the US, leads to the adoption of antitrafficking policies that criminalize prostitution and sex sectors, and to a greater alignment with the US TVPA than with the UN Trafficking Protocol.

The sex trafficking discourse underpins end-demand campaigns and claims success in decreasing the incidence of prostitution in countries where new legislation has criminalized the client. It is also the selling point for multiple Hollywood films and TV documentaries and dramas about the harms of the international movement of young women into sex sectors, as well as the basis for many antitrafficking organizations and several UN Goodwill Ambassadors. Moreover, the concept of sex trafficking is integral to notions of "modern slavery" that emerged at the turn of the twenty-first century, constituting in this framework, a severe form of economic exploitation (O'Connell Davidson 2015). In this way, it has given rise to antisex trafficking activities, such as the Somaly Mam Foundation, that have as aims "the eradication of slavery and empowerment of its survivors" (see http://www.somaly.org/), whereby the notions of slavery, human trafficking, and prostitution are collapsed and conflated, and where sex trafficking is defined as sexual slavery. In this way, the sex-trafficked woman comes to represent the epitome of the enslaved victim. Such conflation returns the twenty-first-century discourse to the earlier preoccupation with prostitution as slavery, and as moral and social evil (see Goldman 1969 [1911]).

Sex trafficking and race

The conflation of slavery and trafficking in sex trafficking discourse has been found to elide the significance of blackness in the making of transatlantic slavery, as well as the legacy of that anti-black racism that manifests today in the forms of racialized wage gaps, the millions of black people incarcerated, racial profiling, militarized policing, and enduring poverty in black communities. It obscures, then, the ongoing power relations of slavery (see, for example, Beutin 2017; Brewer Stewart 2015). It has also been noted that the new antislavery and antitrafficking movements appropriate black suffering and trade in "the pornography of pain" in the campaigns through the use of images of suffering of Africans in the past that show manacles, barred windows, half-naked enslaved women, or supplicating victims (Beutin 2017; Brewer Stewart 2015). The appropriations of black suffering in contemporary antitrafficking and antislavery work "have important stakes for how we understand what racial chattel slavery was, the ways in which it continues to structure contemporary culture through its legacies of anti-black racism and oppression, as well as for how we understand what causes trafficking, and thus, what would be effective approaches to ending it" (Beutin 2017, p. 15). Moreover, this kind of focus redirects attention away from understanding and addressing anti-blackness in the present, and it leads to supporting campaigns that often reproduce the racialized and capitalist logics that underpinned transatlantic slavery. At best, this antitrafficking, modern slavery abolitionist work trivializes past histories of the enslavement of black people in the Americas.

Moreover, the discourse can also be read as an expression of a white savior complex – of the "white (wo)man's burden" (Kempadoo 2015) to save the non-Western world from uncivilized practices and cultures, as feeding into the Western "helping imperative" that is more about "feeling good" about Self than about the Other (Heron 2007). Modern slavery abolitionist movements and antitrafficking campaigns are also led predominantly by rich white men and women – philanthrocapitalists and celebrity humanitarians – in Global North countries, especially in Britain, the US, Canada, and Australia (see also Dotteridge 2017). The contemporary modern slavery and trafficking discourses are thus also fundamentally about constructions of whiteness, and white supremacy and are ultimately also about the production of white subjectivity (Durisin 2017). White power and privilege are deeply infused in contemporary antislavery and anti(sex)trafficking campaigns, positioning white women as innocent subjects who will either be the saviors to others or are themselves in need of protection by the state, and non-white men (including those seen as "white but not quite" – i.e. the postsocialist subject) as criminals, such as the procurers, pimps and traffickers. Hypersexualized women – women of color, postsocialist women, lesbians, or prostitutes – are positioned as never really, fully innocent; they are suspect or considered "risky," existing on the border between criminal and victim.

Convergences and Divergences

As the global sex worker rights movement and academic research has complicated understandings of prostitution, sex work, sexual labor, trafficking, and slavery, the transnational legal and political response has largely ignored these analyses and relies heavily on the notion of sex trafficking. The sex trafficking discourse narrowly addresses effects without tackling the underlying factors and causes, or without acknowledging everyday human struggles and strategies designed to overcome exclusions, exploitation and oppressions, or to explore nonnormative sexual relations and subjectivities. It is in favor of a push for a radical transformation of patriarchy, but without the participation of those in sex work.

This global trend has intensified the criminal regulations surrounding sex work and led to increased human rights violations (Amnesty International 2016). Negative social impacts of antitrafficking are being documented worldwide – the so-called collateral damage (GAATW 2007). These include the strengthening of antiprostitution/sex work ideologies; infantilizing rescue missions to save women and girls deemed to be "innocent victims"; greater police surveillance of the sex trade; new antitrafficking legislation that often replicates existing labor, child protection, immigration, and anticrime laws; programs and trainings to identify and catch "traffickers" who are invariably identified as men of the Global East or South; and extensive border controls to prevent "aliens" from entering wealthy areas of the world coupled with a greater number of detentions and deportations of "illegal" migrants. The new legislation for the criminalization and stigmatization of clients of sex workers as well as for the legalization of prostitution has also created new boundaries between sex workers who may work legitimately and publicly and those who cannot. These impacts are felt and documented around the world, and harm many people who live in the margins or who are engaged in undocumented sexual labor, especially racialized migrant women, men, and transgenders.

The discourse has also created a generalized panic about the idea of human trafficking that is causing anxiety especially amongst young women seeking to travel abroad or migrate. Moreover, it ignores the varied sexual-economic arrangements which exist outside of formal sex work arenas, and exerts control over many governments and their populations through such policies as those coming out of the US State Department. Rather than being a vehicle for gender and social justice for sex workers, these legal, policy, and discursive trends also must be understood in relation to their usefulness to states in controlling migration (Gallagher 2001) and the informal labor market, as well as shoring up national identity (Mattson 2016).

In addition, work on antitrafficking and modern slavery discourses link to questions that scholars such as Sylvia Wynter pose about relationships between gender, race, and notions of the human. Scott (2000) for example, notes that today's genre of the human is premised on a specific construction of "Man" that emerged under modernity in conjunction with an economic system predicated on notions of material redemption. This construction of the human, it is argued, centers the Western bourgeois episteme while "dyselecting" those of human Others (see also Wynter 2003; Scott 2000; McKitterick 2015). That the antitrafficking and modern-slavery frameworks neither challenge reigning relations of power around race or gender, nor seek to expand human rights, must signal a politics that maintains the status quo. In this way, the concept of sex trafficking, which is grounded in Western epistemologies and is fundamental to both the human trafficking and modern slavery discourses, operates not only as a form of control and regulation over nonnormative racialized and sexualized subjectivities and bodies, but as a dehumanizing logic. The sex work discourse attempts to counter such control as well as the dehumanization that is foundational to the discourse.

However, this is not to suggest that kidnapping, forced labor, undocumented migration, smuggling, and new forms of indentureship in sex sectors do not exist or are not recognized in the discourse of sex work. On the contrary, social, political, and economic disparities are increasing in the twenty-first century, with larger numbers than ever of people in poverty, underemployment, and extreme vulnerability, with technological advances limiting formal work options around the world. Wars and continued dispossession from the land continue to produce large displaced populations and refugees, who also seek employment and security. Sex work has thus become more relevant to whole families and communities, in formal and informal ways, with tourism and entertainment industries relying increasingly on racialized sexualized labor. An increasing number of scholars are therefore taking up the issue of sexual labor and sex work around the globe, and the sex worker rights movement continues to organize autonomously and to push for recognition, decriminalization, and respect.

Conclusion

The conceptualization of sex work and sex trafficking has produced two distinct discourses, which when examined carefully, appear to stand far apart, mostly in opposition to each other. Nonetheless attempts are being made to bridge some of the divide and to bring the two discourses into conversation through a recognition of both sexual labor and forced labor. For example, sex worker-allied and feminist sex worker-allied organizations – such as the Global Network of Sex Work Projects (NSWP) and Global Alliance Against the Traffic in Women (GAATW) – seek to address harms that sex workers face; they offer ways to think about the violence and harm encountered in sex sectors that do not require the abolition of sex work, but rather call for decent work, safer sex, the nondiscrimination of sexual-economic practices, and social and economic justice for marginalized, vulnerable populations. Besides these two large globally networked organizations, both of which produce their own materials and publications including the open-access journals *Sex Work Research* and the *Anti-Trafficking Review*, networks such as BTS (Beyond Trafficking and Slavery)[4] have also emerged, joined by older established international agencies, such as Amnesty International. Thus, while the separation between the two discourses of sex work and sex trafficking was established at their conceptualization and appears, especially at the legal, political, and ideological levels, fully entrenched globally, shifts and spaces are discernable, especially in wider networks and alliances in this continued critical intersectional analysis. This takes constructions of sexual labor together with contemporary labor and economic relations and the ways in which colonial legacies and white supremacy shape the local and hegemonic notions of desire and human value. Such analysis is needed to destabilize the polarization that has arisen around the concepts of sex work and sex trafficking. A major problem that remains is how to develop a critical discourse about forced labor and sexual violence without referencing the concept of human trafficking.

It is also in the nexus of new spaces and shifts that the topic of young people in sex sectors, particularly those under the age of 18, comes to the fore, for it is here that many of the unresolved tensions between agency and victimization in debates surrounding adult sex work are placed into relief. Like individuals over the age of 18, young people from all parts of the world are not spared economic hardship and have perhaps the fewest options available to them for safe and well-paying work – for many selling or exchanging sex becomes a way to solve the practical problems of meeting material needs. Research indicates that young people deal with a range of complex and contradictory experiences and feelings around selling or exchanging sex, and discourses circulating in international law and policy discussions often do not account for these complexities (NSWP 2016), often couching them in reductive notions of domestic sex trafficking or child sexual abuse (Montgomery 2009; Musto 2016). However, the current approach is resulting in rampant human rights violations through arrest, denial of life-saving harm-reduction commodities and healthcare, and violence at the hands of authorities who are supposed to be offering help and protection; thus researchers and practitioners in the field are beginning to attend to the diverse experiences and needs of young people themselves (NSWP 2016). There is, then, an important move toward more nuanced, youth-centered research and theorizing that addresses difficult matters surrounding young people and sex, as that intersects with persistent (neo)colonialisms, economic survival, violence, desire, and subjectivity (see also Showden and Majic 2018). It is in this very complicated space, coupled with the importance to humanity of empowering its young, that we expect to see a new generation define the debate in the future and push the boundaries well beyond the discourses of both sex trafficking and sex work.

Notes

1 Radical feminism has not, to date, theorized prostitution as work or labor, and hence is not part of this discussion. However, it is reviewed in relation to the concept of sex trafficking.
2 Truong draws, in particular, on Alison Jaggar's 1983 work on feminist frameworks for her thinking about the organization of sexual needs, and on Gayle Rubin's 1975 essay on the traffic of women about the lack of universality in the organization of sexuality.
3 Some writers, such as Durisin, van der Meulen, and Bruckert (2018), avoid the term "abolitionist" when referring to advocates who seek to abolish prostitution, attempting to trouble the linkage in this feminist perspective between the movement to end chattel slavery and that which defines prostitution as sexual slavery. Others, however, self-identify as abolitionists and explicitly connect chattel slavery and sexual slavery.
4 BTS is a network of critical antitrafficking, sex worker-allied scholar/activists. See https://www.opendemocracy.net/beyondslavery.

References

Aggleton, Peter, ed. 1999. *Men Who Sell Sex: International Perspectives on Male Prostitution and HIV/AIDS*. Philadelphia, PA: Temple University Press.

Aggleton, Peter and Richard G. Parker, eds. 2015. *Men Who Sell Sex: Global Perspectives*. New York, NY: Routledge.

Agustín, Laura Maria. 2007. *Sex at the Margins: Migration, Labour Markets and the Rescue Industry*. New York, NY: Zed Books.

Amnesty International. 2016. Amnesty International Policy on State Obligations to Respect, Protect and Fulfil the Human Rights of Sex Workers. POL 30/4062/2016, May 26. Available at: https://www.amnesty.org/en/documents/pol30/4062/2016/en/ (accessed December 10, 2019).

Andrijasevic, Rutvica. 2010. *Migration, Agency and Citizenship in Sex Trafficking*. Basingstoke: Palgrave Macmillan.

Barry, Kathleen. 1981. "Female Sexual Slavery: Understanding the International Dimensions of Women's Oppression." *Human Rights Quarterly* 3(2): 44–52.

Barry, Kathleen. 1984. *Female Sexual Slavery*. New York, NY: New York University Press.

Bell, Shannon. 1994. *Reading, Writing and Rewriting the Prostitute Body*. Bloomington: Indiana University Press.

Bernstein, Elizabeth. 2005. "Regulating Sex – An Introduction." In *Regulating Sex: the Politics of Intimacy and Identity*, edited by Elizabeth Bernstein and Laurie Schaffner, xi–xxiii. New York, NY: Routledge.

Bernstein, Elizabeth. 2007a. *Temporarily Yours: Intimacy, Authenticity, and the Commerce of Sex*. Chicago, IL: University of Chicago Press.

Bernstein, Elizabeth. 2007b. "The Sexual Politics of the 'New Abolitionism.'" *Differences* 18(3): 128–151.

Beutin, Lyndsey P. 2017. "Black Suffering for/from Anti-Trafficking Advocacy." *Anti-Trafficking Review* 9: Special Issue –The Lessons of History.

Bindel, Julie. 2017. *The Pimping of Prostitution: Abolishing the Sex Work Myth*. London: Palgrave MacMillan.

Blanchette, Thaddeus and Laura Murray. 2016. "The Power of Putas: The Brazilian Prostitutes' Movement in Times of Political Reaction." In *Sex Workers Speak: Who Listens?*, edited by P.G. Macioti and Guilia Garofalo Geymonat. Beyond Trafficking and Slavery Series. Available at: https://drive.google.com/file/d/0B2lN4rGTopsaSldZNW4tUzVEUFk/edit.

Boris, Eileen and Rhacel Salazar Parreñas. 2010. *Intimate Labors : Cultures, Technologies, and the Politics of Care*. Stanford, CA: Stanford University Press.

Brewer Stewart, James. 2015. "The 'New Abolitionists' and the Problem of Race." In *On History*, edited by Joel Quirk and Genevieve LeBaron. Beyond Trafficking and Slavery Series. Available at: https://drive.google.com/file/d/0B2lN4rGTopsaZms5dFQ3WlI3WEE/view.

Brock, Deborah. 1998. *Making Work, Making Trouble: The Social Regulation of Sexual Labour*. Toronto: University of Toronto Press.

Brooks, Siobhan. 2010. *Unequal Desires: Race and Erotic Capital in the Stripping Industry*. Albany, NY: State University of New York Press.

Brussa, Licia. 1991. "Survey on Prostitution, Migration and Traffick in Women: History and Current Situation." Strasbourg: European Committee for Equality between Women and Men. Council of Europe.

Cabezas, Amalia Lucía. 2009. *Economies of Desire: Sex and Tourism in Cuba and the Dominican Republic*. Philadelphia, PA: Temple University Press.

Cabezas, Amalia and Ana Alcázar Campos. 2016. "Trafficking Discourse of Dominican Women in Puerto Rico." *Social and Economic Studies* 65(4): 33–56.

CATW. 2011. "*Prostitution is Not 'Sex Work.*'" New York, NY: Coalition Against the Traffic in Women.

Chapkis, Wendy. 1997. *Live Sex Acts: Women Performing Erotic Labor*. New York, NY: Routledge.

Chuang, Janie. 2006. "The United States as Global Sheriff: Using Unilateral Sanctions to Combat Human Trafficking." *Michigan Journal of International Law* (27)2: 437–494.

D'Cunha, Jean. 2011. "Demand for Legitmising of Prostitution in the West: A Critique." In *Sex Work*, edited by Prabha Kotiswaran. 67–93. New Delhi: Women Unlimited.

Davies, John. 2009. "'My Name Is Not Natasha': How Albanian Women in France Use Trafficking to Overcome Social Exclusion (1998–2001)." *IMISCOE dissertation*. Amsterdam University Press.

de Alburquerque, Klaus. 1999. "Male Sex Workers and Female Tourists in the Caribbean." *Journal of Sexuality and Culture* 2.

Delacoste, Frédérique and Priscilla Alexander. 1988. *Sex Work: Writings by Women in the Sex Industry* [in English]. London: Virago.

De Lisio, Amanda. 2017. "How Brazil's Sex Workers have been Organised and Politically Effective for 30 Years." *The Conversation*, December 15. Available at: https://theconversation.com/how-brazils-sex-workers-have-been-organised-and-politically-effective-for-30-years-88903.

Ditmore, Melissa. 2005. "Trafficking in Lives: How Ideology Shapes Policy." In *Trafficking and Prostitution Reconsidered: New Perspectives on Migration, Sex Work and Human Rights*, edited by Kamala Kempadoo. 107–126. Boulder, CO: Paradigm.

Doezema, Jo. 2010. *Sex Slaves and Discourse Masters: The Construction of Trafficking*. London/New York: Zed Books/Palgrave Macmillan.

Dotteridge, Mike. 2017. "Eight Reasons Why We Shouldn't Use the Term 'Modern Slavery.'" In Beyond Trafficking and Slavery: Open Democracy. Available at: https://www.opendemocracy.net/beyondslavery/michael-dottridge/eight-reasons-why-we-shouldn-t-use-term-modern-slavery

Durisin, Elya M. 2017. "*White Slavery Reconfigured: The 'Natasha Trade' and Sexualized Nationalism in Canada.*" PhD dissertation. York University, Canada.

Durisin, Elya M. and Rob Heynen. 2015. "Producing the 'Trafficked Woman': Canadian Newspaper Reporting on Eastern European Exotic Dancers During the 1990s." *Atlantis: Critical Studies in Gender, Culture & Social Justice* 37(2): 8–24.

Durisin, Elya M., Emily van der Meulen, and Chris Bruckert. 2018. *Red Light Labour: Sex Work Regulation, Agency, and Resistance*. Vancouver: UBC Press.

Enloe, Cynthia. 1989. *Bananas, Beaches and Bases: Making Feminist Sense of International Politics*. Berkeley: University of California Press.

GAATW. 2007. *Collateral Damage: The Impact of Anti-Trafficking Measures on Human Rights around the World*. Bangkok: Global Alliance Against Traffic in Women.

Gallagher, Anne. 2001. "Human Rights and the New UN Protocols on Trafficking and Migrant Smuggling: A Preliminary Analysis." *Human Rights Quarterly* 23(4): 975–1004.

Rubin, Gayle. 1975. "The Traffic in Women: Notes on the 'Political Economy' of Sex." In *Toward an Anthropology of Women*, edited by Rayna R. Reiter, 157–210. New York NY: Monthly Review Press.

Goldman, Emma. 1969 [1911]. "The Trafficking in Women." In *Anarchism and Other Essays* edited by Emma Goldman. New York and London: Dover Publications.

Goodyear, Michael and Ronald Weitzer. 2011. "International Trends in the Control of Sexual Services." In *Policing Pleasure: Sex Work, Policy, and the State in Global Perspective*, edited by Susan Dewey and Patty Kelly, 16–30. New York, NY: New York University Press.

Grant, Melissa Gira. 2014. *Playing the Whore: The Work of Sex Work*. London: Verso Books.

Groes-Green, Christian. 2013. "'To Put Men in a Bottle': Eroticism, Kinship, Female Power, and Transactional Sex in Maputo, Mozambique." *American Ethnologist* 40(1): 102–117.

Gülçür, Leyla and Pinar Îlkkaracan. 2002. "The 'Natasha' Experience: Migrant Sex Workersfrom the Former Soviet Union and Eastern Europe in Turkey." *Women's Studies International Forum* 25(4): 411–421.

Guy, Donna J. 1991. *Sex and Danger in Buenos Aires: Prostitution, Family, and Nation in Argentina*. Lincoln: University of Nebraska Press.

Heron, Barbara. 2007. *Desire for Development: Whiteness, Gender and the Helping Imperative*. Waterloo: Wilfred Laurier University Press.

Hochschild, Arlie Russell. 1983. *The Managed Heart : Commercialization of Human Feeling [in English]*. Berkeley, CA: University of California Press.

Hunt, Sarah. 2015. "Representing Colonial Violence: Trafficking, Sex Work, and the Violence of Law." *Atlantis: Critical Studies in Gender, Culture & Social Justice* 37(2): 25–39.

Jaggar, Alison M. 1983. *Feminist Politics and Human Nature*. Totowa, NJ: Rowman & Allanheld.

Jaggar, Alison. 1997. "Contemporary Feminist Perspectives on Prostitution." *Asian Journal of Women's Studies* 3(2): 8–29.

Jeffreys, Sheila. 1997. *The Idea of Prostitution*. Melbourne: Spinifex.

Kang, Miliann. 2010. *The Managed Hand: Race, Gender, and the Body in Beauty Service Work*. Berkeley CA: University of California Press.

Kaye, Julie. 2017. *Responding to Human Trafficking : Dispossession, Colonial Violence, and Resistance among Indigenous and Racialized Women*. Toronto: University of Toronto Press.

Kempadoo, Kamala, ed. 1999. *Sun, Sex, and Gold: Tourism and Sex Work in the Caribbean*. Lanham, MD: Rowman and Littlefield.

Kempadoo, Kamala. 2001. "Women of Color and the Global Sex Trade: Transnational Feminist Perspectives." *Meridians* 1(3): 28–51.

Kempadoo, Kamala. 2004. *Sexing the Caribbean: Gender, Race and Sexual Labor*. New York, NY: Routledge.

Kempadoo, Kamala. 2015. "The Modern-Day White (Wo)Man's Burden: Trends in Anti-Trafficking and Anti-Slavery Campaigns." *Journal of Human Trafficking* 1(1): 8–20.

Kempadoo, Kamala and Jo Doezema, eds. 1998. *Global Sex Workers: Rights, Resistance, and Redefinition*. New York, NY: Routledge.

Koné, Mzilikazi. 2016. "Transnational Sex Worker Organizing in Latin America." *Social and Economic Studies* 65(4): 87–108.

Kotiswaran, Prabha. 2011.*Dangerous Sex, Invisible Labor: Sex Work and the Law in India*. Princeton, NJ: Princeton University Press.

Kulick, Don. 2005. "Four Hundred Thousand Swedish Perverts." *GLQ: A Journal of Lesbian & Gay Studies* 11(2): 205–235.

Leigh, Carol. 1997. "Inventing Sex Work." In *Whores and Other Feminists*, edited by Jill Nagle. 223–232. New York and London: Routledge.

Levy, Jay and Pye Jakobsson. 2014. "Sweden's Abolitionist Discourse and Law: Effects on the Dynamics of Swedish Sex Work and on the Lives of Sweden's Sex Workers." *Criminology & Criminal Justice* 14(5): 593–607.

Lim, Lin Leam, ed. 1998. *The Sex Sector: The Economic and Social Bases of Prostitution in Southeast Asia*. Geneva: International Labour Office.

Longo, Paolo Henrique. 1998. "The Pegação Program: Information, Prevention and Empowerment of Young Male Sex Workers in Rio De Janeiro, Brazil." In *Global Sex Workers: Rights. Resistance and Redefinition*, edited by Kamala Kempadoo and Jo Doezema, 231–239. New York, NY: Routledge.

Lowman, John. 2000. "Violence and the Outlaw Status of (Street) Prostitution in Canada." *Violence Against Women* 6(9): 987–1011.

Mai, Nicola. 2012. "The Fractal Queerness of Non-heteronormative Migrants Working in the UK Sex Industry." *Sexualities* 15(5–6): 570–585.

Mattson, Gregor. 2016. *The Cultural Politics of European Prostitution Reform: Governing Loose Women*. New York, NY: Palgrave Macmillan.

Maynard, Robyn. 2017. *Policing Black Lives: State Violence in Canada from Slavery to the Present [in English]*. Halifax and Winnepeg: Fernwood Publishing.

McKitterick, Katherine, ed. 2015. *Sylvia Wynter: On Being Human as Praxis*. Durham, NC: Duke University Press.

Mies, Maria. 1986. *Patriarchy and Accumulation on a World Scale* London: Zed Books.

Miller-Young, Mireille. 2014. *A Taste for Brown Sugar : Black Women in Pornography*. Durham, NC: Duke University Press.

Mitchell, Gregory. 2011. "Organizational Challenges Facing Make Sex Workers in Brazil's Tourist Zones." In *Policing Pleasure: Sex Work, Policy, and the State in Global Perspective*, edited by Susan Dewey and Patty Kelly, 159–171. New York, NY: New York University Press.

Montgomery, Heather. 2009. "Are Child Prostitutes Child Workers? A Case Study." *International Journal of Sociology and Social Policy* 29(3/4): 130–140.

Musto, Jennifer. 2016. *Control and Protect: Collaboration, Carceral Protection, and Domestic Sex Trafficking in the United States*. Berkeley, CA: University of California Press.

NSWP. 2016. "Policy Brief: Young Sex Workers." Global Network of Sex Work Projects. Available at: http://www.nswp.org/sites/nswp.org/files/Policy%20Brief%20Young%20Sex%20Workers%20-%20NSWP%2C%202016.pdf

O'Connell Davidson, Julia. 2015. *Modern Slavery: The Margins of Freedom*. UK: Palgrave McMillan.

Padilla, Mark. 2007. *Caribbean Pleasure Industry : Tourism, Sexuality, and Aids in the Dominican Republic*. Chicago, IL: University of Chicago Press.

Papayanis, Marilyn Adler. 2000. "Sex and the Revanchist City: Zoning out Pornography in New York." *Environment and Planning D: Society and Space* 18(3): 341–353.

Pheterson, Gail, ed. 1989. *A Vindication of the Rights of Whores*. Seattle, WA:Seal Press.

Piscitelli, Adriana. 2007. "Shifting Boundaries: Sex and Money in the North-East of Brazil." *Sexualities* 10(4): 489–500.

Raymond, Janice G. and Donna M. Hughes. 2001. "Sex Trafficking of Women in the United States: International and Domestic Trends." Coalition Against Trafficking in Women.

Sanchez, Lisa E. 2004. "The Global E-rotic Subject, the Ban, and the Prostitute-Free Zone: Sex Work and the Theory of Differential Exclusion." *Environment and Planning D: Society and Space* 22(6): 861–883.

Scott, David. 2000. "The Re-Enchantment of Humanism: An Interview with Sylvia Wynter." *Small Axe: A Caribbean Jorunal of Criticism* 8: 119–207.

Schulman, Sarah. 2013. *The Gentrification of the Mind: Witness to a Lost Imagination*. Berkeley, CA: California University Press.

Seshu, Meena Saraswathi and Laxmi Murthy. 2013. "The Feminist and the Sex Worker." In *The Business of Sex*, edited by Laxmi Murthy and Meena Saraswathi Seshu, 16–44. New Delhi: Zubaan.

Showden, Carisa R. and Samantha Majic. 2018. *Youth Who Trade Sex in the U.S.: Intersectionality, Agency, and Vulnerability*. Philadelphia, PA: Temple University Press.

Slamah, Khartini. 1998. "Transgender Sex Workers." In *Global Sex Workers: Rights, Resistance and Redefinition*, edited by Kamala Kempadoo and Jo Doezema, 210–214. New York, NY: Routledge.

Suchland, Jennifer. 2015. *Economies of Violence: Transnational Feminism, Postsocialism, and the Politics of Sex Trafficking*. Duke University Press.

Truong, Thanh Dam. 1990. *Sex, Money and Morality: The Political Economy of Prostitution and Tourism in South East Asia*. London: Zed Books.

Van der Veen, Marjolein. 2001. "Rethinking Commodification and Prostitution: An Effort at Peacemaking in the Battles over Prostitution." *Rethinking Marxism* 13(2): 30–51.

van der Meulen, Emily, Elya M. Durisin, and Victoria Love, eds. 2013. *Selling Sex: Experience, Advocacy and Research on Sex Work in Canada*. Vancouver/Toronto: UBC Press.

Weitzer, Ronald. 2005. "The Growing Moral Panic over Prostitution and Sex Trafficking." *The Criminologist* 30(5): 1–5.

Weitzer, Ronald and Melissa Ditmore. 2009. "Sex Trafficking: Facts and Fiction." In *Sex for Sale*, edited by Ronald Weitzer, 325–352. New York, NY: Routledge.

Wijers, Marjan and Lin Lap-Chew. 1997. *Trafficking in Women, Forced Labor and Slavery-Like Practices in Marriage, Domestic Labor and Prostitution*. Utrecht: STV.

Williams, Erica Lorraine. 2013. *Sex Tourism in Bahia: Ambiguous Entanglements*. Urbana, Chicago and Springfield: University of Illinois Press.

Wynter, Sylvia. 2003. "Unsettling Coloniality of Being/Power/Truth/Freedom: Towards the Human, after Man, Its Overrepresenation – an Argument." *The New Centennial Review* 3(3): 257–337.

Zatz, Noah D. 1997. "Sex Work/Sex Act: Law, Labor, and Desire in Constructions of Prostitution." *Signs* 22(2): 277–308.

Zelizer, Viviana A. 2005. *The Purchase of Intimacy*. Princeton, NJ: Princeton University Press.

Part VII
Human Rights and Social Justice Movements

23

Sexual Rights and Globalization

SHWETA M. ADUR

Introduction

The contemporary conceptualization of *sexual rights* marks the extension of the human rights framework to issues of sex and sexuality. The Universal Declaration of Human Rights (hereafter UDHR) was adopted by the United Nations General Assembly in 1948 in response to the lives lost during, and the gross brutalities of, World War II. The Declaration outlined a set of 30 rights that all human beings are entitled to on the basis of being born human. These rights were forged on the foundational tenets of universality, inalienability, and indivisibility (for more, see United Nations 1948). The doctrine since has successfully influenced international law, and global and regional institutions across the world, thereby becoming a veritable force in itself. The many changes of the 1980s–1990s – marked by the intensifying forces of globalization, rapid expansion of neoliberal economic systems, shifts in sovereignty of the nation-state, rise of non-governmental organizations (NGOs), and unprecedented flows of global migration – made human rights and its potential for adjudicating justice particularly crucial. Consequently, a number of social justice claims were reframed within a human rights agenda.

The concept of "sexual rights" is relatively recent – the controversial and contentious nature of these rights prevented them from being mainstreamed for a long time. However, in the last couple of decades, especially since the 1990s, the concept has slowly and steadily but visibly seeped into activist, academic, and policy circles around the world. This chapter seeks to provide an overview of the mainstreaming of sexual rights, beginning with its emergence and deployment through global United Nations (hereafter, UN) platforms and concludes with some thoughts on its local ramifications and the obstacles that continue to encumber sexual rights claims in the contemporary world. I mainly review the work that has been done at, by, and through the United Nations for a couple of reasons. Partially because it is important to

---

Companion to Sexuality Studies, First Edition. Edited by Nancy A. Naples.
© 2020 John Wiley & Sons Ltd. Published 2020 by John Wiley & Sons Ltd.

streamline the discussion given the expansive and complex nature of the topic of sexual rights, but predominantly because in this era of globalization, the UN is an agenda-setting organization. Globally, the resolutions made at the UN level become instructive, not only as a barometer to gauge the level of consensus on any issue at the international platform level but also because they come with veritable political weight. The UN's resources and diplomatic ties grant it a reach that no individual organization or nation-state could possibly have. Finally, the sprawling organizational web of the UN bodies allows it to effectively translate global policies into local actions in several places concurrently.

What is New about Sexual Rights?

Rosalind Petchesky (2000b) famously referred to the sexual rights agenda as the latest entrant in the quest for human rights, or the "newest kid on the block." Is it really that new? The answer is yes and no, depending on who you ask. On the one hand, sexuality and its disciplinary power has been prolifically debated, reviewed, and written about (Foucault 1978; Halperin 1989; Rubin 1993 etc.). Halperin (1989, p. 257) suggests that:

> Sex has no history. It is a natural fact, grounded in the functioning of the body, and, as such, it lies outside of history and culture....Unlike sex, sexuality is a cultural production: it represents the appropriation of the human body and of its physiological capacities by an ideological discourse. Sexuality is not a somatic fact; it is a cultural effect.

Thus, the social construction and organization of sexuality is context-driven, dynamic, and ever-shifting. Sometimes cultural shifts are so slow that they are barely discernible, yet at times so rapid that they create noticeable upheavals. During periods of upheaval, intense politicization results in the renegotiation of the mores of sexual and erotic expression and freedom. In the modern era, the consolidation and entrenchment of Victorian morality, through its extensive social, medical, and legal apparatus, restructured erotic and sexual life and its footprint is perceptible even to this day (Rubin 1993; Foucault 1978). Foucault (1978, p. 24) emphasized that "in the eighteenth century, sex became a 'police' matter – in the full and strict sense given the term at the time: not the repression of disorder, but an ordered maximization of collective and individual forces." He contended that when demographic targeting and population control were tied to the political and economic fate of the nation-state "between the state and the individual, sex became an issue, and a public issue no less; a whole web of discourses, special knowledges, analyses, and injunctions settled upon it" (Foucault, 1978, p. 26). State power came to bear upon the regulation of bodies, sex, and sexuality. Sex became subsumed to the utilitarian purpose of procreation. Anti-miscegenation laws reinforced the parameters of partner choice and inheritance. Morality crusades of the time obsessed over chastity, exalted monogamy and virginity (especially for women), and demonized prostitution (in effect, while sex work persisted sex workers were disenfranchised). It deemed sexual interest and freedom as pathological and criminalized homosexuality. Access to birth control, contraceptive education, and abortion was zealously regulated and extreme measures were taken to prevent sexual curiosity and exploration among children. Rubin (1993,p. 4) writes, "to protect the young from premature arousal, parents tied children down at night so they would not touch themselves; doctors excised the clitorises of onanistic little girls." The scrutiny extended to fashion, art, and literature as paintings, manuscripts, and sculptures that were deemed obscene were burnt and expunged in the perceived interest of social morality and public safety. For example, around the same time, Paragraph 175 in the German Penal Code also criminalized sexual activity between men.

The value system – Victorian morality or what Foucault (1978) dubbed bourgeois hypocrisy – stealthily spread to the other parts of the world via colonialism and missionary work on the pretext of a "civilizing mission." Modern-Western binaries of sex, gender, and sexuality replaced and marginalized precolonial sensibilities. For example, in India, the earliest state regulation of prostitution dates back to Contagious Diseases Act of 1860. The British colonial government introduced the Act in an effort to contain rising fears regarding venereal diseases afflicting imperial soldiers stationed there (Lakkimsetti 2014). The law facilitated the arrest of sex workers who could then be detained or forcibly presented to intrusive medical examination. Section 377 was also introduced by the British colonial power in several of its colonies (Gupta 2008). Though Britain has the more successful record in spreading antisodomy laws in the colonies, the French and the Germans did their part as well. Curiously, while France decriminalized consensual homosexual conduct in 1791 it imposed sodomy laws on some French colonies such as Benin, Cameroon, and Senegal Gupta (2008, p6). It is hardly unsurprising, then, that even to this day lesbian, gay, bisexual, and transgender (LGBT) activists around the world continue to wrestle with colonial-era sodomy laws that criminalize same-sex sexuality.

Yet just as the history of sexuality has been a zealous history of suppression, opposition to the repressions have been equally fervent and awe-inspiring. In 1897 Magnus Hirschfeld's Scientific Humanitarian Committee campaigned for the decriminalization of homosexuality even though they were suppressed viciously during the Nazi regime. As Giami (2015, e46) noted, even in 1929 the International League for Sexual Reform made an attempt to legitimize extramarital birth and to provide birth control and necessary information regarding sexual health, and prevention and transmission of sexually transmitted infections (STIs).[1] It even sought to medicalize homosexuality in a bid to protect against criminal prosecutions prevalent at the time. Thus, in this sense, politicization of sex and sexuality is not new. Ideas of sexual liberation and sexual freedom have graced our past whether or not we have recognized it and/or explicitly linked it to the language of rights.

Nevertheless, sexual rights, in its most contemporary globally acknowledged articulation – as a movement for sexual rights in the dynamic post World War II era embedded in the rising importance of a transnational political apparatus, neoliberal economic shifts, and transnational advocacy networks– is definitely new. This explicit connection of sexuality and rights is therefore comparatively recent. The post-World War II articulation of sexual rights is traced to interconnected yet overlapping historical moments. The 1960s and the 1970s saw the upsurge of countercultural anti-establishment movements – the women's movement, LGBT rights movement, Civil Rights movement, student movement, and anticapitalist movement. Sexual revolution was an extension of the revolutionary thinking of the time.

It challenged draconian Victorian attitudes toward sex, sexuality, and intimate relationships as it sought greater autonomy in partner choice and reproductive decision-making, and pushed back against demographic targeting. Though the countercultural movements are largely associated with the US and Western world, they were by no means isolated to the West. Progressive political movements spilled over to other parts of the world even if they appeared due to their own circumstances. These movements socialized a generation of social justice stalwarts whose tireless striving loosened the noose of Victorian/colonial morality. As I demonstrate in the paragraphs below, it is primarily the transnational women's movement and LGBT rights activism that forged the path for the rise of sexual rights in the global arena.

Forging a Path: From "Women's Rights as Human Rights" to "Sexual Rights as Human Rights"

At the UN platform, ancillary references to sex and sexuality entered the human rights discourse in part driven by the development imperative (tied to population control and public health) and partially on account of the growing prominence of the transnational women's movements. At the First International Conference on Human Rights held in Tehran, Iran (1968) the declaration under the section "Human Rights Aspects of Family" explicitly connected the fulfillment of socioeconomic human rights to population control. It said:

> the present rapid rate of population growth in some areas of the world hampers the struggle against hunger and poverty, and in particular reduces the possibilities of rapidly achieving adequate standards of living, including food, clothing, housing, medical care, social security, education and social services, thereby impairing the full realization of human rights.
>
> (A/CONF/32/41, 15; United Nations 1968)

In the same section it expounded "that couples have a basic human right to decide freely and responsibly on the number and spacing of their children and right to adequate education and information in this respect" (A/CONF/32/41, 15; United Nations 1968). Sexual and reproductive health was viewed as a means to an end, i.e. socioeconomic development and the language of sexual rights per se were yet to emerge.

According to Corrêa (1997), it was at the 1994 International Conference on Population and Development (ICPD) in Cairo, Egypt that the term "sexual rights" first appeared in negotiations among representatives of governments UNFPA. 2004). At Cairo, it was declared that universal access to sexual and reproductive health services was a significant development objective and a basic human right. The ICPD Programme of Action adopted at Cairo in 1994 (2004, p. 45) affirmed that having reproductive health implies "that people are able to have a satisfying and safe sex life, the capability to reproduce, and the freedom to decide if, when and how often to do so." The cursory nod to a "satisfying and safe sex life" marked a subversive shift toward delinking sex from the imperative of procreation. It also bravely ventured into the arena of equality in intimate relationships by adding that, "responsible sexual behavior, sensitivity and equity in gender relations .....enhance and promote respectful and harmonious partnerships between men and women (UNFPA 2004, p. 56). Despite the fresh attitude toward sex, sexuality, and gender relations, the declaration was formulated from the standpoint of population control and family planning. Sexual health and reproductive health were conflated. The heterosexual couple and family remained at the center.

The Second World Conference on Human Rights held in Vienna in 1993 witnessed the UN's growing commitment toward girls' and women's rights (even though it was at the behest of fierce feminist transnational and grassroots activism). At the conference, the Declaration on the Elimination of Violence against Women (A/RES/48/104) prioritized the elimination of violence against women in public and private life. The Declaration defined, violence against women as:

> any act of gender-based violence that results in, or is likely to result in, physical, *sexual* [italics, mine] or psychological harm or suffering to women, including threats of such acts, coercion or arbitrary deprivation of liberty, whether occurring in public or in private life.

Sexual violence, unlike before, was named, recognized and squarely described as an impediment to realizing full human rights. The notion of sexual rights – as bodily integrity and freedom from violence – began to crystallize from within this conceptualization. It was noted that violence against women encompasses, but is not limited to

> (a) Physical, sexual and psychological violence occurring in the family, including battering, sexual abuse of female children in the household, dowry-related violence, marital rape, female genital mutilation and other traditional practices harmful to women, non-spousal violence and violence related to exploitation; (b) Physical, sexual and psychological violence occurring within the general community, including rape, sexual abuse, sexual harassment and intimidation at work, in educational institutions and elsewhere, trafficking in women and forced prostitution; (c) Physical, sexual and psychological violence perpetrated or condoned by the State, wherever it occurs. (A/RES/48/104)

While the Cairo conference acknowledged sex for pleasure by subtly delinking sex from procreation, the Vienna conference made the darker side of sex visible – gendered sexual violence in peace and in war, sexual harassment, coercion, and sex for profit. The commitment to *women's rights as human rights* was solidified at the Fourth World Congress on Women in 1995 where the Beijing Platform of Action was announced and declared that, "The human rights of women include their right to have control over and decide freely and responsibly on matters related to their sexuality, including sexual and reproductive health, free of coercion, discrimination and violence" (UN Women 1995). The document emphasized the importance of "informed consent" in the context of decision-making.

Both the Vienna and Beijing conferences have been hailed as a victory for women's rights. They shifted the paradigm by acknowledging women's particular vulnerability, including sexual vulnerability, and consequent subordination in the global patriarchal society. The assiduous work done by transnational women's activist groups had finally paid off. Citing their role, Radhika Coomaraswamy (1999, p. 173) – a former United Nations Special Rapporteur on Violence against Women – noted "it is no secret that certain international women's groups have lobbied governments heavily to place this issue on the international agenda." Yet, despite their avant-garde stance on women's human rights, both conferences continued to be heterosexist in their leanings. It is said that when some countries and the Holy See expressed concern over language in the draft documents referring to sexual orientation, the language was perfunctorily dropped. Close on the heels of the momentum generated by these conferences, the World Health Organization (WHO) – a specialized UN body focused on public health – provided a *working definition* of the sexual rights in 2002 (it was published much later; WHO, n.d.). The working definition noted that sexual rights are an extension of human rights and include the right of all persons, free of coercion, discrimination and violence, to:

1. the highest attainable standard of sexual health, including access to sexual and reproductive health care services;
2. seek, receive and impart information related to sexuality;
3. sexuality education;
4. respect for bodily integrity;
5. choose their partner;
6. decide to be sexually active or not;
7. consensual sexual relations;
8. consensual marriage;
9. decide whether or not, and when, to have children; and
10. pursue a satisfying, safe and pleasurable sexual life.

Even though the working definition established a vast number of rights that indicate an openness toward the choice of partners, consensual sexual relations, etc., it still failed to specifically reference sexual orientation or gender identity (hereafter, SOGI) or intersex categories in its conceptualization. Those rights are only derivative. At most the generalized openness could be used to allude to same-sex partner choice and marriage but it would not be guaranteed. For example, even as there was widespread acceptance of reproductive rights and self-determination, doctors and medical professionals continued to deny lesbians access to reproductive technologies because of their sexual preference.

In 2005, Petchesky called for the broadening of the conceptualization of sexual rights. She noted that what was advanced within the women's rights framework in Cairo, Vienna, and Beijing exclusively privileged women as victims and bearers of sexual rights while – citing evidence from Abu Ghraib, Guantanamo, and the Gujarat Riots – the realities of war and violence consistently depict sexualized torture of male bodies. Despite the limitations, the transnational women's movement acted as a precursor to the articulation of sexual rights. Cementing the influence of women's rights advocacy on transnational activism for LGBT rights, Thoreson (2014, p. 191) argues that the "spaces opened by women's movements provided opportunities to articulate inclusive understandings of rights, and encouraged brokers to connect claims under the sexual rights rubric."

LGBT Activism and SOGI Rights on the Global Stage

While same-sex sexuality and behavior has existed in recorded history, the creation of an identity and its subsequent politicization is a more recent phenomenon. The normalization of heterosexuality led to the consequent condemnation of homosexual behavior and its criminalization (Foucault 1978; D'Emilio 1993) which, in turn, was diffused through European imperialist interests in reorganizing gender and sexuality in non-European societies (Altman 2002; Gupta 2008). Many years later, the conduit would reemerge with the making of an international gay and lesbian movement.

The emergence of the homosexual identity in the Western industrialized countries is credited to the contingencies of capitalism and wage labor. Once the primary site of production was relocated from the rural heterosexual nuclear family to urban factories, it allowed people freedom to embark on sexual exploration far from the prying gaze of the family and community (D'Emilio 1993; Rubin 1993). After World War I, small politicized homosexual groups formed in major cities even though many were disbanded due to Nazi reprisals. Later, the end of World War II witnessed a reappearance of same-sex groups such as the Shakespeare Club in the Netherlands, Arcadie in France, and the Mattachine Society and the Daughters of Bilitis in the US. Though groups remained largely covert, in the 1960s the countercultural movements provided a space and opportunity structure for public mobilization. The gay movement in the West emerged from this space of contention. In the 1970s, sexuality became an "important arena for the production of modernity and 'gay' and 'lesbian' identities acted as markers for modernity" (Atlman 2002, p. 419). Processes of globalization, especially the growth of computer- mediated communications, ensured that gay and lesbian identities and liberation groups sprouted in different parts of the world.

In addition, the AIDS pandemic of the 1980s had a paradoxical bearing on the gay rights movement. On the one hand, the epidemic was a setback as deceptive and politically manipulated messages were circulated to demonize gays and blame the public health crisis on the gay lifestyle. For example, AIDS in its initial phase was even called Gay Related Immune Deficiency (GRID). This misconception wasn't discarded until much later when public health officials grappled with rapid rates of transmission in heterosexual population. Still, on the other hand, the crisis led to the rise of homosexual organizing in a number of developing countries (Altman 2002, p. 421) and the reinjection of funding and resources into research on sexuality (Parker 2001). For example, groups such as Pink Triangle (Malaysia) and Triangulo Rosa (Costa Rica) emerged as de facto homosexual organizations directly on account of the pandemic. AIDs research also captured these shifts. In its initial phase the research was directed at biomedical interventions geared toward examining individual behaviors of gay men's lifestyle in Western industrialized countries. But by the 1990s, as developing parts of the world registered unabated rates of transmission, there was "growing interest in understanding the role of gender and sexuality structures in promoting HIV vulnerability, particularly among heterosexually active women and men" (Parker 2001 p. 170). These years saw the rise of cultural, anthropological, and ethnographic studies that were attentive to both cultural and political economic factors. The popularity of the methods of participatory interventions in public health circles, likewise required the cooperation of previously stigmatized populations such homosexuals and sex workers. Based on her research on sex workers in India, Lakkimsetti (2014, p. 202) found that the AIDS pandemic compelled a shift in official attitudes as "the state's need to bring sex workers into these projects transformed their relationship with the state and allowed sex workers to make effective claims of the state." She noted that similar trends had been observable in other parts of the world such as Thailand, the Philippines, and Senegal. Comparable shifts in queer claims on the state were observable in other parts of the world as "sexual citizenship"[2] became a prism through which belonging was contested and rights were claimed.

Just as it was the case with the feminist movement, grassroots organizing and transnational advocacy networks were largely responsible for a number of progressive statutes and declarations. The "Yogyakarta Principles on the Application of International Human Rights Law in relation to Sexual Orientation and Gender Identity(2007)" (hereafter, the Yogyakarta Principles) was a similar win as it extended the human rights standards to protect LGBTI populations from abuse, inequality, discrimination, violence, and unequal representation encompassing arenas political, social, and economic life. The preamble of the Yogyakarta Principles noted that:

> respect for sexual rights, sexual orientation and gender identity is integral to the realization of equality between men and women and that States must take measures to seek to eliminate prejudices and customs based on the idea of the inferiority or the superiority of one sex or on stereotyped roles for men and women, and noting further that the international community has recognized the right of persons to decide freely and responsibly on matters related to their sexuality, including sexual and reproductive health, free from coercion, discrimination, and violence. ...The policing of sexuality remains a major force behind continuing gender-based violence and gender inequality.
> (2007, p. 6)

The Yogyakarta Principles were also instructive about a hitherto neglected question of queer migration and asylum, both of key importance to LGBTI mobility. Principles 22 and 23 reaffirmed freedom of movement. While Principle 22 proclaimed that "sexual orientation and gender identity may never be invoked to limit or impede a person's entry, egress or return to or from any State, including that person's own State," Principle 23 vouched for the "Right to seek asylum." This made it incumbent upon the states not only to recognize SOGI as ground for refugee and asylum status but also to ensure that such policies do not discriminate in terms of SOGI and that queer refugees and asylum-seekers are not returned to states where they have a well-founded fear of persecution.

Moving beyond the mere statement of intentions and policy directives, the United Nations High Commissioner for Human Rights conducted a fact-finding mission. The findings presented at the Human Rights Council reiterated the gross human rights violations endured by LGBTI communities across the world and the sheer urgency for protecting queer lives. The report (A/HRC/19/41, United Nations 2011.) demonstrated the high rates of violence, everyday forms as well as state-sponsored, that mar all aspects of queer lives. For example, it was reported that more than 76 countries around the world still have sodomy laws criminalizing consensual, adult same-sex sexual relations and in at least five there were provisions for the death penalty. It found that only a small group of countries grant asylum on SOGI criteria and, among those, many fall short of acceptable standards. Furthermore, irregular and inconsistent review of applications, mandatory detention in facilities where violence – physical, mental, and sexual – is rampant, forcible return to countries with the advice to remain "discreet" to avoid persecution were not uncommon (A/HRC/19/41, p. 13, United Nations 2011). In a widely publicized case, Aderonke Apata – an LGBT rights activists from Nigeria and an asylum petitioner in UK, was told by the barrister Andrew Bird that "You can't be heterosexual one day and a lesbian the next day, just as you can't change your race." The barrister's erroneous comprehension of sexuality and assertion was based on the fact that Apata had been in a heterosexual relationship in the past and had had children. Bird chose that fact over copious other evidence – 30,000 signatures from British public supporting her claim, submission of explicit video footage and photographs of Apata and her lesbian partner (Bennett 2015). The case shows that sexual identity is not only hard to prove but often the evidence can easily be rejected.

In 2013, the Office of the United Nations High Commissioner for Human Rights (OHCHR) launched UN Free & Equal, a global campaign designed to promote equal rights and fair treatment of LGBTI people. In addition to affirming same-sex relationships, the campaign recognized the violence experienced by transgender communities deprived of legal recognition as well as the medically unnecessary procedures on intersex children.

In July 2016, in a follow-up to the resolutions in 2011 and 2014, the United Nations adopted a resolution for the appointment of an independent expert whose mandate was to monitor and evaluate the implementation of international human rights law in protection of sexual orientation and gender identity (SOGI; Human Rights Watch, 2016).

Thus, both women's and LGBTI movements have argued that the binary renditions of sex and gender, patriarchal norms as well as the idealization of "toxic masculinity"[3] contribute to rampant sexual rights violations around the world. These movements coalesced to produce the present-day understanding of sexual rights. Thus, sexual rights range from those geared toward sexual and reproductive health, against discrimination, and for protection from gender-based violence to the celebration of sexual privacy, pleasure, and the honoring of bodily integrity. Consequently, the quest for equitable sexual rights morphs into various issues that include, yet are not limited to, age of consent, access to comprehensive sex education, contraception, safe and legal abortion, reproductive healthcare, and education to prevent and manage STIs/STDs. Prevention of sexual coercion, rape, sexual harassment, female genital cutting, crimes of honor, street harassment, rape, and other forms of gender-based violence are all deemed violations of sexual rights. More recently, these rights have expanded to include gender and sexual identity, bodily integrity, and expression and orientation, i.e. LGBTI and sexual minorities' rights.

Sexual Rights: Achievements, Aspirations, and the Way Forward

On the global platform, then, these concerted moves confirm that sexuality is politicized and politics is sexualized. The linguistic framing of sexual rights as human rights meant that sexual rights were now protected by a number of conventions, treaties, and documents that are extensions of the UDHR. As a result, it is not only incumbent upon governments to protect their subjects from human rights violations but also to remain accountable and open to transnational monitoring, evaluation, and adjudication. While these shifts have been critical in establishing the salience of sexuality and sexual rights on the world stage, this has not been accomplished without intense contentions and paradoxes. Some of these issues, which I describe in the paragraphs below, relate to (i) the definitional quagmire that makes the implementation of sexual rights problematic, (ii) the problem with Western hegemony and the role of transnational justice networks, and (iii) when rights collide with culture, religion, and tradition.

The definitional quagmire

The definition of sexual rights remains contentious, thus making its implementation problematic not only because it is new but also because of how radical it is and how expansively its reach was envisioned. For example, while the WHO's working definition of sexual rights is widely accepted and quoted, the organization acknowledges the definition's limitation with an unequivocal disclaimer noting that the definitions are "a contribution to ongoing discussions about sexual health, but do not represent an official WHO position, and should not be used or quoted as WHO definitions." As evident, subsuming sexual rights to "ongoing discussions of sexual health" creates problems of its own as scholars continue to debate the pros and cons of merging sexual health and rights with reproductive choice and health (Corrêa 1997). Miller (2001) writes, "'Health' cannot be presumed to be a benign site for sexuality – especially homosexuality," given the history whereby medicalized talk has been used to persecute homosexuality and the fact that the medical community continues to have a complicated relationship with transsexuality (Miller 2001) and intersexuality (Davis 2015). The problem even extends to the conceptualization of SOGI in the Yogkyakarta Principles. Waites (2009) illustrates that the current rendition of SOGI in Yogyakarta Principles leans toward fixity and threatens to marginalize asexual, bisexual, and transgender populations. The definitional quagmire thickens further given sexual life is deeply embedded in sexual contexts which are essentially diverse across the world and, therefore, imposing a strict standardized definition onto diverse local contexts is not without tensions (Altman 2002). This extends to issues that are non-SOGI related as well. For example, what constitutes the legal age of consent varies not only across countries but within states in a particular country and is enforced even more irregularly. Marital rape, yet another example, is not criminalized in many parts of the world and even where there is a blanket criminalization, prosecution is rare.

Transnational justice networks and Western exceptionalism

In this era of globalization, on the one hand transnational justice networks and NGOs have proven indispensable in the struggle for sexual rights (Keck and Sikkink 1998); on the other hand, Petchesky (2000a) warns that "NGO activism may become merely another link in the chain of privatization that further weakens state power, and thus dilutes state responsibility, in the era of globalization." More importantly, transnational justice networks are known to have been mediated by differences of power that privilege the North/Euro-American groups (for more, see Thoreson 2014; Merry 2006, Naples 2002). According to Massad (2002), the "Gay International" – which includes the Western (US and European) human rights organizations, Western gay rights activists, feminist organizations and publications, and NGOs – is but another form of Western imperialism that reinforces the indigenes' civilizational inferiority. Furthermore, a West-centric and universalizing discourse ignores the diversity and particularity of human experience across race, class, nationality, religion etc. For instance, the idea that homosexuality is a 'Western vice' or feminism is Western is often found in developing countries (however debatably misleading and ahistorical the notion is) and if one is not cautious in their maneuverings, even well-intentioned support may fail. Altman and Beyrer (2014, p. 1) demonstrate this by pointing out that:

> indignation and even threats to cut development assistance from donors too often backfire. When David Cameron, the British Prime Minister, mooted withdrawing aid from African countries because of their anti-homosexual policies, gay groups in those countries rightly pointed to the fact this was likely to increase persecution and the perception that they were, indeed, a foreign import.

These concerns with the discrepancies in power between the North and South or West and non-West indeed call for caution to be exercised.

Important alternatives, located in and inspired by queer, feminist, and postcolonial frameworks, have been proposed to move past the archaic notion of Western sexual exceptionalism. These interventions note, that culture is contentious and the battle for (sexual) rights is nonlinear, uneven, and irregular around the world (Merry 2006). For example, in less than a year after India had recriminalized Section 377 (its antisodomy law from British colonial era) it made exemplary strides toward recognizing and institutionalizing rights for the third-gender community. In 2014, the Supreme Court of India mandated reservation in education and jobs and provided exhaustive protections (Writ Petition (Civil) No.400 Of 2012). The judgment referenced the UDHR, various human rights treaty bodies, the Yogyakarta Principles, and the Constitution of India. Justice K.S. Radhakrishnan, added that the "recognition of transgender as third gender is not a social or medical issue but a human rights issue". It took the Supreme Court of India another 4 years to finally decriminalize Section 377. Pakistan has similar protections for "eunuchs" yet continues to wrestle with Section 377 – an archaic colonial vestige. On the other hand, while the US recognizes same-sex marriage and has institutionalized a host of protection and non-discrimination laws, it still lags behind when it comes to transgender and intersex rights. And while Iran has a terrible record when it comes to persecuting gays, Ayatollah Khomeini issued a fatwa allowing sexual reassignment surgery (SRS) way back in 1987. However problematically, the government recognizes only transgender populations who have undergone SRS; the law fails those who do not opt for SRS (Ansari 2017). The conception that the West is essentially at the forefront of sexual rights is not only erroneous and divisive but this arrogance leaves many of its own failures uninterrogated and stymies progress. For example, while about 99% of maternal mortality occurs in developing countries, the US has one of the fastest growing rates of maternal mortality and morbidity among Western industrialized nations. Again, though the scourge of child marriage is attributed to the poor non-Western nations of Latin America, Asia, and Africa, several of US states permit marriage before the age of 18 under some circumstances. According to Human Rights Watch, between 2001 and 2010 around 3,850 children under the age of 18 married in the state of New York (Human Rights Watch 2014).

Collision of rights with culture and tradition

The Human Rights framework has often been viewed as a modern-Western import, professing liberal individualism that is antithetical to traditional cultures. Progress on women's rights and sexual rights has too often been challenged in the name of family, culture, tradition, and religion. In a letter articulating objections to the Cairo Conference of 1994, the Holy See exemplifies the stance:

> The idea of sexuality underlying this text is totally *individualistic* [italics mine], to such an extent that marriage now appears as something outmoded. An institution as natural, fundamental and universal as the family cannot be manipulated by anyone.... Indeed, reading this document – which, granted, is only a draft – leaves the troubling impression of something being imposed: *namely a lifestyle typical of certain fringes within developed societies, societies which are materially rich and secularized* [italics mine].
>
> (The Vatican 1994)

The resurgence of conservative, reactionary, and extremist movements around the world is particularly troubling for sexual rights (Petchesky 2005; Imam 2011). In 2016, Xulhaz Mannan and Mahbub Rabbi Tonoy were hacked to death by extremists for promoting LGBT rights in Bangladesh (Ta* 2017). Scholars have attributed a variety of causes to the rise of extremism such as geopolitical tensions, socioeconomic uncertainties, neoliberal policies, and government corruption but there is resounding consensus that each time a nation/society takes a turn to the right, it has led to the reversal of women's rights and sexual rights. Interestingly, in this era of globalization, extremist values are also exported by those with the wherewithal: a conservative Indian diaspora is culpable in its support of Hindutva; and Kaoma (2013) describes the role played by American anti-LGBTQ evangelical conservatives, particularly Scott Lively, in exporting homophobia to Uganda.

But even in secular circles, sexual rights have been under siege. The extension of human rights to include SOGI rights has been the particularly divisive. Thoreson writes:

> Skeptics routinely cite LGBT rights to illustrate how absurd or unprincipled the human rights discourse has become....the seeming specificity of SOGI has fostered the belief that LGBT persons demand "special rights" or "new rights," framings that have proven persuasive in debates in the North and the South alike. By implication, the rhetoric of new or special rights contrasts LGBT rights with universal human rights, making it seem selfish or trivial for advocates to spend time, energy, and resources securing them.
>
> (2014, p. 93)

Nevertheless, scholars, activists and practitioners have been vocal in pushing back against the rhetoric that human rights, especially for women and sexual minorities, contradict cultural values and tradition (Coomaraswamy 1999; Imam 2011; Erturk 2007). They note that neither tradition nor culture or religion are immutable, they have been interpreted to endorse a culture that privileges heterosexual masculinity at the expense of sexual rights of women and sexual minorities, and hence they can be reinterpreted. The former UN Secretary-General Ban Ki-moon has reiterated the stance by saying "let there be no confusion, where there is tension between cultural attitudes and rights, rights must carry the day" (UN News Center 2010).

Conclusion

The foregoing paragraphs provide a concise and incisive review of sexual rights as envisioned and institutionalized by the United Nations. The chapter begins with the disclaimer that the politicization of sexuality is not new yet the contemporary strategic linguistic framing of sexual rights as human rights has many advantages. This is the first time in history that sexual rights have come with the political backing of the Universal Declaration of Human Rights and the United Nations, a fact that demonstrates the aspirational move toward progressive values. Yet despite obvious strategic gains, the battle for sexual rights is far from over. Definitional inconsistencies, problems with implementation, Western hegemony, pushback in the name of tradition and culture, and the rise of extremist movements continue to hold it hostage.

Now more than ever it is necessary to remain vigilant so the hard-fought gains aren't lost, because while it may have taken years to achieve a semblance of these rights, they can be hijacked in a flash.

Notes

1. Though pathbreaking at the time, many of provisions of the declaration are rather conservatively redundant for contemporary sensibilities on sexual rights. For example, the medicalization model of homosexuality, which was proposed as alternative to the criminalization model, nevertheless pathologized same-sex sexuality as a deviance. The American Psychological Association removed homosexuality from its list of mental disorders in 1973: the World Health Organization removed it from the list of diseases in 1991.
2. The concept of sexual citizenship demonstrates the influence of a person's sexuality on their level of belonging and inclusion in a society. The more conventional understanding limits itself to analyzing the state's role in granting or denying sexual right but Bernstein and Naples (2010, p. 134) call for a more expansive definition wherein state is "one institution among many (albeit a very important institution) that is itself fused with notions of heteronormativity and linked to various other institutions."
3. Toxic masculinity refers to the notion of masculinity that narrowly ascribes manliness to heterosexuality, aggression, violence and hypersexuality. Feminine traits such as emotional vulnerability are denigrated as unmanly.

References

Altman, Dennis. 2002. "Globalization and the International Gay/Lesbian Movement." In *Handbook of Lesbian and Gay Studies*, edited by Diane Richardson and Steven Seidman, 415–424. Thousand Oaks, CA: Sage.

Altman, Dennis and Chris Beyrer. 2014. "The Global Battle for Sexual Rights." *Journal of the International AIDS Society* 17(1): 19243.

Ansari, Azadeh. 2017. "Transgender Rights: These Countries are Ahead of the US." *CNN News*, February 23. Available at: http://www.cnn.com/2017/02/23/health/transgender-laws-around-the-world/index.html.

Bennett, Claire. 2015. "U.K. Authorities Routinely Humiliate LGBT Asylum Seekers." *Slate*, March 5. Available at: http://www.slate.com/blogs/outward/2015/03/05/lgbt_asylum_seekers_in_the_u_k_are_routinely_humiliated.html (accessed November 14, 2018).

Bernstein, Mary and Nancy Naples. 2010. "Sexual Citizenship and the Pursuit of Relationship-Recognition Policies in Australia and the United States." *Women's Studies Quarterly* 38(1): 132–156.

Coomaraswamy, Radhika. 1999. "Reinventing International Law – Women's Rights as Human Rights in the International Community." In *Debating Human Rights: Critical Essays for United States and Asia*, edited by Peter Van Ness, 167–183. New York, NY: Routledge.

Corrêa, S. 1997. "From Reproductive Health to Sexual Rights Achievements and Future Challenges." *Reproductive Health Matters* 5(10): 107–116.

D'Emilio. John.1993. "Capitalism and Gay Identity." In *The Lesbian and Gay Studies Reader*, edited by Henry Abelove, Michele Aina Barale, and David M. Halperin, 467–476. New York, NY: Routledge.

Davis, Georgiann. 2015. *Contesting Intersex: The Dubious Diagnosis*. New York, NY: New York University Press.

Erturk, Yakin. 2007. "Intersections between Culture and Violence against Women." Report of the Special Rapporteur on Violence against Women – Its Causes and Consequences. Available at: http://www.refworld.org/pdfid/461e2c602.pdf (accessed September 2014).

Foucault, Michel. 1978. *The History of Sexuality, vol. 1, An Introduction*, translated by Robert Hurley. London: Allen Lane

Giami, A. 2015. "Sexuality, Health and Human Rights: The Invention of Sexual Rights." *Sexologies* 24(3): E45–E53.

Gupta, Alok. 2008. "This Alien Legacy: The Origins of 'Sodomy' Laws in British Colonialism." *Human Rights Watch Report*. Available at: https://www.hrw.org/sites/default/files/reports/lgbt1208_webwcover.pdf.

Halperin, David. 1989. "Is There a History of Sexuality?" *History and Theory* 28(3): 257–274.

Human Rights Watch. 2014. "US: In New York, Children as Young as 14 Can Marry End Child Marriage in New York State" Available at: https://www.hrw.org/news/2017/02/14/us-new-york-children-young-14-can-marry.

Human Rights Watch. 2016. "UN Makes History on Sexual Orientation, Gender Identity Human Rights Body Establishes an Independent Expert." Available at: https://www.hrw.org/news/2016/06/30/un-makes-history-sexual-orientation-gender-identity (accessed November 13, 2018).

Imam, Ayesha. 2011. "Women, Muslim Laws and Human Rights in Nigeria." Occasional Papers, Woodrow Wilson Center. Available at: https://www.wilsoncenter.org/publication/women-muslim-laws-and-human-rights-nigeria (accessed July 17, 2017).

Kaoma, Kapya J. 2013. The Marriage of Convenience: The U.S. Christian Right, African Christianity, and Postcolonial Politics of Sexual Identity. In *Global Homophobia: States, Movements, and the Politics of Oppression*, edited by Meredith L.Weiss and Michael J. Bosia, 75–102 Champaign: University of Illinois Press.

Keck, Margaret E. and Kathryn Sikkink. 1998. *Activists Beyond Borders: Advocacy Networks in International Politics*. Ithaca, NY: Cornell University Press.

Lakkimsetti, Chaitanaya. 2014. "'HIV is Our Friend': Prostitution, Biopower, and the State in Postcolonial India." *Signs* 40(1): 201–226.

Massad, Joseph. 2002. "Re-Orienting Desire: The Gay International and the Arab World." *Public Culture* 14(2): 361–386.

Merry, Sally Engel. 2006. *Human Rights and Gender Violence: Translating International Law into Local Justice*. Chicago, IL: The University of Chicago Press.

Miller, A.M. 2001. "Uneasy Promises: Sexuality, Health, and Human Rights." *American Journal of Public Health* 91(6): 861–864.

Naples, Nancy. 2002. "Changing the Terms: Community Activism, Globalization and the Dilemmas of Transnational Feminist Praxis." In *Women's Activism and Globalization: Linking Local Struggles and Transnational Politics*, edited by Nancy Naples and Manisha Desai, 1–14. New York, NY: Routledge.

Parker, R. 2001. "Sexuality, Culture, and Power in HIV/AIDS Research." *Annual Review of Anthropology* 30(1): 163–179.

Petchesky, Rosalind. P. 2000a. "Reproductive and Sexual Rights: Charting the Course of Transnational Women's NGOs." Occasional Paper No. 8. Geneva: United Nations Research Institute for Social Development (UNRISD).

Petchesky, Rosalind. 2000b. "Sexual Rights: Inventing a Concept. Mapping an International Practice." In *Framing the Sexual Subject: The Politics of Gender, Sexuality and Power*, edited by Richard Parker, Regina Maria Barbosa, and Peter Aggleton, 81–103. Berkeley, CA: University of California Press.

Petchesky, Rosalind P. 2005. "Rights of the Body and Perversions of War: Sexual Rights and Wrongs Ten Years past Beijing." *International Social Science Journal* 57(2): 301–318.

Rubin, Gayle. 1993. "Thinking Sex: Notes for a Radical Theory of the Politics of Sexuality." In *The Lesbian and Gay Studies Reader*, edited by Henry Abelove, Michael Aina Barale, and David M. Halperin, 3–44. New York, NY: Routledge.

Ta*. 2017. "One Year after the Murders of Xulhaz Mannan and Mahbub Rabbi Tonoy." *Amnesty International*, April 25. Available at: https://www.amnesty.org/en/latest/news/2017/04/one-year-after-the-murders-of-xulhaz-mannan-and-mahbub-rabbi-tonoy/ (accessed November 12, 2018).

The Vatican. 1994. "Letter of His Holiness John Paul II to the Secretary General of the International Conference on Population and Development," March 18. Available at: https://w2.vatican.va/content/john-paul-ii/en/letters/1994/documents/hf_jp-ii_let_19940318_cairo-population-sadik.html (accessed November 14, 2018).

Thoreson, Ryan. R. 2014. *Transnational LGBT Activism: Working for Sexual Rights Worldwide*. Minneapolis: University of Minnesota Press.

UN News Center. 2010. "Universal Decriminalization of Homosexuality a Human Rights Imperative – Ban." *UN News*, December 10. Available at: http://www.un.org/apps/news/story.asp?NewsID=37026#.WWv199PyvOR (accessed November 12, 2018).

UN Women. 1995. "Beijing Platform of Action." Available at: http://www.un.org/womenwatch/daw/beijing/pdf/BDPfA%20E.pdf (accessed November 17, 2018).

UNFPA. 2004. "ICPD Programme of Action adopted at the International Conference on Population and Development, Cairo 5–13 September, 1994." Available at: https://www.unfpa.org/sites/default/files/event-pdf/PoA_en.pdf (accessed November 13, 2018).

United Nations. 1948. "Universal- Declaration of Human Rights." United Nations. Available at: http://www.un.org/en/universal-declaration-human-rights/

United Nations. 1968. "Final Act of the International Conference on Human Rights. Tehran, 22 April to 13 May 1968." Available at: http://legal.un.org/avl/pdf/ha/fatchr/Final_Act_of_TehranConf.pdf (accessed November 13, 2018).

United Nations. 1993. A/RES/48/104. 1993. "Declaration on the Elimination of Violence against Women". Available at: https://www.un.org/en/genocideprevention/documents/atrocity-crimes/Doc.21_declaration%20elimination%20vaw.pdf.

United Nations. 2011. A/HRC/19/41. "Discriminatory Laws and Practices and Acts of Violence against Individuals Based on their Sexual Orientation and Gender Identity." United Nations High Commissioner for Human Rights (UNHCHR). Available at: http://www2.ohchr.org/english/bodies/hrcouncil/docs/19session/A.HRC.19.41_English.pdf (accessed July 14, 2018).

Waites, M. 2009. "Critique of 'Sexual Orientation' and 'Gender Identity' in Human Rights Discourse: Global Queer Politics beyond the Yogyakarta Principles." *Contemporary Politics* 15(1): 137–156.

World Health Organization. n.d. "Sexual and Reproductive Health." Available at: http://www.who.int/reproductivehealth/topics/sexual_health/sh_definitions/en/ (accessed November 13, 2018).

Yogyakarta Principles. 2007. "Yogyakarta Principles on the Application of International Human Rights Law in relation to Sexual Orientation and Gender Identity." Available at: https://yogyakartaprinciples.org/introduction/.

24

The Global LGBT Workplace Equality Movement

APOORVA GHOSH

Introduction

The post-Stonewall era has raised expectations for sexual rights and institutional opportunities for lesbian, gay, bisexual, and transgender (LGBT) identified persons. In the workplace, these expectations have driven the struggle for equality and the inclusion of LGBT employees. The resulting activism has challenged both heteronormative culture and employment policies (Creed and Scully 2000; Raeburn 2004; Briscoe and Safford 2008; King and Pearce 2010; Ghosh 2012). The struggle for equality in the workplace has evolved into a branch of the LGBT social movement known as the Global LGBT workplace equality movement.[1] This chapter contends that to be truly global in nature, this movement must encompass and embrace sociopolitical, cultural, and economic idiosyncrasies across the world to produce an inclusive model that allows organizations and activists to pursue location-specific goals using the strategies that best suit their local contexts.

Urvashi Vaid has laid out three contextual factors of the Global LGBT workplace equality movement.[2] According to her framework, the issue of LGBT freedom and equality at work is both legal and cultural in nature. To gain respect and equality for the LGBT community, LGBT activists must work toward making employment policies inclusive, but they must also challenge the "moral condemnation" that marginalizes LGBT persons at work. From a sociological perspective, this view draws on the New Social Movement, which argues that social movements often aspire for instrumental and expressive goals (Armstrong and Bernstein 2008). Instrumental goals pertain to tangible outcomes, such as adopting a policy or a set of policies, extending employment benefits, and making structural changes in the organization. Expressive goals, on the other hand, seek to bring cultural changes through affirming and inclusive attitudes toward LGBT persons in the workplace.

LGBT workplace activists pursue instrumental goals – such as nondiscrimination policies and health benefits – not only in the workplace but also at the level of state law. After convincing numerous corporations to enact nondiscrimination policies, US activists are now focusing their energies on the congressional bill for the Employment Non-Discrimination Act (ENDA), which would make sexual orientation and gender identity protected categories in employment across the nation (Giarattana 2015). The goals of LGBT affirmation at work, which activists pursue through programs like "Building Bridges" (begun by the Out & Equal Workplace Advocates), are equally important. Programs like these dispel myths about LGBT persons and the phobias that surround them (Baillie and Gedro 2009).

Although the simultaneous pursuit of instrumental and expressive goals for LGBT employees has worked in the US, it remains to be seen whether this strategy can be extrapolated to other nations. National culture refers to "the set of [shared and widely accepted] norms, behaviors, beliefs, and customs that exist within the population of a sovereign nation" (Lin 2014, p. 369). Is it topical for LGBT workplace activists – as entities nested within their national cultures – to fight for goals situated in, and defined by, the US and the Global North? How might the pursuit of instrumental and expressive goals vary across nations? These questions will be assessed cross-nationally while discussing the goals of the global LGBT workplace equality movement.

Second, a global movement must be inclusive of diverse sexualities, racial categories, ethnicities, and nationalities. The LGBT migrants from the Global South have long felt that "gay" communities in the Global North, especially in the Anglo-Saxon world, have been underrepresentative of people of color and immigrants. According to them, these communities have paid little attention to the unique challenges faced by LGBT people of color in foreign countries. These experiences of exclusion have compelled LGBT migrants to form their own ethnically identified networks and activist organizations (Joseph 1996). The institutional valorization of a homonormative white gay identity also constricts the spaces of activism for nonhomonormative and gender-questioning LGBT persons (Rumens 2016). Social movements hardly succeed when people participating in them are divided. Whether divisions based on cultural differences, race, and ethnicity fragment a movement and preclude sexual, racial, and ethnic unity among movement participants is another topical issue that merits discussion.

And third, the movement must strive to encourage more participation than it currently receives. The proportion of LGBT persons who participate in, or contribute to, any form of LGBT activism is usually low, partially because of the "outing costs" involved – costs that are unique to participating in an LGBT social movement because LGBT identities may be more easily concealed than "visible" identities like race, gender, and ethnicity (McClendon 2014). At work, these costs may outweigh the perceived benefits of participation and may be augmented when the jobs of movement participants are at stake because of the dual stigma associated with engaging in activism and being an LGBT person (Ragins et al. 2007; Taylor and Raeburn 1995). It is important, therefore, to explore ways to offset the costs of participating in the movement. In contrast to the US, where LGBT people are encouraged to "self-identify" and be "authentic" about their sexuality (Mattison and McWhirter 1995), how might LGBT people in cultures that have ambivalent or repressive attitudes toward sexuality (Boyce 2006; Tamale 2007) come forward and participate in this movement?

This chapter examines these three interrelated questions from international and cross-cultural perspectives. The questions might apply to LGBT social movements in general, but through an examination of cases from across the world, I will make the case that considering local cultural contexts is vitally important to the success of the LGBT workplace equality movement.

Cross-National Variations in Goals

The LGBT workplace movement in the Anglo-Saxon world – the English-speaking countries in the Global North, notably the US and the UK – has expended a considerable amount of energy achieving instrumental goals. Such goals have largely focused on nondiscrimination laws (Giarattana 2015) and nondiscrimination employment policies; mechanisms for addressing grievances in the workplace; health benefits for domestic partners; family benefits like bereavement leave, parental leave, and travel benefits (Raeburn 2004; Colgan et al. 2007); and transgender-inclusive restrooms at work (Husemann 2016). Instrumental goals have generally been framed as the "culturally and socially appropriate thing to do" for employers (Briscoe and Gupta 2016, p. 698). Expressive goals have also attracted considerable attention. To make the workplace more inclusive, LGBT employee caucuses or the insider LGBT activists often strive to establish networking groups, mentoring opportunities, and career development programs for LGBT employees. They also foster equality training for managers and senior executives, promote LGBT role models, and encourage acknowledging same-sex partners and spouses at company social gatherings (Bond et al. 2009). Pursuing both kinds of goals may help LGBT employees come to terms with their own sexuality. Training and mentoring programs, in particular, may help them grow into compassionate professionals while navigating the day-to-day joys, excitements, sorrows, opportunities, and challenges related to their sexuality (Gedro 2009).

Pursuing expressive goals may also help in achieving instrumental goals. The LGBT social movement in the US targets multiple institutions. In addition to the state and the workplace, the movement has successfully made numerous church denominations LGBT-inclusive. These denominations provide LGBT persons with a sense of community through religious affiliation (Kane 2013). The Presbyterian Church, United Methodist Church, General Board of Church and Society, Episcopal Church, United Church of Christ, Justice and Witness Ministries, and the Union of Reform Judaism are some of the religious congregations that explicitly affirm LGBT persons. The affirmation of these denominations has formed part of the basis for the US federal government's decision that its contractors, too, must provide employment protection to their LGBT employees. President Obama added sexual orientation and gender identity as protected categories in Executive Order 11246, which mandated that federal contractors become Equal Opportunity employers. In a press release issued on July 21, 2014, the White House cited affirmation from religious denominations as one of the reasons that the administration took this step (The White House 2014).

The LGBT workplace equality movement organizations in the US have often pursued expressive goals in corporations. The Building Bridges program, formed by Out & Equal workplace advocates in 1990, is one example. This program helped employers in the San Francisco Bay Area understand LGBT diversity during the formative period of LGBT workplace activism. Out & Equal also developed a climate survey tool to measure attitudes toward LGBT employees in organizations. A group formed in 1995, known as Progress, was established to provide leadership resources and training to LGBT employee activists in corporations (Baillie and Gedro 2009). In the 1990s, Brian McNaught, a pioneer in LGBT diversity training, made a business case out of LGBT social justice issues, and this approach made many employers aware of LGBT diversity within their organizations. Scholars generally share the view that the North American LGBT workplace activism movement has led the way in promoting cultural inclusion of LGBT employees at work in addition to promoting nondiscrimination employment policies (Colgan 2015).

Activists from other countries also feel that merely asking for tangible benefits and policies cannot bring about equality for LGBT employees and that it is also important to make the workplace culture inclusive. In Sweden, for example, the overt exclusion and stigmatization of LGBT employees has been addressed by nondiscrimination policies. However, such policies may not be very effective in masculinist organizational cultures, like those of law enforcement agencies, and they may fail to tackle the marginalization of LGBT persons in such organizations (Rennstam and Sullivan 2016). In Hungary, although legal frameworks exist for the protection of LGBT persons at work and a few corporations have adopted diversity policies, the workplace culture is often described as homophobic because it generally rejects LGBT persons and offers limited avenues to LGBT employees for finding out their legal rights. Although an Equal Treatment Authority was established in 2005, cases of reported LGBT harassment were very rare (as low as five per year), and they were usually reported after the employee had left the workplace (Takács 2016). A similar situation exists in Poland, where LGBT discrimination occurs due either to the absence of nondiscrimination policies or to hostile attitudes in the workplace that supersede any legal protections (Golebiowska 2016). In Chile, LGBT employees face normalized forms of mockery and verbal violence which, according to Jaime Barrientos and his colleagues, are unique to the Chilean context (Barrientos et al. 2016). The movement is considering the need for expressive changes in Brazil too. Góis et al. (2016) have observed that Brazilian corporations have historically been "endogenous" in their operations and that they take an orthodox view of workplace culture. With the growing activism around equality for women, LGBT people, people with disabilities, and people of color; however, corporations are gradually becoming more open to broader social contexts and global norms regarding diversity. Activists are now achieving expressive changes in Brazilian companies, as reflected in statements from top management supporting LGBT employees; the existence of diversity training and education on sexuality in the workplace; and employee participation in diversity days, events, and pride marches. Activist groups in the Global South have begun to affirm that bringing about cultural changes to the workplace may be as important as the adoption of inclusive employment policies. Unless the culture of an organization becomes more inclusive of LGBT identities, workplaces may remain hostile for LGBT people in spite of nondiscrimination policies.

In addition to pursuing expressive goals, LGBT workplace activism in the US has also pursued instrumental goals that, in their context, were *interrelated* with each other. Although activists have primarily focused on employment nondiscrimination policies and domestic partner benefits since the late 1980s (Raeburn 2004), the goal of marriage equality has been integrated into LGBT activism more recently. In 2012, corporations were pressured to support marriage equality. The goal of the marriage equality movement was to strike out the provisions of a federal law, the Defense of Marriage Act of 1995, which legally defined marriage as existing solely between a man and a woman. Although marriage equality was a legal issue that was *indirectly* related to the workplace, activists pursued marriage equality as a "proxy goal" (Walker et al. 2008) and focused their activism on corporations that, with their economic and institutional clout, were well-equipped to persuade the state to recognize same-sex marriage. In March of 2012, around 273 large- and medium-sized corporations filed an amicus brief in the Supreme Court supporting marriage equality. They provided secular reasons for supporting marriage equality – almost all the employers operated in states where same-sex marriage was legal under state law; therefore, many of their employees had same-sex spouses. These corporations advocated for marriage equality because they had to incur additional administrative costs related to the federal taxation of employees based on the gender of their spouses. They also believed that the additional tax burden on healthcare benefits for same-sex spouses made it difficult to retain accomplished employees at their US locations. Support for marriage equality did not come automatically from the corporations. With the support of external advocates, insider LGBT employee activists played an instrumental role in bringing these employers into the pool of the amici curiae (Bernstein and Ghosh 2015).

These cases from the US tell a success story of interrelating employment policies and marriage equality to achieve both goals. Cases from elsewhere, however, suggest that doing so in other contexts may not always be welcomed by activists. French scholars and activists, for example, have argued that given the political and social environment in France, the pursuit of marriage equality would generate even more backlash for LGBT employees. Yohanne Roszéwitch, the President of SOS Homophobie, for example, argued that debates on same-sex marriage have polarized French society on LGBT issues and that LGBT employees have faced more harassment and bullying at work as a result of those debates (Lloren and Parini 2017).

Even within the Anglo-Saxon world, different political circumstances have shaped the movement's goals in distinct ways. In the US, activists pursued equality in employer-sponsored healthcare benefits and nondiscrimination policies at work due to the absence of federal policies mandating them. In the UK, in contrast, activists pursued nondiscrimination and antiharassment policies at work in accordance with a law enacted in 2003, known as the Employment Equality (Sexual Orientation) Regulation (Colgan et al. 2007). The pursuit of such policies was akin to the efforts of civil rights activists in the US who demanded that the Equal Employment Opportunity policies (EEO) of organizations meet the requirements of the Civil Rights Act in the 1960s and 1970s (Meyerson and Scully 1995; Kelly and Dobbin 1999).

Originating from the Anglo-Saxon contexts, the LGBT workplace equality movement is now spreading its global reach through efforts to achieve equality in multinational corporations. In 2016, the Human Rights Campaign decided that only corporations that had adopted nondiscrimination policies related to sexual orientation and gender identity at their domestic as well as foreign locations could receive a rating of 100% on the Corporate Equality Index (Human Rights Campaign 2017). This bar was not raised suddenly, however; the global diffusion of LGBT workplace activism that led to such victories had only started at the beginning of the current decade. In India and Hong Kong, for example, Goldman Sachs, IBM, and Google collaborated with local LGBT activists, the Human Rights Campaign, and Out & Equal Workplace Advocates to provide resource guides on LGBT equality and inclusion to employers (Banerji et al. 2012; Kaplan 2010). These resource guides provide country-specific accounts of the status of LGBT equality and inclusion in workplaces and possible means of achieving them in the respective countries.

Regarding India and Hong Kong specifically, these resource guides suggest that the activists have not pursued instrumental and expressive goals simultaneously. In India, expressive goals were pursued before instrumental goals whereas in Hong Kong, it was the opposite. In India, the pursuit of policy-related goals has generally been rare, although such efforts have met with success in more recent times. The battle to decriminalize sodomy and the work of pro bono legal organizations, like the Alternate Law Forum, to provide legal services to LGBT people are examples of such efforts. Corporations in India have generally been ambivalent about implementing LGBT nondiscrimination policies, and they have mostly cited the ongoing legal battle surrounding homosexuality as the reason for not adopting such policies. This battle ended recently with the Supreme Court's decision to decriminalize homosexuality in *Navtej Singh Johar v. Union of India* on September 6, 2018. According to media reports, many diversity experts and legal professionals at Indian corporations feel that this court order will have far-reaching effects on the workplace and employment policies in India.[3] Although the instrumental opportunity structures of the movement have only expanded more recently, the cultural opportunity structures of the movement have been expanding since the 1990s. The pioneering LGBT organizations in India began their struggle by pursuing primarily expressive goals. The Humsafar Trust's drop-in centers and counseling activities for gay/queer men and their families, Stree Sangam's mobilization of lesbian women, the establishment of Azaad Bazaar (the first LGBT store), and the numerous pride marches of the past decade have aimed to create more inclusive spaces for LGBT persons in India. Mainstream media, such as TV and the cinema, have also played a pivotal role in the movement by making the topics of queerness and different sexualities popular among the masses (Banerji et al. 2012). As in India, the media and online communities in Vietnam are also opening cultural spaces for the discussion of LGBT equality in the workplace. Since LGBT issues are not politically sensitive, LGBT communities are thriving and the social norms and attitudes toward homosexuality are gradually changing, even if that change is largely limited to urban centers like Ho Chi Minh City and Hanoi. Despite the conspicuous absence of LGBT-inclusive employment policies in corporations, the social acceptance of LGBT persons at work is on rise in these cities (Oosterhoff et al. 2014).

In contrast to the situation in India and Vietnam, corporations in Hong Kong are more open to adopting LGBT-inclusive policies, like health benefits for same-sex partners, because of the presence of a global workforce (Kaplan et al. 2010). Advocacy for equal opportunity policies such as LGBT-inclusive diversity training, and health benefits for same-sex partners is more explicit here. Many corporations have LGBT employee caucuses as well. Since attitudes toward sexuality may be different in Asian countries than in the US, LGBT initiatives should be approached more cautiously in Hong Kong and other industrialized nations in Asia. For example, LGBT employees in Hong Kong may not feel as encouraged to come out and self-identify as gay or transgender as they might feel in a US business context. In contrast to an American corporation, where LGBT employees may ask the human resource department to send a public call for the formation of an LGBT caucus (Creed and Scully 2000; Ghosh 2012), Hong Kong employees may begin their involvement with the movement more cautiously by promoting the work of other LGBT networks and exploring the possibilities for affirming their LGBT identities at work (Kaplan et al. 2010). At IBM, for example, a senior executive who was openly gay initiated talks on LGBT diversity in managerial meetings and conducted several roundtables in mainland China, Hong Kong, and Taiwan. Doing so encouraged numerous local employees to champion the formation of an LGBT employee network in the company, and many of them also came out as LGBT persons. At Goldman Sachs, employee activists published LGBT advocacy-related content in the corporation's diversity newsletters. They also used the company's intranet portals to create the basis for the formation of an LGBT caucus (Kaplan et al. 2010). These cases suggest the possibility of pursuing both instrumental and expressive goals in Asian contexts. The models of LGBT advocacy followed in the US and other Anglo-Saxon nations may also be pursued in industrialized nations in Asia – but with a caveat that these approaches ought to be followed more cautiously in other regions, keeping in mind the inter-cultural variations within Asian countries on attitudes toward non-heterosexual and non-binary gender identities. These contexts may require that instrumental and expressive goals are pursued one after the other, and not simultaneously.

In religiously oriented countries (e.g. Pakistan, Bangladesh, and Malaysia) where LGBT persons are absolutely denounced under the state-sponsored religion, or in countries where the state otherwise encourages homophobic/transphobic laws (e.g. Russia, Uganda, and Nigeria) LGBT workplace activism may be pursued more radically, with a focus on first changing the policies. In Pakistan, Bangladesh, and Malaysia, the silencing of transgender employees, absence of job security, and the existence of fewer opportunities for promotion have required that instrumental goals be pursued more urgently than expressive ones; however, the pursuit of the latter could be the next strategic step in activism in these countries (Al Mamun et al. 2016). The success of transgender activists in India in getting legal recognition for the third gender in 2014 suggests that affirmative action and instrumental changes may be the first steps in extending employment to socioeconomically and educationally marginalized sexual communities (Ghosh 2015). Such steps may also apply to other countries like Thailand, where homosexuality is decriminalized but legal/workplace protection for non-gender-binary individuals and same-sex couples is almost nonexistent (Suriyasarn 2016). In Vietnam, where the state delegitimized same-sex marriage in 2000 following the public attention given to same-sex weddings, activists are fighting against such delegitimization on a more urgent basis. That this delegitimization is ambiguous, inconsistent, and conflicts with numerous other laws (that even the enforcement authorities may not always remember) makes this fight more difficult. At best, the activists view the delegitimization of same-sex marriage in 2000 as a "work-in-progress" law that leaves wide gaps for the local authorities to interpret it and enforce it selectively based on the location (rural versus urban) and socioeconomic class of individuals (Oosterhoff et al. 2014).

Instrumental goals could be considered a work-in-progress in the Global North too, however. The protracted battle regarding the federal ENDA since the 1990s highlights the reality that, despite the mass diffusion of LGBT nondiscrimination policies in the corporate world, US lawmakers are still hesitant to adopt a federal law that protects LGBT persons in the workplace. The chronology of events in the battle surrounding this bill in the US Congress can be found in the archives of the Human Rights Campaign, but lately the battle has become even more contentious in the wake of the Supreme Court's decision on the *Hobby Lobby* case in 2014. This decision restored the religious freedom guaranteed under the US constitution to privately owned corporations, meaning that corporations could decide not to employ LGBT persons if employing them conflicted with their religious beliefs. This decision is the result of apprehension that the way the ENDA bill was drafted violated the right to religious freedom. A religious exemption was therefore added to the ENDA bill to grant religious and religiously oriented organizations the freedom to retain employees based on whether they represented the "religious beliefs" of the organization. Several major LGBT activist organizations rescinded their support from the amended bill, arguing that this exemption could be used by employers as a "hop, skip, and jump" plan for discriminating against LGBT employees (Giarratana 2015, p. 94). Many argue that the newly amended bill can hardly facilitate the passage of the ENDA. The religious exemption in the bill also does little to protect LGBT clergy members who are employed by individual congregations and denominations (Rodriguez and Etengoff 2016).

Clearly, the goals of the LGBT workplace equality movement vary across nations. Although the Anglo-Saxon world, especially the US, has more experience with this movement than most other countries, the goals pursued by activists in the US may not be applicable everywhere. As sociopolitical contexts vary between nations – the US and France, for example – goals that align well in one context may conflict with each other in another. In countries like India, where societal attitudes toward homosexuality are more ambivalent than homophobic, pursuing expressive goals might lay the groundwork for pursuing instrumental goals. In contrast, for marginalized queer and transgender communities, instrumental outcomes may be more urgently needed to make education and the workplace accessible to them. LGBT workplace equality movements are generally embedded in the social structures and national cultures where they are carried out; therefore, the activists themselves may be in the best position to decide which goals to pursue in their own locations.

Intersectionality and Inclusivity in the Movement

LGBT persons indeed have intersectional identities due to divisions along racial, ethnic, gender, class, and other lines. According to Valocchi (1999), the term "homosexual," and its more recent variant "gay," emerged in predominantly white middle-class urban communities. These categories coexisted with the alternative taxonomies used by the working class, black communities, and other racially/ethnically marginalized groups. Valocchi further states that the social categories of homosexual/gay drew largely on two things: one, the psychiatric understanding of sexuality that aligned with sex of object choice, which was popularized at the expense of myriad other forms of sexual articulation that were based on sexual practices and behaviors, many of which had indigenous or non-white origins; and two, the need to address the anxieties of the middle-class, white-collar, same-sex attracted men who were scared of being relegated to "feminine" occupations. To reassert their "masculinity" in the workplace, the blanket categorization of "gay" or "homosexual" was used to unify middle-class, predominantly white, men who engaged in a range of same-sex sexual behaviors. This category was embraced by middle-class same-sex-attracted men so that they could identify as a nonthreatening minority group. This classification occurred, however, at the cost of consigning numerous other sexual communities – with diverse, rich histories and practices – to the margins (Valocchi 1999).

LGBT workplace activism in the US – most visibly in large corporations – leverages the competitive capitalism that appeals to a homogeneous "gay" identity to promote its programs on workplace diversity and inclusion (Rumens 2016). These appeals often ignore the diverse contexts of LGBT persons that result from gender, race, ethnic, and class-related differences. Only in times when the agents of social control punished *all* sexual communities by labeling them as "queer" (as when the law criminalized sodomy) did the "respectable" categories of "homosexual" and "gay" achieve resonance across diverse sexual communities, which otherwise followed their own norms, practices, and behaviors (Valocchi 1999).

Regarding gender identification, the tendency to homogenize transgender and gender-nonconforming persons may constrict our understanding of diversity within these groups. In South Asia, for example, the blanket assumption that transgender persons live in a separate "community" – as the Hijras and the Khwaja Siras do in India and Pakistan, respectively (Nisar 2018) – may undercut the rights of transsexuals and transgender *individuals* who do not belong to any community but face conditions similar to those faced by community-identified transgender/queer persons. The Supreme Court of India order that legalized the third gender in education and employment used the categories "Hijra" and "transgender" almost interchangeably, although the former refers to a culturally and historically identified queer community while the latter refers to a person who identifies with a gender different from the one assigned at birth (Bahadur and Kumar 2016).

On the other side of the spectrum, the understanding of transgender issues in the workplace is heavily driven by Western transgender identifications (such as male-to-female and female-to-male) that do not help much to mitigate the range of problems that transgender activists wish to address (Husemann 2016). For example, sex reassignment procedures and its coverage in the health insurance may not appeal to transgender communities in the Global South that embrace gender fluidity instead of the gender binary. Transgender employees in the Global South may, instead, seek their employers' investment in the education of people living in their communities. These investments may be considered the corporate social responsibility of the organizations, and in many regions, they are mandated by the state. Therefore, discussions of transgender issues drawing on Western concerns – focused heavily on only a few issues (like restrooms) – may overlook the other substantive struggles faced by community-identified and socioeconomically marginalized queers of color in the Global South (McFadden and Crowley-Henry 2016). Hence, it may be hard to fight for the workplace equality of transgender individuals at a global level without accounting for variations based on individual-versus-community identifications, racial/cultural affiliations, and diverse social/economic/educational statuses.

When various social groups feel excluded from a movement, they may contest the norms of the dominant groups within the movement and fragment it. For example, economically marginalized and lower-caste LGBT groups in India contested the regulatory practices and exclusionary mechanisms within the LGBT movement that treated them as "unworthy" subjects in need of training in civility and respectable citizenship. Such dissidence may give rise to subcultures of radical activism that counter the neoliberal streaks of activism within the movement (Dutta 2012). Research proves that social solidarity is likely to produce favorable outcomes in the LGBT social movement. Hetland and Goodwin (2013) draw our attention to the link between social democracy and LGBT rights in seven countries – the Netherlands, Belgium, Norway, Sweden, Spain, Canada, and South Africa. These countries legalized same-sex marriage on or before 2009, and each of the seven countries had either a strong tradition of social democracy or a history of labor rights. These two characteristics have enhanced social solidarity in those societies, and social acceptance for same-sex marriage has resulted primarily from such solidarity.

The LGBT workplace equality movement, too, has an emerging wave that is intersectional and is building bridges with several non-binary sexual categories – such as the intersexed and queer persons – who were originally left out of the movement. This wave is inclusive to black feminism and the poststructural/queer analysis of sexual behaviors and practices that account for the historical, geographical, and cultural diversity among LGBT persons (Colgan 2015). LGBT workplace activists are increasingly becoming aware of the specific experiences of LGBT persons that relate to their gender, race, ethnicity, nationality, disability, occupation, and education. This may be viewed as a healthy move for creating social solidarity within the movement and making the movement stronger (Bond et al. 2009).

Challenges still exist in making the movement intersectional and inclusive, however. The multiracial and multicultural LGBT movements may experience "identity contests" (Bernstein 2008) wherein the perceived or real features of being LGBT are challenged. For example, persons of African origin may view homosexuality as a legacy of European colonialism and as a remnant of the apartheid regime which treated homosexuality as a white offense – a stigma that people of African origin may not want to assume. Challenges like these have emerged in ex-apartheid countries such as South Africa, where homosexuality is often viewed as a mechanism for emphasizing similarities with whites and threatening multiracialism (Currier 2010). Nevertheless, initiatives like the Out & Equal Workplace Advocates' "building bridges" model have had visible success in promoting multiculturalism, multiracialism, and multinationalism within the movement (Baillie and Gedro 2009). LGBT workplace activism has, indeed, worked to bring people from different regions together to promote respect for cultural differences. This is as worthy a goal for the movement as the goal of LGBT equality is, and the trend of embracing multiculturalism could be a way to build social solidarity within the movement.

Participation in the Movement

The LGBT workplace equality movement may be broadened by including sexually diverse and gender-diverse individuals while simultaneously acknowledging their multicultural backgrounds (Currier 2010). A group of scholars and activists who take that view is also critical of the participation of LGBT employee caucuses in the movement, contending that the caucuses are creating "gay-friendly closets" for homonormative LGBT persons. Supervised by professional leaders trained in business schools, these caucuses can be considered a means of prioritizing and enforcing gender-conforming, monogamous, professional, apolitical, middle-class ways of deploying (homo)sexuality. The homonormative "lesbians and gay men" who conform to these characteristics often foreshadow LGBT people with non-binary sexual and gender identities who may not embrace the normative ideals of homosexuality in their day-to-day lives. Their excessive visibility and participation in the movement could potentially result in "normative violence" against diverse sexualities, gender identities, and other queer forms of expression (Williams et al. 2009; Rumens 2016).

Another group of scholars and activists takes a diametrically opposed view on LGBT employee caucuses by presenting them as the "insider activists" whose advocacy and access to organizational channels leads to the successful adoption of LGBT nondiscrimination policies, domestic partner benefits, and other inclusive practices – such as LGBT-oriented diversity training – in corporations. Within their own corporations, these activists persuade their employers to adopt these policies and practices by developing a business case for doing so. Outside their corporations, they form inter-corporation networks of LGBT employees. In those networks, they share strategies and tactics to diffuse the best policies and practices to their employers' peer corporations. They work with LGBT workplace movement organizations like the Human Rights Campaign, GLAAD, and the Out & Equal workplace advocates to learn diversity strategies and implement them in the workplace. The caucuses also help these organizations in setting LGBT diversity benchmarks and periodically raising those bars upon successful achievement of outcomes (Creed and Scully 2000; Raeburn 2004; Ghosh 2012, 2019; Briscoe and Gupta 2016).

Despite having staunchly different approaches, both queer and homonormative perspectives on LGBT employee caucuses do not deny that these caucuses were successful in achieving an extensive geographical reach for the movement and incorporating participation from LGBT persons employed in a wide range of industries. LGBT caucuses may also attract movement participation from other employee caucuses in the corporation through "transversal coalition politics," whereby distinct identity groups partake in pursuing their goals together; this is important because achieving equality and fighting discrimination are common goals for LGBT persons, women, racial/ethnic minorities, disabled people, and other underprivileged groups in the workplace. These groups often work together to celebrate "diversity days" as joint events. Interestingly, employee caucuses with differing ideologies, such as the religious caucus and the LGBT caucus, have also come together to run events like the faith and sexuality conference to find ways for religion and sexuality to coexist harmoniously at work (Colgan 2016).

Labor unions

Labor unions, too, have served as active sources of movement participation. In the late 1980s, when LGBT employee caucuses were in their infancy in the US, LGBT workplace activism in the UK was carried out by LGBT unions operating mainly in the public sector and voluntary organizations. When LGBT caucuses started forming in the UK during the first decade of this century, the relationship between the unions and the caucuses was somewhat harmonious and the unions were generally supportive of the "new" LGBT voices raised in them. The two groups generally complemented each other's work, but the caucuses were generally expected by the unions to not overrepresent managerial perspectives on LGBT issues or undermine the trade union representation of LGBT employees. Sometimes tensions erupted between the two groups because of the individualist, pro-business attitude of the caucuses and the pro-worker, collectivist stand of the union (Colgan and McKearney 2012).

The unions' involvement in LGBT issues has generally been higher in Scandinavian countries because of their Social Democratic institutional framework. In countries like Spain, Canada, and South Africa, LGBT workplace activism has been carried out by unions because of the presence of strong labor movements (Hetland and Goodwin 2013). In general, unions have taken up LGBT workplace activism when they had a weak relationship with the state and when they experienced a demographic shift or loss in their membership. In the Netherlands, the shift in the balance of union membership from the industrial working class to other professional classes helped the unions take up several social causes that were traditionally not taken up by unions; LGBT workplace equality was one of them (Rayside 1999). Canadian unions have also embraced progressive policies for transgender employees and LGBT nondiscrimination clauses in their collective bargaining agreements. They worked on creating local grievance mechanisms for LGBT employees that were more efficient than the procedures involved in human rights appeals. The coverage of transgender issues has generally been much lower than that of sexual orientation issues in the collective bargaining agreements of Canadian unions, however. In numerous instances, the language for transgender rights was not well-developed in those agreements and issues of gender expression were superseded by issues of gender identity (Hunt and Pelz 2016).

Union participation in LGBT workplace activism is not uniform worldwide, however. Unions in the United States have generally been unsupportive of LGBT workplace activism because the "masculine" institutional structures within unions often silence LGBT voices and devalue their issues (Bell et al. 2011). For example, the adoption of transition-related health benefits for employees has been found to be significantly lower and delayed in corporations that have a unionized workforce (Ghosh 2019). In Brazil, unions have not become involved much with LGBT issues because of their hostile perception of the business culture and capitalistic order. This helps little in initiating dialogue between unions and management on emerging issues – like LGBT equality – that are historically not taken up by the unions (Gois et al. 2016).

Self-identification (and alternatives for visibility)

Self-identifying as an LGBT person at work can be viewed as the third avenue of movement participation. Self-identification can be useful for evaluating the LGBT initiatives within a corporation. Professional activists argue that to evaluate the work on LGBT diversity, the data needs to be collected confidentially and privately. Therefore, to measure the impact of diversity initiatives on LGBT employees, questions on self-identification are generally designed and integrated with climate surveys administered to employees. Self-identification can also be done voluntarily in confidential human resource records. Self-identification may help in identifying eligible employees for same-sex domestic partner benefits and gender transition-related health benefits. When self-identification is encouraged by an organization under its diversity initiatives, it can instill confidence in LGBT employees to advocate for LGBT equality (Baillie 2010).

Self-identification has its perils too. In organizations that are learning the ropes of diversity (where the work environment could be hostile), self-identification may backfire on LGBT employees and can lead to anxiety, exclusion, and even job loss. The legal protection of LGBT employees varies across jurisdictions and countries, and this often counts as a factor in deciding whether to self-identify (Bond et al. 2009; Jones 2016). When data protection is inefficient, the risk of leakage of confidential human resource data also jeopardizes the good intentions behind self-identification (Kaplan et al. 2010). In situations like these, self-identification may not serve its intended purpose and the activists may come up with alternate avenues for employee participation.

LGBT persons and their heterosexual/cisgender allies may be skeptical of participating in the movement if they do not feel safe talking about or supporting LGBT issues at work. They may also feel the burden of defining and defending their positionality in this movement – as an LGBT person or ally – while supporting it. In the initial stages, when movement actors document LGBT-inclusive workplace policies/practices and advocate for them, the movement may attract more people because the burden of positionality moves from an individual's sexual identity to their sociopolitical views. In hostile workplaces, LGBT and ally activists may build awareness by anonymously creating and sharing online material on antihomophobia or antitransphobia at work (Jones 2016). When the organization is supportive, activists may create resource guides on LGBT diversity at work or publicize the existing resource guides to build the initial momentum for activism. Activists may also persuade their employer to explicitly publicize that LGBT persons are welcome to apply for job(s) in recruitment advertisements. New employees may also be informed in their orientation that they may form an officially recognized LGBT employee caucus within the organization and that they would be encouraged to do so (Bond et al. 2009).

Isomorphic processes

Institutional theorists suggest that LGBT activists may exponentially enhance movement participation by winning over the influential organizations in a field. These organizations may be industry leaders or leaders of the professional cartels that other organizations emulate when adopting best policies and practices. When LGBT employee caucuses are formed and recognized by the influential organizations, it may create a domino effect whereby opportunities for the creation of similar caucuses are made available at peer corporations in those industries. For example, when LGBT employee caucuses were formed in leading organizations like United Airlines and AT&T, peer corporations in their respective industries became more open to the formation of such employee networks in their own organizations (Raeburn 2004). Similarly, organizational identities may be intimately tied to the success of activism, whereby the formation of LGBT employee networks in activism-resistant corporations may give indirect legitimacy to the formation of similar networks in other corporations in the field (Briscoe and Safford 2008). At the international level, movement participation may be enhanced through normative isomorphic pressures from international nongovernmental organizations. Arguably, the advocacy of Amnesty International helped to diffuse transgender human rights policies in Germany, Ireland, Australia, Japan, and India (Al Mamun et al. 2016).

Considering the role of employee caucuses, trade unions, isomorphic processes, and other avenues in making LGBT issues visible, participation in LGBT workplace movements has undoubtedly increased worldwide over the past few decades. However, disparities still exist. While participation has increased in the Anglo-Saxon world and other parts of the Global North, such as Western Europe and Scandinavia, it lags in the regions of the Global South, such as Asia, Latin America, and Africa. Variations exist within the Global North too. Activism has met with more success in the US and the UK through employee caucuses, for example, whereas trade unions are a bigger source of participation in Scandinavian countries and in non-Anglo-Saxon Europe. Similarly, self-identification may not be the best approach for encouraging the involvement of LGBT employees in the movement where conservative organizational cultures and inefficient data-protection practices are an issue. Movement participation may take a massive leap forward when influential organizations in a field are targeted, thus creating institutional opportunities for the movement in other organizations in the field.

Conclusion

This chapter has traced the goals of, and participation in, the LGBT workplace equality movement by making international and cross-cultural comparisons. In doing so, it has highlighted how the movement's characteristics vary internationally. It argues that the global character of this movement is envisaged best when these variations are acknowledged and accepted. Since movement goals and participation can be location-specific, imposing "uniformity" on the movement and replicating the movement's practices in the US may unnecessarily create more tension and less global unity within the movement.

The chapter has also delved into ongoing debates on the "respectability" of this movement: one group of scholars and activists critique it for being excessively oriented toward the homonormative middle class while marginalizing queer persons and people of color, while the other draws attention to the visible, measurable outcomes of this movement by highlighting its professional approach and speaking to the rationalities of movement targets. Within the dominant discourse in LGBT movement studies that continues to widen this rift (e.g. Ward 2008; Williams and Giuffre 2011), a more recent view says that some of these divisions created in the scholarly world might be more imaginary than real. Activists in the field may decide to take a more pragmatic approach, synchronizing these differences in their activism. In doing so, they might pay attention to the global practices of the movement and how those practices could be localized in their own contexts (Ghosh 2015). The LGBT workplace equality movement is growing and becoming global, and activists must be open to learning from global developments while paying attention to their local contexts.

Notes

1. Coined by the Out & Equal Workplace Advocates; see https://pt.usembassy.gov/lgbti-workplace-equality-speaker-selisse-berry/ (accessed January 29, 2018).
2. See http://urvashivaid.net/wp/?p=470 (accessed January 31, 2018).
3. See, for example, Entrepreneur India at https://www.entrepreneur.com/article/319807; India Corporate Law at https://corporate.cyrilamarchandblogs.com/2018/10/section-377-judgment-lgbt-employer-india/ (accessed October 25, 2018).

References

Al Mamun, Abdullah, Mariano L.M. Heyden, and Qaiser Rafique Yasser. 2016. "Transgender Individuals in Asian Islamic Countries: An Overview of Workplace Diversity and Inclusion Issues in Pakistan, Bangladesh, and Malaysia." In *Sexual Orientation and Transgender Issues in Organizations: Global Perspectives on LGBT Workforce Diversity*, edited by Thomas Köllen, 167–180. Switzerland: Springer.

Armstrong, Elizabeth A. and Mary Bernstein. 2008. "Culture, Power, and Institutions: A multi-Institutional Politics Approach to Social Movements." *Sociological Theory* 26(1): 74–99.

Bahadur, Animesh and Kunal Kamal Kumar. 2016. "I Am the Man for the Job: The Challenges of Coming Out as a Female-to-Male Transgender in the Indian Organizational Space." In *Sexual Orientation and Transgender Issues in Organizations: Global Perspectives on LGBT Workforce Diversity*, edited by Thomas Köllen, 43–61. Switzerland: Springer.

Baillie, Pat. 2010. "How Self-Reporting for LGBT Employees Can Benefit Companies: The Metrics at the End of the Rainbow." *The Diversity Factor* 18(4): 35–41.

Baillie, Pat and Julie Gedro. 2009. "Perspective on Out & Equal Workplace Advocates Building Bridges Model: A Retrospect of the Past, Present, and Future of Training Impacting Lesbian, Gay, Bisexual, and Transgender Employees in the Workplace." *New Horizons in Adult Education & Human Resource Development* 23(2): 39–46.

Banerji, Aparna, Kevin Burns, and Kate Vernon. 2012. *Creating Inclusive Workplaces for LGBT Employees in India*. Hong Kong: Community Business. Available at: https://www.communitybusiness.org/latest-news-publications/creating-inclusive-workplaces-lgbt-employees-india-resource-guide-employers.

Barrientos, Jaime, Manuel Cárdenas, Fabiola Gómez, and Monica Guzmán. 2016. "Gay Men and Male-to-Female Transgender Persons in Chile: An Exploratory Quantitative Study on Stigma, Discrimination, Victimization, Happiness and Social Well-Being." In *Sexual Orientation and Transgender Issues in Organizations: Global Perspectives on LGBT Workforce Diversity*, edited by Thomas Köllen, 253–270. Switzerland: Springer.

Bell, Myrtle P., Mustafa F. Özbilgin, T. Alexandra Beauregard, and Olca Sürgevil. 2011. "Voice, Silence, and Diversity in 21st Century Organizations: Strategies for Inclusion of Gay, Lesbian, Bisexual, and Transgender Employees." *Human Resource Management* 50(1): 131–146.

Bernstein, Mary. 2008. "The Analytic Dimensions of Identity: A Political Identity Framework." In *Identity Work in Social Movements*, edited by Jo Reger, Daniel J. Myers, and Rachel L. Einwohner, 277–301. Minneapolis: University of Minnesota Press.

Bernstein, Mary and Apoorva Ghosh. 2015. "'It's a Win-Win for Everybody:' Social Movement Strategies in Institutions as Repertoires of Alignment." *American Sociological Association Annual Meeting*, Chicago, IL.

Bond, Sue, Emma Hollywood, and Fiona Colgan. 2009. *Integration in the Workplace: Emerging Employment Practice on Age, Sexual Orientation and Religion or Belief*. Manchester: Equality and Human Rights Commission.

Boyce, Paul. 2006. "Moral Ambivalence and Irregular Practices: Contextualizing Male-To-Male Sexualities in Calcutta/India." *Feminist Review* 83(Sexual Moralities): 79–98.

Briscoe, Forrest and Abhinav Gupta. 2016. "Social Activism in and around Organizations." *The Academy of Management Annals* 10(1): 671–727.

Briscoe, Forrest and Sean Safford. 2008. "The Nixon-in-China effect: Activism, Imitation, and the Institutionalization of Contentious Practices." *Administrative Science Quarterly* 53(3): 460–491.

Colgan, Fiona. 2015. "Voice and Visibility: Tackling the 'Invisibility' of the Sexual Orientation Strand in UK Organization Equality and Diversity Research." PhD dissertation. London Metropolitan University.

Colgan, Fiona. 2016. "LGBT Company Network Groups in the UK: Tackling Opportunities and Complexities in the Workplace." In *Sexual Orientation and Transgender Issues in Organizations: Global Perspectives on LGBT Workforce Diversity*, edited by Thomas Köllen, 525–538. Switzerland: Springer.

Colgan, Fiona and Aidan McKearney. 2012. "Visibility and Voice in Organizations: Lesbian, Gay, Bisexual and Transgendered Employee Networks." *Equality, Diversity and Inclusion: An International Journal* 31(4): 359–378.

Colgan, Fiona, Chris Creegan, Aidan Mckearney, and Tessa Wright. 2007. "Equality and Diversity Policies and Practices at Work: Lesbian, Gay and Bisexual Workers." *Equal Opportunities International* 26(6): 590–609.

Creed, W.E. Douglas and Maureen A. Scully. 2000. "Songs of Ourselves: Employees' Deployment of Social Identity in Workplace Encounters." *Journal of Management Inquiry* 9(4): 391–412.

Currier, Ashley. 2010. "The Strategy of Normalization in the South African LGBT Movement." *Mobilization: An International Quarterly* 15(1): 45–62.

Dutta, Aniruddha. 2012. "Claiming Citizenship, Contesting Civility: The Institutional LGBT Movement and the Regulation of Gender/Sexual Dissidence in West Bengal, India." *Jindal Global Law Review* 4(1): 110–141.

Gedro, Julie. 2009. "A Personal Narrative of LGBT Identity and Activism." *New Horizons in Adult Education & Human Resource Development* 23(3): 51–54.

Ghosh, Apoorva. 2012. "Leveraging Sexual Orientation Workforce Diversity Through Identity Deployment." In *Handbook of Research on Workforce Diversity in a Global Society: Technologies and Concepts*, edited by Chaunda Scott and Myrtle Byrd. IGI Global, 403–424.

Ghosh, Apoorva. 2015. "LGBTQ Activist Organizations as 'Respectably Queer' in India: Contesting a Western View." *Gender, Work & Organization* 22(1): 51–66.

Ghosh, Apoorva. 2019. "The Politics of Alignment and the 'Quiet Transgender Revolution' in Fortune 500 Corporations, 2008 to 2017." Unpublished paper.

Giarratana, Giovanni P. 2015. "The Employment Non-Discrimination Act after Hobby Lobby: Striving for Progress-Not Perfection." *Stetson Law Review* 45: 91–118.

Góis, João, Francisco Duarte, João Pinheiro, and Kamila Teixeira. 2016. "Sexual Orientation Diversity Management in Brazil." In *Sexual Orientation and Transgender Issues in Organizations: Global Perspectives on LGBT Workforce Diversity*, edited by Thomas Köllen, 493–512. Switzerland: Springer.

Golebiowska, Ewa E. 2016. "Tolerance in the Polish Workplace Towards Gay Men and Lesbians." In *Sexual Orientation and Transgender Issues in Organizations: Global Perspectives on LGBT Workforce Diversity*, edited by Thomas Köllen, 451–466. Switzerland: Springer.

Hetland, Gabriel and Jeff Goodwin. 2013. "The Strange Disappearance of Capitalism from Social Movement Studies." *Marxism and Social Movements*, edited by Colin Barker, Laurence Cox, John Krinsky, and Alf Gunvald Nilsen, 86–98. Boston, MA: Brill.

Human Rights Campaign. 2017. Corporate Equality Index Report. Available at: https://www.hrc.org/resources/corporate-equality-index-archives (accessed January 31, 2018).

Huesmann, Monika. 2016. "Transgressing Gender Binarism in the Workplace? Including Transgender and Intersexuality Perspectives in Organizational Restroom Policies." In *Sexual Orientation and Transgender Issues in Organizations: Global Perspectives on LGBT Workforce Diversity*, edited by Thomas Köllen, 539–552. Switzerland: Springer.

Hunt, Gerald and Michael Pelz. 2016 "Transgender Rights in Canada: Legal, Medical and Labour Union Activities." In *Sexual Orientation and Transgender Issues in Organizations: Global Perspectives on LGBT Workforce Diversity*, edited by Thomas Köllen, 133–147. Switzerland: Springer.

Jones, Tiffany. 2016. "Female-to-Male (FtM) Transgender Employees in Australia." In *Sexual Orientation and Transgender Issues in Organizations: Global Perspectives on LGBT Workforce Diversity*, edited by Thomas Köllen, 101–116. Switzerland: Springer.

Joseph, Sherry. 1996. "Gay and Lesbian Movement in India." *Economic and Political Weekly* 31(33): 2228–2233.

Kane, Melinda D. 2013. "LGBT religious Activism: Predicting State Variations in the Number of Metropolitan Community Churches, 1974–2000." *Sociological Forum* 28(1): 135–158.

Kaplan, Mark, Mark King, Roddy Shaw, and Sam Winter. 2010. *Creating Inclusive Workplaces for LGBT Employees*. Hong Kong: Community Business. Available at: https://www.communitybusiness.org/latest-news-publications/creating-inclusive-workplaces-lgbt-employees.

Kelly, Erin and Frank Dobbin. 1999. Civil Rights Law at Work: Sex Discrimination and the Rise of Maternity Leave Policies. *American Journal of Sociology* 105(2): 455–492.

King, Brayden G. and Nicholas A. Pearce. 2010. "The Contentiousness of Markets: Politics, Social Movements, and Institutional Changei Markets." *Annual Review of Sociology* 36: 249–267.

Lin, Hsien-Cheng. 2014. "An Investigation of the Effects of Cultural Differences on Physicians' Perceptions of Information Technology Acceptance as They Relate to Knowledge Management Systems." *Computers in Human Behavior* 38: 368–380.

Lloren, Anouk and Lorena Parini. 2017. "How LGBT-Supportive Workplace Policies Shape the Experience of Lesbian, Gay Men, and Bisexual Employees." *Sexuality Research and Social Policy* 14(3): 289–299.

Mattison, Andrew M. and David P. McWhirter. 1995. "Lesbians, Gay Men, and their Families: Some Therapeutic Issues." *Psychiatric Clinics of North America* 18(1):123–137.

McClendon, Gwyneth H. 2014. "Social Esteem and Participation in Contentious Politics: A Field Experiment at an LGBT Pride Rally." *American Journal of Political Science* 58(2): 279–290.

McFadden, Ciarán and Marian Crowley-Henry. 2016. "A Systematic Literature Review on Trans* Careers and Workplace Experiences." In *Sexual Orientation and Transgender Issues in Organizations: Global Perspectives on LGBT Workforce Diversity*, edited by Thomas Köllen, 63–81. Switzerland: Springer.

Meyerson, Debra E. and Maureen A. Scully. 1995. Tempered Radicalism and the Politics of Ambivalence and Change. *Organization Science* 6(5): 585–600.

Nisar, Muhammad Azfar. 2018. "(Un) Becoming a Man: Legal Consciousness of the Third Gender Category in Pakistan." *Gender & Society* 32(1): 59–81.

Oosterhoff, Pauline, Tu-Anh Hoang, and Trang Thu Quach. 2014. Negotiating Public and Legal Spaces: The Emergence of an LGBT Movement in Vietnam. No. 74 IDS Evidence Report. Available at: https://opendocs.ids.ac.uk/opendocs/handle/123456789/3976 (accessed August 29, 2018).

Raeburn, Nicole Christine. 2004. *Changing Corporate America from Inside Out: Lesbian and Gay Workplace Rights*. Minneapolis: University of Minnesota Press.

Ragins, Belle Rose, Romila Singh, and John M. Cornwell. 2007. "Making the Invisible Visible: Fear and Disclosure of Sexual Orientation at Work." *Journal of Applied Psychology* 92(4): 1103–1118.

Rayside, David. 1999. *On the Fringes of the New Europe: Sexual Diversity Activism and the Labor Movement: Laboring for Rights: Unions and Sexual Diversity across Nations*. Philadelphia, PA: Temple University Press.

Rennstam, Jens and Katie Sullivan. 2016. "The Limits of Inclusion: Stories from the Margins of the Swedish Police." In *Sexual Orientation and Transgender Issues in Organizations: Global Perspectives on LGBT Workforce Diversity*, edited by Thomas Köllen, 339–352. Switzerland: Springer.

Rodriguez, Eric M. and Chana Etengoff. 2016. "Religious Workplaces: The Joys, Trials and Tribulations of LGBT Clergy." In *Sexual Orientation and Transgender Issues in Organizations: Global Perspectives on LGBT Workforce Diversity*, edited by Thomas Köllen, 181–196. Switzerland: Springer.

Rumens, Nick. 2016. "On the Violence of Heteronormativity within Business Schools." In *Sexual Orientation and Transgender Issues in Organizations: Global Perspectives on LGBT Workforce Diversity*, edited by Thomas Köllen, 389–404. Switzerland: Springer.

Suriyasarn, Busakorn. 2016. "Discrimination and Marginalization of LGBT workers in Thailand." In *Sexual Orientation and Transgender Issues in Organizations: Global Perspectives on LGBT Workforce Diversity*, edited by Thomas Köllen, 197–215. Switzerland: Springer.

Takács, Judit. 2016. "LGBT Employee in the Hungarian Labor Market." In *Sexual Orientation and Transgender Issues in Organizations: Global Perspectives on LGBT Workforce Diversity*, edited by Thomas Köllen, 233–252. Switzerland: Springer.

Tamale, Sylvia. 2007. "Out of the Closet: Unveiling Sexuality Discourses in Uganda." In Africa After *Gender*, edited by Catherine Cole, Takyiwaa Manuh and Stephen Miescher, 17–29. Bloomington, IN: University of Indiana Press.

Taylor, Verta and Nicole C. Raeburn. 1995. "Identity Politics as High-Risk Activism: Career Consequences for Lesbian, Gay, and Bisexual Sociologists." *Social Problems* 42(2): 252–273.

Valocchi, Steve. 1999. "The Class-Inflected Nature of Gay Identity." *Social Problems* 46(2): 207–224.

Walker, Edward T., Andrew W. Martin, and John D. McCarthy. 2008. "Confronting the State, the Corporation, and the Academy: The Influence of Institutional Targets on Social Movement Repertoires." *American Journal of Sociology* 114(1): 35–76.

Ward, Jane. 2008. *Respectably Queer: Diversity Culture in LGBT Activist Organizations*. Nashville, TN: Vanderbilt University Press.

White House, The. 2014. Fact Sheet: Taking Action to Support LGBT Workplace Equality is Good for Business. Available at: https://whitehouse.gov (accessed June 26, 2018).

Williams, Christine and Patti Giuffre. 2011. "From Organizational Sexuality to Queer Organizations: Research on Homosexuality and the Workplace." *Sociology Compass* 5(7): 551–563.

Williams, Christine L., Patti A. Giuffre, and Kirsten Dellinger. 2009. "The Gay-Friendly Closet." *Sexuality Research & Social Policy* 6(1): 29–45.

25

Reproductive Justice

MICHELE EGGERS-BARISON AND CRYSTAL M. HAYES

Introduction

This chapter is about the far-reaching struggle for reproductive justice. Reproductive justice (RJ) is defined as a theoretical paradigm that centers the experiences of marginalized Black[1] women and other Women of Color (WOC) and issues related to their bodies, sexuality, and reproduction as a human right. It theorizes on three primary interconnected reproductive human rights: "(1) the right to have a child under the conditions of one's choosing; (2) the right not to have a child using birth control, abortion, or abstinence; and (3) the right to parent children in safe and healthy environments free from violence by individuals or the state" (Ross 2017, p. 290). While we tell the story of RJ primarily through the lens and history of women who helped to pioneer the movement for RJ in the United States and poor women in the Global South navigating and negotiating regressive reproductive politics, embedded in their stories is our own journey and pathway to reproductive freedom. We tell these stories as two women who understand what it means to live in a world where women's bodies are treated with contempt and scrutiny, and where law is created specifically to control women's bodies. As Clare Hemmings et al. (2011) tell us, stories matter. We use this chapter as an opportunity to highlight the stories and history that we think connect our collective struggles for liberation and RJ while reimagining a world where the most vulnerable women among us get to live free in their bodies without violation or fear, and where RJ is the norm and not the exception. We bring our full selves to this project. We bring both the parts of our identity and experience that have been targeted and repressed as well as an awareness of our enormous privileges as two women with advanced degrees in social work with access to the tools and resources to use our voices to honor the voices of women who are routinely silenced.

For full transparency, we share our identities as an important part of our story. We believe this is a core way to hold ourselves accountable to the power we hold. It is also our way of being sure to never forget how our experiences and identities are shaped by belonging to a group of women who have their human rights regularly violated. Our understanding of the struggle for RJ is woven together and rooted in what it means for women to have reproductive choices made for them based on their identity as poor working class WOC, immigrant and undocumented women, lesbian women, transgender men and women, and women with physical and mental disabilities.

We are two women. One who self-identifies as a cis-straight Black woman and the other a Latina born in the US of Chilean immigrant parents. We grew up in a post *Roe v Wade* world in the United States. However, that alone does not tell the full story of how we experience our reproductive bodies or our journey towards reproductive freedom. Between us we have had four abortions and two live births. One of us became a mother, and one of us gave the gift of motherhood to another woman and her family. Our experiences are not solely explained or shaped by *Roe* and access to reproductive "choice," which includes abortion and contraception, but also by a paternalistic dominant discourse and culture that does not fully respect WOC and young, poor, and immigrant women as human beings with the capacity to determine their destiny. While growing up in a post-*Roe* world mattered in some significantly important ways for us, it does not tell the full story of our lives or the women like us who belong to groups who have been historically and systematically marginalized. To fully tell those stories, and what it means to claim ownership over our own reproductive bodies and sexuality, we have to tell the story of violence, sexual assault, poverty, fear, and racist and sexist stereotypes that are used to maintain patriarchy and the racial social order.

We are both the survivors of sexual violence, poverty, and other forms of gender-based violence. We both belong to a group of women with a history of reproductive oppression that stretches from the United States to the Global South. We bring to bear that history in this chapter about RJ. I would like to begin by situating myself in relation to my Black grandmother, Charley-May Phinizy, who was a poor working-class domestic worker, followed by a brief look at the life and work of Loretta Ross, one of the founders of the RJ movement and praxis. Black women's stories are at the heart of the struggle for reproductive freedom in the United States. To begin with the complex lives of Black women help to root us in the vastness of RJ as one that encompasses everything from economic and racial justice, to educational opportunities, healthcare, housing, and gender-based violence, including racialized, gender-based, state-sanctioned and sponsored violence.

In the United States, being born on the cusp of *Roe* was a good time to be born a Black girl. In fact, growing up a 1970s baby after the Civil Rights Act was passed and just before *Roe v. Wade* was made into law meant that I had the capacity to control my reproductive body and live in a world where my civil and political rights were intact. While I was positioned to have access to more freedoms than my mother or grandmother, I was not free from systemic racism or poverty that so often plagues the lives of WOC no matter when they are born.

Nonetheless, the 1960s and 1970s, overall, was an exciting time for women positioned to take full advantage of all the professional and educational opportunities opened to them by the women's movement. Some women were positioned to enter college and chose careers, rather than feeling obligated to be married with children, something that would have been impossible for my poor working-class grandmother, Charley-May. Like so many other Black women during this period, my grandmother worked as a domestic worker in a culture that did not respect her as a woman or mother. She was parenting in a culture where she was not welcomed, belonged, or expected to exist outside the racial hierarchy. How she became pregnant and a mother, where she gave birth, how she gave birth, whether or not she had doctors who could hold her humanity, and her entire birth and mothering experiences were driven by the racial hierarchy in the United States. Her experiences help to tell not only her story, but also *the* story of reproductive oppression in the United States for Black women. Despite working full-time cleaning the homes of affluent white families, she lived without healthcare and died from cancer at only 42 years old – younger than I am now. She lived in a boarding house where she rented a single room for herself and my mother in Harlem, New York, while sharing a bathroom and kitchen. She died when I was only two-years old so she did not live to see the widespread growth in contraceptive technology that gave women options to separate sex from reproduction, and marriage from children.

This period of discovery, freedom, and incredible opportunities for (some) women should not overshadow the world that women like my grandmother faced who could not afford basic living expenses, healthcare, or safe affordable housing. The poverty my grandmother struggled with is just another form of reproductive violence that continues to persist today as deep racial disparities dating back to slavery continue to harm Black women and other marginalized women in the United States (Davis 1983). Reproductive oppression is racialized and institutionalized when poverty, inadequate housing, poor healthcare, failing school systems, and environmental pollution and degradation disproportionately impact poor working-class WOC. During the early 1990s the movement for RJ was informed by the material conditions of Black women's lives. They set out to identify and respond to the differential and difficult challenges faced by women on the margins who struggled to parent their children, like my grandmother, as well as address other broad social inequalities that disproportionately impact WOC.

Black women in particular helped to lead the RJ movement that changed the way we talk about reproductive rights as solely an issue of "choice" to one that includes the barriers that get in the way of choice, resources, and power. Loretta Ross's own story of forced sterilization led her to become one of the founding pioneers of the RJ movement where she helped to coin the term "reproductive justice" in 1994 with several other Black women (Price 2010). Catapulted by her own personal experiences, Ross defined and theorized reproductive justice with a group of 11 other Black women after returning from the 1994 Conference on Population and Development in Cairo, Egypt (Ross 2017). RJ was born in response to the need to address the politics of population control around the world, and in response to proposed healthcare policy reforms in the United States which ignored women's reproductive health, while promoting reductive claims that reproductive freedom is solely dependent upon the ability to make "good" choices (Ross 2017).

Ross and others helped to redefine reproductive politics beyond ending racial disparities in healthcare and the right to privacy claims promoted by those in the pro-choice movement (Price 2010; Ross 2006a; Ross et al. 2001). Ross and Solinger (2017) reminds us that:

> Roe v. Wade and its legalization of choice had guaranteed nothing to women who could not pay for reproductive options. These women remained dangerously vulnerable. After Roe, many poor women of color suffered coerced sterilization, were denied public assistance if they had one "too many" children, and were targeted for other methods of population control. The anti-civil rights, anti-war political culture depended, after Roe, on the symbol of the hyperfertile woman of color as toxic reproducer, as a female unfit for rights or choices.
>
> (p. 121)

Shifting the discourse of reproductive politics from struggles over contraception and abortion to social justice issues like political power, access to resources, and RJ as a human right, were some of the main goals of the RJ movement. They offered new analytic tools that applied a human rights framework as an alternative to the legal system in the United States. It was a model that allowed a bridge between RJ to the Universal Declaration of Human Rights (UDHR) and to a global community of other WOC:

> The term Reproductive Justice was coined in 1994 by women of color shortly after Cairo. We were envisioning from the perspectives of women of color engaged in both domestic and international activism, and attempting to create a lens applicable to the United States with which to interpret and apply the normative (but not universally agreed) understandings reached at Cairo. In particular, we offered a critique of the way that opposition to the fundamentalists and misogynists strengthened the problematic alliance between feminists and the population control establishment. As activists in the U.S., we needed an analysis to connect our domestic issues to the global struggle for women's human rights that would call attention to our commitment to the link between women, their families, and their communities.
>
> (Ross 2006a)

Drawing on UDHR's eight categories, RJ advocates believed that the human rights framework allowed RJ to be operationalized in ways that would be otherwise limited within the legal systems in the US. The eight categories are:

1. Civil Rights – nondiscrimination, equality
2. Political Rights – voting, speech, assembly
3. Economic Rights – living wage, workers' rights
4. Social Rights – health care, food, shelter, education
5. Cultural Rights – religion, language, dress
6. Environmental Rights – clean air, water, and land; no toxic neighborhoods
7. Sexual Rights – right to have or not to have children; right to marry and when.
8. Same-sex Rights. Trans-gender rights. Right to birth control and abortion. Right to sexual pleasure and define families.

Ross and others understood the implications of ignoring legal systems that failed to protect women's reproductive rights as human rights and brought to bear an important understanding of the social justice and human right issues that regularly limit individual liberty for women, particularly poor women from marginalized groups. In many ways, Ross taught us that RJ lies at the heart of one's capacity to enjoy their full humanity. For us, RJ is an unapologetic edict and struggle against white supremacy and all forms of oppression that flow from it, or what bell hooks describes as "imperialist white supremacist patriarchy" (hooks 2010, p. 4). RJ is a theoretical response to the different interlocking systems of oppression that are used to maintain women as a subjugated group, particularly Black women and other WOC (Ross 2017).

RJ theory purposely integrates intersectionality, by calling attention to the ways race, class, and gender shapes the lives of Black women and other WOC and how they experience their bodies. Intersectionality is a term officially coined by Black feminist scholar Kimberle Crenshaw that explains how people are impacted by multiple forms of oppression (Crenshaw 1997, 1989). RJ also incorporates self-help strategies that invite Black women to see themselves as experts and leaders with valuable experiences to share with the world as movement builders (Ross 2017, 2006a). In this way, RJ is not just a theory, but a praxis that shifts our understanding of reproductive politics and individual struggle to control one's body, to one that directly engages issues of power, identity, race, borders, migration/immigration, the environment, and all other forms of human rights violations collectively experienced by Indigenous women, poor women, and immigrant and/or undocumented women (Crenshaw 1991; Ross 2017). Combining theoretical Black radical feminist frameworks with human rights and the practice of self-help that comes directly out of the National Black Women's Health Project (NBWHP), now known as the Black Women's Health Imperative (BWHI), Rose et al. helped to change reproductive politics from a movement that focused solely on choice to broad social inequalities (i.e. poverty, housing, jobs, inadequate education, and domestic violence) that extend beyond the individual bodies and the ability to make choices.

Loretta Ross's story leading up to her work as a pioneer of RJ helps to illuminate how multiple forms of oppression operate in the lives of WOC and its implications for their reproductive rights. Ross began her life much like other Black women during her time. Ross was born in 1953 in Temple, TX to a blended family. She was the sixth child in a family of eight children. Her father was a Jamaican-born immigrant and her mother owned a music store and supplemented the family's income as a domestic worker. Ross's family was typical in many ways and she was raised within a two-parent family. Her mother was a housewife during Loretta's childhood while her father, a retired Army Drill Sergeant, worked at the Post Office while also taking on multiple side jobs to support his family.

What was not typical, however, or perhaps not typically talked about was the history of sexual violence that swirled around Ross as a young African American girl growing up in the segregated South during the civil rights movement. When Ross was 11 years old she was raped by a stranger who was never prosecuted, but that was only the beginning of her abuse. At 15 years old she was the victim/survivor of incest, and became pregnant by her 27-year old cousin. Ross had a son by her cousin, and she has often described the experience of her own incest and the broader implications of incest and sexual abuse in the Black community in her work (Nelson 2010; Ross 2018; 2006b).

As Ross's story suggests, RJ includes a range of issues including sexual assault and rape. Choosing when and with whom we will partner and have sex is often not a choice for women. WOC are at high risk for sexual assault and are vulnerable to sexual violence, such as the silence in the community and failure of the legal system to protect them. According to a study by the Black Women's Blueprint, 60% of Black girls will experience sexual abuse before turning 18 years old and the vast majority never report it (Axtell 2012). The Department of Justice estimates that for every white woman who reports her rape, at least five white women do not report, while for every Black woman who reports her rape, there are at least 15 Black women who do not report (Axtell 2012). Why are Black women not reporting at the same rates? Racist and sexist stereotypes about Black men as sexual predators and Black women as insatiable "Jezebels" (Harris 2015) who cannot control their own sexual appetites or fertility present special challenges for Black women when seeking help for sexual violence from the very social service systems that discriminate against them (Axtell 2012). Ross survived the sexual violence from her childhood, but she would later learn that Black women's reproductive bodies were under attack in ways that she had yet to discover.

Ross was 23 years old and a student at Howard University when she was presented with a form of birth control that was easy to use and readily available (Kolata 1987; Roepke & Schaff 2014). It was the early 1970s and the Dalkon Shield, a new intrauterine contraceptive device (IUD), hit the market by storm and was especially popular among young married women and college-aged women who wanted a non-hormonal based form of birth control that was reversible (Goldberg 2012). Abortion was only made legal in 1973 and still not available to poor women who could not afford it, so the idea of an unintended pregnancy was not something that Ross was ready to consider as a young college student with a long life, and many reproductive years, ahead of her.

Ross used the IUD for nearly three years until she began to experience some unpleasant symptoms and subsequent complications. She sought medical help, but her symptoms were ignored and misdiagnosed by white male doctors as a sexually transmitted disease (STD) for more than six months. After nearly dying in her apartment she woke up in a hospital bed to the news that the doctors had performed a total hysterectomy. Ross's doctors had not paid sufficient attention to her pain or her repeated attempts to convey that there was something else and not merely an easily treatable STD going on. This neglect nearly cost Ross her life. To save her life, doctors were forced to perform a hysterectomy, permanently altering Ross's reproductive choices for the rest of her life. Ross, already the mother of a child born of rape, would never experience the birth of children free from violence. Her health was permanently altered from the loss of her reproductive organs coupled with the hormones used to regulate her body.

For Ross, this moment was pivotal and marked her political interests in issues of forced sterilization and sterilization abuse that targeted all the women in her family and other mostly poor working-class WOC (Ross 2017). Ross was not the only woman injured and almost killed by the Dalkon Shield. The Dalkon Shield caused injuries to more than 300,000 women, including an unknown number of infertility cases and some deaths, and it remains today the largest personal injury case in United States history (Roepke and Schaff 2014). However, what is different about Ross is that nearly every woman in her immediate family had an unnecessary and preventable hysterectomy, and all before they were 30 years old. Ross immediately began to understand her own experience of sterilization as part of the larger history of forced sterilization and abuse experienced by WOC. At 23 years old, inspired by her own experiences, Ross entered the reproductive rights movement opposing sterilization abuse and filed the first ever civil complaint against the company that produced the Dalkon Shield. She won her case and received a substantial settlement, which led to other cases and the company's ultimate bankruptcy, and propelled her as a leader in the RJ movement, altering the way that we understand reproductive rights forever. When it comes to RJ, Black women helped to pioneer and expand the idea of reproductive rights and justice, but remain to this day the least likely in the US to receive adequate reproductive healthcare or to live in communities with the resources to choose when and if they will parent (Ross 2017). Black women remain extremely vulnerable to domestic and state-sanctioned police violence (Crenshaw 2015; Mogul, Ritchie, Whitlock 2011; Ritchie 2006), high rates of poverty, and other forms of systemic oppression with major implications for their overall health and well-being. Black women pioneered the movement for RJ, but have yet to benefit directly from it. For example, Black women in the United States have the highest rates of maternal and pediatric mortality, far exceeding white women and other women throughout the world (CDC 2017). Several scholars have noted that this is due to multiple factors including a history of systemic cultural racism and ensuing racism perpetrated in the medical community (Callaghan et al., 2006; MacDorman, Marian, and Mathews 2008).

Cultural, political, and legal strategies to oppress reproductive bodies that do not fit into the white patriarchal heteronormative cisgendered model leave WOC and other marginalized women under constant threat of violence and oppression. The historic and neocolonial nature of reproductive politics transcends borders. Our own familial histories reflect the importance of being in solidarity with women across geographic boundaries in response to local to global dominant mechanisms of reproductive oppression.

Reproductive Justice in the Global Context

No country in the world has committed to a vision that can guarantee the physical security of women (WomenStats Project 2014). Our writing is rooted in our experiences of being the targets of sexual and physical violence, of being witness to personal and state violence against our family members, and of being part of a culture and systems that constantly reinforce lack of agency and choice with our own bodies. Living free from violence is a human right. However, globally, women and girls experience high rates of sexual violence, including sex trafficking, intimate partner violence, and femicide. Further, layers of socially constructed gender norms within a given culture manifest as lack of political will at various levels of government. For example, very few legal state efforts have gone into investigating the murdered and missing Indigenous women in Canada and the young women in Ciudad Juarez, Mexico, reinforcing permissive practices of violence against women (Ensalaco 2006; Walsh 2017). Across the globe, women lack equal access to education, economic opportunities, political participation, and health and reproductive health (UN

Women 1995). Reproductive injustice is a global crisis. Thus, applying an RJ framework in a global context helps to deconstruct complex systems of gender inequity sustained through transnational social, economic, and political processes.

Rooted in colonialism, neoliberal globalization reinforces systemic control over economic trade, natural resources, land, labor practices, and the construction of race, class, gender, sexuality, and citizenship norms in achieving political and economic dominance (Parekh and Wilcox 2018). The dominant discourse on neoliberal policies proclaims to reduce poverty, increase living standards and work opportunities, and strengthen economic growth. However, neoliberalism has been shown to extend the gap between the rich and poor, increase militarism instigating the conditions for war and internal conflicts, exploit natural resources, and privatize needed social services, such as health and education. Women most marginalized, who are poor, young, member of an ethnic minority, Indigenous, or immigrant, are unjustly impacted (Jaggar 2009). Women are disproportionately vulnerable to economic and political marginalization, exploitation, poverty, and violence. As a woman with roots in Chile, I have been drawn to understand the dynamics of inequity across borders. I have documented mobilization efforts in Ciudad Juarez, Mexico in response to the missing and murdered young women, many of whom relocated to work in the Maquiladoras. I have also documented environmental harms from Global North mining companies in Honduras, that have resulted in widespread health and reproductive health issues. In both these situations, neoliberal policies and practices instigated significant internal and international gender displacement (Ganguly-Scrase, Vogl, and Julian 2005).

Chile

Using Chile as a case study from dissertation research conducted between 2013 and 2014, this section will focus on and address the complex systems of inequity experienced by immigrant women. In using excerpts from my research, the aim is to shed light on the link between local and global mechanisms of inequity in order to understand the impact of this on women's reproductive lives. As the daughter of Latin@ immigrants, I felt personally connected to other women who shared their stories of isolation and discrimination, and of strength and resistance. Through an ethical commitment to the women in this study, my goal is to highlight their stories to inform our understanding of RJ. Thus, the following analysis will center on the experiences of immigrant women in Chile, whose lives are embedded within a web of global, national, and local policies and practices.

Historical perspective on reproductive health policies

Chile's reproductive health policies can be traced over three distinct time periods, each situated within a global and historic context, which determine immigrant women's reproductive health experience. The first period, before the 1973 coup d'état, draws attention to how social medicine led to universal healthcare and how Cold War and overpopulation discourses shaped women's reproductive health experiences in both positive and negative ways. The introduction of social medicine in Chile instigated a movement toward the implementation of policies to address the rising health issues due to poverty. With the introduction of social medicine and public healthcare, by the 1960s Chile had developed one of the most progressive reproductive health programs in the Americas (Moenne 2005; Shepard & Casas Becerra 2007). In part, this was instigated by US foreign policy to decrease poverty and population growth, which were seen as social, economic, and political destabilizing forces in Latin America. In addition, Chile was responding to the high rates of maternal mortality from unsafe abortion. Within the context of overpopulation and public health concern for women's lives, Chile became one of the first in the region to implement a state-subsidized family planning program (Moenne 2005; Casas 2004; Shepard & Casas Becerra 2007). The focus of family planning policies during the 1960s was on the reduction of maternal mortality from unsafe abortion, but not to liberate women from the dominant cultural expectations and gender norms: "Then family planning was not considered a right" (Casas and Herrera 2012, p. 142).

The second period, during the dictatorship from 1973 to 1989, illustrates how anticommunist sentiment and the introduction of economic neoliberalism shaped 17 years of repressive and restrictive reproductive health policies, specifically targeting poor women. Under Pinochet's *Política de Populación* (population policy), restrictive population control policies were developed and administered as a measure to protect national security (Casas 2004; Moenne 2005). During the dictatorship, women were at risk of military violence. Women were detained, tortured, sexually assaulted, and killed (Fried 2006). Further, as part of the neoliberal economic agenda, there was a reduction in social service spending, which greatly impacted the state-subsidized family planning program that was implemented the decade before. Isadora, an activist at a feminist non-governmental organization (NGO), remembered the withdrawal of contraceptives to women by the public health system.

> I remember listening to many women that went to the shantytowns to these organizations… they didn't receive the pill… they had it before, [but] it was not given to them anymore. I remember that. And that might have been two or three years after the coup. It was very soon after.

Poor women who accessed public health services were specifically impacted by changes in policies during the dictatorship. These included the forced removal of women's IUDs. Isadora, recalled,

> They were taking out the IUDs. I know cases, I myself interviewed women at that time they had their IUDs taken [without their consent]… I can tell you, incredible, incredible testimonies of women at that time. [It was] poor women. Very poor women… women from the poor neighborhoods.

Francesca, a community member in a *población* (low-income neighborhood) also remembers the removal of IUDs from women in her community,

> Did you know a matter that happened during the dictatorship that was very strong here? All the women in this area went to the *consultorio* [public health clinic] and suddenly, the doctors in the clinic removed the contraceptive. So, there were women 40 to 45 years old who [found themselves] pregnant. They took out the [IUD] without authorization of the woman.

The third and final time period, the return to democracy from 1990 to the present, highlights the aftermath of Pinochet's population and neoliberal economic policies. Neoliberal policies continue to reinforce privatization in multiple systems, such as education and health, and subsequent inequity for poor, Indigenous, immigrant, and young women from low-income sectors. For example, over 15% of all births in Chile are to adolescent mothers, with the highest percentage located within the low-income sector (Human Rights Watch 2011). Estrada (2009) states there were 80.9 births per 1,000 teenage girls in a La Pintana, a *población* in Santiago, versus 6.9 births represented in a higher income area in Santiago within the same age group (para. 10). Thus, it is not the reproductive needs of women that have changed over time, but rather the social, economic, and political context in which women's reproductive experiences are embedded.

Neoliberalism and the demand for domestic workers

As global economic neoliberal policies and practices transcend geographic borders, so does the increase in internal and international migratory flows of people. Consequently, a transnational pool of labor is created and sustained. Understanding the underlying social, economic, and political conditions of migratory patterns provides a deeper analysis of how neoliberalism sustains instability within home and host communities. Often those who are migrating have limited, or no, access to education, health, or employment in their home countries. They suffer from poverty, discrimination, and/or state or interpersonal violence, forcing global migration and displacement to areas where they continue to experience inequity, exploitation, and marginalization.

The northern part of Chile in the municipalities of Antofagasta and Calama, is home to multiple mining operations, including Chuquicamata, the largest copper mine in the world (Jarroud 2015). Thousands of immigrant women, mostly from bordering Peru and Bolivia, as well as Colombia and Ecuador, are drawn to the area by the mining industry, which creates the need for domestic workers and subsequent conditions for the exploitation of domestic labor.

The Bolivian women who I spoke with in this region had migrated to the area to escape violence and poverty. Because of the mining industry, they had heard of Calama as a place where they could find employment. There are many uncertainties for these women. Young women who come to Calama by themselves and are unfamiliar with the area are at risk of abuse, economic exploitation, and forced prostitution. Johanna, a young Bolivian woman, professed that she felt lucky because she found employment within four days with a "good boss." She had heard stories of other women with bad experiences. She stated that sometimes bosses are not nice and that women are forced to work on the street as sex workers. Johanna traveled to Chile by herself and, although the journey was difficult, she had a friend in Calama who greeted her, thus she was not on her own like many other women when they first arrive. Still, Johanna's situation was precarious. She entered Chile on a three-week tourist visa and she had already been in the country for two months. She wanted to return to Bolivia for a 10-day vacation to see her three children who were living with family in Bolivia, but she was worried what might happen at the border, both in leaving Chile and in trying to enter again after violating the conditions of her visa.

For Colombian immigrants, the internal and subsequent international displacement emerged as a consequence of political violence, which was strengthened by the US initiative, Plan Colombia, to arm military and paramilitary antidrug forces (Paley 2014; Segovia & Lufin 2013). Afro-Colombians make up one-third of the internally displaced persons in Colombia (Alzate 2008). Internally displaced women are at high risk for maternal mortality, gender-based violence, unintended pregnancies, complications from unsafe abortion, and sexually transmitted diseases, including HIV (Alzate 2008; Austin et al. 2008). Thus, Afro-Colombian women who are fleeing conflict take significant risks in order to arrive in a safe place (Black et al. Gupta 2014).

Francisco, a psychologist in the north of Chile, told me that when Afro-Colombians migrated to Calama, it was the first time local Chileans had seen a Black person.

> We are seeing Black people we've never seen our whole lives. We don't have Black people here in Chile... and the most incredible thing is they're Chileans, they're born here in Chile, so in the future they will be Chileans just like us. They will speak the same as us, not with the Colombian accents. It's a very new thing, so there is a lot of exclusion... [as soon as] they put a foot here in Chile, they are excluded and discriminated against.

When internally or internationally displaced, women lose access to critical social and cultural networks (Austin et al. 2008). In Chile, a country with deep historic and systemic racism, Afro-Colombians are regularly the target of discrimination constructing further social and economic marginalization, with women being stereotyped either as drug traffickers or prostitutes.

In Calama, prostitution is a distinct part of the economy. This is due, in part, to the exploitation of women within a highly structured patriarchal capitalist sex work industry in a mining town. Rojas (2012) defines areas in Calama as moral zones. These moral zones are areas that are condemned for moral reasons by middle- to upper-class Chileans. For example, Francisco explained that "downtown is a moral zone so we can always find prostitutes and we can find bars and drinking places." Moral zones are portrayed as frequented by outsiders, however Rojas revealed that this is a social belief not grounded in actual practice. Moral zones are typically patronized by local Chileans, but the blame for the social contamination is placed on immigrants, specifically on immigrant women. Shepard (2006) identifies this as a double discourse, whereby individuals promote "traditional and repressive sociocultural norms publicly, while ignoring – or even participating in... these norms in private" (p. 15). In exploring this further, I discovered that the majority of sex workers in Calama are Chileans and that the majority of immigrant women migrate to Calama to work in the service industry. However, still a hierarchy of inequality was revealed within the sex work industry, with immigrant women being most at risk. Alma explains,

> There were two figures here in prostitution... those women who have devoted all their lives in prostitution and work in places that can exercise prostitution, [such as] nightclubs, beer halls, or house dates... almost all are Chilean girls working in the *choperia* or *café* with legs, what they are called here in Chile... the majority have some college education. This other group has not completed basic education. They are women who have left school who started working very very young and are illiterate. In this group there are more immigrant women.

Intersectional systems of oppression, such as race, class, gender, and nation, shape a woman's agency within multiple contexts, including that of sex work. Not only are immigrant women blamed for the moral contamination of an area, they are also relegated to a lower strata within the sex work industry, making them more at risk of experiencing sexually transmitted diseases, including HIV, unwanted pregnancies and subsequent unsafe abortions, discrimination, and violence.

Luisa, a social worker from a health organization in a *población* south of Santiago's city center, explained that the biggest expression of inequality for women in Chile is violence: "gender violence is present in all areas of the state." Women are discriminated against, used to traffic drugs, and are insulted, raped, abandoned, hit, humiliated, and degraded. She added that women suffer from direct violence, but also violence from gender and race inequality such as inappropriate sexual conduct from the police or racial discrimination by border agents when they are detained.

According to Alma, a *matrona* [midwife] in a *consultorio* in Calama, Servicio Nacional de la Mujer (National Women's Service, SERNAM) reported that approximately 80% of the women in Calama are victims of some form of abuse. In Alma's *consultorio* alone, roughly 50% of the women they see have experienced some degree of violence. She explains,

> There is physical and psychological violence here. Pregnant women still suffer from physical violence. Here is a mining town where men come to work. Here it is very macho and still men beat women to feel more macho. Women suffer some degree of violence either psychological or physical… there are extreme cases like pregnant women that we have here who are still beat up.

Paloma, an immigrant woman from Peru, was 13 years old when her husband threatened if she did not marry him, he would kill her father. This man was 11 years her senior. Paloma was pregnant at 14 years old with their first child. When she was seven months pregnant, he started hitting her. Then he started sleeping with other women and inviting them to the house and being with them in front of her. Sometimes he would disappear for a week at a time and return with no money and no reason for why he was gone. When she started working, he questioned why she came home so late, accusing her of sleeping with other men. Insulting and beating her became an evening ritual when she got home from work. Sometimes he would come home drunk in the middle of the night and she would wake to him pulling her outside by her hair, including while she was pregnant with their other children. He was violent with her in every way, including sexually, repeatedly raping her. This type of abuse was an everyday occurrence. When she came to Chile in search of work, he followed her and the daily violence continued for many years. At the time of the first interview with her, she was trying to separate from him. She was staying at a friend's house, but it was very difficult for her to be away from her youngest, who at this time was 14 years old. She always put her children first and often went without eating in order to feed them. She has four children from this marriage and has had four abortions in total, two of which occurred in Chile.

Alma reported that immigrant women are discriminated against on all levels, "it's a pyramid and each [level] starts when they arrive in Chile undocumented."

Alma declared, "Those who are pregnant are actually discriminated against and undermined to the fullest. There is no law that will protect them." Employers do not always see domestic workers as human and there is fear of denouncement as domestic work is in the private sphere with little to no regulation (Masi De Casanova 2013; Segovia and Lufin 2013). The immigrant women who I interviewed suffered from overt racism, which often included verbal and physical abuse, and were exploited by their employers. Multiple women shared stories of having to work over their maximum hours or on their days off if they were live-in domestic workers. Not having time off or working late hours made it difficult for these women to receive health and reproductive healthcare. Paloma left for work at 6:00 am and did not return home until 7:30 pm. When she got home from work, she cooked and cleaned and washed her children's clothes until 1:00 am. As a domestic worker, Paloma often took care of other women's children in addition to her own. Paloma's employer stated that if she got pregnant, she would lose her job, which she needed to support the four children she already had.

The decision to terminate a pregnancy in a highly criminalized environment most often was connected to concerns about motherhood and family. Paloma, for example, had no control within her relationship to manage family planning. Nor did she have control in her work environment where she would lose her job if she became pregnant. Keeping her job in order to support her children meant that Paloma could not become pregnant again. Yet, Paloma had no control within her relationship of whether or not she became pregnant. Paloma's decision, like the decisions of other women interviewed in this study, to terminate her pregnancies was in response to economic and social inequality in which her life and the context of her decisions are embedded. The dominant cultural discourse on abortion in Chile declares that women who terminate their pregnancies have acted against the social norm of being a mother. However, often it is in the commitment to motherhood that abortion becomes the alternative for women.

According to Segovia and Lufin (2013), women migrating in search of work opportunities, involves the broader family context. Over 80% of Colombian immigrants in Chile have children living in their home country, linking economic and political dynamics of displacement with family responsibility and obligation. Thus, immigrant women in Chile are faced with distinct challenges. These women are confronted with state and interpersonal violence, exploitation, loss of leaving their families and children behind, lack of state support and protection, and immigration policies that restrict their mobility and access to resources.

I visited a Catholic Church in Calama where the Sisters provided support to immigrant women. Sister Maria reiterated that undocumented women constantly face social and economic difficulties. Further, Sister Maria stated there is limited prenatal care for undocumented women, so these women show up at the hospital when they are due to deliver, impacting both maternal and infant mortality rates. According to Nuñez and Torres (2007), in 2002 there were approximately 23,000 Peruvian women in Chile, of which over 75% were of reproductive age. These statistics show how large segments of the population are at risk of not receiving needed reproductive health services. Of the births delivered at the hospital in Calama, 40% are born to immigrant women (Jarroud 2015). Alma added, "In Antofogasta, the majority of stillbirths are born to foreign women" because they cannot access healthcare, "so these are very serious matters."

In theory, Chilean women with limited financial resources can access reproductive healthcare because there is some level of state protection. Participants highlight that this is not the case for immigrant women. Alma attributes this to both inherent inequities in society as well as lack of political will to allocate resources for immigrant women,

> There is discrimination and racism [and] there is a stereotype of the user population, especially women across the border. Then there is abuse, much, much abuse and because the system is, say, this system has no guidance to ensure the rights of the people... I think that [is] the underlying problem. It is a political decision that you want to keep the focus... on containing state spending.

Undocumented women in Chile face social and economic difficulties, not unlike other poor Chilean women. However, with the added component of immigrant status, there are multiple intersecting systems of oppression, which limit agency and choice. These difficulties are the result of everyday violence, such as poverty, racism, sexism, and lack of access to quality employment, education, and health and reproductive health services (Nuñez and Torres 2007). The existing structures of inequality impact women's lives and serve as the context in which reproductive health choices are limited and controlled.

Racism, classism, and sexism are deeply embedded in contemporary cultural attitudes in Chile as a result of historic structures and processes. Paola, a feminist researcher, reflects,

> I would say that inequality is something that's been present all along in the history of Chile... Mapuches are not equal to the Chileans... poor people are not equal to the rich ones... women are not equal to men, but that's normal. So, what's normal? It's not equality; it's inequality.

The normalization of inequality is not unique to Chile, but rather a representation of how cultural attitudes and beliefs sustain systems of inequality. In Chile, this plays out in profound and distinctive ways, such as the limitation and denial of access and opportunities within multiple systems.

An RJ framework sheds light on mechanisms of inequality as indivisible from embodied experience, highlighting how women negotiate their reproductive lives in a complex system of distinct interlocking forms of oppression. The case study of immigrant women in Chile underscores the multiple ways that women lack agency within global to local mechanisms of social, economic, and political power structures and resultant inequity. Inequity and parallel human rights violations, such as being the target of political violence, discrimination and exploitation in employment, interpersonal and sexual violence, forced prostitution, internal and international displacement, and lack of access to needed health and reproductive health services as highlighted in the case study, limit control over choice around having a child, not having a child, or being able to raise the children that a woman already has. Thus, to achieve reproductive freedom elicits a multidimensional response.

Conclusion

As we move into a new era of reproductive politics we will need to think about how to ensure that the framework that was designed specifically to empower Black women and girls, does empower them and other WOC who live under the constant threat of violence and the daily violation to their human rights. We also need to reaffirm our commitment to poor women, undocumented women, and immigrant women, Indigenous women, and trans-women, and other gender nonbinary people who are constantly mis-gendered and often the victims of violence at a higher rate than all other women.

Reproductive justice is a theoretical frame to understand the complex system of interlocking forms of oppression in which women's reproductive relations are embedded. Having an understanding of the multiple systems of inequity (social construction of laws, policies, cultural attitudes, poverty, discriminatory practices, violent harms against women) that impact women helps the ability to deconstruct inequity in order to change it. Reproductive justice is also a Black feminist praxis (Ross 2017). Inequity is embodied. Thus, marginality is not only a place of social exclusion, but also a place of resistance. One of the many principles that make up a reproductive justice frame includes political power and participation from those most impacted as necessary to achieve RJ (p. 301). Situating the narratives of marginalized individuals and communities in the center of analysis helps to change the politics of knowledge production. Further, it helps to foster a space of critical reflection to make visible and change harmful power structures and to acknowledge the strength of women's resistance within the context of inequity. Mohanty (2003) states, "This particular marginalized location makes the politics of knowledge and the power investments that go along with it visible so that we can then engage in work to transform the use and abuse of power" (p. 231).

Note

1 We capitalize Black in the tradition of the Black press and scholars like W.E.B. Dubois, who argued that Black always be capitalized as a form of respect when talking about the Black experience (Tharps 2014), We choose to also capitalize Women of Color. We do so as a sign of respect and to center their humanity in a world dominated by racism and gender-based violence. In this chapter we will also capitalize not only Black but also Indigenous and Women of Color (and not white when referring to white people or white communities) to not only pay People of Color respect, but to also politically call attention to the use of power that is embedded in language. Capitalizing Black and not white helps to signal the ongoing need to demarginalize Blackness and decenter whiteness in the face of enduring white supremacy and racial inequality.

References

Alzate, Monica. 2008. "The Sexual and Reproductive Rights of Internally Displaced Women: The Embodiment of Colombia's Crisis." *Disasters* 32(1): 131–148.

Austin, Judy, Samantha Guy, Louise Lee-Jones, et al. 2008. "Reproductive Health: A Right for Refugees and Internally Displaced Persons." *Reproductive Health Matters* 16(31): 10–21.

Axtell, Brooke. 2012. "Black Women, Sexual Assault and the Art of Resistance." *Forbes Magazine*, April 25.

Black, Benjamin O., Paul A. Bouanchaud, Jenine K. Bignall, et al. 2014. "Reproductive Health During Conflict." *The Obstetrician & Gynaecologist* 16(3): 153–160.

Callaghan, W.M., M.F. MacDorman, S.A. Rasmussen, et al. 2006. "The Contribution of Preterm Birth to Infant Mortality Rates in the United States." *Pediatrics* 118(4): 1566–1573.

Casas, Lidia. 2004. "Women and Reproduction: From Control to Autonomy? The Case of Chile." *Journal of Gender, Social Policy & the Law* 12(3): 427–519.

Casas, Lidia and Tania Herrera. 2012. "Maternity Protection vs. Maternity Rights for Working Women in Chile: A Historical Review." *Reproductive Health Matters* 20(40): 139–147.

Crenshaw, Kimberle. 1989. "Demarginalizing the Intersection of Race and Sex: A Black Feminist Critique of Antidiscrimination Doctrine, Feminist Theory and Antiracist Politics." *University of Chicago Legal Forum*. Art. 8.

Crenshaw, Kimberlé. 1991. "Mapping the Margins: Identity Politics, Intersectionality, and Violence against Women." *Stanford Law Review* 43(6): 1241–1299.

Crenshaw, Kimberle. 1997. "Intersectionality and Identity Politics: Learning from Violence against Women of Color." In *Reconstructing Political Theory: Feminist Perspectives*, edited by Mary Lyndon Shanley and Uma Narayan, 178–193. University Park, PA: Pennsylvania State University Press.

Crenshaw, Kimberlé, Andrea J. Ritchie, et al. 2015. "Say her name: Resisting police brutality against black women."African American Policy Forum, Center for Intersectionality and Social Policy Studies, Columbia Law School.

Davis, A.Y. 1983. *Women. Race and Class*. New York, NY: Vintage.

Ensalaco, Mark. 2006. "Murder in Ciudad Juárez: A Parable of Women's Struggle for Human Rights." *Violence Against Women* 12(5): 417–430.

Estrada, Daniela. 2009. "*Chile: Teen Pregnancy, A Problem That Won't Go Away.*" *Inter Press Service News Agency*. Available at: http://www.ipsnews.net/2009/11/chile-teen-pregnancy-a-problem-that-wonrsquot-go-away/.

Fried, Gabriella. 2006. "Piecing Memories Together after State Terror and Policies of Oblivion in Uruguay: The Female Political Prisoner's Testimonial Project (1997–2004)." *Social Identities* 12(5): 543–562.

Ganguly-Scrase, Ruchira, Gillian Vogl, and Roberta Julian. 2005. "Neoliberal Globalization and Women's Experience of Forced Migrations in Asia." In *Proceedings of the Social Change in the 21st Century Conference*, edited by C. Bailey and K. Barnett, 2–14. Brisbane, Australia: Queensland University of Technology, Centre for Social Change Research, School Humanities & Human Services.

Goldberg, K. 2012. "Designing the Popularity of the Dalkon Shield." Unpublished Master's thesis. Case Western Reserve University. Available at: https://etd.ohiolink.edu/!etd.send_file?accession=case1333737047&disposition=inline.

Harris, Tamara Winfrey. 2015. *The Sisters are Alright: Changing the Broken Narrative of Black Women in America*. Oakland, CA: Berrett-Koehler.

Hemmings, C., I. Grewal, C. Kaplan, and R. Wiegman. 2011. "Why Stories Matter: The Political Grammar of Feminist Theory. Durhm, NC: Duke University Press.

hooks, bell. 2010. *Understanding Patriarchy*. Louisville, KY: Louisville Anarchist Federation Federation.

Human Rights Watch. 2011. "World Report 2011: Chile." Available at: https://www.hrw.org/world-report/2011/country-chapters/chile.

Jaggar, A.M. 2009. "The Philosophical Challenges of Global Gender Justice." *Philosophical Topics* 37(2): 1–15.

Jarroud, Marienela. 2015. Antofagasta Mining Region Reflects Chile's Inequality. *Inter Press Service News Agency*. Available at: http://www.ipsnews.net/2015/09/antofagasta-mining-region-reflects-chiles-inequality/.

Kolata, G. 1987. "The Sad Legacy of the Dalkon Shield." *New York Times*, December 6. Available at: https://www.nytimes.com/1987/12/06/magazine/the-sad-legacy-of-the-dalkon-shield.html.

MacDorman, M.F. and T.J. Mathews. 2008. "Recent Trends in Infant Mortality in the United States." NCHS data brief, no 9. Hyattsville, MD: National Center for Health Statistics.

Masi de Casanova, Erynn. 2013. "Embodied Inequality: The Experience of Domestic Work in Urban Ecuador." *Gender & Society* 27(4): 561–585.

Moenne, Maria Elena A. 2005. "Embodying Memory: Women and the Legacy of the Military Government in Chile." *Feminist Review* 79: 150–161.

Mogul, Joey L., Andrea J. Ritchie, and Kay Whitlock. 2011. *Queer (In)justice: The Criminalization of LGBT People in the United States*, vol. 5. Boston, MA: Beacon Press.

Mohanty, C.T. 2003. *Feminism Without Borders: Decolonizing Theory, Practicing Solidarity*. Durham, NC: Duke University Press.

Nelson, Jennifer. 2010. "'All This That Has Happened to Me Shouldn't Happen to Nobody Else': Loretta Ross and the Women of Color Reproductive Freedom Movement of the 1980s." *Journal of Women's History* 22(3): 136–160.

Núñez, Nuria R. and Carmen E. Torres. 2007. "Mujeres Migrantes Peruanas y Salud Reproductiva: Usarias de Consultorios de Salud de la Zona Norte de la Region Metropolitana." Documento de trabajo. Fundación Instituto de la Mujer/UNFPA, Santiago de Chile.

Paley, Dawn. 2014. *Drug War Capitalism*. Oakland, CA: AK Press.

Parekh, Serena and Shelley Wilcox. 2018. "Feminist Perspectives on Globalization." In *The Stanford Encyclopedia of Philosophy*, edited by Edward N. Zalta, Spring edn. Available at: https://plato.stanford.edu/archives/spr2018/entries/feminism-globalization/.

Price, K. (2010). What is Reproductive Justice?: How Women of Color Activists are Redefinding the Pro-Choice Paradigm. *Meridians* 10(2): 42–65.

Ritchie, Andrea J. 2006. "Law Enforcement Violence against Women of Color." In *Color of Violence: The INCITE! Anthology*, edited by INCITE! Women of Color Against Violence, 138–156. Durham, NC: Duke University Press.

Roepke, C.L. and E.A. Schaff. 2014. "Long Tail Strings: Impact of the Dalkon Shield 40 years Later." *Open Journal of Obstetrics and Gynecology* 4(16): 996–1005.

Rojas, Pablo. 2012. "La Construccion del Centro de Calama Como Region Moral." Unpublished doctoral dissertation. Universidad Católica del Norte, Facultad de Humanidades, Escuela de Psiocología, Antofagasta, Chile.

Ross, Loretta. 2006a. "Understanding Reproductive Justice: Transforming the Pro-Choice Movement." *Off Our Backs* 36(4): 14–19.

Ross, Loretta J. 2006b. "A Personal Journey from Women's Rights to Civil Rights to Human Rights." *The Black Scholar* 36(1): 45–53.

Ross, Loretta. 2017. "Reproductive Justice as Intersectional Feminist Activism." *Souls* 19(3): 286–314.

Ross, Loretta J. 2018. "Teaching Reproductive Justice: An Activist's Approach." *Black Women's Liberatory Pedagogies*, edited by O. Perlow, D.I. Wheeler, S.L. Bethea, and B.M. Scott, 159–180. Cham: Palgrave Macmillan.

Ross, Loretta J., Sarah L. Brownlee, Dazon Dixon Diallo, et al. 2001. "The 'Sistersong Collective': Women of Color, Reproductive Health and Human Rights." *Latina American Journal of Health Studies* 17(2): Research Library 79.

Ross, L. and R. Solinger. 2017. *Reproductive Justice: An Introduction*, vol. 1. Berkeley: University of California Press.

Segovia, Jimena Silva and Marcelo Lufin. 2013. "Approaches to the Afro-Colombian Experience in Chile: South-South Immigration Toward the Northern Regions." *Journal of Black Studies* 44(3): 231–251.

Shepard, Bonnie. 2006. *Running the Obstacle Course to Sexual and Reproductive Health: Lessons from Latin America*. Westport, CT: Praeger Publishers.

Shepard, Bonnie and Lidia Casas Becerra. 2007. "Abortion Policies and Practices in Chile: Ambiguities and Dilemmas." *Reproductive Health Matters* 15(30): 202–210.

Tharps, L. 2014. "The Case for Black with a capital B." *New York Times*, November 18. Available at: https://www.nytimes.com/2014/11/19/opinion/the-case-for-black-with-acapital-b.html.

UN Women. 1995. The United Nations Fourth World Conference on Women, Beijing, China. Available at: https://www.un.org/en/events/pastevents/women_conf_beijing_1995.shtml.

Walsh, Jenna. 2017. "The National Inquiry into the Missing and Murdered Indigenous Women and Girls in Canada: A Probe in Peril." *Indigenous Law Bulletin* 8(30): 6–10.

WomenStats Project. 2014. "WomenStats Maps." Available at: http://www.womanstats.org/maps.html.

Index

abolitionist feminism, 417
abortion, 13, 50, 150, 182, 207, 210, 211, 286, 337, 430, 437, 464, 465, 467, 469, 472, 474–476
acquiescence, 391, 399
adoption, 10, 49, 109, 181, 186, 187, 191–192, 194, 340, 348, 350, 413, 418, 448, 455, 456
adultery, 41, 42, 287, 344, 378
affirmative defense, 401
Africa, 14, 30, 42, 44, 62–64, 66, 68, 71–73, 185, 195, 210, 216, 243, 265, 267, 268, 343, 362, 365, 411
Afro-Columbian women, 474
AIDS, 8, 72, 74, 80, 81, 100, 165, 192, 207, 234, 292, 294, 312, 328, 329, 331, 363
AIDS Pandemic, 363, 364, 413, 435, 436
allies, 4, 123, 124, 131, 132, 233, 244, 252, 262, 306, 457
Allison, Dorothy, 299
allyship, 123
Alternate Law Forum, the, 450
American Association of University Women (AAUW), 391
American Native two-spirit identified, 213
Amnesty International, 345, 412, 419, 421, 458
Anglo-Saxon world, the, 446, 449, 452, 458
anti-black racism, 418

anti-discrimination law, 243, 247, 252, 389, 395, 396
anti-homophobia, 124, 125, 129–132, 135
antiquity, 302, 306
anti-sex trafficking movements, 417
antisodomy laws, 61, 67, 73, 347, 362, 431
Argentina, 14, 25, 27, 28, 185, 186
Asia, 44, 62, 66, 68, 185, 265, 268, 270, 343, 347, 348, 365, 381, 411, 413, 440, 451, 453
Asia-Pacific, 343, 346, 348
assault, 61, 292, 361, 375, 389, 390, 395, 396, 399, 465, 469, 472
Assisted Reproductive Technology (ART), 184
Australia, 111, 151, 185–187, 243, 245, 246, 249, 338, 339, 342, 346–348, 360, 365, 374, 376, 381–384
Azaad Bazaar, 450

Badgett, M. V. Lee, 251
Bahamas, 61, 71
Baker, N. Carrie, 405
Bara, 318, 319, 321, 324–328, 330, 331
Barad, Karen, 225, 236
Bauer, Heike, 24, 29, 30, 144, 147
Beauvoir, Simone de, 282
Beccalossi, Chiara, 25, 27, 28, 144, 145, 147
Bechdel, Alison, 318, 328–331
BE HEARD, 400

Companion to Sexuality Studies, First Edition. Edited by Nancy A. Naples.
© 2020 John Wiley & Sons Ltd. Published 2020 by John Wiley & Sons Ltd.

Beijing Platform of Action, 433
Berdache, 44
Berlin, 23, 24, 50, 146, 149
Bible Belt, 206
binding arbitration, 400
biotypology, 27
birth control *see* contraceptives
bisexuality, 181, 216, 285, 286, 312 *see also* sexual identities
black radical feminism, 468
black women, 7, 13, 66, 288, 465, 466, 468–470
Black Women's Health Imperative (BWHI), 468
Bolivian women, 473
Boys' love, 318, 319, 326–327
brahmachaya, 34
Bray, Alan, 307
breast/chestfeeding, 180, 195, 196
Brian McNaught, 448
Buddhism, 43, 213, 343
Building Bridges program, the, 448
Burke, Tarana, 396
Burlington Industries, Inc., 401
Butler, Judith, 6–8, 80, 87, 103, 283, 284, 290, 302, 341

Canada, 64, 185, 186, 188, 214, 243, 245, 250, 265, 270, 338, 339, 341, 342, 365, 382, 409, 410, 412, 419, 454, 456, 470
Caribbean, 65, 66, 68, 149, 150, 265, 267, 268, 411
castration, 43, 44 *see also* Eunuchs
Catholicism, 14, 211
Catholics, 209
censorship, 50, 152, 306, 307, 318–322, 324
Central Europe, 24
Chauncey, George, 24, 33, 49, 301
chestfeeding, 180, 195, 196
children, 10, 41–44, 46–48, 165, 166, 182, 186, 191–193, 195, 197, 229, 230, 249, 265, 270, 313, 330, 366, 372, 375, 376, 379–381, 432, 433, 440, 464, 466–469, 473, 475, 476
child sexual abuse, 376–377
Chile, 13, 448, 471–477
Chilean women, 477
China, 25, 34, 41, 42, 45, 260, 271, 346, 347, 403, 451

Christianity, 43, 44, 61, 66, 206, 211, 213, 343
Christian Right (and Religious Right), 207, 364, 417
cisgender, 75, 122, 123, 134, 179, 180, 193, 252, 292, 457
Civil Rights Act of 1964, 244
classism, 131, 477
class oppression, 309
clergy, 24, 43, 208, 364, 452
climate survey tool, 448
Coalition Against Trafficking in Women (CATW), 380
Cold War, 27, 50, 471
Colgan, Fiona, 242, 250, 447–449, 454–456
colonial, 7, 12, 24, 30, 34, 61–75
colonial governance, 62
colonialism *see* postcolonialism
comics, 11, 318–331
Comics Code Authority (CCA), 321, 326
coming of age, 313, 330
coming out, 84, 112, 180, 248, 252, 292, 293, 312, 313, 420
Committee for the Study of Sex Variants, 31
common sense, 306, 397, 398, 403
communism, 22, 28, 50 *see also* socialism
comparative sexual citizenship, 40–51
conception, 67, 83, 85, 101, 126, 144, 146, 148, 149, 181, 188, 189, 337–341, 343, 344, 346, 348, 350, 361, 435, 439
Conference on Population and Development, 432, 466
confidentiality, 404
confucianism, 343
congregations, 207, 208, 212, 215, 447, 452
Connell, Catherine, 129, 249, 268, 361, 417, 418
consent, 61, 172, 361, 362, 371, 376, 380–383, 399, 404, 437, 438
conservative Christianity, 206
constructionism, 80, 82–83, 282
consultorio, 472, 475
consumerism, 47–48
contact zones, 64
Contagious Diseases Act of 1868, 362, 431
contraceptives, 47, 149, 150, 430, 466, 469, 472
cross-dressing, 24, 44, 45
Cruse, Howard, 328–330

cultic prostitution *see* sacred prostitution
curriculum, 14, 123, 127, 129, 132–134, 230–233, 235
cycle, 27, 181, 189
Czechoslovakia, 28, 33, 35, 148

Dalkon Shield, 469, 470
dangerousness, 374, 375
Daoism, 43
data analysis, 95, 107–111
David, Emmanuel, 252
death penalty, 252, 344, 383
Declaration on the Elimination of Violence against Women, 433
decolonizing education, 135
deconstructionism, 79, 88
de facto partnerships, 342, 350
Defense of Marriage Act, the, 449
de Lauretis, Teresa, 8, 80, 91, 97, 288, 290
Dellinger, Kirsten, 248, 250
deviant sexualities, 66, 69, 72, 321, 385
dignity, 182, 390, 401–404
discourse, 5, 6, 8, 24, 30–34, 64, 69, 71, 72, 74, 81, 83–86, 88, 90, 91, 97, 99, 124, 125, 133, 182, 229, 233, 260, 266, 288, 308, 309, 342, 344–346, 362, 366, 385, 410, 411, 413, 416, 418–421, 430, 432, 439, 440
discrimination, 10, 73, 82, 124, 131, 180, 181, 188, 193–196, 243–247, 250–252, 340, 342, 379, 390, 392–397, 400, 403–405
divorce, 42, 48, 50, 329, 330, 338
domestic labor, 11, 258–260, 262–265, 473
domestic worker, 264–266, 269, 271, 411, 465, 466, 468, 473–477
dominant discourse, 458, 465, 471
Donna Haraway, 153
dowry *see* marriage payments
Drobac, Jennifer, 394, 398, 403
Drydakis, Nick, 246, 247

Eastern Europe, 30, 143, 148, 343, 411
East Indian Company, 361
economic and racial justice, 465
Ellerth, 401
Ellis, Havelock, 23–26, 34, 144, 146, 188, 189, 294, 310
emotional labor, 251, 259, 265, 267, 270, 414

Empire, 7, 24, 145, 342, 360–363
employer liability, 390, 397, 400–401
Employment Equality (Sexual Orientation) Regulation Act, 2003, 449
Employment Nondiscrimination Act (ENDA), 244, 446
Equal Employment Opportunity Commission (EEOC), 393
equality, 13, 33–35, 45, 48, 50, 68, 81, 90, 99, 148, 170, 208, 233, 249, 341, 347, 360, 364, 384, 402, 432, 445–459, 467, 474–477
equal opportunity employers, 447
equal opportunity policies (EEO), 450
essentialism, 180, 285, 288, 301, 311
ethics, 9, 95, 107–111, 206, 228, 234, 310, 410
eugenics, 27, 29, 147
eunuchs, 363, 439
Euro-American colonialism, 62
evangelical abstinence campaigns, 209, 210
evolutionary psychology, 3, 91, 161
expressive goals, 445–452
extramarital sex, 50, 66

Facebook, 286, 396
familial rejection, 313
family-making, 179, 182, 187–193
Faragher, 398, 400, 401
fascism, 22, 147
father, 32, 41, 42, 44, 47, 194–196, 330, 347, 468, 475
Fausto-Sterling, Ann, 6, 104, 282, 283
female dominance *see* matriarchy
femicide, 470
feminism, 6, 7, 33, 46, 50, 100, 270, 285, 287, 288, 414, 417, 439, 454
fertility, 43, 63, 71, 143, 144, 148–151, 180, 182, 188, 194, 366, 469
Fine, Michelle, 169
Fisher, Kate, 25, 229
Fitzgerald, Louise, 391
forced labor, 261, 420, 421
forced sterilization, 466, 469, 470
Foucault, Michel, 5, 7, 21, 22, 27, 31, 80–84, 88, 125–127, 144, 206, 285, 301–303, 307–310, 357–359, 374, 430, 431, 435
France, 14, 27, 186, 243, 245, 342, 365, 390, 431, 435

Frühstück, Sabine, 28, 144, 147
Fuller, Larry, 319
Funayama, Sanshi, 325

Gametes, 179, 181, 187–190
Gay and Lesbian Alliance Against Defamation (GLAAD), 294, 384, 455
gay and lesbian studies, 8, 79–82, 86–88, 91, 100, 281, 301
gayness, 365
gay rights movement, 207, 435
gay-straight alliances (GSA), 130, 233
gender, 3–5, 7–9, 14, 31, 33, 35, 43, 44, 48, 49, 61, 63–65, 67–69, 71, 82, 83, 86, 87, 98, 100, 101, 103, 107, 108, 111, 123–126, 128, 130, 133, 148, 164, 168, 172, 179–182, 187, 188, 193, 195, 196, 206, 209, 211, 213, 215, 231, 233, 244, 247, 259, 282–285, 288, 300
gender based violence, 433, 436, 437, 465, 474, 478
gender equality, 33, 35, 148, 236, 364
gender identity, 8, 44, 51, 213, 214, 233, 243, 244, 253, 283, 300, 301, 313, 320, 330, 339, 347, 349, 434, 436, 446, 450, 456
gender inequality *see* patriarchy; matriarchy
gender nonconformity, 49, 128, 244 *see also* cross-dressing
Germany, 7, 26, 32, 49, 145–147, 149, 243, 245, 365, 381, 390, 458
gestational parent, 188, 189
Giuffre, Patti, 242–253
The Global Alliance Against Traffic in Women (GAATW), 380, 421
global gay, 72
global intimate, 258, 271
globalization, 11, 12, 51, 74, 251, 259, 272, 358, 363–367, 410, 412, 413, 415, 429–441
Global Network of Sex Work Projects (NSWP), 413
global north, 8, 14, 71, 252, 259–261, 264, 265, 268, 358, 364, 365, 367, 412, 413, 417, 419, 447, 458, 471
global positioning systems (GPS), 376
Global South, 8, 12, 14, 122, 259, 261, 262, 265–267, 269, 270, 364, 367, 410–412, 416, 446, 448, 453, 454, 458

Goffman, Erving, 283
Go, Hirano, 325
Go, Mishima, 325
governance, 12, 62, 74, 348–349, 371, 372, 374, 383
governance (of sex and sexualities, bodies), moral governance, regulation, 372
Great Britain, 24

Hall, Radclyffe, 310
Halperin, David, 51, 97, 127, 307, 320, 430
harassment, 12, 13, 124, 129, 131, 242, 243, 365, 390–398, 400, 402–405
Harlem Renaissance, 311
Harris, 167, 169, 233, 294, 398, 469
Harvey Milk High School, 134
Hawai'i, 61, 62
Hawai'ians, 61, 62
health, science, and psychology, 9–10
Hearn, Jeff, 163, 242, 339, 381
Herzog, Dagmar, 34, 50, 145, 149
heteronormative, 10, 11, 65, 66, 88, 98, 107, 126, 128, 131, 179, 180, 182, 187, 188, 192, 193, 248, 251, 252, 269, 270, 339, 347, 362, 366, 368, 371, 372
heteronormative culture, 131, 252, 445
heteronormativity, 5, 8, 89, 98, 113, 123–125, 127, 129, 130, 132, 135, 232, 233, 248, 250, 252, 282, 284, 291, 341, 347
heterosexism, 68, 123, 124, 126–131, 160, 232, 360
heterosexuality, 3, 4, 10, 14, 23, 65, 72, 86, 87, 98, 104, 123, 125–131, 209, 215, 282, 284, 285, 306, 339, 358
heterosexual privilege, 123, 132, 233
Hijras, 181, 363, 453
Hill, Anita, 395
Hinduism, 43
Hirschfeld, Magnus, 7, 23–25, 29, 30, 32, 144–147, 149
history of sex and crime, 3–7, 33, 51, 83, 281, 300–305, 307, 358
HIV/AIDS, 8, 72, 74, 100, 165, 192, 234, 328
Hobby Lobby case, 452
homonormativity, 8, 73, 104, 112, 129–132, 249–251, 415

homophobia, 61, 73, 124–127, 129–134, 195, 207, 228, 232, 233, 236, 249, 252, 313, 329, 330
homosexuality *see* sexual identities
Hong Kong, 267, 346, 348, 450, 451
hostile work environment, 400, 401
human rights, 12–14, 122, 132, 244, 260, 348, 349, 413, 419, 420, 429, 432–434, 437–441
Human Rights Campaign, the, 450, 452
human sexual response, 27, 152
Humsafar Trust, the, 450
hypersexual, 66, 182, 287, 323, 324, 379, 415, 416, 419
hysteria, 46

Iceland, 186, 243, 346
identity contests, 454
illegitimacy, 362
immigrant women, 13, 465, 471, 473–478
immigration, 12, 46, 270, 272, 339, 340, 348, 360, 362, 365, 384, 419, 468, 476
Immigration Reform and Control Act of 1986, 360
India, 25, 34, 42, 43, 63, 64, 67, 71, 181, 190, 195, 346, 347, 361–363, 403, 431, 439, 440
indigenous, 13, 44, 63–66, 71, 135, 301, 303, 416, 468
indigenous peoples, 30, 64, 66, 135, 304
individual liability, 397
Indonesia, 210, 243, 244, 331, 349, 403
industrialization, 47–48
inequality between men and women *see* patriarchy; matriarchy
infertility, 27, 180, 181, 188, 189, 194, 469
insider activists, 455
Institute for the Study of Sexual Pathology in Prague, 24
Institute of Sex Research, 4, 23
instrumental goals, 445–447, 449, 451, 452
intercultural awareness, 45–46
internally displaced, 474
International Conference on Population and Development, 432
International League for Sexual Reform, 431
internationally displaced, 474
International Marriage Broker Regulation Act (IMBRA), 261–263
International Marriage/"Mail Order Bride", 262
International Organization of Migration (IOM), 359
intersectionality, 9, 14, 51, 153, 162–164, 167, 172, 452–454, 468
intersex, 49, 83, 180, 339, 347, 384, 393, 434, 437–439, 454
intimacy, 42, 258–272
intimate citizenship, 338, 341, 345
intimate industries, 259–262, 264, 265, 271
intimate labor, 10, 11, 15, 259–265, 267, 272
intrauterine contraceptive device (IUD), 469
intrauterine insemination (IUI), 151, 189
in-vitro fertilization (IVF), 10, 151, 189, 194
involuntary labor trafficking, 11, 260
Iran, 69, 166, 206, 216, 403, 439
Irvine, Janice, 26, 33, 46, 148, 170, 207
Islam (or Muslims), 42, 171, 206, 211, 213
Israel, 12, 186, 190, 207, 390, 402, 403
Italy, 25, 27, 193, 249, 311, 365
It's On Us, 401

Japan, 11, 25, 28, 34, 262, 267, 318–321, 323–327, 329–331, 346–348, 458
Jewish, 41, 46, 206, 214, 215, 329, 402
Johnson, Virginia, 4, 8, 9, 27, 33, 341, 342

Kaiser Family Foundation, 390
Kamasutra, 43
Kamir, Orit, 402, 403
Khwaja Siras, 453
Kimberle Crenshaw, 163, 468
Kinsey, Alfred, 4, 26, 27, 33, 146, 147, 152
The Kinsey Project, 125
kinship, 181, 192–193, 363
Krafft-Ebing, Richard von, 7, 21–24, 31, 32, 144, 145

lactation, 180, 195–197
Lanser, Susan, 301, 304, 305
Latin America, 14, 206, 265, 411, 413, 440, 458, 472
lesbian, gay, bisexual, and transgender (LGBT)
 bestseller, 305, 314
 employee caucus, 457
 global context, 12, 233, 252, 304, 470–471

history, 311
literary history, 302, 308, 311
military index, 345
representation, 302, 303, 306, 314
rights, 431, 432, 434, 437, 440, 454
studies, 127, 300–305, 311, 313
unions, 456
lesbian, gay, bisexual, trans, and queer/
    questioning (LGBTQ), 318
    rights, 29, 181–187, 243, 244, 253, 330
lesbian, gay, bisexual, trans, queer+
    (LGBTQ+) *see* gayness; lesbianism;
    bisexuality, transgender; two-spirit;
    homosexuality; sexual identities
lesbianism, 293, 305, 306, 384 *see also*
    sexual identities
limitations, statutes, 404
linkages, 64, 65, 422
Lišková, Kateina, 28, 33–35, 148
Lišková, Kateřina, 28, 33–35, 148
Lloren, Anouk, 243, 245, 449
Loretta Ross, 465, 466, 468

Macao, 346
Mackinnon, Catherine, 282, 284, 392, 393,
    400, 402
Magnus Hirschfeld, 7, 23, 29, 32, 145, 431
Māhū, 61, 63, 74, 181
Malawian, 207
Malaysia, 342, 346, 347, 362, 435, 451
male dominance *see* patriarchy
male sex work, 312, 415
manga, 11, 318, 319, 321, 322, 324,
    326–328, 330, 331
marginalization, 5, 62, 84, 122, 131, 367,
    412, 448, 471, 473, 474
market, 27, 35, 36, 73, 152, 258–260, 263,
    264, 266, 321, 324, 382, 396, 469
marriage
    ages of marriage, 42, 45
    arranged marriages, 344
    ceremonies, 41, 346
    companionate marriages, 48
    equality, 170, 208, 341, 384, 449
    remarriage, 50, 63, 361
    temporary marriages, 42
marriage payment, 41
masculinist organizational cultures, 448
Masters, William, 4, 9, 33, 146, 147, 152

masturbation, 46, 144, 165, 210, 229, 398
material feminism, 414
matriarchy, 40
matrona, 475
McCarren-Walter Act, 362
McCloud, Scott, 320
McNaught, Brian, 448
medical-therapeutic approaches, 308
memoir, 309, 313, 329–331
Meritor Savings Bank, 394, 397, 399, 400
methodology, 9, 95, 96, 101, 104–106, 111,
    225, 246, 376, 381
#MeToo, 13, 389–396, 399, 404
migration, 11, 12, 46, 259–263, 268–272,
    348, 357–368
Milano, Alyssa, 396
Millett, Kate, 282
miscarriage, 194, 195
miscegenation, 286, 357, 430
Mishel, Emma, 247
modernity, 63, 64, 69–71, 74, 148, 271, 304,
    420, 435
modern language of sexuality, 23
monasticism, 43, 309
monogamy, 68, 69, 153, 430
moral panic, 236, 375
mother, 13, 47, 166, 188, 189, 193, 195,
    265–266

National Black Women's Health Project, 468
national culture, 70, 446, 452
nationalism, 70, 71, 145, 149, 347, 454
Navtej Singh Johar v. Union of India, 450
neoliberal globalization, 11, 413, 471
neoliberal/neoliberalism, 22, 73, 134, 150,
    251–252, 259, 260, 411
Nepal, 344, 345, 347
New Age movements, 213
New Social Movements, 445
New View Campaign, 36
The New York Times, 395
New Zealand, 185, 191, 243, 338, 342, 347,
    348, 350, 365, 384
non-binary, 13, 49, 180, 181, 192, 304, 478
non-disclosure agreements, 400, 404
non-heterosexualities, 383–385
North America, 46, 47, 49, 100, 134, 307,
    341, 360, 411, 413
North Korea, 345

objective, 27, 36, 85, 100, 102, 104, 108, 234, 394, 398, 432
Office for Civil Rights (OCR), 394
Oliveri, Rigel, 391
Oncale, 397, 398, 403
ontology, 103, 104, 236, 285
Oosterhuis, Harry, 7, 21, 23, 31, 32, 145
orientalism, 62, 63
Orzechowicz, David, 250–252
Osman, Diriye, 299, 312, 313
outing costs, 446

pansexual, 398
parenthood, 149, 179–187, 190–193, 195, 196
parenting, 10, 179–197, 466
Parini, Lorena, 243, 245
Parkin, Wendy, 242
patriarchy, 40, 43, 129, 287, 288, 306, 419
pedagogy, 123, 124, 126–127, 131, 132, 134, 227, 232
pederasty (historical), 30, 45, 322
performative, 87, 104, 126, 282–284
Peruvian women, 476
pervasive, 72, 99, 128, 153, 246, 360, 391, 394, 396, 397
perverse press, 321–323
Phallic worship, 43
physique magazines, 321–323
pleasure, 22, 33, 36, 43, 66, 203, 228, 233, 234, 288, 291, 309, 310
población, 472, 473, 475
Poland, 27, 33, 207, 448
policy, 5, 11–12, 131, 170, 231, 233, 260, 282, 347, 396, 421
polyandry *see* polygamy
polygamy, 41, 47, 66
polygyny *see* polygamy
popular culture, 11, 107, 226, 281–295, 340
population control, 34, 71, 150, 430–433, 466, 467, 472
pornography, 382–383
positionality, 9, 95, 107–111, 164, 457
postcolonial, 7, 8, 12, 24, 61–75
postcolonialism, 46, 61, 62–65
postmodernism, 91, 102
postsocialism, 25, 148
poststructuralism, 80, 81, 83–85, 87, 91

poverty, 13, 29, 41, 263, 267, 418, 420, 432, 465, 466, 468, 471–473, 478
power, 7–9, 22, 24, 27, 30, 31, 33, 36, 64, 67, 69, 85–87, 103–105, 125, 126, 129, 131, 133, 134, 153, 164, 187, 193, 236, 268, 287, 306, 365, 378, 420, 430, 438, 466, 468, 477, 478
practices, 3–5, 8–13, 15, 25, 61, 66, 68, 69, 88, 101, 111, 112, 124, 132, 170, 171, 205–207, 210, 215, 233, 260, 284, 286, 287, 304, 347, 361, 364, 367, 399, 453, 455, 457–459
pregnancy, 13, 148–150, 169, 170, 188–191, 194, 195, 230, 289, 329, 367, 469
premarital sex, 208, 210, 212
privacy, 73, 187, 312, 348, 383, 402, 437, 466
privilege, 84, 105, 112, 122–124, 128–130, 134, 164, 192, 233, 236, 311, 316, 390, 398–399
procedure, 189, 401, 404
prostitute/sex worker, prostitution, sex work (and Harm) (and female subordination/ objectification), 25, 45, 67, 417, 419
prostitution, 12, 43–45, 50, 66, 67, 70, 125, 214, 263, 272, 287, 360, 373, 380, 411–414, 416–419, 431, 433
protestantism, 206, 211, 216
proxy goal, 449
psychoanalysis, 5, 30, 81, 88, 145, 146
Psychopathia Sexualis, 7, 21, 23, 32, 144, 145
public nudity, 371
public spaces, policing of, 194, 308, 346, 371, 372, 374, 385
pulp fiction, 311, 312

quantitative methods, 101, 107
quee pedagogy, 122–135
queer, 6–9, 11, 30, 49, 62, 65, 73, 79–92
  conversion, 215
  pedagogy, 123, 124, 126–127, 132, 134, 135
  research, 103–105, 108–114
  studies, 7, 62, 65, 99, 112, 122, 215, 232, 251, 302, 357
  theory, 6, 8, 9, 79–92, 95–100, 123–127, 135
workplaces/labor, 247

queering, 9, 87, 96–100, 129, 132–134, 251, 252
queer methodologies, 9, 95, 96, 100–111
Queer Nation, 8, 96
queer-only schools, 134
quid pro quo, 400

race/racial/racialization, 7, 8, 22, 24, 29, 31, 65, 70, 74, 91, 108, 110, 163, 164, 166, 172, 242, 244, 247, 259, 264, 283, 288, 301, 319, 359, 367, 368, 394, 446, 453
racial disparities, 466
racial hygiene, 22, 28, 29, 36
racialization, 6
racial oppression, 108
racism, 3, 7, 22, 29, 30, 70, 131, 150, 310, 313, 329, 360, 415, 418, 465, 474, 476, 477
radical feminism, 287
radical lesbian feminism, 125, 329
reasonable, 376, 394, 398, 401
reception of oocytes from partner (ROPA), 189
reflexivity, 9, 107–111
relationships, 8, 11, 24, 27, 34, 35, 40, 49, 74, 87, 89, 90, 129, 145, 161, 163, 166, 171, 180, 192, 193, 195, 207, 210, 212, 214, 216, 228, 229, 245, 251, 258, 262, 263, 265–272, 293, 308, 313, 337, 340, 341, 343, 344, 348, 358, 360, 361, 367, 372
religion/spirituality, 3, 4, 10, 13, 15, 22, 43–44, 46, 70, 74, 81, 85, 161, 170–171, 205–216, 244
reproduction, 4, 10, 85, 105, 151, 165. 179–197, 235, 338, 340, 348, 349, 410, 414, 466
reproductive freedom, 464–466, 477
reproductive health, 191, 197, 349, 432, 433, 436, 437, 466, 470–473, 476, 477
reproductive justice, 13, 464–478
reproductive politics, 13, 464, 466–468, 470, 478
reproductive rights, 13, 50, 434, 466–468, 470
reproductive violence, 466
resistance, 8, 28, 30, 62, 64, 73, 97, 123–126, 129, 135, 164, 211, 284, 289, 339, 471, 478

retaliation, 404
reverse dowry *see* marriage payments
Rhode, Deborah, 344, 399
Rich, Adrienne, 104
Robbins, Trina, 326, 328
Roe v. Wade, 465, 467
romance, 48, 252, 268–270, 281
romantic friendships, 49
Roszéwitch, Yohanne, 449
Rubin, Gayle, 5, 6, 282, 285, 307, 359
Rule 412, 399
Rupp, Leila, 45, 181, 301, 303, 306, 358
Russia, 24, 25, 146, 243

sacred prostitution, 43, 44
sadomasochism, 324–326
same-sex marriage, 14, 42, 50, 61, 62, 170, 209, 243, 252, 290, 339, 341–343, 346–348, 350, 384
Sappho, 305, 306
science, 3, 9–10, 22, 24, 26, 27, 29, 32, 46, 96, 99, 101, 102, 143–153
Scientific-Humanitarian Committee, 7, 24, 29, 146, 431
scripting theory, 10, 162–164
seclusion of women *see* women-seclusion
Section 377, 362, 363, 431, 439
Sedgwick, Eve, 91, 291, 295
selective incapacitation, 374
self-identification, 161, 162, 308, 456–458
separate spheres, 396
settler colonialism, 63, 64, 66, 135
settler privilege, 122
Seventh-day Adventists, 209
severe, 104, 150, 394, 397, 417, 418
sex crimes, 385
sex education, 27, 50, 123, 167, 169, 170, 207, 210, 229, 281
sex/gender system, 282, 303
sexism, 131, 150, 160, 313, 329, 360, 477
sex offender registers, 375
sex offenders, 374–377
sex of object choice, 83, 253
sexology, 3, 7, 9, 21–37 *see also* science
  commodification of female sexuality, 35
  cross-disciplinary and cross-cultural translation, 26
  de-pathologization of homosexuality, 33, 34

sexology (cont'd)
  and homosexuality, 4, 312
  and literature, 305
  Nazism and Fascism, 29
  pioneers, 30
  progressiveness and conservatism, 368
  and racism, 150
  and rights, 360
  and sexual deviation, 145
sex reassignment, 453
sex trafficking, 260, 262, 337, 378, 380, 381, 385, 409–422
sexual assault, rape, 361, 395, 396, 469
sexual attraction, 161
sexual citizenship, 228, 337–350
sexual diversity, 5, 26, 227, 232–233
sexual essentialism, 285
sexual ethics, 206
sexual harassment, 12, 168, 389–405
sexual identities, 3, 4, 7, 8, 22, 23, 48, 49, 70, 82, 87, 89, 104, 124, 146, 206, 213–215, 287, 303 see also sexual nonconformity
sexuality/sexualities
  education, 10, 225–236
  influences on education, 10
  influences on government, 170
  influences on peers, 166
  influences on policy, 101
  influences on religion, 205–216
  media influence, 167
  parental influence, 166
  and parent/child communication, 230
  research, 1 3, 4, 9, 68, 101, 108, 162, 228, 236, 364
  socialization, 10, 161–172
  studies, 3–15
  transmitted diseases, 45, 70, 362, 379, 474, 475
sexual labor, 11, 258–263, 266–269, 271, 272, 371, 381, 409–417, 419
sexual liberalization, 22
sexual liberation, 33, 49, 50, 364, 431
sexual nonconformity, 49
sexual orientation, 4, 10, 48, 49, 73, 147, 161, 165, 179, 180, 182, 193, 209, 243–250, 303, 346, 349, 358, 394, 436, 437, 447, 450
sexual perversion see sexual nonconformity

sexual politics, 62, 65, 73, 74, 340, 364
sexual respectability, 70, 74
sexual revolution, 152, 311, 312, 431
sexual rights, 12–14, 30, 32, 51, 348, 349, 429–441, 445
sexual science, 24, 26, 34, 143–148, 151, 153
sexual violence, 74, 146, 379, 382, 421, 433, 465, 468–470, 477
sex work see prostitution
Shinto, 43
Shunga, 322
Singapore, 72, 211, 271, 342, 346, 347
slavery (female sexual, modern, transatlantic), 366, 416, 418–422, 466
Slovenia, 186, 207
Smith, Christine, 330
Smith, Howard W., 393
socialism, 148 see also communism
social justice movements, 3, 12–14, 301
sociobiology, 3
sociology, 89, 100, 125, 338
sodomy, 66, 293, 307, 347, 362, 363, 373, 383, 384, 436, 450
sodomy laws, 362, 383, 431, 436
Somerville, Siobhan B., 29, 320
SOS Homophobie, 449
South America, 143, 185, 341, 345, 411
South Korea, 345, 348
Spain, 25, 65, 66, 454, 456
standpoint theory, 79, 82, 306, 433
State fair employment and practice statutes (FEPS), 392
statistical prevalence, 389
statistics, 376, 377, 381, 390, 399, 476
stereotype, 66, 71, 72, 84, 163, 182, 188, 210, 215, 231, 247, 250, 266, 268, 293, 322, 325, 366, 367, 392, 394, 465, 469, 477
Stoler, Ann L., 24, 29, 68
Stoller, Robert, 282
Stop Enabling Online Sex Trafficking Act (SESTA), 261
Stop Street Harassment, 390
straight privilege, 123, 124, 130
Stree Sangam, 450
subjective, 105, 170, 248, 394, 398
Supreme Court, 61, 170, 243, 287, 294, 342, 347, 350, 383, 384, 397, 401, 439, 449

surrogacy, 10, 181, 182, 187, 189–191, 195, 259, 263, 340
surrogate, 44, 189–191, 194
Sutton, Katie, 32
symbolic interactionsim, 162

Tagame, Gengoroh, 318, 321, 325, 328, 330
Taïa, Abdellah, 299, 312
Taiwan, 267, 271, 345, 347, 367, 451
technology, 9, 143–153
television, 50, 167–169, 285, 287, 289, 291–295
temple prostitution *see* sacred prostitution
Terry, Jennifer, 31, 147
Thailand, 143, 195, 243, 263, 345, 346, 365, 366, 436, 451
third gender, 74, 304, 347, 439, 451, 453
Thomas, Clarence, 395
Tiefer, Leonore, 27, 33, 35, 36
tipped wage, 400
Title IX, 294, 392, 394
Title VII, 244, 392–402, 404
Title VIII, 392
Tom of Finland, 318, 322, 324, 325, 330
tradition, 13, 14, 28, 40, 44, 69, 74, 148, 209, 216, 417, 438, 440–441
trafficked, 45, 260, 271, 362, 366, 380, 381, 417, 418
trans, 6
transgender *see* gender nonconformity; cross-dressing
transgender-inclusive restrooms, 447
transition-related health benefits, 456
transnational, 190, 259
  history, 22
transnational justice networks, 364, 438, 439
transnational mothering, 265–266
transversal coalition politics, 455
transvestism *see* cross-dressing
The Triangle Project (Toronto), 134
Triptow, Robert, 319, 328, 329
Trump, Donald, 14, 294, 396, 404
Twentieth-century literature, 309
Twitter, 396
two-spirit, 44, 182 *see also* berdache

UN Convention Against Organised Transnational Crime, 380
underreporting of sex offences, 377

United Kingdom, 193, 243, 245, 248, 338, 342, 365, 376, 377, 383
United Nations, 13, 69, 243, 252, 261, 344, 349, 365, 380, 416, 429, 432, 434, 436, 437, 441
United States, 27, 29, 31, 49, 81, 96, 112, 145, 148–150, 187, 191, 206, 207, 216, 229, 243, 318–326, 328, 338, 350, 374
Universal Declaration of Human Rights, 429, 441, 467
The Universal Declaration of Human Rights, 429, 441
unwelcome, 194, 366, 389, 391, 394, 397–399, 404, 411
UN Women, 390, 404, 433
urbanization, 47
US Department of Education (ED), 394
US imperialism, 63, 265

validity, 33, 95, 107–110
veiling of women, 69, 70
Viagra, pink, 35
victim/victimization, 377–379, 421
Victorian morality, 430, 431
Vienna, 24, 433, 434
Vietnam, 345–347, 366, 411, 450, 451
Vinson, Mechelle, 397
violence (sexual, colonial, against women), 349, 380, 416, 417
virginity, 41, 210, 327, 430
von Krafft-Ebing, Richard, 7, 21, 144, 145

wages/wage discrimination, 246, 247
The Washington Post, 390
Waters, Chris, 32, 33
Weeks, Jeffrey, 21, 22, 301, 302, 359, 382
Weinstein, Harvey, 395
Western Europe, 14, 27, 143, 144, 147, 148, 270, 410, 411, 417, 458
Western exceptionalism, 438–440
Western hegemony, 13, 367, 438, 441
whiteness/white supremacy/white power, 179, 251, 419, 421, 468, 478
white supremacy, 179, 251, 419, 421, 468, 478
widowhood, 42, 44, 361
Wilde, Oscar, 285, 308–310

Wings, Mary, 326
Wislocka, Michalina, 33
Wittig, Monique, 103, 282
Woman question, 65
women of color, 13, 150, 163, 259, 261, 263, 264, 288, 419, 464, 467, 478
Women's Rights as Human Rights, 432–434
women-seclusion, 41
World Bank, 70, 364, 412
World Health Organization, 73, 434, 441
World League of Sexual Reform, 23, 146
World Policy Analysis Center (WORLD), 403, 404

yaoi, 318, 319, 327
yin and yang, 43
Yogyakarta Principles, 349, 436, 438, 439
Young people, 10, 12, 165, 227–236, 331, 377, 421

Zionism, 207